SPECIAL EDITION

USING PHOTOSHOP® 3 FOR MACINTOSH®

Bill Harrel

Rob Sonner

Darien Kruss

Ted Padova

Ted Evangelakis

Elizabeth Brown Lawler

Jeff Foster

Cyndie Klopfenstein

Rick Wallace

que

Special Edition Using Photoshop 3 for Macintosh

Copyright ©1995 by Que® Corporation

Library of Congress Catalog No.: 94-69626

ISBN: 1-56529-614-1

97 96 95   3 2 1

Interpretation of the printing code: the rightmost double-digit number is the year of the book's printing; the rightmost single-digit number, the number of the book's printing. For example, a printing code of 95-1 shows that the first printing of the book occurred in 1995.

This book is based on Photoshop 3 for the Macintosh.

Publisher: *David P. Ewing*

Associate Publisher: *Stacy Hiquet*

Associate Publisher—Operations: *Corinne Walls*

Publishing Director: *Brad R. Koch*

Managing Editor: *Sandy Doell*

Credits

Publishing Manager

Thomas H. Bennett

Acquisitions Editor

Cheryl D. Willoughby

Product Directors

Stephanie Gould
Jim Minatel
Lisa A. Bucki

Production Editor

Noelle Gasco

Copy Editors

Kelli Brooks
Nicole L. Rodandello
Maureen Schneeberger
Theresa Mathias
Lisa Gebken
Danielle Bird
Linda Seifert
Nanci Sears Perry
Julie A. McNamee
Geneil Breeze
Wendy Ott
Charles Bowles

Technical Editors

Matt Brown
Christopher Ehren

Figure Specialist

Cari Ohm

Book Designer

Sandra Stevenson

Cover Designer

Dan Armstrong

Operations Coordinator

Patty Brooks

Editorial Assistant

Andrea Duvall

Aquisitions Assistant

Ruth Slates

Production Team

Stephen Adams, Claudia Bell,
Stephen Carlin, Maxine Dillingham,
Karen Gregor, Daryl Kessler,
Bob LaRoche, Elizabeth Lewis,
Michael Thomas, Tina Trettin,
Marvin Van Tiem

Indexer

Michael Hughes

Composed in *Stone Serif* and *MCPdigital* by Que Corporation

Photo Credits

All photos used in chapters 1–4 come from the Adobe Photoshop tutorial.

The Wristwatch photo used for figures 8.3, 8.15, and 8.27 comes from 21st Century Media Photo Disk.

The Parrots photo that appears throughout chapter 9 and in the color section, "Photoshop in Color!," comes from the Kodak Photo CD.

Figure 9.7 comes from the Adobe Photoshop Tutorial.

Figures 9.40 and 9.41 are Image 1 from the Kodak Photo CD.

Photos used in chapters 14 and 15 are credited as follows:

"Trees," "Austria," and "Boat on Vistula" by Matt Brown, Mountain View, California;

"the Flower Girl," "Osiana," and "Rose Bouquet" by Nick Bonura, Louisville, Kentucky;

"Caroline Pouting" and "Robinson at Christmas" by Peggy C. Strickler, Louisville, Kentucky;

"Silly Kitty" and "San Fransisco Street" by Keenan Lawler, Louisville, Kentucky;

"Painted Rose" by Jeff Robinson, Fairfax, Virginia;

"Old Style Clock" and "Katie the Beagle" by Bob and Bonny Manning, Louisville, Kentucky;

Bryce Landscapes and other graphics by Elizabeth Brown Lawler.

Dedications

To Maria and Peter, my favorie Tristan players, and to Richie, for listening to all those esoteric monologues about the alchemical properties of alpha channels.

Ted Evangelakis

To Suban, Lis, Ang, Subaan, Bren, Becca, and the other teenagers who shared their teenage years with me, so I could go on to become a successful adult.

Cyndie Klopfenstein

About the Authors

Bill Harrel has written hundreds of articles covering graphics and desktop publishing for leading computer magazines, such as *Publish* and *PC World*. He has also authored or co-authored nine books, including *Using QuarkXPress for Macintosh* (Que) and *Using the Macintosh* (Que). Before becoming a freelance writer, Harrel owned a Southern California-based design firm with clients such as Johnson & Johnson, Executone, and AT&T.

Rob Sonner works for HSC Software, Inc. in Carpinteria, California, in Product Development and Support. In prior lives Rob has worked for Apple Computer, Inc., Viking Office Products, World Media, Inc., and Tri-County Publishing, as well as writing for the *Los Angeles Times* and the *LA Weekly*.

Darien Kruss began mastering the technology of computers in 1981, when he purchased his first Apple II. Since the introduction of the Lisa in 1983, he kept pace with the entire line of Macintosh computers to become a recognized "guru" of the trade. His talents in course development, consulting, training, and his understanding of the prepress environment are currently utilized by the Wace Resource Center in Chicago, Illinois.

In his continuing pursuit of cutting-edge technologies, Darien is becoming more involved in three-dimensional modeling, rendering, animation, and digital video projects. He has created several multimedia presentations for corporate use, and an interactive training program utilizing text, graphic, audio, and video components.

Darien is an active participant in several forums on CompuServe (76344,1352) and America OnLine (Darien M).

Ted Padova is President/CEO of Graphic Traffic Digital Imaging Centers in Ventura and Thousand Oaks, California. He has co-owned and operated digital imaging service bureaus for five years. His ventures include: teaching Electronic Design and Application Software classes at several universities, teaching private classes on Photoshop, page layout, etc., at Graphic Traffic, authoring a feature column for the L.A. MacDigest, and speaking engagements at schools, user groups, and computer manufacturing facilities. He holds a Master of Arts degree from California State University at Bakersfield in Clinical Counseling.

Ted Evangelakis is a multimedia developer living and working in Coral Gables, Florida. He has a Bachelor's Degree in Architecture, a Bachelor of Fine Arts in Photography, and a Master of Fine Arts in Photography. After spending half his life in high school, he is now a partner in a multimedia design company specializing in interactive presentations, CD-ROM development, and video animation. In the fall of 1993, Ted was selected as one of two winners of the NBC "Homegrown Peacock" competition, and his Peacock animation was aired nationally in December 1993.

Elizabeth Brown Lawler is a graphic artist and Mac consultant with six years experience ranging from PC presentations to Mac animation. She loves creating digital portraits, and hopes to get into special effects for film. She lives with her new husband and three cats in Louisville, Kentucky.

Jeff Foster is the President of Foster Digital Imaging, Inc., a high-tech design studio in Brea, California. Foster has over nine years experience in technical & illustrative design, with companies like McDonnell Douglas, Universal Studios-Hollywood, and FOX Television. He specializes in illustrative photo composition for print, 3-D modeling design-animation, and special effects for film, video, and multimedia.

Cyndie Klopfenstein's background comes entirely from the printing and publishing industries—but the Macintosh has forced that focus into new directions. After putting in time as a typesetter, designer, press operator, stripper (not tabletop), and even a sign painter, she has settled on training for the prepress industry. With eight books and a series of videos to her credit, she has become a sought-after trainer for corporations making the switch to desktop. United Airlines, the Children's Diabetes

Foundation, and the Mayor's Office of Economic Development for the City of Denver rank among companies which have employed Cyndie's expertise. The Klopfensteins own and operate one of Denver's oldest and largest service bureaus.

Rick Wallace spent 20 years as an award-winning reporter, investigator, and news director in the radio and television news business before discovering computers. In the 10 years since then, his voyage of computer curiosity has given him opportunities to become president of a company that produced videotape tutorials on computers and software, produce seminar programs to help real estate agents get computerized, write a series of books on computer-aided law practice management, create custom training materials and newsletters for some of the largest companies in the computer industry, write and produce uncountable user's manuals for various computer peripherals and software, serve as a writer— and de facto computer support person—for a crisis management consulting company, and write or contribute to Que books on PageMaker, QuarkXPress, CorelDRAW!, Windows, and, of course, Photoshop.

Acknowledgments

Many thanks go out to all involved who made this possible on my end: Julie Sigwart for the wonderful proofreading and additional insight; Dan Prochazka for letting me borrow his CDs as well as his CD-ROM drive in a pinch; Scott Hawthorne for letting me at his vast Photo-CD collection; Mark Elpers at the T/Maker Company and Lance Gilbert at Second Glance for their kind contributions; the whole gang at HSC, especially Phil Clevenger and Kai Krause for the "Cool, you're going to do what?" support; and last, but not least, Gene "Using the Macintosh" Steinberg for the original invitation to be a part of it all.

Rob Sonner

Much of my continuing education and learning is inspired by and received from two important sources: my PostScript Ninja employees— Robert Bulger, Brian Fitz-Gerald, Mike Soprano, Jeff Sell, and Brian Pardini—and my Ventura College and UC Santa Barbara students— among whom include, Sherry Tyler of Sherry Tyler Design in Ventura, California; Barbara Obermeier of Obermeier Design in Ventura, California; Ron Sellers, student at Art Center College of Design in Pasadena, California; Rosario Gilson of Gilson Design in Ventura, California; and Luis Ramirez, student at Art Center College of Design in Pasadena, California.

Special thanks for inspiration, tidbits of wisdom, and patience during the writing of this book goes to Maureen Antonio of Antonio Design in Ventura, California.

Much appreciation and thanks go to one of my co-authors, Bill Harrel in Ventura, California.

A special thanks for much assistance and support throughout this pro-ject goes to Cheryl Willoughby, Acquisitions Editor at Que Publishing.

Ted Padova

Sometimes it's people from the past that become part of your future—my father Eldridge—and other times it's people who've been there all along— Suban—who make you what you are today.

Cyndie Klopfenstein

Trademarks

All terms mentioned in this book that are known to be trademarks or service marks have been appropriately capitalized. Que cannot attest to the accuracy of this information. Use of a term in this book should not be regarded as affecting the validity of any trademark or service mark.

Photoshop is a registered trademark of Adobe Corporation.

Contents at a Glance

Part VII: Learning from the Pros

Part VIII: Appendixes

Contents

Contents

Part II: Acquiring Images   113

Contents

Part IV: Working with Color   359

Part V: Filters, Plug-Ins, and Special Effects   441

Contents

Contents

Contents

Contents

Contents

Contents

Introduction

There's no sense in redoing the Adobe documentation. It's good the way it is, and besides, what's the point of duplicating it? Instead, the objective of this book has been to take the same kind of information to its ultimate goal—the process of using Photoshop to edit images. You learn all about the Photoshop commands, but you see them through a prism of practicality, where all the information has been stuck into place with glue formulated from day-to-day usage.

INTRODUCTION

Using Photoshop for Macintosh • Using Photoshop for Macintosh • Using Photoshop for Macintosh

What Special Features Does This Book Contain?

The information in this book is organized by the following features.

Tips

Tips have been constructed on a foundation of the practical. Of course, every computer book has tips, but there's been a special effort to tune these to the working world.

Notes

Notes provide you with additional information.

Cautions

Cautions warn you about potential problems.

Tactics Recipes

Tactics Recipe sections throughout the book work in a way similar to extended tips, giving you a complete "cookbook" to a particular image editing task. These sections set out all your choices and leave the final decision up to you, while making a guiding recommendation.

Learning from the Pros

If one working pro can give you good advice, how about five of them? The "Learning from the Pros" chapters are extensive interviews with professionals who use Photoshop in their work with real world examples. You'll get solid tips and an overall view of the creative process.

Design Notes

There's no sense having Photoshop unless you produce a good-looking image from it. To help, Design Notes are placed at strategic points throughout the book.

Really Useful Appendixes

Speaking of the appendixes, these have some valuable stuff. There are appendixes that tell you how to transfer Photoshop files between Mac and Windows machines, use ATM, and create the ultimate Photoshop machine.

Two 4-Color Sections

Photoshop's color potential is illustrated in two exciting 4-color sections of the book called "Photoshop in Color!" which contains images from throughout the book, and "Learning from the Pros," which contains images from the "Learning from the Pros" chapters. The color effects demonstrated in these pages are referenced and explored in-depth.

Who Needs This Book and What Should You Read First?

There's no way you are going to read every page of this book. Well, maybe eventually, but it's not exactly a mystery-thriller-adventure-spy novel, is it? So, here's a guide to help you find your way and to help you explore Photoshop's power.

Help for Beginners to Image Editing

Not only have you never used Photoshop, but you've never used image editing software before. Start with chapter 3, "Photoshop Basics," to get an overview of the whole image editing process and computer graphics concepts.

After getting your feet wet in chapter 2, "Exploring What's New in Photoshop 3," take the plunge by jumping into chapter 1, "Touring Photoshop." It will increase your knowledge and give you a context for everything that follows.

After learning the basics, you'll want to find all the places where you can get images for editing in Photoshop, such as scanning, clip art, stock photograph collections, and Photo CDs. Part II, "Acquiring Images," is all about where to find images for use with Photoshop.

Part VII, "Learning from the Pros," contains several high-end tips, as well as material on the nature of the creative process—the basic ways professionals get the most from Photoshop.

From there, you have as many routes to follow as there are types of images. Your best approach may be to decide what kind of image you want to edit or create first, and follow each chapter one-by-one. The chapters are organized in the order you need to edit an image.

Graphics Professionals Looking for the Meat of the Program

Start with chapter 1, "Touring Photoshop," for a quick introduction on how the program works. You'll notice that Photoshop provides you with a wealth of paint and touch-up tools, just like the studio you work in now. That's one reason Photoshop has been so immensely popular among graphics professionals and photographers who are migrating to the computer.

Next, you may enjoy reading how other designers use Photoshop. That's Part VII, "Learning from the Pros." Five graphics professionals tell you how they make use of the program in their everyday work.

Most graphics professionals seem to have a particular working style. Some work with color, and some work with grayscale images. Others work with both. Some use their images in desktop publishing layouts and others use them in presentations. You'll find extensive information for tuning Photoshop images for the type of work you do in Part VI, "Publishing."

From there, you'll want to move into Part III, "Creating and Touching Up Images." This section covers the nuts and bolts of using Photoshop. It provides an in-depth look at the tools and how to use them.

Power Photoshop Users Looking for More and More

Check out the tips that appear throughout the text. This special hot information is set off in shaded boxes so that you can find it easily as you flip pages. And chapter 2, "Exploring What's New in Photoshop 3," lists every single new feature for version 3.

You'll be tempted to skip chapter 1, "Touring Photoshop," but it's worth a look even if you don't want to actually take the tour. It acts as a visual cross-reference to the rest of the book so that you can see where to go to find out about features of specific interest, like the new previews and proxies.

With version 3's new layering facilities, you'll want to spend some time in chapter 10, "Working with Layers."

See how your views match up with five other professionals in Part VII, "Learning from the Pros."

There's a lot of tweaky thoughts on pushing the contours of the Photoshop interface in chapters 17 through 20, which concentrate on special effects.

Power users tend to gravitate towards scripting, which is explained in chapter 25, "Automating Photoshop." This part includes information on using QuicKeys and other utilities to automate your Photoshop power.

How Is This Book Organized?

Overall, you'll probably notice that information flows in building block style. For example, Part II, "Acquiring Images," begins with importing images, and then moves on to more complicated issues such as scanning and creating your own Photo-CD collection.

Part I: Getting Started

This is the section for everybody, no matter what your background.

There's a quick-start tour in chapter 1, "Touring Photoshop." The new features in version 3 are presented in chapter 2, "Exploring What's New in Photoshop 3." Read how to set up Photoshop to work the way you do in chapter 4, "Setting Up the Photoshop Environment." And an overview of computer graphics and Photoshop basics are in chapter 3, "Photoshop Basics."

Part II: Acquiring Images

Where do you get images for touching up in Photoshop?

Chapter 5, "Importing and Exporting Images," explores importing images from other programs, digital cameras, and stock photograph collections. Chapter 6, "Scanning Images," provides an in-depth look at scanning.

Chapter 7, "Photo-CD Images," covers the exciting new world of Photo CDs, with information on how to use them in Photoshop and how to create your own Photo-CD collections.

Part III: Creating and Touching Up Images

Here's the nuts and bolts discussion of Photoshop and its sheer brute image-editing prowess.

Painting and editing tools are discussed in chapter 8, "Drawing, Painting, and Editing." This chapter also shows you how to use the icons in the toolbox.

Chapter 9, "Selecting Objects in Photoshop," explores selecting and editing specific objects in a Photoshop image, and also covers moving objects within an image, duplicating selections, and applying colors to selections.

Chapter 10, "Working with Layers," explores the most exciting new feature in Photoshop 3—layering. You'll be amazed at the power this new feature provides for image editing.

Chapter 11, "Drawing and Editing Paths," looks at a common graphics program function, *paths*, and Photoshop's approach to this critical concept.

Masking is the ability to exclude specific areas from editing (similar to using masking tape when painting a room in your house). Chapter 12, "Using Masks and Channels," looks at this important function and how to use it.

Part IV: Working with Color

You'll need a good understanding of color to get the desired results from Photoshop and other publishing packages. Chapter 13, "Understanding Color," provides a crash course in using color in a publishing environment.

The concepts involved in color are explored further in chapter 14, "Using Color Correction Tools," where advanced topics, such as color mapping, adjusting hues and saturation, and adjusting brightness and contrast, are discussed.

Part V: Filters, Plug-Ins, and Special Effects

In addition to editing and touching up images, Photoshop allows you to perform a variety of exciting special effects.

Chapter 15, "Using Photoshop's Plug-In Filters," discusses the concept of plug-ins, along with an explanation of the plug-in filters that ship with the program and how to use them. Chapter 16, "Third-Party Plug-Ins," looks at third-party plug-ins that provide even more functionality to the program.

Chapters 17 through 20 cover creating special effects in specific applications. The topics are:

▶ Chapter 17, "Creating Special Effects with Video"

▶ Chapter 18, "Creating Special Effects with Channels"

▶ Chapter 19, "3-D Modeling Special Effects"

▶ Chapter 20, "Text Special Effects"

Part VI: Publishing

This real-world Photoshop section covers using the program in various applications.

Photoshop was originally created to work in conjunction with desktop publishing programs, such as PageMaker. Chapter 21, "Photoshop for the Desktop Publisher," looks at using images for importing into DTP layouts. Digital designers will find help in chapter 22, "Photoshop for the Digital Designer," and presenters can turn to chapter 23, "Photoshop for the Presenter," for information on using the program to edit images for presentations.

Professional photographers who want to use Photoshop for enhancing and touching up their work, or for cataloging and creating Photo-CD portfolios, should turn to chapter 24, "Photoshop for the Professional Photographer."

Computers are supposed to make work easier and faster. Power users will want to automate repetitive tasks with the features discussed in chapter 25, "Automating Photoshop." The Mac operating system comes with several automation features, including AppleScript and Publish and Subscribe. System automation utilities, as well as third-party products such as QuicKeys, are discussed in chapter 25.

Part VII: Learning from the Pros

Five professionals tell you how they put Photoshop to work.

In chapter 26, "Scanning Objects: Instant Art from Real Life," Denny Knittig talks about developing art for Pillsbury's *Fast and Healthy* magazine.

In chapter 27, "Deconstructing Reality: Photo Manipulation," Randy Sizemore, Senior Designer at the Newsletter Factory, shows how he uses Photoshop to prepare images for newsletters.

Scott Lipsit talks you through designing a line of sports watches with Photoshop in chapter 28, "Achieving a Retail Vision: Product Design to Billboards."

Bert Monroy shows you how to create a photorealistic illustration from scratch, beginning in Adobe Illustrator and then moving the image to Photoshop in chapter 29, "Thinking Photorealistically: Is It Real, Or Is It Paint?"

In chapter 30, "Designing Printable Pieces: When Paper Meets the Press," Andy Fulp of Kennickell Printing reveals several common mistakes designers make when preparing art for the printing press.

Part VIII: Appendixes

If all the information in the bulk of the book isn't enough, you'll find some really helpful information in the appendixes, such as the following:

- In Appendix A, " Photoshop and Your Hardware," you learn what hardware you'll need to make Photoshop sing.

- Appendix B, "Resources," provides a list of additional resources to help you get the most from the program.

- Appendix C, "Installation," is an overview of the installation process.

- Appendix D, "Keyboard Shortcuts," is a table of keyboard shortcuts and special characters.

- Appendix E, "Swapping PC and Mac Photoshop Files," discusses swapping PC and Photoshop files.

- Appendix F, "Installing and Using Adobe Type Manager," discusses how to install and use Adobe Type Manager.

PART

I

Getting Started

Touring Photoshop

Are you new to Photoshop? If so, you're embarking on an exciting new course—image editing software. Of all the tasks we perform on computers, few are more entertaining and awe-inspiring. This chapter is the first leg of the trip— your introduction to the application and its basic functions.

Seasoned Photoshop users can relax here. While much of this may seem like old hat, version 3 has undergone some significant interface changes. As we progress through the tour, I'll be pointing out what's new. For a thorough discussion of new features in Photoshop 3, check out chapter 2, "Exploring What's New in Photoshop 3."

by Bill Harrel

CHAPTER 1

Besides a hands-on guide through the new Photoshop, this chapter also provides you with a visual index. The illustrations throughout this chapter point out the primary chapters and sections where those items are covered in-depth. (However, a few basic items, such as switching between background and foreground brush mode, don't get much cross-referencing. That's because these features are so fundamental to using Photoshop that their main coverage is handled right here.)

Taking the Quick Tour

Hold on to your hat! This section zooms through the Photoshop interface. If you need more detailed information on any point touched on here, check out the cross-references in the figures. They'll guide you to appropriate chapters that contain more detailed information on specific issues. In the meantime, let's get moving.

By the way, most of this tour uses one of the sample images, Portrait, located in the Tutorial folder on your program disks. When you install Photoshop, Install gives you the option to install the tutorial. If you did not install it, you can go back and run the installation program again. Then you can follow along as I take you on a quick tour.

Opening an Existing Image

Unlike other Macintosh programs, such as desktop publishing and word processing programs, instead of starting from scratch with a new document, most of the work you do in Photoshop will be on existing images. Photoshop is more of an image-editing and touch-up application, rather than a document creation program.

To launch Photoshop, double-click the Photoshop 3.0 icon, shown in figure 1.1. You'll find it in the Photoshop 3.0 folder.

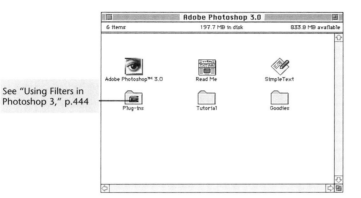

See "Using Filters in Photoshop 3," p.444

Fig. 1.1

Double-click the Photoshop 3.0 icon to launch Photoshop.

Getting Started

Tip

Launching Photoshop from the Apple Menu

Wading several folders deep to launch an application can be time-consuming and cumbersome. System 7.x provides a convenient alternative—launching from the Apple menu. To do so, you must first put the program on the Apple menu. The procedure is as follows: Select the program icon, then use Make Alias on the Finder File menu to make a copy of the icon. (You can rename the icon if you want. *Photoshop 3 alias* is a bit much.) Drag the alias icon into the Apple Menu folder in the System folder. The next time you open the Apple menu, you'll see the Photoshop 3 icon. If you're using System 7.5, you can use the Add Alias to Apple Menu script in the Useful Scripts option on the Apple menu.

After Photoshop finishes opening, pull down the File menu and choose Open to open an image, as shown in figure 1.2.

Fig. 1.2

Opening an
existing image
with the Open
command.

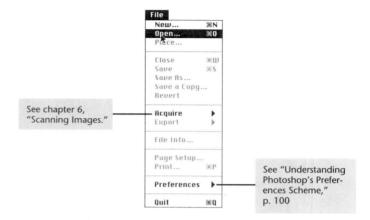

See chapter 6,
"Scanning Images."

See "Understanding
Photoshop's Prefer-
ences Scheme,"
p. 100

You get a relatively standard Macintosh dialog box for opening files
(see fig. 1.3).

Fig. 1.3

Use the Photoshop
Open dialog box to
open existing files.

Thumbnail

Click here to
create a
thumbnail
preview

Click here to see
thumbnail preview

See "Other Graphics
Formats," p. 80

The Open dialog box lists all of the files in the selected folder that
Photoshop supports. Basically, you use this dialog box to open files. You
open a supported image (see chapter 3, "Photoshop Basics," for information on supported file formats) the same way you do in any other
Macintosh application: select it and click Open, or double-click the file
name. To make finding files easier, Photoshop provides several features to
help you find the file that you're looking for. You'll find these features
particularly helpful when you're looking in folders that contain many
files.

Getting a Thumbnail Preview

When scrolling through a list of file names, it's not always evident what each file contains. Photoshop 2.5.1 and later help solve this problem by allowing you to save thumbnail previews with the image file. The thumbnail preview is displayed in the Open dialog box when the Show Thumbnail check box is selected. Figure 1.3 shows the dialog box with the thumbnail displayed.

Tip

Saving a Thumbnail with Image Files

You can tell Photoshop to save thumbnails with virtually any supported graphics format by selecting the Save Previews check box in the General Preferences dialog box. Setting Preferences is discussed in chapter 4, "Setting Up the Photoshop Environment," in the "Using the Preferences Command" section.

Another advantage to Photoshop's thumbnail feature is that the thumbnails also display as file icons in folders, as shown in figure 1.4. This helps you find files easier. Plus, you can open any Photoshop file by double-clicking the icon. Note, though, that the folder window must be set to Icon on the View menu to see the thumbnail.

Note

The Files BCY Green 1 and BCY Green 2, in figure 1.4, do not show icons because they have not been saved with the Save Thumbnail feature turned on.

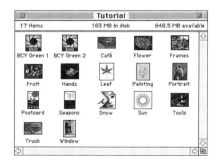

Fig. 1.4

Photoshop file icons saved with thumbnails in the tutorial folder.

Creating a Thumbnail Preview

If, as discussed in the preceding tip, you make sure that Save Previews in the General Preferences dialog box is selected, Photoshop will always save images with thumbnails that you can display in the Open dialog box. For images saved from other graphics applications or earlier versions of Photoshop, you may be able to create a thumbnail on the fly by clicking the Create button in the Open dialog box. However, for this to work, QuickTime must be running, and you must have a PICT image. All other formats—TIFF, Photo CD, EPS, and so on—must be opened in Photoshop and re-saved. Remember also, that General Preferences/Save Previews must be selected.

Tip

Finding Files with Find

If you're like me, you have so many files on your computer that you sometimes forget where you put them. If you know the file name—or at least part of it—you can use Find in the Open dialog box to locate it. Simply begin at the top of the folder structure, where the file might be. For example, I keep my work in a folder called "Documents." So I know that if I begin there, the file I'm looking for will be somewhere in that set. To find the file, simply type the first few letters in the file name (or any other part of the name), and then click Find. Photoshop moves down the folder structure until it finds the first occurrence of that text string. To move further down the structure, simply click Find again. Repeat this process until you find the file.

Overview of the Photoshop Application Window

Now that we have an image, let's take a look at the application window shown in figure 1.5. (Note that Photoshop opens with palettes open and in the same place they were when you last closed the program. If you're following along with the quick tour, your screen may look slightly different from figure 1.5.)

Toolbox   Menu bar   Title bar

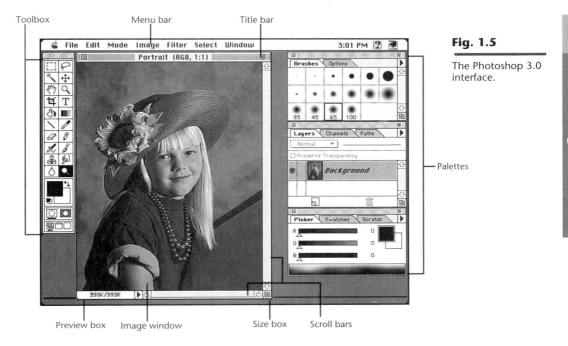

Preview box   Image window   Size box   Scroll bars

Fig. 1.5

The Photoshop 3.0 interface.

Palettes

Getting Started

Let's take a look at the components of the interface.

Design Note

Breaking Down the Photoshop Interface

This section looks at all of the labeled portions of figure 1.5. Palettes, which include the three unlabeled windows at the right of the screen, are discussed a little later in this chapter, in the section "Opening, Arranging, and Using Palettes."

Toolbox

All graphics and desktop publishing applications have toolboxes. As you can see, Photoshop's is extensive. The tools in the toolbox help you edit and touch-up images. There's a lot of power here. We'll look more closely at the toolbox later in this chapter, under "Getting to Know the Toolbox."

Image Window

The image window holds the image. Like the document window in a word processor or any other application, this is where you view images and perform your work. Besides displaying the image, the image window has three important parts: scroll bars and buttons, the title bar, and the preview box.

Scroll Bars and Scroll Buttons

Almost all Mac applications have scroll bars and scroll buttons. Scroll bars are the gray bands at the bottom and right side of the image window. If the image is larger than the window containing it, you can use the scroll bars and scroll buttons to move the image around in the window.

At the lower-right corner of the image window, where the scroll bars meet, notice the Size box. Use this box to resize the image window manually with your mouse.

Title Bar

The title bar displays the file name and zoom ratio. (Zoom factor and ratio are described later in this chapter, in the section "Navigating the Application Window.") The title bar contains the close box, for closing the image without quitting the application, and the zoom box, for maximizing the image window.

Preview Box

The preview box shows the file size and the amount of RAM that the image is using. As you begin working with large 24-bit image files, these numbers will become more important. The figure in the preview box displaying the memory size is new to version 3. For more about RAM requirements, see the "Using Scratch Disk (Memory Setup)" section in chapter 4, "Setting Up the Photoshop Environment" and Appendix A, "Photoshop and Your Hardware."

Getting to Know the Toolbox

As you can see in figure 1.6, Photoshop's toolbox is loaded with options. One of the more challenging aspects of learning to use the program is remembering which tool does what. After you finish reading this section, it'll make a lot more sense. Pay special attention to the cross-references; they direct you to locations in this book where you can find more detailed information.

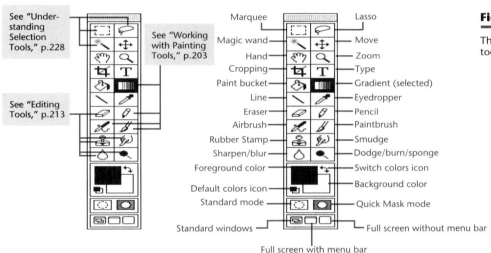

Fig. 1.6

The Photoshop toolbox.

In all, the toolbox contains 20 tools, with additional tools behind tools that you get to by holding the Option key as you click on a tool. For example, clicking on the Dodge/burn/smudge tool while holding Option toggles between the three tool modes. Some of Photoshop's palettes also contain tools. Palettes are discussed later in the section "Opening, Arranging, and Using Palettes."

Tools

Seasoned Photoshop users will notice that the tools are in a slightly different order, and that the Elliptical Marquee tool is now part of a Marquee tool.

Marquee. This is Photoshop's main selection tool. To select a rectangular area, simply drag the tool around the section. The selection is then enclosed inside a moving line of dashes, sometimes called marching ants. Figure 1.7 shows the Marquee tool in action. You can use the Options palette to change the shape of the marquee selection to elliptical or to single row or column. (Note that this is different from previous versions, which had separate rectangular and elliptical tools.)

Fig. 1.7

The dashed rectangle on the child's face marks the area selected with the Marquee tool.

Tip

Constraining Selections

In Photoshop, and most other Mac applications, you can constrain a selection tool by holding the Shift key as you drag the mouse. To draw perfect squares with the Marquee tool in rectangular mode, simply hold Shift as you drag. Likewise, to draw perfect circles, hold Shift while dragging the Marquee tool in elliptical mode. You can also constrain drawing tools.

 Lasso. The lasso is a free-form selection tool. Use it to select irregular shaped areas by drawing around the area.

Magic Wand. This tool selects contiguous areas of the same or similar color. You also can use it to select multiple discontinuous areas of the same or similar color by Shift-clicking one area and then another, until all desired areas are selected.

Move. New to version 3, the Move tool allows you to move selected, or "floating" sections. To use it, simply select a portion of an image (or paste in an object), select the Move tool, and drag the selection.

Hand. Use the Hand tool to drag, or scroll, an image around in an image window. This is similar to PageMaker's Grabber Hand. You also can double-click the tool on the image to maximize or reduce the image window.

Zoom. This is a simple tool to use. Click the tool on a portion of an image to enlarge it. Option-clicking the tool zooms out, or reduces the image. You can return the image to 100 percent, or 1 to 1, by double-clicking the Zoom tool in the toolbox. You also can zoom in on a selected area by dragging the Zoom tool around the area, as shown in figure 1.8.

Fig. 1.8

To perform a marquee zoom, drag the Zoom tool cursor around the area you want to zoom in on, as shown here.

Cropping. *Cropping* is the cutting away of outer areas. To crop an image, use this tool to drag a rectangular selection around the area you want to keep. (Corner handles on the crop-tool selection allow you to resize the selection.) Simply click inside the selected area to cut away the outer area.

Type. Use this tool to enter text onto your image canvas. Click the Type tool in the general area where you want the text to appear. The Type Tool dialog box appears (see fig. 1.9), allowing you to enter the text and format it. Be careful, though. This tool is a one way street. Once you place and deselect text, you can't go back and edit it. The only recourse is to erase the text and start again. (Note that with the new layering feature, you can place text on a separate layer, which makes working with text much easier. Layers are discussed in chapter 10, "Working with Layers.")

Fig. 1.9

Use the Type Tool dialog box to enter text onto your canvas.

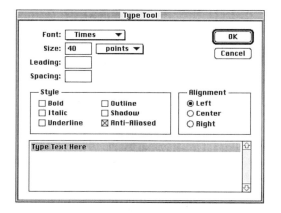

 Paintbucket. Use this tool to fill a contiguous area of similarly colored pixels with the current foreground color.

Gradient. A *gradient* (or *gradation*) is a transition from one color to another. In Photoshop, the gradient consists of one color gradating to another. To create a gradient, simply drag the Gradient tool over the area where you want the gradient.

 Line. Use this tool to draw a straight line. Just drag where you want the line to appear.

 Eyedropper. The Eyedropper picks up color. Using the Eyedropper, click a color in an image to make it the foreground color, and Option-click a color to make it a background color. (For a discussion of foreground and background colors, read the next section, "Controls.")

Eraser. Here's another simple one. When the background color is white, the Eraser paints white, in effect erasing whatever you drag it over, as shown in figure 1.10. When you Option-drag, the cursor changes to the Magic Eraser, which returns the area you drag over to what it was before the image was last saved.

Fig. 1.10

Here the Eraser tool removes part of the image.

Pencil. Use this tool to draw lines. Just drag your line. The Pencil tool is a freehand pencil, meaning you can draw any kind of line, providing you have a steady hand.

Airbrush. The Airbrush tool creates an airbrush effect. When you drag it over an area, it draws feathered, or "airbrushed," lines that blend into the image.

Paintbrush. Similar to the Pencil tool, the Paintbrush tool draws lines. The difference is that the Pencil tool draws smooth lines and the Paintbrush tool draws blurry lines. If you think of the difference in the way pencils and paintbrushes work, this should be easy to fathom. But just in case it's not, figure 1.11 shows the difference.

Fig. 1.11

This shows the difference between Pencil tool lines and Paintbrush tool lines.

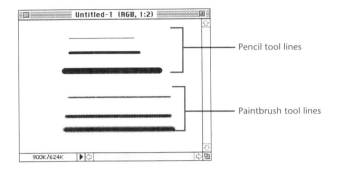

Rubber Stamp. The Rubber Stamp tool is a cloning tool. To use it, Option-click it in the area you want to duplicate and then drag it to the area where you want to place the duplicate. Figure 1.12 shows an example of an effect achieved by using the Rubber Stamp tool.

Fig. 1.12

An example of what you can do with the Rubber Stamp tool.

Smudge. Use this tool to smudge, or blend, two colors together. This is great for fixing cracks or correcting areas. Just drag the cursor over the area you want to smudge.

Sharpen/blur. Drag this tool over an area you want to blur or sharpen. To toggle between these, Option-click the icon in the toolbox.

Dodge/burn/sponge. Dodge lightens the area you drag; burn darkens an area; and sponge (new to version 3) increases or decreases saturation. The concept of saturation is discussed in the "Editing Tools" section of chapter 8, "Drawing, Painting, and Editing."

Controls

The bottom section of the toolbox contains a series of icons known as *controls*, or *toolbox controls*. This is a hodgepodge of handy buttons for controlling foreground and background color (see fig. 1.13), quick masks, and screen display options. Again, if the brief descriptions here aren't enough for you, check out the cross-referenced sections.

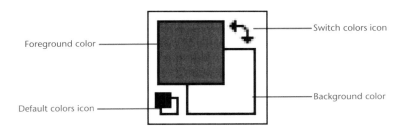

Fig. 1.13

Foreground and Background color controls.

▶ **Foreground color.** The Pencil, Paintbrush, Airbrush, and Paintbucket tools paint in the foreground color. When you click the foreground icon, the Color Picker dialog box appears (see fig. 1.14). Select the color that you want most of Photoshop's brushes to use.

▶ **Background color.** The background color is, of course, the opposite of the foreground color. It is the color used by the Eraser. When you click the background color icon, the Color Picker dialog box appears (see fig. 1.14), allowing you to choose a new background color.

▶ **Default colors.** Click this icon to return Photoshop's foreground and background colors to their defaults, black and white, respectively.

▶ **Switch colors.** Click this icon to swap the foreground and background colors. You'll find this handy for making the foreground color white.

Standard mode. Click this icon to exit the Quick Mask mode. (You enter Quick Mask mode by clicking the icon next to this one.) Masks are a bit too complicated to discuss during this brief tour. For now, it is enough to know that they are used to select objects and areas in an

Getting Started

image. They are discussed in detail in chapter 12, "Using Masks and Channels."

Fig. 1.14

Use the Color Picker dialog box to select fore-ground and background colors.

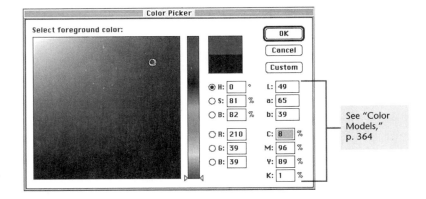

See "Color Models," p. 364

Quick Mask mode. Click this icon to enter Quick Mask mode. Masks are a bit too complicated to discuss during this tour. They are discussed in detail in chapter 12, "Using Masks and Channels."

Standard windows/Full screen with menu bar/Full screen without menu bar. These three icons along the bottom of the toolbox control the appearance of the screen, or desktop. The three modes are displayed in figure 1.15.

Fig. 1.15

The three display modes accessible from the toolbox. They are: Standard windows, full·screen with menu bar, and full screen without menu bar.

Standard windows

Full screen with menu bar

Full screen without menu bar

Opening, Arranging, and Using Palettes

In version 2.5, Adobe introduced floating palettes. Palettes are, in essence, floating dialog boxes. Unlike dialog boxes, however, palettes remain open on-screen until you close them, instead of closing each time you perform an action. So, in that respect, they are more like toolboxes than dialog boxes. Open the Window menu and choose Palettes, as shown in figure 1.16, to access palettes. Palettes contain options for modifying tools, adjusting color channels, and a wealth of other features (see fig. 1.17).

Fig. 1.16

Showing and hiding palettes is toggled from the Palettes submenu.

Fig. 1.17

Photoshop's ten palettes.

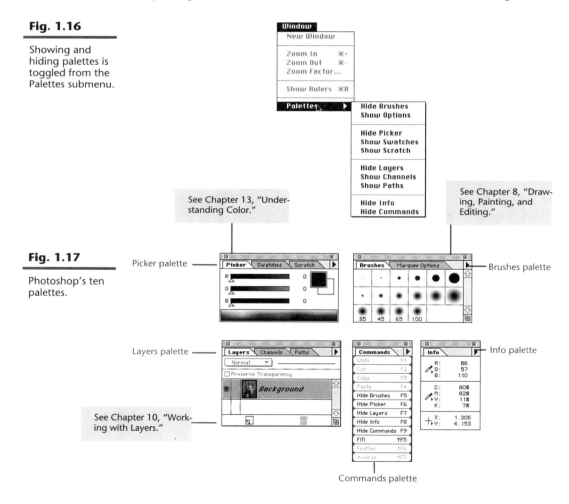

See Chapter 13, "Understanding Color."

See Chapter 8, "Drawing, Painting, and Editing."

Picker palette

Brushes palette

Layers palette

Info palette

See Chapter 10, "Working with Layers."

Commands palette

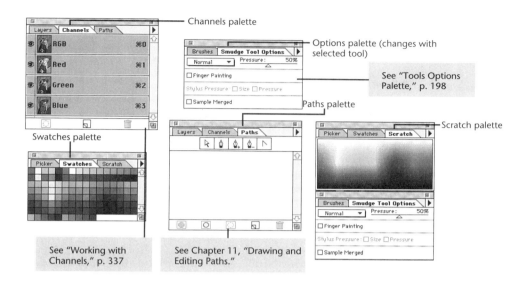

Channels palette

Options palette (changes with selected tool)

See "Tools Options Palette," p. 198

Paths palette

Scratch palette

Swatches palette

See "Working with Channels," p. 337

See Chapter 11, "Drawing and Editing Paths."

I

Getting Started

Look confusing? Depending on the palette, of course, you control a variety of functions from each one. The Brushes palette, for example, controls the size and shape of brushes. Notice also the folder-like tabs at the top of each palette. These are for selecting the individual palettes within palettes, which change the context of the palette. The Brushes palette, for instance, doubles as the Marquee Options palette. When you click the Marquee tool, the palette changes to allow you to set marquee selection options.

Note

New to version 3 is the Commands palette, which is discussed in more detail in the "Taking in Some Special Sights" section of this chapter.

Palette Elements

All 10 palettes contain some basic features, such as pop-up menus, options, zoom boxes, and so on, as shown in figure 1.18. This section describes the common features of the palettes and how to use them. Features common to most Macintosh windows, such as scroll bars and size boxes, are not discussed here.

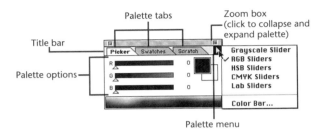

Fig. 1.18

Elements of a
Photoshop palette.

▶ **Palette menu.** Depending on the palette, this menu provides a number of options for modifying the appearance of the palette or using various aspects of the palette or tools modified by the palette. To use the menu, click the pop-up arrow and then drag to the desired option.

▶ **Zoom box.** Use this option to collapse, or roll up, the palette. As shown in figure 1.19, this provides more viewing area on your monitor. It also expands the palette.

Fig. 1.19

An example of
collapsed palettes.

▶ **Palette options.** These are the controls for the palette's functions. They are different for each palette.

Note

The options in palettes are extensive. Be sure to refer to the cross-references to find specific information on each one.

Arranging Palettes

Everybody loves choices, right? The beauty of palettes is that you can move them anywhere on the screen simply by dragging on the palette's title bar. You can collapse some palettes and leave some open. You can hide some palettes and show others. Photoshop lets you choose how to configure your work environment. Yet another convenience is the program's ability to remember how and where you left palettes from session to session. When you close the program, it notes the placement and arrangement of each palette. Then, when you open Photoshop again, the palettes are displayed as you left them.

Using Palettes

If you've been using computers for any length of time at all, you'll remember the days when virtually every option was hidden away in some obscure dialog box. Photoshop is no exception. In versions prior to 2.0, most features are tucked away in dialog boxes. After you make a change, you have to close the dialog box to see the change, and then reopen it to make additional changes. The few palettes there are, such as Brushes, are stationary and provide very few options.

Version 3's palettes not only float, they are feature-rich and often context-sensitive as well. When you click one of the paint tools, for example, the palettes options open ready to help you fine-tune that specific tool.

As mentioned, the file folder tabs at the top of the palette allow you to quickly jump from feature to feature. The Layers palette, for example, also is grouped with the Channels and Paths palettes. In addition to clicking the tabs, you also can open a palette from the Window/Palette menu to the desired option. The options on the Palette submenu are grouped by the topics in the respective palette. Show Layers, Show Channels, and Show Paths, for instance, are grouped together on the palette's pop-up menu.

How each palette operates, of course, depends on the respective palette and the tool selected. However, basic operation is similar. You select an option and use the palette to modify the option. In figure 1.20, for example, I used the Brushes palette to select a brush size for the paintbrush. You can either choose from the palette of brush sizes, or choose Show Options from the Palette menu, and then use the Brush Options dialog box to precisely adjust your brush size. You can even create and save your own brushes or add brushes to the palette.

Fig. 1.20

This is an example of selecting a brush size with the Brushes palette.

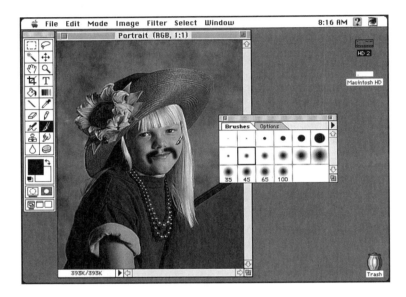

The point is palettes are powerful and versatile. I hate to keep harping on this, but you should use the cross-references to find specific descriptions of each palette. I strongly suggest that you keep this book handy while working in Photoshop, and use the cross-references each time you venture into new territory.

Rearranging and Regrouping Palettes

Yet another interesting feature is the ability to rearrange and regroup palettes. You can, for example, change a palette's tab position inside a palette group, drag a palette from inside one group to become a separate group, or drag it to another group.

This is just one more way Photoshop allows you to configure your desktop to your own specific needs. Say, for instance, that you use the Brushes, Layers, and Command palettes often. Wouldn't it make more sense to have them all in the same palette group, rather than having three separate groups open at once?

The procedure for rearranging and regrouping palettes is easy. Simply drag the palette tab to the desired position. To move a palette from one group to another, drag the palette tab out of the old group into the new. To create a separate or new group for a palette, simply drag the palette tab to the desktop. You can then add other palettes to the new group as desired by dragging them by the tab into the new group.

Navigating the Application Window

Are you new to Photoshop? Then this is the section for you. Most Mac applications operate similarly. Why, then, are there so many programs? Applications usually diverge at the point where the tasks they perform are achieved. Hence, Photoshop is necessarily different from, say, Microsoft Word at the point where the image editing begins. Otherwise, the interface is the same. Both programs, for example, open and save files similarly. Both have cut and paste options for moving objects from place to place, or from document to document.

This section is a short overview of the Photoshop application window, or interface. We begin at the image-editing level, rather than the Mac interface level. This section assumes that you know how to use your Mac. (If you don't, check out Que's *Using the Macintosh,* Special Edition.)

Key Concept: Getting a Better View

Due to the nature of the application, image editing requires you to see your documents from several different zoom levels. To touch up specific areas, for instance, you need to zoom in very close on that area. On the other hand, to see the overall effect of your work, you must view the entire image.

Photoshop lets you adjust the "zoom ratio" to any level. *Ratio* is measured in relationship to the size of the image. A ratio of 1:1 (one-to-one) is actual size; 2:1 is magnified twice, and so on. You can make the picture very small, or you can blow it up by several hundred percent, allowing you to work on your images at the pixel, or dot, level. Figure 1.21 shows the same image at various zoom levels.

Keep in mind that the 1:1 view of an image is based on screen resolution, rather than the actual dimensions. Images display on a screen at about 72 dots (or pixels) per inch. Documents with higher resolutions than 72 pixels per inch display larger than they print. When you use the Zoom tool, you are only changing the size of the view, not the size of the document.

Fig. 1.21

Examples of zoom levels.

Notice in the example that in the lower-right corner, you can actually see the dots that make up the image, allowing you to edit the image at the pixel level. Notice also that the zoom ratio is displayed in the title bar of each image window (for example, 1:1, 2:1, and 4:1).

When the number to the right of the colon is larger than the number to the left of the colon, the image is reduced. The opposite is true when the number to the left is larger than the number to the right; then the image is enlarged.

Zooming In and Out

Basically, there are two ways to zoom in and out on drawings. (*Zooming in*, of course, means magnifying, and *zooming out* means reducing.) You can use the Zoom In and Zoom Out commands on the Window menu (or their ⌘-(+) and ⌘-(–) keyboard shortcuts), or the Zoom tool.

To use the Zoom commands, simply make sure the image window is selected, and then choose the command. The Zoom tool provides a little more versatility. To zoom in on a specific area, select the Zoom tool and drag (marquee select) around the area you want to zoom in on, as shown in figure 1.22.

Fig. 1.22

Marquee selecting an area with the Zoom tool.

If you make a mistake, or zoom out too far, simply double-click the Zoom tool in the toolbox to return to 1:1 view. You also can hold down the Option key and click the portion of the image you want to zoom out on. Notice that when you hold Option with the Zoom tool selected, the plus inside the magnifying glass changes to a minus symbol. (Many tools can be modified this way.) Finally, for less precise zooming, you can simply click the Zoom tool directly on the portion of the image you want to zoom in on.

Getting Started

Adjusting the Zoom Ratio

When you use the Zoom In and Zoom Out commands, or click an image with the Zoom tool, Photoshop magnifies the image by the zoom ratio. The zoom ratio is set in the Zoom Factor dialog box, shown in figure 1.23. To open this dialog box, choose Zoom Factor from the Window menu.

Fig. 1.23

Use the Zoom Factor dialog box to set the zoom ratio used by the Zoom In and Zoom Out Commands, and the Zoom tool.

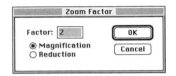

Photoshop's default zoom ratio is two, which means that the image doubles in size each time you zoom in or reduces by a factor of two each time you zoom out. Zoom factor allows you to set the ratio for magnification and reduction separately. As you become more familiar with Photoshop, you'll get a better idea of the ideal zoom ratio. Photoshop provides up to 31 zoom ratios, ranging from 1:16 to 16:1.

Scrolling Around

Large images, or those you zoom in on, often take up the entire screen. If you're working on several images at once, your windows are small. In both of these cases, you will often need to scroll in the image window to view and edit various areas.

Photoshop provides a number of ways to move around in the image window. The most common method is to use the scroll bars and scroll buttons. The other options include the Hand tool, the keyboard, and reference windows.

Using the Hand Tool

 Perhaps the easiest way to get around in the image window is to use the Hand tool. To use it, simply select it from the toolbox, and then drag the image around inside the window.

Scrolling with the Keyboard

As you become more proficient at using Photoshop, you'll learn several shortcuts for performing many functions. One of the program's more useful features is its numerous keyboard shortcuts, several of which enable you to scroll around in the image window. You'll find them especially helpful for working on large images.

In all, there are six keyboard-scroll shortcuts. The key combination depends on your keyboard. On an extended keyboard, for example, you press Page Up to scroll up one screen and Page Down to scroll down one screen. The same functions are performed on a standard Mac (small) keyboard by pressing Control-K and Control-Shift-K, respectively. You'll find a complete list of scrolling keyboard shortcuts, and all other keyboard shortcuts, in Appendix D, "Keyboard Shortcuts."

Using a Reference Window as You Scroll

A problem with scrolling around in magnified view is that it's often difficult to keep your bearings. An easy way to stay oriented is to create a *reference window*. As shown in figure 1.24, reference windows also show the changes you make in the zoomed-in view. This allows you to see how your edits affect the appearance of the overall image.

Fig. 1.24

You can use a reference window to keep your place when working in zoomed-in views.

To create a reference window, simply select the image window you want to duplicate and then open the Window menu and choose New. Photoshop creates a new window containing a copy of the image, and treats both windows as one. Changes made in either window are reflected in the other.

Turning on Rulers

Another way to stay oriented inside image windows is with rulers. Like almost all other graphics programs, Photoshop can display intersecting rulers along the left and top of the image window. To turn them on, simply select Show Rulers from the Window menu. Not only do the rulers keep you informed as to where you are in the image, but you also can use them to measure objects within images as you create and edit. To do so, use the zero intersection point feature.

Changing the Zero Intersection Point

The *zero intersection point* is the place in the image where the ruler tick marks, or measurement markers, intersect. Photoshop's default is the upper-left corner of the image window. But you can change it easily enough. (Many designers, especially magazine and newspaper layout people, are trained to measure pages from the bottom up.)

To change the zero intersection point, just drag it from the upper-left corner, as shown in figure 1.25. You can place it anywhere on the image. To return it to the default setting, simply click in the upper-left corner, where the rulers meet, or where you began.

Tip

Changing the Unit of Measurement

Many designers and publishers measure their images and documents in picas or points. You can change how Photoshop measures your images in the Unit Preferences dialog box. Changing measurement systems and other preferences are discussed in chapter 4, "Setting Up the Photoshop Environment," in the "Using the Preferences Command" section.

Dragging the zero intersection point

Fig. 1.25

Changing the zero intersection point.

Measuring Objects

Now that you know how to use the zero intersection point, let's find a use for it (other than measuring pages from the bottom). I like to use it to get precise measurements of objects in drawings.

For example, the hat in figure 1.26 looks big. Do you wonder just how big it is? To find out, all you do is drag the zero intersection point to the left edge of the hat, as shown in figure 1.26. When you let go, the ruler measures from the edge of the hat. To get an exact measurement, simply place the mouse pointer on the right edge. The dotted line shows you how wide the hat is. To find out how tall the hat is, place the cursor at the bottom of the hat. (It measures 3 1/4-inch x 2 3/4-inch.) You also can find the measurement in the Info palette, providing you have it displayed.

Fig. 1.26

Measuring objects
with the rulers.

New Zero
intersection
point

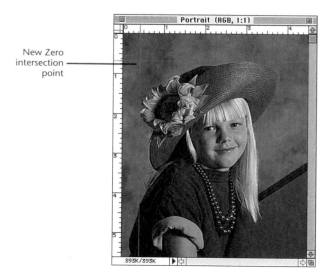

Adding Text to Images

Unlike Illustrator and other draw-type graphics programs, bitmap paint
editors, such as Photoshop, are not ideal for entering paragraphs of text.
You can, though, successfully add a few words for some great special
effects. The possibilities are limitless, so be sure to read chapter 20, "Text
Special Effects," for a complete discussion of using text with images. This
section briefly discusses the mechanics of using the Type tool.

Entering text onto your image is a breeze. All you do is click the Type tool
(I-beam) in the area where you want the text, and then type the text in the
Type Tool dialog box (see fig. 1.27).

Tip

Changing Text Color

If you want the text to be a color other than the current foreground
color, you should define the color and make it Foreground before
creating the text.

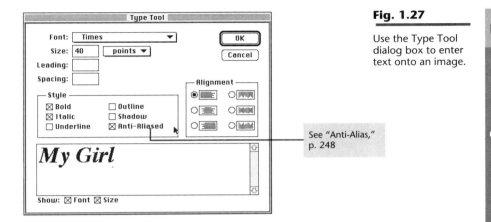

Fig. 1.27

Use the Type Tool dialog box to enter text onto an image.

Notice that the Type Tool dialog box also lets you format text, by changing the font, size, and weight. These options work the same as in any other Macintosh application. You also can make the text outlined or shadowed. (The Anti-aliasing option tells Photoshop to smooth the edges of the text. You'll seldom turn it off.). Now, in version 3, you can align text vertically, instead of just left, right, and center. This a handy option for creating posters and other effects, and for using non-Latin alphabets like Japanese.

When you click OK, Photoshop enters the text on the image where you clicked, as shown in figure 1.28. You can use the Move tool (or arrow keys) to move the text around on the image. Be careful, though, not to click the Type tool in the image area away from the text, or you'll deselect the text. The only way to get rid of type once it's deselected is to erase it, which is not an easy process. You also can select it with a Selection tool and delete it, but you'll seldom get the desired effect. (If you perform other actions after text is placed, you cannot use Undo to delete the type. This is discussed in the "Backing Out of Trouble" section in this chapter.)

If you haven't saved the image after you deselected the text, you can use the Magic Eraser tool (Option-Eraser) to return the area where the text is placed to its last saved version.

Fig. 1.28

Text placed with
the Type tool.

> ## Tip
>
> ### Use Layers to Place Type
>
> A disadvantage to placing type on a Photoshop image is that once
> the type is deselected, you can no longer move it or delete it. If you
> want to get rid of it or edit it, you must erase the text and start over.
> Unfortunately, the text blots out, or paints over, the objects beneath
> it. When you erase the text, you get white space (or the current Back-
> ground color) underneath. Version 3's new layering feature provides
> an alternative. Simply place the text on its own layer, making it an
> individual object you can edit and change separately. For more on
> layers, see the "Taking in Some Special Sights" section in this
> chapter.

After the text is placed as desired, you can click the Type tool or a selection
tool in the image area (away from the text) to deselect it.

Backing Out of Trouble

As you're working on an image, you'll often wish you hadn't performed a certain action. Maybe, for instance, you painted or erased an area inadvertently. Don't panic; Photoshop gives you a couple of ways out: Undo and Revert. (One other way is the Magic Eraser tool, which, when you drag it over an edited area, returns to the previously saved version. Providing, of course, that you haven't saved the image since making the change you want to reverse.)

Undo

Undo is common to most Mac programs. It's a simple command. All it does is reverse the last action. If you paint a line in the wrong place, for example, Open the Edit menu and choose Undo to reverse it. You must remember, though, that Undo only affects the last action. If you draw a line, release the mouse button, and then draw another line, Undo will undo only the last line you drew. But, all is not lost.

Revert

Revert returns the image to its last saved version. So, if you totally screw up your image, simply open the File menu and choose Revert to start over. You'll want to be careful with this one, however, because you can lose a lot of work. After you've successfully performed an action, save your work. Another way to avoid messing up an image is by working on a duplicate of the image, which is discussed in the "Using the Duplicate Command" section later in this chapter.

Magic Eraser

Remember that text I put on Portrait in an earlier section? In figure 1.29, I use the Magic Eraser to get rid of it. This is very handy. But remember that it only restores back to the most recently saved version of the image.

Fig. 1.29

The Magic Eraser
returns areas to the
last saved version.

Making Working Copies

Often, it's advantageous to work on a copy of an image to avoid damaging the original. There also are several other reasons to duplicate all or a portion of an image. You may, for example, want to place part of an image within another image. Two methods Photoshop provides for making copies of images and parts of images are duplicating and cloning. (And, of course, there's always the good ol' Macintosh standby: Cut, or Copy, and Paste.)

Using the Duplicate Command

The Duplicate command on the Image menu allows you to make an exact copy of an image. Simply make sure the image window that contains the image you want to duplicate is active, and then open the Image menu and choose Duplicate. You are then asked to name the duplicate (or accept the default name), and Photoshop creates a copy. You can then close the original and work on the duplicate.

Using the Rubber Stamp Tool

 Cloning is done with the Rubber Stamp tool. You can clone within an image or to another canvas. You saw an example of cloning within the same image earlier in this chapter. You can clone part of an image to another image, as shown in figure 1.30, by Option-clicking the Rubber Stamp tool in the original and then dragging in the new canvas.

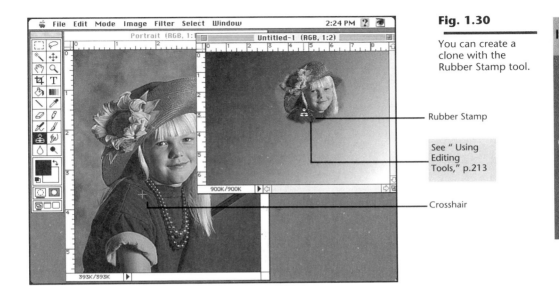

Fig. 1.30

You can create a clone with the Rubber Stamp tool.

Rubber Stamp

See " Using Editing Tools," p.213

Crosshair

Notice, in the figure, that the crosshair cursor in the original shows you which part of the original you are currently cloning. Use it to guide your movements in the new canvas.

Understanding Plug-Ins

An extension of Photoshop's brute power, *plug-ins* are small software applications that provide functionality to the program. This concept is not unique to Photoshop. Other applications provide similar options, such as QuarkXPress' XTensions and PageMaker's Additions. For more information about plug-ins, see chapter 15, "Using Photoshop's Plug-In Filters," and chapter 16, "Third-Party Plug-Ins."

Scanner plug-ins, for example, allow you to interface with a specific scanner. Filter plug-ins allow you to perform enhancement and special effects routines on images. Other types of plug-ins perform different functions. In figure 1.31, for instance, I used the Emboss filter (or plug-in) on Portrait.

Fig. 1.31

Example of an
effect achieved
with a filter
plug-in.

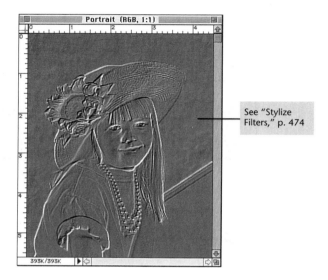

See "Stylize
Filters," p. 474

Usually, plug-ins install themselves on the Filter or File/Acquire menus.
Photoshop ships with several, and there are many third-party plug-ins
available. Scanner vendors, for example, often supply plug-ins, and some
software vendors create special effects plug-ins.

Unless you change the location of plug-ins, they are kept in the Plug-ins
folder in the Adobe Photoshop 3 folder. As you can see in figure 1.32, plug-
ins can include filters, file import and export converters, and can support
a whole host of other functions. For extensive information on plug-ins, be
sure to see chapters 15 and 16.

Fig. 1.32

The contents of the
Plug-ins folder.

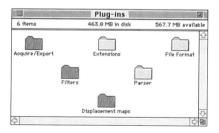

Printing

Printing from Photoshop is similar to printing from any other Mac application. You use the Page Setup command to set up your printer parameters, and then use the Print command to print. However, getting the desired quality is another issue. If you're printing a grayscale image on a laser printer, the procedure is a snap. Printing to desktop color printers is also relatively foolproof. Things get sticky, though, when you need color separations for an offset press. More often than not, the images you process in Photoshop will finally wind up as part of a larger document, such as a layout or presentation. In these situations, you print from other applications, such as PageMaker, QuarkXPress, or Persuasion. These issues are covered in depth in Part VI, "Publishing."

This section covers the basics of printing from Photoshop.

Printing to a Grayscale Printer

Grayscale printers are typically black-and-white laser printers. They come in all shapes and sizes, with resolutions from 300 dots per inch (dpi) to 1200 dpi and beyond. While you can get passable results from lasers, most often you'll use the output for proofing. Some publishers use laser output for newspaper-quality ads and photographs. But seldom is laser output used for high-end jobs, such as magazine spreads and fancy posters. You'll find a wealth of information on preparing images for layouts in the "Preparing Images for Layout" section of chapter 21, "Photoshop for the Desktop Publisher."

(Imagesetters are also grayscale printers. *Imagesetter* output is used for high-end jobs headed for the print shop. Preparing images for a print shop run is an intricate process that is a bit too advanced for this overview. Chapter 21 contains information on imagesetter output.)

After you make sure that your Mac is set up to print properly—the printer should be selected in Chooser and the desired settings made in Page Setup—you print in Photoshop as you do from any other Macintosh application (by choosing Print from the File menu).

Figure 1.33 shows the Print dialog box. If you set up your printer properly, usually all that you need to do in this dialog box is click the Print button. You should make sure, though, that the Gray radio button is selected in the "Print in" option at the bottom of the dialog box.

Getting Started

Fig. 1.33

Use the Print
dialog box to print
your images.

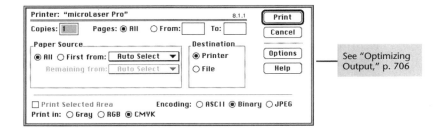

See "Optimizing
Output," p. 706

Looking at this dialog box, it's easy to see that you have several options. Most of them do not apply to simple printing on a laser printer. If you need additional information, be sure to check out chapter 21, "Photoshop for the Desktop Publisher."

Printing to a Color Printer

As with laser printers, there are several types of color printers. They range from $200 inkjets to $500,000 printers capable of turning out dazzling kiosks and posters, with all sorts of other devices in between and beyond. This section primarily discusses desktop color printers, which like laser printers, are most often used for proofing. If you plan to use Photoshop for high-end image editing or digital design, a number of places in this book can be very helpful. You should pay close attention to all of the chapters in Part VI, "Publishing." Chapter 13, "Understanding Color," also provides useful information.

When you print to a desktop color printer, about all you need to do is make sure that the proper color model is selected in the Print In option at the bottom of the Print dialog box. Color printers print by mixing percentages of colors—either red, green, and blue (RGB), or cyan, magenta, yellow, and black (CMYK). Before printing to your color printer, you should determine which model your printer uses. Again, the concept of color models is covered in chapter 13, "Understanding Color."

Printing Color Separations

Frankly, printing color separations, either from Photoshop or a desktop publishing program, such as QuarkXPress, is a fairly complicated procedure—much more so than I can cover in this overview.

To mass produce color output from a computer, most print shops require color separations. You can't simply take the printout from your color printer down to the corner shop and get a million copies. You'll find extensive information on producing color separations in Part VI, "Publishing." Chapter 13, "Understanding Color" also contains valuable help.

> **Tip**
>
> **Improving Color Output with Calibration**
>
> An important consideration when printing color from a desktop graphics application is calibration. You can greatly improve print quality by calibrating your printer and monitor so that the two types of output match more closely. Photoshop has a rudimentary calibration routine. You also can use third-party calibration hardware, Photoshop's built-in color management system, or a third-party color management system to calibrate your monitor, printer, and scanner. These topics are discussed in the "Calibration" section of chapter 13, "Understanding Color."

Taking In Some Special Sights

A few of the major features of Photoshop 3 deserve a special look; that's what this optional special sights tour is all about—some hands-on experimentation with these major improvements.

Checking Out Multiple Layers

Layering? If you're a seasoned Photoshop user, you're probably thinking that it's about time. Most other image editing packages have had layering for a while now, especially on the Windows side.

Borrowed from vector draw programs, layering is an easy concept to understand. Think of *layers* as clear acetate sheets on which you place the objects in your image and then stack the sheets to complete the image. Layers are managed from the Layers palette. Each layer can be locked, which means you cannot select or edit objects on that layer until you unlock it. Only one layer can be active at a time, which means you cannot select or edit objects on that layer until you make it active. And you can make layers invisible, or non-printable. Each image starts with a background layer, and you can then add as many as 99 layers.

In a paint-type graphic, when you add objects to a drawing, they weld into the bitmap, making further editing difficult. The primary reason for layering is to keep the objects in your image organized and separated. In a poster, for example, you can keep text on a separate layer to render it easier to move, delete, or edit. Again, layers keep objects separate, or stop them from becoming a permanent part of the background.

Perhaps figure 1.34 can help illustrate this concept. In the image on the left, I use a layer to enter the text. In the figure on the right, I place the type on the image, or background layer. Later, I decide that I want to see how the image looks without the text. In the left image, I simply hid the layer to get rid of the text. In the right image, I have to erase the text, making a mess that will take some time to fix. The only way to get the text back is to go through the entire text placing process again. Maybe you can't tell by looking at the figure, but there's a lot of work involved here.

Fig. 1.34

Example of how layered and non-layered objects behave. In the image not displaying any text, the text layer is hidden.

See "Understanding Layers," p. 268

Along the same lines, if I decide to delete the text altogether, in the left image, I just delete the layer. In the right image, well, I've got my work cut out for me. The more time you spend touching up an image and getting it just right, the more you'll appreciate layering.

As you add objects, the image becomes more complicated. Hiding layers makes the image less cluttered, making it easier to work on objects on other layers. Making layers non-printable (hiding) lets you print portions of your image for proofing. It also allows you to print your images on transparent overlays that you can stack during a presentation.

The Layers palette is extensive, providing a wealth of options, including: tinting all the objects on a layer, changing their color, or making them transparent. This section looks at the basics of adding a layer, hiding and showing a layer, and so on. The intricacies of the Layers palette are discussed in chapter 10, "Working with Layers."

Adding a Layer

Few things are more simple than adding layers to a Photoshop image. Just make sure the image window you want to create a layer for is active, and then select New Layer from the Layer palette menu, as shown in figure 1.35.

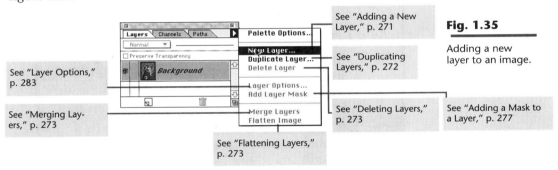

See "Adding a New Layer," p. 271

See "Layer Options," p. 283

See "Duplicating Layers," p. 272

See "Merging Layers," p. 273

See "Deleting Layers," p. 273

See "Adding a Mask to a Layer," p. 277

See "Flattening Layers," p. 273

Fig. 1.35

Adding a new layer to an image.

Then, in the New Layer dialog box, you can name the new layer, as shown in figure 1.36. If you elect to use the default, layers are named Layer 1, Layer 2, and so on. Usually, you should give layers a more descriptive title. (The other options in this dialog box are discussed in Chapter 10, "Working with Layers.")

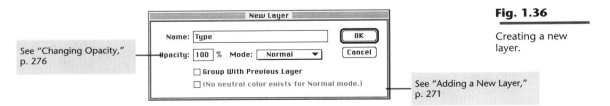

See "Changing Opacity," p. 276

See "Adding a New Layer," p. 271

Fig. 1.36

Creating a new layer.

Adding Objects to Layers

Virtually any function available in Photoshop can be performed on a layer. You can create text, paste objects, and edit objects with the paint and touch-up tools. To do so, make sure the layer that you want to work on is selected in the Layers palette, and get to work. In figure 1.37, I'm adding type to the Type layer that I created. Notice that the Type layer is highlighted in the Layers palette.

Fig. 1.37

Adding type to a layer.

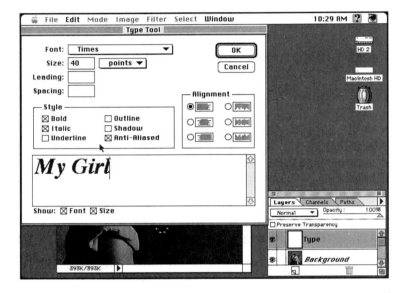

As you work on separate layers, it seems as though you are making changes to the image (background) itself. The changes actually occur on a clear overlay, allowing you to work and make mistakes at will, without ruining the objects on other layers.

Hiding Layers

Another aspect of layers is that you can hide them when you don't need them. There are many advantages to hiding layers. Basically, hiding a layer removes the objects on the layer from sight and makes it non-printable. You can, for example, easily print several versions of the same image. Some Photoshop images can be quite large; keeping several versions of the same file can eat up hard disk real estate quickly.

Hiding layers is easy; simply click the eye next to the layer name in the Layers palette, as shown in figure 1.38. To show the layer, click in the same spot again.

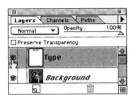

Fig. 1.38

Hiding a layer.

Deleting Layers

As touted several times in this chapter, the most beneficial aspect of layering is the ability to add objects to images without disturbing the image itself. After you learn to use the layering feature, you'll wonder how you lived without it.

> **Tip**
>
> **Getting a Better Layers View**
>
> As you can see from the screen shots in this section, the layer thumb-nails are often too small to see what's on some of them. Take heart. You can adjust the size of the icon with the Palette Options command on the Layers palette menu. You have three options: small, medium, and large. You can also turn thumbnails off to increase speed.

Deleting a layer is as easy as hiding and adding a new one. Just choose Delete Layer from the Layer palette menu.

Assigning Commands to the New Commands Palette

Okay, so the new palette structure is great. But anything a software developer can do to make the program easier to use is a welcome addition. For example, wouldn't it be nice to perform often-used actions by simply pressing a function key? Photoshop lets you do this, but how do you remember which functions are assigned to which keys? Version 3 comes to the rescue. Not only can you assign commands to function keys and

Shift-function key combinations, you also can display a palette that constantly reminds you which keys execute which commands.

All of this new functionality is packed into the new Commands palette, displayed in figure 1.39. As you can see, Photoshop comes with a default function key scheme. You can use it, modify it to suit your needs, or create multiple schemes for certain types of projects. If, for example, you routinely perform a series of functions on images before bringing them into your layout, you can create a Commands scheme for working specifically with those images, another one for other types of layouts, and so on.

Fig. 1.39

Use the Commands palette to assign often-used commands to keystrokes.

Adding Commands

You can add commands to the default command list or any others you create by choosing New Commands from the Commands palette menu, which opens the New Command dialog box shown in figure 1.40. In this dialog box, you name the command, choose the key to assign it to and, if you want, assign a color to the command. Adding a color causes the command name to appear in color on the palette.

Fig. 1.40

The New Command dialog box allows you to assign and change commands on the Commands palette.

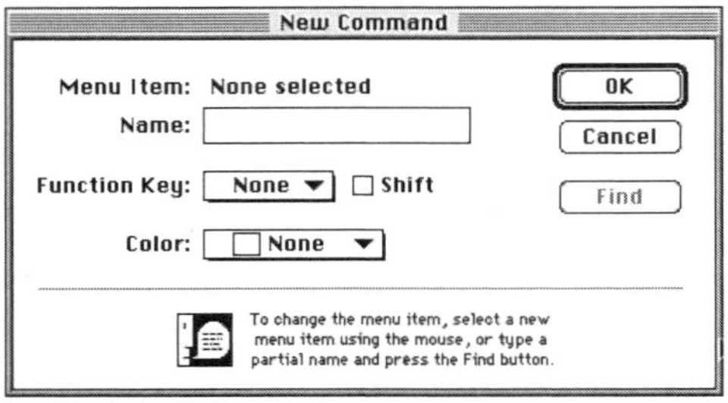

Photoshop won't let you assign commands to keys already in use. To change a key's command assignment, you should use the Edit Commands option in the Commands palette menu, discussed next.

Editing Commands

The Edit Commands option in the Commands palette menu opens the Edit Commands dialog box, shown in figure 1.41. This dialog box allows you to make changes to the entire Commands palette scheme. You can add new commands, edit existing commands, delete commands, and change the world. Have a ball!

Fig. 1.41

The Edit Commands dialog box allows you to make changes to your Command Palette scheme.

Saving Commands

If you use Photoshop for several different types of image editing, you can create and save several different command schemes with Save Commands on the Commands palette menu, which opens the Save Commands dialog box (see fig. 1.42). To load a command scheme, use Load Commands on the Commands palette menu. You also can append (add to) a saved command scheme with Append Commands on the Command palette menu.

Fig. 1.42

Use the Save
Commands dialog
box to save
Command palette
command
schemes.

Proxies and Previews

Applying filters to large images can take some time. Wouldn't it be nice if
you could see what the filter will do to your image before you apply it?
With Photoshop 3, you can. Many of the filter dialog boxes now have
proxies and previews. *Proxies* allow you to make filter changes interactively, by making adjustments with your mouse. *Previews* show you what
the changes you're making will do to the image.

Simple enough, right? Let's look at an example. In figure 1.43, I'm making
adjustments in the Lighting Effects dialog box with my mouse (adjusting
the lighting effects). Because the Preview check box (bottom-left) is
selected, the changes are simulated and displayed. As you can imagine,
this approach saves a lot of time as opposed to the old method of making
adjustments (waiting for the filter to make the changes to the image, and
then, if you don't like the effect, undoing it and starting over).

Fig. 1.43

Using proxies and
previews to adjust
and view filter
modifications.

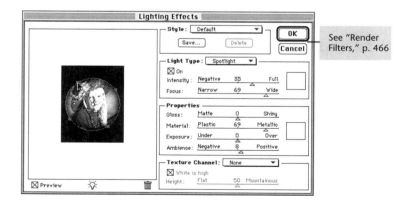

See "Render
Filters," p. 466

Drag and Drop between Images

One of the more flashy buzz-phrases of modern computing is "drag and drop." Well, far be it from Photoshop to be left out. That's right. You can now drag and drop portions of one image to another, as shown in figure 1.44.

Fig. 1.44

Dragging and dropping between images.

Flower will appear here in Portrait image

Primarily, this feature is a time-saver because it eliminates steps from the copy-and-paste process. Using it in combination with layers is a great way to combine elements of multiple images to create new images or alter existing ones.

Getting More Help

If, after going through the tutorial, the Photoshop manual, and this book, you still can't find the answer to a question or solve a problem, all is not lost. Plenty of additional help is available. Or, perhaps you're like many Photoshop users who just want to get all the functionality and creativity possible out of the program. In either case, check this list of resources for getting more support and tips on using Photoshop.

Adobe Systems

Where else than the source? Nobody knows Photoshop better than its creators, and Adobe's technical support team is one of the best in the business. The company provides several support options, including:

▶ **Technical Support.** Adobe provides one free call to technical support. The phone numbers are listed on the Roledex card (and in several other places) in the Photoshop package. After that, you can purchase additional support time or call a 900-number.

▶ **Fax Request Line.** You can get unlimited, free support on Adobe's 24-hour automated fax line. The number for all Adobe products is: 408-986-6560.

▶ **Automated Technical Support.** This is a full-time, computer-driven diagnostic system that provides answers to the most commonly asked questions. The number for all Adobe products is: 408-986-6587.

▶ **Electronic Bulletin Board.** Here's a treasure chest. Abode's BBS is an electronic meeting place for downloading drivers and filters, getting tips, and finding out about issues confronted (and often solved) by other Photoshop users. The phone number for all Adobe products is: 408-562-6839.

On-Line

On-line services, such as CompuServe, provide a wealth of information on using Photoshop (and millions of other computer issues). The ones listed here are not only a good source for solving technical problems, they're also a good place to exchange design and technique ideas with thousands of Photoshop users, desktop publishers, and digital designers.

▶ **Adobe Forum.** Adobe Systems has a strong presence on CompuServe, in both the PC and Mac sections. You can find them easily with CompuServe's GO command. Simply type **GO ADOBE**.

▶ **DTP Forum.** Another information-packed resource is the desktop publishing forum on CompuServe. Here you can exchange ideas with some of the world's most successful and experienced desktop publishers. You'll also find thousands of helpful files, including images, fonts, filters, and lots of tips and techniques. Get there with **GoDTP**.

▶ **Photoshop Forum.** For Photoshop-specific issues you'll find a wealth of information in the Photoshop Forum on America Online. This forum also has images, fonts, filters, and lots of tips for downloading. The keyword is **Photoshop**.

Publications

Few software applications are more widely used among Macintosh users than Photoshop. You'll find monthly advice, tips, and techniques on getting the most from Photoshop in the leading Macintosh trade magazines. Other indispensable resources are magazines devoted to desktop publishing.

▶ *MacUser*. Published by Ziff-Davis, MacUser is a monthly magazine containing a hands-on desktop publishing section that often highlights features and procedures in Photoshop. You can find *MacUser* on many newsstands, or get a subscription by calling 800-627-2247.

▶ *MacWorld*. Published by MacWorld Communications, Inc, *MacWorld* often carries tips and techniques on Photoshop in the magazine's "Graphics" section. You can find *MacWorld* on many newsstands, or obtain a subscription by calling 800-288-6848.

▶ *Publish*. Published by Integrated Media, *Publish* is the leading desktop publishing magazine. Its features and make-over sections often carry useful information on using Photoshop in digital design. You can get a subscription to *Publish* by calling 800-685-3435.

Where To Go from Here

▶ If you're a seasoned Photoshop user, be sure to check out chapter 2, "Exploring What's New in Photoshop 3."

▶ Hungry for more information on getting started with Photoshop? Chapter 3, "Photoshop Basics," takes up where this chapter leaves off. You'll learn the concepts behind computer graphics, such as file formats and the different types of images you can process and export from Photoshop to other applications, such as desktop publishing and presentation programs.

▶ If you just loaded Photoshop and are new to using it, you'll want to configure the program and calibrate your monitor. Chapter 4, "Setting Up the Photoshop Environment," takes you through the setting preferences and calibration procedures, which allow you to set up the program to best suit your needs and working environment.

Exploring What's New in Photoshop 3

Are you tired of wimpy to-the-right-of-the-decimal-point incremental upgrades? Photoshop 3 won't waste your time. There's a lot of new features included to make your work easier. This chapter introduces you to these new features.

by Bill Harrel

CHAPTER 2

Working Faster

A common complaint with Photoshop for Macintosh is the program's sluggishness. Graphics processing (image editing), especially Photoshop filters to giant image files, is one of the most demanding processes your Mac performs. New Apple technology, of which Photoshop 3 takes full advantage, gives image editing a huge shot in the arm.

▶ **Native PowerPC.** Everybody is excited about Apple's new PowerPC (Power Macintosh) technology. The PowerPC chip in the new Power Macintosh has the potential to provide the extra power boost for which image editors, desktop publishers, and digital designers clamor. Photoshop 2.5.1 came with a PowerPC accelerator plug that adds some speed to the program. Version 3 is written from the ground up as native PowerPC code, providing optimal performance on the Power Macintosh. Note that you still can use Photoshop on a conventional Mac. The install program knows which version to place on your hard disk.

▶ **ATM 3.8.1.** For Power Macintosh to run optimally, all software running on it should be native PowerPC. Since the release of Power Mac, a complaint among desktop publishers, designers, and others who use Type 1 fonts with Adobe Type Manager has been that version 3.6 is non-native. These users contend that Adobe's Type Manager slowed down Power Mac processing. Tests by leading Macintosh magazines show that ATM does, indeed, degrade Power Macintosh performance by as much as 20 percent. With Photoshop 3 you'll find the latest native PowerPC-ready version. If you have a Power Mac, install ATM. (If you're not using a Power Mac, you still can install ATM 3.8.1 for additional performance and functionality.) You'll also find several Type 1 fonts on the CD-ROM disc.

Getting Even More Creative

Photoshop and its support of plug-ins is famous in the design world for versatility. With some imagination, users can achieve levels of creativity unheard of before image editing came to the desktop. Version 3 continues the legacy. Exciting new enhancements can bring out the eloquent designer in you.

▶ **Multiple Layers.** Hands down, multiple layers support is the most important enhancement to this new version of Photoshop. Basically, layers allow you to place objects on clear overlays, similar to acetate sheets. The layers keep objects separate and stop them from blending into the background level of the image. This makes adding, editing, and deleting objects much easier. Layers can be hidden and made nonprintable, allowing for tremendous editing and proofing power. You also can change the opacity and blending of layers, allowing for interesting special effects.

▶ **Dust & Scratches Plug-In.** Have you ever scanned a photograph only to find that glaringly obvious dirt and scratches have all but ruined it? The Dust & Scratches plug-in helps alleviate this problem. Software has not yet reached the ability to determine what should be on the image and what should not be, but the Dust & Scratches plug-in does a reasonable job of eliminating defects in the image.

▶ **Color Range.** The new Color Range command lets you easily create anti-aliased masks based on selected colors. If you're new to image-editing software, this probably sounds like mumbo-jumbo. Basically, Color Range makes it easy to select all areas of an image based on similar colors. You can then apply changes to the mask. There's a lot more power here than this simple explanation covers, but basically you'll find this command beneficial for working with images containing scattered occurrences of the like colors.

▶ **Filter Factory.** Here's a simple but powerful idea. The Filter Factory lets you design and name your own Photoshop plug-ins. Here's your opportunity to save the design effects you use often.

▶ **Lighting Effects Plug-In.** This new filter lets you apply multiple light sources, and add textures to an image, and modify textures. You can choose from a range of colors, intensities, and angles. This is a special effects filter that allows you to add artistic enhancements to an image based on light (or tinted light), and set from where that light (or multiple sources of light) emanates.

▶ **Mezzotint Filter.** Previously, Mezzotint was an effect available only at a production house. The Mezzotint filter renders color or grayscale images into a series of stylized dots, lines, or strokes. This is one more way to add automatic special effects to your images.

Getting More Work Done Faster

Nowadays, everyone is in a hurry. We want everything in our lives to happen right now. In part, computers are responsible for our impatience. Image editing on a computer is hundreds of times faster than by hand. We've come to expect (and applaud) features that reduce steps and save time. Photoshop 3 contains several new features designed to make your life easier and allow you to spend more time with your family and pets.

▶ **CMYK Preview.** Monitors display images by mixing percentages of red, green, and blue (RGB). Printers and printing presses mix cyan, magenta, yellow, and black (CMYK). To get the best results from a CMYK printer, it's often necessary to change the color mode of an image from RGB to CMYK with Mode, CMYK Color. When you do this, however, sometimes colors shift, or change. It can take some time to perform an RGB-CMYK conversion of large image files. CMYK Preview lets you see a screen representation of the mode change before you actually invoke the CMYK Color command.

▶ **Gamut Warning.** When a printer can't print a certain color, that color is said to be out of the printer's *gamut*. The colors that can't be printed are especially subject to color shifts. Invoking Gamut Warning (Mode menu) highlights all the areas outside the printer's gamut, allowing you to make edits that are more likely to ensure successful printing.

▶ **File Information Tags.** This feature lets you assign information tags to image files, such as photographer's name, date and location of the photograph, caption, and other information required by the IPTC worldwide standard for newspapers. The information you can tag to image files is extensive, including origin, category, keyword search terms, and so on.

▶ **Replace Color.** Somewhat similar to Color Range, Replace Color allows you to create a mask based on specific colors and then correct the color by adjusting hue, brightness, and saturation levels. Replace Colors works on selected portions of the image or the entire image. This is a quick and dirty way to replace colors throughout an image or selection. It works similar to search and replace.

▶ **Selective Color Correction.** Selective Colors allows you to edit images or selections by adjusting ink amounts of individual color channels or separation plates. Basically, this means you can correct or change colors individually throughout an image or selection. This is a good way to bring colors into a printer's gamut range.

▶ **Sponge Tool.** The Sponge tool allows you to interactively saturate and desaturate colors, or adjust grays. *Saturation* means less gray, and *desaturation* means more gray. Increasing gray in bright or intense colors generally dulls them. You'll find this another effective way to bring colors within a printer's gamut range.

Interfacing with Photoshop

If you hate change, you're probably not too happy with the ever-evolving interfaces of computer software. Just when you get used to doing things one way, somebody releases a new standard. But if you think about it, most often the new way is easier and more effective. Photoshop 3 has several interface changes that alter the way you interact with the program. This section takes a look at the new interface changes.

▶ **Brush Size Preview.** A drawback in Photoshop 2.5.1 and previous versions is that no matter what size you set your brush, the cursor stays the same size. This is misleading and awkward, making it difficult to apply the brush precisely. Photoshop 3 allows you to set your brush cursor to the exact size in the Brushes palette. Now, when you erase, you'll erase precisely instead of being forced to guess where the action will land in relationship to the cursor.

▶ **Commands Palette.** Use this new palette to assign frequently-used commands to keys or keystroke combinations. You can then display the assignments on a floating palette. The commands can be arranged in the palette in any order, and you can color code the commands and display them in multiple columns. You can also save task-specific Commands palette schemes and load them at will.

▶ **New Palette Design.** Palettes can be resized and arranged anywhere on the desktop. You can also modify the way some palettes look. The Layers palette, for example, lets you adjust the size of layer thumbnails. You can also collapse palettes into the title bar. This lets you further eliminate clutter and free up image-editing real estate. You can also recombine palettes into new groups and drag them into their own palettes as you need to.

▶ **Drag and Drop.** Drag and drop means pretty much what it says: to drag an object or selection from one place and drop it at another. In this case, though, you drag and drop from image window to image window, or from document to document. Basically, this feature is a shortcut that replaces using cut and paste or importing into images.

▶ **Proxies and Previews.** A drawback to using filters on large image files is that, depending on your computer, it can take several minutes for Photoshop to convert the file. Proxies and previews allow you to see how the changes you make in filter dialog boxes affect the images—before you click OK. Some dialog boxes have filters that contain preview windows right in the dialog box, letting you make changes interactively on the preview with your mouse. Other filters show the preview directly on the image, by manipulating the pixels in the screen image without actually changing the file. Some of the filters show changes in the dialog box and the image window.

Deluxe CD-ROM Edition Features

If you own a CD-ROM drive, you'll find a few extras on the Deluxe CD-ROM Edition disc included with Photoshop 3. This section looks at the additional items on the CD-ROM disc.

▶ **Adobe Acrobat Reader.** An exciting new development in computing is the portable document approach to creating documents. While (as of this writing) it hasn't really caught on yet, a major portable document platform contender is Adobe's Acrobat. Basically, Acrobat provides a way to transfer and share files electronically, complete with colors, pictures, tables, and so on, regardless of the platform or applications in which the document originated. Acrobat converts files to Adobe's Portable Document Format (PDF). The inclusion of Acrobat Reader in Photoshop 3 allows you to view and print PDF files on your Mac.

▶ **Stock Photography and Digital Art Show.** For the first time, Adobe is including a collection of stock photos on CD with Photoshop. In all, you get several images from top collections, such as PhotoDisc, Digital Media, and others. Be mindful of the copyrights, though. Many of the images are not offered without restrictions.

▶ **Multimedia Tutorial.** If you've seen the Deluxe CD-ROM Edition of Adobe Illustrator, you're already impressed with Adobe's multimedia tutorials. The tutorials consist primarily of several hands-on sessions narrated by the designers of the program. Version 3 of Photoshop also has a multimedia tutorial. In other words, the people who wrote and designed Photoshop show you how to use it. Imagine that!

▶ **Third-Party Plug-Ins.** Part of Adobe's brute strength is the ability of third-party vendors to design plug-ins that add functionality to the program. Included on the CD-ROM disc, you'll find a collection of sample plug-in filters for creating special effects and other functions. You can use these plug-ins to enhance your documents, to get an idea of what's available in the plug-in market, and to get information on where to buy additional plug-ins.

▶ **Other Utilities.** You'll also find the following utilities on the CD-ROM disc: the PostScript printer driver 8.1.1, an upgrade to the latest version; several plug-ins from third-party vendors, such as Alien Skin Software, Aldus, Kai's Power Tools, and several others; several textures for use with the new Lighting filter; the latest version of Apple QuickTime (version 2); a folder full of technical notes from Adobe; and on-line documentation in Adobe Acrobat format.

Getting around What's Not in Photoshop 3

No program is perfect—even if thousands of Photoshop users would disagree. This section is a wish list of missing features that would add even more versatility to the program. It also includes some suggestions for working around the missing features.

▶ **Better Spot Color Support.** If you're familiar with the leading desktop publishing (PageMaker and QuarkXPress) and illustration (FreeHand and Illustrator) programs, you know that they contain excellent spot color support. When you import an image containing spot colors, for example, the colors are added to the Color palette. Each program can print spot color separations. While Photoshop 3 has a PANTONE palette and you can assign PANTONE spot colors to images, you cannot print spot color separations. One way to get around this is to use In Software's Plate Maker plug-in, which allows you to export the spot color definition in a PostScript format and print it from another program. Plug-ins are discussed in chapter 15, "Using Photoshop's Plug-In Filters," and chapter 16, "Third-Party Plug-Ins."

▶ **Fractal Painter-Like Brush Effects.** If you're familiar with Fractal's fantastic special effects package, Painter, you may be wondering how to get the same fancy brush effects in Photoshop. If you're not familiar with Painter, it goes beyond most image editing software by providing several of the brush tips and other effects often found in high-end production houses. For example, Painter's brush tips include charcoals, pastels, watercolors, and many others. Creating such custom brushes in Photoshop would be a real chore, and in some cases impossible. The remedy (other than using Painter) is to buy Xaos Software's Paint Alchemy, which is a collection of predesigned Photoshop brush palettes.

Where To Go from Here

▶ For more information on layering, turn to chapter 10, "Working with Layers."

▶ The new plug-ins, and plug-ins in general, are discussed in chapter 15, "Using Photoshop's Plug-In Filters," and chapter 16, "Third-Party Plug-Ins."

▶ Converting images to CMYK and using the CMYK preview are discussed in chapter 13, "Understanding Color" and in Part VI, "Publishing." You'll also find information on gamuts in chapter 13 and Part VI.

▶ The new Sponge tool is discussed in "The Editing Tools" section of chapter 8, "Drawing, Painting, and Editing."

▶ Setting the new brush size option and other preferences are discussed in chapter 4, "Setting Up the Photoshop Environment."

Photoshop Basics

Not long ago, computer graphics were blocky, jagged, and clumsy looking. They looked as if a machine had drawn them—not a very smart or talented machine, at that. Seemingly overnight, computers have reached a new level of ability. Almost every graphic you see now—from simple flyers to the weather and commercials on television—comes from computers. The personal computer is as essential as paint, ink, and easels (also products of technology).

by Bill Harrel

CHAPTER 3

To get the most from Photoshop, you should understand the differences between the two basic graphics formats, vector and bitmapped, and when to use which type. This chapter also looks at the various graphics types supported by Photoshop. It explains which types you should use when exporting to other applications, such as desktop publishing and presentation programs.

When you finish this chapter, you can move on to chapter 4, "Setting Up the Photoshop Environment," where you will make informed choices about how to configure the program for the work you plan to do.

A Computer Graphics Primer

Computer graphics come in two basic formats: *vector* and *bitmapped*. The differences between the two are like night and day. Photoshop is a bitmap graphics program (bitmap editor) that deals primarily with bitmaps. To create and edit vector graphics, you should use a draw program, such as Adobe Illustrator.

Graphics programmers didn't create the two types to confuse you. As you will see from the following discussion, the two types are quite necessary.

Vector Graphics

Draw programs, such as CorelDRAW! (Windows), MacDraw, or Adobe Illustrator, create vector graphics. Vector graphics are drawn mathematically, using lines and curves, rather than the multiple fixed dots used in bitmaps. The immediate advantage of this format is that the files are generally much smaller than bitmaps and usually don't take as long to print.

More important than file size and print time, however, is that vector graphics are scaleable and can support many artistic qualities better than bitmaps. When an image is scaleable, you can resize it without losing quality. Vector graphics are very adept at handling drawings that consist of lines and arcs, or images where elements are well defined (see fig. 3.1).

The vector graphics format used by Illustrator is more efficient at creating graphics with intricate details, such as text and smooth lines.

Notice the detail of the drawings in figure 3.1. Fine lines are truly fine, as are text and flat surfaces. The vector format's ability to support high

Fig. 3.1

Examples of vector graphics.

resolution allows more control over detail, which makes it ideal for technical drawings and diagrams.

Vector graphics provide more control over the final output resolution. Because they are device independent, they do not have a fixed resolution. In other words, you can print the graphic at whatever resolution (measured in dots per inch [dpi]) your final output device supports. Bitmapped graphics, on the other hand, retain the resolution at which they were created.

Often, the quality of a graphic depends largely on the resolution. There are many reasons for this. The most significant is that as resolution increases, dots get smaller, which allows for more flexible dot placement within an image. This translates into smoother lines and evenly spread fills.

Vector graphics also are better at high-resolution fountain fills, such as the Illustrator linear and radial fills and blends shown in figure 3.2, and all sorts of other special effects you can't achieve with the same level of success in bitmapped graphics.

Fig. 3.2

Example of effects more suitable to vector graphics: linear gradient, radial gradient, and a blend.

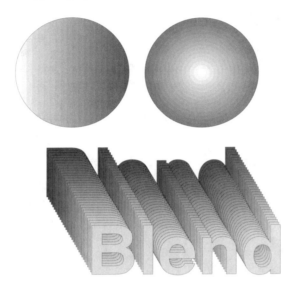

Another advantage of vector graphics is that many of them, such as Illustrator's Encapsulated PostScript (EPS), Designer's DRW files, and some others, provide direct support for Type 1 and TrueType fonts. What this means is that, like a word processor or desktop publishing file, you can open and close the file as often as you like, even import it into other programs, and the text remains editable.

When you use type in a bitmap editor such as Photoshop, it becomes part of the graphic, a bitmap itself, and is no longer editable as a text string.

Because they are drawn mathematically and retain their resolution, vector graphics, unlike bitmapped graphics, can be resized without losing quality. (To a certain extent, bitmapped images can be reduced without loss of quality. However, reducing them too much can cause them to lose clarity. You will have little or no luck, however, enlarging them in your layouts.)

PostScript Graphics

Adobe's Encapsulated PostScript (EPS) graphics format is the most widely used and most versatile vector graphic. It is the graphics format of choice for desktop publishers and designers. Besides, PostScript is the language used in today's high-resolution typesetting equipment. As you will see in the discussion of graphics output in chapter 21, "Photoshop for the Desktop Publisher," it is a must for reproducing quality four-color documents on an offset printing press.

Opening EPS Images in Photoshop

By the very nature of object-based vector graphics, they are not really conducive to extensive editing in Photoshop. Paths and separate objects, and the relationship between them, are not maintained. When Photoshop opens an EPS image, it converts, or "renders," it into a Photoshop, or bitmapped image. You can then edit it as bitmap, but, after you save it, the image's vector qualities are lost forever.

Another thing to remember about Photoshop and EPS files is that the program can open only EPS images saved from Illustrator. You cannot open images saved from Aldus FreeHand or CorelDRAW! without first saving them to Illustrator format.

When you open an EPS image in Photoshop, the Rasterize Adobe Illustrator Format dialog box, shown in figure 3.3, appears. From here, you choose in which mode (color, grayscale, and so on) to open the image, as well as several other parameters. You also can control image size, resolution, and anti-aliasing in this dialog box. Resolution and basic color issues are discussed a little later in this chapter. You can find an in-depth discussion of color in chapter 13, "Understanding Color." Discussions of resolution can be found in chapter 21, "Photoshop for the Desktop Publisher."

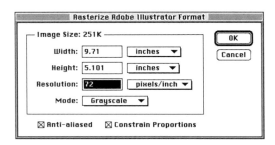

Fig. 3.3

The Rasterize Adobe Illustrator Format dialog box allows you to control how Photoshop displays PostScript images.

Getting Started

You should pay special attention to the Anti-aliased check box at the bottom of the dialog box. Remember that anti-aliasing smoothes object edges, thereby cutting down on jaggies. This works especially well with text and other clearly delineated objects. When opening EPS files at low resolutions—under about 150 pixels (dots)—you should turn anti-aliasing on. At higher resolutions, jaggies are less of an issue.

Tip

Use Place To Import EPS Images as a Floating Selection

When you open an EPS image, it opens as a background, as does any other image. To bring EPS images into an existing image as a floating selection that you can move, edit, and color before placing permanently, open the File menu and choose Place. For further versatility, place the EPS file on a separate layer.

Saving EPS Files from Photoshop

The main reason to save a Photoshop image as EPS is to import it into Illustrator. Unfortunately, Illustrator doesn't support any other formats. When importing or placing bitmapped images in Illustrator, your editing options are limited. You should make most of your changes in Photoshop, because Illustrator can do little other than change the colors in an image, display, resize, and print the file; you will have to use it primarily as is.

When you choose EPS in the Save As dialog box, the EPS Format dialog box opens, providing several options for saving the image. These options primarily control the appearance of the bitmapped header saved with the EPS file. Let's look at the options in the EPS Format dialog box (see fig. 3.4).

Fig. 3.4

Use the EPS Format dialog box to choose the type of image preview that saves with the file.

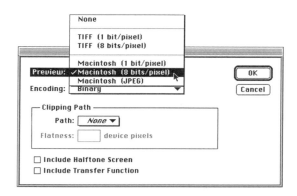

▶ **Preview.** By themselves, PostScript graphics cannot display on a monitor. To do so, the image file must include a bitmapped preview. This option controls the appearance of that preview. There are five options: two (TIFF) previews for PCs and three Macintosh formats. The bit depth (bits-per-pixel is discussed later in this chapter) designates the number of colors: 1-bit is black and white and 8-bit is 256 colors. Macintosh JPEG creates a 24-bit (16.7 colors) preview and compresses it to save disk space.

▶ **Encoding.** This option tells Photoshop to which code scheme to export: binary or ASCII. When exporting to Illustrator, use binary. It compresses the file by using a shorter encoding scheme. ASCII stands for American Standard Code for Information Interchange. This is simply a big term for text file. ASCII creates larger files, but it is compatible with more programs and printers, including several PC programs. (Also, when you're saving a CMYK EPS [CMYK stands for cyan, magenta, yellow, and black] file, you can choose whether to save the file with a JPEG compression scheme, making the file even smaller.)

▶ **Clipping Path.** The Path option in the Clipping Path area of the dialog box saves the clipped path with the EPS file. You can find a detailed discussion of clipping paths in chapter 11, "Drawing and Editing Paths."

▶ **Include Halftone Screen.** An advantage of saving an image from Photoshop as an EPS file is that EPS can maintain halftone screen settings, which can be vital to getting the desired printing results. Halftone screens are discussed in several places throughout this book, including the "Resolution and Screen Frequency" section of this chapter.

▶ **Include Transfer Function.** This option interacts with an option in the Page Setup dialog box. The Photoshop Page Setup dialog box allows you to adjust an image's contrast and brightness when clicking the Transfer button. All this check box does is allow you to save the Transfer settings from Page Setup with your EPS file. Simple enough, right?

QuarkXPress DCS Images

Before the TIFF 5.0 graphics format (discussed later), there really was no way to color separate bitmapped images in a layout program. So, Quark came up with EPS/DCS (Desktop Color Separations) files. Basically, what

DCS does is preseparate the image and save it into five separate PostScript files—one for each CMYK plate, and one for the image preview.

When you open the EPS Format dialog box while saving a CMYK image, Photoshop gives you the option of saving the file as DCS (see fig. 3.5). While this technique works, sometimes it requires four or five times the disk space. Since the advent of TIFF 5.0, or CMYK TIFF, it's not really necessary to use DCS format. However, not all versions of layout programs support DCS; it's good to know that you now have an alternative.

Fig. 3.5

The Desktop Color Separations EPS Format option.

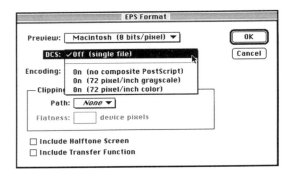

Bitmapped Graphics

Bitmapped graphics are created in bitmap editors, or paint programs, such as Photoshop. Nowadays, however, most paint programs are referred to as image-editing, photograph touch-up, or digital darkroom software. Granted, most of them have become much more adept at photograph enhancement; but no matter what you call them, they're still bitmap editors.

As you've seen, vector graphics have several advantages over bitmapped graphics. Bitmapped graphics consist of a series of dots in fixed patterns and print in blobs, much like a rubber stamp. Each dot is programmed into a computer file. If the graphic contains a lot of grayscale or color information, the file can be gigantic and take a long time to print. Depending on the image, bitmapped graphics also can lack some artistic features of vector formats. Low-resolution bitmaps do not, for example, reproduce curved and fine lines or text nearly as well. Nor are they as flexible in creating intricate shading and certain special effects. High-resolution bitmaps can create large, unruly files.

Bitmapped graphics are device dependent, which means that they retain the same resolution, regardless of the capabilities of the device you use to print them.

This is not to say that bitmapped formats are bad. In fact, they are essential to many types of desktop publishing and design. It is the same characteristics that make them unsuitable for some images that make them better for others. The way they use dots makes them ideal for lifelike images, such as photographs, some sketches, and painting-like graphics.

Grayscale and color photograph scanning requires bitmapped formats. In fact, print shops have used a similar procedure to prepare photographs for printing for years. Using special cameras (today, many shops use scanners), they turn the photograph into a halftone (or color separations for color pictures). A *halftone* is a translation of the picture in dots, which makes it possible for the printing press to reproduce it. A closer look is taken at halftoning in chapters 22, "Photoshop for the Digital Designer," and 23, "Photoshop for the Presenter," where preparing images for printing and layout are discussed.

Figure 3.6 shows a few examples of bitmapped graphics. Notice that the chair is more of a paint or charcoal sketch with smudges and thick paintbrush-like lines.

TIFF Graphics

When working with bitmapped images for importing into layouts, TIFF (Tagged Image File Format) is ideal. Developed by Aldus to standardize scanning, TIFF has become highly useful and reliable. TIFF supports CMYK color separations and LZW (Lempel-Ziv-Welch) compression, and can be brought into virtually any layout, presentation, database, or word processing program. Photoshop opens TIFF files directly, exactly as they're saved. Exporting them is almost as straightforward. You don't have to make many decisions.

When you save a Photoshop image as a TIFF file, the TIFF Options dialog box appears (see fig. 3.7). This dialog box has only two options: Byte Order and LZW Compression. Byte order refers to whether the image is saved as PC or Macintosh. LZW toggles on and off compression.

Fig. 3.6

Example of types of images suitable to bitmapped formats and image editing software.

Fig. 3.7

The TIFF Options
dialog box.

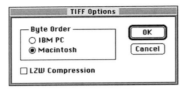

▶ **Byte Order.** Here's an easy one. Mac and PC TIFF formats are slightly different (though neither platform has trouble reading one or the other). If you plan to use the image on a Mac, select Macintosh. To use the image on a PC, choose IBM PC.

▶ **LZW Compression**. Because image editing files can be so large, compression is a significant issue. LZW compression is a routine built right into the TIFF format that substitutes frequently used code strings for shorter codes strings. The beauty of the LZW approach is that, unlike other compression routines, you don't lose image quality, and most major DTP programs, including FreeHand, QuarkXPress, and PageMaker, support it.

Other Graphics Formats

Basically, graphics formats fall into either the vector or bitmap categories. In Photoshop, most supported formats are bitmapped. Photoshop supports a slew of file formats; you can open and save about 20 different kinds of image files from the Open and Save dialog boxes, and you can expand on these through plug-ins, which place additional formats on the File, Acquire and File, Export command submenus. In this section, we look briefly at each of the more significant formats and their uses. As you will see, often these other formats simply provide compatibility with other programs and platforms, rather than give you any more versatility than found in the TIFF and EPS formats.

Photoshop Native Formats

You may be wondering how Photoshop's native format found its way deep into this subcategory. Well, the native format is important, but only to Photoshop, (except for Specular Collage, which will read and produce Photoshop files.) You can't use it anywhere else. If you want to use Photoshop images in another application, you will have to save the images in TIFF, EPS, or one of the other formats discussed in this section.

Photoshop 3 supports two formats: Photoshop 2.0 and 3. Use the previous version to share files with other people who have not yet upgraded.

There are many benefits to the Photoshop 3 format. It saves each image with any channel, layer, path, or other program-specific changes you may make, which are not supported by other formats. You should save images in native Photoshop while editing, and leave them in said format until the image is exactly as you want it before exporting to another, more compatible file type.

PICT

PICT is the standard native Macintosh picture format. It is based on the Mac's QuickDraw language that interprets and displays data on your monitor. It's an apt format that's almost as versatile as EPS, but it does not handle fonts as well. PICT is one of the few formats that can handle both vector and bitmapped objects. PICT allows you to save images at any bits-per-pixel depth or resolution. PICT also supports 32-bit images, which means that you can save a mask channel with RGB images. (Pixel depth is discussed a little later in this chapter. Masks are discussed in chapter 12, "Using Masks and Channels.")

When you save a PICT file from Photoshop, the PICT File Options dialog box appears (see fig. 3.8). From here, you choose the bits-per-pixel rate (16 or 32) and the JPEG compression rate (only if QuickTime is installed). Keep in mind when choosing compression that JPEG can degrade image quality at higher rates. On the other hand, the higher the quality, the larger the file. Life has so many trade-offs.

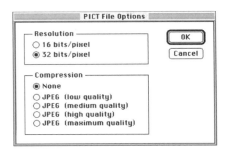

Fig. 3.8

The PICT File Options dialog box lets you control how the PICT image is formatted.

PCX

Created by Z-Soft for use with its once-popular PC Paintbrush, PCX is the oldest PC bitmapped format. In many ways, it's quite similar to TIFF, but does not support CMYK separations. It does, however, support 16.7 million colors.

JPEG

JPEG stands for Joint Photographic Experts Group, which is the committee that created this file format. This format is desirable because you can compress images when you save them. However, unlike TIFF's LZW compression scheme, depending on the rate of compression, you sacrifice quality for image size.

Known as a lossy compression scheme, JPEG loses data as it compresses. But, at least you can control how much data is lost. When you save a JPEG image, the JPEG Options dialog box appears (see fig. 3.9), allowing you to choose one of four settings. Until you learn more about compression, you should probably use the highest setting, or maximum quality.

Fig. 3.9

The JPEG Options dialog box lets you control the compression rate.

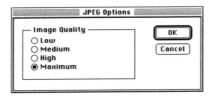

Image compression saves disk space (and allows for shorter transmission times). However, when working on images—especially when applying filters—the routine of opening, editing, saving, reopening, and so on, can greatly degrade them. My advice is that you use compression only when necessary, and that you use it only to store files after all of the editing is performed.

Finally, you've probably noticed that PICT, EPS, and a few others support JPEG compression. The above advice goes for them, too.

Photo-CD

An increasingly popular image format is Kodak's Photo CD. (This section is just a brief mention of this format; you will find an extensive discussion in chapter 7, "Photo-CD Images.") Basically, this format allows you to take images and negatives to a Photo-CD service bureau and have images scanned and saved on a CD-ROM disc. The images are saved in several resolutions and bits-per-pixel depth.

Photoshop can open Photo-CD images directly, but you cannot save in this format. When you open a file saved in this format, the Photo-CD Options dialog box displays, allowing you to set pixel depth and a few other options, such as color mode.

While many DTP programs—PageMaker, QuarkXPress, and others—support Photo CD, they cannot color-separate them. When using these images, you will need Photoshop to convert them to a more compatible format, such as CMYK, TIFF, or EPS, or, when using a prepress separation program, RGB TIFF.

CompuServe GIF

This format is used primarily on CompuServe for viewing and transmitting images on-line. Like TIFF, it uses LZW compression. But, unlike TIFF, it supports only 256 colors.

Premier Filmstrip

Adobe's Premier is a QuickTime movie editing program. While it allows you to perform several special effects—merge frames, fades, and others—you cannot edit individual frames. Here's where Photoshop comes in. You can bring a Filmstrip format into Photoshop, as shown in figure 3.10, change the background frame-by-frame, add objects, and have a ball.

Note that for this procedure to work, the Filmstrip format must first be saved from Premier. You cannot open a QuickTime movie in Photoshop. Note also that you can save only Filmstrip format images back to that format; other images cannot be saved as Filmstrips.

Fig. 3.10

An Adobe Premier filmstrip brought into Photoshop for editing.

Caution

Don't Resize Premier Filmstrips

Don't change the size of Filmstrip documents in Photoshop. If you do, you will not be able to convert them back to Filmstrip format. Edit them to your heart's content, but do not alter them with Image Size or Canvas Size. You also cannot make mode changes.

Other Formats

In addition to the formats discussed above, Photoshop supports several other non-mainstream image formats, such Amiga's IFF and HAM, Window's Paint BMP, Scitex, and others. Again, these formats primarily provide compatibility between platforms and other programs.

You can find information on using images from other programs and platforms in chapter 5, "Importing and Exporting Images." Scanning and editing scanned images are discussed in chapter 6, "Scanning Images." Mac to PC and back issues are discussed in Appendix E, "Swapping PC and Mac Photoshop Files."

But remember, when preparing images for layout in other programs, most of the time you will wind up with a TIFF or EPS file. They keep you compatible with the world and provide the best results.

Resolution and Screen Frequency

Each output device—laser printer, monitor, slide recorder, and image setter—works differently and requires you to prepare graphics uniquely. Each reproduction device also has its own requirements, as do the media—paper, slides, transparencies, and so on—that it prints on. For example, a grayscale photograph printed on newsprint requires line screens and resolution settings different from those used to print the same photograph on glossy paper.

More than any other variable, resolution and screen frequency play essential roles in how well your graphics reproduce. The purpose of this section is to familiarize you with these terms and to present an overview of their importance. The next sections discuss screen frequency and resolution in each type of graphics reproduction.

Color (or bits-per-pixel) depth is discussed in the section "Color Basics."

> **Note**
>
> Most of the discussion of graphics output in this chapter pertains not only to Photoshop but also to all graphics applications in general, and all DTP applications.

Resolution

Most computer users are familiar with printer resolutions. For those who are not, let's do a brief refresher. Hard copy output devices—printers, imagesetters, slide recorders, and plotters—print at various rates of dots per inch (dpi). Most laser printers, for example, print at 300 or 600 dpi. Imagesetters (photo-quality typesetters) print from 900 dpi up to 3,000 dpi and beyond. The benefit of higher resolution is smaller dots. Smaller dots mean more detail and subtleties—sharper lines and curves—and, more importantly, cleaner halftone screens and photographs.

A combination of screen frequency and resolution affects image quality. Resolution is important because it determines the printer's ability to print higher screen frequencies.

Screen Frequency

Screens and *halftones* (these terms are often used interchangeably) are percentages of solids. When you tell a program to shade a box at 20 percent, you are creating a screen. Grayscale photographs, where shades of gray are made up of percentages of black, are also screens. So are the percentages of colors that make up a four-color drawing or photograph. Four-color images are created on a printing press by mixing percentages of cyan, magenta, yellow, and black (CMYK). These concepts are developed fully in chapter 13, "Understanding Color."

Conventionally, halftones are created with a camera. Fine-mesh screens (measured in lines per inch, or lpi) are laid over the object to be screened. The mesh separates the image into lines of tiny dots. The size and frequency of the dots determine where the printing press puts ink on paper, thus creating halftones.

Computers and scanners have all but eliminated the need for the fine-mesh screens, but printing presses still work primarily the same. It is important to consider screen frequency when preparing documents for the printing press, for a variety of reasons.

The most important consideration is how ink spreads on different paper types. For example, taking into account the difference in how soft newsprint and coated glossy paper accept ink is crucial. On soft paper, ink soaks in and spreads, causing the ink to run together. Glossy paper is much more forgiving.

To compensate, halftones printed on newsprint require a *loose* screen (about 75 to 90 lpi), so ink dots do not spread together, muddying the image. Coated paper, where ink spread is minimal, works best at 133 lpi or higher so that the coarseness of the screen is not noticeable. (Good examples of these two paper types are the pages in this book. The text pages, like this one, are soft and coarse. The color insert pages are glossy and less absorbent.) The trick is to match the lpi to the paper's absorbency so that as little as possible of the screen's coarseness shows, without degrading the halftone through ink spread.

Another aspect of halftone printing affected by lpi (and resolution) is grayscale. Manipulating screen frequency and grayscale can make a tremendous difference in the quality and clarity of *each* photograph.

You will find extensive information on resolution and screen frequency in chapter 21, "Photoshop for the Desktop Publisher."

Tip

Avoid Mistakes by Rubbing Shoulders with the Professionals

When preparing a document for slide recorders and the print shop, work closely with your service bureau and print shop. Before creating the graphics and laying out the document, decide on what medium(s) the work will be reproduced (i.e., paper type, slides, copier, etc.). Then consult your service bureau and print shop regarding the best resolution and lpi settings for that medium. Don't worry about seeming like a beginner. All professional designers work very closely with their vendors to assure the best results.

Computer Color Basics

Perhaps even more confusing than image resolution is color depth. Images (and computer display systems) are rated by the number of distinct colors they can display. The range is from 1 (black and white) to 16.7 million colors, with 256 being the most common. The number of colors an image can contain is referred to as its *color depth*.

The number of colors a display system is capable of depends on its bits-per-pixel rate. Four-bits-per-pixel, for example, provides 16 colors; 24-bits-per-pixel provides 16.7 million colors. (When talking about computer image color, a discussion of display systems also is pertinent. The number of colors an image is saved at coincides with display system bits-per-pixel rate.)

The 16-color model is the easiest one to use to demonstrate this concept. Since there are four bits-per-pixel, you have 4 x 4 (16) possible RGB combinations. As the number of bits per pixels increases, the possible combinations also increase substantially.

Today's graphics cards come in five color standards, as depicted in table 3.1.

Table 3.1   Bits-per-pixel rates

Bits-Per-Pixel	Color Mode Name	Number of Colors
1-bit	Black and white	2
4-bits	Minimum color	16
8-bits	Pseudo color	256
16-bits	Hi-color	32,768
24-bits	True-color	16.7 million

For most applications, 256 colors are fine. Image editing requires at least Hi-color. Most Photoshop users need 24-bit color.

Note

Just because a display is capable of only 16 or 256 colors, that doesn't mean unsupported colors do not display. For example, when an image calls for more colors than the graphics card is capable of, the additional colors are displayed through a process called *dithering*. Dithering mixes two or more solid colors to form another. If your display doesn't support many colors, you've probably noticed that some hues seem coarse, or speckled. This is the result of dithering. In many applications, dithering is not a problem, but in graphics and photograph processing, where color purity is critical, it's hard to work with and mostly not acceptable.

Figure 3.11 shows an example of three grayscale images displayed at various color depths. Notice the dithering. You get even more unsightly dithering when working with images containing thousands or millions of colors.

Grayscale images use the same color depth, or bits-per-pixel ratings, as do color images, except that images are rated in shades of gray. Four-bits is 16 shades of gray; 8-bits produces 256 shades of gray.

Fig. 3.11

Examples of gray-scale at 1-bit, 4-bits, and 8-bits.

Finally, as with everything else in life, there are trade-offs for these beautiful, high-resolution displays. The more colors and the higher the resolution, the more computing required by your CPU, which slows down your system. You can get around the demand that high resolution and numerous colors place on your computer by choosing an accelerated graphics card, which is discussed in Appendix A, "Photoshop and Your Hardware."

> **Caution**
>
> **Beware of Color Depth Claims**
>
> Just because a display adapter claims 32,768 or 16.7 million colors doesn't mean that it supports them at all resolutions. When you increase the number of colors, the display adapter needs more memory to store the additional information. When looking at a card's color (and resolution) specifications, make sure it's capable of the number of colors you need at the desired resolution. Sometimes you can add RAM to a graphics card to increase resolution and color capabilities.

Color Models

A *color model* is a method for representing color as data. In the computer and publishing world, color models provide consistent ways of describing color with number values. Photoshop supports several color models. This section looks at the ones used most often: RGB, CMYK, and PANTONE Matching System (PMS). You will find an in-depth discussion of color models in chapter 13, "Understanding Color."

RGB

RGB stands for red, green, and blue. By mixing these three colors, you can create just about any color possible. RGB is the model used by your monitor. The screen mixes colors by illuminating red, green, and blue phosphorous lights with an electron gun at the back of the monitor. Varying the intensity of each light produces different colors.

Graphics applications vary in the number of combinations you can mix. Photoshop lets you use percentages of colors, as shown in figure 3.12, or select a color by eye. Either procedure allows for thousands of RGB combinations.

Fig. 3.12

Selecting a color from the Color Picker dialog box.

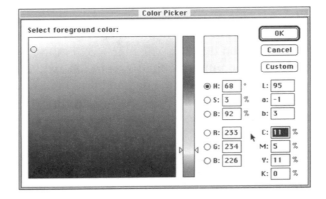

CMYK

CMYK stands for cyan, magenta, yellow, and black. CMYK is the process used by most print shops for full color, or process color print documents. Photoshop and other applications, such as Illustrator and QuarkXPress, separate the four colors into plates, one for each color. The printing press then prints percentages of the colors, one over the other, to mix the desired colors.

Note

Printing CMYK separations is discussed in chapter 13, "Understanding Color." When printing separations from Photoshop, the program automatically converts RGB information to CMYK. This also is true when you export your drawings from a draw program to EPS format. However, if you export to a bitmap format, such as PCX or TIFF, RGB values are maintained. Whenever you export from any graphics application to a DTP layout, you should use either EPS or CMYK TIFF.

PANTONE Matching System (PMS)

PMS is the spot color matching system used in most print shops. When you choose a color from a swatch book at your local printer, it is usually PMS.

Photoshop has a complete PANTONE color system built-in. But the program does not support spot color separations, nor can you export images with PANTONE colors defined in them, as you can from many draw-type programs. Instead, the program mixes CMYK values to create PMS colors, which does not always work well. (By the way, PhotoSpot from Second Glance or InSoftware's PlateMaker both export spot colors.)

To use Photoshop's PANTONE system, you must switch to the Custom Colors dialog box, shown in figure 3.13, by clicking the Custom button in the Color Picker dialog box. Usually, PANTONE colors are matched by the numbers displayed beneath each color swatch.

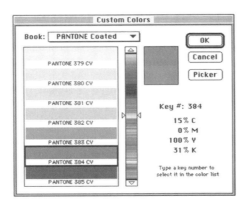

Fig. 3.13

Use this dialog box to select Pantone colors.

> **Tip**
>
> **Use a Swatch Book To Match PANTONE Colors**
>
> Few monitors are capable of displaying colors exactly as they print. You should use a PANTONE Matching System swatch book, or, when using the Pantone Process option, use the Pantone process color guide, available at your print shop or graphics supply store, to assure that you get the colors you want.

Most People Don't Print from Photoshop

While a few high-power designers use Photoshop to create and print fancy book covers, brochure covers, posters, and a host of other documents, most of the work you do in the program winds up in another application, such as a presentation or desktop publishing layout. When saving an image for these types of jobs, you must be aware of several nuances specific to each application.

This section looks briefly at the basics of graphics output. You will find more specific information in several chapters throughout this book, including chapters 21 through 25 in Part VI, "Publishing."

Preparing Graphics for Your Monitor

The devices covered here are computer screens, television monitors (including videotape), and overhead slide projectors that you connect to your display adapter. Since preparing graphics for each device is identical, the word *monitor* is used in this discussion to cover them all.

The two drawbacks to creating graphics incorrectly for monitors are slow screen redraws and bad coloring. The first problem can slow down your presentation, making you and your audience wait too long for transitions between slides. The pace and timing of a presentation are very important. The second problem ruins the quality of your presentations.

Of all the different output devices, preparing graphics for your monitor is easiest. There is no extra processing between what you see on-screen and what comes out of the printer or off the offset press—what you see is what you get. (As you will see later in this chapter and throughout this book, getting what displays on your monitor to reproduce properly on paper is not nearly as simple.)

Remember, there are two basic graphics types: vector and bitmap. Vector graphics are device independent, meaning that they'll print or display at the resolution of the output device. Bitmaps are device dependent. They print or display at their own resolution, regardless of the resolution of the output device.

How can you display a 300-dpi image on a 75-dpi monitor? There's the rub. You can't. The image displays at 75 dpi. The problem is that your Mac's CPU must process the image at 300 dpi, which requires several more times the data processing time—for absolutely no gain.

This is why it takes so long for Photoshop to display 300-dpi images. It is also why PageMaker, QuarkXPress, and other layout programs display low-resolution replicas of the graphics you bring into your layout—to speed up screen redraws.

Adjusting Resolution in Photoshop

Adjusting the resolution of an image in Photoshop is simple. Open the image, and then choose Image Size from the Image menu. The Image Size dialog box in figure 3.14 is then displayed. Simply type in the new resolution and then click OK. Adjusting resolution downward can greatly affect file size. Smaller images display much faster. In order for the changes to take effect in other applications, though, you must save the image after making resolution changes.

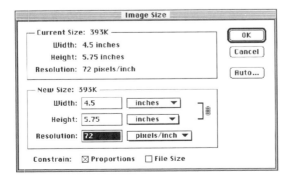

Fig. 3.14

Use the Image Size dialog box to resize images and resample resolution.

Also notice that you can change image size in the Image Size dialog box. When changing image size and resolution, be mindful of the Proportions and File Size check boxes. Proportion maintains the image quality by not allowing distortion; it forces changes to occur in relation to the X and Y axes. The only time you would deselect this option is if you want to change the shape of the image.

File Size affects the image in several ways, but primarily it affects resolution and size. If, for example, you decrease the image size with File Size selected, resolution increases. With File Size deselected, the file size decreases. Conversely, if you change resolution with File Size selected, you will change the size. The foolproof way to change resolution and size is to deselect File Size, and then make size and resolution changes simultaneously.

Tip

Color Depth also Affects Screen Redraw Speed

The speed with which your Mac redraws images during an electronic presentation also is affected by an image's bits-per-pixel rate. If, for example, you plan to show the presentation on a Mac display system capable of only eight-bit color, nothing is gained by using 24-bit images, except that you get unsightly dithering and slower redraws. You can solve this overkill problem by indexing colors, as discussed in the "Converting between Color Modes" section of chapter 13, "Understanding Color."

Graphics and Slide Recorders

Slide recorders, of course, print documents as 35mm slides. When using vector—device-independent graphics—don't worry about resolution. The image will print at the highest possible setting. The only type image you should treat differently is bitmapped. The image you see on your monitor is reduced several times to fit on a slide. Remember, making an image smaller increases quality.

When scanning or resampling an image for slides, be it a line drawing or 24-bit photograph, consult your sevice bureau. Higher settings can slow down the slide recorder. If you set the resolution too high, you could overload the slide recorder, causing it to crash. To get the slides to print, you will have to go back and lower the resolution of the bitmaps. You don't have to worry about screen frequency. A slide's line screen is set from the presentation program. (Note that printing to slide recorders is discussed in-depth in chapter 23, "Photoshop for the Presenter.")

Laser Printers

In the early and mid-1980s, it was common to use 300-dpi laser sheets for camera-ready art. When I first started publishing, I used my laser printer to print text and line art and let the print shop shoot the tricky stuff—screens and halftones. At first, I did not know I had an alternative. Then I noticed service bureaus with something called imagesetters springing up all over the place. One of them offered to print out a sample document, and I was hooked.

There is a tremendous difference between 300-dpi laser output and 1,200-dpi (or higher) imagesetter output. Today, I use my laser printer primarily for printing proofs. Only for occasional small jobs that consist of text and a few rules do I use a laser sheet for the final output. As you will see, 300- and 600-dpi printers cannot print screens and halftones very well. However, the latest round of PostScript Level 2,600-dpi printers are getting much better at it. But they're still not suitable for most Photoshop output.

High-Resolution Laser Printers

Some high-resolution laser printers boast 600, 800, 1,000, even 1,200 dpi. However, this can be misleading. Often, the processors in these machines are simply fooled into squeezing more toner into smaller areas. And that's the problem with laser printers in general; they use toner—they spread powder on paper. This is an inherent limitation. The dots are big at any resolution, which restricts their ability to create halftones.

However, the output from some of them is much crisper and cleaner than 300-dpi machines. Edges are smoother and sharper. Screens are tighter. Often, it is quite acceptable. Whether you should use one for final camera-ready grayscale output depends on if you are pleased with the results. I do not use them for photographs. However, if you have one in-house, and the output is acceptable, that is an entirely different situation.

> **Caution**
>
> **Don't Use Laser Output for Four-Color Output**
>
> You should never attempt to use laser printer output for four-color documents. Dot placement is not precise enough.

Color Printers

Color printers are used by publishers and designers for transparencies and proofing during the layout process. Some people also use them for short mass production runs (say, less than 50 copies). However, they really are not suited for publishing hard-copy documents.

Exceptions are display makers and dye sublimation printers that designers often use to make only one or a few copies of a document, such as, say, a point-of-sale poster. Depending on the job and device, optimal resolution and screen settings vary. You will get the best results by consulting with the service bureau where you output these jobs.

Grayscale Images and Laser Printers

Just because your scanner, monitor, and graphics package are capable of up to 256 shades of gray doesn't mean that that many will come out of your printer. For example, 300-dpi printers can achieve only about 25 shades of gray because of their resolution and screen frequency restraints. Their highest screen frequency, before quality degradation, is about 60 lpi. The dots are too big to set screen frequency any higher.

You can calculate what grayscale level an image will print at by using the formula shown in figure 3.15.

Fig. 3.15

Formula for figuring grayscale levels.

$$\text{Gray} = \left(\frac{\text{Printer resolution}}{\text{screen frequency}}\right)^2 + 1$$

In other words, 60 lpi on a 300-dpi printer will give you 25 levels of gray. There are a number of reasons for adjusting shades of gray, the most important being continuous tone quality, or how well graduating shades of gray run together. Other reasons include file size and printing time. The higher the resolution and lpi, the bigger the computer file and the longer it takes to print.

If you set line screens higher than 60 lpi on a 300-dpi printer, the image can become muddied, or blotchy ("posterized"). You can set screen frequency somewhat higher on higher resolution devices and get improved quality, but for top quality grayscale images, you should use an imagesetter for the final output.

Imagesetter Output

Imagesetters are never used as mass reproduction devices. Instead, they are used for printing camera-ready art for an offset printer or for silk-screening processes.

Throughout this book, the terms *printers* and *imagesetters* are used interchangeably. However, there is a big difference between them. Imagesetters are the output devices of choice for desktop publishers. Unlike laser printers, they do not use toner. Instead they use a process similar to photography. The page, a plastic-coated paper (or film), is developed in chemicals. The result is higher resolution (because dots are much smaller). This means cleaner output—crisp and clear lines and type, as well as fine screens and halftones.

Another important difference is subtlety. Laser printers print bold and black. They are not capable of hairlines and crisp, small (under 8 point) text. Imagesetter output contains finer lines and more detail.

Today, there are several makers of imagesetters, but their output quality is comparable. They print at several resolutions from about 900 dpi to over 3,000 dpi. The higher resolution is more expensive and takes longer to print.

Beyond Camera Ready

Another very powerful desktop publishing option is printing *to film*. This is exactly what it sounds like; the document comes out of the imagesetter as a negative. This procedure is not much different from printing positive paper sheets on a high-resolution imagesetter, and the benefits are many.

> **Note**
>
> To get accurate four-color reproduction, printing to film is required. Another option is to have the print shop make the color separations with the conventional camera separation method.

No matter how good your print shop's camera (and the person operating it) is, some clarity and detail are lost during shooting. Printing to film ensures the best possible reproduction of your layout (except for, perhaps, full-color photographs, which are still a bit tricky to reproduce on a computer).

Screens and halftones are screened exactly as you set them. It eliminates the possibility of underexposure or overexposure, camera alignment problems, and any number of conditions influenced by human intervention. Once you learn the intricacies of printing to film, there is no substitute for transferring print data directly from your computer to a negative.

Where To Go from Here

▶ Before getting your hands dirty editing images in Photoshop, you should first setup your work environment as delineated in chapter 4, "Setting Up the Photoshop Enviroment."

▶ Color issues are discussed in-depth in chapter 13, "Understanding Color." These are important issues that you will need to know to succeed in printing color photographs.

▶ Monitor calibration is vital to color output. It is covered thoroughly in the "Calibration" section of chapter 13, "Understanding Color."

▶ You will find detailed information on output, line screens, resolution, and paper type in chapter 21, "Photoshop for the Desktop Publisher."

Setting Up the Photoshop Environment

Not all desktop publishers and designers work the same way. Specific tasks require different work environments and work habits. Any graphics program worth its salt lets you adjust program parameters to help customize the program to work the way you do. Photoshop provides extensive controls over the program and its interface.

Some people, for example, work with large images, requiring large blocks of RAM and virtual memory on the system hard disk. Some designers prefer to work with inches as their measurement standards. Others prefer points and picas. Photoshop provides control over these environment options and many others.

by Bill Harrel

CHAPTER 4

You can, for example, permanently change the way a tool works or adjust the tool's size and shape. Additionally, you can save the changed settings. You can control the way CMYK composites display. You can make sure that Photoshop always saves in a version 2.5-compatible format in order to maintain compatibility with other users who have not upgraded. The list goes on and on.

Note

This chapter specifically covers customizing general program parameters, such as memory usage and units of measurement. Other preference options, such as color separation setup, monitor setup, and calibration, are discussed in other chapters. You can find references to the appropriate chapters in the "Using the Preferences Command" section of this chapter.

Understanding Photoshop's Preferences Scheme

As you saw in chapter 1, "Touring Photoshop," you can add keystroke shortcuts to the new Commands palette, save sets of keystroke command schemes, and so on. This is one way to customize your environment. Photoshop provides three other ways. You can customize tool actions by double-clicking the tool in the toolbox, make changes to application preferences from the Preferences command on the File menu, or simply move and rearrange the palettes.

When you change a tool or adjustment in the Preferences dialog boxes, Photoshop saves the changes in a file called Photoshop 3.0 Prefs, which is located in the Preferences folder in your System folder (see fig. 4.1). Unlike desktop publishing programs, such as QuarkXPress and PageMaker, Photoshop does not let you save separate sets of preferences for specific documents or globally for the application in general. However, the program does remember which palettes were open and where they were placed the last time you closed the application.

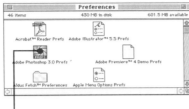

Fig. 4.1

Photoshop saves
and remembers
preference settings
in Photoshop 3.0
Prefs.

Photoshop 3.0 Prefs icon

Tip

Returning to the Default Preferences Scheme

Adobe ships Photoshop with a set of default preferences that are an
ideal starting point for many jobs. As you work on different projects
and make changes to the interface as you go, you can get pretty far
from the original default scheme. To return Photoshop to the default
scheme at any time, simply delete Photoshop 3.0 Prefs from the
Preferences folder located in your System folder.

Using the Preferences Command

When you select Preferences, located on the File menu, you see a submenu
of options that can be tailored to your liking (see fig. 4.2). The following
list describes these options and where they are discussed in this book.

▶ **General.** This opens the General Preferences dialog box and provides
access to several often-changed items, such as tool cursor shape,
CMYK composite display, and several others. General preferences
are discussed in the next section of this chapter, "Using General
Preferences."

▶ **Gamut Warning.** Color output devices (printers, monitors, scanners) and printing presses have limitations. Some cannot print all the
colors available in Photoshop. When a color is out of a printer's range,
it is said to be beyond the device's gamut. This option lets you adjust
the opacity and color of the program's built-in gamut alarm. For more
information on gamuts, check out chapter 13, "Understanding Color."

▶ **Plug-ins.** This lets you change the location of the folder containing Photoshop's plug-ins. The Plug-ins folder is located, by default, in the Adobe Photoshop 3 folder. Plug-ins are discussed in chapter 15, "Using Photoshop's Plug-In Filters," and chapter 16, "Third-Party Plug-Ins."

▶ **Scratch Disks.** This controls Photoshop's use of memory and virtual memory. Scratch disks are discussed later in this chapter, in the "Using Scratch Disk (Memory Setup)" section.

▶ **Transparency.** This controls Photoshop's canvas grid. It's covered in the "Using Transparency" section, later in this chapter.

▶ **Units.** This controls the measurement system Photoshop uses, such as inches, picas, and so on. This is discussed in the "Using Units of Measurement" section, later in this chapter.

▶ **Monitor Setup.** This calibrates the monitor. You can find complete instructions for calibrating your monitor in chapter 13, "Understanding Color," in the "Calibration" section.

▶ **Printing Inks Setup.** This lets you adjust output for printers and printing presses. This is another form of calibration. Ink setup instructions are in chapter 13, "Understanding Color," in the "Calibration" section.

▶ **Separation Setup.** This is another form of calibration that allows you to adjust color separation output. You also can find color separation setup instructions in chapter 13, "Understanding Color," in the "Calibration" section.

▶ **Separation Tables.** This allows you to create and select different tables to control separation output. Complete separation setup information is in chapter 13, "Understanding Color," in the "Calibration" section.

Using General Preferences

Out of all the Photoshop preferences options, you can change the General Preferences most often; they have the most effect on the general interface. When you select Preferences from the File menu, and then select General from the submenu, the General Preferences dialog box opens (see fig. 4.3).

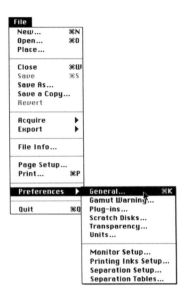

Fig. 4.2

Set Photoshop's various environment options from the Preferences submenu.

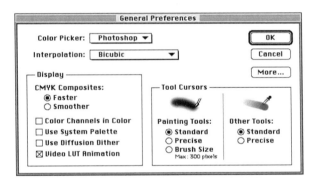

Fig. 4.3

Set Photoshop preferences from the General Preferences dialog box.

The following list describes the available options in the General Preferences dialog box.

▶ **Color Picker.** Use this option to choose which color picker—Photoshop's or Apple's—pops up when you click the foreground or background color swatches in the toolbox. If you're familiar with other Mac graphics applications, you may be used to the Apple color picker. But you'll probably find Photoshop's more powerful. Both color pickers are shown in figure 4.4.

Fig. 4.4

The Apple and
Photoshop color
pickers.

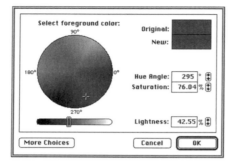

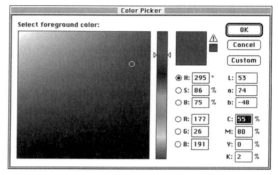

▶ **Interpolation.** This controls how Photoshop enlarges or rotates images. When Photoshop enlarges an image, it must fill in—or interpolate—pixels to close the gaps. There are three options: Nearest Neighbor, Bilinear, and Bicubic. Nearest Neighbor is the fastest interpolation method; it simply duplicates the pixel next to the gap. Bilinear, a little slower, smoothes the display by creating intermediary shades. Bicubic is the slowest but most effective method; it increases contrast between pixels, eliminating some of the blur that can occur during interpolation.

▶ **Display.** These options control how Photoshop displays images on your monitor. Each option has a different purpose and effect, as discussed below:

 • **CMYK Composites.** Monitors display in the RGB color model and printing presses and printers print in CMYK. When you edit a CMYK image in Photoshop, your computer must do some horrific calculations to get it to the monitor in RGB. Faster provides fast screen redraws, but sacrifices image quality and accuracy. Smoother forces Photoshop to create closer conversions between the actual CMYK colors and those displayed on your monitor. Depending on your system and the size of the image, this can be a very slow process.

- **Color Channels in Color.** Photoshop separates images into color channels. RGB has three channels and CMYK has four channels— one for each color. In the Channels palette, Photoshop displays each channel in grayscale. With this option turned on, the program tries to simulate the channel in the respective color. A cyan channel, for instance, is displayed in cyan. Truthfully, this doesn't help you edit channels. It's really difficult to determine when you might use this.

- **Use System Palette.** If you use an 8-bit (256 colors) display, this option tells Photoshop to use the Macintosh system color palette. By default, Photoshop tries to simulate the best colors in the foreground, or active, image window. Frankly, it's next to impossible to accurately edit photographs on an 8-bit system. You really should use at least a 16-bit display—24-bit is even better.

- **Use Diffusion Dither.** This lets you switch back and forth between Macintosh system QuickDraw dithering and Photoshop's diffusion dithering. The Photoshop method is a little more accurate but can cause flaws around object edges.

- **Use Video LUT Animation.** Unless this option causes problems with your video card, leave it on. *LUT* stands for *lookup table.* To speed up 24-bit displays, Photoshop uses a color lookup table. This option primarily affects previews when working in color manipulation dialog boxes.

- **Tool Cursors.** Photoshop 3 allows you to adjust the size and action of your cursor. With paint tools, you can choose many different cursors: the standard Photoshop cursor used in previous versions; the Precise cursor, a target-like cursor that draws exactly in the center of the target; or the Brush Size cursor that adjusts to the size of the brush—up to 300 pixels. Figure 4.5 shows the difference in the three cursors for the Paintbrush tool. You also can set other tools, such as Selection and Mask, to Precise.

Fig. 4.5

Standard, Precise, and Brush Size tool cursor preferences.

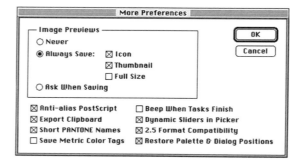

When you click More in the General Preferences dialog box, you get the More Preferences dialog box, shown in figure 4.6. The following list describes the options in More Preferences.

Fig. 4.6

Use the More Preferences dialog box to set additional preferences.

▶ **Image Previews.** Photoshop can save image previews as file icons and as previews for the Open dialog box. Use Image Previews to control when and how the previews are saved. The options include never saving a preview, always saving a preview, or instructing Photoshop to ask when saving the file whether to save a preview. There are three types of previews: Icon, Thumbnail, and Full Size. Selecting Icon saves a preview for the file icon. Thumbnail saves previews for the Open dialog box. Full Size saves a 72 dpi screen preview for use in layouts.

▶ **Anti-alias PostScript.** Anti-alias smoothes the edges of objects, which eliminates jaggies. This option simply tells Photoshop to anti-alias PostScript objects you import into the program.

▶ **Export Clipboard.** Photoshop supports two clipboards: its own internal clipboard for transferring among images, and the system clipboard for transferring between applications. Turning this option on simply lets you cut and paste between applications. Even when this option is turned off, however, you still can import into Photoshop from other applications.

▶ **Short PANTONE Names.** If you plan to import Photoshop images into a desktop publishing or draw program layout, select this object to make sure Photoshop uses the same naming conventions used by these applications.

▶ **Save Metric Color Tags.** Use this option only if you use EFI's EfiColor for Photoshop. It helps you coordinate screen and printer calibration between Photoshop and QuarkXPress. When this option is turned on, Photoshop uses EfiColor's separation tables when saving the image. In turn, QuarkXPress (when using EfiColor) uses the same table, allowing for better color calibration. This option works only when you also use EfiColor with QuarkXPress.

▶ **Beep When Tasks Finish.** This tells Photoshop to beep your Mac when an operation, such as an execution of a filter or when a preview finishes redrawing, is complete. Use this option when you want to turn to another task while waiting for Photoshop to complete an operation. The beep tells you when to come back to the computer.

▶ **Dynamic Sliders in Picker.** This tells Photoshop to provide dynamic sliders in the Picker palette. By default, the slider colors change as you drag the slider, which can take some time for an older Mac's redraw. Use this option to turn off dynamic sliders.

▶ **2.5 Format Compatibility.** Use this option to assure that Photoshop 3 images can be opened in Photoshop 2.5. Photoshop 2.5 does not support such file attributes as layers, proxies, and previews.

▶ **Restore Palette & Dialog Positions.** When this option is selected, Photoshop remembers where you left palettes and dialog boxes and opens them in the same position the next time they're accessed. When this option is turned off, palettes and dialog boxes return to their default positions.

Using Scratch Disk (Memory Setup)

Photoshop files can require enormous amounts of memory, often more than you have in your Mac. A scratch disk allows you to work with files larger than you have the memory to accommodate. Scratch disk memory is much slower than RAM, however, so you should give Photoshop as much system RAM as you can.

Tip

Give Photoshop Room To Spread Out

Scratch disk is another term for *virtual memory*. Virtual memory is space on your hard disk that the computer treats as additional RAM—or memory. In addition to using your Mac's virtual memory (set up in the Memory Control Panel), Photoshop also can use its own section of the hard disk. When working with large files in Photoshop, you should make sure you have several free megabytes of space open on the scratch disk. You also can improve performance by using a disk optimizer, such as Mac Tools, to provide Photoshop with contiguous disk space.

Giving Photoshop Its Fair Share of RAM

The key to getting the best performance from Photoshop is making sure the program gets plenty of RAM in which to work. You control how much memory the program uses with the Adobe Photoshop 3.0 Info dialog box, shown in figure 4.7. To open the dialog box, simply select the program icon in Finder, open the File menu, and choose Get Info.

Fig. 4.7

Use the Adobe Photoshop 3.0 Info dialog box to set a program's memory options.

The Memory Requirements section has three options: Suggested Size, Minimum Size, and Preferred Size. Suggested Size tells you how much RAM Photoshop should ideally have allocated, providing that you have enough system RAM. You get the best performance by allocating at least this much memory to the program. The minimum size is the least amount of memory the program claims when it opens. When you boot, if this much RAM (including virtual memory) is not available, the program cannot open. You can make this figure lower if you plan to run Photoshop on a system with low RAM or if you are running several other applications.

Preferred Size is how much RAM the gluttonous Photoshop really wants. If this much memory is available when the program boots, Photoshop claims and uses it. You also can change the preferred size, if you have enough memory available—which you should if you plan to use Photoshop with large images. The number of plug-ins you use can also affect how much memory Photoshop needs.

The point is, Photoshop needs as much memory as you can give it. When your Mac runs out of memory, Photoshop creates a scratch disk.

Setting Up a Scratch Disk

The Scratch Disk option lets you set the location of the scratch disk. In figure 4.8, for example, you can see that I have two hard disks and a Bernoulli removable on my system from which I can choose a scratch disk location. The default is the startup disk. When you choose a scratch disk, make sure it has enough free space to accommodate large files and is fast. On my system, the two hard disks are pretty fast—the Bernoulli, on the other hand, is not. Besides, it's not a good idea to set up scratch disks on removables; it can cause Photoshop to fail.

Fig. 4.8

Setting memory options with the Scratch Disk Preferences dialog box.

The Secondary option allows you to choose a secondary, or overflow scratch disk, which Photoshop uses when the primary disk is full.

Using Transparency

Transparency simply puts a grid in the clear, or transparent, areas of an image. A grid makes it easier to precisely place objects in a document by providing visual guides. Photoshop's grid is a checkerboard (see fig. 4.9).

Fig. 4.9

An example of a Photoshop trans-parency grid.

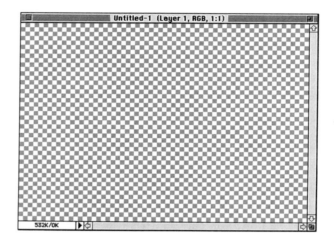

Grids are set up in the Transparency Options dialog box, shown in figure 4.10. Open the File menu, choose Preferences, and select Transparency to access this dialog box. You can adjust the size and color of the grid, or choose None to have no grid at all.

Fig. 4.10

Set Photoshop's grid from the Transparency Options dialog box.

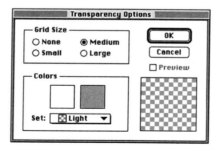

When the grid is turned on, transparent portions of images display the checkerboard grid. You can tell Photoshop to display the grid on new canvases by selecting Transparent in the Contents area of the New dialog box, as shown in figure 4.11. For this option to work, however, the grid must be turned on in Transparency Options.

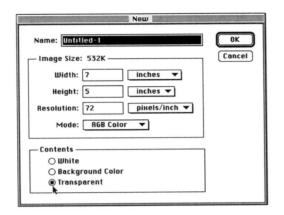

Fig. 4.11

You can select the Transparency option in the New dialog box.

Using Units of Measurement

Depending on your background, you may prefer units of measurement different from Photoshop's default inches. Newspaper layout people, for example, often prefer points and picas. You can change Photoshop's units of measurement. Open the File menu, and choose Preferences, Units to open the Units Preferences dialog box (see fig. 4.12).

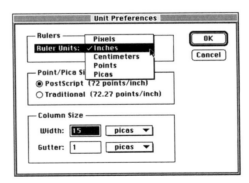

Fig. 4.12

Use the Units Preferences dialog box to set up the measurement system.

To change the measurement scheme used on the rulers, simply select an option from the Ruler Units pop-up menu. If you're used to the traditional 72.27-points-per-inch convention, instead of the new 72-points-per-inch now used in PostScript computer typesetting, choose the Traditional setting in Point/Pica Size.

Use the Column Size option to indicate a column size. Some layout programs, such as Corel Ventura, use column widths to display images across columns. This setting is used by Image Setting and Canvas Setting when resizing images.

Where To Go from Here

▶ If you plan to do high-end design and color printing of Photoshop images, you need to set up other preference options, including Monitor Setup and Separations Setup, to get professional results. Be sure to check out the information in the "Calibration" section of chapter 13, "Understanding Color."

▶ You can find more information on memory requirements of Photoshop in Appendix A, "Photoshop and Your Hardware."

▶ Now that you have Photoshop all set up and ready to go, you can get to work editing images. Chapter 5, "Importing and Exporting Images," discusses bringing images into Photoshop.

PART

II

Acquiring Images

Importing and Exporting Images

It's hard to imagine that the ultimate Macintosh program was thought up just over five years ago—time moves so quickly! Photoshop brought to reality the powers of a virtual desktop darkroom. In addition to Photoshop's powerful capabilities for image enhancement, it also opens many graphics file formats from different imaging applications.

This chapter will first look at setting up the Photoshop environment and then examine the many file formats supported by Photoshop. We'll look at the various methods of opening or acquiring images and the file formats used to export images.

by Rob Sonner & Ted Padova

CHAPTER 5

Preparing the Photoshop Environment

There are several ways to open or import images into Photoshop. Before you import images, however, you may want to make some adjustments to the way Photoshop is set up.

The first thing you will notice when you open a Photoshop image is a grid flashes on your screen. If you create a new file, you may see the appearance of a grid covering the document window. For many users this grid will, at first, be an annoyance.

The grid view is controlled by opening the File menu and choosing Transparency. A dialog box will appear providing many choices for either a grid display or viewing documents without a grid (see figure 5.1). In addition to the grid sizes displayed in the dialog box, you can choose any color to represent the grid. Several choices are available from a pop-up menu where the default is listed as light. In addition to the preset grid colors, you can customize the grid color by clicking on either of the swatch squares in the dialog box. Selecting either of these squares will present the color picker for selecting any color to represent a checkerboard look to the grid.

Fig. 5.1

The Transparency Options dialog box provides many choices for displaying the transparency grid.

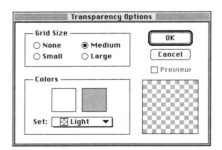

It is important for you to understand the uses and purpose of the grid. The people in Mountain View did not put this feature in Photoshop to annoy you, so there indeed must be some important reason for the grid's existence. When you open an image in Photoshop, the document will appear on a background. As you add shapes to your document you can place the new shapes on additional layers. All information on a layer by default will appear opaque. The area surrounding a shape may contain no information and appear transparent. You cannot immediately discern the difference between transparent and opaque views unless there is some indicator for viewing transparency—hence, your grid.

The transparency grid displays a nonprinting grid to indicate which areas of the document are transparent. The view may at first appear annoying, but once you become familiar with it, the grid will be helpful in constructing your Photoshop images. Therefore, the first step in setting up your Photoshop environment is to be certain the transparency grid is active and the display is suited to your individual preference. For more information on the transparency view and how it is used with layers, see chapter 10, "Working with Layers."

Opening a File in Photoshop

Photoshop is the ultimate program for opening graphic image files on either the Macintosh or PC platform. When you open the File menu and choose Open (see fig. 5.2), a dialog box will appear. Notice the choices available for Format. The default for opening a file is to view the Thumbnail of Photoshop files. All files appearing in the dialog box will be native Photoshop documents. When you select the Show All Files check box, a number of file formats will appear under a pop-up menu.

Fig. 5.2

Open the File menu and choose Open.

Photoshop can open virtually any graphic file format you choose, provided it's coded in the program or you have the equivalent file format plug-in for the less common formats not specifically native to Photoshop. Examples of non-native Photoshop formats are MacPaint and PixelPaint. For more details on this and other formats, continue reading this chapter. On the other hand, any file saved from an application and used exclusively by that application is known as a *native file*. Figure 5.3 illustrates the Open dialog box for a native Photoshop image.

Fig. 5.3

The native Photoshop files can show a thumbnail preview of an image before you open the document.

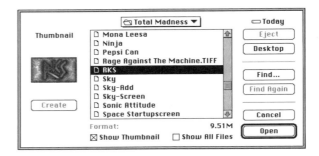

Opening files is very easy; highlight the file you want and click the Open button. You see the files that Photoshop can read at a glance. Photoshop 3 supports 22 file types. In addition, there are several Acquire plug-in modules that allow for custom image editing and manipulation; detailed information is available in the section, "Acquiring Images In Photoshop," later in this chapter. If the file is not in the dialog box, it probably came from a program or a file format that Photoshop does not recognize. Select the Show All Files check box at the bottom of the Open dialog box (see fig. 5.4) to show the available files with the corresponding file type in a pop-up list (see fig. 5.5). This is similar to the traditional Open As dialog box in Photoshop 2.5.1.

Fig. 5.4

The Photoshop Open dialog box with the Show All Files check box selected.

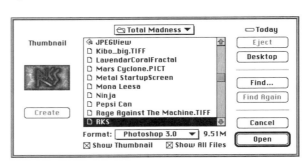

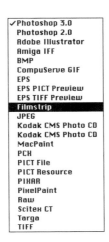

Fig. 5.5

A list of the available file types in Photoshop 3.

If Photoshop cannot open an intended file, a warning box appears that describes the pending problem. If this happens, check the origin of the image's format. Photoshop is capable of opening many bitmap files native to Macintosh, as well as some of the more common PC formats.

Key Concept: Importing Object-Oriented Art into Photoshop

Programs like Adobe Illustrator and Adobe Dimensions are superb drawing programs designed to draw art as objects. There are almost endless opportunities to use artwork that originates in these and similar programs, and then import the artwork into Photoshop for additional editing. One example of such a design is creating line art in Adobe Illustrator, and then using the line art as a template to colorize in Photoshop. Object-oriented art from PostScript drawing programs can be brought into Photoshop in several ways. We'll examine the methods of importing Encapsulated PostScript (EPS) art into Photoshop to see how you can combine these methods for effective design purposes.

Opening Adobe Illustrator Files

Adobe Illustrator is a vector based program that draws art as objects. Photoshop, on the other hand, is a raster based, or bitmap based, program that describes its artwork as pixels. When you open an Illustrator image into Photoshop, the artwork will be *rasterized,* which simply means the vector objects will be turned into pixels. Illustrator files can be opened in Photoshop by opening the File menu and choosing Open. When you open an Illustrator file, a dialog box appears, as illustrated in figure 5.6.

Fig. 5.6

Opening Adobe Illustrator files in Photoshop provides several choices for rasterizing the image.

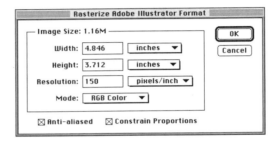

When you open an Illustrator file, you can choose the mode and resolution in the Open dialog box. In figure 5.6 the mode selected is RGB while the resolution is 150 ppi (pixels per inch).

Tip

Accelerating Photoshop Performance

When you work with line art images for illustration purposes, set the document resolution to 72 ppi for rough editing, much like the rough sketching that occurs with paintings like watercolor or oils. Before you begin the detail work, resample the image in resolution to match your output requirements. The resampling will be interpolated resolution, but not a problem for the rough areas of the image. Perform the detail work at the desired output resolution. By working first in the lower resolution modes, Photoshop's performance will be much faster. For a complete explanation on optical and interpolated resolutions see chapter 6, "Scanning Images."

After you accept values entered in the Open dialog box, Photoshop will rasterize the image. A progress bar will be displayed on-screen showing the percentage of completion as the image progresses with rasterization. This process may take some time depending on the size and resolution entered in the dialog box.

Using Illustrator Art as Templates

If you decide to use line art images created in Adobe Illustrator as templates, the new Layers features of Photoshop will be a great asset. For a thorough explanation of layers and how to use them, see chapter 10, "Working With Layers." For now, let's look at opening an Illustrator file and using it as a template.

▶ *Create the Illustrator artwork.* Adobe Illustrator is much more suited to creating line art, illustrations, and perspective drawings than Adobe Photoshop. When creating the artwork, do not apply colors or fills to objects. Keep the artwork as a line art drawing.

▶ *Save the Illustrator file as an EPS file.* Photoshop cannot open or import native Adobe Illustrator files. You must first save Illustrator files as EPS. When using Adobe Illustrator 5.5, you can save the file as EPS with the 8-Bit Macintosh preview and the Illustrator 5.5 Compatibility. Photoshop 3 does not require Illustrator 3 format compatibility, as was the case with previous versions of Photoshop.

▶ *Open the Illustrator EPS file.* In Adobe Photoshop, open the File menu and choose Open. Select the Illustrator file and open it by either double-clicking on the file name or selecting the Open button in the dialog box. A progress bar is displayed while Photoshop rasterizes the image.

▶ *Open the Layers palette.* The Illustrator artwork will appear on a default layer 1. To view the layer, open the Window menu and choose Palettes, then Show Layers. The layers palette shows the default layer 1 and a thumbnail of the artwork on this layer.

▶ *Create a layer for the Photoshop artwork.* Click the New Layer icon in the Layers palette to create the new layer. The new layer is transparent and the line art is in view from the first layer behind our new layer. Figure 5.7 shows an Illustrator file opened in Photoshop with an additional layer added.

Fig. 5.7

Layer #2 can use
layer #1 line art as
a template.

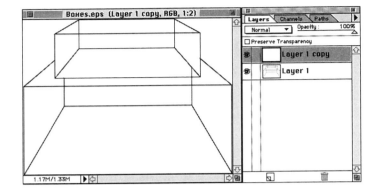

▶ *Apply paint and coloring to the new layer.* Select the new layer and apply
paint and fills to this layer. If you need to select areas defined by the
line art, move to the first layer and create the selection. When you
move back to the second layer, the selection will be active and all
painting can be applied within the selection. For more information
on working with selections, see chapter 9, "Selecting Objects in
Photoshop."

Tip

Compensating for Line Art Strokes

If you use line art as a template, selections within the lines will not
include the lines. If you select an area and apply color, adjacent areas
of the image will appear with gaps. To avoid this problem, create a
selection between lines with the Magic Wand tool. Open the Select
Menu and choose Modify, Expand. Set the expansion value in the
dialog box to 2. Apply the fill in the desired layer. The expansion of
the selection will compensate for the stroke value of a one-point line.
If more than a one-point line is used, set the Expand value higher.
Figure 5.8 illustrates blends created in Photoshop to a perspective
Adobe Illustrator drawing.

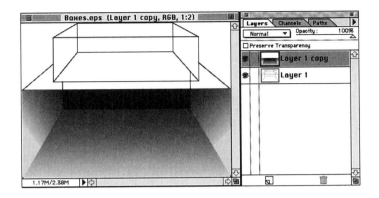

Fig. 5.8

By expanding selections you can create smooth transitions between adjacent colors.

Placing Illustrator Art

Another means of importing EPS artwork into Photoshop is with the Place command. When you have a document window in view, open the File menu and choose Place. When you place an Illustrator EPS file, the image maintains proportions and conforms to the size of the document window without distortion. If, for example, you place an Illustrator EPS file that is eight-inches wide into a Photoshop image three-inches wide, the Illustrator file will be placed at three-inches width while the proportions are maintained. The EPS file will be rasterized at the resolution of the document where it is placed.

Figure 5.9 illustrates an EPS file placed into a Photoshop file. Notice the placed image is represented by a bounding box rectangle. When the cursor is placed inside the bounding box, an icon appearing as a gavel will indicate the image can be stamped down into the document. If you decide not to place the image, moving the cursor outside the bounding box will display an international *no symbol* (a circle with a diagonal line). Clicking outside the bounding box will return you to the document window without the image placed.

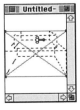

Fig. 5.9

When you place an EPS image in Photoshop, the bounding box around the image will be displayed.

II

Acquiring Images

Pasting EPS artwork

Another method of importing EPS artwork is through Copy and Paste commands. You can copy artwork in PostScript illustration programs and paste the artwork into Photoshop documents. Pasting EPS artwork provides more flexibility when importing into Photoshop files. Artwork can be imported into Photoshop as either a raster image or as paths similar to the way it was created in the original illustration program with Bézier curves, anchor points, and direction lines.

Pasting as Pixels

When you copy artwork from an EPS editing application, and paste it into a Photoshop document by opening the Edit menu and choosing Paste, a dialog box appears. The dialog box, as illustrated in figure 5.10, provides an opportunity to paste the information as pixels or as paths.

Fig. 5.10

Pasting EPS files in Photoshop documents enables you to choose how the information will be imported.

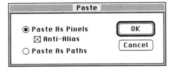

A nice feature of Photoshop is the ability to create a document at a size ratio of 1:1 to the clipboard information. If, for example, you copy an EPS image in Adobe Dimensions with a width of 3.72 inches and a height of 2.89 inches, the new document default specifications will be presented with the same dimensions. These dimensions are visible when you open the File menu and choose New. The height and width are displayed in the New document dialog box so there is no guesswork regarding the size.

Figure 5.11 illustrates an Adobe Dimensions image pasted as pixels in a newly created document window. Notice the 3-D effect would be difficult to illustrate in Photoshop. In addition to the Copy and Paste commands, Adobe Dimensions files can be opened and placed in the same manner as Adobe Illustrator files.

Fig. 5.11

3-D objects, created in programs like Adobe Dimensions, can be pasted into Photoshop documents.

Pasting as Paths

When you open the Edit menu and choose Paste for EPS artwork, the Paste as Paths option can be selected in the dialog box. When Paths are pasted, the artwork appears similar to the way it was illustrated in the EPS drawing program. All the anchor points, Bézier curves, direction lines, and direction points are available as paths in Photoshop. The advantage of pasting objects as paths is the ability to redefine the paths in Photoshop by moving anchor points and changing the curves. Figure 5.12 illustrates an Adobe Illustrator image pasted as paths.

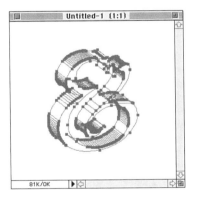

Fig. 5.12

When you Paste as Paths, the paths can be edited in Photoshop much like editing in illustration programs.

II

Acquiring Images

Another advantage of pasting as paths is apparent when working with type. When you create outlines with type in Adobe Illustrator, the type can be pasted as paths in Photoshop. Once pasted as paths, the paths can be edited to stylize the type and create many interesting effects.

Design Note

Importing Large Text Blocks

When large bodies of copy are to be imported into Photoshop, create the copy in programs designed to handle text formatting, such as layout applications. You can export a page from programs like PageMaker and QuarkXpress as EPS files and import them into Photoshop. If EPS images from layout applications have difficulty rasterizing in Photoshop, place them in Adobe Illustrator and save the file out of Illustrator as an EPS before importing into Photoshop. EPS exports can also be distilled in Adobe Acrobat and opened in Adobe Illustrator and finally saved as EPS files. Not all programs exporting as EPS files can be opened in Photoshop. If you have difficulty getting the file in Photoshop, try any number of these means to get the file into Illustrator and exported from Illustrator as an EPS file. Figure 5.13 shows an EPS export of a text block that was created in PageMaker and printed to disk as an EPS file. The image was opened in Photoshop and placed on a second layer. The shadow was made by duplicating the text layer and offsetting it from the original type. The shadow was blurred with the Gaussian Blur filter.

Fig. 5.13

Large text blocks can be exported from layout applications as EPS files and opened in Photoshop.

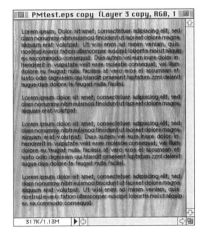

Acquiring Images in Photoshop

Acquiring images in Photoshop is another way of importing your artwork, and is generally for those special circumstances that cross your desktop from time to time: scanning, Quick Editing, and the like.

In order to acquire an image, you must have an accompanying Photoshop Acquire plug-in module. While several ship with Photoshop 3 itself, many more are available from public on-line services, such as America Online in the Mac Graphics forum's Photoshop SIG file libraries.

When you open the File menu and choose Acquire, you see the Acquire submenu as shown in figure 5.14. Anti-Aliased PICT, PICT Resource, Quick Edit, TWAIN Acquire, and TWAIN Select Source are the built-in Photoshop options. Other items listed in the menu are third-party modules which were installed.

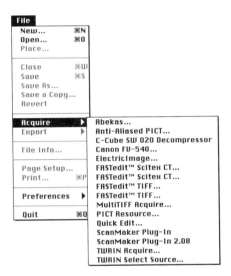

Fig. 5.14

When you open the File Menu and choose Acquire, a submenu reveals all the accessible acquire plug-ins.

II

Acquiring Images

Acquiring Anti-Aliased PICT Files

When you open the File menu and choose Anti-Aliased PICT, you can access files exported as PICT. Programs like MacDraw, Canvas, and SuperPaint support PICT formats. Some programs supporting the PICT format, like MacDraw, can perform architectural drawings and technical illustrations with as much ease as Adobe Illustrator or Aldus FreeHand in the hands of experienced users. Until just a few years ago, Knight-Ridder created all their illustrations in MacDraw. If you look at newspapers with charts, graphs, and illustrations from a few years ago, all the Knight-Ridder illustrations sent over API wire services were MacDraw files. Remember the Desert Storm campaign? The charts of missiles, tanks, maps of the Middle East, and so on, were all drawn in MacDraw. To an Illustrator or FreeHand user, seeing these drawings and knowing they were created in

MacDraw would make them seem impossible. Yet the Knight-Ridder staff could whip out a drawing faster than most of us can create an autotrace in Illustrator.

If you don't use programs like MacDraw, you may need to bring a file created by someone else into Photoshop for editing, coloring, or maybe creating shadows on objects. The Anti-Aliased PICT command is designed to anti-alias edges of PICT images to provide them with a smoother appearance. Fills will appear similar to tones created in EPS illustration programs or Photoshop. However, if you want to preserve the fills and attributes of PICT images, you can copy the artwork in the illustration program and paste it into a Photoshop document or simply open the PICT file in Photoshop. Either way, the image will appear more rough and crude over the anti-aliased image.

In the Anti-Aliased PICT dialog box (see fig. 5.15), you set the file size prior to opening the file or choose to constrain its proportions. Selecting the Constrain Proportions box ensures that the file you acquire will not have distorted proportions from the original file's proportions.

Fig. 5.15

The Anti-Aliased PICT dialog box enables you to control image dimensions and modes.

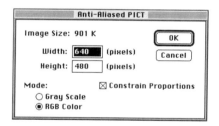

Acquiring and Opening a PICT Resource File

To open and edit resource PICT files in Photoshop is as easy as opening any other file format. Perhaps the most common use of a PICT resource file is creating startup screens. A *startup screen* will display an image when you boot up your computer. The exporting of PICT resources is explained later in this chapter in the section "Other Formats Available." If you have a PICT resource file you wish to edit, you can open the File menu and choose Acquire, PICT Resource.

The standard Open command for opening PICT resource files looks inside all readable files and opens the first PICT Resource it sees, if one is available. It's best to use the Open PICT Resource for opening files such as Startup Screens that contain a single resource PICT. Saving as a PICT

Resource is simple. When doing so, you're presented with a dialog box to give the resource file a Resource ID number and a resource name, which is optional and different from the file name itself. You can combine PICTs multiple resource into one resource file with ID numbers just as you can with ordinary Macintosh program applications.

Acquiring PICT resource files is different in one major way: you can open a Resource file with multiple PICT resources, scroll through them via ID number, and then choose which one to Open and Edit. Figure 5.16 is a screen capture of an Open Scrapbook (a PICT resource data file with multiple PICT resources) using the Photoshop PICT Resource Acquire plug-in module. To edit and access one of the resources, simply scroll through the list, find the one you want, and click the OK button.

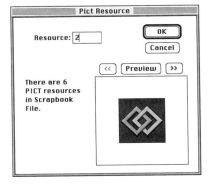

Fig. 5.16

The PICT Resource Acquire plug-in module interface.

II

Acquiring Images

Open the contents of Scrapbooks, open almost any application file, and scroll through the list of PICT resources and icons. For example, you can open the Photoshop application itself and attempt to pull out the actual on-launch splash screen.

Quick Edit Acquire Plug-in

With a sandwich, there are two basic ways to slice it: diagonally or straight through the center. The same goes for opening most files. If you find yourself working on files that might as well be the size of the North American continent, the Photoshop Quick Edit Acquire plug-in might be right for you. It lets you edit a small part of a file. It's not for everyone, but the timesaving aspect is a definite advantage.

Take one particular scenario: the 150MB TIFF file you are preparing for separations needs one small airbrush retouch to the lower-left corner. Opening the file would be another forced 15-minute coffee break. The quicker option is to use the Quick Edit Acquire module and be done in a flash.

The Quick Edit Acquire module supports CMYK, RGB, Lab, and grayscale images in TIFF and Scitex formats. It maintains all the necessary and important values of these file formats when you re-save back to the original file. The same goes for when you work with the SCITEX CT file format, although it must be in CMYK mode.

Note

Quick Edit does not support LZW compressed TIFF files. If your TIFF file is already saved in an LZW compressed format, you need to take an extended lunch hour to open the file (this depends on the size, of course), and re-save it with the LZW compression turned off. At this point in time, you may as well just make the necessary change while the TIFF is open. Plan ahead next time to save yourself from such situations.

To set up Quick Edit selections is simple. Open the File menu and choose Acquire, Quick Edit. A dialog box will appear, as illustrated in figure 5.17. The initial selection area does not have to be too precise because the selection area you set is made from a preview window that generously is larger than most other utility or plug-in thumbnail previews.

Drag your marquee to select an area to edit, click the Open button, and you're off and running. When you make your selection, notice how the window updates with the ideal specs of your selection in both pixel size and proportional file size. You can update your selection at any time.

Another option is to work in a gridline squared-off selection area. This is very useful on larger images where you want to systematically apply the same effect to all areas of the image but don't have the available memory.

When you're finished with your selective file editing, open the File menu and choose Export, Quick Edit Save. This quickly and effortlessly saves your selected work back to the original file.

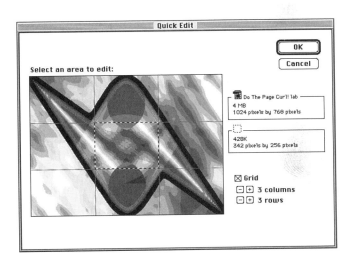

Fig. 5.17

You can define the area to be edited in the Quick Edit dialog box by drawing a selection marquee.

Acquiring Scanned Images

There are a number of third-party plug-ins that accompany scanners that appear in the Acquire submenu when they are installed. These plug-ins are specific to hardware devices such as scanners. For a complete discussion on scanner plug-ins and acquiring the plug-ins, see chapter 6, "Scanning Images." One plug-in that ships with Photoshop and is used for acquiring scanned images is the Twain Acquire plug-in.

Opening Photo CD Files

Photo CD is growing so rapidly in popularity that there is a separate chapter dealing exclusively with Photo CDs. See chapter 7, "Photo-CD Images" for a complete explanation on opening them in Photoshop.

Opening Filmstrip Files

Filmstrip files are excellent for rotoscoping, such as applying uniform filter effects or making a color correction adjustment in Photoshop.

II

Acquiring Images

To make a filmstrip, you need to have the Adobe Premiere QuickTime Movie Editing software. When you export your clip movie to a filmstrip file, you can set the different preferences for the particular file. These preferences include the movie format size and how many frames per second (FPS) to export.

Filmstrip files are generally large in size, depending on the length of the movie or excerpt. Because of this, you need to take all the usual large file size concerns into consideration, such as available RAM and sufficient scratch disk space. A 320×240 pixel filmstrip that is one minute in length takes up more than 180MB of hard disk space in file size.

When you view the filmstrip file in Photoshop, you can see every frame in one huge file that is many times the size of your screen in length. At the 1:16 view ratio, the thumbnail previews are about the size of an ant. The layout is six frames wide across the screen, and many more times that in sheer length from top to bottom—depending on the total actual number of frames in the filmstrip.

Each frame in the filmstrip has a frame number below the gray separation zone in the right corner of each frame, and it's corresponding SMPTE (Society of Motion Picture and Television Engineers) timecode base corresponding to its time and place in the film sequence (see fig. 5.18). Edit, draw, paint, doodle, and manipulate each frame in the movie to your heart's desire just as you would any other Photoshop document. Or you can apply a filter effect to the entire movie clip.

Tip

Preserve Filmstrips with Alpha Channel Masks

Here is a particularly handy note when you are creating a filmstrip for use in Photoshop: Premiere includes an alpha channel selection mask you can choose to load before making any changes to the file itself. Doing this preserves the filmstrip borders. Load this selection in the ordinary fashion by opening the Select menu and choosing Load Selection.

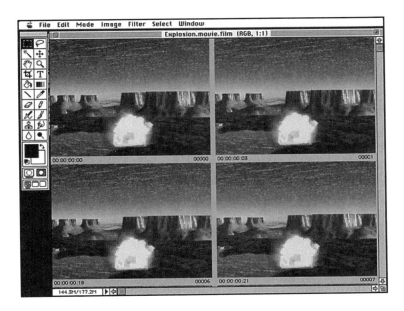

Fig. 5.18

This is what a typical filmstrip file in Photoshop looks like on the inside.

Caution

Don't Alter File Size, Dimensions, or Resolution

Be careful not to alter the physical file size dimensions or resolution in any way because that makes it impossible for the filmstrip file to be imported back into Premiere as a filmstrip movie. If you change these specs—even slightly—Photoshop doesn't let you save the file in the filmstrip format.

Opening Raw files

The Raw file format is the savior of bringing in files of unknown format, origin, or type to the Macintosh desktop. This is particularly useful if you want to open a file in raw binary format such as those produced on mainframes.

The welcoming user interface is not something that's meant to purposely confuse you. Buttons like Swap and Guess are there for your advantage and to assist you with its capability to second guess. Don't worry, with the state of computer graphics on the whole, it's doubtful you'll ever have to open a Raw file. But in case you do, I'll do my best to explain it in layman's terms and not step on anyone's toes while doing so.

Raw files are the "bare bones" of a graphics file. "Raw" itself is not a graphics format, but rather a description of undocumented file formats that consist only of binary information. Raw data files generally are devoid of the typical information that specifies the image dimensions, bit depth or the mode—such as RGB, CMYK, or grayscale. Other files that Photoshop only can open in Raw format do have headers and all of the defining parameters, but they are in a format that is unknown to Photoshop.

Use these steps to open a file with the Raw format:

1. Open the File menu and choose Open. In the dialog box that appears select the Show All Formats check box. Click on the pop-up menu and scroll down to select RAW.

2. Determine how tall and wide the file is. The Raw Options dialog box asks you to provide several parameters to format the data (see fig. 5.19). The image size is entered in the Width and Height fields. The Swap button switches the Height and Width values.

Fig. 5.19

The Raw Options dialog box presents a series of buttons that can save a file or present a difficult puzzle if you're missing the vital information.

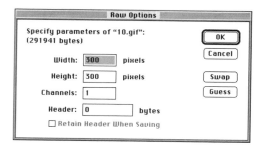

3. Specify how many channels the document contains. The number of channels in the image is specified in the Channels field. For an RGB image, enter the number 3, because an RGB image has three channels: red, green, and blue. A CMYK document has four channels, and a Grayscale image has one channel.

4. Figure out the header size if one exists. The Header field allows you to enter the number of bytes that compose the header (if there is one). This option tells Photoshop how many bytes to skip before interpreting the raw image. If this header is not ignored when opened in Raw, your image will look like a mess of seemingly random noise.

   To save the header information that is included with the original, select the Retain Header When Saving check box. This way, if it is a format that Photoshop does not recognize, you can preserve the file format information.

5. If you are missing information on size of file or header, click the Guess button. If you can specify the height, width, and how many channels the image contains, Photoshop calculates how many bytes the header contains by counting the remaining bytes of information. Because this is described as a "guess," it shouldn't surprise you that it doesn't always work; you may be presented with a misinterpreted garbage-soup image.

Take special note when you open CMYK files as Raw: you must convert them in Photoshop. When you open CMYK files using Raw, Photoshop creates the new file in RGB with an additional channel. All the CMYK information is there, but it needs to be reassembled to be properly viewed. To do this, convert the RGB file into a multichannel document and then convert the file to CMYK. At this point, your image appears inverted, so invert the file to see the image properly.

Opening PC Files

Cross-platform capability between Macintosh computers and PCs is one of Photoshop's true strong points. Files may be transferred between systems in a variety of file formats compatible to both platforms. In this section, we'll examine many file formats for exchanging Macintosh and Windows application files.

Opening Windows' Graphics File

With the ever-expanding Windows market of computing software, and more and more graphics being created in Windows programs, there is plenty of opportunity to bring these over to the Macintosh through Photoshop.

Before you attempt to open or import a Windows file, make sure you saved it in a cross-platform file format such as TIFF (Tagged Image File Format), JPEG-JFIF (non-QuickTime based) format, BMP (Color Bitmap-Windows), PCX (from the DOS/PC Paintbrush days), Targa (TGA/NuVista), CompuServe GIF (Graphics Interchange Format), or Scitex (universal high-end image-processing file format).

Perhaps one of the best opportunities for file exchanges is in the native Photoshop format. Photoshop 3 supports both versions 2.5 and 3 for exporting files. If you need to open a Photoshop image in Windows, save it as a native Photoshop file. Regardless of whether the Windows user is working with version 2.5 or 3 he or she will be able to open the file.

Tip

When Other Formats Fail

If you experience file corruption problems when exchanging Photoshop files between platforms, use the Photoshop format. If, for example, you save a file from the Macintosh and open the file on a Windows machine, export it from Photoshop in Windows as TIFF, EPS, or whatever format you may ultimately use. Sometimes TIFF files become corrupted and cannot be used when exchanging files. Resaving from within Photoshop on the desired platform may solve the problem.

If files cannot be placed in layout or illustration programs when transferred across platforms as TIFF or EPS, try opening the file in Photoshop on the destination platform. If the file opens, open the Image menu and choose Duplicate. Save the duplicate image in the desired format. Sometimes the duplicate image re-saved will rescue a potentially corrupted file.

Importing Graphic Formats from Adobe Photoshop for Windows

The available cross-platform formats included with Photoshop offer one of the most comprehensive of all applications software found on either the PC or Macintosh. File formats included with Photoshop that can read their respective formats are BMP, CompuServe GIF, PCX, and Targa. These formats can be opened with the standard Photoshop Open command.

You can find more information on the these formats in the section "Exporting Images" later in this chapter.

Acquiring Images from Other PC Imaging Programs

Photoshop can read images created in standard PC formats from PC applications like Aldus Photostyler, Fauve Matisse, Fractal Design Painter, Micrographx Picture Publisher, and PicturePress. However, Photoshop cannot read the proprietary formats of these programs.

One particular all-time favorite of designers and graphic artists is TIFF (Tagged Image File Format). The TIFF file is a continuous tone RGB or CMYK graphics file that's very similar in file format structure to a PICT. TIFF is perhaps the most popular file format and is used extensively by desktop publishers and digital design professionals on both PCs and Macintosh computers.

In Photoshop 3, TIFF files are saved either with a Mac header or with a PC header for easier porting to Windows applications. If you're exporting to a PC, make certain you stick to the DOS/Windows file naming convention that is eight characters long, with the appropriate three-character extension (in this case TIF).

Exporting Images

Photoshop provides the user with a number of file formats that you can export to use with many applications—on both the Macintosh and PC platforms. If you need to use your digital files to import in different applications, it is helpful to understand the various formats supported by Photoshop. To see the available file format types, open the File menu and choose Save or Save As. The first time you save an untitled document, you're prompted for a file format in the Save As dialog box (see fig. 5.20). After you select a format and a file name, all subsequent saves update the file. To change a format from a saved file, you must choose the Save As option. (All references to Save or Save As in this section apply to the File menu and the respective choices for saving files.)

II

Acquiring Images

137

Fig. 5.20

Photoshop 3's file
format options in
the Save As dialog
box.

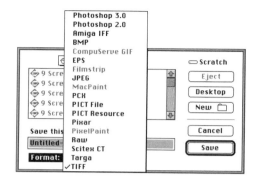

Native Formats

As stated earlier in this chapter, any file saved from an application and
used exclusively by that application is known as a *native file*. The Photoshop
3 format is a native format for Adobe Photoshop; thus, a file saved as
Photoshop 3 can be opened and edited in Photoshop 3. Previous versions
of Photoshop are also supported. If, for example, you need to provide a file
to a user who has not upgraded to Photoshop 3 and still uses Photoshop
2.5.1, the file can be saved in a format which supports the earlier version.

Photoshop 2.5.1 support is provided in the General Preferences settings.
Open the File menu and select Preferences, General. Click the More
button. Select the 2.5 Format Compatibility check box to save all Photoshop
files as Photoshop 3 and to include the 2.5 compatible format (see fig.
5.21). If you work exclusively in Photoshop 3, it is best to disable the 2.5
compatibility. Photoshop 3 files saved without the 2.5 format take up less
disk space.

Fig. 5.21

Photoshop 2.5
compatibility
enabled in the
More Preferences
dialog box.

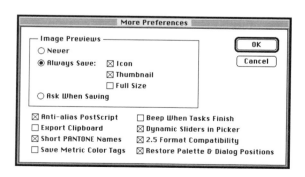

In addition to Photoshop 2.5, there is a separate file format compatibility for the earlier version of Photoshop 2.0. This is a separate format available in the Save options. All of the Photoshop file formats fall within the description of native formats and cannot be used in other applications.

The Photoshop 3 format is essential if you work on documents with layers. The Photoshop 3 format is the only format that supports the preservation of layer information, so that the layers can be preserved for additional editing sessions. If the Photoshop 3 format is saved with 2.5 enabled and the document is opened in the earlier version, all layers are flattened into a composite image. For more information about layers and preserving them, see chapter 10, "Working with Layers."

BMP

BMP is a Windows Bitmap format native to Microsoft Paint. This format is widely supported by a number of Windows and OS/2 applications. The format has been around for a long time and is supported by many applications for both the business and graphics worlds. You can save BMP files in 24-bit color (16 million colors) from RGB images or eight-bit color from indexed color images. Fewer bits can be saved from grayscale and bitmap files.

When the BMP format is chosen, the BMP Options dialog box appears (see fig. 5.22). In this dialog box, you can define the bit depth of the image and whether you want to compress the image. If you select the Compress (RLE, or Run-Length Encoding) check box, the file is compressed with the RLE scheme. RLE is a lossless compression for saving BMP files. Compression schemes are usually referred to as lossy or lossless. A *lossy compression* eliminates pixels during the compression and often reduces its quality when it is uncompressed and printed. A *lossless compression*, on the other hand, does not deteriorate an image.

Fig. 5.22

When you export BMP files, you can describe compression schemes and bit depth.

CompuServe GIF

CompuServe is one of the oldest and most successful bulletin board services in the world. Years ago, CompuServe was made up of industrial reports, airline ticket orders, and chitchat among computer users. As the industry grew and graphics became popular on our desktop computers, CompuServe developed GIF (Graphics Interchange Format) for compressing eight-bit images that could be telecommunicated to their service and exchanged among users. Some became quite creative in uploading images that bordered on X-rated graphics!

EPS

Encapsulated PostScript (EPS) is simply one of the best formats for digital prepress and high-end imaging. EPS is supported by top-notch applications for professional uses, such as Adobe Illustrator, Aldus FreeHand, Aldus PageMaker, and QuarkXPress. In some instances, EPS files have truer images in color representation than even TIFF files. EPS exports from Photoshop have a number of options for encoding, masking, and halftoning. When the EPS option is selected during the file save process, the EPS Format dialog box appears, which describes the nature of the EPS export (see fig. 5.23).

Fig. 5.23

The EPS export format is one of the best file types used in high-end prepress.

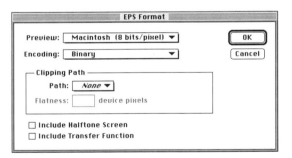

EPS files can be exported with a number of *previews*; these describe the view of the image on-screen. Macintosh users should choose the Macintosh view (PICT), and files exported to PCs should include the TIFF preview. For video work, use the JPEG option. The bit depth given with the preview options relates only to the display of the image. The higher the number of bits, the better the screen appearance. Regardless of the screen view, the image produces equally well on printers.

Tip

Speeding Up Performance

Whenever screen views are optimized to provide the best possible views, the computer performance is reduced. As the computer takes longer to refresh the screen, the waiting period between editing documents becomes greater. Unless it is essential for your layout, always choose screen views with just enough information to accurately accomplish your designs.

If you experience printing problems with images previewing in color and higher bit depths, re-save the file without color previews and try to print the image again. Sometimes the file prints with less information in the preview.

Another item to choose when you save an EPS file is the Encoding scheme. The choices are ASCII (American Standard Code for Information Interchange), binary, and JPEG (Joint Photographic Experts Group). During earlier versions of some of the page layout and illustration software, some applications preferred ASCII encoding while others preferred binary encoding. QuarkXPress has typically preferred binary while Aldus PageMaker used ASCII. Today, if you use these applications in their most recent versions, almost all use the binary encoding. Binary encoding is much preferred because it takes almost half the storage space of an ASCII encoded file. Consult your user manual for preferred formats and encoding for all your applications. JPEG is a lossy compression scheme; it should be reserved for video work and not for documents designed for printing. If you work in print, don't use JPEG or any other lossy compression. After you lose pixels in an image, you can't get them back.

If a path has been saved, the path name can be selected from the Path pop-up menu, in the Clipping Path area of the dialog box. Whenever a clipping path is used, be certain to set the flatness available in the EPS dialog box. Flatness settings for laser printers should be set at 3. Imagesetters printing between 1200 and 3600 dpi should have flatness settings in the document no less than 7. Clipping paths are difficult to image on PostScript devices. Flatness settings help the imaging of files with clipping paths.

The check boxes for Include Halftone Screen and Include Transfer Function should *always* be left deselected unless you're a very experienced user. Selecting these prevents any overriding at the imagesetter or by the person printing your file. For a complete explanation on setting screens and functions, refer to chapter 22, "Photoshop for the Digital Designer."

EPS files are ideal for color separation work. When a document is converted to CMYK color, Photoshop can perform separations through the DCS (Desktop Color Separation) format. The DCS option appears only with CMYK color images (see fig. 5.24). DCS files create five separate documents. Each of the four separated files, such as cyan, magenta, yellow, and black, are used when printing the image. The fifth file is a composite view of low resolution for position only (FPO). The FPO is placed in a document for separating and the other files are sent to the printer as each separation is imaged.

Fig. 5.24

The EPS Format dialog box with the DCS option enabled.

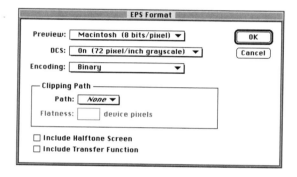

EPS formats also work well with bitmap images. When black line art images need to appear without the white background—as if they were masked, the EPS format renders all white areas transparent. Transparency in the white areas only applies to bitmap images. When an image is in bitmap mode and the file is saved as EPS, the Transparent Whites check box appears in the EPS Format dialog box (see fig. 5.25). Selecting the check box makes all white areas transparent.

Fig. 5.25

The EPS Format dialog box with Transparent Whites selected.

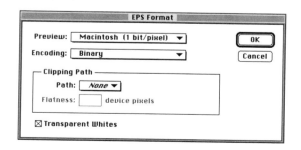

Filmstrip

Filmstrip is a file format for exporting video files that are used for rotoscoping from programs such as Adobe Premiere. Files can be imported from Premiere, edited in Photoshop, and exported back out as a filmstrip file. When the file is used back in Premiere, the video clip appears with any edited frames performed in Photoshop.

JPEG

JPEG (Joint Photographic Experts Group) is a lossy compression scheme most often used with video. JPEG files offer very high compression rates that can store large files economically on disk. JPEG discards data from the file which might appear fine when viewing video, especially with repetitive frames that contain the same colors. In such a case, the viewing of the video is not noticeable to the user. With printed material, however, it is most often undesirable and should be avoided for professional imaging.

TIFF

Aldus Corporation developed TIFF (Tagged Image File Format) specifically for saving scanned images; it is now one of the most widely used formats in the graphics world. TIFF is ideal for file exchanges among systems and applications supporting the format. If you're looking for the most problem-free format for file exchanges, TIFF works like a champion.

TIFF is also excellent for grayscale imaging and produces excellent quality halftones. Color separations are also excellent, but for the most critical eye, the EPS DCS files noted earlier are the optimum choice.

TIFF also supports a compression scheme that can be used when exporting the file in this format. The LZW (Lempel-Ziv-Welch) compression is a lossless scheme and doesn't reduce image quality by a single pixel.

Other Formats Available

In addition to the popular formats previously mentioned, Photoshop supports some exports for several other file types. This section takes a brief look at the remainder of the formats available for exporting from within Photoshop.

II

Acquiring Images

Amiga IFF

The Amiga Interchange File Format (IFF) is used to save a file in a format that the Amiga Commodore computer can use. Perhaps the most popular use of these computers is the support for NewTek's Video Toaster. In addition to Amiga computers, the IFF format is also supported by several paint programs on PCs, such as DeluxePaint from Electronic Arts. When you create Photoshop formats on the Mac and transfer the files to other platforms, it is important to know what format is preferred by the application receiving the Photoshop file. In the above example, the IFF format is ideal.

Another variation of the IFF format is the Amiga HAM (Hold and Modify) format, which is a compressed version of the Interchange File Format. HAM images conform to only two fixed image sizes, 320×200 pixels or 320×400 pixels. All other sizes distort the image and make it appear stretched out.

The HAM export is not found in the Save dialog box. To save a file in Amiga HAM, open the File menu and choose Export. The Export submenu provides an opportunity for third-party vendors to include plug-in modules to export proprietary formats and add additional functionality to Photoshop when transferring files to other applications or systems. Figure 5.26 shows the formats shipped with Photoshop 3.

Fig. 5.26

The Export submenu can accommodate additional plug-ins for third-party file exports.

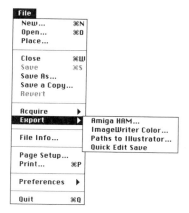

MacPaint

MacPaint was originally introduced with the Macintosh in 1984 when the computer shipped with MacPaint and MacWrite. It was the first graphics application on the Macintosh and, at the time, astounded users by what it could do with illustration. By today's standards, and when compared to Adobe Photoshop, it is slightly amusing and crude. MacPaint images are limited to 72 dpi and produce bitmapped images with a noticeably jagged edge regardless of the device used where the file is imaged. Today, professional designers use it mainly as a template for PostScript illustration programs.

Paths to Illustrator

The Paths to Illustrator choice is available when you open the File menu and choose Export. This format is unique to Adobe Illustrator, where paths drawn in Photoshop can be exported as Bézier curves and edited in Illustrator. When you open Adobe Illustrator, you see crop marks that begin at the lower-left corner of the document window. Be certain to view the document in keyline view. The exported paths default to no stroke and no fill. At first, it may seem like the paths are not there. However, when you view Artwork only, the paths are displayed.

PCX

PCX is used by many PC and Windows applications. Originally, it was developed by Zsoft for PC Paintbrush and now includes support for most PC Windows graphics applications. Because the format is so widely used among PC applications, it is often chosen first by many users. It should, however, be avoided if you are a professional designer, especially when you use CMYK color for separations. The preferred choices for color separating are EPS and TIFF formats.

PICT File

The PICT (Picture) format is native to the Macintosh. It first appeared in August, 1984, with the introduction of Apple Computer's MacDraw. Since that time, PICT has been used by many applications, especially when images are designed for screen previews. PICT is ideal for presentations, screen displays, and video work. PICT is a disaster when printing to PostScript devices. The PICT format should be completely avoided when files are to be imaged with PostScript interpreters. Some printing devices, such as film recorders, prefer PICT formats for imaging and all QuickDraw

II

Acquiring Images

printers also prefer PICT files. Laser printers with PostScript RIPS (raster image processor) and high-end imaging equipment, like imagesetters, dyesub printers, and high-end inkjet printers, all print EPS and TIFF images faster and more efficiently.

PICT Resource

PICT Resource permits the user to export files that can be used as startup screens. For example, I recently downloaded a file from America Online of film actress Sela Ward, saved it out of Photoshop as a PICT Resource, and placed it in my system folder. Every time I boot my computer, she appears during the startup. The startup screen replaces the Macintosh welcome screen and displays any image you save as a PICT Resource. The resource file has an ID number specified in the Save dialog box. The startup screen should include the default ID of zero (0).

PIXAR

The PIXAR format was designed to transfer files to PIXAR workstations. These are high-end workstations used for 3-D imaging and high-end graphics. Photoshop files can be ported over to the PIXAR workstation and used with the 3-D renderings created by these machines. PIXAR developed applications for the Mac such as MacRenderMan, Showplace, and Typestry. The company's most notable applications remain with the high-end imaging on their proprietary systems.

PixelPaint

At one time, PixelPaint from Pixel Resources was a strong complement to Photoshop. It actually preceded Photoshop as the first sophisticated pixel-based editing program. As Photoshop grew in acceptance in the user community, it became the *de facto* standard as a design and photo-editing tool; thus, PixelPaint lost market share and is now almost non-existent in the professional design community. The PixelPaint format is still supported for transferring files, but is of little use to those who work with and exchange Photoshop files.

Raw

Raw is most often used to transfer files to mainframe computers and across computer platforms. When the format is chosen and you save a file as a Raw image, the Raw Options dialog box appears (see fig. 5.27). This dialog box must hold some precise information for the file to be usable.

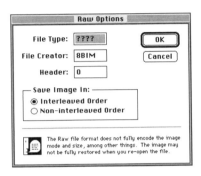

Fig. 5.27

The Raw Options dialog box must be used for entering precise information about the file.

The File Type relates to Macintosh files only. PICT, Text, TIFF, and others are common file types for the Macintosh. If the file is to be transferred to another computer, anything entered in the File Type box is fine because no other system uses this information.

File Creator defaults to the Photoshop ID, which is 8BIM. If you change this, Photoshop is not able to re-open the image. For all practical purposes, leave the default value undisturbed.

The Header is specified in the number of bytes appearing at the beginning of the file. If no header is used, the file can be edited with utilities such as Norton Disk Doctor or MacTools to replace the zeros with header information.

The Order is either Interleaved or Non-interleaved. The Interleaved Order describes color values by channel in a sequential order. The first pixel is red, the second pixel is green, the third pixel is blue, and so on. When the Non-Interleaved Order is used, the first byte is red, the next byte represents the next red pixel, and so on until the red is fully described. Then the green pixels are described, and then the blue pixels are described.

II

Acquiring Images

Scitex CT

Scitex CT (Continuous Tone) is a proprietary format for Scitex imaging systems. Photoshop supports files scanned on Scitex equipment and saved in the Scitex CT format. Depending on the service bureau, some bureaus may prefer that you save in native Photoshop format and let the Scitex shop convert the image to their system. At the user level, it is more important for you to be able to open high-end scans saved as Scitex CT than to have the ability to save in the format. When using a service with Scitex or any other equipment, you should first consult with the imaging specialists about how they prefer to receive your files for imaging to their systems.

Targa

Truvision's Targa or TGA format is more common on PCs than Macintosh computers. Truvision developed the format to support their line of video cards which enabled saving files in 32-bit mode and included the eight-bit video alpha channel. Service bureaus see many files in this format from users who dump video frames to their computer and want to produce color images from the video captures. Don't let the extra bits fool you though, these images are less than ideal for digital imaging and don't produce quality color prints or separations. For professional work, rely on high-end scanners.

Where To Go from Here

▶ When you save files you must be aware of the layer information and how the file is treated when exported. Look at chapter 10, "Working with Layers," for a complete understanding of layers.

▶ This chapter discussed many different Acquire modules. Almost all scanners ship with Photoshop plug-ins. Look at chapter 6, "Scanning Images," to understand the methods of acquiring scanned images.

▶ This chapter briefly touched on Photo CDs. Look at chapter 7, "Photo-CD Images," for a comprehensive view of using this technology.

▶ See Part VI, "Publishing," to learn how images are prepared and ultimately saved or exported. Look at chapter 21, "Photoshop for the Desktop Publisher," chapter 22, "Photoshop for the Digital Designer," and chapter 24, "Photoshop for the Professional Photographer," for more information on when to use one format over another.

Scanning Images

For many, this chapter on scanning might be considered one of the most important chapters in this book. Once we develop an understanding of using Adobe Photoshop, the issue of scanning becomes an important concern to anyone preparing images for viewing on-screen, in print, or in video presentations. Scanning is the essential companion of Photoshop and it is often one of the most difficult and misunderstood procedures in digital imaging. We are quite often faced with questions like, "At what resolution do I scan the image? What file format do I choose to save my scanned image?" and "Should I use the line art or grayscale mode when scanning my image?" These and many more questions are a mystery in the desktop imaging industry for the novice and professional.

Using Photoshop for Macintosh • Using Photoshop for Macintosh • Using Photoshop for Macintosh • Using Photoshop for Mac

by Ted Padova

CHAPTER 6

This chapter on scanning addresses the questions above, explains the scanning process, and describes how to create good scans for editing in Photoshop 3. We'll first look at the different types of scanners and then examine the scanning process. We'll look at scanning different types of images such as line art, black-and-white photos, and color photos. We'll also look at how scans are used and when to use one scanning device over another. So hold on, pick a comfortable place to curl up with this book, and we'll try to solve the scanning mystery.

Understanding Scanning Hardware

Scanning devices come in several varieties and vary in price considerably. Just stop and think of the scanner you can purchase with a street value of $600 and compare that cost to a high-end scanner at $100,000. With this much variation in cost, is there really a difference between images scanned with low-end machines and images scanned with expensive high-end devices? Unfortunately, every time we ask such a question with respect to scanning, the answer will typically be *sometimes*. Sometimes we will need to obtain a high-end scan. Sometimes we can use scans from low-end devices. Knowing the differences between the scans on such devices is the first key to understanding the scanning process. Without getting into too much technobabble, let's take a look at the different types of scanners and examine their strong and weak points.

Handheld Scanners

Handheld scanners are at the lowest end of scanning devices. They were more popular during the early days of desktop publishing when flatbed models were much more expensive. A handheld scanner is dragged over a photo or artwork to achieve the scan. The usability of the scan is often determined by how steadily you can smoothly drag the device over the image to be scanned.

Considering the cost of flatbed models today, which can be purchased for a price lower than the retail price of Adobe Photoshop, you should dismiss any consideration of buying a handheld scanner. Handheld scanners will soon end up in a museum with the pet rock and hula-hoop, which is where they should remain for our amusement. If you own one, contribute it to the Smithsonian and purchase a flatbed scanner.

Flatbed Scanners

The most common scanner today is the desktop flatbed scanner. I hesitate to comment about price since we'll probably see many more price reductions before Photoshop 4.0 arrives. As of this writing, some flatbeds are below $600 street cost and are still moving downward. If price is the single, most important consideration for you, there are several models from which to choose within this price range. Prices for flatbed models can vary considerably depending on the manufacturer and scanning capability. To understand why these prices vary so much, let's take a look at the technology and components of the flatbed scanners.

Flatbed scanners are CCD (Charge-Coupled Devices). These tiny little light-sensitive electronic chips measure light reflected from the object being scanned to produce the digital image. The number of CCDs in a scanner is reflected in the price. Obviously, the more CCDs, the heavier the price tag. Manufacturers will advertise scanners as being capable of scanning resolutions from 300 ppi (pixels per inch) or dpi (dots per inch) to 1200 or more ppi. The resolutions of the scanning device are related to the number of sensors in the scanner.

What this means for you, the end user, is a need to know the differences so that you can make a wise purchase. A 300 ppi scan on one device will be noticeably different on another, more expensive device. To fully understand the differences between scanners, we need to look at several issues related to image quality.

Bit Depth

Bit depth is how many grays or colors a scanner can produce. A one-bit scanner will produce two grays: black and white. Scans of one-bit in depth are sufficient for line art and illustrations. They are not sufficient for photographs or color images. Four bits produce a 16 gray level scan, eight-bit scanners produce 256 gray levels or colors. Both of these scanner types were marketed several years ago and are rapidly becoming extinct. The 24-bit scanners produce over 16 million colors. These scanners capture eight bits per channel. For example, the scan produces 256 grays for the Red channel, 256 for the Green channel, and 256 for the Blue channel. The result is an RGB color image. When you multiply $256 \times 256 \times 256$ you get over 16 million possible color variations. Most of the lowest priced flatbed scanners are 24-bit scanners.

Unfortunately, there are many differences in image quality between 24-bit scanners. One scanner might produce excellent scans with images that show a lot of detail in the highlight and shadow areas, while another scanner will produce dark images in the shadows with less detail. So you wonder, "If I have a 24-bit scanner, how come my photos appear murky and flat?" Well, there's more to this scanner issue. It's called *dynamic range*.

Dynamic Range

Scanners that capture the shadow details are known to have a good dynamic range. Having a good dynamic range produces images with more detail in shadows and less overall black in the dark areas of the image. The reason there is a problem with the dynamic range of CCD scanners is the nature of the photosensitive elements. CCDs have a *linear response* while the reflection of the photograph has a *logarithmic response*. Think of a gradient created in Photoshop that begins with black and graduates to white. A linear progression is made from the black to the white in equal stepping. As you progress down the gradient, the grays become more apparent. The first part of the gradient is intensely black and less discernible. A logarithmic blend, on the other hand, creates the first part of the gradient in more distinct steps and then graduates to white in a smooth transition. The result is more detail in the black areas with discernible grays.

Scanner manufacturers are attempting to resolve the problem of poor dynamic range by producing scanners with higher bit depths captured during the scanning process. The 32-bit and 48-bit scanners attempt to produce tonal correction and sharpening before an image is sampled down to 24 bits (*downsampling* an image is the process of lowering the resolution). In essence, the extra bits are used to correct the problem of the dynamic range. The final result will be a 24-bit image with more detail in the shadows and an overall strong dynamic range.

More Is Not Always Better

So here you are, the artist or designer who doesn't give a hoot about CCDs, electronics, or technology. You just want a decent scan, and you want to buy a scanner for yourself or the office. What will be your determinant in acquiring a model for home or office use?

The primary misconception in scanning is to think *more is better*. The more ppi (pixels per inch) scanned, the better the image, right? No, not always. As mentioned earlier, the dynamic range must be considered too if you want to produce good quality images. I have a 1200 ppi scanner at the office and a 400 ppi scanner at home. If I were to scan anything, I would always choose my 400 ppi scanner. It produces far better images with much more dynamic range. Don't be fooled by the thought that the more samples you can obtain, the better the quality of the image produced.

If this is true, how do you go about purchasing a scanner? There are some steps to follow when making a scanner purchase which you should consider.

Purchasing a Desktop Scanner

If you're in the market for purchasing a scanner, there are some inexpensive steps you can take to make a good decision and eventually save yourself some money.

▶ *Know your scanning needs.* If you are an artist who needs to create scans for templates and line art which will eventually be colorized and illustrated in Adobe Photoshop, the tonal ranges and dynamic ranges of a scanner carry little importance. Line art is black and white, so the higher resolution scanners are the most useful for you.

If you scan photographs for producing halftone images, grayscale scanning is critical and dynamic range is necessary to capture shadows in detail.

If most of your work is reflective art from photographic prints, a flatbed model is the scanner of choice. If your source material is 35mm slides, a slide or transparency scanner is preferable to a flatbed outfitted with a transparency adapter.

▶ *Read the reports.* Many magazines have testing labs where they perform tests and write special articles on various hardware equipment. Magazines such as *MacWorld, MacUser, MacWeek,* and *Publish* produce reports from their testing labs. Find issues that compare the testing of flatbed or transparency scanners. Usually, they produce images in grayscale and color in the reports for visual comparisons.

(continues)

153

▶ *Perform scanning tests.* Some service bureaus and digital imaging centers rent time on computers and scanners. Try to find service centers in your area where you can rent time on a computer and scanner. Scan images of the type of work you do and have the images output on the various printing devices you use. Try to use an assortment of images with different lighting conditions and tones.

▶ *Take a computer class.* Many universities, state colleges, and community colleges have extension programs offering classes in digital design and the visual arts. You can take advantage of computer labs outfitted with computers and scanners, as well as tap into the knowledge of the instructors. In addition, the classmates and colleagues you meet provide an excellent network for obtaining information on many different scanner models and types. People become fanatics with respect to their computers and will defend them, regardless of any problems with the hardware. With third-party hardware, they will be much more honest and admit the shortcomings of the instruments they use.

Transparency Scanners

Transparencies, like 35mm slides and 4 × 5 film, can be scanned on flatbed scanners outfitted with a transparency adapter or on scanners dedicated to scanning only transparencies. Where flatbeds provide some good results for reflective images, such as photographic prints and line art, they fall short with transparency scanning. Scans from transparencies are much better if they're produced with dedicated transparency scanners.

Transparency scanners offer much higher resolutions than flatbed scanners and they typically capture more than eight bits per channel, which gives the scans a much better dynamic range. Don't let the resolution fool you. Slide scanners producing 2700 to 3500 ppi are capturing images at a high resolution, so the image can be sized up from 35mm. The image may appear in a document window at 14-inches-by-10-inches with a 72 ppi resolution. When sized to express 266 ppi, the image will be a little more than 3-inches-by-2-inches.

Transparency scanners, for 35mm scanning only, have broken the $2,000 barrier. The Coolscan by Nikon is a popular desktop transparency scanner that provides good quality scans. Kodak makes some excellent slide scanners as well. If you need to scan 4 × 5 transparencies, the Leaf 45 is designed to support 35mm, 2 1/4, and 4 × 5 transparencies. The Leaf scanner is higher priced; it's usually out of the price range for individual users and small agencies. Leaf scanners may be available in photo labs where scans are performed by service professionals and sold on a per scan or per megabyte fee.

Kodak Photo CD

We have included a separate chapter on Kodak Photo CD; those interested in knowing more about it should look at chapter 7, "Photo-CD Images." It is mentioned here merely as a possible alternative to purchasing a scanner or as a means of obtaining better color images than you could using your flatbed scanner.

High-End Scanners

Most high-end scanners use photo-multiplier tubes (PMTs) instead of CCDs. High-end scanners begin at around $30,000 in price and exceed $100,000. These scanners are usually in prepress houses, print shops, and service bureaus. Scan orders are placed at the service center and technicians perform the scanning, color correcting, and cleaning up of the digital images. The most common high-end scanners are drums where the artwork is either taped to a cylinder or placed inside a cylinder that spins rapidly. The PMTs move across the images as the cylinder is rotated. There are also some CCD systems in the high-end range that produce equally good scans. These scanners are much more sophisticated than the flatbeds and provide excellent tonal ranges and good quality scans.

High-end scans are used by professional artists and printers when color separations are needed. For any quality work that needs to be separated, high-end scanners should be your only choice. If you try to color separate flatbed scans, the results will be disappointing to both you and your client. Don't accept jobs without the budget to support quality work. Most often it will cost you more money when scrapping the low-end scans and redoing the job with higher quality images. My advice to anyone with a client who won't budget high-end scans for color separations is to walk away from the job. In the end, you'll be glad you did.

II

Acquiring Images

155

Using Scanning Software

So far, you have learned that you should not use handheld scanners and that high-end scanners are not within your reach financially. For those of you who wish to perform your own scans, let's assume your scanning tasks will be completed on either the flatbed models or slide scanners. The remainder of this chapter addresses the scanning process for these models.

Scanners are only half the equation for acquiring images into your computer. The other half rests with the software. Two varieties of software are used with scanners. One is a Photoshop plug-in supplied by the scanner manufacturer; the other is the application software designed for scanning.

Photoshop Plug-Ins

Ever since Photoshop's introduction, manufacturers of scanners have provided plug-in software modules to allow their scanners to be accessed from within Photoshop. Even the high-end drum scanners provide Photoshop plug-ins for scanning on the sophisticated systems. Anyone who scans on flatbeds or slide scanners usually prefers scanning with a Photoshop plug-in.

Photoshop scanner plug-ins are installed by copying the plug-in to the Acquire/Export folder. When Photoshop 3 completes its installation, the application will be stored in a folder along with three other folders titled Plug-ins, Tutorial, and Goodies. Inside the Plug-ins folder will be a number of other folders including the Acquire/Export folder. To install a scanner plug-in, drag the plug-in to the Acquire/Export folder. From this point, you can access the scanner from within Photoshop; open the File menu, choose Acquire, and select the scanner plug-in. When you access the plug-in, a dialog box appears which enables you to make various selections about the scan. Figure 6.1 shows some of the choices available for the LACIE Silverscanner II plug-in module.

Most scanner plug-ins are sophisticated in that they enable you to specify how scans are made. Many of the plug-in choices are covered in the following sections.

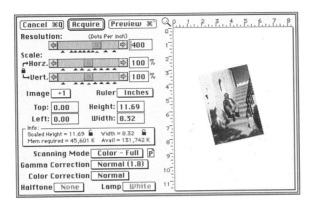

Fig. 6.1

The LACIE Silver
Scanner II plug-in
provides a number
of options for user
choice on how a
scan is to be
performed.

Scanner Resolution

Scanner resolutions are measured in two areas. The true or optical resolution of the scanner and the interpolated resolution. It is important to understand the difference between optical and interpolated resolutions. *Optical resolution* is the actual number of pixels a scanner can acquire during the scanning process. *Interpolated resolution* is a means of mathematical guesswork where pixels will be created mathematically and added to the image.

Tip

Use the Proper Resolution Settings when Scanning

There are two simple rules to follow when scanning images with respect to resolution. First, never scan grayscale or color images above the optical resolution. In other words, don't use interpolated resolutions when scanning for these modes. Second, when scanning line art, always scan at the highest interpolated resolution. When you obtain a line art scan, you can downsample or drop the resolution in Photoshop to match the printer's resolution.

Scaling

Scanning plug-ins provide scaling options where the image may be sized up or down during the scan. When images are sized up, the resolution should accommodate the sizing. For example, if you wish to size an image up 200 percent and want 200 pixels per inch resolution, the scan should

II

Acquiring Images

157

be made at 400 ppi. In this case, the higher resolution will accommodate the scan without interpolation.

Scanning Mode

The scanning mode permits choices between color, grayscale, and line art scans. If you wish to scan line art, be certain to scan the image in this mode. Likewise, grayscale images should be scanned in the grayscale mode. If you choose 24-bit color and change the mode to grayscale or line art, the original color scan will be extraordinarily large and take substantial time to convert the mode in Photoshop.

Gamma

Gamma controls the midtones in the image. When you increase the gamma, the midtones appear lighter. When you decrease the gamma, the midtones appear darker. Also, you need to consider the output device to which the image will be printed. If you intend to print to a laser printer, the gamma will need to be set to a higher setting than an imagesetter. When you experiment with gamma adjustments, try settings of 2.0 for laser printers and settings of 1.6 for imagesetters.

Preview Image

A Preview button appears in all plug-in software. The *preview* is a quick pass of the scanner that displays a mini-view of the scanner bed. This view is important; it helps you determine where cropping is needed. In addition, you can use the preview to determine whether you need to adjust the brightness or contrast settings before scanning.

Cropping Boundaries

All scanner plug-ins enable you to designate the area you want to scan. Some software is not intuitive when you want to crop an area of the image. You might not see a selection marquee or tool to create a rectangle where the scanned area is to be defined. In many cases you just drag the selection arrow as if it were a Selection Marquee tool to define the boundaries of the area that will be picked up by the scanner. Always be certain to crop the image as closely as you can. The less area scanned, the smaller the file size.

Brightness and Contrast Adjustments

Most scanner plug-ins enable you to adjust the brightness and contrast settings before the scan occurs. If at first you don't notice some of the controls that are discussed here, you might search through any menus or buttons in your scanning plug-in to see if other dialog boxes appear that enable you to make adjustments. With the Silverscanner II, the brightness and contrast settings appear in a second dialog box, as illustrated in figure 6.2.

When you adjust brightness and contrast on an existing image in Photoshop, you lose information. Photoshop takes two values and maps them into one value, which eliminates pixels. When you adjust the brightness and contrast during the scanning process, the scanning software redistributes pixels and you do not lose information. After scanning, you can perform the final tweaking of the image inside Photoshop.

Tip

Make All Adjustments for the Best Image Quality before You Scan the Image

Even with all the marvelous features of Adobe Photoshop available to us, Photoshop has difficulty resurrecting bad scans. Photoshop can't work with information that's not in the image. If a loss of detail or tones occurs during the scan, Photoshop is unable to create what is not present. Always make adjustments with the scanning plug-in to achieve the best possible image before you bring it into Photoshop.

When you purchase a scanner, study the manual accompanying the plug-in software. Be certain of all the plug-in capabilities and understand the controls. Experiment with adjustments so you completely understand how to achieve the best scans with your hardware and software. Once you achieve a good scan, you can use all of the wonderful capabilities of Photoshop to enhance or modify your images.

Fig. 6.2

The Silverscanner II plug-in provides a second dialog box to control the brightness and contrast controls.

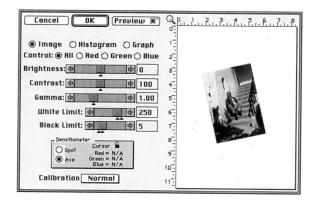

Ofoto by Light Source

Some third-party software on the market is dedicated to scanning outside Photoshop. The most popular scanning application that is not a plug-in module is Light Source's Ofoto. Ofoto for some time only supported grayscale scanning. Its most recent version now supports 24-bit color and grayscale scanning. One of the most impressive features of Ofoto is its capability to straighten images during the scanning process. Ofoto automatically adjusts an image so that you don't have to rotate it when you bring it into Photoshop. Another feature of Ofoto is its capability to scan images from printed pieces without a moiré pattern. All images with dots or halftoning appear with a moiré when you scan the material. Ofoto eliminates the moiré when performing the scan. In addition to these features, Ofoto provides support for a vast number of scanners and includes some impressive calibrating options for output to printers and imagesetters.

Twain

Twain (Technology Without An Important Name) is a standard developed by Aldus, Hewlett-Packard, and some other vendors to scan images from within other applications. Perhaps one of the best uses for Twain is batch scanning for FPO (For Position Only) images in layout applications to create some rough layouts. There was an attempt to create a standard with the Twain modules by the various vendors involved. However, it has not become as popular as the many plug-ins available for Adobe Photoshop. Hewlett-Packard uses the module with many of the scanners it ships, and you may see it as a plug-in module for other applications software.

> **Caution**
>
> **Respect the Rights of Others**
>
> Upon occasion, there are legitimate reasons and proper conditions for scanning printed pieces. If you own the rights to the source material, scanning printed pieces is permissible. If, however, you scan someone else's material and use it, you are in violation of copyright law. At the least, using the material is unethical. A photographer is very much an artist, as is any illustrator, designer, or painter. To respect their rights, use your own photographs or purchase CDs with stock photos that permit unlimited use. Creating designs from your own photos is much more satisfying and you will avoid any legal trouble. If you need stock photos, several sources provide them with unlimited use and royalty free. All you have to do is purchase the CD used to store the images. One of my favorites is the Vivid Details series of CDs. They use drum scans at high resolutions and have a wonderful collection.

II

Acquiring Images

Understanding the Scanning Process

Obtaining good quality scans is a matter of practice; quality improves as you become familiar with your hardware and software. We can provide some general guidelines to start you off on the road to better scanning, but after you learn those, scanning requires practice, practice, and more practice. To get you started in the right direction, let's examine some of the issues you need to control when doing any scanning.

Resolution

The first consideration of scanning an image is to decide what the optimum resolution is for your scan. Resolution requirements depend on the type of artwork that you are scanning. Line art, for example, has different requirements than grayscale or color art. The next sections examine each type of artwork independently.

Line Art Scanning

Line art refers to line illustrations, black and white artwork, text characters, logos, and similar artwork. There are only two color values with line art, black and white. The advantage of scanners claiming high resolutions of 1200, 1600, or 2400 ppi is most evident when performing line art scans. My preference for scanning line art is to scan it at the highest resolution of the scanner's capability and then downsample the image in Photoshop to suit my needs. In the case of my Silverscanner II, which I dearly love, I scan line art at the highest resolution, 1600 ppi. When I have my scan in Photoshop, I drop the resolution to match my printing device. For example, if I intend to print at 600 dpi, I resample my image to 600 dpi. If, on the other hand, I wish to print my file on an imagesetter, I resample the image to 1200 dpi. To resample an image in Photoshop 3, open the Image menu and choose Image Size. Figure 6.3 shows the Image Size dialog box with the available settings for width, height, and resolution.

Fig. 6.3

The Image Size dialog box enables you to down-sample an image to lower resolutions.

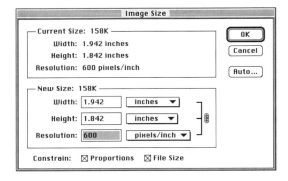

Tip

Choose the Proper Resolution for Line Art

Line art resolution should match the printing device resolution. Printing line art at 1200 dpi to a 600 dpi printer will not produce a better image than printing the same file at 600 dpi to the same printer. When outputting to imagesetters, using resolutions of 1200 dpi is sufficient regardless of whether you wish to print at 1200, 2400, or 3600 dpi.

When you scan in a line art mode from your plug-in software, the file mode is bitmap. If you change the mode to grayscale, the file size will increase eight times over the bitmap mode. Both modes will print exactly the same and there will be no advantage in converting to grayscale. Keep the file in the bitmap mode and export the image as an EPS or TIFF to import into layout or illustration programs.

Caution

If You Want Your Files To Print, Read This!

There's nothing that will drop a $200,000 imagesetter to its knees faster than a 1200 dpi bitmap sized down and rotated in a layout or illustration program. Sizing placed files in other programs is always going to cause you problems. Don't ever do it, under any circumstances. When you need to size and/or rotate images, perform all these functions in Photoshop. Save the file and place it into the layout or illustration application at a 1:1 ratio and leave it alone. If you need to adjust it, reopen Photoshop, perform your adjustments in Photoshop, and then update your links.

Grayscale Scanning

You should always scan grayscale images within the optical resolution of the scanner. Determining resolution is related to the halftone frequency of the printed image. 300 dpi laser printers have a maximum attainable halftone frequency of 60 lines per inch (lpi). If you don't understand frequencies, open up the yellow pages of your phone book and look at the photos. Most of them were printed at 65 lpi. Take a look at a magazine and compare the photographs to the yellow pages. The magazine quality images were printed at 133 to 175 lpi. The obvious difference between them is that there are noticeable dots in the lower frequency images. All digital images require a frequency setting when you output to imagesetters or laser printers.

Image resolution is directly related to halftone frequency. The most common formula to use is resolution = frequency $\times$ 2. In our laser printer example, the frequency is 60, so the resolution should be no more than 120 dpi. A 300 dpi produces no better quality when imaged to a 300 dpi laser printer than the 120 dpi imaged on the same printer. In most cases, the dpi resolution can be even lower than twice the frequency. To determine the best resolution for your images, try multiplying the frequency times 1.25, 1.5, or 1.75. Run a series of tests to decide which formula works best for your scanner and the output devices you use.

Many plug-ins enable you to target resolutions at the precise number you desire. For example, my Silverscanner II enables me to scan at 266 dpi, if I so desire. The target resolution works well with this scanner. With some scanners, it might be advantageous to scan at the highest optical resolution and to downsample the image as we did with line art scans. Again, you should test the procedures on your equipment to see which method achieves the best results.

Color Scanning

Scanning color images follows the same rules as scanning grayscale images. Resolutions for color images require the same calculations. When scanning color for output to imagesetters for film separations, the flatbed scanners and even the low-end slide scanners do not produce the quality needed for separated film. Use service bureaus or print shops that have high-end systems.

For output to color printers, you can scan color images on flatbeds to create layout proofs. These proofs are helpful when you want to examine the colors before acquiring high-end scans. Once again, the principles follow the same as those outlined for grayscale images. Continuous-tone printers, like dye sublimation, provide excellent results with surprisingly low frequencies and low resolutions. A continuous tone provides an image without the appearance of dots that looks like photographic quality. The 3M Rainbow printer, for example, requires no more than 150 dpi with a 60 lpi frequency to provide continuous tones. If you use photo labs or service bureaus to obtain higher end color prints, check with the service personnel to determine what resolution and frequencies you need to use for their devices.

Once you obtain scans from your scanner, you then can defer the control for clean-up and image improvement to Photoshop. Obviously, not all images will be perfect when you examine the source material. In most cases, you will need to use Photoshop's tools and commands to enhance the image. Depending on the type of material scanned and your desired output, you may choose to perform several enhancements in Photoshop. The next section describes some typical problems and provides solutions.

Key Concept: Getting the Best from Line Art Scans

Before we begin the process of acquiring better scans, let me say that there is continual learning needed to perfect your design skills, whether working in Photoshop or any other application. Sometimes you can find traveling seminars which arrive at major metropolitan communities near you that provide many helpful solutions. This was recently the case for me when I visited a *Thunder Lizard Productions* seminar on scanning. *Thunder Lizard Productions* provides many excellent seminars offered by top notch people in the industry. I was most fortunate in once again attending a seminar provided by Steve Roth, who is known for great works on scanning, halftoning, and many of his *Real World* publications. Steve recently discovered a technique for line art scanning that I will share with you.

Scanning Line Art

As noted earlier in the section on Line Art Scanning, I recommend scanning at the highest interpolated resolution of the scanner. This is fine if you have scanners equipped to handle 1200, 1600, or 2400 dpi interpolated resolutions. But what if your scanner is maxed out at 300 or 600 dpi? Well, there is a solution. You can use Steve Roth's technique on low-end and medium range flatbed scanners to achieve good quality line art:

1. *Scan in grayscale.* Rather than scan your image in the line art mode, scan in grayscale at the highest resolution capable from your scanner.

2. *Double the resolution.* Open the Image menu and choose Image Size. Enter a value for Resolution twice the size of the original scan. If you scanned at 600 ppi, increase the resolution to 1200 ppi. The increase in the resolution will be interpolated. However, this doesn't matter because your artwork is line art. Upsizing at interpolated resolutions is recommended with grayscale or color images.

3. *Apply an unsharp mask.* Open the Filter menu and choose Sharpen, Unsharp Mask. A dialog box appears that enables you to set the sharpening effect. For Amount, enter **400**; for Radius, enter **1**; and for Threshold, enter **4**.

4. *Reapply the unsharp mask.* Whenever you apply a filter, you can apply it again by opening the Filter menu and by choosing the first option available. This first option changes according to the last filter applied. If you followed the directions in the preceding bullet, this option is Unsharp Mask. When you select Unsharp Mask at this position in the Filter menu, the filter will reapply the values last entered in the dialog box. In this case, an Amount of 400, a Radius of 1, and a Threshold of 4.

5. *Adjust the threshold.* The scanned image contains grays because you scanned it in grayscale mode. To strip the grays and render the image black and white, access the Threshold settings. Open the Image menu and choose Map, Threshold. The Threshold dialog box appears. Enter a value of **2** in the dialog box.

6. *Convert to bitmap.* The image is still in grayscale mode. All line art scans ultimately end up in bitmap mode. To convert to bitmap, open the Mode menu and choose Bitmap. A dialog box appears with various descriptions of how the bitmap conversion is to be made. You

should keep the image in a black and white mode with no screening or dithering, so choose 50% Threshold from the available radio button choices in the dialog box.

This method works exceptionally well on detailed drawings and type of small point sizes. Regardless of the scanner you may use, try the above method and experiment with techniques to achieve the best scans. Everything goes better when you start with good quality originals to scan. However, sometimes that is not possible and you need to perform some clean-up.

Cleaning Up Line Art

We all have an uncle Harry or Joe living in some place like Chicago or Des Moines who, twenty-five years ago, designed the logo for his plumbing company. Uncle Harry heard you are a computer whiz and great designer, so he faxes his 32nd generation logo to you because he needs some new business cards. Uncle Harry thinks, "Well, you're going to put it on the computer, so you should be able to just whip it out." You take one look at the fax and think this is going to be a nightmare. Well, let's see if we can save both you and Uncle Harry.

Figure 6.4 is a symbol scanned from the yellow pages. A yellow page symbol appears as rough as Uncle Harry's fax and both require some clean-up to improve the image. The scanning plug-in can address the brightness and contrast issues, but it can't sharpen the image. We need Photoshop to clean it up.

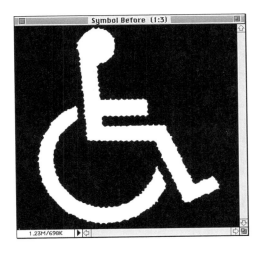

Fig. 6.4

Line art images are not always perfect and many need some clean-up.

II

Acquiring Images

1. *Scan the image at the proper resolution.* For line art that requires clean-up, use the same scanning principles you use for any other line art scans—scan the artwork at the highest interpolated resolution.

2. *Downsample the image.* You should match the device resolution. If you intend to image the file on an imagesetter, the resolution needs to be downsampled to 1200 dpi. If you choose a laser printer for your final output, you need to downsample to that device's resolution. The key operative here is *final output.* If you ob-

tain laser proofs before imagesetting, you need to target the resolution at the imagesetter and let the laser proofs print at that resolution. The alternative is to create two separate files, one for the laser printer resolution and one for the imagesetter. In this case, you must be certain you supply the file with the higher resolution to the service bureau for imagesetter output.

3. *Size the image to the final output dimensions.* To size the physical height and width, open the Image menu and choose Image Size. Set the size in the dialog

box with the Proportions option selected to maintain proportional sizing without distortion.

4. *Convert to grayscale.* Many of Photoshop's tools and commands do not work in bitmap mode. You need to use both the Filter menu and the Adjust options to clean up your scan. Neither of these menu commands are available for bitmap images.

5. *Blur the image.* This sounds somewhat paradoxical because your image needs to be cleaned up and sharpened, not blurred. If you have jagged edges on line art, the first objective is to anti-alias the edges. Think of *anti-aliasing* as smoothing the edges. Essentially, you add pixels to fill in gaps in the artwork.

To blur the image, open the Filter menu and choose Blur, Gaussian Blur. Figure 6.5 illustrates the Gaussian Blur dialog box that provides an image preview of the blurring effect. The amount of the blur depends on the image you have scanned. In some cases, only a slight blur is necessary. In the example, the image is so poorly degraded, a strong blur with a radius of 25 was applied.

Fig. 6.5

Line art scans with severe degradation require a strong blur.

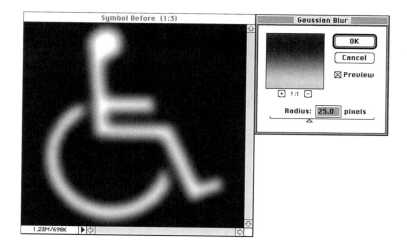

6. *Sharpen the image.* Once you have used the Gaussian Blur to fill in the gaps with pixels, you can sharpen up the image by returning it to black and white and by eliminating all gray values. You can achieve this task by adjusting the brightness and contrast in the Levels dialog box. To access Levels, open the Image Menu, and choose Adjust, Levels. As you move the input levels sliders, the contrast changes and the image looks sharper. Both of the end input sliders move inward toward each other, as illustrated in figure 6.6. By moving the sliders with the Preview option selected in the Levels dialog box, you can observe dynamic updating of the image.

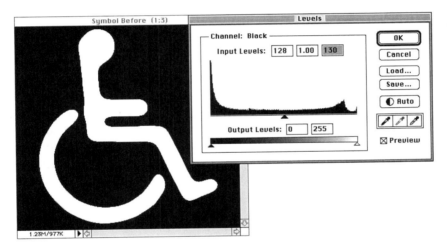

Fig. 6.6

Adjusting the Levels sliders sharpens the blurred image.

7. *Change the mode to bitmap.* Once the image is cleaned up, return to bitmap mode. To convert the grayscale image to bitmap, open the Mode menu and choose bitmap. The file size in bitmap mode is approximately one-eighth the size of the grayscale image.

8. *Save the file in an appropriate format.* If you are going to place the file in a layout or illustration program, save it as a TIFF or EPS file. Be certain the destination program supports the file format you use.

When you perform these steps, you can greatly improve images from source material that gets faxed to you or is provided from many generations of photocopying. Figure 6.7 shows the difference between the original image and the edited version of the same image.

II

Acquiring Images

169

Fig. 6.7

Fig. 6.7

A comparison of
the original scan
and the edited
image.

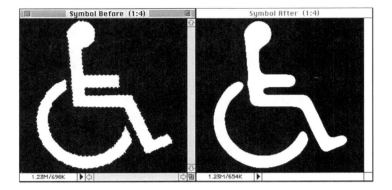

Working with Crooked Scans

When you scan images on flatbed scanners, a light, which is typically a
fluorescent bulb, travels below the scanner platen and passes through the
length of the scanner bed. When you position the artwork on the scanner
platen, I recommend that you do not position the artwork in the top or
bottom corners. If the light intensity is weaker in these areas, the scan
suffers on the edges. Positioning the artwork in the center of the scanner
bed will most assuredly render a scan crooked. Fortunately, Photoshop
provides the necessary tools to easily straighten the image after it has been
scanned. Figure 6.8 illustrates an image that was placed in the center of the
scanner platen and then scanned at an angle.

Fig. 6.8

Artwork placed in
the center of the
scanning bed
needs to be
straightened.

To straighten a crooked scan, use Photoshop's Cropping tool. When you choose the Cropping tool and notice the palette options available to this tool, you can select many options for cropping the image. Figure 6.9 illustrates the options available in the Cropping Tool Options palette. For example, you can fix the size so the cropped image conforms to a physical dimension. You can also establish the output resolution, either together with the physical dimensions or independent from the dimensions. When choosing the resolution, be certain the cropped image will not be interpolated up from the original size. If for example, you scan an image at 120 ppi at 3 × 2 inches and you crop it to 4 × 5 inches, the upsizing of the image will be interpolated if you keep the resolution at 120 ppi. If you disable the Fixed Size option in the Cropping Tool Options palette, the image will be cropped at a 1:1 ratio with no interpolation.

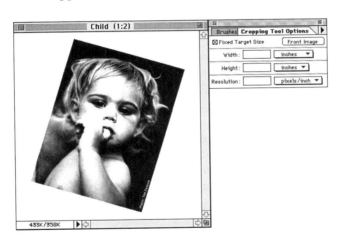

Fig. 6.9

The Cropping Tool Options palette provides many options to describe how an image is cropped.

The Cropping tool can rotate and crop the image in a single motion. To perform the task, take the Cropping tool and drag it in the document window. When you release the mouse, a rectangle with handles appears. Each of the handles can be moved to reshape the rectangle. If you press the Option key while dragging a handle, the Cropping Rectangle rotates. Releasing the Option key will again permit you to reshape the rectangle. When cropping a crooked image, try to position the Cropping Rectangle in a position similar to that illustrated in figure 6.10. When the cursor is positioned inside the rectangle, the icon changes to a scissors icon signifying that you can crop. When you click the mouse while the scissors icon is present, the image is rotated and cropped in a single step.

Fig. 6.10

Rotate the
Cropping Rect-
angle by holding
the Option key
down while
moving a handle.

Using Film Recorders

If you want 35mm transparencies or negatives enlarged to 16 × 20, or
larger, photographic prints, the final prints will lose detail and appear
grainy when enlarged from 35mm. Photoshop can help us achieve better
results by scanning the 35mm transparency and then by returning the
output to a film recorder on a 4 × 5 or 8 × 10 sheet of film. If photographic
quality and detail are important, you should perform the scan on a drum
scanner at a service bureau. Resolutions on drum and high-end scanners
are high enough to accommodate sizing an image to much larger sizes
than the original. Typically, film recorders will print to transparencies and
negatives from sizes larger than the final output size. For example, the
AGFA Forte film recorder images a 4 × 5 sheet film from a digital image size
of 10.514 × 7.889 inches. When the file is imaged to the film recorder, it
is downsized to the output film size.

Perhaps the least standard devices in the industry are film recorders.
When you attempt to prepare a file for a service bureau offering film
recorder output, always check to see what sizes they prefer for their
devices. Also, the resolutions of film recorders do not consider halftone
frequencies. When you output to a film recorder, there is no presence of
dots or halftoning. To determine the proper resolution, you should always
check with the service bureau offering the film recorder service. The
resolution of the film recorder also deviates from other printing devices.
Film recorders offer resolutions in lines per inch such as 2000, 4000, 8000,
and some at 16,000. These measurements are not the same as lpi noted
earlier when discussing halftoning.

Scanning for Presentations

The easiest scans to create are those intended for screen and video presentations. The advantage of these images is that what you see on-screen is what you get. There are no considerations for gray levels, tones, or halftoning. The resolution of your monitor is 72 ppi. Any images scanned and saved at higher resolutions are unnecessary. Target your resolution for 72 ppi and examine the results. If you have 35mm transparencies to scan, the quality rendered from the low-end slide scanners is superb for screen presentations. Scanning from these devices is much preferred over scanning from flatbeds with transparency adapters.

Where To Go from Here

▶ Chapter 13, "Understanding Color," discusses calibrations and calibrating for output devices. This chapter is a must for those who wish to print scanned images on any printing device.

▶ Chapter 21, "Photoshop for the Desktop Publisher," and chapter 22, "Photoshop for the Digital Designer," elaborate on when to obtain high-end scans, how to prepare images for output to a variety of printers, and how to create files for color separations.

▶ Chapter 24, "Photoshop for the Professional Photographer," covers much more on output to film recorders and printing to various color printers.

II

Acquiring Images

Photo-CD Images

Getting your work from, or to, a Photo CD is easy. In this chapter you'll learn the basics of Photo CD and:

- ▶ How to open a stored photo
- ▶ How to store your photos on a CD
- ▶ Viewing options
- ▶ The importance of resolution
- ▶ The protection of copyrights

Photo CD is the digital form of a photograph stored on a compact disc—much like scanning a photo and saving it to your hard disk. In 1990, Kodak developed the Photo-CD technology using a medium that has been around for two decades. The CD was currently in use by other industries, most notably the music industry, but Kodak developed the first usage of the CD for visual storage. Using CDs made sense. The amount of data that could be stored is massive compared to other popular media such as the floppy disks, removable cartridges, and tape systems. A CD can store as many as 100 35mm photos or about 25 8 × 10 photos. Photo-CD images can be viewed on a television or computer screen without the need for a darkened room, large viewing screen, or even much in the way of special equipment, hardware, or software.

by Rob Sonner and Cyndie Klopfenstein

CHAPTER 7

Almost immediately, Kodak and Phillips developed simple-to-operate viewing systems that connected directly to televisions with minimal resolution requirements. The resolution for photos displayed on television is low (by desktop publishing standards), so many images can be stored and viewed much like you would view a slide show. The technology makes it interesting, and the ease of use makes it a feasible alternative to typical home viewing of pictures or mass storage for low-resolution desktop publishing photos. The quality when first developed was not quite there, and perhaps still isn't, for very high-end four-color work, but all of us that participate in the publishing fast lane know the quality isn't far behind.

Photo-CD Basics

The CD-ROM is the technology behind the music CD. This type of disc has the information stored or written to the disc, which is then read or played repeatedly.

WORM (write once, read many) is the type of CD that Photo-CD technology subscribes to. Data can be added in separate sessions when using a multiple-session disc. This means that you can store a series of photos and then return the CD to have more photos added at a later date. There are special CD players that enable you to read multiple-session CDs.

Photo CDs are stored in a format called YCC. This format, like PICT, TIFF, and others, is simply a definition of the data stored. The YCC format uses the infinite color space theory, which is related to Photoshop's LAB format. LAB was invented in the 1930s and is still used today.

In Photoshop's LAB, the L channel represents the Luminosity aspects of an image, while the A and B channels store color values to fill out the rest of the information to display the final image on your monitor. Working in LAB provides a wide open field of possibilities for image variables; the largest contingent of all color modes takes into account all shades and hue variations available from both CMYK and RGB.

The three channels of the YCC format that are similar to the LAB format are: Y, C1, and C2. Each channel has eight data bits assigned to it. However, the zero points range and differ depending on what values are actually present.

For the technically and color-advanced Photoshop user, the YCC image encoding on a Photo CD allows for approximately a 50 percent overrange in overall luminance. With the corresponding RGB values where R255, G255, and B255 are white, there is a small problem with conversion of the reflective highlights if the color range is not clipped and tweaked properly. The result may be either muddy, low-light shades in the shadowed areas or washed-out highlights in the areas of high contrast and extreme brightness.

Creating Photo CDs

Many of the same places that you might go for typical photo processing can provide you with Photo-CD services. You may wish to have the photos printed to 35mm slides first so that you can choose only the best images and order them in logical succession. Some service bureaus won't accept 35mm slides. They'll only accept rolls of negatives since they process much faster. (Make sure you call the service bureau first. As with most service industries, there is usually a charge for specific ordering of photos.) You might find that your local drugstore, photo processing center, or instant print shop provides Photo-CD services. Though it is sometimes performed by the same companies that process your regular photo film, the equipment and process is quite different.

The system required for storing photos to CD is expensive; it's not something the general public has the capital to invest in. Because the technology licenses belong to Kodak, all processing stations are either created by Kodak or bear their license. As is the case with most hardware licensing, this makes the hardware expensive. For about $7,000 you can store your own Photo-CD discs. This might not seem such an unlikely investment for an advertising agency or photography studio.

Photo CDs range in price from fifty cents to about $2.50 per image and usually take less than an hour to actually capture per 100 images. However, this doesn't mean you can have the images back in an hour. Many service centers have not made the investment in the hardware and they may need to send it out of state to have the CD images saved. In cases such as this, it may take a week or more to have the CD made. Plan for this as you create your artwork in Photoshop on a tight schedule. A CD typically stores about 100 images—some more, some fewer.

II

Acquiring Images

177

The Players

There are two primary methods for viewing your stored photos: on television or on your computer monitor. Working with Photoshop, our primary interest is in the computer monitor, but the television method does bear mentioning. After all, once you've created those morphed digital images and you need to make a presentation, a large television might be more accessible than crowding six clients around your 16-inch SuperMatch monitor.

As mentioned above, Kodak and Phillips manufacture Photo-CD players for the television. Kodak also has a portable version. Each of the different players offers specific features. The portable version is, of course, the most limited in the feature department.

CD-ROM Drives

To play the Photo CDs on your computer, you need a CD-ROM drive. These types of players are getting to be fairly reasonably priced. The major purchasing factors for you will be: speed, multiple or single session, and probably, price. Most of the newer drives are multi-session, so this may not be a factor much longer. If you own an older single-session drive, you will only be able to access the first session of a multi-session disc.

When working with a CD drive, the most desirable feature for many is not having to juggle discs. Storing 100 images on removable cartridges may mean that you have six SyQuests that you need to shuffle through. Or, if you're lucky, you have a gigabyte hard disk that you can copy them onto. With a 600M CD, there is a great deal of space for storing your photos, but not for saving them once they have been edited. Remember, you're working from a write once, read many disc (yes, multiple sessions mean that you write more than once, but that's a different definition of writing and is not considered writing more than once since it does not write to the same space on the CD twice), so you must store edited photos somewhere else.

Photoshop—The Editor

Once you've accumulated the necessary hardware (the CD-ROM drive) and the necessary software (the Photo CD), you're ready to begin editing the photos in Photoshop. In the next section, you'll work through the steps for actually opening, editing, and saving your images.

Using and Saving Images

Opening Photo-CD images in Photoshop is the same as opening other more common image types. The steps below walk you through what is now, or will become, very familiar territory.

> **Note**
>
> You should have QuickTime installed in the System folder to access Photo-CD images. If you completed a full install of the Photoshop program, QuickTime was installed for you.

1. Open the File menu and choose Open. The Open dialog box appears, as shown in figure 7.1.

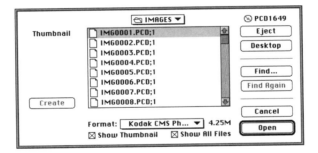

Fig. 7.1

From the Open dialog box, you can open a Photo-CD format directly into Photoshop.

2. Kodak CMS Photo CD is listed as the type of Format. If no files appear, try choosing Show All Files and then selecting a format type from the Format pop-up menu.

3. Double-click the file name in the list window. A new dialog box appears, as shown in figure 7.2.

Fig. 7.2

You can choose a resolution to work from in the Resolution pop-up menu.

4. Choose a resolution from the Resolution pop-up menu.

5. Choose Source. The Choose Source Precision Transform dialog box appears (see fig. 7.3).

Fig. 7.3

You select a Source and Destination profile in this dialog box.

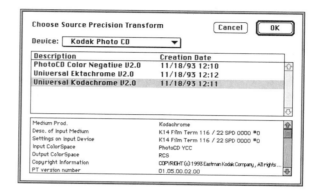

If this is the first time you have opened the file, no Source and Destination profiles are selected. These profile choices (also called PTs) are based on the profiles that are installed in your System folder. Your choices will remain the default until you change them.

6. Choose a device from the Device pop-up menu and a description of the film you made the CD from in the Description list.

7. Click OK and you will return to the primary dialog box.

8. Click OK. The image is displayed in the window and ready for editing.

Once the image is open in Photoshop, you can confirm its size and pixel ratio, and change the settings as you see fit using standard Photoshop methods. Choose Image Size from the Image menu; the Image Size dialog box appears (see fig. 7.4). Notice that the image size displayed also shows there are 144 pixels per inch. If you select either of the unit's pop-up menus, you can select Pixels or another unit of measurement to see the immediate equivalent.

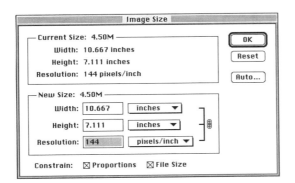

Fig. 7.4

Using the Image Size dialog box, you can adjust the physical size and file size, or both of an open photo.

> **Tip**
>
> **Resetting Image Size**
>
> When setting up an image resize, if you want to go back to the original numbers in the dialog box, simply hold down the Option key and the Cancel button becomes a Reset button, allowing you to reset the settings.

Defining Resolution

Images stored on a Photo CD are of varying resolution. You may be given up to five different resolutions in a bundle referred to as an ImagPac. These resolutions offer quality ranges from thumbnail size to 6144×4096 pixels. The higher resolution files are saved in a Kodak compressed file format—something similar to LZW or Stuffit formats that are automatically decompressed when you open them. You will want to select a resolution that is appropriate for the intended use of the photo. For instance, if you plan only to view the image on a television, a low resolution will be sufficient. If the final project is a four-color, high-gloss annual report, a very high resolution will be necessary. As with all scanned, illustrated, or Photo-CD images, the higher the resolution, the more disc space the image will consume.

The resolution options are as follows:

▶ 128×192 are used for thumbnail index images printed on each Photo-CD sleeve jacket and for image retrieval preview purposes.

▶ 256 × 384 images are used for previewing images on your monitor.

▶ 512 × 768 pixel images are used for standard NTSC imagery.

▶ 1025 × 1536 are reserved for High-Definition Television (HDTV) signals.

▶ 2048 × 3072 pixel images are for output in high-quality printing situations, such as slides or full-page 8 × 10 composite proofs.

▶ In some special circumstances, a Photo-CD service center may offer 6144 × 4096 pixel images on the disc. This is the highest possible resolution. You may choose to use it if you intend to enlarge the image a great deal.

Each ImagePac on the CD uses between three and six megabytes of disc space with each of the different available sizes.

Tip

Resolution Reductions

If you intend to enlarge the photo, the resolution choice must increase proportionately. Typically, the resolution will be 1.5 to 2 times the screen ruling or lpi. For instance, if you intend to print the photo at 133 lpi, the resolution will be about 200 or so. Any resolution amount beyond this is virtually useless information that just consumes disc space. Conversely, if you intend to reduce the photo, you should also reduce the required resolution and maintain the 1.5/2:1 ratio. Otherwise, here again, you are embedding excess information into the file that will not be visible.

Stock Art

You are not limited to only those images that you have captured yourself. One of the first moves that Kodak made after releasing the Photo-CD technology was to publish a disc of stock imagery. These images, like those you shoot yourself, can be opened, manipulated, and combined in Photoshop. For special effects, you might try combining stock imagery with your own shots and varying the resolutions of the images as you combine them. Photo CD has certainly helped to reduce the costs associated with creating photo designs.

Protecting Copyrights

When using a provided CD—what you believe to be stock—be sure that you have permission. Many Photo CDs have been created for the purpose of your unlimited use, much like the clip art of the not-so-distant past. But even clip art might have some limitations on when and where it can be used. Photo CDs might also. Photo CDs can be protected by the copyright of the person who shot the photos, or by the person who contracted the CD to be made; at any rate, it may not be for unlimited general use.

Protecting Your Copyrights

By the same token, your photos might also come with limitations. Make sure that those who have access to your CDs fully understand their right to use them. Establishing a written policy and making sure that your clients, or people who may be using your photos, completely understand the restrictions is a good way to avoid misunderstandings. You want your copyrights protected in the same manner that you protect those of others. Though Photo CD has certainly opened up a whole new type of electronic picture world, it has brought with it new challenges about ownership and usership for those who take advantage of the technology.

Where To Go from Here

▶ After you have your image, you'll want to check out Photoshop's new layering facilities in chapter 10, "Working with Layers."

▶ See chapter 12, "Using Masks and Channels," to learn how to use these important functions.

▶ In order to get the most out of Photoshop, you'll want to learn more about color in chapter 13, "Understanding Color."

II

Acquiring Images

183

PART

III

Creating and
Touching Up Images

Drawing, Painting, and Editing

Everyone has some creativity inside them that is just itching to get out. Some people express themselves with photography—finding just the right scene, adjusting the lighting, and correcting contrast. Other people may yearn for an artist's palette—the opportunity to experiment with paint and brushes. Photoshop offers both of these opportunities at the same time.

The program incorporates over a dozen specialized tools and numerous floating palettes for enhancing scanned images or creating original digital art. This chapter introduces you to the capabilities of these tools and suggests some ways of combining them for additional effects.

by Darien M. Kruss

CHAPTER 8

Using Common Tool Options

Photoshop plays two main roles in graphics: it acts as a photo-retouching tool and a digital canvas on which to create original art. While most of the menu commands within the program deal with photo-retouching, most of the tools in the toolbox deal with artwork creation—which will be referred to as *painting*.

Brushes Palette

Just like the traditional artist maintains a plethora of brushes to achieve every imagined effect, the digital artist also has a wide variety of brushes from which to choose. To view the Brushes palette, choose Palettes, Show Brushes from the Window menu. The palette may be resized and dragged around on the desktop. You also can drag palettes onto each other to combine them. For more information on working with palettes, see the section "Opening, Arranging, and Using Palettes," in chapter 1.

The Brushes palette retains the brush shape for each one of these painting and editing tools separately: Pencil, Paintbrush, Airbrush, Eraser, Rubber Stamp, Smudge, Focus, and Toning tools. Selecting a new tool from the toolbox will change the active brush shape to the last one used with that tool. Always choose a tool first, and then click the brush size you want to use with that tool.

Brushes under 28 pixels in diameter are displayed at their actual size; larger brushes are shown at a reduced view with their diameter (in pixels) shown beneath (see fig. 8.1). The currently selected brush is identified by a thick border around it.

Fig. 8.1

The Brushes palette displays the current set of brushes with a border around the currently selected size.

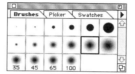

Selecting a Color

The Pencil, Paintbrush, Airbrush, Line tools, and occasionally the Smudge tool use the current foreground color to paint with. The Eraser uses the background color, and the Gradient tool can use both the foreground and background colors.

There are several methods for selecting the foreground and background colors. You can use the Eyedropper, the Color Picker, the Picker palette, and the Swatches palette. While you are experimenting with the painting tools, you will want to change your colors frequently to see the results of different settings. Methods for picking colors are discussed later in this chapter.

Eyedropper

When trying to match a color from an existing image, it is easiest to use the Eyedropper tool. Select the Eyedropper from the toolbox and click any part of any document that is currently open to select a foreground color (see fig. 8.2). If you hold the mouse button down while you drag inside a document, the foreground color control in the toolbox (and the Picker palette, if it is open) will constantly update to show the current color.

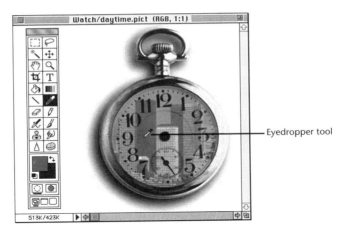

Eyedropper tool

Fig. 8.2

Use the Eyedropper tool to sample the color in an existing document.

Tip

Working Efficiently with Colors

While using any painting tool (Type, Paintbucket, Gradient, Line, Pencil, Paintbrush, or Airbrush), hold down the Option key to temporarily activate the Eyedropper tool. Clicking the mouse button will sample colors from any open document, even if that document's window is not active. While working in Photoshop, you might want to consider keeping a small artist's palette-type document open that contains a selection of your most often used colors.

III

Creating and Touching Up

To set the background color with the Eyedropper, hold down the Option key while clicking the mouse button. You will see the results in the background color control of the toolbox (and the Picker palette, if it is open).

The Eyedropper can be configured to sample a single pixel from an image, or the average of a 3×3 or 5×5 matrix surrounding the selected pixel. To view the Options palette, choose Palettes Show Options from the Window menu. The Eyedropper Options appear in the Eyedropper Options palette (see fig. 8.3).

> ### Tip
>
> **Displaying the Options Palette**
>
> Double-clicking any tool in the toolbox will open the Options palette for that tool and bring it to the front, if necessary.

Choose a Sample Size from the Options palette pop-up menu to determine the method for selecting color with the Eyedropper. For a more precise, crosshair-shaped pointer while sampling a color, press the Caps Lock key on your keyboard so that it is in the locked position.

Fig. 8.3

The Eyedropper tool can provide a point sample or the average of the surrounding pixels.

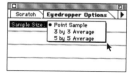

Color Controls

Near the bottom of the toolbox are several controls for manipulating and setting the foreground and background colors (see fig. 8.4). Because many tools rely on these settings, it would be a good idea to become very familiar with the following options:

▶ *Foreground color selection box.* Click here to display the color picker and set the foreground color.

▶ *Background color selection box.* Click here to display the color picker and set the background color.

▶ *Default colors.* Click this icon to set the foreground and background colors to black and white, respectively. (Press the letter "d" on the keyboard to set the colors to their defaults.)

▶ *Switch colors.* Click this icon to swap the current foreground and background colors. (Press the letter "x" on the keyboard to switch the colors.)

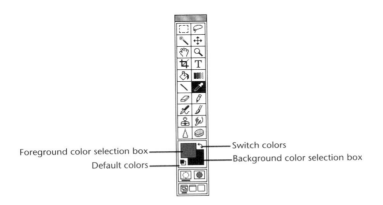

Foreground color selection box
Default colors
Switch colors
Background color selection box

Fig. 8.4

The color controls provide a quick indicator of the current color settings.

Clicking either the foreground or background color selection boxes will open the Color Picker dialog box. The Photoshop Color Picker dialog box provides a comprehensive method for selecting color from a variety of color spaces (see fig. 8.5). HSB (Hue, Saturation, Brightness), RGB (Red, Green, Blue), Lab, and CMYK (Cyan, Magenta, Yellow, and Black) colors can all be specified from this one location.

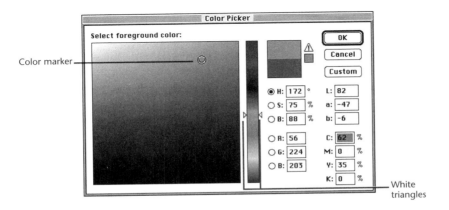

Color marker
White triangles

Fig. 8.5

Photoshop's comprehensive Color Picker dialog box.

III

Creating and Touching Up

191

To specify a color, follow these steps:

1. Click in the color slider (the narrow vertical bar in the center of the dialog box) to position the white triangles.

2. Click in the color field (the large square on the left side of the dialog box) to position the small circular color marker.

   The information shown in these color controls varies depending on which of the radio buttons H, S, B, R, G, or B has been selected on the right side of the dialog box.

3. Clicking one of these radio buttons places that color component into the narrow vertical bar. The remaining two color components are distributed in the large square—one on the horizontal axis and one on the vertical axis.

While you adjust colors, one of two rectangles near the top of the dialog box will change showing the newly selected color. The rectangle below it does not change because it represents the original color that had been previously selected.

An alternate method for specifying color values is to enter them numerically into the appropriate fields in the dialog box. The color field and color sliders will update as the values are entered. This is the only way to specify colors for the Lab and CMYK color spaces.

The Custom button displays an additional dialog box for selecting colors from popular manufacturers such as ANPA, Pantone, Toyo, Focoltone, and TruMatch (see fig. 8.6). Choose the manufacturer from the Book pop-up menu and type in the color's number or code to select it. Alternatively, you can scroll through the listing of colors by clicking either the up or down scroll arrow, or by clicking anywhere in the colorful scroll bar.

It is important to realize that although you may be picking colors based on special inks, the colors are converted to *approximations* in your current color space, and may not print with the exact specifications of the color manufacturer.

To go back to the standard Photoshop picker, click the Picker button in the Custom Colors dialog box. Some find it useful that Photoshop displays the nearest CMYK equivalent to the selected custom color in the lower portion of the dialog box. By switching back to the standard picker, it is also possible to extract the nearest HSB, RGB, and Lab values for the selected color.

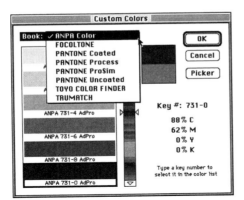

Fig. 8.6

Custom colors are chosen from a scrolling list or by typing numbers.

Picker Palette

Another method used for selecting colors is found in one of Photoshop's palettes. Choose Palettes, Picker from the Window menu. The Picker palette appears (see fig. 8.7). The controls for selecting colors consist of one, three, or four sliders—depending on the color model with which you choose to work. The same foreground and background swatches are available here as in the toolbox, and a color bar provides a more generalized selection.

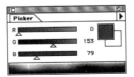

Fig. 8.7

The Picker palette provides a convenient way to select colors.

Note

In the Picker palette, one of the two color swatches (foreground or background) is always active and identified by a border. When this palette is visible, the Eyedropper tool will, by default, select a new color for the active swatch. Hold the Option key while using the eyedropper to select a new color for the inactive swatch. Click a swatch in the Picker palette to activate it—click again to display the Color Picker dialog box.

III

Creating and Touching Up

To change the color space of the picker—but not the color of your current document—choose an option from the Picker palette Options menu (see fig. 8.8). You may choose between grayscale, RGB, HSB, CMYK, and Lab color sliders.

Fig. 8.8

All palettes (except the toolbox) have an Options menu at the right side of the title bar.

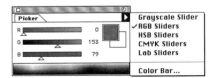

If the option is selected in Photoshop's preferences, the sliders will dynamically show the range of colors each is capable of. Choose a color by clicking anywhere on a slider, or by dragging the triangle along the slider's length. The value for that slider is displayed to its right. For more information in setting preferences see the section "Using General Preferences," in chapter 4.

Each of the slider's values differ and it may not be possible to specify an exact value using them, as the following list illustrates:

▶ **Grayscale** values range from 0 (white) to 100 percent (black).

▶ **RGB** values each range from 0 (no color, or black) to 255 (full strength color) representing red, green, and blue.

▶ **HSB** sliders are shown with hue from 0° to 360°, with pure red at 0 and yellow at 60. Saturation and brightness can each be set between 0 and 100 percent.

▶ **CMYK** values range from 0 to 100 percent for each of the process colors: cyan, magenta, yellow, and black.

▶ **Lab** sliders describe luminance (a measure of brightness) between 0 and 100 and two chrominance values (green to red and blue to yellow) between -120 and +120.

The color bar at the bottom of the picker can be changed by selecting Color Bar from the Picker palette's Options menu. You have the choice of RGB, CMYK, Grayscale, and foreground to background spectrums. If you choose to display the spectrum between foreground and background colors, the option to lock these colors is available as a check box. Selecting the check box will continue to present the current color spectrum, even if the foreground and background colors change.

To select a color from the color bar, simply point to the color and click—the pointer changes to the Eyedropper upon entering the bar. Hold down the Option key and click in the color bar to set the background color (or inactive color if the Picker palette is visible). Click inside the current color bar with the Shift key down to cycle through the four color bar options.

Swatches Palette

While probably most useful to multimedia developers, the Swatches palette is extremely useful for anyone who must constrain their color choices to a limited selection. Open the Window menu and choose Palettes, Swatches to display this palette.

This color-picking palette consists of a grid of small squares or swatches, sixteen to a row and any number of rows. Colors from the swatches can be selected for the foreground or background color. New colors can be added or inserted as swatches, and existing swatches can be deleted. All of these actions require that you hold down one or more keys while clicking on a swatch. The default swatches are shown in figure 8.9.

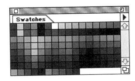

Fig. 8.9

Store and retrieve your most often used colors as swatches.

Modifying Swatches

There are several actions available from within the Swatches palette by holding down specific keys. But be careful because none of these actions can be reverted with the Undo command.

To initiate certain actions, do the following:

▶ Select a new foreground color (or active color if the Picker palette is visible) by clicking on a swatch.

▶ Select a new background color (or inactive color if the Picker palette is visible) by holding Option and clicking on a swatch.

▶ Add the current foreground color to the palette by holding Shift and clicking on an empty swatch. If there are no empty swatches left, increase the size of the palette by dragging the size box.

III

Creating and Touching Up

▶ Replace an existing swatch with the current foreground color by holding Shift and clicking on it.

▶ Insert the current foreground color into the palette and nudge all other swatches over by holding the Shift and Option keys together and clicking on a color.

▶ Delete a swatch by holding the Command key (⌘) and clicking on a swatch.

Saving and Loading Color Sets

After you have created a set of color swatches, you may want to store it on disk for future use. To save the current set of colors, choose Save Swatches from the Swatches Palette Options menu (see fig. 8.10). A directory dialog allows you to choose a name and location for the colors file.

Fig. 8.10

Color swatches can be saved to disk and retrieved later.

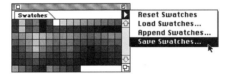

To load one of your own color files, or one of the several that ship with Photoshop, choose Load Swatches from the Swatches Palette Options menu. A directory dialog appears which only displays color files. The selected file's colors will replace those currently in the Swatches palette.

If you would like to have access to both the current set of colors, as well as an additional set that you load from disk, choose Append Swatches from the Swatches Palette Options menu. The color file that you open in the resulting directory dialog will be added to the end of the currently displayed swatches.

Picking Custom Color Swatches

Photoshop is installed with several color files consisting of predefined colors provided by major manufacturers: ANPA, Pantone, Toyo, Focoltone, and TruMatch. These can be found within the Photoshop folder, inside the Goodies folder, inside the Color Palettes folder. By loading or appending these colors into your Swatches palette, they can be picked in much the same way as clicking the Custom button in the Color Picker dialog. Pointing to a custom color swatch causes that color's name to be displayed in place of the word "Swatches" in the title bar of the palette (see fig. 8.11).

Color name

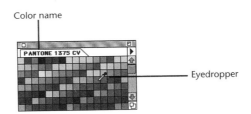

Eyedropper

Fig. 8.11

Custom color swatches are identified by their names.

Although you can't name your own colors or select colors by typing in their numbers, the name as shown in the palette's tab is useful when trying to match colors in your image to colors in a vendor's swatch book.

Palette Options

Each of the painting tools has settings that affect the way that tool behaves. Because you will be changing these settings frequently, it is a good idea to make sure the Options palette is either grouped with a palette you will not need to access frequently, or is separated on its own. To display the Options palette, open the Window menu and choose Palettes, Show Options. To separate a palette from others it is grouped with, drag its name tab away and release it somewhere else on the desktop (see fig. 8.12).

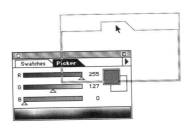

Fig. 8.12

Separate a palette from a group by dragging its name tab.

III

Creating and Touching Up

If your screen seems cramped with a multitude of floating palettes, you may want to combine palettes together that will most likely not be used at the same time. For example, group the Options palette and either the Swatches or Scratch palette together by dragging one palette's name tab onto another visible palette.

Reset Tool/Reset All Tools

When the Options palette is visible, choose Reset All Tools from the Options Palette Options menu. This will ensure that all the tools are behaving with their default settings for such things as mode, pressure, and fade. Click OK when the dialog box appears asking you to confirm your action.

Each time you begin a new project in Photoshop, you may want to reset all the tools so that they function the way you expect them to. If not, the option to reset only the currently selected tool is also available in the Option Palette Options menu.

Tool Options Palette

A quick way to bring up the Options palette (see fig. 8.13) is to double-click on any tool in the toolbox. Except for the Text tool and the Move tool, all other tools have settings which can be changed in the Options palette. Some of the more common settings are discussed first, and additional settings specific to each tool are discussed under that tool's name.

Fig. 8.13

The Options palette contains settings which affect the way a certain tool (in this case, the Paintbrush) functions.

Mode

The Mode pop-up menu in the Options palette determines the method by which new color is added to existing color while painting. The interaction depends on the relationship between any existing color in the image and the foreground color that is being used to paint with. A visual guide to the modes is presented in figure 8.14. A similar mode menu is available in the Layers palette that affects the interaction of an entire layer with those layers underneath.

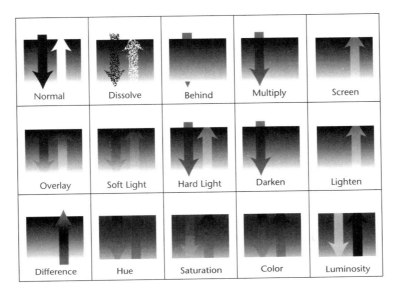

Fig. 8.14

Various painting modes illustrated on light and dark backgrounds.

The following blending modes are available in the Options palette for the painting tools, and in the Layers palette.

▶ **Normal mode** replaces existing color with the current foreground color. This is the default mode.

▶ **Dissolve mode** produces a splattered effect by randomly diffusing the foreground colored pixels based on the current opacity setting.

▶ **Behind mode**, when applied to transparent areas in a layer, adds pixels only to space not presently occupied by color—as if painting on the back of a sheet of acetate.

▶ **Multiply mode** always produces a darker color by performing a multiplication of the values of the existing and foreground colors. Painting on or with white produces no results, while painting on or with black produces black.

▶ **Screen mode** always produces a lighter color by performing a multiplication of the inverse values of the existing and foreground colors. Painting on or with white produces white, while painting on or with black produces no results.

▶ **Overlay mode** examines the existing color and multiplies or screens it with the new color being applied. Highlights and shadows are least affected, and the resulting color is a mix of the existing color and the foreground color.

▶ **Soft Light mode** either multiplies or screens by examining the value of the foreground color and its relationship to the existing color. If the foreground color is lighter, then the result is lighter (as with the Dodge tool). If the foreground color is darker, then the result is darker (as with the Burn tool). The effect is similar to shining a diffused light on the image.

▶ **Hard Light mode** is essentially the same as Soft Light mode, but results in a more intense color shift. The effect is similar to shining a bright light on the image. Painting with black or white results in black or white, respectively.

▶ **Darken mode** only replaces pixels in those areas of the image that are lighter than the current foreground color.

▶ **Lighten mode** only replaces pixels in those areas of the image that are darker than the current foreground color.

▶ **Difference mode** evaluates the values of the existing pixels and foreground color and produces an inverse of the two based on the result. Lighter pixels result in a more complete inverse effect, while darker pixels produce less of a color change. Black produces no results. With the Paintbrush and Airbrush tools, an "edge" appears around the painted strokes as the brush's hardness decreases.

▶ **Hue mode** paints over any existing colored pixels with only the hue of the foreground color. The saturation and luminance remain the same.

▶ **Saturation mode** paints over any existing colored pixels with only the saturation of the foreground color. The hue and luminance remain the same. Painting on any shade of gray (no saturation) produces no results.

▶ **Color mode** applies the saturation and hue of the current foreground color to any existing colored pixels while retaining their luminance. Because highlight and shadow areas are maintained this mode works well for coloring monochrome images or changing the color, but not detail, of colored images. Painting on white produces no results.

▶ **Luminosity mode** paints over any existing colored pixels with only the luminosity of the foreground color. The hue and saturation remain the same. The results here are the exact opposite of those achieved with color mode.

Opacity, Pressure, or Exposure

The slider that appears in the Options palette when a painting tool is selected controls the opacity, pressure, or exposure for that tool. Values are measured in percent from 1 to 100, and can be changed in 1 percent increments by dragging the triangle to the left or right. This setting determines the amount of effect that a tool has on the image (see fig. 8.15).

60%

100%   30%

Fig. 8.15

Several strokes made with the paintbrush tool at various opacity settings.

The greater the percentage, the more visible the effect is.

The following tools use the opacity setting: Paintbucket, Gradient, Line, Eraser, Pencil, Paintbrush, and Rubber Stamp. The tools using pressure are: Airbrush, Smudge, Sharpen/blur, and Sponge. The Dodge and Burn tools use an exposure setting.

Tip

Changing Slider Values with the Keyboard

The opacity, pressure, or exposure of the currently selected tool (including the Paintbucket, Gradient, Line, Eraser, Pencil, Airbrush, Paintbrush, Rubber Stamp, Smudge, Sharpen/blur, and Dodge/burn/sponge) can be set in 10 percent increments by pressing one of the keys, 0-9, on the keyboard or numeric keypad. Each numbered key represents 10 times its value except "0," which represents 100. Pressing the numbered keys while any other tool is selected (including the Marquee, Lasso, Magic Wand, Move, Hand, Zoom, Cropping, Type, and Eyedropper tools) will change the opacity of the currently selected layer.

Fade

Unless the fade setting is selected, it will not affect the way paint is added to the document. When selected, you must enter a number into the field that determines the number of steps it will take before the current brush has faded completely (see fig. 8.16). The pop-up menu provides the option to fade to transparent or to the background color. Each step corresponds to the spacing value that has been set up for the particular brush in use.

Fig. 8.16

The brushstroke on the left fades in 100 steps and the stroke on the right fades in 50 steps.

For instance, the stroke on the right of figure 8.16 is a 20 pixel diameter brush with a 25 percent spacing (or 5 pixels) set to fade out in 50 steps. After moving 250 pixels, the brush no longer adds paint to the image.

Stylus Pressure

If your Macintosh is equipped with a pressure-sensitive stylus and tablet, such as those manufactured by Wacom and CalComp, you have additional options available in the Options palette.

The pressure applied to the stylus can be linked to any number of these brush attributes: size, color, and opacity/pressure/exposure (depending on the type of painting tool that is selected).

The following three types of painting attributes may be associated with a pressure-sensitive pen and tablet:

▶ **Size** decreases the size of the chosen brush as the pressure applied to the stylus is reduced. The size of the current brush never exceeds its set size in the Brushes palette.

▶ **Color** increases the saturation of the selected foreground color if the stylus receives greater pressure, and reduces the saturation if the stylus receives less pressure.

▶ **Opacity/Pressure/Exposure**, depending on the tool selected, controls the amount of effect that the selected tool has on the image. When this option is checked, the opacity/pressure/exposure never exceeds the current setting in the Options palette.

Working with Painting Tools

Following are descriptions of the many painting tools that are available in Photoshop. Some have extra options that were not covered in the previous section. Each one requires some experimentation and practice before you become proficient in its use. Keep in mind that the painting tools can produce infinitely different results based on the current mode setting, foreground color, image color, brush attributes, opacity/pressure/exposure setting, and stylus pressure setting (if available). The illustration(s) following each tool are meant to demonstrate only the most basic use of the tool.

All tools are selected by clicking the appropriate icon in the toolbox. Next, move the pointer into the document where you want to begin painting. While some tools can be activated with a single click, most tools are used by pressing the mouse button and dragging to form a path or line. Release the mouse button when the path or line is finished. If you move the mouse

III

Creating and Touching Up

too fast, the computer's display may not be able to keep up with you, but Photoshop will maintain a certain degree of accuracy in reproducing your motions. You will find, however, that at high resolutions or with large brushes, it is best to move the mouse very slowly to avoid sharp corners where there should be smooth curves.

Design Note

Creating Straight Lines

To create a perfectly straight line with any painting or editing tool, click once where you would like the line to start; then hold down the Shift key and click where you would like the line to end. The currently selected tool will modify the image (either by painting or editing) in a straight line between the two points. To continue creating straight line segments, hold the Shift key and click at each point where you want the line to be drawn.

The pointer that many tools display while painting is the same as that tool's icon in the toolbox. Pressing the Caps Lock key on the keyboard will display a crosshair for more precise positioning of the brush or line. An additional option in the Preferences dialog box (Choose Preferences, General from the File menu) allows you to specify that the pointer becomes the shape and size of the currently selected brush in the Brushes palette. Choosing to view the actual size of the brush makes it easier to determine exactly where paint will be applied to the image. For more information on setting these preferences, see the section "Using General Preferences" in chapter 4.

Pencil Tool

 The Pencil tool provides a hard-edged brush stroke that appears jagged when magnified (see fig. 8.17). All the pixels produced by the Pencil are the same opacity and color. The Pencil is the fastest of the painting tools in terms of response time and therefore is the preferred tool for making rough sketches or quick annotations.

The Pencil tool options consist of the standard settings mentioned above, plus a check box for Auto Erase. When selected, the Auto Erase option will watch the existing colors in the image to see if they are the same as the current foreground color. If the Pencil is clicked on a pixel that is the current foreground color, Auto Erase will paint that pixel with the current background color. This is most useful when editing bitmapped images or icons at a high magnification where it is desirable to change individual pixels between the two colors.

Fig. 8.17

Use the Pencil tool for fast and rough sketches.

Line Tool

When you need a straight line from one point in your image to another, use the Line tool. Besides the standard mode and opacity setting, the Line tool Options palette provides settings to change the line's width (measured in pixels). Type a number from 1 through 1000 into the field to specify the thickness of the line. A width of 0 (zero) will not draw a line, but is useful for measuring distances and angles between two points. In order to read the results, be sure to first open the Info palette by choosing Palettes, Info from the Window menu.

The Anti-aliased check box softens the edges of the line if selected, or leaves them hard and possibly jagged if not selected. The difference is apparent in figure 8.18.

Fig. 8.18

Enlarged to 200%, these lines show the effects of not selecting (left) and selecting (right) the Anti-aliased check box.

III

Creating and Touching Up

Arrowheads may be added to the start and/or end of any line by checking the appropriate box(es). To configure the size and shape of the arrowheads, click the Shape button. You are presented with three options to define the shape and size of the arrowhead:

▶ **Width** of the arrowhead is measured in percent of the line's weight and can range from 10 to 1000.

▶ **Length** of the arrowhead is also measured in percent of the line's weight and can range from 10 to 5000.

▶ **Concavity** of the arrowhead's body is measured in percent of the line's weight from –50 to +50.

Design Tip

Place Lines on Layers

When creating lines or arrowheads in your image, it is sometimes difficult to place them exactly where you want them. Instead of fussing with the lines until they are right, simply create a new layer to hold the lines. Now they can be easily selected and moved without disrupting the image around them. Also, draw lines with the Info palette visible so that their angles and lengths are displayed.

Paintbrush Tool

The Paintbrush functions almost the same as the Pencil. One difference is that the edge of a paintbrush stroke has a softer, more diffused look rather than the harsh and jagged edge of the pencil (see fig. 8.19). The setting which affects the amount of edge of a particular brush is its hardness value, which can range from 0 to 100 percent. The hardness can be set by double-clicking on a brush in the Brushes palette.

The second difference is that rather than the ability to Auto Erase, the Paintbrush has a feature called Wet Edges which can be selected in the Tool Options palette. When the Wet Edges check box is selected, the amount of color applied to the image is about 40 percent less than what the same opacity setting would produce when using normal mode. Additionally, the extreme outer edges of painted strokes are darker than the main color.

Fig. 8.19

Paintbrush strokes, in general, are softer than those made by the Pencil, yet harder than those made by the Airbrush.

Each time paint is applied to an area of the image, the resulting color gets darker, as if the paint were building up.

Airbrush Tool

Both the Pencil and Paintbrush tools dispense all the paint they are capable of as soon as the mouse button is clicked. The Airbrush, however, dispenses paint slowly over time as long as the mouse button is held down. Similar to a real airbrush, the Airbrush tool produces very soft, diffused strokes that can be built up by passing the brush over the same area multiple times (see fig. 8.20).

Fig. 8.20

Like a real airbrush, strokes are soft and can build up.

The Airbrush is especially useful when applying a custom brush shape to an image—a starburst, for instance—because the longer the mouse button is held down, the more visible the shape becomes. The Airbrush tool uses the same options as the Paintbrush except that the opacity slider is replaced by a Pressure slider. The greater the pressure, the faster paint flows out of the brush while the mouse button is held down.

Paintbucket Tool

The Paintbucket is used to fill a contiguous area with the same color or pattern. A contiguous area is defined as any single space in an image of a similar color that is touching. The range of color that is considered

III

Creating and Touching Up

"similar" depends on the value entered into the Tolerance field of the Tool Options palette. As the value increases (between 0 and 255) the number of pixels that Photoshop is likely to change also increases. The Contents pop-up menu lets you choose whether the area you click is filled with the current foreground color or with the currently defined pattern.

> **Note**
>
> A pattern is defined by making a rectangular selection in an image and choosing Define Pattern from the Edit menu. When filling or painting an area with a pattern, the selection is repeated or tiled, similar to wallpaper or gift wrap.

In figure 8.21, the image on the left was filled with a pattern with the Paintbucket set to a tolerance of 32, while the image on the right was filled with the tolerance set to 70.

Fig. 8.21

Increasing the tolerance affects more similar colors.

When the Anti-aliased check box is selected, fringe pixels are added to fill in any gaps where some color already exists. Figure 8.22 shows the effect of filling an area with anti-aliasing off (left) and on (right).

Fig. 8.22

Anti-aliasing smooths filled area edges.

As with all painting tools, the Paintbucket only affects the currently selected layer of a document. When working on a multiple-layer document, selecting the Sample Merged check box will force the Paintbucket tool to "see through" the layers in a document and behave as if all the colors on all the layers are on a single layer. Any new colors or patterns added to the image are added to the active layer only.

Gradient Tool

The Gradient tool can create two types of shapes and five styles of blends. It is most often used to create backgrounds or special effects, or to fill in selections. The five styles are listed in a pop-up menu in the Tool Options palette. They include: foreground to background, foreground to transparent, transparent to foreground, clockwise spectrum, and counterclockwise spectrum.

The first three styles are straightforward transitions between the foreground and background colors, or the foreground color and nothingness. The last two create gradients whose hues move clockwise or counterclockwise around the colorwheel between the foreground and background colors.

All gradients are defined by dragging the gradient pointer across the document window to form a defining line. Where the line starts is where the foreground color begins to make a transition. The angle and distance at which the line is drawn determine the angle and distance of a linear blend, if that option is chosen in the Tool Options palette. The point at the end of the line is where the background color or transparency has been imaged to its full effect.

The Midpoint slider (range 13 to 87 percent) determines at what point along the drawn line the transition is one-half complete. A lower value causes the background color or transparent part of the gradient to be longer, while a higher value causes the foreground color part to be longer. If you set the midpoint too close to their extreme values, you might clip the gradient. Figure 8.23 shows four gradients that run from black to white with differing midpoint values.

When the Type pop-up menu is set to Radial, the Gradient tool creates a blend in the shape of concentric circles from the center outward. In addition to the midpoint slider that determines the half-completion point, a Radial Offset slider determines how long to "hold" the foreground color before beginning the transition. The left side of figure 8.24 shows two radial gradients with differing offset values. The right side of the figure shows similar gradients created with the foreground and background colors reversed.

Fig. 8.23

Midpoint values
determine the
sharpness of
change that
appears in a
gradient.

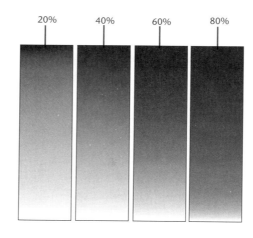

Fig. 8.24

Increase the radial
offset to hold the
foreground color
longer.

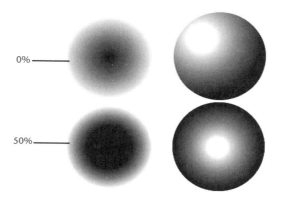

Design Note

Creating Spheres

To create a realistic looking sphere, start by making a circular selection with the Elliptical Marquee tool. Select the Gradient tool and
change its Type to Radial in the Options palette. Set the Style to
Foreground to Background, and be sure the current foreground color
is lighter than the current background color. Drag inside the circular
selection with the Gradient tool from the highlight spot to the opposite side of the circle (the shadow spot). Try changing the midpoint
and radial offset values to achieve different results.

Normally, gradients are produced in bands, each with a slightly different shading. In some cases, especially when enlarged or distorted, these steps can become too obvious and distract from the overall look of the gradient. Selecting the Dither check box in the Gradient Tool Options palette causes a small amount of noise to be added to each step, diminishing the likelihood that the banding will be noticeable.

Type Tool

If at all possible, type should be created in an application that supports vector-based (also called object-oriented) type for the highest quality and best control. This would include both PostScript and TrueType fonts. For special effects, however, raster type (the kind created by pixels) created in Photoshop is sometimes necessary. To achieve smooth text at large sizes, you must be using either TrueType fonts or Type 1 fonts with Adobe Type Manager installed. If not, any text you create will appear bitmapped and jagged on-screen and when you print.

Before creating text, choose the desired foreground color because it will be used to initially draw the text on-screen. You may also want to create a new layer to hold the text until you have styled it the way you want. Unlike other programs, text created in Photoshop becomes part of the raster image once deselected and cannot be altered (as far as changing font, size, style, or characters is concerned).

Text is inserted into the active layer by choosing the Type tool and clicking the document in the approximate location where you want the text to appear. The Type Tool dialog box appears (see fig. 8.25).

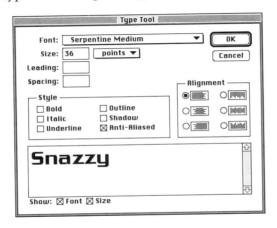

Fig. 8.25

Text is entered and formatted in the Type Tool dialog box.

In this dialog box, you can choose formatting options for the text you are about to create. Use the pop-up menu to pick a font, and type values into the fields to set the size, leading, and spacing for the text. *Leading* is the amount of space between lines of text and *spacing* is the amount of space between characters.

Choose one or more of the Style options by clicking the appropriate check boxes: Bold, Italic, Underline, Outline, or Shadow. Unless you have a reason not to (such as creating very small type or trying to mimic type on a computer screen), always select the Anti-Aliased check box to create text with softer edges.

There are six different radio buttons, each one corresponding to one type of text alignment. The first column has options for aligning text horizontally: flush left, centered, and flush right. The second column has options for aligning text vertically: top, centered, and bottom. Figure 8.26 shows horizontal text and vertical text.

Fig. 8.26

Horizontal text reads left-to-right while vertical text reads top-to-bottom.

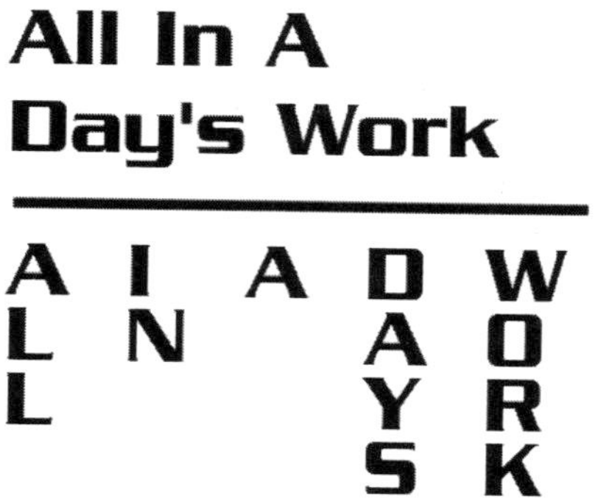

The actual text you want to create is typed into the scrolling field near the bottom of the dialog box. There is no practical limit to the amount of text that can be entered at one time. To see the text in the actual font and size specified at the top of the dialog box, select the Show Font and Show Size check boxes underneath the text entry field. Without these selected, text appears in the system font (default), usually Chicago, size 12.

Click OK or press the Enter key to place the text onto the active layer of your document. The text becomes a floating selection that can easily be made into its own layer by dragging the floating selection name onto the New Layer icon (page) in the Layers palette. As long as the text is still selected, it may be removed by pressing the Delete key, or by choosing

Clear from the Edit menu. By using the Type tool, Move tool, or any of the selection tools, it is possible to drag selected text around on the screen. For more information on selecting parts of an image, see "Creating Selections" in chapter 9.

Although kerning is not available as an option, text can be kerned by selecting each letter and nudging it to the left or right with the left and right arrow keys on the keyboard.

Using Editing Tools

The tools described in this section will only function properly if there is already some paint or an image in your document. These are the editing tools, and their purpose is to modify the pixels that already exist in your image without necessarily adding new ones. Included in this section are: Eraser, Rubber Stamp, Smudge, Sharpen/blur, and Dodge/burn/sponge.

Eraser Tool

It makes sense that if Photoshop allows you to paint onto an image, it should let you remove paint from an image. That's exactly what the Eraser is for. On a single-layer (or background-only) image, the Eraser paints with the background color. It's practically the same as using the Pencil, Paintbrush, or Airbrush tools. In fact, the Mode pop-up menu in the Tool Options palette allows you to select which of these three styles you would like to use when erasing. A fourth behavior, called Block, is simply a squared-off version of a pencil-like brush.

The Brushes palette remembers the last brush you used for each of the different modes. As a reminder, the pencil tool creates hard, jagged edges while the Paintbrush and Airbrush have softer, more diffused edges. Each mode except for Block, has the appropriate opacity or pressure slider, as well as a fade control. To cycle through the four modes of the Eraser tool, hold the Option key as you click the eraser icon in the toolbox.

Clicking the Erase Layer/Erase Image button in the Tool Options palette erases the active layer or the entire image, if no layers exist. Layers erase to transparent while an image without layers erases to the current background color. Figure 8.27 shows an image on a layer being erased to display the checkerboard pattern signifying transparency.

Fig. 8.27

Erasing on a layer replaces the image with transparency, which is identified by a checkerboard pattern.

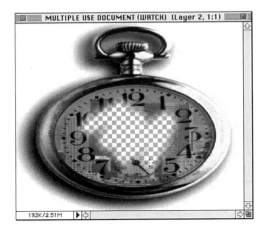

Selecting the Erase to Saved check box causes Photoshop to erase portions of the image to the last saved version of the image. If the image has changed color modes or dimensions since it was last saved, this option will not function and a dialog box will alert you to this fact.

The Erase to Saved function of the Eraser tool brings back the last image saved to disk wherever it is used. The result is identical to the Rubber Stamp's option named From Saved in the Rubber Stamp Options palette when normal mode is selected. The Rubber Stamp provides additional modes, such as Dissolve and Multiply.

Rubber Stamp Tool

The Rubber Stamp tool combines several interesting image manipulation and painting features in one location. They include: Clone, Pattern, From Snapshot, From Saved, and Impressionist. The mode is chosen from the Option pop-up menu in the Tool Options palette.

Clone (aligned) allows you to select a point in a document from which you want to "pick up" an image and then begin to paint with that image in the same or another document. It is useful for retouching projects where you might want to copy an element from one image onto another. Or, as shown in figure 8.28, the poster is removed from behind the child's head by cloning an empty wall into its place. The same technique could just as easily have created a two-headed child, or one with three eyes and two noses.

Poster   Wall cloned over poster

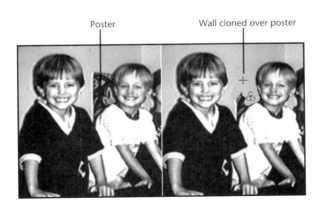

Fig. 8.28

Cloning paints one image onto another.

To begin cloning, move the Rubber Stamp pointer set to clone mode to the place where you want to "pick up" an image. This can be the same document you are working on, a different layer in the same document, or even a different document. Hold the Option key and click the mouse button once. This defines the starting point or origin of the image you will be painting with. Next, move to the place where you want to begin painting and create brush strokes just as you would with the paintbrush.

A crosshair cursor follows the image that you "picked up," so you know what you are painting with. The aligned mode refers to the fact that when you release the mouse button and begin painting again, you will continue painting exactly where you left off—the image will be aligned with the one you just painted. This is most useful when painting a single object into your image from another document, because you can change brush shapes and sizes without affecting the newly painted image.

To change the origin at any time, hold the Option key and click the mouse button where you want to "pick up" a new image. By default, Photoshop will only clone the currently selected layer onto itself, ignoring any paint on layers above or below. To force Photoshop to "see through" all visible layers of the source document, select the Sample Merged check box in the Tool Options palette. The Rubber Stamp tool will then clone paint from all visible layers onto the currently selected layer.

Clone (non-aligned) works the same way as above, except that each time you release the mouse button and press it again, you are painting from the previous origin point. This is useful when painting an object several times onto your image from another document. For example, perhaps you have "picked up" a flower from one document and want to place it into another image in five different places. Each time the mouse button is pressed, the origin will snap back to the flower so it can be painted in its new location.

III

Creating and Touching Up

215

Pattern (aligned) paints the currently defined pattern using a paintbrush-like stroke. The aligned option ensures that the tiles always line up with each other, even if the mouse button is released. Figure 8.29 illustrates painting with a pattern.

Fig. 8.29

Using the Rubber Stamp tool to paint with a pattern.

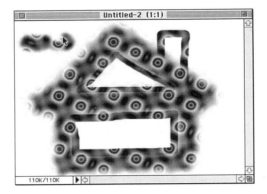

Pattern (non-aligned) works the same as above, except that each time you release the mouse button and press it again, the pattern starts over from the current mouse location. This causes tiles not to align properly, creating a more random, broken look to areas where it is applied.

From Snapshot paints the image last saved into Photoshop's snapshot memory. To save the current layer into snapshot memory, choose Take Snapshot from the Edit menu. The result is basically the same as using the Eraser tool with Erase to Saved selected, or using the From Saved option (described next), but it is not necessary to save your document to disk if you take a snapshot.

From Saved paints the image last saved to disk. The advantage of using this method rather than the Eraser tool's Erase to Saved option is that many additional painting modes are available, such as dissolve or multiply.

The impressionist option for the Rubber Stamp brings the image saved to disk back onto the screen as a pseudo-impressionistic style. The most common application of this technique is to save a photograph to disk, and then erase the entire image on-screen. Using a small to medium-sized brush, begin to repaint the image with short, straight strokes. Pretty soon you have a reproduction of the photograph that appears to have been drawn with oil paints. An example of this technique is illustrated in figure 8.30.

Fig. 8.30

Simulate an oil painting with the Rubber Stamp's Impressionist option.

Smudge Tool

The Smudge tool, when applied to an image, has the effect of pushing or smearing pixels in the direction of your brush stroke, as if you are dragging your finger through wet paint (see fig. 8.31). Increase the pressure value to allow longer drags, and decrease the pressure value to force shorter drags.

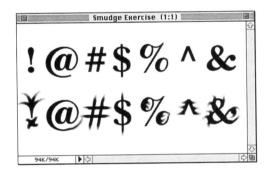

Fig. 8.31

Smudging distorts the image by smearing pixels together.

When the Sample Merged check box is selected, smudging will read the pixels from all layers, although only the active layer is affected.

To use the Smudge tool as a painting tool, select the Finger Painting check box in the Tool Options palette. The Smudge tool uses the current foreground color to create smeary strokes on your image. Figure 8.32 shows an example of painting with the Smudge tool.

Fig. 8.32

The Smudge tool in finger painting mode can create interesting looking brushstrokes—and is less messy than giving paint to a child!

Tip

Mixing Sampled Paint

An alternative way to create new colors from existing areas in your document can be achieved by mixing sampled paint. Use the eye-dropper tool to select colors from your image and paint them into the Scratch palette or an empty area of your document; or clone colors into the Scratch palette using the Rubber Stamp tool. Place the sampled colors right next to each other. The idea is then to use the Smudge tool in your document or in the Scratch palette to smear two or more colors together. This has the same effect as mixing paints on an artist's palette.

Focus Tools

Two functions in the toolbox share the same location. These are the Blur and Sharpen tools, which are collectively called the Focus tools. Found in the last tool in the first column of the toolbox, you can choose the function you want to use from the Tool pop-up menu in the Tool Options palette. You can also hold the Option key and click the Focus tool in the toolbox to toggle between the Blur and Sharpen tools. While similar commands appear under the Filter menu, these tools can apply the same effect using painted strokes.

The Blur tool decreases the contrast between adjacent pixels, causing an area to appear out of focus (see fig. 8.33). Each time Blur is applied to an image, more detail is lost and it cannot be returned by using the Sharpen tool. You can use the Erase to Saved function of the Eraser tool, however, to bring the last saved area of an image back.

The Sharpen tool increases the contrast between adjacent pixels, causing an area to appear crisper (see fig. 8.33). Each time Sharpen is applied to an image, the contrast is increased, and eventually pixels will become fully saturated as red, green, blue, cyan, magenta, yellow, black, or white. You cannot return an image to its original state by applying the Blur tool after the Sharpen tool. You can use the Erase to Saved function of the Eraser tool, however, to bring the last saved area of an image back.

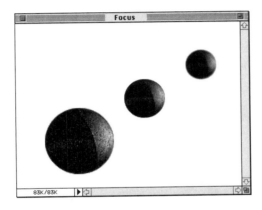

Fig. 8.33

The largest sphere was sharpened and the smallest sphere blurred to give the illusion of depth.

When the Sample Merged check box is selected in the Tool Options palette, the Blur and Sharpen tools create new pixels on the active layer to simulate the effect of blurring or sharpening the actual image.

Toning Tools

There are three other functions that share a common tool. This is the Dodge/burn/sponge tool, which is collectively referred to as the Toning tools. Found in the last tool of the second row of the toolbox, you can choose the function you want to use from the Tool pop-up menu in the Tool Options palette. You can also hold the Option key and click the Sharpen/blur tool in the toolbox to toggle between the Blur and Sharpen tools. Commands that perform similar functions are available elsewhere in Photoshop, but these tools can be applied using painted strokes.

The Dodge tool is used to lighten an area of an image, as in correcting underexposed photographic film. The Dodge tool uses an exposure setting to determine the amount of effect that is applied to the image—the lower the exposure, the less the effect. A Mode pop-up menu in the Tool Options palette is used to control which areas of an image are most affected by the Dodge tool: shadow, midtones, or highlight.

The Burn tool is used to darken an area of an image, as in correcting overexposed photographic film. The Burn tool uses an exposure setting to determine the amount of effect that will be applied to the image—the lower the exposure, the less the effect. A Mode pop-up menu in the Tool Options palette is used to control which areas of an image are most affected by the Burn tool: shadow, midtones, or highlight.

When used correctly, the Dodge and Burn tools together can be a powerful weapon against unwanted highlight and shadow areas in a photograph. Figure 8.34 illustrates the use of the Dodge tool to remove a shadow from the right side of the subject's face, while the Burn tool is used to eliminate intense highlights on the subject's forehead and nose.

Fig. 8.34

Portions of the original photo (left) have been corrected with Dodge and Burn (right).

 The Sponge tool is used to either increase or decrease the saturation in part of an image. Choose which function you want the tool to perform from the Mode pop-up menu in the Tool Options palette. Saturating an image will cause any color already there to become more intense and vivid. Desaturating begins to remove color from an image, until eventually you are left with only a grayscale photo.

Mastering the Brushes Palette

While the various features and capabilities of the many painting and editing tools are extensive, they would all be useless without the capability to select from an array of different brushes. The Brushes palette provides the access for many tools to be used in an artistic or expressive way. Display the Brushes palette by choosing Palettes, Brushes from the Window menu.

Tools that can utilize brushes include the Eraser, Pencil, Airbrush, Paintbrush, Rubber Stamp, Smudge, Sharpen/blur, and Dodge/burn/sponge. Each time one of these tools is selected, the Brushes palette will draw a thick border around the brush that is currently active for that tool. To select a different brush, click on its icon.

Changing Brush Sets

The Brushes palette options menu provides four commands to help you manage the plethora of brushes that are available to Photoshop. By default, only 16 brushes are available in the Brushes palette (see fig. 8.35). A preview of each brush is shown in one of the six spaces allocated to each row of the palette. To display more spaces, simply make the palette larger by dragging its size box down. The first row consists of brushes with a harder edge than the second row. The third row of brushes all have numbers underneath the brush previews. The numbers refer to the diameter of the brush in pixels.

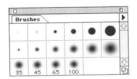

Fig. 8.35

The default brushes that come with Photoshop vary in hardness and size.

Choose the appropriate commands from the Brushes Palette Options menu to perform the following functions:

▶ Choose Reset Brushes to revert the Brushes palette to its default set of 16 round brushes.

▶ Choose Load Brushes to replace the current set of brushes with a new set from disk.

▶ Choose Append Brushes to add all the brushes from a set on disk to the currently available brushes.

▶ Choose Save Brushes to write the currently available brushes to disk as a set that can be loaded or appended in the future. This is especially useful to facilitate the sharing of brush sets among many users.

Making a New Brush

Any existing brush may be edited by double-clicking on its preview. A new brush may be created by clicking once in an unused space in the Brushes palette or by choosing New Brush from the Brushes Palette Options menu. The New Brush dialog box is displayed so that you can specify the attributes of the new brush (see fig. 8.36). This identical dialog box also appears when editing an existing round brush.

Fig. 8.36

These settings control the attributes of a round brush.

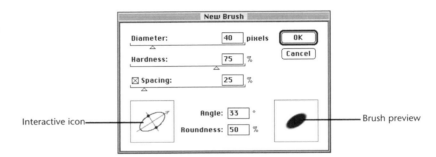

Interactive icon

Brush preview

The controls that are available for a round brush are as follows:

▶ **Diameter** is a measure of the brush's size. The allowable range is from 1 pixel to 999 pixels. Drag the slider or enter a value into the field. A preview is shown in the lower-right corner of the dialog box. If the preview is too large to fit in the available space, its scale will be shown just above the box.

▶ **Hardness** determines the type of edge that a brush will have. Drag the slider or enter a value into the field. The minimum value is 0% which results in the softest, most diffused edge. The maximum hardness value of 100% gives a sharp, crisp edge while still maintaining an anti-aliased brushstroke.

▶ **Spacing**, if the check box is selected, controls how often paint is placed into the image when this particular brush is dragged with the mouse. When spacing is not active, paint is applied whenever the pointer moves a single pixel. With spacing active, the percentage (from 1 to 999) is a factor of the diameter of the brush. A spacing of 100% will apply paint to the image only when the pointer has moved the same distance as the brush's diameter. The smaller the spacing, the smoother the resulting brushstroke. The larger the spacing, the more spread out the individual applications of paint will be.

▶ **Angle** is the rotation of the brush measured in degrees from –180 to +180. The angle has no effect on a perfectly round brush, but can create a calligraphic effect on narrower brushes. Change the angle by entering a value into the field or by dragging the head or tail of the arrow in the interactive icon.

▶ **Roundness** is a measure of how close the brush shape comes to a perfect circle. A roundness of 100% is a perfect circle, and a roundness of 0% is extremely thin. Change the roundness by entering a value into the field or by dragging the small round dots that appear on either side of the interactive icon.

Click the OK button to accept the changes. The brush preview will be updated in the Brushes palette if necessary.

Defining A Brush

Besides creating round brushes, Photoshop has the ability to turn any rectangular area of an image into a brush. It is common to use small illustrations or text dingbats as brushes. Areas with a high amount of contrast work better than areas with little or no contrast because the brush will be converted to grayscale during the process.

To create a custom brush, follow these steps:

1. Open the image that contains an element you want to make into a brush. You may also draw or import artwork directly into a document window. (In figure 8.37, text dingbats have been typed in the document.)

2. Use the Rectangular Marquee to create a selection around the object or area that will become a brush. The Marquee Options palette must not be set to feather.

3. Choose Define Brush from the Brushes Palette Options menu (see fig. 8.37). The new brush will appear in the next available space in the Brushes palette. In some instances, the preview may appear cropped to the upper-left corner of the area you selected even though the entire brush was stored correctly. You may also need to scroll down in the palette to see the new brush if it is not immediately visible.

III

Creating and Touching Up

Fig. 8.37

Custom brushes
are defined from
a rectangular
selection.

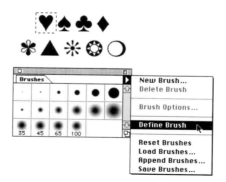

To paint with a custom brush, just choose any of the painting tools that support brushes and click on the custom brush icon in the Brushes palette. Custom brushes have all the same capabilities as round brushes when it comes to opacity, pressure, exposure, fade, wet edges, and spacing. To set the spacing for a custom brush, double-click the brush's preview in the Brushes palette. The Brush Options dialog box appears (see fig. 8.38).

Fig. 8.38

Setting the options
for a custom brush.

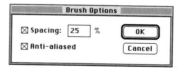

If the brush you defined originally came from a bitmap document (just black and white pixels, no shades of gray), you may want to select the anti-aliased option of the brush to soften the edges.

Figure 8.39 shows three brushstrokes created by a custom brush. The first stroke uses the default spacing of 25%. Notice how there are small gaps between the shapes of the brush. The second stroke uses a spacing of 125%. The third stroke also uses a spacing of 125%, but it is set to fade to transparent in 10 steps.

Deleting a Brush

To delete brushes that are no longer necessary, select the brush from the Brushes palette and choose Delete Brush from the Brushes palette options menu. The shortcut is to hold the Command (⌘) key down while clicking on a brush preview. Be careful when deleting brushes because the operation cannot be undone.

Fig. 8.39

Several brush-
strokes made with
a custom brush.

Where To Go from Here

▶ Chapter 9, "Selecting Objects in Photoshop," explains how to restrict
and control where paint is applied in your document.

▶ Chapter 11, "Drawing and Editing Paths," discusses the use of vector-
based tools as drawing aids.

▶ Chapter 17, "Creating Special Effects with Video," covers painting on
QuickTime movies and touching up bluescreen images.

III

Creating and Touching Up

Selecting Objects in Photoshop

There's one simple thing to know about Photoshop. When you master selections, you master Photoshop. If you're new to Adobe Photoshop, this chapter is the most important one in this book. For the Photoshop user upgrading to version 3, there are some very nice, new methods of creating a selection and this chapter is equally important for you. Regardless of your level of experience, creating a selection is essential, and the better you get at it, the faster and more precise all your Photoshop sessions will be.

Using Photoshop for Macintosh • Using Photoshop for Macintosh • Using Photoshop for Mac

by Ted Padova

CHAPTER 9

Unlike object-oriented programs that permit the selection of objects by means of a simple click, Photoshop requires its objects, which are represented by pixels, to be encompassed within a selection marquee. With the many different colors or shades of gray in images, creating selections can be difficult. Fortunately, Photoshop provides the user with many different approaches to creating, manipulating, and editing selections. This chapter explores Photoshop's means of creating selections and explains how to work with selected regions of images.

Understanding Selection Tools

Before we look at the tools available for creating a selection in Photoshop, let's look at why selections are necessary. MacPaint, a pixel-based application, awed early Mac users. When creating an item in MacPaint, such as shapes and text, the user needs to select the item to move it, alter its gray value, delete it, or add to it. To change shapes, the user depends heavily on the use of the Rectangular Marquee to surround the pixels. The user applies changes to the selection with the toolbox or menu options, but the rest of the image is undisturbed. This principle continues with the advanced application software professionals use today.

Selections are vital in Photoshop where specific regions of an image need to be changed, edited, or manipulated to create the desired design effects. Photoshop is much more complicated than a simple paint program like MacPaint; not only due to its advanced features and tools, but also because there are so many shades of colors and grays to work with. Selecting a region where the end of a color or gray stops and another shade begins is not easy. Crude selections make an edited image look artificial. Precise selections make the end result appear authentic and genuine.

Fortunately, Photoshop has a number of methods for creating selections both from tools in the tool palette and from menu options. In addition, you can work with channels and layers, and save selections for later use. The next few sections cover the uses of selection tools from the toolbox.

Rectangular Marquee Tool

 The Rectangular Marquee tool is one of the best known instruments to Macintosh users. Rectangular Marquees are used in almost every graphic application on the Macintosh, whether it be a specific tool from a toolbox or a selection arrow on the desktop. Photoshop's Rectangular Marquee tool works like a rectangular marquee in any other program, with the addition of options for specifying marquee shapes and sizes. Each of the marquee tools in the toolbox has an associated Options palette where the attributes of the tool can be further defined. With respect to the Rectangular Marquee tool, you can constrain the aspect ratio, establish a fixed size, and create a feather radius (see fig. 9.1).

A Marquee Options palette is available when you select the tool in the Photoshop toolbox. To view the palette, open the Window menu and choose Show Options. The palette options will appear for the tool selected in the toolbox.

Fig. 9.1

When you view the Rectangular Marquee Options palette, the palette provides several choices for creating selections.

Elliptical Tool

The Elliptical Marquee tool works like the Rectangular Marquee tool, except that it creates oval or elliptical selections. The Elliptical Marquee tool is accessed in the Marquee Options palette from the pop-up menu, as illustrated in figure 9.2. Once you choose Elliptical from the Marquee Options palette, all other options are identical to those available to the Rectangular Marquee tool.

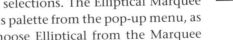

Fig. 9.2

In addition to the same options for the Rectangular Marquee tool, the Elliptical Marquee Options palette provides an anti-aliasing feature.

III

Creating and Touching Up

Lasso Tool

 The Lasso tool is used for creating selections around irregular shapes. Use of the tool is much like a freehand drawing tool where the edges of the shape are traced to create the selection. This tool functions a bit differently than previous paint programs where the selection shrank to the object being selected. With Photoshop, the tool stays fixed at the position where the trace of the object is performed. In addition, the Lasso tool has some palette options that can be used for feathering and anti-aliasing (see fig. 9.3).

Fig. 9.3

Lasso Options palette.

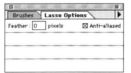

Magic Wand Tool

 The Magic Wand tool was introduced in the first version of Photoshop. This tool selects a contiguous group of like pixels within a specified tolerance range. The tool samples the position where the mouse button is depressed and travels from that point throughout a range adjacent to the sample. Pixels of similar value in nonadjacent positions are unaffected. Like the other selection tools, the Magic Wand tool has choices available in an Options palette (see fig. 9.4). The Magic Wand Options palette has many different choices than the Rectangular Marquee or Elliptical Marquee. For example, to set ranges for how wide a selection will occur, the Tolerance Setting accepts values between 0 and 255. The higher the number, the wider the range of values that will be selected.

Of all the selection tools, the Magic Wand seems to attract the attention of the beginning Photoshop user the most. It appears somewhat magical in use, but at times can be impractical, especially with large image files. As the Magic Wand travels through a document, it analyzes each pixel to determine its value and to decide whether the pixel in question will become part of the selection. To do this, much time is expended in the evaluation of the pixels. The Magic Wand is used less frequently once the beginner knows more selection techniques.

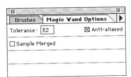

Fig. 9.4

The Magic Wand Options palette includes a user definable tolerance specification for ranges between 0 and 255.

Pen Tool

The Pen tool in the Paths palette functions like a pen tool in illustration programs for drawing Bézier paths. Once the path is created, it can be converted to a selection. The Pen tool functions are so extensive, chapter 10 deals with paths and path operations exclusively. We mention it now because the Pen tool can be used for creating selections. Rather than Options palette features, the paths operations have a separate palette for additional features. Figure 9.5 shows the palette available when choosing Paths.

Fig. 9.5

The Paths palette has a number of options for creating paths and selections.

Menu Selections

In addition to the tools for creating selections, Photoshop has a menu specifically used for working with selections. The Select menu has a number of features to assist the user in creating, manipulating, and working with selections. The first three items in the menu deal with more basic selection functions. Several menu selections will be examined in more detail in the section, "Editing Selections." For now, let's look at examining menu commands and understand what they mean.

To select the entire image area, open the Select menu and choose All. Some of Photoshop's features are not enabled unless there is an active selection. If you want to apply an effect to the entire image area, use the Select All feature from the menu. The Select All option has the keyboard equivalent of ⌘-A. This Command key combination is easy to remember because many other applications have the same one.

III

Creating and Touching Up

To deselect any active selection, open the Select menu and choose None. The keyboard equivalent is ⌘-D. Commit this keyboard equivalent to memory because you will probably use it frequently. Some caution should be noted, however, when you deselect regions that haven't been saved. Photoshop allows a single Undo operation for the last action. If you use Select None or ⌘-D, you can Undo the operation and regain the selected area. If you work fast and deselect, and then use a tool or menu operation, the selection will be lost. Photoshop cannot regain access to performing Undo and bring back the selection.

The Inverse operation in the Select menu is used to inverse a selected area. This menu function does not have a keyboard equivalent. The ⌘-I keystrokes will invert an image. *Invert* and *Inverse* are very different operations and should not be confused. Inverse is beneficial when all of an image needs to be selected except for an object or objects. A good example might be a human figure against a background. The figure may be represented with different colors or tones and the background may be a single color value. In performing selections with several tools, it is easier to select shapes with common color values. Therefore, if we want to select the human figure, we might first select the background, and then use Inverse. Photoshop inverses our selection of the background and selects the figure. In essence, Inverse deselects the current selection and selects all that was previously not selected.

Creating Selections

Photoshop, the feature rich application that it is, has a multitude of ways to use the selection tools independently and in conjunction with each other. Knowing how the tools operate helps the user determine how to approach a selection. By understanding tool operations, one can evaluate shapes and determine which method will work best in creating the desired selection. The tools quite often can be used together to create selections through a combination of techniques.

In order to properly evaluate your approach to creating a selection, you need to learn how to use tools together. You can combine tool operations to add to and subtract from selections. This adds much more flexibility in achieving precise selections. This section covers a more in-depth look at creating selections and combining selection tool operations.

Geometric Selections

Geometric selections work well with shapes of a geometric design. Squares, rectangles, circles, ellipses, and polygon shapes fall within geometric shapes. Tools such as the Rectangular Marquee, Elliptical Marquee, and even the Lasso tool are common to selecting geometric shapes. Geometric selections include:

▶ *Constraining* a selection to create a square or circle. As with other Macintosh applications, to create perfect squares and circles, press the Shift key and use the Rectangular Marquee or Elliptical Marquee tool.

▶ *Drawing from center.* Depress the Option key and drag outward with the Rectangular and Elliptical Marquees.

▶ *Rows and columns* of single pixel widths. Select the single row or single column items from the Options palette available with the Rectangular Marquee tool. Use the single pixel horizontal and vertical lines when edges of a geometric selection are rough and need to be straightened.

▶ *Constraining aspect ratio* is a means of controlling the relationship of the horizontal width to the vertical height. If the height is to be twice the width, fixing the aspect ratio enables you to create a marquee that will always result with the height twice the width. To accomplish this, select the pop-up menu from the Options palette and select the Constrained Aspect Ratio feature. The boxes below the pop-up menu permit user-definable height and width values for the constraint.

▶ *Fixed size* is another feature available in the pop-up menu and is a great tool for sizing documents to the same physical size. When Fixed Size is enabled, you can enter dimensions for width and height. When you create a rectangular marquee, the rectangle will pop into the document area at the fixed size. If the document area is larger than the selection, you can move the selection around to encompass the desired image area. After you select the image, you can crop it by opening the Edit menu and choosing Crop. This is particularly helpful when sizing images for video frames. By setting a 320-by-240 pixel fixed size, you can crop all images to size and use them in a program like Adobe Premiere.

Lasso Selections

You can use the Lasso tool in two ways: as a free-form tool for creating irregular-shaped selections and as a geometric tool for creating polygon selections. To create a free-form selection, use the Lasso tool like a pencil and trace the edges of an object. As you use the Lasso tool, especially in creating selections around large areas, don't be concerned about missing the edges. You can polish up the edges later. The important thing to remember is to trace an edge and move around the object without stopping until you get to the point of origin (don't release the mouse button until you trace around the selection completely). A lasso selection is illustrated in figure 9.6.

Fig. 9.6

The bird on the left was selected with the Lasso tool.

 Constrain the Lasso tool to a straight line by using it in combination with the Option key. At first it may seem a bit awkward because the sequence of actions must be performed in a precise order. Look at a step-by-step sequence of creating straight lines with the Lasso tool.

▶ Position the Lasso tool in the document area and depress the mouse button.

▶ While holding the mouse button down, press the Option key and release the mouse button. As you move the mouse while pressing the Option key, a rubber band effect enables you to pivot on the point where the coordinates were first established.

▶ Move to another location and click the mouse button. Each click of the mouse button establishes new coordinates.

▶ Return to the point of origin and release the mouse button and the Option key. The selection will be made. If you don't navigate to the point of origin, Photoshop completes the selection by drawing a path from the mouse release to the point of origin.

A combination of the two uses of the Lasso tool is helpful in creating selections on objects where a side may be a straight line and other sides are irregular shapes. In figure 9.7, if you wish to select the window shades, you would use a combination of methods. The sides of the window shades are straight lines, while the top of the window shades is made up of arcs. In such a case, you need to create both a straight line and free-form selection.

Fig. 9.7

The Lasso tool is used for free-form and geometric shapes.

To use a combination of the methods, the straight lines are created in the same manner as noted above. When the free-form operation begins, you simply drag the mouse around the irregular area and then continue to create straight lines when needed. All of this is best accomplished while keeping the Option key depressed. When you drag the mouse, it acts as a free-form tool. When you release the mouse button, you enable the geometric operation.

Add and Subtract Selections

If you were limited to using a tool to create a selection and not to alter the selection in any way, Photoshop would not be much better than the lower-end paint programs. Fortunately, greater control is available by means of adding to or eliminating from a selected area. When using a tool like the Lasso tool, if the free-form object is not precisely selected, you can add any areas that you missed to your selection. You can also delete from the selection any areas that went astray during the trace. To add to a selection, use the Shift key with any of the selection tools. Use the Command key (⌘)

III

Creating and Touching Up

and any of the selection tools to delete from a selection. Use of either tool requires the respective key to be depressed before the tool is used. Failure to do so eliminates the current selection when you click the mouse button.

  Figure 9.8 shows an image where the Magic Wand tool was used to select an area, and additional selections were made with the Shift key depressed. The different color ranges were added to the selection. The Magic Wand was unable to select some areas within the object. To include the area inside the object, the Lasso tool can be used in combination with the Shift key. As the inside image area is surrounded with the Lasso, it becomes part of the selection. When you use several tools with the Shift or Command key, you can facilitate the selection process. If you use a single tool to create selections, it will be much more difficult.

Fig. 9.8

Several colors on the parrot on the left were selected with a combination of the Shift key and multiple uses of the Magic Wand tool.

Tip

The Shrinking Lasso

Paint programs have used a Shrinking Lasso to create a selection around an object. The Shrinking Lasso hugs the object when it is marqueed. If, for example, a marquee is created around a black rectangle and the marquee includes white background around the edges of the rectangle, the Shrinking Lasso eliminates the white background and selects only the rectangle.

To create the same effect in Photoshop, marquee an object as illustrated in figure 9.9. With the Magic Wand tool selected, press the Command key (⌘) and click inside the marquee. The white area is eliminated from the selection, leaving the object selected, as illustrated in figure 9.10.

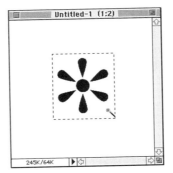

Fig. 9.9

Selection marquee around an object.

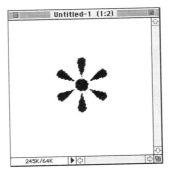

Fig. 9.10

Selection created with Command key (⌘) and Magic Wand.

Magic Wand Tolerances

The Tolerance Setting in the Magic Wand Options palette controls the values within the specified range for the brightness of the sampled pixel. Brightness values range from 0 to 255. If a tolerance of 32 is set in the Options palette and a pixel is sampled at the 128 level of brightness, the Magic Wand will include all pixels with brightness values between 96 and 160. Thirty-two is added to and subtracted from 128 for the range of brightness values included. All pixels in a contiguous area are selected.

In color images, the brightness values are measured in each channel. An RGB image, for example, has brightness values of 0 to 255 in each of the three channels. Therefore, if a pixel is sampled with red at 30, green at 110 and blue at 90, the Magic Wand would read each of the values and add/subtract from their respective values. The contiguous range of the selection would include pixels with red ranges between 0 and 62; green ranges between 74 and 142; and blue ranges between 54 and 122. As the tolerance is increased in the Options palette, a wider range of pixels are selected.

III

Creating and Touching Up

237

The Tolerance Setting in the Options palette controls not only the Magic Wand tool but also the menu options in the Select menu. The Grow and Similar menu options in the Select menu respond to the Tolerance Setting in the Magic Wand Options palette.

Grow

Grow expands the selection in a contiguous area. When you have used the Magic Wand or any other tool to create a selection, you can use the Grow command to stretch out the selection according to the Tolerance Setting in the Magic Wand Options palette. At any time, the tolerance may be changed so that the Grow command selects more or fewer adjacent pixels. This feature is particularly helpful when you need to expand the edges of a selection to include pixels of similar value to the current selection.

Grow has the Command key equivalent ⌘-G, which is helpful in successive repetition of the command. When the tolerance is set to a lower value, successive uses of Grow expands the selection outward. When the selection reaches out to an undesirable selection, simply Undo the last command to bring it back.

Similar

Similar, like Grow, is controlled by the Tolerance Setting in the Magic Wand Options palette. Similar differs from both the Magic Wand tool and Grow because you can use it to select pixels throughout the image area. Similar is not restricted to a contiguous range and will find pixels anywhere in the image with a similar value to the sample.

Similar does not have a keyboard equivalent. If successive uses of the command are necessary, you can develop a custom function key or QuicKey. See chapter 25, "Automating Photoshop," for more information on QuicKeys.

Color Ranges

One of the new additions to Photoshop in version 3 is the Color Range command in the Select menu. When you open the Select menu and choose Color Range, a dialog box appears as illustrated in figure 9.11. Color Range functions like a combination of the Magic Wand tool and the Similar command. A sample is measured when you click in the image. Color Range locates all pixels of similar value to the sampled color.

The tolerance is measured by a slider indicating Fuzziness. The two radio buttons in the dialog box toggle between the image view in the dialog box and the area that will be selected. Selected areas appear white in the preview box.

Fig. 9.11

The Color Range dialog box enables you to sample a color that will be converted to a selection.

The Color Range dialog box defaults with the Select pop-up menu set to Sampled Colors. This option enables you to place the Eyedropper tool on the document window and sample a color value or sample a color in the preview box. When you click OK, the sampled color is selected throughout the image. To add or subtract sampled colors from the current range, use the Eyedropper tools from the dialog box with the + and – symbols denoting add and subtract. In addition, you can use the keyboard equivalents: the Shift key to add and the Command key (⌘) to subtract. While the image is selected for selection, the only visible area in the preview box is the color or colors that have been selected. At times, it may be necessary to view the image, sample a color, and view the selection. Photoshop makes the task easy by permitting a toggle between views with the Control key. When the Selection radio button is active, depressing the Control key displays the image in the preview box. Likewise, when the Image radio button is selected, depressing the Control key displays the selection.

The pop-up menu reveals several choices for the color values to be selected, as seen in figure 9.12. As mentioned, the default is set to Sampled Colors, which provides the user an ability to define the value to be selected from a sample in the image. The preset color values of reds, yellows, greens, cyans, blues, and magentas enable selections of the respective color.

Once you select a color—for example, red—and click the OK button, all the red color values in the image are selected. When you access the dialog box again, and select another color, such as yellow, the yellow color is

III

Creating and Touching Up

added to the red and both colors appear selected. Figure 9.13, in the color section, illustrates the selection of two colors successively with the Color Range command. The first selection on the left parrot was yellow and the second selection on the right was made by choosing the red color. With each successive color new additions or subtractions are performed on the selection.

Fig. 9.12

Color Range dialog box with Select color options.

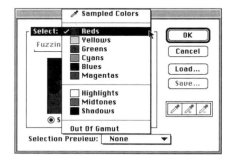

Fig. 9.13

(See color section.)

You can perform additional combinations to narrow the selection for different results. For example, you can select cyan, and then select Out of Gamut. The result will be a selection of all cyan colors that are out of gamut. In addition, Highlights, Midtones, and Shadows are included in the ranges. Likewise a selection of yellow and a subsequent selection of Highlights results in all yellow highlight colors.

The Color Range command provides for several previews to be displayed while making selections. Adjacent to the word Preview is a pop-up menu where you may choose how to view your selections. When a selection is made with the None preview, all the selected pixels will appear white. Figure 9.14 shows the preview set at None and the corresponding selection appearing in white in the dialog box.

The Grayscale item in the pop-up menu displays the document window in grayscale view. The grayscale view is particularly useful when viewing Highlights, Midtones, and Shadows (available in the Select pop-up menu). The Black Matte displays the document window against a black background for representing all deselected areas. The White Matte functions the same as Black Matte with the deselected areas appearing in white. The last item, Quick Mask, displays the deselected area in the Quick Mask mode. See the section "Quick Mask" later in this chapter for further discussion of the Quick Mask mode.

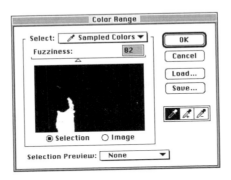

Fig. 9.14

All that appears white in the preview box will be selected.

Color Range also enables you to select colors within predefined selections. Figure 9.15 shows a selected area created with the Lasso tool. When you open the Select menu and choose Color Range, the area within the selection appears in the preview box (see fig. 9.16).

Fig. 9.15

Selection created with the Lasso tool.

The Color Range dialog box displays a portion of the image within the active selection. This feature can be useful in targeting regions of an image where an object needs to be selected. By eliminating many similar color values in other parts of the document, the selection may be easier to accomplish by narrowing the range to a defined area.

III

Creating and Touching Up

Fig. 9.16

Color Range
applied to the
selected region.

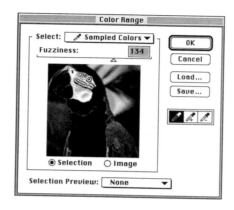

Selections and Channels

It's difficult to talk about selections without mentioning channels and some channel operations. This chapter introduces some channel operations with respect to saving and loading selections. For an in-depth look at channels and how they are used, refer to chapter 12, "Using Masks and Channels."

Saving Selections

If you assume creating a selection will be a complex task and may require some time to complete the perfect selection, you need a means of preserving the selection. If you click with a selection tool anywhere in an image, any current selection is lost. If you quit Photoshop and reopen at another time, any selection created is likewise lost. Therefore, you need to save the selection in order to regain it or work on it in subsequent Photoshop sessions. Photoshop provides a means for saving selections by using the Select menu. Once you save a selection, you can bring it back in its entirety by loading the selection from the Select menu.

When you save a selection, it is stored in an alpha channel. The *alpha channel* is a holding place for selections. You can move to the alpha channel, edit, and manipulate it, and change your selection. To save a selection, open the Select menu and choose Save Selection. The Save Selection dialog box appears (see fig. 9.17).

If a selection has not yet been saved, the dialog box only enables you to save the current selection in an alpha channel. If a selection has been saved, you can add to the channel, subtract from the channel, intersect with the channel, or create a new channel. If two documents of the same size and pixel depth are open, you can save a selection from one document to a channel in another document. Figure 9.18 shows a selection saved to a channel, with the channel displayed in the document window.

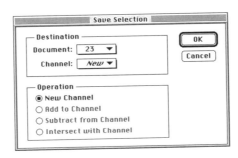

Fig. 9.17

When you save a selection, Photo-shop provides a dialog box to offer many choices on how the selection will be saved.

Fig. 9.18

An alpha channel created from a selection.

Once the channel has been created, you can save the Photoshop document with the channel information. In a subsequent Photoshop session, you can open the document and regain the selection from the channel.

Loading Selections

When a selection is saved, the selected area appears white and the deselected area appears black. When you open the Select menu and choose Load Selection, all the white in the channel becomes the selection. As you move through the channels in the document, you will notice the selection is active in all channels. You can use the Load Selection command regardless of the channel displayed in the document window. For example, if you move to the Red channel in an RGB image, you can load the selection. Likewise, you can load the selection in the composite channel, green, blue, or another alpha channel. If you loaded the selection while in the composite view, you can move to any of the other channels to display the selection.

You can load selections between documents as long as the document is the same size and pixel depth. For example, a 320-by-240 pixel RGB document of 72 dpi can load a selection from a grayscale document 320-by-240 and 72 dpi. If the dpi resolution is not exactly the same, the channel operations will not work between the documents. Likewise, if one document has a width of 320 pixels and another has a width of 321 pixels, you cannot use the channel operations. The mode, however, is incidental. RGB, CMYK, and grayscale images, as long as they meet the necessary criteria of size and pixels, will work together.

You can load a selection to another alpha channel. This is particularly helpful when creating a selection of one object, saving the selection, and then creating a selection of another object. To merge the selections into a single selection, one of the saved channels can be the currently active document area. When you open the Select menu and choose Load Selection, the selection from another channel can be added to the current channel. Figure 9.19 shows a document viewed in a fourth channel. The Load Selection command was used to load the selection in channel #5. The selection appears in channel #4 aside the first selection. To enable both shapes to be loaded into the composite channel, the area must be white. Make the selected area white by striking the Delete key. Be certain the color of the background is identified as white in the toolbox. When the selection is loaded, all of the area becomes the selection (see fig. 9.20).

Fig. 9.19

A selection loaded
into an alpha
channel.

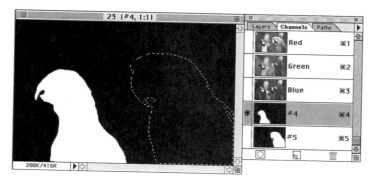

Fig. 9.20

A selection merged
in an alpha channel.

Gradient Selections

The opportunities for working with selections in alpha channels are almost endless. You can edit the channels with any of the tools in the toolbox; you can reshape, add to, or subtract from them with many of Photoshop's tools and menus. One of the most impressive uses of an alpha channel is to create a gradient selection.

A *linear gradient* has more of one color or gray value at one end of the gradient than at the opposite end. A selection that is *graduated* has a more intense area selected at one end of the gradient and a lesser amount of selection at the other end. You can create a gradient selection in an alpha channel with the Blend tool (see fig. 9.21).

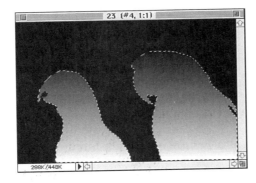

Fig. 9.21

Gradient created in
an alpha channel.

III

Creating and Touching Up

To understand gradient selections, let's look at a step-by-step procedure for creating them.

1. Create a selection in a document. In this example, select the two parrots in figure 9.22.

245

2. Select the alpha channel from the Channels palette. Selecting the channel is performed by clicking on the channel name in the palette. In this example, channel #4 is the alpha channel.

3. Open the Select menu and choose Load Selection. You want just the selected area to be filled with a gradient blend.

4. Select the default foreground black color and background white color in the toolbox.

5. Select the Gradient tool from the toolbox.

 6. Click at the top of the selection and drag to the bottom of the selection. The selected area will fill with a gradient.

7. Select the RGB channel in the Channels palette. While in the composite view, you can load a selection from any channel.

8. Open the Select menu and choose Load Selection. Choose channel #4 and click OK. Figure 9.22 illustrates a graduated selection loaded into the RGB composite image.

Fig. 9.22

A Gradient selection can be loaded into the RGB composite channel.

Photoshop cannot visually display a graduated selection so it finds a brightness value of 128 and displays the selection from that point to the brightness value of 0. In essence, the selection starts at a 1 percent white and continues to 100 percent white, even though the display may not appear selected. At this point, you can apply any of the filters or editing operations of Photoshop to the gradient. Striking the Delete key displays the image stronger at the top and ghosting to white at the bottom, as illustrated in figure 9.23.

Fig. 9.23

Strike the Delete key in a gradient selection to obtain this effect.

Editing Selections

Once a selection has been created, it can be moved, edited, touched up, and refined. Selections can be a nuisance to view on-screen with the *marching ants* look of the selection marquees. It is particularly disturbing when you need to refine the edges of a selection. Photoshop provides a means for holding the selection and hiding the marquee. To hide the selection marquee without disturbing the selection, open the Select menu and choose Hide Edges. The keyboard equivalent is ⌘-H and should be committed to memory. Once you work with selections, you will use this key command frequently.

Tip

When the Tools Don't Work

If you find the tools in the tool palette don't work properly, especially when painting or using the Rubber Stamp tool, press ⌘-H. Once a selection is hidden, it can easily be forgotten. If you use Photoshop's tools with an active selection, the tool functions are only applied to the selected area. If the cursor is outside the selection, no effect takes place on the image.

You can edit selections in several ways. Most often the edges of pasted or modified selections need to be tweaked to prevent the appearance of an artificial look. Photoshop provides a number of functions that you can use to edit selection marquees.

Anti-Alias

The Options palette for the selection tools has an anti-aliasing switch to toggle for choosing whether the selection will be anti-aliased. To *anti-alias* a selection is to smooth its edges. The actual operation of the anti-aliasing process is based on calculating the edge at twice its size, and then reducing the enlarged portion with interpolation to fill in pixels. This provides an illusion of a smooth edge. This is most obvious when you look at type anti-aliased against a white background. At actual size, it appears smoother. When you zoom in on the pixels you see an addition of gray pixels at the edges of black type. Figure 9.24 shows type characters enlarged. The window on the left is not anti-aliased. The window on the right is anti-aliased. Notice the gray pixels at the edges of the character. When both windows appear at actual size, the anti-aliased type appears much smoother.

Fig. 9.24

Type without anti-aliasing (left) and with anti-aliasing (right).

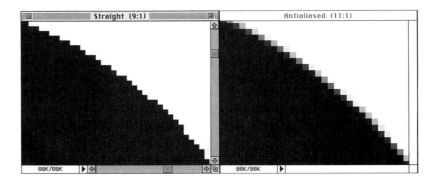

When the selection tools are used with anti-aliasing, the curved edges appear sharper through the same means of creating the anti-aliased effect. Poorly selected edges cannot always be compensated for with anti-aliasing.

Feather

Feathering edges is another means of smoothing which is handled much differently than anti-aliasing. Feathering adds a ghosting effect to the boundary of the selection based on the value set in the feather radius control. If a feather radius is set to 3, the edge of the selection moves 3 pixels in and 3 pixels out from the selection marquee, fading as it moves. You can control the amount of feathering in the dialog box that appears, as illustrated in figure 9.25. Too much feathering makes the object look like it has a halo.

Fig. 9.25

Feathering can
be set to ranges
between 1 and 250
in the dialog box.

You can apply feathering from the Options palette when using selection tools, or from the Select menu. The Select menu feather is not available until an active selection is made in the document window. The feathering on the edges of a selection is not immediately apparent when you apply it. Feathering appears only when a selection is cut, pasted, moved, or filled. Figure 9.26 illustrates a selection filled without feathering and one with feathering applied. The image on the right has a feather radius of 7 pixels. Whenever you use feathering, keep in mind that the feathering will be twice the value specified. The illustration shows the feathering inside the selection at 7 pixels and the feathering outside the selection marquee at 7 pixels.

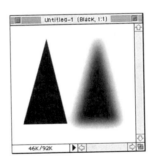

Fig. 9.26

Selections filled
without feathering
(left) and with
feathering (right).

Border

The Border command in the Select, Modify menu, like the Feather command, only works when there is an active selection in the document window. When the Border dialog box appears, as illustrated in figure 9.27, enter a value between 1 and 64.

When a border is created, the selection moves from center outward, in both directions, one half the value specified in the dialog box. A border of 8 pixels moves the selection rectangle out 4 pixels and in 4 pixels. The result looks like two selections have been created. Figure 9.28 illustrates a border created with 8 pixels around a triangle.

III

Creating and Touching Up

Fig. 9.27

Fig. 9.27

The Border dialog box accepts ranges between 1 and 64.

Fig. 9.28

A border with an 8 pixel width.

Border can be used to smooth edges of a selection by defining a small border and opening the Filter menu and choosing Blur, Gaussian Blur. Although a Gaussian Blur filter is not as effective as anti-aliasing or feathering, the resulting redistribution of pixels being blurred can be useful.

Expand

One of the new additions to Photoshop 3 is the Expand command. Open the Select menu and choose Modify, Expand. The Expand Selection dialog box lets you specify between 1 and 16 pixels. Figure 9.29 shows the Expand Selection dialog box in which you enter the desired range.

Fig. 9.29

The Expand Selection dialog box enables you to define the expansion of a selection from 1 to 16 pixels.

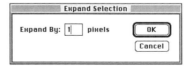

Expand is very useful for increasing the selection by one or two pixels to include pixels that you may not have selected with other tools. Expand moves the selection outward the number of pixels specified in the dialog box. If the Magic Wand tool or Color Range is used, the selection may leave a few pixels behind that should otherwise be part of the selection. When using either the Magic Wand tool or Color Range, Expand will no doubt be used more often than not.

Contract

Contract has the opposite effect of the Expand command. Instead of moving outward, Contract moves the selection inward, reducing it by the value specified in the dialog box. Figure 9.30 shows a dialog box similar to that you observed with Expand.

Fig. 9.30

The Contract Selection dialog box lets you specify a range to contract a selection, from 1 to 16 pixels.

To access Contract, open the Select menu and choose Modify, Contract. The range of values is the same as those mentioned with Expand. Contract can be defined with a range between 1 and 16 pixels. The use for Contract is also similar to that of Expand, which will be helpful when using tools like the Magic Wand tool or the Color Range command.

Tip

Editing Feathered Selections

If you create a feather and want only the inside or outside portion of the feather to remain, you can combine Feather with Expand and Contract. For example, create a feathered selection at 8 pixels and fill it. The Feather function moves the selected area to a range of 8 pixels in and 8 pixels out from the original selection. Next, Inverse the selection.

Choose the Expand command and enter a value of 5, and then press the Delete key. The remaining image appears with a feather appearing inward. Figure 9.31 illustrates the original feathering filled on the left and the Expand/Delete operation on the right.

III

Creating and Touching Up

Fig. 9.31

A feathered selection filled and an Expand/Delete applied.

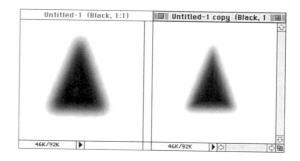

Grow

Sometimes moving a selection in or out from the existing selection is not enough to select some irregular adjacent shapes that you want to include with the selection. You can use Grow to include common values in the selection where the other commands do not work. To access the Grow command, open the Select menu and choose Grow. After you use the Grow command, use Expand or Contract to add or eliminate edge pixels. If the first attempt at using Grow includes too much image area, apply the Undo command. Keep in mind that Grow is directly linked to the Tolerance Setting in the Magic Wand Options palette. Change the tolerance and apply the Grow command again. Several attempts at undoing and changing tolerances may narrow or expand a range to include a more desirable selection.

Similar

Although Similar does not affect edge pixels alone, you can use it in some cases where there are no other similar values in the image than the object being edited or there are values in regions that can simply be deselected. For example, if you wish to select more area adjacent to your object, you can use the Similar command and deselect any other area outside the object that may have been included with using Similar. Open the Select menu and choose Similar to access the command. You can use Similar, like Grow, with successive Undos and tolerance changes in the Magic Wand Options palette. Sometimes, it may be helpful to use Grow and Similar on the same selection to create the desired result.

Mattes and Selections

Photoshop 3 has two new features that improve the appearance of selected edges. The Remove Black and White Matte commands in the Select, Matting menu are used with pasting selections or when saving selections in channels. When you copy and paste a selection, frequently there are some undesired pixels at the edges of the selection. An image that you copy and paste on a black background sometimes shows white pixels at the edges. To remove them, open the Select menu, choose Matting, and then choose Remove Black Matte. Choose Remove White Matte to remove black pixels from the edges of an image you paste on a white background. When pasting an image on a black background, Remove Black Matte eliminates a ghosting effect often created on black backgrounds. When pasting an image on a white background, Remove White Matte eliminates ghosting at the edges of images on white backgrounds. The use of black or white mattes does not depend on the background color. You can use Remove Black Matte, for example, with a white background as well as a black background. Matting effects are most obvious when you feather a selection and then choose one of the matting commands.

Quick Mask

The Quick Mask mode creates a selection mask. Using Quick Mask is not a selection procedure, but a masking procedure for selections. You can edit and reshape masks to create a new selection or an edited version. Apply the Quick Mask feature from the toolbox. The lower-left icon shows a selection oval which represents the Standard mode, the lower-right icon shows the Quick Mask mode. You can toggle back and forth between the modes.

Quick Mask takes effect only when there is an active selection in the document window. When a selection is present and you choose the Quick Mask mode from the toolbox, the deselected portion of the image gains a red, translucent overlay. The overlay represents a mask and displays a protected area of the image. To open a dialog box that enables you to control the appearance of the mask and the selection, double-click the Quick Mask icon in the toolbox (see fig. 9.32).

The radio buttons provide choices for displaying the selected areas as masked or unmasked. They also provide choices for displaying the deselected portions of the image as either masked or unmasked.

By default, the overlay covers the protected area of the image. If you want the selection to appear with the overlay, choose the radio button for Selected Areas. This option displays the selection with a red overlay.

Fig. 9.32

The Quick Mask Options dialog box provides you with several choices on how masks can be viewed.

The default color for masks is red, but it can be changed by clicking on the color swatch in the Quick Mask dialog box. When you click on the swatch in the Quick Mask dialog box, the Color Picker appears. From this point, choose any color to represent the mask. If the color red is not easily distinguishable from the selected region, you change the color by accessing the Color Picker. You can define the opacity of the color or keep the default opacity, 50 percent. If you want an opaque mask, change the opacity to 100 percent.

When a mask is visible in the document window, you can add more mask area or eliminate portions of the mask. When the mask changes, the selection changes when you return to the standard mode. One wonderful feature of the Quick Mask mode is that you can use any of the painting tools to edit the mask and, ultimately, the selection. This feature provides much greater control than the Lasso tool. With a selection active and the view in Quick Mask mode, you can use the Paintbrush with any of the brush tips to apply more mask overlay to the image. When the foreground color is black and you apply the painting tools to the selected region, the selection becomes smaller and more protected area is added. Figure 9.33 shows additional masking that was applied to the selected area by using the Paintbrush tool. To add to a selection which will eliminate portions of the mask, change the foreground color to white. When you use the painting tools with a white foreground, a portion of the mask overlay is eliminated during painting; this results in an expanded selection.

In the Quick Mask mode, you can easily toggle between a display of selected areas and a display of masked areas. To see the overlay on the masked areas, hold down the Option key and click the Quick Mask icon in the toolbox. Hold down the Option key and click again on the Quick

Mask icon in the toolbox to observe the overlay as a selection. Repeat the sequence and you return to the other view. When you're editing the mask, toggling back and forth can help you see the selection's location.

Fig. 9.33

Editing the selection in Quick Mask mode.

Defringe

When you create, edit, move, or paste selections, a halo effect often results. Removing the black or white matte, or expanding or contracting selections may not be enough to eliminate the halo. Defringe replaces the edge pixels with colors similar to the adjacent pixels immediately surrounding the selection. Open the Select menu and choose Matting, Defringe. A dialog box appears that enables you to set the range between 1 and 64 (see fig. 9.34).

Fig. 9.34

Set the range between 1 and 64 in the Defringe dialog box.

Like other matting functions, Defringe is not accessible when a selection is created. If you move or paste a selection, the matting functions are accessible. You can create a floating selection if you need to apply a defringe to an image area without moving or pasting. To do this, open the Select menu and choose Float. Matting commands are accessible with floating selections. Defringe works well with selections created with anti-aliasing, but it is best not to use this command on feathered selections. To feather an image and then to defringe it is contradictory and defeats the purpose of feathering. Defringe also works well when you use Expand and Contract. When you contract and float a selection, Defringe will smooth the appearance for a more desirable effect.

Moving and Duplicating Selections

After you create selections, you can move them, duplicate them, copy them, paste them, add them to documents, or delete them from documents. Understanding some of the aspects of replication and movement of selections and what to do with a selection once it has been created is part of the selection process. Features discussed thus far have been reserved to creating and improving selections. The next few sections cover how you can actually use selections.

Floating Selections

When a selection is created, it is fixed over the background area. You can change or alter all pixels within the selection marquee and permanently change the image when you perform more than one operation. You can duplicate a selection and create a floating selection in a variety of ways. A *floating selection* is an identical set of pixels hovering over the original selection. You can manipulate, change, and delete floating selections and leave the original image area undisturbed. To create a floating selection, execute one of the following commands:

▶ *Float.* Open the Select menu and choose Float to apply this command to any selection which will create a floating selection. The Command key equivalent is ⌘-J which toggles between float and defloat, depending on whether the selection is floating at the time you execute the command.

▶ *Paste.* When you paste an image by opening the Edit menu and choosing Paste, it automatically becomes a floating selection. The selection marquee is present and the image inside the marquee floats over the region where you pasted the selection.

▶ *Clone.* Depress the Option key and move the selection. The new selected object is a duplicate of the original selected object. Cloning has an advantage over copying and pasting because it doesn't require memory to hold the copy. Cloning can also be accomplished by depressing the Option key and using the direction arrows on the keyboard. This method is helpful when precise movements are needed.

▶ *Move.* When you move an image by clicking and dragging the selection, the selection floats (see fig. 9.34). Note that the original selection does not float and only becomes a floating selection after it is moved. If just the selection marquee is moved, the new selected area does not float. See the section "Moving Selections," later in this chapter.

You can apply matting functions only to floating selections. Using the matting commands does not affect the floating of the selection. In other words, if you apply the matting commands to a floating selection, the selection continues to float.

Whenever a selection is floating, it can be defloated by opening the Select menu and choosing Defloat. Additionally, you can defloat selections by executing any of the following commands:

▶ *Defloat.* Open the Select menu and choose Defloat. Once a floating selection appears in the document, the Select menu option for Float changes to Defloat (⌘-J).

▶ *Tools.* Using the selection tools from the toolbox creates a selection that is defloated.

▶ *Loading Selections.* Open the Select menu and choose Load Selection. When a selection is loaded from a channel or layer, the selection is defloated.

▶ *Modifying.* Open the Select menu and choose Modify. Then choose any of the modify commands. When you open the Select menu and use the Modify submenu commands, they all defloat a floating selection. Border, Expand, Contract, and Smooth all create defloated selections.

▶ *Adding.* Adding to a selection with the selection tools from the toolbox defloats an image. Eliminating parts of a selection with selection tools from the toolbox preserves the floating selection.

▶ *Stroking.* Open the Edit menu and choose Stroke. Adding a stroke from the Edit menu defloats a selection.

III

Creating and Touching Up

257

▶ *Paths.* Open the Window menu and choose Show Paths. Select the Paths pop-up menu from the Paths palette and choose Make Path. Converting to paths defloats a selection and defloats a selection from a path. Returning to the selection from a path causes the selection to be defloated.

▶ *Quick Mask.* Select the Quick Mask tool in the toolbox. Moving to the Quick Mask mode defloats a floating selection. When returning from the Quick Mask mode to the Selection mode, the selection is also defloated.

You can use floating selections in hundreds of ways to create special effects and improve images. Some of the effects are discussed in chapter 10, "Working with Layers."

Moving Selections

When you create and move a selection, the selected image's pixels are moved with the selection, but the background color is left behind. By default, the background color is white. There is an apparent hole in the image when a selection is moved. Figure 9.35 illustrates a selection moved away from the area originally positioned in the document. A floating selection, on the other hand, is like a duplicate copy hovering over the selected area. When you move a floating selection, it leaves the background intact and undisturbed. Figure 9.36 illustrates a floating selection moved in the same way as figure 9.35.

Fig. 9.35

When you move a non-floating selection, the background color is revealed.

Fig. 9.36

When you move a floating selection, the background remains intact.

You can move the selection marquee in an image without bringing the contents of the selection with it. To move a selection marquee in this manner, hold the Option and Command keys down while moving the selection with one of the selection tools or the Move tool. Figure 9.37 shows a selection moved without the contents of the selection moved.

Fig. 9.37

A selection marquee is moved without disturbing the image area.

Use the Info palette to make precise movements of a selection. To access the Info palette, open the Window menu and choose Show Palettes, Show Info. When you place the cursor in the document window, the x, y coordinates are displayed in the palette. The width and height of a selection are denoted by the W and H at the bottom of the palette (see fig. 9.38).

For precise movements measured numerically, the Info palette creates additional display information when you move a selection. During a move with a selection tool or the Move tool, the Info palette displays the angle of movement represented by A and the distance of movement represented by D (see fig. 9.39). The X and Y in the palette denote horizontal and vertical distances moved. Using the Info palette, you can move either the selection marquee or the selection to precise locations in the document. As you move the selection, new values are registered in the Info palette.

Fig. 9.38

The Info palette displays the x, y coordinates and the width, height of the selection.

Fig. 9.39

The Info palette displays when a selection is moved.

Cloning Selections

To create a clone in an image, depress the Option key while dragging a selection. The moment you move the selection with the Option key depressed, the selection becomes a floating selection. Cloning is preferred over copying and pasting because it doesn't use the clipboard and, therefore, does not occupy memory as does a copy operation. This is particularly helpful with slower computers and with computers with limited RAM, especially when you work with large images.

Cloning is helpful when you make repeated duplications, or when you apply large image selections to other parts of a document. In figure 9.40, if you want to eliminate the window shade on the left side of image and replace it with brick to match the siding, you could use a clone operation.

Fig. 9.40

Photo image
before clone.

If you marquee select an area of brick and depress the Option key, you can move the newly created floating selection over the area to be replaced. By holding down the Shift key, you can constrain the movement to a precise horizontal direction. The result of cloning and moving the selection appears in figure 9.41.

Fig. 9.41

Photo image
after clone.

Caution

Know the Sequence of Steps

When using the keyboard keys and the selection tools, it is important to know the sequence of the steps applied. If, for example, you click the mouse button before you depress the Option key, the clone does not work properly. The selection moves, but it isn't cloned.

III

Creating and Touching Up

The sequence for the above example is:

1. Depress the Option key.

2. Depress the Shift key.

3. Click and drag the mouse while keeping both keys down.

The sequence of numbers 2 and 3 can be reversed. If a little movement occurs before you hold down the Shift key, Photoshop snaps the selection to be moved into position after you press the Shift key. Step number 1, however, must be the first step in the sequence.

Copying and Pasting

Familiar to all Macintosh users, Copy and Paste are often the first menu commands used when duplicating shapes and objects. Because Photoshop has so many other features that perform the same action, this method should be the last used. The Copy command requires the use of memory and slows Photoshop performance. If you use drum scans of 40, 50, or more megabytes, you need to avoid slowing down the computer in every way possible.

You can use Copy to transfer the file to the system clipboard. If, for example, you want to copy and paste into the Scrapbook or other application, the Copy command is one choice available to you. When you copy in Photoshop, the program stores the information in a program buffer. Application clipboards are not the same as a system clipboard. The Macintosh system clipboard maintains files in a PICT format. Programs like Adobe Illustrator have application clipboards for copying and pasting EPS formats between documents. When you copy a selection in Photoshop, it uses the application clipboard to store the information. When you quit Photoshop, the information is transferred to the system clipboard and is converted to PICT. Sometimes, you will notice a pause in Photoshop when you quit because it is converting the clipboard to a PICT file.

When you copy information in Photoshop and create a new file, the new file size matches the size of the clipboard file. This can be helpful in creating new documents that require the same exact size. When you copy in other applications and open Photoshop, you can paste the clipboard information into Photoshop.

If you want to copy in Adobe Illustrator and paste in Photoshop, you can choose between two paste operations. You can rasterize and anti-alias the information or you can paste in and preserve paths. When you choose to paste the information in a new document, Photoshop presents the Paste dialog box, which enables you to select the paste method (see fig. 9.42).

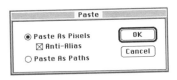

Fig. 9.42

Pasting Adobe Illustrator art provides opportunities to describe how the pasted objects will appear.

If you choose the Paste As Pixels option, Photoshop rasterizes the image at the resolution of the document where the paste occurs. If you choose the Paste As Pixels option, any type or path created in Illustrator is rasterized. Figure 9.43 illustrates a Paste As Pixels function enabled.

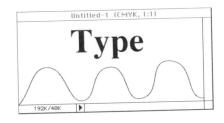

Fig. 9.43

Pasting Adobe Illustrator paths as pixels.

If you enable the Paste As Paths option in the Paste dialog box, the type does not appear. Photoshop cannot render PostScript type that has not been converted to outlines or paths when the Paste as Paths option is enabled. The Illustrator paths, however, are pasted into the new document as paths. You can edit them by using the path operations. The paths pasted into a new document, illustrated in figure 9.44, is the same file pasted in figure 9.43.

When type is converted to outlines in Adobe Illustrator, Paste As Paths pastes the type with the paths available. Notice that figure 9.45 contains the same text, but it is converted to outlines. When you convert type to outlines in Adobe Illustrator, the type appears pasted in Photoshop the same as Illustrator paths pasted in Photoshop.

III

Creating and Touching Up

Fig. 9.44

Only the Illustrator
paths appear
pasted on the new
document.

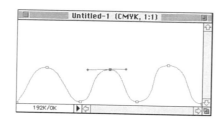

Fig. 9.45

The type, converted
to outlines, appears
with paths
available.

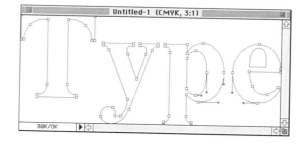

Dragging and Dropping Selections

An alternative to the copy and paste functions is the Drag and Drop
method new to Photoshop 3. To perform Drag and Drop, select any of the
selection tools, or the Move tool, and drag a selection from one document
window to another. When the item is being dragged to a second document
window, the cursor appears as a grabber hand. Unlike channels, Drag and
Drop works between documents of different resolutions and image sizes.
It also works between different modes. For example, an RGB image can be
dropped into a grayscale image. Figure 9.46 illustrates a selection dragged
from the larger document window to the smaller one.

Fig. 9.46

The bird figure is
dragged from the
original document
window to a new
document window.

With documents of the same size, Drag and Drop positions a selection at the same coordinates in the destination document as the selection was originally positioned in document of origin. This is handy for precise positioning of elements that would otherwise be copied and pasted. Drag and Drop, when used with the Move tool, is not restricted to dragging a selection. The Move tool takes the entire image in a document and grabs it, without the need for a selection marquee.

> **Tip**
>
> **Drag and Drop for Mode and Image Changes**
>
> At first, the user may be tempted to use Drag and Drop to change modes, image sizes, or resolutions. In most cases, using Drag and Drop is slower than using the Mode or Image Size menus. Use the Mode menu to change a document mode and use the Image Size dialog box to change sizes and resolutions.

Drag and Drop doesn't work with moving a selection within another selection. For this operation, open the Edit menu and choose Paste Into. Paste Into pastes the contents of the clipboard into a selection. Another paste function is Paste Layer, also available in the Edit menu. Paste Layer is discussed in chapter 10 "Working with Layers."

Where To Go from Here

▶ Chapter 8, "Drawing, Painting, and Editing," describes how you can use painting tools with selections.

▶ Chapter 10, "Working with Layers," deals with layer selections as well as layer operations. You can combine many layer operations with operations described in this chapter to perfect the selection methods.

▶ Chapter 12, "Using Masks and Channels," describes creating selections with alpha channels. Saving and loading selections are other features used with alpha channels, which are detailed in chapter 12.

▶ Chapter 13, "Understanding Color," is essential for specifying and painting colors in selections. You should understand the fundamentals of color before you begin a project.

▶ Check out chapter 15, "Using Photoshop's Plug-In Filters," for some fun and serious work with filters and selections.

III

Creating and Touching Up

265

Working with Layers

The single most exciting new feature of Adobe Photoshop 3 is the introduction of *layers*. Layers provides a whole new dimension in working with Photoshop images and adds much more flexibility to an already feature-rich application. Photoshop users who worked with advanced features of earlier versions of Photoshop may need to rethink their approach to working with selections and channels as a means of accomplishing specific tasks. With the inclusion of layers, new approaches to preparing Photoshop images are necessary. If you are startled by the reorganization of some of Photoshop's other features, hold your judgment until you can explore and understand layers and how to work with them.

Using Photoshop for Macintosh • Using Photoshop for Macintosh • Using Photoshop for Macin

by Ted Padova

CHAPTER 10

This chapter deals with understanding and using layers and focuses on some new approaches to editing images in Photoshop.

Understanding Layers

When an image is opened in Photoshop 3, the document opens with a *background*. A background, in Photoshop terms, is like a canvas under a painting. The canvas can be white, hold color, or display a full painted image. All Photoshop files of previous versions open with the image on the background. When you create a new document in Photoshop 3, you have a choice as to how the layer information will appear, as illustrated in figure 10.1. The New dialog box gives you three choices for how to represent the layers contents.

Fig. 10.1

The New dialog box provides options for de-scribing layer contents.

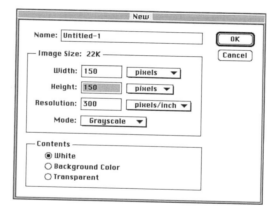

Layer descriptions are represented in the Contents section. If you select White, the document contains a white background. If Background Color is selected, the document contains a background that is the same as the background color identified in the Photoshop toolbox. If you select Transparent, the document opens with a layer and not a background. Backgrounds are different than layers.

A background, similar to a canvas, cannot be repositioned. It is always in the background. Layers, on the other hand, can be reorganized, moved, added, and deleted from a document. Shapes and color values can be moved from the background to other layers, but the background itself is fixed and must remain as the first layer in the document. If you create a document with the Transparent option in the New dialog box, the layer can be moved after adding new layers.

The background and all subsequent layers can accept all of Photoshop's editing tools and features. You can paint, draw, edit, paste, create selections, and redistribute artwork on each layer. Layers can be grouped, merged, and flattened. New layers can be added and deleted. When a Photoshop file is exported in any format other than the native Photoshop format, the layers are flattened and all layers merge into a background.

When a layer is added to a document, the layer is transparent. It's like placing a sheet of acetate over a drawing; it remains clear until you paint, draw, paste, or add pixels to the layer. By default, edited areas of a layer appear opaque while the unedited portions remain transparent. Information on the layers share the same file attributes as all other layers. They have the same number of pixels, the same resolution, the same channels, and the same image mode such as grayscale, RGB, CMYK, and so on.

Memory requirements increase with the addition of layers. However, unlike channels that increase image size proportionately with the addition of each channel, layer additions add file memory according to the amount of information positioned on the layer.

Displaying Layers

When a layer is added to a document, it appears in the Layers palette with a thumbnail displaying all information on the layer. You can adjust the thumbnail sizes by selecting Palette Options, from the Layers pop-up menu, which is available by pressing the arrow in the upper-right corner of the Layers palette. The Layers Palette Options dialog box appears, displaying three choices for the thumbnail size (see fig. 10.2). In addition to the thumbnail size, the None option displays the layer name without a thumbnail view.

Several layers in the Layers palette appear with a scroll bar to scroll layers in view. As a layer is edited in the document window, the thumbnail is dynamically updated.

III

Creating and Touching Up

Fig. 10.2

Choose from these
palette options in
the Layers Palette
Options dialog box.

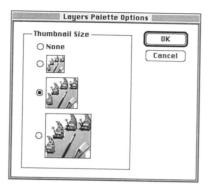

Tip

Hide Thumbnails To Speed Performance

When thumbnails are displayed in the Layers palette, they dynamically update the layer information. The updating of the thumbnail
view is like a screen refresh and slows the performance of Photoshop,
especially when you're working with large files and limited memory.
To accelerate Photoshop's performance, select None from the Layers
Palette Options dialog box to view the layers without the thumbnail
views. By naming layers with descriptive names for the layer contents, the thumbnail isn't always necessary.

Sometimes, it helps to temporarily hide a layer while working on a
document. The view icon, represented by an eye in the Layers palette, can
hide a layer or background from view in the document window (see fig.
10.3). When a layer is hidden, the document window does not show any
of the layer pixels, but the thumbnail still displays all information on that
layer. To display the layer again in the document window, click in the
same column where the view icon appears.

Fig. 10.3

The background is
hidden in the
document window.

Adding a New Layer

There are several ways to add layers to documents. The pop-up menu from the palette includes a New Layer option to add a layer. The icon that appears at the bottom of the palette creates a new layer and prompts the user to enter a name for the layer in a dialog box. This is the preferred method for adding new layers because creating and naming the layer can be accomplished in one action.

When you choose New Layer from the pop-up menu, the layers are added as layer 1, layer 2, and so on. Photoshop continues this numbering sequence with the addition of each new layer. After the layer appears in the Layers palette, you can name it by double-clicking on the layer name in the Layers palette. The Layer Options dialog box appears. If you want to rapidly create layers but don't want to name them, you can bypass the dialog box by Option-clicking the new layer icon. This creates a new layer and names it in the sequence mentioned above.

A layer is also added through drag and drop actions. Any selection or layer from a second document can be dragged with the Move tool to the active document window. When you drop the image, it is placed on a new layer. Unlike channels, where the documents have to be the same pixel depth and physical size, drag and drop with layers requires no attribute similarities. A 72ppi image at CMYK color, for example, can be dragged and dropped to a 300ppi grayscale image and vice versa. The source information accepts the mode and resolution of the destination document. If the resolution of the source document is less than the destination document, the image is interpolated when dropped.

When you open a document from earlier versions of Photoshop or a scanned image, the information appears on the background. The background is fixed at the first position in the Layers palette and cannot be moved. If you want to have the background treated as any other layer, you

III

Creating and Touching Up

can convert it from the background element to a layer. Double-click the background in the Layers palette to bring up the Make Layer dialog box, which is unique to the background (see fig. 10.4). The default name appears as Layer 0. When you click the OK button, the background is converted to a layer.

Fig. 10.4

You can convert a background to a layer in the Make Layer dialog box.

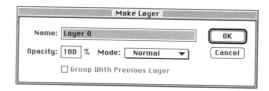

At this point, you can add a user-definable name and convert the background to a layer by clicking the OK button. The background, as a layer, can be repositioned and treated like any other layer.

Duplicating Layers

Drag and drop can also be used in the same document for duplicating a layer. To duplicate a layer, drag the layer from the Layers palette to the new layer icon. When the layer is duplicated, it appears with the word copy added to the layer name. For example, if you duplicate a layer named Text, the name Text copy appears. To duplicate a layer and have the dialog box appear, you can use the Duplicate layer feature in the palette pop-up menu.

Interesting special effects can be added by duplicating layers; it blends the modes and filters. You easily can create drop shadows by duplicating a type layer.

Tip

Converting Channels to Layers

One way to convert a channel to a layer is to copy and paste the channel into the layers. Another way is to split the channels of one document, and then drag and drop the channel to the other document. When you view layers, the source channel becomes a layer in the destination document. To conserve memory and speed up Photoshop's operations when drag and drop is performed, the clipboard is not used.

Deleting Layers

You can delete layers by accessing the Options Palette in the Layers pop-up menu and choosing the Delete Layer option. When a selection is active in the document window, Delete Layer changes to Delete Selection. A floating selection needs to be defloated before it can be deleted.

Another means of deleting layers is through drag and drop. Grab the layer from the Layers palette and drag it to the Trash icon (in the lower-right corner of the palette window). When you drag and drop a layer to the Trash icon, Photoshop automatically defloats the image when you grab the layer and move it.

When a layer is deleted, it is possible to undo the operation and regain the layer; however, you are limited to one level of Undo. Which means that if you perform another action after deleting the layer, it is lost and must be re-created. Also, if you move the layer and elect not to trash it, the selection is lost.

Merging Layers

As you work with an image composition, you can add new layers and create temporary work areas to use for merging, manipulating, and editing image elements. As new layers are added, the file size requirements grow according to the information contained on the layers. When two or more layers are completed with their composition, you can merge them into a single layer. When the layers are reduced in an image, the file requirements likewise are reduced. To merge any number of layers, make sure you have all of the layers visible. All layers that you do not want to merge should be hidden; hide them by selecting the view icon in the Layers palette. With the visible layers, select Merge Layers from the Layers pop-up menu in the Layers palette (see fig. 10.5).

Flattening Layers

When a Photoshop document contains layers, it can only be saved as a Photoshop 3 document. Opening the document in Photoshop 2.5.1 displays the image as a composite with no layers. The composite image is created by *flattening* the layers. Only the Photoshop 3 file format can contain layers; all other formats automatically prompt the user to flatten layers when you choose Save from the File menu. Among other things, this

III

Creating and Touching Up

273

is Photoshop's safeguard against problems associated with file exports. Imagine if you were to submit a file to a service bureau as a TIFF for digital imaging and the layers were active. Whatever layer was last active would be imaged, disregarding the rest of the image.

Fig. 10.5

Merging layers by choosing the option from the Layers pop-up menu.

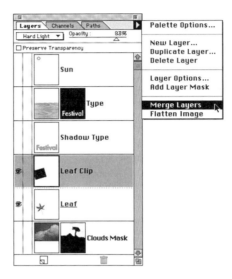

If you want to print a proof and intend to continue editing your document, use the Save a Copy command under the File menu. When you use the Save a Copy command, the dialog box in figure 10.6 appears.

Fig. 10.6

You can save a copy of your document in this dialog box.

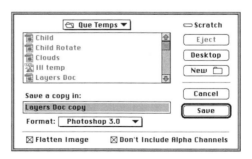

The Save a Copy dialog box has a check box for flattening an image. If the file format is other than Photoshop 3, the flattened image automatically is enabled. When you use the Save a Copy command, the image is saved as a copy and returns you to the original document with the layers present. Save a Copy is handy when you want to continue editing a file with the layers.

You also can flatten an image in the Layers palette pop-up menu. When you choose flatten layers, you lose all of the layers in a document and it's rendered as a composite image. This command should only be used when you don't want to do any further editing to the document.

Caution

Submitting Native Photoshop files

When you submit native Photoshop files to digital imaging centers, make sure you flatten the image. If a native Photoshop 3 file is printed from Photoshop, only the visible layers are imaged. By flattening the image, you ensure appropriate proofing after viewing the flattened image and reduce any chances for error.

Repositioning Layers

As new layers are created, they are positioned on top of the last layer in the document. At times, you may need to rearrange the order of the layers. For example, if you create text on a new layer, and then duplicate the layer and create a shadow, the shadow appears on top of the text. The order of these two layers needs to be changed.

To reposition a layer, click and drag the layer to be moved up or down in the Layers palette. As you move a layer on top of another layer in the Layers palette, a solid line appears above the layer. When this line is visible, release the mouse button to accept the new order of the layers.

The background cannot be moved to another layer position in the palette. In order to move the background, it must be converted to a layer. Convert the background by double-clicking in the Layers palette. When you click OK to accept, the background is converted to a layer and can be moved to another layer position.

III

Creating and Touching Up

Changing Opacity

Although it is much more appropriate to hide layers by selecting the view icon in the Layers palette, layers also can be hidden by setting the opacity slider to zero. You can adjust the opacity of any layer in the document. The background can be adjusted to a one percent opacity by double-clicking the layer in the Layers palette. Figure 10.7 shows the resulting Layer Options dialog box. Adjusting the opacity of the background is a nice way to ghost the image when you want foreground shapes and text to appear on a background or texture. This method works much better than adjusting output levels or filling with white at different opacities.

Fig. 10.7

You can adjust the layer opacity in the Layer Options dialog box.

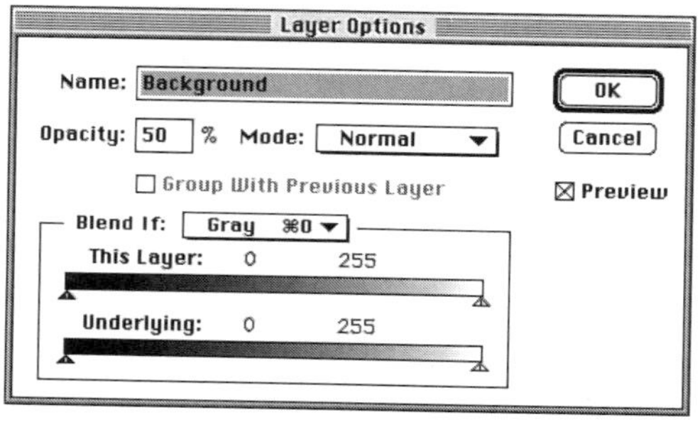

By default, all new layers are added at 100 percent opacity. A layer added to a document appears on top of the other layers and, with no information on the new layer, is transparent. If a layer is copied, pasted, or duplicated, the information on the layer is opaque for all layers below it. Any layer in the document can have the opacity changed for the entire layer area by adjusting the opacity slider in the Layers palette. The opacity adjustment applies to the entire layer. You can create selections on the layer and apply change in the opacity only to the selected regions.

Tip

Keyboard Opacity Adjustments

Use the number keys on the keyboard to set the opacity slider to fixed 10 percent increments. Press 1 to set the opacity at 10 percent, 2 for 20 percent, 3 for 30 percent, and so on. Zero (0) sets the opacity to 100 percent. When you duplicate a layer by the drag and drop method, set the opacity first, and then drag and drop the layer to create a duplicate at the specified opacity.

You also can adjust opacity in the Layer Options dialog box; access this by double-clicking the layer. Add a new layer or select one from the pop-up menu in the Layers palette.

Layer Masks

Layer masks are similar to a combination of the Quick Mask mode and the Alpha channels. Layer masks can be used for trying out many different effects before you actually apply the effect to the layer and ultimately to the image. To imagine how you might use a layer mask, think of words that have a texture or pattern fill. You want the texture to be applied to the text only and the text to appear on top of another layer in the document. To create such an effect, you can use a layer mask. At first, creating a layer mask might seem complicated, but after you understand how to create the masks, you'll use them frequently. In the following sections, you'll examine some of the principles in creating layer masks.

Adding a Mask to a Layer

Layer masks are added to individual layers. To add a layer mask, you must select the layer to make it active. Only layers can have a mask. The background cannot have a layer mask unless it's converted to a layer. With the layer active, choose the pop-up menu from the Layers palette. Choose Add Layer Mask from the pop-up menu choices. When the mask is added, as illustrated in figure 10.8, a thumbnail appears in the Layers palette adjacent to the layer thumbnail.

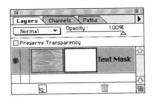

Fig. 10.8

Try out different effects by adding a mask to a layer.

You can make each of the thumbnails active by clicking the respective icon. When the layer mask is created, a black border surrounds the thumbnail. Click the layer thumbnail to display it with a black border. It is important to note whether the layer or the mask is selected while working in this mode.

Understanding Layer Mask Attributes

To use the layer mask, you need a basic understanding of the mask attributes. When a layer mask is created, the mask is an eight-bit file representing only gray levels. It functions similar to a channel; the mask is represented by white and the area isolating the mask is represented by black. When a layer mask is created, the mask appears white. This means that the mask and the layer are at a 1:1 ratio and the layer can be viewed completely through the mask. To hide a portion of the layer, the mask must be opaque. All areas changed to black hide the underlying layer. The only way to change the white value in the mask to black or gray is to invert, use the fill command, or the painting tools. Even if the background color is originally black when the mask is created, the mask can still be filled white. If the mask contains a gray level, the layer is masked at a different level of opacity.

Without complicating things too much, just look at a simple mask. For example, if you want the layer information to appear inside some type created in the mask, the type should be rendered white and the surrounding area should be rendered black. To create such an effect, follow these steps:

1. Open a document with a pattern or texture.

2. Convert the background to a layer by double-clicking it in the Layers palette.

3. Choose Add Layer Mask from the Layers pop-up menu. The layer mask is active when it is created.

4. Choose Map, Invert from the Image menu (⌘-I). Invert turns the background from white to black.

5. Deselect the mask. Choose white for the foreground color in the toolbox by reversing the foreground/background.

6. With the mask still active, choose the Type tool from the toolbox and click in the document window. Notice that the document window, while displaying the mask, appears white. This indicates that there is no masked object in view.

7. Type some text in the text box. The type is filled with the foreground color, which is currently white. When the image is displayed in the document window, the texture appears inside the text added to the mask (see fig. 10.9).

Fig. 10.9

When a mask is
added to the layer,
only the masked
area appears in
the layer.

Figure 10.10 shows the various layer mask options accessible by double-clicking the layer mask in the Layers palette.

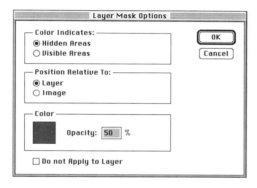

Fig. 10.10

The Layer Mask
Options dialog
box.

The first area of the dialog box, Color Indicates, shows the Hidden Areas selected by default. Figure 10.11 shows the mask and the layer information contained in the mask.

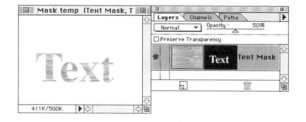

Fig. 10.11

A layer mask with
hidden areas
displayed.

III

Creating and Touching Up

If the Visible Areas option is selected, the display reveals what colors change if the mask is applied as above. This option can be used as a display only to view the changes or it can be used when you apply the layer mask. If the Visible Areas option is accepted when the mask is applied, it appears reversed out (see fig. 10.12).

Fig. 10.12

A layer mask with
visible areas
displayed.

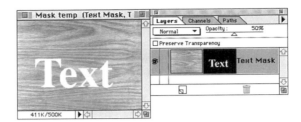

The second set of options, in the Position Relative To section, defaults at a position relative to the layer. When this option is selected, the layer and the layer mask move together when repositioned with the move tool. The Image option moves the layer information while the mask remains stationary. When you are moving in either mode, it is necessary to make the layer active and not the mask in the Layers palette.

The opacity setting and color relate only to the display of the mask and not the editing of the image. Opacity settings range between one and 100 percent, and color can be changed by clicking the color swatch to make color selections from the picker. Visibility of the opacity settings and color are only apparent when viewing in Quick Mask mode or when viewing channels. Each layer or channel can have a different opacity or color setting to represent the selected or unselected region of the respective layer or channel.

If you select the Do not Apply to Layer check box, a mask is created without applying the mask to the layer. This is handy for creating and editing selections. The mask application can be toggled by holding the Command key (⌘) down and clicking the mask. When the mask is not applied to the layer, a red X is placed on the mask. If you want to create a selection, you can work on the mask, Command (⌘)-click the mask, and go to the Select menu to load the selection. Figure 10.13 shows a graduated selection created in the mask and loaded in the layer.

Fig. 10.13

Selection loaded
from the mask.

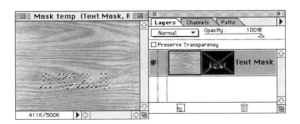

When a layer mask is created, it appears not only in the layer window, but also in the Channels palette. By viewing the Channels palette, you can see the layer mask temporarily created as a channel. If the mask is applied to the layer, the channel is lost. Deleting the channel prompts the user to apply or discard the layer mask. From the Channels palette, you can use channel operations and apply them to the document or other documents adhering to the requirements of using channels. Figure 10.14 shows the Channels palette illustrated after the layer mask is created. For specific functions and uses with channels, see chapter 12, "Using Masks and Channels."

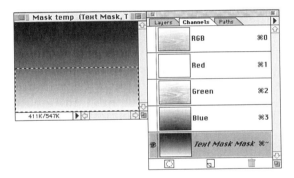

Fig. 10.14

The Channels palette with the layer mask displayed in alpha channel.

Clipping Groups

Clipping groups are a form of masking; they add more power and flexibility to using layer operations. A clipping group clips the layers above the layer performing the clipping operation. One or more layers can be clipped to a given layer. In addition, multiple clipping groups can be created in a document.

When you create clipping groups, it is important to remember that all layers to be clipped must reside above the clipping layer. In the Layers palette, the default view of each layer is displayed by a solid line separating the layers. The solid line is an indicator that no clipping was applied to the layer. You clip layers by pressing the Option key and clicking the solid line separating the layers. Figure 10.15 shows the icon presented when the Option key is pressed.

When you place the cursor on the line and click the mouse button, the line changes from solid to dotted—indicating that clipping was applied to the layer. In order to create a clipping group where the layers are to be clipped to the background, the background must be converted to a layer. A comparison of an image with and without clipping is shown in figures 10.16 and 10.17. Figure 10.16 illustrates a document without clipping applied and 10.17 illustrates the same document with the clipping applied. Each layer was added to the clipping group individually by pressing the Option key and clicking each of the dotted lines displayed in the Layers palette.

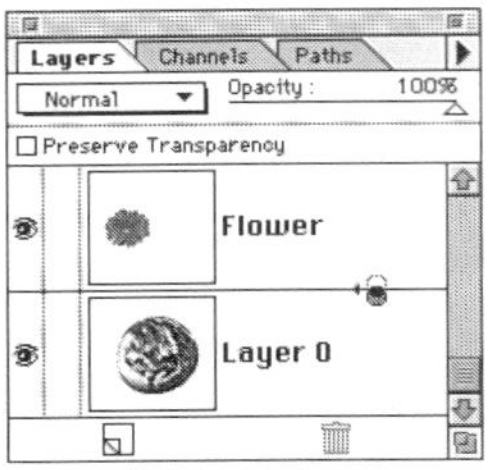

Fig. 10.15

When you press the Option key with the cursor positioned between two layers, the cursor appears with an icon that indicates a clipping will occur.

Fig. 10.16

Document and Layers palette without clipping.

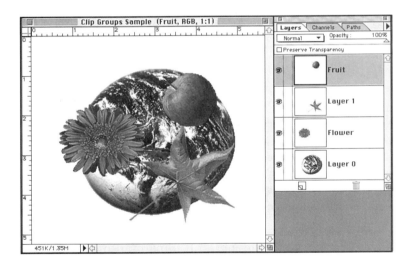

You can have as many clipping groups as you have disk space to work on an image. New clipping groups can be created and subsequent layers can be clipped in separate groups. The clipping group feature works with images that need several items contained in a mask. By keeping the items in individual layers, you have more flexibility in editing the image.

In addition to using the Option key, double-click a layer in the Layers palette to access the Layer Options dialog box (see fig. 10.18). Select the check box called Group With Previous Layer; this performs the same function as Option-clicking in the Layers palette. Each time the box is selected, the layer is included in the clipping group. Disabling clipping groups also can be performed by the Option-click method or by disabling the check box in the Layer Options dialog box.

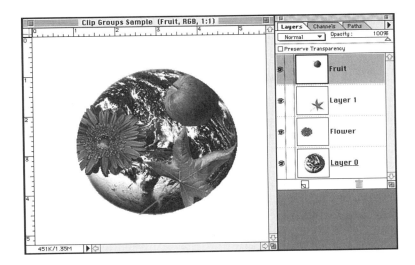

Fig. 10.17

Document and Layers palette with a clipping group.

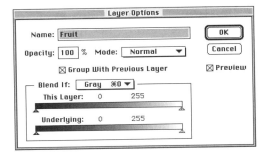

Fig. 10.18

The Palette Options dialog box with clipping group enabled.

Layer Options

When you double-click a layer, a dialog box appears. If the background is active, the double-click action presents a Make Layer dialog box. This operation enables you to convert the background into a layer. By default, a document opened has a background. Because the background cannot be reorganized among the other layers, it is fixed at the background position. When you convert the background to a layer, it behaves as any other layer in the document.

III

Creating and Touching Up

When you double-click a layer, the Layer Options dialog box appears providing a number of layer options (see fig. 10.19).

Fig. 10.19

The Layer Options dialog box provides several editing features.

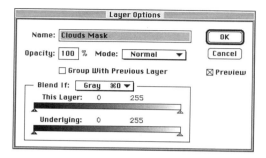

The Layer Options include the following:

▶ **Name.** When layers are created they can be named. During the editing of the image, the layer appearance may be different than the description applied to the name when the layer was first created. The name of the layer can be changed to accommodate design changes at any time.

▶ **Opacity.** The opacity can either be changed in the dialog box or the Layers palette by moving the opacity slider. Striking the number keys changes the opacity at 10 percent increments.

▶ **Mode.** The Mode pop-up menu provides for the selection of the various calculate functions described in chapter 9, "Selecting Objects in Photoshop." In addition to the previously discussed mode operations, there are two calculations unique to layers. The Behind and Clear operations only are available when a layer is active.

   ▶ **Behind.** Behind puts a pasted shape behind the information in the layer. If the entire layer is filled with pixels, the pasted image appears as a selection when you choose Behind from the Mode pop-up menu. Transparent areas of the layer reveal the pasted object. Figure 10.20 illustrates a shape pasted in a layer with the behind mode selected.

   ▶ **Clear.** Clear makes all the pixels in a pasted object in a layer appear transparent. When the layer is viewed with the transparency active from the Preferences menu, the clear areas are more distinctive. Figure 10.21 shows a shape pasted into a layer with the clear mode.

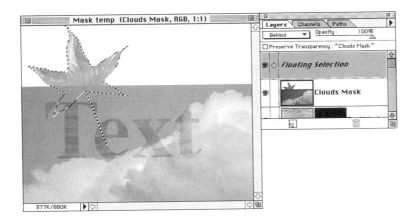

Fig. 10.20

The pasted object
is positioned
behind the other
layer shapes.

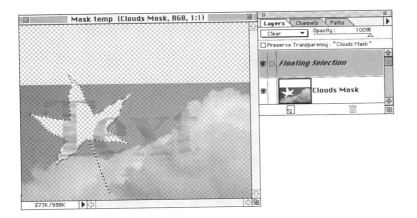

Fig. 10.21

Clear renders the
selected area
transparent.

▶ **Group With Previous Layer.** This is the same as using the clipping
group function by pressing the Option key and clicking between
layers in the Layers palette. Enabling this check box creates the
clipping group as described earlier.

▶ **Blend If.** Gives you a choice for gray pixel ranges and the color
channel pixel ranges. The Gray option provides a range for all pixels
in the image from a composite view. The individual color channels set
the range for each channel. When a mode is changed, for example
from RGB to CMYK, the channel choices reflect the new mode
changes. After the colors for blending are selected, adjustments can be
made on the sliders below the pop-up menu.

III

Creating and Touching Up

▶ **Adjustment Sliders.** The adjustment sliders affect blending changes for the layer being adjusted and the information in the underlying layer. The black triangles on the left side control the darkest pixels in the image while the slider on the right controls the lightest pixels in the image. The top row of sliders for *This Layer* appears as though pixels are eliminated from the layer. The bottom row of pixels for *Underlying Layer* appears as though more of the underlying layer is viewed through the current layer.

The sliders can be split by pressing the Option key (see fig. 10.22) and dragging one half of the sliders. This function provides a smooth transition between a range of pixels between two values and displays only part of their original colors.

Fig. 10.22

Layer Options with the adjustment sliders split.

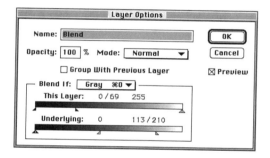

Tip

Understanding the Color Range Adjustments

To provide a thorough understanding of what is happening to the pixel values as you move and split the adjustment sliders, create a gradient from black to white over a background image. Make adjustments to each of the sliders noting the elimination of pixels when adjusting the This Layer option and the appearance of the Underlying layer when adjusting the bottom row of sliders. Hold the Option key down and split the sliders by moving them back and forth independently. Because the gradient has a full range of grays, the adjustments provide a visual explanation of the relationships between the layers when moving the sliders.

Layer Operations

Now that you understand the nature of layers and the many functions and features of layer commands, take a look at layer operations (lay-ops). You see how the previously described features work effectively with layers, and learn some new concepts and layer functions.

When you work with layers, there are two potential problems that you might experience until you are completely familiar with layers. The first and most common problem is not addressing the layer to which you intend to apply the action. When things don't seem to work properly, always double-check to make sure that you selected the layer in the Layers palette where you want to apply your editing. This is something that easily can be overlooked and most often is the source of a problem.

The second area where you might experience some problems is with preserving transparency. First, look at layer operations to understand the Preserve Transparency setting in the Layers palette.

Preserve Transparency

The Layers palette has a check box at the top called Preserve Transparency. When you create a layer and place a shape on it, all the transparent areas can be distinguished by setting the Transparency view from the Preferences dialog box. The first inclination for users is to toggle this option off by selecting None. When None is selected, the transparent areas of the layer are represented in white. This representation does not provide the user with immediate feedback on what is transparent and what is the image area. This is especially true when only a single layer is viewed in the document. If the transparency view is None, then extra care is necessary when working on a layer in order to know what effects are applied to the shapes.

Preserve Transparency is similar to a selection mask. When the check box in the dialog box is enabled, the transparent areas of the layer do not accept editing features. If, for example, you want to edit type on a layer that appears above a texture, pattern, or other image, you can edit the type with or without the transparency preserved. If you select the type layer and apply paint with one of the painting tools, the paint is applied to the entire layer. If you enable Preserve Transparency in the Layers palette, only the type is affected. Figure 10.23 shows painting applied without Preserve Transparency enabled.

Fig. 10.23

Painting applied
without Preserve
Transparency.

The same effect is applied to figure 10.24, except the Preserve Transparency option is enabled.

Fig. 10.24

Painting applied
with Preserve
Transparency.

Preserve Transparency can be used with a number of Photoshop commands and features. Pasting, color correction and balance, brightness and contrast adjustments, some filter applications, and so on, can all be applied with or without preserving transparency. When you use this option, it is critical to verify whether the Preserve Transparency check box is enabled. If you accidentally overlook the check box setting, mistakes easily can be corrected by choosing Edit, Undo. Be certain to let the screen refresh and review the results before going to another command which might disable the Undo operation.

> **Caution**
>
> When something appears to go awry in creating a design while working on layers, first check the Layers palette for the active layer. If the layer is not selected, editing cannot be applied to that layer. Use the Undo command when you accidentally apply commands and functions to the wrong layer.
>
> Get in the habit of selecting a layer and observing the Preserve Transparency check box. When you first start with layer operations, practice creating effects with and without Preserve Transparency selected until you become familiar with the results. Practice to a point where you can anticipate the result before the action is applied. Any subsequent mistakes easily are recognizable and can be corrected when you know why a result occurred different than what you expected.

Copy and Paste in Layers

You can copy information from other Photoshop files or from the same file and paste it to a number of areas in a document. You have as many choices as the alternatives you have available in performing layer operations.

Pasting into a Layer

Pasting information in a layer places the clipboard image on the selected layer. When the paste command is exercised, the information is held in a floating selection. From this point, you can apply the pasted information in a number of ways. By defloating the image, the information is made part of the active layer; it adheres to the opacity and mode specified in the Layers palette. Figure 10.25 illustrates a pasted image that appears as a floating selection in a layer.

When the image from figure 10.25 is defloated, it appears with a 50 percent opacity as specified for this layer in the Layers palette. If the opacity of the pasted information is to appear different than the layer, it is better if you define the pasted area as its own independent layer. As a new layer, you can apply different opacity or mode changes. To create a layer for the pasted information, you need to choose Make Layer from the

III

Creating and Touching Up

Layers palette pop-up menu (see fig. 10.26). Whenever a floating selection is created in a document, the New Layer option in the Layers palette pop-up menu is substituted with Make Layer. Defloating the image returns to the New Layer option.

Fig. 10.25

Pasting in a layer.

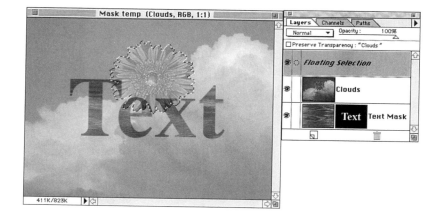

Fig. 10.26

Make a layer from a floating selection.

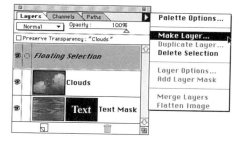

When Make Layer is selected, a dialog box identical to the New Layer dialog box appears that lets you name the layer, set the opacity, and set the mode.

Copy and paste perform in the same manner as drag and drop when it relates to selections. If a layer is dragged from a document without a selection and dropped into the destination document, a new layer automatically is created and the image is defloated. Selecting an entire layer from one document and pasting it into another is the same as an object in a layer that is selected, copied, and pasted.

Pasting into a Layer with a Mask

When you paste information into a layer where a layer mask has been created, the pasted information is applied to the mask and placed on the previously defined masked object. The pasted information appears as a floating selection. The floating selection can accept editing changes without affecting the underlying layer information until it is defloated. For example, you can adjust the brightness of the floating selection in the levels dialog, and apply filters and painting functions while the selection is floating. Any changes applied to the floating selection do not change the masked area of your image. Figure 10.27 shows a floating selection on the layer where a layer mask was created. The floating selection was adjusted in the Levels dialog box and the Pixelate filter was applied.

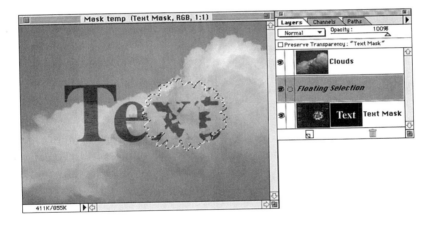

Fig. 10.27

A pasted image in a layer with a mask.

Notice that the pasted region adheres to the masked area, which is defined in the layer mask. When defloated, the pasted image is applied as it is viewed in figure 10.27. After it is defloated, the selection cannot be edited apart from the masked region.

Pasting into the Layer Mask

Pasting also can be performed on the layer mask and can be added to the mask to create a different one. To paste into the mask, be certain that the mask thumbnail on the right of the layer thumbnail is selected and choose Paste. The shape is pasted into the mask. You can view the mask exclusively by pressing the Option key and selecting the mask thumbnail. If the pasted information is to be included in the mask, you must render

III

Creating and Touching Up

the portion of the selection white. By selecting white foreground color and striking the Option and Delete keys, the selection fills with white. Make sure you don't strike the Delete key—thinking that the background color will be placed in the selection. While the selection is floating, striking Delete eliminates the pasted information, including the selection. Figure 10.28 shows a pasted image in the mask.

Fig. 10.28

A pasted image in a layer mask.

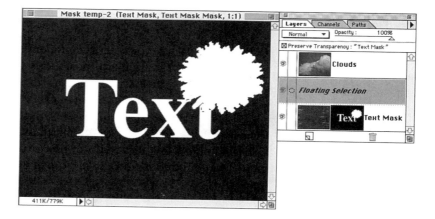

You can adjust the opacity of a floating selection separate from the rest of the mask. In figure 10.28, the opacity for the selection is set to 50 percent; the text mask remains at 100 percent opacity. The results are illustrated in figure 10.29.

Fig. 10.29

A pasted image in a mask with a 50 percent opacity setting.

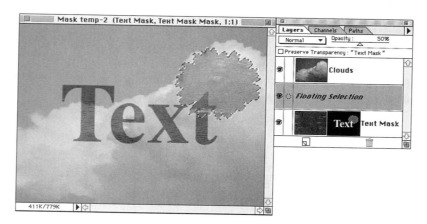

Notice that the mask includes both the text and the new pasted image all masking the texture in the layer. The text appears darker because the opacity is set at 100 percent, the image region of the mask appears lighter due to the 50 percent opacity setting.

Pasting in Clipping Groups

Clipping groups accept pasted images much the same as layer masks. When an image is pasted into a clipping group, the image comes into the layer and can be moved inside, partially inside, or outside the clipped region. The image comes into the document at the same level of opacity; this can be misleading at times. The opacity slider for the floating selection that appears when the image is pasted reads 100 percent. However, the appearance of the pasted information assumes the same level of opacity as defined for the layer. While the selection remains floating, additional editing can be performed to the selected region only. Some darkening of the pasted shape can be performed by adjusting levels, burning in, or painting.

Pasting in a clipping group is an excellent opportunity to use the Behind mode. If you want the newly pasted object to appear behind the current layer information, you can select Behind from the Layers palette mode choices. While the selection is floating, additional editing features can be applied without affecting the other information in the layer. For example, opacity adjustments, filters, and painting can be applied only to the selected region. In addition, you can mask the pasted information with the layer information when selecting the Preserve Transparency check box in the Layers palette.

Next, examine a step-by-step view of using paste with clipping groups. Figure 10.30 illustrates a document with several layers. Each of the layers is clipped to the triangle so that all image boundaries are contained in the triangle.

If you want to paste an image in the Sun layer, which is a part of the clipping group, select the layer and choose Paste from the Edit menu. The pasted image appears on top of the sun image. If you select Behind from the mode pop-up menu in the Layers palette, you can reposition the pasted image behind your original layer shape. If you want the opacity to appear different on the pasted image than the layer, you can change opacity while the selection is floating. Figure 10.31 shows the result.

III

Creating and Touching Up

293

A document with
several layers and
a clipping group.

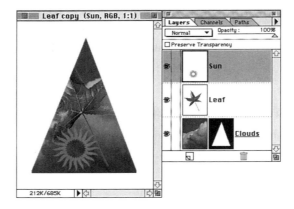

A pasted image in
a clipping group.

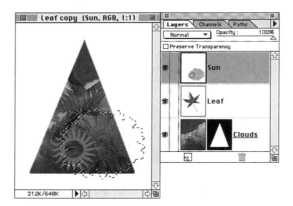

Pasting a Layer

Pasting operations also can be performed by choosing the Paste Layer command in the Edit menu. This command differs from the Paste function you use when you paste into a layer by activating the document and the layer where you want the information to appear. In this case, when you paste, the information is placed in composite with the current layer. The Paste Layer command, on the other hand, creates a new layer and places the clipboard information on that layer.

When Paste Layer is selected from the Edit menu, a dialog box, identical to the dialog boxes with New Layer and Make Layer, appears. User defined input for the layer name and opacity can be performed in this dialog box. The Paste Layer operation differs from Paste with respect to the selection. When the image is pasted as a layer, there is not a selection. It performs similar to the drag and drop operation. Paste Layer is handy because it uses the dialog box to prompt the user to make the name and opacity changes. Drag and drop requires activating the dialog box by double-clicking the layer or choosing the layer options in the Layers palette. The disadvantage of using Paste Layer is the memory requirements for copying to the clipboard before the paste can be used.

Paste Into

Paste Into, from the Edit menu, is used with a selection. After you create a selection in a layer, Paste Into regards the selection as a mask and pastes the clipboard information into the selection (see fig. 10.32). Paste Into is helpful when you need to combine selections or create a feathered selection and paste an image into the feathered selection.

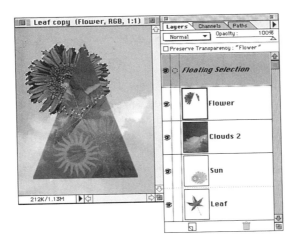

Fig. 10.32

An image pasted into a selection.

Linking Layers

When two or more layers are created in a document, they can be linked together by selecting the linking column in the Layers palette. The second column from the left is used for linking layers. To link, add to a link, and delete from a link, perform the following steps:

1. Select a layer to be included in the link.

2. Click in the link column adjacent to the second layer to be included in the link. Do not select the layer, just click in the link column. The second layer is linked to the selected layer.

III

Creating and Touching Up

3. Move to another layer and click in the link column. Once again, do not select the layer. The third layer is added to the link.

4. Move to any layer with three or more links in the document and click the Link icon to exclude the layer from the link. If two layers are linked, clicking the Link icon breaks all links in the document.

5. When a link is present, click and drag in the link column to include multiple layers in the link. Click and drag multiple links to eliminate them from the link.

Figure 10.33 illustrates multiple layers linked together.

Fig. 10.33

The Linked layers are displayed with the Link icon in the second column in the Layers palette.

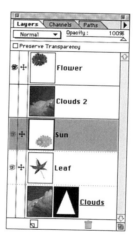

To fix the relationship between elements as they are repositioned in a document window, it is useful to link the layers. This is particularly helpful with type and drop shadows. After the type is created on one layer and the shadow on another layer, link them to reposition both in the document window.

TACTICS RECIPE

Moving Layers Accurately

You can move layer information with the Move tool. To constrain the movement, press the Shift key to move a layer or several layers linked. For precise movement of layers in small increments, use the arrow keys on the keyboard. If you need to move several layers to a specific position in the document from a reference at the original position, create a reference on a new layer. If, for example, you want to move an object precisely 72 pixels up and 36 pixels to the right, follow these steps:

1. Duplicate the layer you want to move by dragging it to the New Layer icon in the Layers palette. A copy of the layer is created as a new layer.

2. Click the Marquee tool and choose the Rectangular option. In the Marquee Options palette, choose Style, Fixed and set the Width to 72 and the Height to 36 pixels.

3. Place the cursor at the top-left corner of the object to be moved and click to display the selection marquee.

4. Press ⌘-Delete to fill the rectangle with the foreground color. A solid rectangle appears

above the object and measures 72 pixels up and 36 pixels across.

5. Select the original layer to make it the active layer.

6. Move the layer so that the bottom-left corner of the object rests on the top-right corner of the rectangle.

Other references can be created on new document layers by using the single-row and single-column shapes in the Marquee Options palette. By pressing ⌘-Delete, a line only one pixel wide can be established. Rows and columns can be created to form a grid for referencing the positions of objects on other layers. By combining fixed size selection marquees, the Info palette, and single-row and column-marquee shapes, precise reference points can be applied and measured.

Making Selections in Layers

A selection made from the non-transparent information in a layer behaves differently than channels and other Photoshop principles. If you load a selection from a channel, for example, the selection appears from the white areas in the channel. Furthermore, when you create a layer mask, the masking region of the layer is represented as white. When you make a selection in a layer, the opposite applies; a black text character is selected when you choose Load from the Select menu. This can be awkward for those who are used to working with channels, but it actually makes sense after you understand the attributes of layers.

III

Creating and Touching Up

When the Transparency Options in the Preferences menu are set to view transparent areas in any view (other than none), the transparent image area is represented by gray squares (see fig. 10.34). At any time, you can observe what area of the image is transparent and what area is opaque. If you create a simple text character at 100 percent opacity in a document window, the text is opaque and the area surrounding the text is transparent. If you choose the Load Selection command from the Select menu, the text character is selected by default. With black text, the black is selected; this is very different from selections with channels.

Fig. 10.34

A text character with transparency set to medium in the Preferences dialog box.

Loading selections in layers makes sense when you understand that the surrounding area that may appear white is empty. Therefore, Photoshop can only select what is on the layer; it selects the image area. When you choose Load Selection from the Select menu, the Load Selection dialog box appears (see fig. 10.35).

Fig. 10.35

You can add a selection from the Load Selection dialog box.

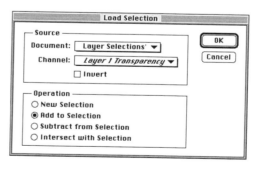

The Load Selection dialog box provides a number of selection choices to create the selection:

▶ **Document.** Selections can be loaded from layers in the current document, or layers from another document. To load selections from another document, the documents must be the same physical size; unlike channels, the pixel depth does not have to be the same. In other words, a document of 72ppi can load a selection from a layer in a document of 100ppi.

▶ **Channel.** The channel can be described as either the layer transparency information or an alpha channel. Layer transparencies and channels can be loaded from other documents as long as the physical size of the image remains the same between them.

▶ **Invert.** When the invert check box is enabled, the selection is inverted. All the image areas of the document become deselected while the transparent areas become selected.

▶ **New Selection.** By default, new is selected. When you choose Load Selection, the layer displays a new selection from the document and channel described in the dialog box.

▶ **Add to Selection.** This is used when an active selection exists in the document and a selection from another source is added to the active selection.

▶ **Subtract from Selection.** The opposite of the Add to Selection occurs. The loaded selection is subtracted from the current selection. In both instances, a selection must be active in the document window.

▶ **Intersect with Selection.** When a selection is active, another selection intersecting the first selection is created. This feature works well with marquee selections created to make a partial selection from a layer object. Figure 10.36 shows the marquee in the document window.

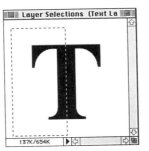

Fig. 10.36

A selection created with marquee rectangle.

III

Creating and Touching Up

299

If you load the selection to create a new selection, the text character becomes selected and replaces the current selection. If the Intersect option from the Load Selection dialog box is addressed, the text character in the marquee rectangle becomes the new selection, as illustrated in figure 10.37.

Fig. 10.37

Load selection with Intersect.

Thorough explanations of creating selections is provided in chapter 9, "Selecting Objects in Photoshop," and chapter 12, "Using Masks and Channels."

Where To Go from Here

▶ Chapter 8, "Drawing, Painting, and Editing," is an excellent beginning for editing features that can be applied to layers.

▶ Chapter 9, "Selecting Objects in Photoshop," provides many detailed explanations of working with selections that can be used with layer operations.

▶ Chapter 12, "Using Masks and Channels," is a continuation of working with selections and layers.

▶ Chapter 16, "Third-Party Plug-Ins," describes many exciting editing tasks that can be completed by applying filters to layers.

Drawing and Editing Paths

At first glance, it may appear strange that a raster image editing program such as Photoshop would have tools which previously were only found in vector-based illustration programs. As you will see, though, there is perhaps no better place for such capable selection and drawing tools.

Chapter 9, "Selecting Objects in Photoshop," covers the topics of making selections, and chapter 12, "Using Masks and Channels," covers working with channels. If you have not already read those chapters, you may want to consider doing so before continuing.

by Darien M. Kruss

CHAPTER 11

Key Concept: Understanding Paths

Paths in Photoshop are a powerful tool for making selections, defining areas to be filled or stroked, and storing masks for later use. Any number of paths can be saved with the documents you create.

In a raster image, a *line* is made up of many pixels placed next to each other that lead from one point in the image to another. To change the length and direction of the line, you must erase the pixels and redraw them somewhere else. In a vector image, as in geometry, a *line* is defined by the shortest distance between two points.

A *path* is made up of anchor points that determine its overall placement. Between anchor points are line or curve segments which define the path's shape. Curve segments also may have direction lines to control their curvature. Figure 11.1 shows a basic path and its anchor points (square shaped) at the beginning and end of each segment. Filled anchor points are selected, while hollow ones are not. Curve segments show their direction lines (round shaped) when selected.

Fig. 11.1

All paths consist of anchor points connected by lines or curves.

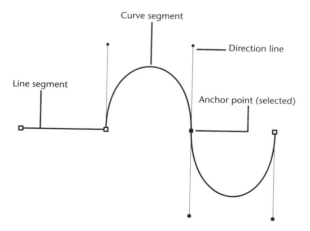

Curve segment

Direction line

Line segment

Anchor point (selected)

Paths are drawn with the *Pen tool*, one of several tools in the Paths palette used to create and edit paths. These drawings are not painted into your image, as with the Pencil or Paintbrush, but rather float above the image in a resolution-independent layer. While in this layer, paths may be edited, moved, and reshaped without affecting any part of the image itself. Because of their resolution-independent nature, paths can reduce the effort required to create accurate selections.

In Photoshop, creating accurate selections around an object can be one of the most important tasks in a painting or retouching project. Even with a plethora of tools that are dedicated to making selections, working accurately in a pixel-based environment can become time-consuming and tedious. Sure, you can become proficient with the Lasso tool or the Quick Mask feature, but to make smooth-flowing shapes or to trace the outline of an object with any amount of precision requires the use of paths.

Working with pixels to touch up a selection with the Lasso tool can sometimes result in rough, jagged edges or soft, blurry ones. On the other hand, paths always create precise, anti-aliased selections. Furthermore, paths are automatically scaled, and rotated with the image.

When To Use Paths vs. Channels

While both paths and channels can be used to store selections and retrieve them at a later time, paths only store coordinate information relating to the position of anchor points and direction lines. Compare this to saving selections as channels that consist of an 8-bit grayscale image the same dimensions as your document. In an RGB image, each saved channel adds one-third the original document size to your storage requirements. CMYK images add one-fourth the original document size, and grayscale images add the full original document size (see fig. 11.2). Hundreds of paths can be stored in just a few kilobytes of space, and, in most cases, perform as well as, or better than, an equivalent channel.

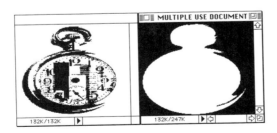

Fig. 11.2

Saving a channel of this grayscale watch nearly doubles the file's size.

Because paths are resolution-independent, they can undergo more changes than channels before showing signs of degradation. For instance, suppose you need to scale an image up and rotate it. A selection saved as a channel will start to become blurry and inaccurate. The same selection stored as a path will remain crisp and on-target.

Paths can store information no longer present in the image because paths that fall outside the boundaries are retained. Channel data that falls outside the boundaries (after cropping, scaling, or moving) is lost.

Paths, like channels, can be filled. Unlike channels, however, paths also can be stroked using any painting tool. Also, paths can be further influenced by selections, whereas selections ignore the presence of paths.

One case where you might not want to store a selection as a path is when the opacity of the selection is an important factor. Paths only store solid masks. Another use for channels is to store extremely small and fine detail, such as a texture in fabric or stars in the sky.

Creating Simple Paths

If you're familiar with PostScript drawing programs, such as Adobe Illustrator and Aldus FreeHand, you may find that this section is a review of concepts you already know. To everyone else, this is mandatory reading in order to fully benefit from the capabilities of these tools.

To use paths, open the Paths palette. Open the Window menu and choose Palette, Show Paths. The Paths palette contains tools and icons for creating and editing paths (see fig. 11.3).

Fig. 11.3

All path tools and operations are accessed from the Paths palette.

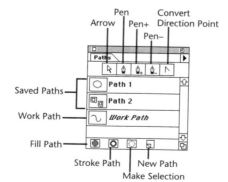

The tools at the top of the Paths palette each perform a specific purpose. Select them the same way you select tools from the toolbox. The icons at the bottom of the palette can be used several ways. To perform the default action on a path, click the icon (if a path is visible) or drag a path's name to the icon. To specify additional options for the action, hold the Option key as you click the icon or drag a path's name to it. These commands also are available in the Path palette's options menu—found by pressing the small triangle on the right side of the palette's title bar.

Each path stored in the palette is given a name. To the left of a path's name is a preview icon showing the contents of the path.

Making Paths of Lines

To begin drawing a path, be sure you have a document open, and then click the Pen tool in the Paths palette.

The Pen tool creates anchor points which connect to form straight lines wherever you click and release the mouse within a document. By clicking and dragging the mouse, anchor points with direction lines are created; these are the foundation for making curves. The Pen tool in Photoshop works just like the Path tool in Adobe Illustrator, with one exception. There is a check box in the Options palette labeled Rubber Band. When this box is selected, the Pen tool behaves proactively and continuously displays the anticipated result of the current path segment. When the box is not selected, path segments are not drawn until the mouse button is pressed.

To draw a path consisting of straight lines, follow these steps:

1. Begin by choosing the Pen tool in the Paths palette.

2. Visualize in your mind where you want to draw the first line.

3. Move the pointer into the image where you want the line to begin and click the mouse button once. An anchor point (black square) appears under the pointer.

4. Move to where you want the line to end and click the mouse button again. You see the line drawn between the two points.

Lines are defined by only two points (see fig. 11.4). You can create additional points along a line, but they don't add any benefit. In fact, additional points make editing more difficult and may cause printing problems if used as a clipping path.

III

Creating and Touching Up

305

Fig. 11.4

Use only two points
to define a line.

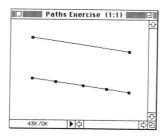

If you want to continue drawing lines from the selected point, move the
pointer and click again.

Tip

Constraining Lines And Nudging Points

To draw lines that are constrained to multiples of 45-degree angles,
hold the Shift key before clicking the mouse button at the end of
each path segment. Constrained lines can be useful when tracing
around regular hard-edged shapes or while creating a path to be
used as a guide for painting. The selected anchor point can be
nudged one pixel at a time by pressing the arrow keys on the keyboard in the direction you want the pixel to move. Hold the Shift
key as you press an arrow key to nudge the selected point 10 pixels
at a time.

There is no practical limitation to the number of segments (both lines and
curves) that can be part of a single path (see fig. 11.5).

Fig. 11.5

An open path
made up of line
segments, the last
four constrained
with the Shift key.

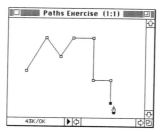

While you are still forming a path, it is possible to take back your last action. Press the Delete key on the keyboard to remove the last point you created (the currently selected point). Use the Pen tool to click a remaining end point of the path to specify a continuation point. Then click the mouse button where you want the next segment.

> **Tip**
>
> **Deleting Entire Paths**
>
> While you are drawing a path, you can press the Delete key twice to erase the entire path. Be cautious when using the Delete key to fill a selection with the background color while a path is visible. The Delete key acts only upon the path and not upon the selection, as might be expected. To fill a selection, you have to deselect the path by clicking away from the path name in the Paths palette.

Making Subpaths

There is no limitation to the number of subpaths that can be stored under one path name. (Because a path usually refers to the entire path layer, *subpath* is used to refer to a single path in the layer.) The following three methods can be used to create a subpath:

▶ Deselect the currently active path by clicking the Pen tool in the Paths palette to reset it. You can begin a new path by clicking anywhere in the document.

▶ Hold down the Command key (⌘) to temporarily activate the Arrow tool and click in an empty area of the document. Release the Command key to begin a new subpath.

▶ If appropriate, close the current path by moving the pointer to the starting endpoint. A small loop appears next to the pointer indicating that you are about to close the path. Click the mouse button to complete the action. After you close a path, you may begin another one in the same layer. Just click the mouse button where you want it to begin.

III

Creating and Touching Up

Making Paths of Curves

To draw curves with the Pen tool, you must always think one step ahead. When making lines, clicking is enough to define the starting and ending points of the segment. For curves, you must drag the mouse in the direction you want the curve to go next. By default, direction lines "teeter-totter" on the anchor points to create smooth transitions between segments.

Suppose you want to follow the shape of the curve shown in figure 11.6. Complete the following three steps after selecting the Pen tool from the Paths palette:

1. Click and hold the mouse button at the left-most endpoint of the curve and drag upward, just slightly higher than the actual curve's height. This defines the starting point of the segment, as well as the curve's direction—in this case, upward.

2. Next, click and hold the mouse button where the curve would form a half-ellipse and drag downward. In this case, it is directly in line with the first anchor point. Notice how direction lines extend in both directions from the anchor point. This ensures a smooth transition between the two curve segments.

3. Lastly, click and hold the mouse button where the second curve segment ends and drag upward, in the direction that the curve continues.

Tip

Direction Line Length

Although the same curve can be formed by direction lines of varying lengths, there is a preferred method of deciding the length of direction lines on either side of a curve. When dragging direction lines for a curve segment, try to make each one an equal length. This simplifies things greatly in case you need to edit the curve in the future.

It only takes two points to define most curve segments. Figuring out where to place them, though, takes some practice before it becomes second-nature. It's a good idea to not get preoccupied with putting the anchor points in the exact location while drawing a curve—rather, go back and edit the curve after you complete its basic shape.

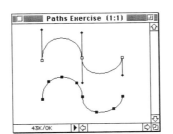

Fig. 11.6

Only place anchor points at the beginning and end of a curve segment—the fewer the better.

Making Cusps

A *cusp* occurs when a curve segment veers off suddenly into a line segment or another curve segment heading in a different direction. Direction lines for cusps don't "teeter-totter" across an anchor point.

To define a cusp while you are drawing a segment, hold down the Option key and drag the direction lines from the anchor points you have just completed (see fig. 11.7). As a reminder, always drag the direction lines in the next direction the curve will go.

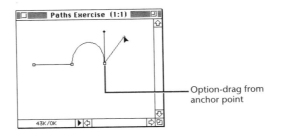

Option-drag from anchor point

Fig. 11.7

Cusps are created by dragging direction lines from existing anchor points with the Option key.

Closing Paths

For the most part, closing paths are optional because Photoshop treats all paths as closed for filling, selection, and masking purposes. However, you may want to purposely close paths for a better visual description of the complete path shape or in order to avoid surprises.

Note

Photoshop does recognize open paths for stroking operations and export to Adobe Illustrator and Adobe Dimensions.

III

Creating and Touching Up

Figure 11.8 shows a path and the result of filling the path. Photoshop automatically closes up the loose end points by the shortest distance possible. Open paths also close automatically when they are converted to selections. Stroking a path does not close it, however.

Fig. 11.8

Open and closed paths are treated the same when filling or making selections.

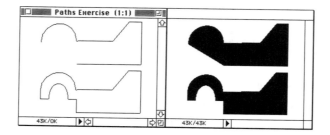

Using the Paths Palette

All of the controls for dealing with paths are found in the Paths Palette Options menu. Some of the commands are manifested as shortcut icons in a row at the bottom of the palette. Usually, the default action can be activated by simply clicking an icon. Holding the Option key down while clicking brings up additional controls for some icons. It is also possible to act upon a path that is not currently visible by dragging its name onto an icon (holding the Option key, if desired) to initiate a response.

Any saved or working paths in the Paths palette may be reordered by dragging their names up or down the list. You may want to group similar paths together to find them more easily.

Changing Path Preview Size

Saved and working paths can display a thumbnail icon to their left in the Paths palette. The thumbnail is updated each time the path is changed. To change the size of the icon, or to disable it, choose Palette Options from the Paths Palette Options menu. You can choose one of three preview sizes—or none—from the Paths Palette Options dialog box (see fig. 11.9).

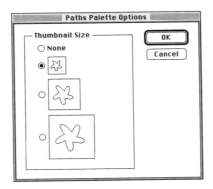

Fig. 11.9

Saved and working paths may have thumbnails to help identify them.

Make New Path

To create a new, empty path for the current document, follow these steps:

1. Click the New Path icon at the bottom of the Paths palette, or choose New Path from the palette's Options menu.

2. Name the path in the resulting New Path dialog box (see fig. 11.10). This path becomes the currently active path and is placed at the top of the list.

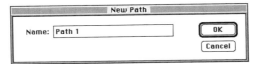

Fig. 11.10

Starting new paths prepares them to be saved.

Saving Paths

It's not necessary to create a new path before you begin to draw a path. When you start drawing without a selected path layer, the path is stored in a temporary *work path* identified by italic type in the Paths palette. The work path can be immediately saved by dragging it to the New Path icon, or by choosing Save Path from the palette's Options menu (see fig. 11.11).

The Save Path dialog box automatically prompts you to name your newly saved path. The default name is the word path followed by the next sequential number that isn't already shown in the Paths palette (see fig. 11.12).

Fig. 11.11

Save all the paths you use; they don't take up much space.

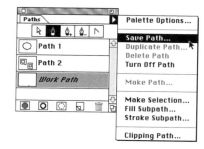

Fig. 11.12

Name your paths descriptively to avoid wasting time later.

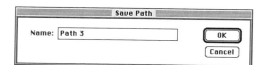

> **Note**
>
> Saving a path with your document does not write the document to disk. You still need to periodically save your image (from the File menu) or you could lose everything.

After creating additional paths or editing existing paths that already were saved in the Paths palette, it is not necessary to save the path in order to retain the changes. Changes made to existing paths are effective immediately.

Showing and Hiding Paths

After you have paths saved in the Paths palette, you can recall one path at a time to the screen for editing or manipulation by clicking its name. The path becomes active on the screen and its name appears highlighted in the Paths palette. To hide a path you no longer want to view, click in an empty area of the Paths palette, or choose Turn Off Path in the Paths Palette Options menu.

Deleting Paths

To permanently remove an entire path, drag the path name to the Trash icon in the Paths palette (see fig. 11.13). You are asked whether you want to apply the path as a selection before it is deleted, or discard the path.

Fig. 11.13

Delete paths by dragging their name to the Trash icon.

Change Path Name

To change the name of a path, double-click the path's name in the Paths palette. The Save Path dialog box appears, allowing you to change the path's name (see fig. 11.14).

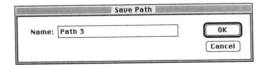

Fig. 11.14

Update path names to accurately describe their contents.

Copying Paths to Other Documents

It is possible to copy paths you drew to other Photoshop documents. You may want to store paths in an archive that you have used for a project, or create libraries of paths that you can use over and over again. Do either of the following to copy your path:

▶ Drag the path name you want to copy from the Paths palette to another visible document window to copy the entire path (see fig. 11.15).

▶ Use the Arrow tool to drag only the selected subpath(s) from one document window to another document window.

III

Creating and Touching Up

313

Fig. 11.15

Copy a path to another document by dragging its name from the Paths palette to the document window.

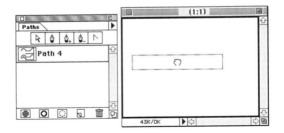

Editing Paths

Besides the Pen tool, all the other tools in the Paths palette are used for editing paths. The first tool, the Arrow tool, is used to select, move, and duplicate anchor points and line or curve segments.

The Arrow tool in Photoshop appears as a hollow shape so it isn't confused with the standard Macintosh arrow pointer. To move a point on a path, click it with the Arrow tool—selected points appear solid, not hollow—and drag it to its new location (see fig. 11.16). A moved point adjusts all the segments connected to it. Unselected points do not move at all.

Fig. 11.16

Drag an anchor point to change a path's shape.

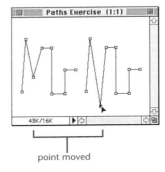

point moved

Tip

Arrow Tool Shortcuts

If you simply want to edit a point or segment on a path while using most other Photoshop tools, hold down the Command key (⌘) to temporarily activate the Arrow tool. Also, pressing the T key on the keyboard toggles between selecting the Arrow tool and the Pen tool in the Paths palette.

Click a line segment to move the entire line, including the connected anchor points (see fig. 11.17).

line moved

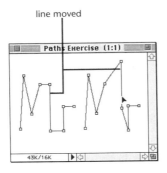

Fig. 11.17

Drag a line segment to move both attached anchor points simultaneously.

To select multiple anchor points that are in close proximity with each other, drag a marquee with the Arrow tool. A *marquee* is a selection formed by clicking the mouse at one corner of an imaginary rectangle that encloses the points you want to select and dragging to the opposite corner (see fig. 11.18). Any movement applied to one point mimics the other selected points. You also can delete all the selected points by pressing Delete.

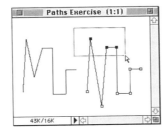

Fig. 11.18

Select nearby points by dragging a marquee around them with the Arrow tool.

To select or deselect individual anchor points, one at a time, hold the Shift key as you click the point (see fig. 11.19). All the selected points follow the movement of any one selected point. You also can delete the selected points by pressing Delete.

Clicking a curve segment with the Arrow tool selects that segment and displays its direction lines. Dragging the segment itself or dragging a single direction line changes the shape of the curve. Keep in mind that direction handles always "teeter-totter" across smooth anchor points.

III

Creating and Touching Up

Fig. 11.19

You can move multiple points simultaneously after selecting each one with the Shift key.

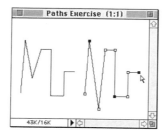

To select an entire subpath, hold the Option key while clicking any part of the path. All the anchor points become solid, indicating selection.

A path can be duplicated in its own document by holding the Option key and dragging the copy to a new location (see fig. 11.20). Release the mouse button before releasing the Option key or the path is simply moved, not copied.

Fig. 11.20

Duplicate paths or segments by dragging with the Option key.

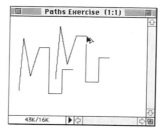

Adding Points

Sometimes you need to place additional anchor points along a path so that it can be shaped the way you want. Use the Pen+ tool to create new anchor points by clicking any line or curve segment once (see fig. 11.21). If you attempt to add a new point to an existing point, or where no path exists, there are no results.

Hold the Command and Option keys with the arrow, or Control and Shift keys with the Pen tool, to temporarily activate the Pen+ tool on a line or curve segment.

Newly added points try to maintain the existing shape of the path as closely as possible. New points are always created with direction lines, even when added to a straight line segment.

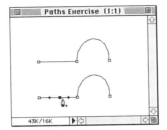

Fig. 11.21

Add new points to
a segment with the
Pen+ tool.

Deleting Points

To remove unwanted or unnecessary points from a path, click them with
the Pen– tool (see fig. 11.22). Clicking anywhere but on an anchor point
produces no results.

Hold the Command and Option keys with the arrow, or Control and Shift
keys with the Pen tool, to temporarily activate the Pen– tool on an anchor
point.

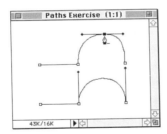

Fig. 11.22

Delete unwanted
points with the
Pen– tool.

The two points on each end of a deleted point join together. Photoshop
attempts to retain the shape of the original path as closely as possible.

Converting Corners

You should be familiar with the difference between line and curve
segments before using the Convert Direction Point tool. The Convert
Direction Point tool can convert anchor points between their two states:
corner and smooth.

Click a corner point with the Convert Direction Point tool and drag the
mouse to extend direction lines from it, making it a smooth point (see fig.
11.23). The direction lines "teeter-totter" across the anchor point.

Fig. 11.23

Drag anchor points
with the Convert
Direction Point
tool to make
them smooth.

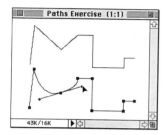

Click a *smooth point* (any anchor point connected to at least one curve segment) with the Convert Direction Point tool to convert it to a corner (see fig. 11.24). All direction lines disappear.

Fig. 11.24

Click smooth
anchor points
with the Convert
Direction Point
tool to make
them sharp.

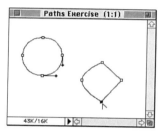

The Convert Direction Point tool also can be used to convert the sharp transition of a cusp to a smooth transition. To change it to a smooth anchor point, click (and drag, if desired) the direction line attached to a cusp (see fig. 11.25).

Fig. 11.25

Drag cusp direc-
tion lines with the
Convert Direction
Point tool to extend
smooth direction
lines.

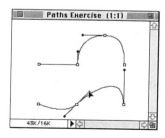

Duplicating Paths

Occasionally, you may want to experiment with a path you saved in the Paths palette. Instead of modifying your only copy of the path, create a duplicate so that the original remains untouched. To duplicate a path, follow one of these steps:

▶ Drag the path name you want to duplicate to the New Path icon in the Paths palette. The new path is the same name as the old path with the word copy appended to the end.

▶ Click the path name you want to duplicate so that it becomes selected. Choose Duplicate Path from the Paths Palette Options menu, or hold the Option key while dragging the path's name to the New Path icon. A dialog box appears where the duplicated path can be named.

Using Paths for Painting

Part of the allure of using paths for painting operations is because the result is always smooth and anti-aliased. To prepare a path for painting operations, it must first be visible. If you just drew the path, it is visible. If you saved it previously, you may need to click its name in the Paths palette first.

If your path layer contains more than one subpath, you may need to specify which subpath you want painted. If none of the subpaths are selected, the entire path layer is painted. If only some of the subpaths have been selected, only those subpaths are painted.

Any paint applied using the following methods becomes part of the currently active layer (highlighted in the Layers palette). You may want to consider creating a new layer before painting any of your paths. Active selections in the document limit the ability of a path to be filled or stroked. The filling or stroking only occurs in the confines of the selection (see fig. 11.26).

Fill Paths

Paths can be filled quickly with the current foreground color. Choose a foreground color using any method with which you are comfortable. Then, click the Fill Path icon, or drag a path name to the Fill Path icon.

The path is filled with the foreground color on the currently active layer in the Layers palette (see fig. 11.27). For more information on selecting foreground colors, see the section "Selecting a Color," in chapter 8, "Drawing, Painting, and Editing."

Fig. 11.26

An active selection affects a path's ability to be filled or stroked.

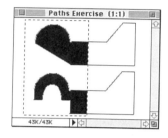

Fig. 11.27

Filling a path adds pixels to your image.

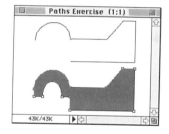

For an additional dialog box to control how the path is filled (see fig. 11.28), choose Fill (sub)Path from the Paths Palette Options menu, or hold the Option key while clicking or dragging a path name to the Fill Path icon.

Fig. 11.28

The Fill Path dialog box provides controls for setting the path's contents, blending, and rendering options.

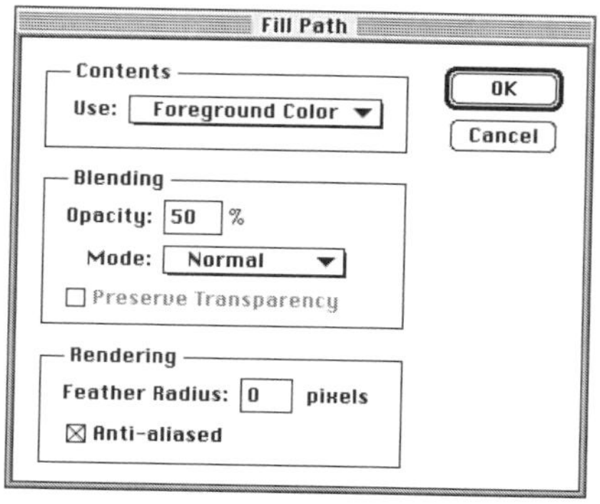

Stroke Paths

The selected path layer or any selected subpaths can be traced, as if by hand, with many of the painting tools found in the toolbox. To stroke a path, follow these steps:

1. Select the path or subpath you want to stroke.

2. Choose the painting or editing tool you want to use to stroke the path: Pencil, Line, Airbrush, Paintbrush, Rubber Stamp, Eraser, Smudge, Blur/sharpen, or Dodge/burn/sponge. Choose the tool you want to use by clicking it in the toolbox.

3. Choose the brush from the Brushes palette that you want to use for stroking the path. The brush follows the path from beginning to end, always staying directly centered on the path itself.

4. In the tool's Options palette, verify the settings available for the tool you have chosen. Do not forget to set a foreground or background color, if your tool requires that, as well.

5. Click the Stroke Path icon or drag the path name to the Stroke Path icon. The currently selected tool, brush, color, and options are used to follow the path (see fig. 11.29). Open paths are observed.

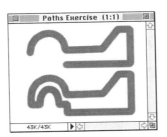

Fig. 11.29

These stroked paths show that stroking does not close loose end-points.

To stroke the same path again, but with a different tool, choose Stroke Path from the Paths Palette Options menu, or hold the Option key while clicking the Stroke Path icon or dragging a path name to the Stroke Path icon. You can choose a new tool from the pop-up menu in the Stroke Subpath dialog box (see fig. 11.30).

III

Creating and Touching Up

Fig. 11.30

Paths are stroked
with the currently
selected tool unless
another tool is
chosen in the
Stroke Subpath
dialog box.

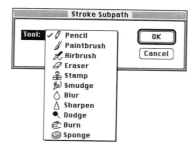

> **Tip**
>
> **Stroking Paths for Special Effects**
>
> There are some effects that can be produced by stroking a path mul-
> tiple times with different sized brushes and varying colors and opaci-
> ties. One of these is glowing neon lights. Start with a larger brush
> and a more saturated color. Stroke the path with the Paintbrush or
> Airbrush tool. Repeat this several times with increasingly smaller
> brushes and less saturated tints of the same color. Finish with a one-
> pixel wide brush set to white.

Creating Complex Paths

Sometimes, a simple open or closed path is not flexible enough for a
particular need. Photoshop allows multiple paths in a path layer
to interact with each other to create more complex paths. It works like
this: if one subpath encloses another, it creates a *compound*, or hole. Filling
a compound path results in an empty space, similar to that shown in
figure 11.31.

Fig. 11.31

Paths that are
enclosed by other
paths become holes
(compounds).

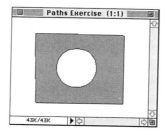

It is not necessary that both paths in a compound even be closed. Open paths that partially enclose or overlap each other are considered closed and can create compounds.

To fill or stroke only one subpath of a compound, click it with the Arrow tool to isolate it from the other subpaths in the path layer. Only selected subpaths are painted.

Using Paths as Selections

The powerful tracing capability of paths makes them the perfect tool for creating and storing selections. Because the path is resolution-independent, you do not have to work tediously in a pixel-based environment trying to get smooth, anti-aliased selections.

Depending on the complexity of your task, you also may opt not to create perfectly curved and ultra-precise masks. In the prepress industry, many workstation operators who use Photoshop cut masks with the path tool by making only straight line segments—not worrying about individual pixels that may not get selected. When the path is converted to a selection, the anti-aliased feature picks up the slack.

Converting Paths into Selections

After you have a path that you want to use as a selection, just click the Make Selection icon in the Paths palette, or drag the path name to the Make Selection icon. The default settings are used to generate your selection.

You can have more control over how the selection is created, and even how it interacts with an existing selection. Choose Make Selection from the Paths Palette Options menu, or hold the Option key as you click or drag a path name to the Make Selection icon. The Make Selection dialog box appears (see fig. 11.32).

In the dialog box, you can specify a feather radius and whether or not to anti-alias the selection. You also can choose how the new selection interacts with an existing selection by choosing one of the options at the bottom of the dialog box. In any case, your path remains visible on the screen until you delete or hide it.

Fig. 11.32

The Make Selection dialog box specifies how selections made from paths look and interact with existing selections.

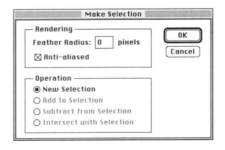

Converting Selections to Paths

If you use another method to make a selection (Marquee, Lasso, Magic Wand, and so on) an easy way to store it—that takes up very little space—is to convert it to a path. Paths, however, only store solid areas of a selection. If your selection is based on different opacities, or if it consists of many small but highly detailed objects—like stars in the sky—then you may want to save your selection as a channel instead.

 To convert a selection to a path quickly, click the Make Selection icon in the Paths palette while your selection is visible on the screen. Photoshop traces the selection with the default settings and displays a path where the selection used to be (see fig. 11.33). Depending on the amount of detail in the selection, converting it to a path may take several minutes.

Fig. 11.33

Any selection can be converted to a path for manipulation or storage.

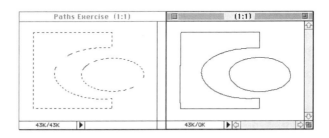

For more control over how the path is created from your selection, choose Make Path from the Paths Palette Options menu, or hold the Option key while clicking the Make Selection icon in the Paths palette. A dialog box appears where you can enter the tolerance (in pixels) that the path should follow (see fig. 11.34). The higher the tolerance, the smoother the path is, at the loss of some detail. The lower the tolerance, the more detail the path contains with added anchor points.

The fewer anchor points there are in a path, the easier it is to edit and manipulate. But to retain much of the detail of the selection, you need to store additional anchor points.

Fig. 11.34

Set the tolerance in the Make Path dialog box to control the smoothness of the path.

To find just the right tolerance on critical projects, you may want to initially store your selection as a channel, and then experiment with a few tolerance values as you convert it to paths—keeping only the one you want and discarding the others, including the channel.

Paths and Other Applications

There are many other applications on the Macintosh platform that support paths. Most of them are drawing or illustration packages, but several 3-D modeling and animation programs use them as well.

Photoshop currently has the ability to read paths that were created in Adobe Illustrator, Adobe Dimensions, and Adobe Streamline. But it can write paths to a format that many other applications recognize and use. Photoshop also can write a special kind of file, called EPS, that contains a *clipping path* (a built-in mask) which page layout programs can greatly benefit from.

Sharing Paths with Other Adobe Programs

Paths created in Illustrator, Dimensions, and Streamline can be copied to the clipboard and pasted into Photoshop. This is currently the only way to import paths into Photoshop. When pasting, Photoshop displays a Paste dialog box that asks if the new path should be added to your image as pixels (and if so, should they be anti-aliased) or stored as paths (see fig. 11.35). Click the appropriate button(s) to specify your choice.

Open the File menu and choose Export, Paths To Illustrator to save paths from Photoshop to an Adobe Illustrator format.

III

Creating and Touching Up

Fig. 11.35

Paths pasted from the clipboard can be rendered as pixels or remain as paths.

In the dialog box, enter the file's name and navigate to the location where you want it to be saved. Choose the path you want to export from the pop-up menu at the bottom of the dialog box (see fig. 11.36). To export all the saved paths at once, choose All Paths from the pop-up menu.

Fig. 11.36

Path export options are displayed in a dialog box.

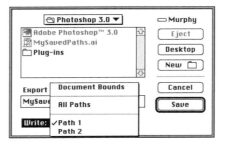

There is another option in the pop-up menu called Document Bounds. Choosing this option—which places a check mark next to it—also writes cropmarks to the Adobe Illustrator file that define the boundary of the current document.

When you open the document from within Adobe Illustrator, you may need to switch to Artwork mode (open the View menu and choose Artwork). All exported paths fill with none and stroke with none, rendering them invisible to most applications.

Defining a Clipping Path

All raster images that export to other applications (such as a page layout program) appear as rectangles. Any white space at the outer edges of an image is recognized as an opaque white and usually obscures anything behind it on the page. Occasionally, you may want to isolate one object from an image without erasing or cropping the rest of the image. To do this, you must create a clipping path.

To begin, use the selection tools or the path tools to create a path that is the shape you want the document to be. If you use the selection tools, you convert your selection to a path. Save the path and name it (see fig. 11.37).

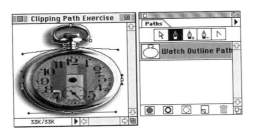

Fig. 11.37

Paths destined to be clipping paths must first be named.

Choose Clipping Path from the Paths Palette Options menu. Choose the path's name from the pop-up menu in the Clipping Path dialog box (see fig. 11.38).

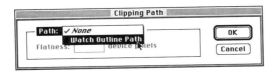

Fig. 11.38

Define the clipping path by choosing its name from the pop-up menu.

Now you must save the file in EPS format. If you have other information in the file, such as channels or additional paths, you may want to use the Save As command so that you won't overwrite your working document. Open the File menu and choose Save (or Save As). Choose EPS from the format pop-up menu and name your file in the directory dialog box. Click Save.

The EPS Format dialog box appears so that you can specify the preview, encoding, and clipping path (see fig. 11.39). If you experience problems printing an exported EPS file, you may need to resave it with an increased flatness (start with numbers between 1 and 10) which affects how dots are mapped to your printer or imagesetter.

When this image is brought into another application that accepts EPS files, the image is transparent outside of the clipping path, instead of an opaque white. In figure 11.40, the image on the left does not have a clipping path, while the image on the right does, isolating the watch face from the rest of the image.

III

Creating and Touching Up

Fig. 11.39

Only the EPS
format supports
clipping paths.

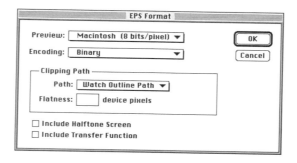

Fig. 11.40

Page layout pro-
grams recognize
when a clipping
path has been
applied.

Where To Go from Here

▶ Chapter 12, "Using Masks and Channels." Because many path operations can be used to make and store selections, a good understanding
of the uses of masks will help you decide when best to use paths or
channels.

▶ Chapter 9, "Selecting Objects in Photoshop." Paths can be used to
supplement or replace some of the selection tools such as the
Marquee, Magic Wand, and Lasso. This chapter describes methods
for adding selections together and subtracting one selection from
another.

Using Masks and Channels

Masks and channels are among Photoshop's most powerful set of tools for manipulating images and creating special effects. You may remember the recent hit movie, *The Mask* starring Jim Carrey. Photoshop masks are not quite the same thing, but they do carry transformational powers similar to Jim Carrey's mask. In fact, the technology used to create *The Mask* is not so different from some of the capabilities you have right in front of you when you use masks and channels in Photoshop.

by Ted Evangelakis

CHAPTER 12

Key Concept: Understanding Masks and Channels

So, what are masks? Essentially, a *mask* is an area of your canvas that is protected. Any area that is masked off cannot be painted, airbrushed, or otherwise modified. Let's say you have an old photograph of your grandfather sitting in a room. You want to colorize him but leave the background in black and white. You can do this by creating a mask of all the areas around him. Then you can add color to his portrait without affecting the background areas at all.

When you learned about making selections in chapter 9, you may not have realized it, but you also learned the basics of creating masks. Essentially, a mask is the opposite of a selection. When you make a selection, the area that is not selected becomes masked—it's literally like putting masking tape all around your selection. This area cannot be affected by any of the paint tools, filters, or other transformational tools in Photoshop. If you want to save a mask for later use, you can save it as an alpha channel.

Channels are used to store image information. There are two types of channels: *color* and *alpha*. Every image has color channels, which are similar to plates in the printing industry. Alpha channels store selections and masks.

Color Channels

Color channels hold the information which builds the color in your images. Because each channel is a 256-color grayscale image, the channel information for a color channel determines the values for the particular color that the channel represents. For example, the Red channel in an RGB image holds the values that are used to determine how much red exists in your color images. When the color channels are combined, Photoshop composites the different values of the color channels to create a color image.

In Photoshop, you can view and edit color channels for CMYK, RGB, or Lab images. If you select Color Channels in the General Preferences dialog box, you also can view those channels in color, but the color information is always based on the 256-color, grayscale values of the channel.

Alpha Channels

When you want to keep a selection that you've created for later use, you can save it into a channel. By doing this, you have a permanent selection that will stay with your document as long as you need it. This saved selection is called an *alpha channel*. It contains the selection and mask information you need to reactivate the selection at a later time. You might, for example, define a complex selection around a few objects in your scene and save that into an alpha channel. When you need to edit that selection again—to change color balance, adjust levels ,and so on—you do not have to re-create the selection from scratch. You simply apply the alpha channel that was generated from the original selection.

Figure 12.1 shows an alpha channel based on the Quick Mask shown in figure 12.4 and the selection shown in figure 12.5. In this illustration, the black area represents the mask and the white area represents the selection.

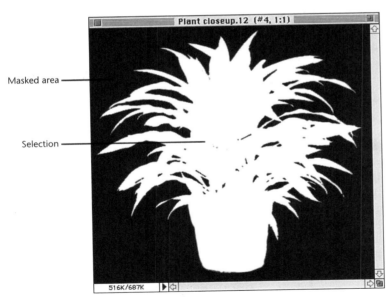

Masked area

Selection

Fig. 12.1

Alpha channel showing mask in black and selection area in white.

III

Creating and Touching Up

Creating a Mask

To create a mask, you need to pick one of the selection tools in the Photoshop Tool palette. You can use the Marquee, the Lasso, or the Magic Wand to make a new selection or modify an existing one. You also can use the Pen tool in the Paths palette to create a selection. Figure 12.2 shows an area that was selected using the Lasso tool.

Fig. 12.2

A selection that was created using the Lasso tool.

Lasso tool

Selected area

Painting and Touching Up Images

After an area has been selected, the masked part of the image is protected. You can begin painting on the area inside the selection without worrying about affecting the masked area. The best way to understand this is through an example:

1. Make a selection using the Lasso tool.

2. Click the Brush tool in the Tool palette.

   If the Brush palette is not visible, select the Window menu, scroll down to Palettes, and choose Show Brushes.

3. Click one of the fat brushes that has a soft edge.

4. Now use your mouse (or tablet) and apply some broad strokes across the selected area. Make sure you cross over into the masked area.

Observe the results. The masked area remains untouched, but the selected area shows the brush strokes. You can see the results in figure 12.3.

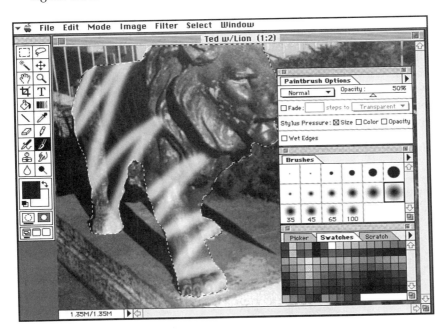

Fig. 12.3

Brush strokes appear in the selection, but not the masked area.

Now that you are comfortable with the idea of masks and selections, it's time to learn more about masks.

Using Quick Masks

Photoshop offers a quick, simple way to create and alter masks. The Quick Mask option, available in the Tool palette, allows you to see exactly what areas are masked by placing a partially opaque color over the masked areas. You can then edit the mask using familiar paint tools like the Paintbrush, Airbrush, and Pencil.

Creating a Quick Mask

Creating a Quick Mask is easy. First, make a selection using one of the standard selection tools. After you finish making your selection, click the Quick Mask mode selector on the Photoshop Tool palette.

When you go into Quick Mask mode, the area that is not selected gets filled with a partially opaque color, indicating that this area is masked (see fig. 12.4). When you are in Quick Mask mode, your selection no longer behaves like a regular selection. This is because you are now *editing the mask*, not the image itself. The tools you normally use to draw or edit your image are now used to edit the mask. Let's take a closer look at this.

Fig. 12.4

The partially opaque areas indicate the masked area of the image.

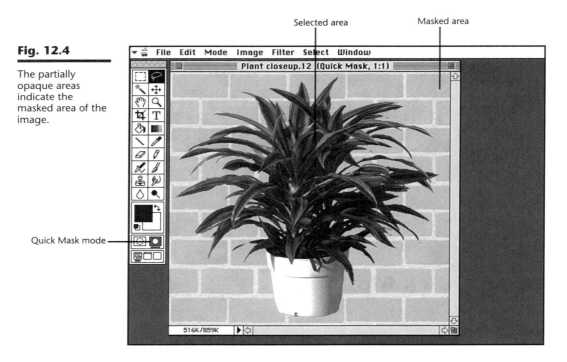

Selected area   Masked area

Quick Mask mode

Adding to a Selection

When you edit your mask in Quick Mask mode, you also are editing your selection. To add to your existing selection, you take away, or remove, part of your mask. To do this, you must select white as your foreground color and paint on the areas you want added to your selection. The mask color is removed from these areas. The process goes like this:

1. When you enter Quick Mask mode, make sure the foreground color is white. If it is not, click the double-headed arrow next to the foreground chip to make the foreground color white.

2. Select one of the painting tools: the Paintbrush, Airbrush, Pencil, Line, Eraser, Smudge, Blur or Sharpen, or Rubber Stamp. See chapters 1 and 8 for a description of these Photoshop tools.

3. Paint your mask in the areas that you want to add to your selection. Notice that the partially opaque color that was there goes away. If you use a subtle tool like Blur or Sharpen, the effect is mild, like a soft feather.

Subtracting from a Selection

Essentially, the process is the opposite of adding to a selection. To subtract from your existing selection, you add to your mask. To do this, you must select black as your foreground color and paint on the areas you want to remove from your selection. The mask color is added to these areas. The process is as follows:

1. When you enter Quick Mask mode, make sure the foreground color is black. If you were previously editing the mask using white, click the double-headed arrow next to the foreground chip to make the foreground color black.

2. Select one of the painting tools: the Paintbrush, Airbrush, Pencil, Line, Eraser, Smudge, Blur or Sharpen, or Rubber Stamp. See chapters 1 and 8 for a description of these Photoshop tools.

3. Paint your mask in the areas that you want to subtract from your selection. Notice that the partially opaque mask color is added to these areas. If you use a subtle tool like Blur or Sharpen, the effect is mild, like a soft feather.

III

Creating and Touching Up

> **Tip**
>
> **Using Quick Masks To Composite Images**
>
> Using your painting tools for Quick Mask editing opens up a world of possibilities. One of these is the ability to create irregularly feathered masks which vary the feather amount, or softness, along the edge of the mask. Using a combination of Airbrush and Paintbrush tools, you can create feathered masks for nearly any application. By helping you create selections with variable feathering, these masks allow you to composite elements from several images in a seamless manner.

Setting Quick Mask Options

The Quick Mask Options dialog box is accessed by double-clicking the Quick Mask mode icon (see fig. 12.5). There are two preference areas available.

Fig. 12.5

The Quick Mask Options dialog box.

First, choose which areas of the image you want overlaid with the partially opaque color—either the masked areas or the selected areas.

Second, choose the color that you want for the overlay by clicking the color swatch. This takes you into a color picker, in which you can select any one of 16.7 million colors. In the opacity box, type in the percentage of opacity to be applied in the overlay areas.

Turning a Quick Mask into a Selection

After you finish editing your mask, you can turn it back into a selection and exit the Quick Mask mode. To do this, simply click the Standard mode icon in the Tool palette. This is located right next to the Quick Mask mode icon. Figure 12.6 shows a Quick Mask turned back into a selection.

Fig. 12.6

Your edited selection appears once again with the marching ants around it.

Standard mode

Selection

After you leave Quick Mask mode, your newly customized selection is available for you to edit in any way you choose. All the Photoshop tools return to their normal way of functioning. You can even take your new selection, which you've labored over for a long time now, and save it as a channel.

Working with Channels

So, now that you know what channels are, you might be wondering how you would use them in your day-to-day work. Let's say, for example, that you are editing an old photograph that has been damaged in several places. You have laboriously gone through the process of defining multiple complex selections that you will need to load throughout the process of restoring the photo —to adjust contrast or brightness levels, to paint on, to fix cracks and dust spots, and so on. Saving each selection into a channel allows you to call that selection up whenever you need to use it. By using channels, you only need to create your selections once.

Photoshop offers several different ways to work with channels. One of the easiest and most efficient ways to deal with channels is to use the Channels palette.

III

Creating and Touching Up

There also are some menu commands in the Select menu that can be used in the process of converting selections into channels and vice versa.

Using the Channels Palette

The Channels palette gives you access to most of Photoshop's channel functions. It is accessed by opening the Window menu and choosing Palette, Show Channels. When you initially open the palette, it is grouped with the Layers and Paths palettes. If you want to separate it from this group, you can click the folder tab at the top, and drag it out to create its own window. Figure 12.7 shows the Channels palette as it appears when you open its window.

Fig. 12.7

The Channels palette showing an RGB image with one alpha channel.

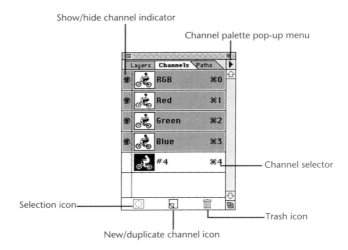

Show/hide channel indicator

Channel palette pop-up menu

Selection icon

New/duplicate channel icon

Channel selector

Trash icon

The Channels Palette Pop-Up

The Channels palette has a series of options available via a pop-up menu at the upper-right corner of the palette. Many of the commands in the pop-up menu are available in the main window of the Channels palette by clicking and dragging icons, but the pop-up menu commands generally have more options.

As you go through the different channel functions in this section, you will learn when it might be preferable to use the pop-up menu commands rather than the click and drag functionality of the Channels palette main window.

The Channels palette pop-up menu is accessed by clicking the small triangle at the upper-right corner of the palette. Figure 12.8 illustrates the pop-up menu.

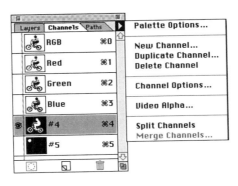

Fig. 12.8

The Channels palette pop-up menu is accessed by clicking the triangle at the upper-right corner of the Channels palette.

There are two preferences that are only available via the Channels palette pop-up menu. These are described below.

▶ *Palette Options.* The Palette Options dialog box allows you to select the size of the thumbnail that displays in the Channels palette. There are three sizes available. You also have the option of showing no thumbnail, which can be beneficial if you have many alpha channels and not much scrolling room. Turning off thumbnails also speeds up Photoshop in general. So, if you don't need to see thumbnails, it might be better to leave them turned off.

▶ *Video Alpha.* Video Alpha is a specialized command that is used with certain 32-bit video cards (for example, TrueVision NuVista, and NuVista+). Geared for video production, this command loads the alpha channel of your choice into the 8-bit mask channel of the video card. This allows you to composite video with computer-generated imagery.

To set your Video alpha channel, choose Video Alpha from the pop-up menu. Then select the channel you want loaded into your graphics card from the pop-up list.

Converting a Selection into a Channel

As you learned earlier, alpha channels are used to store selections for later use. There are two ways to create alpha channels: use the Save Selection option in the Select menu, or use the Selection icon in the Channels palette.

III

Creating and Touching Up

339

To convert a selection into a channel using the Save Selection menu item, follow these steps:

1. Open the Select menu and choose Save Selection. The Save Selection dialog box appears (see fig. 12.9).

Fig. 12.9

The Save Selection dialog box allows you to select a destination channel and a method for creating your new alpha channel.

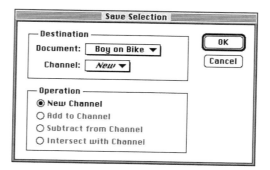

2. Select a Destination from the options in the Save Selection dialog box:

▶ You can choose the Document into which you want to save your selection. The default is the current document, but you also can save your selection into a new document or into another Photoshop file that has the same dimensions as your current document. To select another document, click the pop-up menu and drag to the destination of your choice.

▶ You can choose the channel you want the selection to occupy. The default is to create a new channel. But you also can choose to write over an existing channel. To select an option other than New, click the pop-up menu and drag to the channel you want to copy over.

3. If the destination channel is an existing channel, choose how the current selection will be treated:

▶ *New Channel* disregards what is in the destination channel and creates a new alpha channel defined solely by your current selection.

▶ *Add to Channel* adds the current selection to the destination channel.

▶ *Subtract from Channel* subtracts the current selection from the destination channel.

▶ *Intersect with Channel* keeps only the areas that are common to both the current selection and the destination channel.

To convert a selection into a channel, you also can click the Selection icon in the Channels palette. A new channel appears in the Channels palette.

While the Select menu provides more choices for creating new channels, the Channels palette offers a quick, easy way to create new channels if all you want to do is turn your current selection into a new channel in your current document.

Tip

Using Selections To Modify Channels

The Selection icon allows you to perform some of the same functions that are available in the Save Selection dialog box. To add your current selection to an existing channel, hold the Shift key down while dragging the Selection icon to the channel you want to add it to. To subtract your current selection from an existing channel, hold the Command key (⌘) down while dragging from the Selection icon to the channel you want to subtract from. And to intersect the selection area with an existing channel, hold the Command (⌘) and Shift keys down while dragging from the Selection icon to the destination channel.

Selecting Channels

The Channel Selector in the Channels palette indicates which channels are currently selected for editing. Clicking anywhere on the channel selector highlights the channel and displays it in your image window. If you click the composite color channel (RGB, CMYK, or Lab) for your image, all of the component channels become highlighted and the image is displayed in full color.

You can select multiple channels for viewing and editing. When you select an alpha channel to view in addition to your composite color image, or with other alpha channels, the display of your channels is very similar to a Quick Mask display. A partially opaque color is laid over the masked portion of the image. When you display multiple alpha channels, the different levels of opacity and color assigned to each alpha channel are combined.

To select more than one channel, simply hold down the Shift key while clicking the different channels you want to edit. When multiple channels are selected, any editing you do affects all your channels.

Caution

Editing with Multiple Channels Selected

Be careful when you have multiple channels selected. Anything you do will affect all selected channels. If you're not cautious, you may inadvertently modify a channel without realizing it until it's too late.

Tip

Working with Multiple Channels

Selecting more than one channel to work on allows you to edit image elements spread over several channels at once. If, for example, you want to apply a Noise filter or a Blur filter to channels 5, 7, and 9, you could select those channels by Shift-clicking their channel selectors and then applying the filter. You also could draw with one of the Paint tools on multiple channels. As with many things in Photoshop, the creative possibilities are endless.

Double-clicking the channel selector on an alpha channel brings up the Channel Options dialog box, illustrated in figure 12.10.

Fig. 12.10

The Channel Options dialog box allows you to name your channel and set color options.

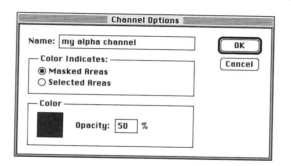

In this dialog box, you can name your alpha channels so that they are easier to reference by following these steps:

1. When you double-click the channel selector, the number of your channel is highlighted in the Name box.

2. To rename the channel, simply type over the number in the Name text box.

There are two other options in the Channel Options dialog box. In the Color Indicates box, you can choose which area of your channel is filled with partially opaque color when that channel is selected for display along with other channels. You can choose either the masked area or the selected area for this option.

The Color box allows you to select a color for the color fill, along with an opacity percentage.

Tip

Rearranging Alpha Channels

If you have multiple alpha channels that you want to rearrange, click the Channel Selector of the channel you want to move, and drag it to its desired location. As you drag, a black highlight bar between channels indicates your current location.

Showing/Hiding Channels

The Show/Hide Channel Indicator is a narrow column on the left side of the Channels palette (see fig. 12.11). This column shows you whether a particular channel is selected for display. It also allows you to select additional channels for display.

If a channel is being displayed, the eye symbol appears in the column. It is possible to have channels selected for viewing and not selected for editing, or selected for editing and not selected for viewing. Figure 12.11 shows an illustration of this possibility. The Blue channel is selected for editing only; alpha channel #4 is selected for editing and viewing; and alpha channel #5 is selected for viewing only.

Why would you choose to select some channels for display but not for editing? Let's say you are working on some screens for use in a video production. You can create a channel that shows rectangles which designate the action and title safe areas of the frame. After you do this, you can select that channel for display only so that your guidelines are visible while you create the screen elements for your video.

Fig. 12.11

The Channels palette showing a combination of viewing and editing possibilities.

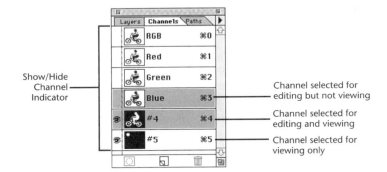

Show/Hide Channel Indicator

Channel selected for editing but not viewing

Channel selected for editing and viewing

Channel selected for viewing only

Remember these rules of thumb as you work with channel selections:

▶ To select a channel for viewing and editing, click the Channel Selector. To select multiple channels, hold down the Shift key while selecting additional channels.

▶ To select a channel *for viewing only*, click the Show/Hide Column. The eye symbol appears in each channel selected for viewing. To select multiple channels *for display only*, hold down the Shift key while selecting additional channels.

▶ To select a channel *for editing only* (not viewing), you must first select it in the normal way using the Channel Selector. Then you can click in the Show/Hide column to remove that channel from the display. When you hide a selected channel, you must have another channel selected before you can use any of Photoshop's tools. When you edit an undisplayed channel, you must be cautious because whatever changes you make to your image affect the undisplayed channel.

▶ You must always have at least one channel displayed. If you try to click the Show/Hide column with only one channel selected for viewing, you will not be able to deselect that channel. You must Shift-click to select additional channels before deselecting the first channel.

Creating New Channels

The New/Duplicate Channel icon at the bottom of the Channels palette allows you to create a new alpha channel for your image. To create a new channel, follow these steps:

1. Click the New Channel icon. The Channel Options dialog box appears.

2. Name your alpha channel and set your preferred options.

3. Click OK.

A new channel is created, and appears in your Channels palette. Whatever channels you had selected previously for viewing and editing are deselected and your new channel appears in the image area, immediately available for editing.

You also can create a new channel by choosing the New Channel option from the Channels palette pop-up menu.

Duplicating Existing Channels

There are many instances where you will want to duplicate an existing channel. A good example of this is when you are creating soft drop shadows for text or other image elements. Usually, you type your text into a new alpha channel (using white as the foreground color). Then you can duplicate the channel and apply an offset and blur to create the drop shadow alpha channel.

This process is very simple using the Channels palette. Drag the Channel Selector of the channel you want to duplicate to the New Channel icon at the bottom of the Channels palette. When the icon is highlighted, release the mouse. You then have a new channel in your palette that is an exact copy of the one you initially selected. The channel is automatically named the same name as the original with the word "copy" appended.

Any channels you had selected previously for viewing and editing are deselected and the duplicate channel appears in the image area, immediately available for editing.

You also can duplicate a new channel using the Duplicate Channel option on the Channels palette pop-up menu:

1. Click the Channels palette pop-up and choose Duplicate Channel. This brings up the Duplicate Channel dialog box shown in figure 12.12.

Fig. 12.12

The Duplicate Channel dialog box allows you to name your Duplicate channel, as well as set its destination.

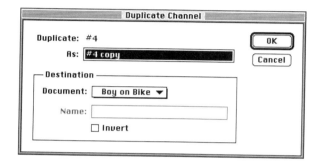

2. The Duplicate Channel dialog box offers several options:

▶ Give your new channel a name by typing over the default name (the name of your current channel with the word "copy" appended) in the As text box.

▶ The default destination is the current document, but you can choose either a new document or another open document from the document pop-up.

▶ If you choose to duplicate your channel into a new document, you have the option of giving your new file a name. Simply type it into the Name text box.

▶ Using the Invert check box, you can invert the alpha channel of the duplicate. Inverting a channel creates a "negative" version of the channel, with black and white values reversed. This is useful if you want to edit areas only outside of the original selection.

Tip

Dragging Channels between Documents

A quick way to copy channels from one document to another is by dragging a channel from the Channels palette to the image area of your destination document. This creates a copy of your source channel in the other document.

Deleting Channels

When you no longer need to keep a channel in your document, you can delete it directly from the Channels palette. The Trash icon at the bottom is used for this purpose.

Drag the channel you want to delete to the Trash icon at the bottom of the Channels palette. When the icon is highlighted, release the mouse, and your channel is deleted.

You can only delete one channel at a time. If you have multiple channels selected, the one that you click and drag is the channel that is deleted.

You also can delete a channel by opening the Channels palette pop-up menu and choosing Delete Channel.

Splitting and Merging Channels

Photoshop offers a set of commands that allows you to split your color or multichannel files into separate files. Why would you want to do this? Well, you might be working on a very large file that needs to be sent to a service bureau for separation. Rather than spring for a high capacity optical drive or DAT, you can separate your file into multiple single channel files that can be placed on lower capacity media (like SyQuest disks). Then, your service bureau can merge the files into one large color file and output the separation.

Splitting Channels

You can separate your Photoshop file into multiple documents using the Split Channels option in the Channels palette pop-up menu. Each channel becomes a one channel document, with the name of the original document appended to the name of the channel. If, for example, you have an RGB file named "Test" with one alpha channel, the Split Channels command will create four files named "Test.Red," "Test.Green," "Test.Blue," and "Test.#4".

Figure 12.13 shows an RGB file before and after being split.

Fig. 12.13

Split Channels divides your multi-channel files into separate files.

Caution

Save Your Document before Splitting Channels

Before you issue the Split Channels command, make sure that you have saved your document. The reason for this is that the Split Channels command does not keep the current document open after it has been split into multiple documents.

Merging Channels

The Merge Channels command allows you to combine channels that have been split using the Split Channels command. You also can use channels other than those generated by the Split Channels command. To do this, you must make sure that the other files are single channel files that have the same dimensions.

Merge Channels allows you to create special effects with channels, or to composite scans created on grayscale scanners using Red, Green, and Blue filters.

To merge channels, you need to begin with either a split file or multiple single channel files. If you have not split a file, you need to create single channel files that have the same dimension as the other files you are planning to merge.

The following steps illustrate how to use the Merge Channels command:

1. Make any of the single channel files active by clicking anywhere in their window.

2. Open the Channels palette pop-up menu and select Merge Channels.

3. In the Merge Channels dialog box, select a mode from the pop-up menu. You have the option of creating an RGB, CMYK, Lab, or Multichannel file.

4. If you are creating a Multichannel file, type in the number of channels that you want in your new document in the Channels box.

5. Click OK.

   The next dialog box that appears is the Merge Mode Channels. Mode indicates the mode of the merged file (RGB, CMYK, etc.).

   Depending on which mode you are merging into, you will have from one to four pop-up menus from which to choose your channel mapping options. In an RGB dialog box, you will have three pop-up menus to set (see fig. 12.14).

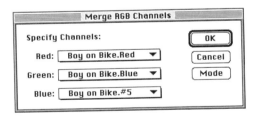

Fig. 12.14

The Merge RGB Channels dialog box, showing the three channel mapping pop-up menus.

6. Select a channel in the Red, Green, and Blue pop-up menus.

7. Click OK and your merged file appears in an untitled window (see fig. 12.15).

III

Creating and Touching Up

Channel mapped to red channel

Channel mapped to green channel

Channel mapped to blue channel

Fig. 12.15

The component channels and the result of the Merge Channels command.

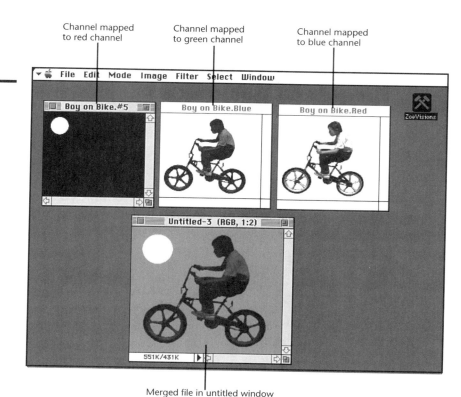

Merged file in untitled window

Converting a Channel into a Selection

When working with channels, keep in mind that your ultimate goal is to use these channels to make selections. Just as there are different ways to turn selections into channels, you have several options when converting a channel into a selection.

There are two basic ways to load channels as a selection: use the Load Selection option in the Select menu, or use the Selection icon in the Channels palette.

To create a selection from a channel using the Load Selection menu item, follow these steps:

1. Open the Select menu and choose Load Selection.

The Load Selection dialog box appears. At this point, you have several options (see fig. 12.16).

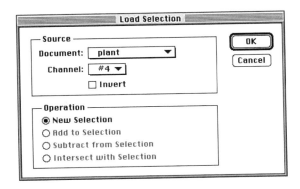

Fig. 12.16

The Load Selection
dialog box allows
you to select an
alpha channel to
turn into a
selection.

2. Select a Source:

▶ Choose the document from which you want to load your selection. The default is the current document, but you also can load
your selection from another document. To select another document, click the pop-up selector and drag to the source file of your
choice.

▶ Select the channel from which you want to load the selection. The
default is the first alpha channel (channel #4), but you can select
any channel in the source document.

3. Select an Operation:

▶ *New Selection.* Disregards what is in the existing selection (if one
exists) and creates a new selection defined solely by the channel
you choose.

▶ *Add to Selection.* Adds the channel to your current selection.

▶ *Subtract from Selection.* Subtracts the channel from your current
selection.

▶ *Intersect with Selection.* Keeps only the areas that are common to
both the channel and the current selection.

Even though the Select menu provides you with more choices for creating
new channels, the Selection icon in the Channels palette offers a quick,
easy way to load selections. To load a selection from a channel using the
Selection icon, drag the channel you want to load from the Channels
palette to the Selection icon. You also can hold down the Option key and
click the channel you want to load. The selection appears in your image
window.

Another method for loading selections that are based on channels 0 through 9 in your current document is to hold down the Option and Command keys (⌘) while pressing the number of the channel that you want to load. Again, the selection appears in your image window.

Tip

Using Channels To Modify Selections

The Selection icon allows you to perform some of the same functions that are available in the Load Selection dialog box. To add a channel to your current selection, hold the Shift key down while dragging the channel to the Selection icon. To subtract a channel from your current selection, hold down the Command key (⌘) while dragging the channel to the Selection icon. To intersect the channel with the current selection, hold down the Command (⌘) and Shift keys while dragging the channel to the Selection icon.

Working with Alpha Channels

Now that you know all about alpha channels, selections, and quick masks, you can begin applying that knowledge to your everyday Photoshop work. As you know, everything you do with these elements will eventually be used to create selections that can be used to perform a variety of tasks—colorizing photographs, collaging multiple image elements, and making color or level adjustments to certain regions of your image.

Often, when working with alpha channels, you will find it necessary to use some of Photoshop's tools directly on a channel to perform a given function. You might, for example, want to enter text directly into an alpha channel so that you can position it precisely before applying it to your image. Or, if you are creating a 3-D button for a presentation, you might apply the emboss filter to an alpha channel to give it depth.

The manipulations you perform in your alpha channels often can be as complex as the ones you use in your image window. But when you are toiling over your alphas, remember that the final results always appear in your composite image (RGB, CMYK, etc.). No matter how complex or beautiful your alpha channels are, it is always the final picture that tells the story. It is the application of the alphas, rather than the alphas themselves, that is most important to your final image.

Saving Channels with Your Document

When you want to save your alpha channels along with your file, you have several options. First, open the File menu and choose Save As to open the Save As dialog box.

▶ If you have multiple alpha channels that you want to save with the file, you can select the Photoshop 3, Photoshop 2.0, Raw, or TIFF formats from the pop-up format selector.

▶ If you have a single alpha channel that you want to save with your file, you can select the Photoshop 3, Photoshop 2.0, PICT File, PICT Resource, PIXAR, Raw, Targa, or TIFF formats from the pop-up format selector.

Using Channel Calculations

One of the most powerful methods of controlling channel information in Photoshop is through the Channel Calculation commands. Channel Calculation allows you to take two channels in any two same-size/same-resolution documents and perform mathematical calculations based on the pixel information in those channels. The result of these calculations is placed in a user-selectable channel.

For example, let's say you create a drop shadow for some text that you've typed into an alpha channel. Then you want to carve your original selection out of that drop shadow. That's when the Calculation commands can be invaluable. In figure 12.17, the image on the left is the original text entry in an alpha channel; the image in the middle is the result of duplicating that channel and applying a blur and an offset; and the image on the right is the result of a channel calculation—subtracting the left channel from the middle channel.

Fig. 12.17

An example of the calculation command using the subtract para-meter. The image on the right is the result.

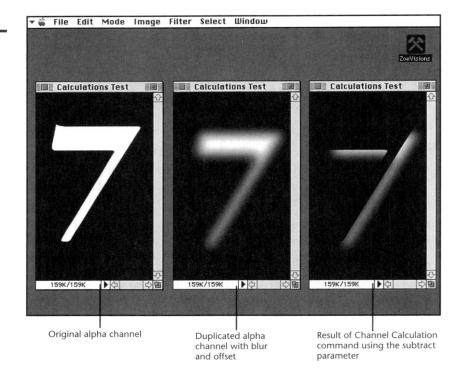

Original alpha channel

Duplicated alpha channel with blur and offset

Result of Channel Calculation command using the subtract parameter

The way channel calculations work is by taking the pixel values from each selected channel and combining them based on the Blending mode you choose. Each pixel in a channel is assigned a value from 0 (black) to 255 (white). The mathematical values of these pixels are what you manipulate when you perform a channel calculation.

Using channel calculations allows you to create special effects channels that can be used to generate glows, shadows, 3-D elements, and many other visual effects.

In Photoshop, there are three menu items which deal with channel calculations: Duplicate, Apply Image, and Calculate.

Duplicate does not really perform any calculations on channels; it simply makes a duplicate copy of your current document, including all the alpha channels. This can be very useful if you are experimenting with different effects and want to keep an unaltered version of your current document active. When you issue the Duplicate command, the duplicate copy is not saved until you issue the Save command.

Apply Image and *Calculations* are similar commands. Both are used to perform calculations on two channels. The primary differences between *Apply Image* and *Calculations* are that *Apply Image* always applies the calculation to the currently selected channel, and it can work on composite channels (RGB, CMYK and Lab). With *Calculations,* you can select any two channels for your calculation, but you cannot select a composite channel.

How To Use Channel Calculations

The first time you open up the Calculations dialog box, you might be a little overwhelmed by all the pop-up menus and check boxes. This section goes through those pop-up menus, one by one, and helps you learn how to navigate this complex, but powerful feature. Before you use the Channel Calculations command, make sure you have one or more same-size/same-resolution documents open. To preview your calculation as you click through the options, click the Preview check box. The following steps outline the process of performing a channel calculation.

1. Open the Window menu and choose Palettes, Show Channels. This allows you to see a list of all the channels in your current document.

2. Open the Image menu and choose Calculations. The dialog box shown in figure 12.18 appears.

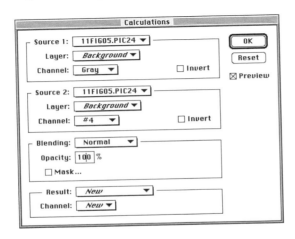

Fig. 12.18

The Calculations dialog box, showing the Source channel pop-up menus, the Blending pop-up menu, and the Result pop-up menu.

III

Creating and Touching Up

3. Make selections from the following options:

▶ *Source 1.* Click here to select the source image from a pop-up menu of all open documents that match the size/resolution of your current document.

▶ *Layer.* Choose the source layer from the next pop-up menu. If layers exist, you have the option of merging layers for the purpose of the channel calculation.

▶ *Channel.* Select the channel on which you want to perform the calculation.

▶ *Invert.* Selecting the Invert check box allows you to invert the channel values.

▶ *Source 2.* Select the second of two channels that you will be combining and also the Layer, Channel, and Invert options.

▶ *Blending.* Here you set the blending parameters that tell Photoshop how you want to combine the channels. A description of the different parameters is detailed in the next section.

▶ *Opacity.* Type in the value you want to give the Source 1 channel (the value you type in applies *only* to Source 1).

▶ *Mask.* If you don't want to use a third source as a mask, leave the Mask check box deselected. If you select the Mask check box, the Mask, Layer, and Channel pop-up menus appear. You also have the choice of inverting the mask by selecting the Invert check box.

▶ *Result.* Select the result document. This can either be an existing document or a new document.

▶ *Channel.* Select the result channel. This can either be an existing channel or a new channel. The result also can be placed into a selection. If you choose Selection, the results aren't placed into a channel.

Channel Calculation Parameters

When you are defining your calculation parameters in the Blending section of the dialog box, several options are available to you. These are similar to the Fill options and some of the brush modes:

▶ *Normal.* Combines the two channels based only on the opacity value typed. If the opacity is set at 100 percent, the result is identical to source 1; if the opacity is 0 percent, the result is identical to source 2. Any values in between result in varying degrees of overlay between source 1 and source 2.

▶ *Multiply.* Multiplies the pixel values of the two source channels and divides the operation by 255. This makes the resulting image darker than the source channels. The effect is similar to laying two positive transparencies over each other on a light box.

▶ *Screen.* Multiplies the inverse of the pixel values of the two source channels. This makes the resulting image lighter than the source channels. The effect is similar to sandwiching two color negatives into an enlarger and printing the image.

▶ *Overlay.* This is really a combination of Multiply and Screen. The highlight and shadow values of the channels are kept as close to the original channels as possible. The other values are mixed according to the opacity value set.

▶ *Soft Light.* Again, this is a combination of Multiply and Screen. The values of the channels are mixed as if a diffused light is shining through them.

▶ *Hard Light.* Combines Multiply and Screen, but the values of the channels are mixed as if a bright spotlight is shining through them.

▶ *Darker.* This calculation compares the pixel values in each of the two channels and places the darker of the two pixels into the result channel.

▶ *Lighter.* Compares the pixel values in each of the two channels and places the lighter of the two pixels into the result channel.

▶ *Add.* Adds the pixel values of the two channels and places the resulting value into the result channel. Using Add is a good way to add selections to existing channels.

There are two value boxes in the Add dialog box. You can set a scale value from 1.000 to 2.000, and you can set an offset value ranging from –255 to 255. The results of the Add calculation are divided by the scale amount, and then the offset value is added or subtracted from

III

Creating and Touching Up

357

this figure. The scale value darkens the image as you go from the lower to the higher value. The offset value lightens the image if the number is positive and darkens the image if the number is negative.

▶ *Subtract.* Subtracts the pixel values of the source 1 channel from the values in the source 2 channel and places the resulting value into the result channel.

Just like the Add calculation, there are two value boxes. You can set a scale value from 1.000 to 2.000, and you can set an offset value ranging from –255 to 255. The results of the Subtract calculation are divided by the scale amount, and then the offset value is added or subtracted from this figure. The scale value darkens the image as you go from the lower to the higher value. The offset value lightens the image if the number is positive and darkens the image if the number is negative.

▶ *Difference.* Compares the pixel values in two channels and returns only the values that are different to the result channel.

Where To Go from Here

▶ Chapter 9, "Selecting Objects in Photoshop." Since channels get their start in life as selections, this chapter gives you all the tools you'll need to master the art of creating selections.

▶ Chapter 17, "Creating Special Effects with Video." Learn how to create perfect masks for working with video production software. This chapter uses many of the principles you have learned in "Using Masks and Channels."

▶ Chapter 18, "Creating Special Effects with Channels." This chapter goes in depth into the world of channel operations. The base knowledge you acquired in "Using Masks and Channels" will help you explore the world of special effects.

PART IV

Working with Color

Understanding Color

I f all your work is designed for screen view, you can skip this chapter; what you see on-screen is what you get. However, if you ultimately want to have images from the screen printed on any output device, this chapter is essential. Working in color begins with understanding the various color models and modes supported in Adobe Photoshop, how these models work together, and when to use one over the other. The biggest variable, and most uncontrollable, in digital imaging is obtaining on your monitor the colors that you will get on an output device.

by Ted Padova

CHAPTER 13

This chapter covers understanding the various color models, changing color modes, and calibrating color for specific output devices. Calibration is one of the most important tasks to achieve in Photoshop. Before you can understand and perform calibrations, you must first understand color and how it is represented on the computer screen.

Key Concept:
Your Computer Monitor Doesn't Match Printing Devices

The first basic principle to remember is that your print-out will never exactly match your monitor, regardless of the device from which the output was generated. In today's technology, you cannot expect exact replication of color values. But what about color calibration systems? Won't they match the monitor view to printouts? Unfortunately, with all the variables to control, exact matching is not possible regardless of the calibration system used.

Stop and think about the human factor alone. One hundred people will interpret 100 shades of purple in slight variances with no consensus of opinion. There will be differences of opinion regarding color matching between individuals because we all see color slightly different. Think of adjustments made to a television set. One person may adjust the color or tint knob and feel the flesh tones are exactly as they should be; while others will make some different adjustments and believe their settings to be perfect. Achieving exact color matching is nearly impossible between individuals viewing the same device.

Add another variable which considers the differences between the way a color monitor projects color and how printed color is perceived. For a single individual to match color on the screen to a printed piece is nearly impossible, let alone the comparison judged by two or more individuals. Look at the variances between monitors. Twenty monitors connected to the same CPU will display slight differences. Even monitors identical in manufacturer and model will display slight differences. Combine this variable with the different ways color is projected between the monitor and printed piece, and the issue becomes more complicated.

Computer monitors display color by projecting light through a phosphor glow in a glass tube. The signals projected are RGB (Red, Green, and Blue). When the intensity of all three colors is at maximum (100 percent of each color) you perceive the resultant color as white. When no light is transmitted from all three guns, the color is black. The computer monitor uses an *additive color* system. As more light is added from each of the three guns, you notice the color change in value.

Offset printing uses a CMYK (Cyan, Magenta, Yellow, and Black) color model. You start with, let's say, a white color of the paper which projects light at full intensity and you perceive it as white. As you subtract from this light by absorbing it, i.e. adding more ink, the white becomes more obscure. No ink applied to paper reveals the paper color, and 100 percent of all inks results in Black. The printed piece is a *subtractive color* system. The process is reverse from the monitor display.

Combine the variable of the various modes available in Photoshop and adjustments applied to those modes together with channel adjustments, and the lid comes off your comparison. In addition, printing inks may vary with mixtures, absorption will be different between papers and roller pressure, and dot gain on printing presses will vary.

These variables put us into an infinite realm of possibilities which will display slight variances of the way color appears from the monitor to the printing press.

Color output devices are no different from printing presses. The color in the ribbons will change, CMYK devices will not translate Pantone colors precisely, and you still have to contend with the differences between the RGB and CMYK modes. Additionally, RGB devices, such as film recorders, will vary with calibrations and film or media types.

If you have all these variables to consider, how do you deal with working on digital images and predictable color results when you go to printing devices? There are several issues to understand and try to control:

▶ Understand there will be variances between the computer monitor and the printed piece, regardless of the device printing the image. With this in mind, attempt to bring the monitor view into a *ballpark* range of predictable color.

▶ Calibrate for every printing device. Run tests on all the devices used. Accept the fact that there will be costs incurred in running the tests, but that they will be necessary to create guides and formulas to be used for each job. Also be aware that this calibration might be different for different output devices and will change over time due to monitor aging.

▶ Always specify color for process separations from a Pantone Process color chart and not the computer screen. Recognize the fact that the computer monitor will always lie to you and you cannot trust the values displayed.

▶ When using Pantone PMS colors or any other matching system, realize the spot colors cannot be accurately displayed on CMY or CMYK color printing devices. Use care in showing color proofs to clients where spot colors will appear, and offer a disclaimer by showing the spot color swatch noting that it will replace the values displayed on the color proof.

Before you calibrate monitors and printing devices, you need to understand the color models used by Adobe Photoshop.

Color Models

The term *color models* is a means of explaining how colors relate to each other and what happens when they are combined. In early school years, we discover color relationships by adding one color value to another to produce a third color. In simplistic terms, Red + Yellow = Orange; Yellow + Blue = Green; and Red + Blue = Purple. Our early childhood years of learning these color relationships are a foundation for understanding more complex issues related to the many color models available to us today.

Rather than understand the science of color theory, it is important to understand there are many color models available because one model does not provide for all the relationships that exist. The RGB and CMYK models are good examples of systems used for specific purposes. The RGB model is used for monitor and television displays and the CMYK model is used for offset printing, desktop color printers, and like devices.

Photoshop has a number of color models from which to choose and each has its own particular uses and attributes. Understanding the models will be your first step in being able to produce accurate color on output devices.

RGB Color

Images acquired through desktop scanners that scan color produce RGB files. You first view the image in an RGB mode and often work in this mode before converting it for printing. RGB color can be displayed on your monitor in 24- bit mode, which produces a range of 16.7 million different color values. RGB is a three-channel color mode with 8-bits of color for each of the three RGB channels.

When looking at color models, it is important to know the channels used to represent the image. Color values are stored in separate channels and, when superimposed, the composite view displays the complete comple- ment of color represented in the image. You can edit images in the composite view or in independent channels. You can control how to view each channel in the General Preferences dialog box (see fig. 13.1). There's an option to view each channel in color or grayscale. If the Color Channels in Color check box is selected, the respective channels will display in red, green, and blue for an RGB image. In general though, it is a bad idea to view channels in color because your eyes see each color with different sensitiv- ity. If you view channels as grayscales, you get a more accurate idea of the brightness values in the channels.

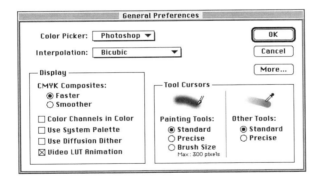

Fig. 13.1

The General Preferences dialog box shows Color Channels in Color disabled.

For most editing purposes, it is best to display the channels in grayscale. The display of color channels does not affect the composite view which remains in color. It merely makes it easier to perform many editing functions. Figure 13.2 shows the Channels palette with the composite image and the three separate RGB channels.

IV

Working with Color

Fig. 13.2

The Channels palette displays the color composite image and three RGB channels in grayscale.

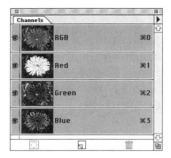

Each of these channels is semi-transparent and can be thought of as an overlay. When plastic sheets are placed atop each other and percentages of color lay on top of another color, additional colors are produced. In effect, this is what happens in Photoshop when you view a composite image made up from several channels.

One advantage of the RGB mode is that it provides for full advantage of Photoshop's tools, palettes, and features. Other modes may not take advantage of some features, or may not be able to export the file in some formats. RGB, on the other hand, provides maximum opportunities for working on and saving files.

CMYK Color

CMYK color is the mode used for process color printing. Photographic images displayed on-screen are converted to the four basic process colors of cyan, magenta, yellow, and black to produce a full color spectrum on the printing press. If it were not for process color printing, we might need a printing press stretching from Los Angeles to Denver to print all the separate colors on individual heads of the press. Fortunately, converting to these primary color values yields a color spectrum by mixing percentages of each value.

CMYK has a major limitation when compared to the RGB color model. The number of reproducible colors in CMYK falls far short of the number of colors available in the RGB mode.

There are colors in the RGB range that cannot be printed. Non-reproducible colors are typically referred to as being out of gamut. A discussion of color gamut is covered later in this chapter in the section "Understanding Color Gamuts." Likewise, there are CMYK values that cannot appear on-screen. It is not possible, for example, to view 100 percent cyan on the computer monitor.

CMYK images are four channel documents with each of the CMYK values displayed in separate channels. Like the RGB images noted previously, overlaying the channels produces the composite view. Photoshop files increase in size according to the number of channels and/or layers created in the document. Therefore, CMYK images will always be larger file sizes than the same document in an RGB mode. For this reason, it may be more desirable to work on an image in RGB, especially with large images. All tasks performed on a three channel file will complete faster than the four channel file. To view and select individual channels, open the Window menu and choose Palettes, Show Channels. Figure 13.3 shows a CMYK image and the four individual Cyan, Magenta, Yellow, and Black channels.

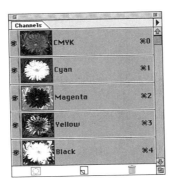

Fig. 13.3

The Channels palette displays the color composite image and four CMYK channels in grayscale.

Working in RGB mode can be a problem if colors applied in the image are not reproducible on CMYK devices or offset printing. Photoshop provides a means of viewing the CMYK color mode while still in an RGB format. Open the Mode menu and choose CMYK Preview to see the color as it translates to CMYK from RGB mode (see fig. 13.4). This means all colors applied will remain in the CMYK range while the file is still in RGB.

Fig. 13.4

Access CMYK Preview from the Mode menu.

Lab Color

In 1931, the Commission Internationale de L'Éclairage (CIE) established a color mode intended to represent all color based on visual perception. Any color in the universe that can be visually perceived is defined mathematically so the colors can exist without regard to any device. As an international standard, the Lab mode is often used to port images between different systems supporting the mode.

Lab color documents are three channel files. The first channel represents the lightness of the image, often referred to as *luminance*. The other two channels control chroma, which consist of the *a* channel for control of the range between green to magenta, and the *b* channel for control of the range of color between blue to yellow. As with other color modes, you can edit a channel individually. In the case of the Lab mode, the lightness, or luminance, of the image can be adjusted without interfering with the color values (see fig. 13.5).

Fig. 13.5

The Lab mode with Lightness and the *a* and *b* channels displayed.

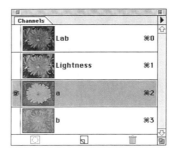

Another advantage of the Lab color mode is that you can save a file from this mode and print it directly to PostScript Level 2 printers. Both EPS and TIFF formats are supported from this mode; therefore, the color can be preserved in its mathematical representation which is independent of any printing device. Theoretically, if the equipment is properly calibrated, the color should be as close to true as possible, regardless of the device imaging the file.

Spot Colors

Photoshop supports a number of color palettes for spot color selection. The most popular is the Pantone Matching System (PMS). When spot colors are applied to an image, the colors are converted to the current mode of the document. Spot colors cannot remain as a spot value in either an RGB or CMYK document. Additionally, spot colors cannot be printed as spot color separations. When the spot colors are used in duotone, tritone, and quadtone images, a mixture of the values will appear similar to the example of overlays previously noted. In other words, each spot color will mix with other spot colors and appear closer to a process separation than to a spot separation (see fig. 13.6).

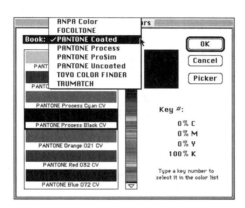

Fig. 13.6

Spot color books available in Photoshop.

For screen printer separations and five or six color jobs, the way Photoshop behaves has always been a problem. Photoshop can only separate four colors. If a six color separation for a silk screener is needed, Photoshop cannot separate all six colors. A third-party plug-in marketed by In Software, called PlateMaker, solves the problem. The plug-in imports or exports color separations from CMYK images and additional colors converted to channels in a DCS 2.0 format. When saved, the file will create the DCS separations into the number defined in the file. This can be four color CMYK with additional channels masking areas for spot colors, spot varnishes, foil stamping, embossing, and so on. Another third-party plug-in producing equally reliable results for multiple color separations is PhotoSpot from Second Glance.

Although Spot color is not a separate mode, it is important to know how the color and printing are treated in order to convert it to the proper mode.

HSB and HSL

Previously, Photoshop 2.0 had a separate mode for displaying HSB color. The HSB mode was eliminated in Photoshop 2.5 with the introduction of the Lab color mode. As yet, HSB is not an available mode in Photoshop 3. As a response to the user community for converting files to the HSB mode, a plug-in was developed to provide for RGB to HSB/HSL conversions and vice versa (see fig. 13.7). The plug-in can be downloaded from many BBS services and works with Photoshop 3.

Fig. 13.7

RGB file converted to HSB with HSB/HSL plug-in.

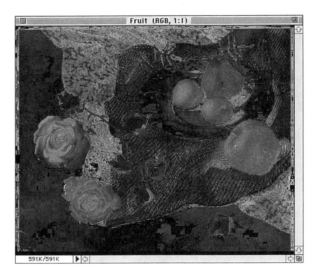

HSB is a three channel mode representing Hue, Saturation, and Brightness. The *Hue* is the color in the image; for example, red, pink, blue, and so on. *Saturation* is a level of gray measured between 0 and 255. When saturation is increased, gray is removed; and when saturation is reduced, gray is added to the image. *Brightness* is measured by reflectance from a color. Intuitively, you know images low in brightness appear flat or dull. HSL, likewise is a three channel image representing Hue, Saturation, and Luminance. *Luminance* controls the brightness values in the image.

Specifying colors in HSB/HSL modes is advantageous over the RGB modes because HSB/HSL modes come closer to human perception of color than do RGB modes. The colors represented are more distinguishable than colors viewed in RGB. To see the relationships between the HSB/HSL values, open the Preferences menu and choose Apple Picker (see fig. 13.8). You can also click on the foreground color in the color selector from the Toolbox to bring up the Picker. From this point, the button noting More Choices reveals color representation in either RGB or HSL color. When the HSL icon is selected, you can make adjustments to the Hue, Saturation, and Lightness.

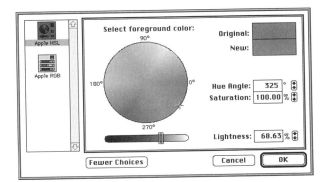

Fig. 13.8

Apple Color Picker
displaying HSL
color controls.

Moving the + symbol around the color wheel provides an understanding
of how the adjustments affect color. As the cursor is moved around the
wheel, the color changes; and as it is moved into the center, more gray is
added. These adjustments relate to Hue and Saturation, respectively. The
lightness slider below the color wheel adjusts the luminance and gives a
brighter or darker appearance to the new color.

Indexed Color

Indexed color has many useful advantages for specific purposes. An
indexed color image is a single channel document (see fig. 13.9). Although
the image appears in color, the single channel file size is much smaller
than any of the three or four channel modes. This makes indexed color
images ideal for multimedia and presentation programs viewed on-screen.

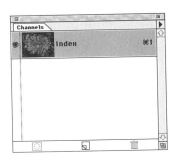

Fig. 13.9

An indexed color
single channel
image.

Indexed color images are reduced to 8-bits when converted, and there are a number of choices available during the conversion process to decide how the 8-bit, 256 color range will be displayed. This is discussed in more detail in the next section, "Converting between Color Modes."

To display various indexed color images, methods of dithering options are available. Indexed color images are used to view color on 8-bit monitors and to bring consistent viewing across a broad range of monitors. For example, a video presentation displayed in RGB mode on 8-bit, 16-bit, and 24-bit monitors appears differently on each monitor. 24-bit is obviously the best quality view. Indexed color images, because they display the same number of bits (usually 8), appear the same across all monitors. This mode can add consistency to viewing presentations on-screen independent of the monitor display.

Converting between Color Modes

All Photoshop images contain channels to represent the color information in the document. The simplest image form is a bitmap file with a single channel. RGB and CMYK documents have three and four channels, respectively, to describe their color information. When images are converted from one mode to another, there may be a loss of color or shifts in color ranges. In the conversion from one mode to another, all layers are flattened and the composite image is represented with only the channel information. Once a mode has been changed and color is lost from the image—when converting from RGB to Grayscale or CMYK, for example—it cannot be regained. Conversion can fortunately be reversed with the Undo command.

Mode conversions are made to prepare an image for printing or display devices. An image may be scanned in RGB and then converted to CMYK for printing; or, the RGB image may be converted to indexed color for video presentations. In addition to preparation for display or printing, images may be converted to apply special design effects. Many interesting image compositions can be made from overlaying a converted image over the original. Regardless of how the mode conversions are made, it is important to understand what happens to the image during the conversion process and what uses will be applied to the converted documents.

Bitmap Mode

Bitmaps are the simplest document form in Photoshop. The format was introduced on the Macintosh with MacPaint when the computer was first sold in January 1984. By today's standards, original MacPaint bitmap files are crude and much less sophisticated than bitmaps used in Adobe Photoshop. Whereas MacPaint files can only attain resolutions of 72 ppi (pixels per inch), Photoshop bitmaps can hold much higher resolutions that are ideal for line art scans. Bitmaps are 1-bit displays with black and white values only. When the file is converted from images with color, all color information is stripped, leaving the black-and-white values to form the bitmap image.

To convert an image to bitmap, the document must be in a grayscale mode. If RGB or CMYK images are to be converted to bitmap, they must first be converted to grayscale, and then to bitmap. When converting a grayscale image to bitmap, Photoshop provides several options to describe how the converted image will appear. To set bitmap options, open the Mode menu and choose Bitmap. The Bitmap dialog box appears (see fig. 13.10).

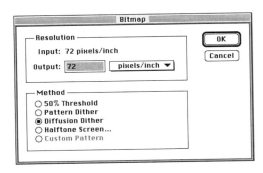

Fig. 13.10

The dialog box appears when you convert from grayscale to bitmap.

Here, you can specify the output resolution. If you specify the output as 200 ppi, the document will appear to become larger in physical size. Open a grayscale image at 72 ppi and convert it to bitmap with output resolution set to 200 ppi (see fig. 13.11). Notice the image magnification. After examining the image size, you'll notice that the physical dimensions are identical to the size before conversion. Photoshop displays the new document at the higher pixel density which only appears magnified.

Fig. 13.11

A view of a bitmap image after it was resampled at 200 ppi.

> **Tip**
>
> **Bitmaps Take Advantage of Interpolated Resolutions**
>
> When a bitmap is converted from grayscale and specified at higher resolutions, it will be interpolated and not true or optical resolution. When dealing with bitmap images, feel free to use interpolated values. Scanning line art, especially, will take advantage of interpolated resolution. Always scan line art at the highest interpolated value. Bitmaps, unlike grayscale or color images, should try to match output resolutions of printing devices.

In addition to output resolutions, the bitmap conversion process permits you to define the type of dithering to appear in the image. *Dithering* is a technique where Photoshop presents an illusion of smoothing tones in color or black-and-white images. In the case of the bitmap, all pixels are black and white. Dithering displays the image with an appearance of gray tones. There are many dithering options available during the bitmap conversion.

50% Threshold

The first dithering option in the bitmap dialog box is the 50% Threshold. Using Threshold will, in essence, be an absence of dithering. Threshold eliminates all gray values in an image and renders it in distinct black and white. Gray values are measured from 0, which is white, to 255, which is black. All gray tones fall between these two ranges; the midpoint is 128. Choosing the 50% Threshold from the bitmap dialog box will evaluate all pixels in the document, and those with values of less than 128 will be converted to white. Values above 128 will be converted to black. The result, as illustrated in figure 13.12, is a black-and-white image of high contrast.

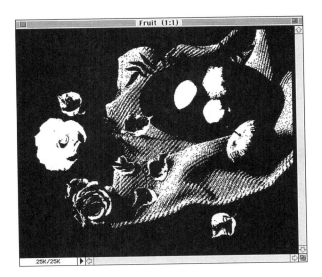

Fig. 13.12

A bitmap conversion with 50% Threshold.

The same result will occur on a grayscale image when you choose Threshold. To choose the Threshold command, open the Image menu and choose Map, Threshold. When 128 is entered in the Threshold dialog box, the image will appear exactly the same as the 50% Threshold feature in the bitmap dialog box (see fig. 13.13).

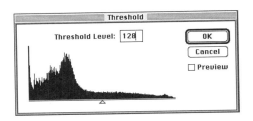

Fig. 13.13

When the Threshold Level is set to 128, the result will be identical to using 50% Threshold in the Bitmap dialog box.

The advantage of using the Threshold setting is that the control can be set to any of the 255 values, and it is not limited to a single setting of 128. As the slider is moved, all pixels below the new value will be rendered white and all pixels above that value will be rendered black.

Pattern Dither

Pattern Dither is similar to what you may have seen displayed on black-and-white monitors, such as the early Mac Plus and SE computers. The dithering process is a geometric organization of the pixels to simulate gray tones. On black-and-white monitors that cannot display gray values, the illusion of creating grays is performed by this dithering. Pattern dither bitmaps can simulate the grays on non-PostScript printers. Dot matrix printers, for example, have difficulty representing gray tones and the printed output is similar to what you might see on a black-and-white monitor. With a pattern dither image, the printer will reproduce an image with an appearance of gray values similar to what is viewed on-screen (see fig. 13.14).

Fig. 13.14

A bitmap with a Pattern Dither.

Diffusion Dither

Whereas Pattern Dither has an appearance of an obvious screen pattern, the Diffusion Dither is a more pleasing view with a film grain look. The dithering process begins at the upper-left corner of the image where the color value is assessed. Any value above the middle gray (128) is changed to white. Values below the middle gray are changed to black. As the conversion works through the image, adjacent pixels are evaluated and converted with reference to the first pixel value. The result is a more desirable dither than that produced with the Pattern Dither option. The only control that the user can exercise is changing the first pixel value. If the first pixel is white, it can be changed to black and vice versa. By starting with a white pixel, the image will appear slightly darker than starting with a black pixel.

Figure 13.15 shows the same image with a Diffusion Dither applied to both images. The image on the left has a black pixel in the upper-left corner, the one on the right has a white pixel in the upper-left corner. The image on the right appears slightly darker than the one on the left.

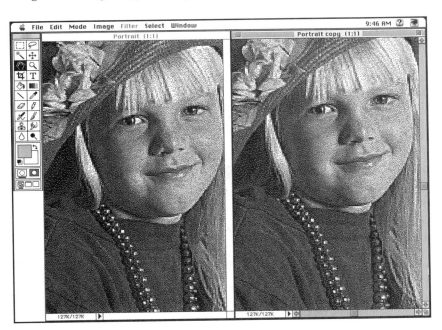

Fig. 13.15

Diffusion Dither has been applied to both of these images. The image on the left started with a black pixel, the image on the right started with a white pixel.

Halftone Screen

The Halftone Screen option in the Bitmap dialog box creates a halftone look to the image with various screen and frequency controls while displayed on the monitor. Halftoning is usually reserved for files output to PostScript devices where the halftone effects are applied while printing.

For non-PostScript devices, simulated halftones with different frequency values can be created. To control the frequency and dot shape for printing to non-PostScript printers, select the frequency from the dialog box after the Halftone Screen option is selected (see 13.16).

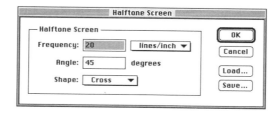

There are several choices for the dot shape from the Shape pop-up menu. The frequency is user-definable between the ranges 1.000 and 999.999. For screen view, there will be no discernible differences between 40 and 999.999. Obvious changes will be visible below 30 lines per inch (lpi). Figure 13.17 illustrates a cross-shaped dot at 20 lpi. At 20 lpi, the dot sizes are large enough to display the dot shape used in the halftone process.

Fig. 13.17

When low values of frequencies are used, the dot sizes will be large and visible.

Custom Pattern

The Custom Pattern option in the Bitmap dialog box provides infinite opportunities to apply textures and pattern effects to an image. In order to properly use this feature, a pattern needs to be defined. Patterns can be any Photoshop image. Some patterns ship with Photoshop 3 and are placed in the Photoshop folder in a sub folder called Goodies; within this folder is another called Brushes & Patterns. The PostScript Patterns folder residing in Brushes & Patterns has a number of Adobe Illustrator drawings that can be opened in Photoshop. When opening an Illustrator EPS file, the size and resolution can be determined in a dialog box which permits Photoshop to convert Illustrator lines and curves to pixels or dots. The conversion of object oriented art from programs like Illustrator to pixel based programs like Photoshop is known as *rasterizing* the image.

Patterns can be full size, so the pattern and image where the pattern will be applied have a 1:1 ratio. In this case, the pattern will appear similar to overlaying one image atop the other. Smaller sizes will create repeating pattern effects. Textures such as marble, wood, and paper can be used as patterns as well as icons and figures. Virtually anything opened in Photoshop can be defined as a pattern.

After the image appears as a Photoshop document, marquee a section or the entire image and choose Define Pattern from the Edit menu. Note that Define Pattern will not be available until a selection is active. Once the pattern is defined, the conversion to bitmap and selection of Custom Pattern will apply what was defined to the bitmap. Figure 13.18 illustrates a custom pattern effect applied to a bitmap. In this case, the Undulating Dot Grain pattern from the Photoshop PostScript patterns was used.

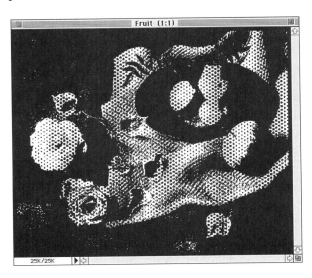

Fig. 13.18

A Custom Pattern was applied to this bitmap during the conversion from grayscale.

Bitmaps are used for two purposes. First, line art images can be preserved in Bitmap mode to either print or use as a template in an illustration program. The advantage of using a bitmap is that the image occupies less space than a grayscale image. Bitmap images are approximately 25% the size of a grayscale image. If a line art scan reaches 1200 ppi or more, the storage requirement for grayscale is much greater than the same image saved from the bitmap mode with no difference visible in image quality.

Secondly, bitmaps can be saved with transparent whites so that all the white appearing in an image is masked out. This is particularly useful when exporting icons and logos to layout programs where a screen or gradient is used in the background. Without masking the white areas of the image, the white pixels will appear and block the underlying background color.

Tip

Use Transparent Whites over Clipping Paths

When line art images are used, always save the file as EPS with Transparent Whites enabled when the image needs to be masked in the white areas. Creating clipping paths as an alternative may present severe printing problems. Images with clipping paths increase in difficulty according to the number of points plotted on a path. The higher the number of points, the more difficult the file will image.

Bitmap files also can be used for design effects with color and grayscale images. In this case, the bitmap will be included in a file using another mode. As an example of using bitmap images with an RGB image, let's presume you want to apply a film grain look to a color image. Using the noise filter will not create the same effect as the Diffusion Dither process explained earlier. Some third-party filters, like Aldus' GE Gallery Effects, have a film grain filter; but even if you don't have them, this procedure still works well.

Create a duplicate copy of any RGB image. Convert the copy to grayscale. Choose Bitmap from the Mode menu and choose Diffusion Dither. Image resolution should match the original from which the copy was made. With the Move tool from the toolbox, drag the bitmap to the open RGB original image. The bitmap will be placed on a layer on top of the background. From the Layers palette, bring the opacity down so the background information is displayed. The image takes an appearance of a grain effect. Further adjustments can be made by choosing any of the Layer mode options for various design effects.

A limitation of bitmap images are the few editing opportunities available while in this mode. Filters, brightness adjustments, many tools, and other Photoshop features are unavailable while in Bitmap mode. In order to take advantage of the many editing features of Photoshop, the image must be converted to grayscale.

Grayscale Mode

Grayscale images have as many as 256 gray levels. Grayscale is distinguished from bitmap by the number of bits represented. While bitmap is represented as a 1-bit file, grayscale images are represented by 8-bits. The number of grays possible in an 8-bit image in binary base-two numbering is a maximum of 256, thus the 256 gray levels. As noted in the explanation of using the Threshold setting, 0 is white and 255 is black. All values in-between represent the number of grays.

Converting images from grayscale to bitmap reduces the image representation to a 1-bit document. Because there is no provision to represent gray levels, various adjustments cannot be made while in Bitmap mode. For example, adjustments to image brightness values by using the Levels or any other Image Adjust features cannot be applied in this mode. In order to make adjustments, a bitmap image has to be converted to grayscale.

When a bitmap is converted from the Bitmap mode to grayscale, a dialog box is presented to indicate a size ratio (see fig. 13.19). If the default size ratio is left at 1, the image size and resolution will equal the size and resolution from the bitmap. If the number is changed to 2, the image resolution remains the same, but the physical document size is one-half the size of the bitmap. Entering 4 in the Size Ratio box reduces image size to one-fourth the original, and so on.

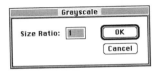

Fig. 13.19

You can change the size ratio in the Grayscale dialog box.

In addition to the obvious uses of grayscale images, such as working in black and white, creating halftones, and scanning grayscale photos, the Grayscale mode is used as an intermediary step when converting modes. This is the case with RGB files converted to bitmap. The Grayscale mode is selected first because you cannot go directly from RGB to bitmap. Grayscale is also an intermediary step in creating duotones from RGB images. Other color modes such as CMYK, Lab, and Multichannel require first converting to grayscale and then to the Duotone mode.

Grayscale does not permit the use of color tools. Changes to Hue/Saturation, Selective Color, Color Balance, and so on, are not available in Grayscale mode. The image must first be converted to RGB or another color mode before these functions can be applied. When the grayscale image is converted to RGB, there will be no change in image appearance. There will, however, be two more channels added to describe color in this mode. As a three-channel document, the file size will grow three-fold. When an image is converted from RGB to grayscale, all color is eliminated. The only way to regain the color is to undo the operation or revert back to the last saved version of the original RGB file. If the conversion is made and the document is converted again from grayscale to RGB, it will not pick up the lost color values.

Halftone effects are applied at the Print or Save operations with grayscale images. Unlike the bitmap halftone screens available with dithering, Photoshop permits grayscale images to describe halftoning functions in the Page Setup dialog box. Once the halftone frequency, angle of the halftone dots, and dot shape have been described in the Page Setup dialog box, the file can be saved with these halftoning descriptions embedded in the file.

To save a file with halftone functions, the file must be saved as EPS with the Include Halftone Screen enabled. Once the halftone frequency is saved with the file, it cannot be altered until a default or different frequency is saved from Photoshop.

Duotone Mode

For our purposes in this section, reference to the Duotone mode shall also include monotone, tritone, and quadtone images. Duotone images are composed of two colors; tritone images include three colors; and, quadtone images are composed of four colors. Traditional duotone images were created by exposing the same image twice on two separate pieces of film. One of the exposures attempted to capture the highlight areas, and the other attempted to capture the detail areas. In addition to giving the appearance of two colors producing an image, duotones have been used to increase the tonal ranges of black-and-white photos. Inasmuch as PostScript can produce 256 distinct levels of gray, the offset press can print a narrower range of tones. When two pieces of film with separate inks are used in the printing process, the tonal range expands providing a much richer looking image.

Duotones should not be confused with spot color, especially with respect to screen printing. Screen printers often require solid colors or shades of a single color to knock out any underlying color. All separations are distinct with no color overlap. Duotone images, on the other hand, will produce separations overprinting the two or more colors used which will create a mixture of the two colors in many areas of the image. The duotone separations appear much like process color separations and should be treated the same.

In converting documents to the Duotone mode, all color in an image must be stripped. This usually occurs by first converting color images to grayscale, and then to the Duotone mode. When Duotone is selected from the Mode menu, the Duotone Options dialog box appears for user-defined duotone options such as duotone, tritone, and so on, and color specification (see fig. 13.20). The options are available in the Type pop-up menu in the Duotone dialog box.

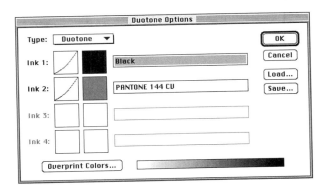

Fig. 13.20

The Duotone Options dialog box.

Color can be specified in many ways. When the color swatch is clicked on for either black or the second color, referred to as Ink 1 and Ink 2, the Color Picker is presented. Custom colors can be identified from the various color systems such as Pantone, Trumatch, Toyo, and so on in the Custom Color Selector. If a color is selected on the Photoshop Picker, the color will automatically be referenced to a corresponding spot color from the active color book. Figure 13.21 shows the Pantone Coated color book selected in the Custom Colors dialog box. Because RGB or CMYK values would not work on a two color separation, Photoshop identifies a color that can be separated as a two color separation.

Fig. 13.21

The Custom Colors dialog box.

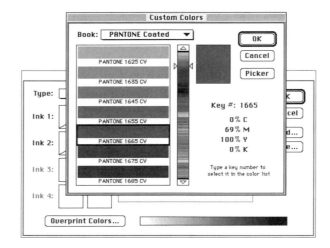

The curves button available for each ink specified in the duotone image will present a dialog box to adjust curve settings for each color. By adjusting the curves, more or less ink will be applied from the respective color to highlight the detail areas of the image. Unfortunately, your monitor view and even desktop color proofing systems will not present an accurate view of what the image will look like when it's printed. Monitor view was discussed earlier in this chapter and is covered in more detail in the section "Calibration," later in this chapter. Suffice it to say, the monitor display will not demonstrate accurate color.

The color printer you choose for a proofing system will undoubtedly use a CMYK printing process. All the spot colors selected for the duotone image will be printed with CMYK inks to simulate the appearance of the spot color. Since neither will be a good indicator for viewing the color before going to press, those with little or no experience in creating duotones should rely on some of the preset curves provided with the Adobe Photoshop program.

During Photoshop's installation, a folder is created where duotone, tritone, and quadtone colors and curves are installed. These settings can be loaded in the Duotone dialog box with predefined curve settings. Using Photoshop's presets will provide for better results than randomly adjusting curves. To load the presets, click on the Load button in the Duotone dialog box. Another dialog box will be presented to enable navigation to the presets folder. The path during installation is Adobe Photoshop: Goodies:Duotone Curves:Duotones:[color book], where [color book] will be either Gray/Black, Pantone, or Process colors. If a spot color is used, the Pantone curves can be addressed. When a curve setting is loaded, the preset values have been optimized to provide for good results in creating duotone images (see fig. 13.22).

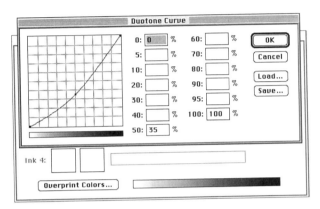

Fig. 13.22

Duotones can have the Curves adjusted for each color.

Caution

Use Exact Color Names When Printing Color Separations

When creating spot color documents of two or more colors, be absolutely precise in noting the naming conventions used for each color. A color defined as PANTONE 144 CV in Photoshop will print on a separate plate from PANTONE 144 CVC in Aldus FreeHand. If the names are not exactly the same, the file will not separate properly and you may be paying for wasted film at the service bureau.

Adobe Photoshop 2.0 used Pantone spot color names from the Custom Picker with a CV suffix. However, the duotone curves had a CVC suffix. This inconsistency was rectified in Photoshop 2.5 where all Pantone spot colors end with a CV by default. Naming conventions can, however, be changed in the Preferences dialog box to display long or short names. This is particularly helpful when other applications default to either the CV or CVC suffix. Due to the critical need for exact color names when printing color separations, always print separations to a laser printer before requesting film from the service bureau.

After a file is converted to a duotone, it can be converted back to grayscale, in which case all color information will be stripped from the image, much like the RGB to Grayscale conversion. Duotone images can also be converted to the many color modes. Converting a duotone image to another mode will eliminate the duotone value and the image could not be separated as a duotone. Once the conversion has been made, none of the color modes permit conversion directly back to the Duotone mode. The process of conversion to grayscale and then redefining the duotone would be necessary.

Indexed Color Modes

Indexed Color mode is used to limit the number of colors to display an image. Converting to Indexed Color can be performed only from the RGB mode. Lab and CMYK modes must first be converted to RGB, and then to Indexed. There are several choices available during the conversion process to describe the bit depth and number of colors to be indexed and dithering method.

When you open the Mode menu and choose Indexed Color, the Indexed Color dialog box appears (see fig. 13.23).

Fig. 13.23

Set Resolution, Palette, and Dither options in the Indexed Color dialog box.

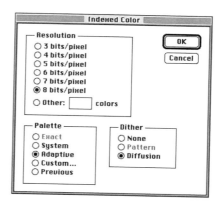

The first item to deal with is the bit resolution, which ultimately produces the number of colors. A 4-bit image, for example, will produce 16 colors that can be simultaneously displayed on the monitor. Some early LCD panels for overhead projection used a 16-color display system. By setting the monitor to 16 colors, the monitor display could more closely resemble the overhead. If 8-bits per pixel is selected, 256 colors will be displayed. The other option provides for a specific number of colors to be displayed. This choice can be useful in dealing with screen printing where a limited number of colors will appear on separate plates.

When the bit resolution has been determined, you can choose one of five color palettes for the conversion.

Exact Palette

The Exact palette is used when there are 256 or fewer colors in the RGB image. The conversion to this mode will exactly match the RGB colors with no dithering applied to the image. Exact will only appear as an available selection if the image contains 256 or fewer colors, otherwise it will appear gray and not selectable. To experiment with this option, open an RGB image and select Indexed Color. If the image has a full range of color, the Exact option will not be available. Crop the image to a small area of similar color and choose Indexed Color again. If the colors are 256 or fewer, the Exact option will be available. The specific number of colors will be displayed in the Indexed Color dialog box (see fig. 13.24).

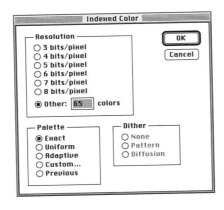

Fig. 13.24

The Indexed Color dialog box with the Exact palette displaying 65 colors.

System Palette

The System palette uses the Macintosh system default 8-bit color display. If fewer than 8-bits are selected to describe the resolution, the System option changes to Uniform. System and Uniform palettes are consistent with any Macintosh application following Apple guidelines for programming. In order to represent a wider color range, the System palette uses one of the dithering options available. The dithering for pattern and diffusion are the same as the explanation provided with bitmap conversions. Selecting None for dithering presents a posterized look to the image.

Adaptive Palette

Adaptive palettes are used to best represent the color range of a given image. When selecting the Adaptive option, Photoshop analyzes all the color values and attempts to create a palette that comes as close to the original colors as possible. This conversion is used often when 24-bit images need to be converted to 8-bit images without losing the color detail. Uses for presentations and multimedia can take advantage of Indexed Color conversions using the Adaptive palette.

Custom Palette

The Custom option provides for a user-defined color palette. This is a palette that you can create and manipulate for a number of uses and save for later use. When the Custom option is selected, the Color Table dialog box appears (see fig. 13.25).

Fig. 13.25

When Custom is chosen in the Indexed color dialog box, a Color Table will appear.

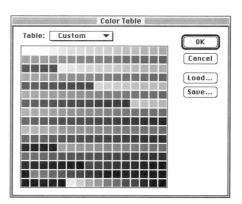

The Color Table dialog box can be modified to suit individual needs for creating color palettes. Creating and manipulating color tables involves the following steps:

1. Select Custom from the Indexed Color options.

2. Click on a single color.

3. The Color Picker will be presented. Choose any color from the Picker and click OK.

4. You will be returned to the Color Table dialog box (see fig. 13.26). From this point, additional colors or color ranges can be selected to continue changing the colors. Click and drag across a color range.

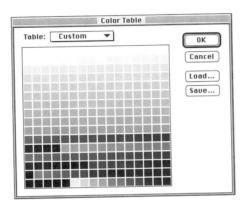

Fig. 13.26

Color Table with a range of colors replaced.

5. The Picker will again be presented. Select a color and click OK. This will be a foreground color.

6. The Picker will be presented again. Select another color and click OK. This will become a background color. Photoshop uses these two colors to create a gradient and replace the color values originally selected in the color table with the gradient colors.

7. When finished replacing colors, click OK.

When two or more colors are selected in the color table, Photoshop will display the Color Picker twice—the first time to select a foreground color and the second to select a background color. Individual colors can be changed by clicking on the single color in the table. After all colors have been changed, the new color palette can be saved as a file. This file can then be loaded at any future session.

Previous Palette

The Previous palette is available only after a Custom or Adaptive palette has been used to convert an image. Using this option provides for consistent color conversion with multiple documents. Once a conversion has been made to a document, open another RGB image. When Indexed Color is selected, the Previous palette selection is available. Choosing this option creates an identical palette as that used in the first conversion.

Color palettes defined in the Indexed mode can be saved and loaded when working on images in other modes. The colors can be appended or loaded into the Color palette and applied to images.

Tip

Creating Custom Colors for Flesh Tones

Custom colors are ideal when colorizing line art drawn in illustration programs and opened in Adobe Photoshop. A good example is creating a palette for flesh tones.

Open an RGB photo with a human figure. Go to an area of skin and marquee a small section. Open the Edit menu and choose Crop. Select the Indexed Color mode and choose Exact. Click OK. The colors will be applied to the Color palette. Open the Edit menu and choose Color Table. Click on the Save button and name the file Flesh tones. Open the line art illustration in Photoshop. Go to the Color palette and choose Append. Select the Flesh tones file and click OK. The colors will be appended to the Color palette.

RGB Color

The RGB Color mode is often the point of origin from which conversions are made to other modes. You begin in RGB when using scans from desktop scanners that provide RGB images. From this mode, you can convert to the many other Photoshop modes such as Grayscale, Duotone, Indexed Color, and CMYK color. Quite often, RGB is a working mode because it contains three channels which makes the file sizes smaller than CMYK images. The RGB composite image displays the three channels superimposed from the red, green, and blue channels. The channels can be viewed separately in either grayscale view or in color, which is determined in the preferences settings.

RGB images are usually 24-bit, with 8-bits for each of the three channels. When viewing a 24-bit image on an 8-bit monitor, pattern dithering is used to simulate tonal ranges for a better quality view. Inasmuch as a monitor may not truly display 24-bit color, the image can be edited in a 24-bit mode. All Photoshop's tools perform 24-bit editing features regardless of the pixel depth of the display system.

You can convert RGB images to many other modes and then back to the RGB mode. In many cases, the original RGB colors will be lost and the only way to regain them is to revert to the previous saved image. You need to look at the RGB conversions individually.

RGB to Grayscale

When RGB images are converted to grayscale, all color is eliminated from the image. Photoshop warns you by displaying a warning dialog box (see fig. 13.27).

Fig. 13.27

The RGB to Gray-scale conversion warning dialog box.

When the OK button is clicked, all color is removed from the image and the channels are reduced from 3 to 1. The original RGB image can be regained by selecting Undo from the Edit menu or by reverting to the previous saved document. Grayscale to RGB conversion increases the channels from 1 to 3, but does not regain the original color information.

RGB to Indexed Color

Converting from RGB to Indexed Color in any one of the modes noted in the indexed color section reduces the number of colors from a possible 16.7 million to 256 or less. Much like the conversion to grayscale, the original RGB colors will be lost. The conversion reduces the 3 channel RGB document to a 1 channel Indexed Color image. When the RGB image is converted to Indexed Color with a dithering effect, converting back to RGB will retain a dithered look to the image. As with the grayscale image, the file would have to be reverted to the last saved version in order to regain the original 24-bit color information.

RGB to CMYK Color

The most frequent conversion applied to RGB images is the RGB-CMYK conversion. Files are often converted to CMYK for printing on CMYK devices and color separations. The RGB color gamut is much larger and contains more color values than the CMYK images; therefore, when conversion to CMYK is made, some colors are changed to the nearest CMYK equivalent. In some cases, it severely changes many color values.

When the conversion has been made, converting back will not regain the original color in the RGB image. Once again, the only way to get back to the original RGB information is to revert to the last saved image.

Since many individuals prefer working in the RGB mode and most often print from CMYK mode, Photoshop 3 has created a useful way to preview CMYK color without disturbing the image. Under the Mode menu there is an option for CMYK Preview (see fig. 13.28). When the CMYK Preview option is selected, the RGB image will preview as if the file was converted to the CMYK color mode. All color shifts will be recognized without disturbing the RGB image.

Fig. 13.28

CMYK Preview from the Mode menu allows you to preview CMYK color without disturbing your image.

For the design professional ultimately printing color separations, one should always remember to never convert to CMYK then back to RGB, then CMYK, and so on. Each time the conversion is made, the color values are recalculated and become less accurate with each conversion.

RGB to Lab Color

Conversion to Lab color is a mode that can be converted to and from with the least disturbance to the color values. An RGB image can be converted to Lab color where adjustments to the brightness of the image can be made without affecting Hue and Saturation. The image can then be converted back to RGB where additional editing can be performed.

RGB to Multichannel

Multichannel is often an automatic conversion that occurs when a channel is deleted from multiple channel documents. With RGB images, if any of the three channels is deleted, the result will be a multichannel document.

RGB images can be converted to multichannel under the Mode menu. A multichannel document will display all three channels in grayscale and the color names will be replaced by numbers. Conversion back to RGB mode can be made without loss of color.

CMYK Color

CMYK color is the mode used for process color printing and process separations. Conversions to CMYK mode are usually made from RGB or Lab color. When converting an RGB image to CMYK, Photoshop uses Lab color as an intermediary step. In other words, the image is converted to Lab color from RGB and then from the Lab mode to CMYK. CMYK mode is most often the final point where an image rests. From this point, no further conversions are made. It's normally the completion of the image preparation for printing and no further mode changes would be necessary.

Lab Color

Lab color will typically be the point of conversion from either RGB or CMYK. Images are converted to Lab mode so adjustments to the luminance or lightness channel can be made without affecting Hue or Saturation. Lab color is also a mode that can be printed directly to PostScript Level 2 devices.

Some systems, like Kodak Photo CD, can be opened directly in the Lab mode. These images may be converted from Lab color to either RGB or CMYK. Because Lab color encompasses both the RGB and CMYK gamuts, color is not altered when converting to or from this mode.

Understanding Color Gamuts

So far, this chapter has referred to the color gamut of several modes. To fully comprehend the meaning of color gamut, look at figure 13.29 in the color section, "Photoshop in Color!"

The large area defined as the Lab color region represents all color that can be perceived. The range is much larger than the ranges of color contained within. Notice the RGB color gamut is larger than the CMYK gamut. When you speak of colors being out of gamut, the reference is made to colors not able to be represented in that particular color mode. When a color is out of gamut, Photoshop displays an alert warning in the Color Picker palette (see. fig. 13.30).

Fig. 13.30

Alert Warning in the Color Picker palette.

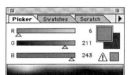

When the alert symbol is clicked with the cursor, the color will move to the nearest color value within the gamut. The alert warns the user that the color, although within our perception of color, cannot be printed from the current color mode. When the alert is selected and the color moves to within an acceptable color range, the new color viewed will more closely resemble what will be printed.

Calibration

You may think by now that trying to get anything on your color monitor to resemble a printed piece is a shot in the dark at best. Actually, it's a shot in the dark at worst! Knowing that you have all these variables to consider, and knowing that printed color will never appear exactly like your monitor, you may think it's impossible to define some predictable color imaging. This is the case if you don't do anything about bringing your monitor view into as close approximation to printing devices as possible. Fortunately, Photoshop does provide tools for calibrating systems to bring these views closer together.

Calibration for Printing Devices

In the early days of desktop publishing, users had marvelous fun creating documents with icons and images integrated with text; and most often they were pleased with whatever result was produced. As more sophisticated devices appeared, users began to cringe at the bitmap dot matrix look when compared to laser printing. During the first days of the QMS thermal color printer, users were awed by the ability to produce color on printed material from our computers. The Mac II was a giant of computer hardware and the monitor display in 8-bits was beyond belief.

As technology has progressed with improved screen and output appearances at geometric rates, users' desires for precise results have exploded to a point of no compromise. With every new development, users have endured an insatiable need for better speed, better performance, and better color. Today, the mere fact that you may come to a close approximation of what you can create on-screen to a printed piece is not enough. Users want more. They want it better and they want it exact.

Unfortunately, individuality is not expressed in the digital prepress world. Computer systems and software are set to generic standards from which the individual must adjust or make adjustments. With respect to color visibly displayed on-screen and resembling a color print, adjustments need to be made to tailor our instruments to our individual perceptions. These adjustments all begin with calibrating monitors, printing devices, and output variables to suit our perception.

As mentioned earlier, our perceptions of color may vary greatly amongst each other. For this reason, you must exercise great care and take the necessary time to calibrate your instruments and bring them together as best you can. Taking control of as many variables as possible will provide for better results. It has already been determined that there will be discrepancies between the computer monitor and printed material. Narrowing the range can be accomplished, and Photoshop provides you with the tools to fine-tune your color adjustments.

(continues)

Monitor Calibration

The first step in calibration is making adjustments to neutralize the monitor. Photoshop ships with a Control Panel utility for calibrating the gamma, color balance, and white-and-black points of your monitor. When Photoshop is installed, the gamma Control Panel is placed in the Photoshop Goodies: Calibration Folder. The file should be dragged to the System Folder where it will be placed in the Control Panels folder.

Gamma Adjustment

Because you already know that all computer monitors display an image differently, the gamma adjustment is made to provide a standardized look of an image across several monitors. Gamma is also used to eliminate color casts inherent in all monitors. Adjusting gamma involves several steps:

▶ *Warm up the monitor.* Be certain the computer monitor has been on for at least 30 minutes. The monitor needs to warm up and stabilize.

▶ *Adjust room lighting.* Ambient light will also have an effect on your view of screen color. Be certain to eliminate harsh light cast on the monitor screen and to set the room lighting to normal working conditions. If light in the room changes—for example, day and evening hours—adjustments should be made for each lighting condition.

▶ *Adjust desktop pattern.* Be certain to set the background color of the monitor to a neutral gray. Don't use bright color patterns for the desktop. Adjacent color brightness will affect your perception of the color in an image. In System 7.5, choose the Desktop Patterns Control Panel and scroll to the neutral gray pattern (see fig. 13.31).

Fig. 13.31

System 7.5 provides a neutral gray pattern in the Desktop Patterns dialog box which should be used for the background desktop color.

▶ *Set the target gamma.* Select the Gamma Control Panel from the Control Panels in the Apple Menu (see fig. 13.32). The Gamma Control Panel defaults at the Target Gamma of 1.8. This setting is recommended for images that will be printed on color printers or for color separations. Higher gamma settings of 2.2 should be used for video and film recorder output.

▶ *Gamma Adjustment.* Move the slider below the Gamma Adjustment in the Control Panel while observing the vertical bars above the slider. Move the slider back and forth to see how the vertical bars appear more or less distinct. The objective is to bring the vertical bars together with a smooth transition between them. Try to position the slider at a point where the bars are the least distinct.

▶ White point adjustment. With the Gamma Control Panel on-screen, hold a white piece of paper up to the side of the monitor so the Control Panel and paper can both be viewed. The paper should be the same as what will be used for printing. For example, if 80-pound coated stock is used for a print job, try to use the same stock type for this comparison. Be certain the radio button in the lower-right corner of the gamma window is selected for White Point. The three sliders above the White Point will adjust the monitor brightness. Move these sliders back and forth while trying to match the screen whites to the paper.

▶ *Color balance adjustment.* The Color Balance adjustment is your next step. By moving the middle slider, you can display more or less color cast on the monitor. If you move the sliders to extremes, you can notice the appearance of color cast. Adjust the sliders so a neutral gray is displayed in the gray bar at the bottom of the gamma window.

Fig. 13.32

The Gamma Control Panel.

(continues)

▶ *Black point adjustment.* Select the Black Point radio button. The black point adjustment will display or remove color tint from the monitor. Once again, move the sliders to extremes to observe the appearance of color tints. Adjust the sliders so all color tints have been removed from the gray bar below the black point.

▶ *Save settings.* Save the settings with a descriptive name. Use the time of day or something descrip- tive to indicate when the gamma adjustments have been made. Save the file to the Photoshop Calibra- tion folder (see fig. 13.33).

Monitor Setup

After the gamma settings have been made, the remainder of the calibra- tions will be performed within Photoshop. Open Photoshop and choose Preferences, Monitor Setup (see fig. 13.34). The Monitor Setup dialog box appears (see fig. 13.35).

Fig. 13.33

Gamma settings should be saved with a descriptive name for easy identification.

Fig. 13.34

From the Prefer- ences submenu, choose Monitor Setup.

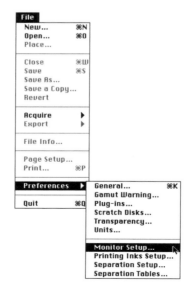

Monitor Setup involves the following several choices:

▶ The first option is the type of monitor used. Click on the Monitor pop-up menu and scroll through the options to find the monitor that matches your brand. If your monitor is not available from the list, you need to select the Other option and refer to the monitor's documentation for chromacity coordinates. Enter the x and y coordinates in the Custom setting for Phosphors (see fig. 13.36). If the documentation is not complete,

place a call to the tech support line of your monitor manufacturer.

▶ If your monitor is available in the pop-up menu, the settings for Gamma, White Point, and Phosphors automatically appear when you choose the monitor type. The only setting you have left to choose is Ambient Light. If the room light is brighter than the monitor, choose High from the pop-up menu. If the room light is not as bright as the screen, choose Low. If the light levels are the same, choose Medium.

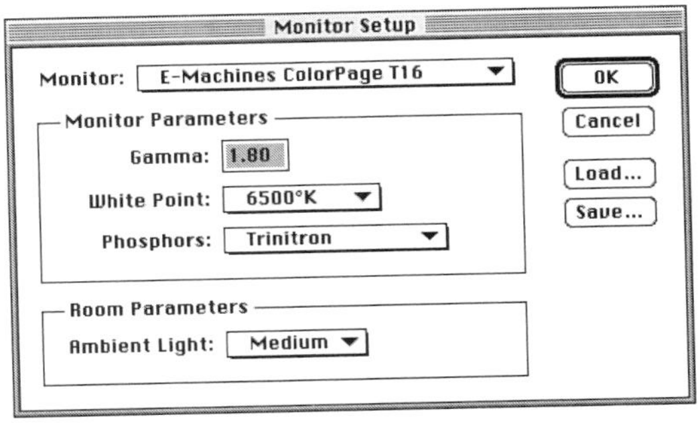

Fig. 13.35

The Monitor Setup dialog box is used to select the monitor type for the individual user.

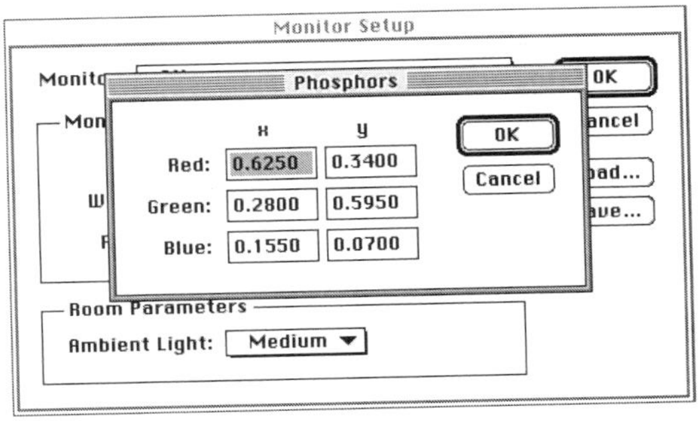

Fig. 13.36

Custom Phosphor settings for RGB x, y coordinates.

(continues)

Printing Inks Setup Adjustments for Color

After the monitor adjustments have been made, you need to adjust the screen view to the printed material and try to bring them together in appearance. For this exercise, it is best to obtain a printed piece from the device(s) you use. For example, if you use a service bureau for film separations and a printer for offset press work, it would be advantageous for you to obtain film separations and a printed piece to perform your calibrations. Obviously, a single piece printed as a four-color job on offset press would be expensive and you may need a starting point to perform calibrations before conducting additional experiments and calibrations. A sample has been provided to first calibrate your printing inks as a starting point. From this point, additional tests should be made with your service bureau and printer.

Figure 13.37 in the color section is a four-color print on 60-pound coated stock. Use this example to perform your first calibration for Printing Inks; but keep in mind your printer will run your jobs on a different press and the film will be separated on different devices than this sample. You will need to perform additional calibrations for devices printing your jobs.

Tip

Preserve Your Test File

The Olé No Moiré file that ships with Photoshop is copied to the Separation Sources folder during installation. This file should remain intact and unedited to perform all your calibration work. Locate the file on your hard disk and select the file. From the File menu, choose Get Info. Select the Locked check box in the info window. Each time the file is opened, the original remains intact because you cannot overwrite a locked file.

Printing Inks adjustments involve the following several steps:

1. Open the Olé No Moiré file. If you lock the file, a warning dialog box will appear indicating changes cannot be saved. Click OK to open the file.

2. With the file open on-screen, be certain no background documents are open. Choose Hide Others from the upper-right corner of your screen under the Photoshop icon.

3. Hold the Olé No Moiré print from your *SE Using Photoshop 3 for the Macintosh* book up to the screen. If you have the means for producing a separation and print from the Olé file, use it instead of the print in the book.

4. Go to the Printing Inks Setup dialog box in the Preferences options under the File menu (see fig. 13.38).

5. Examine the screen view and the print. Your first item to control will be Dot Gain. The default value for Dot Gain is 20 percent. The default ink colors is SWOP Coated (Standard Web Offset Printing). Leave this setting at the default value.

Dot Gain percentages can be adjusted between –10 percent to 40 percent. The higher the number, the more Dot Gain will be applied and the image will appear darker. Conversely, lowering the Dot Gain will lighten the image. The objective is to bring the monitor view and print within close resemblance

to each other. If the print is darker than the screen, increase the Dot Gain. If the print is lighter than the screen view, lower the Dot Gain. Photoshop does not provide dynamic previews for dot gain adjustments. Therefore, each time an adjustment is made, you have to click the OK button.

This procedure will take several attempts to obtain the right setting. Change the Dot Gain, click OK, and observe the results. If the screen image is lighter or darker than the print, make another adjustment and click OK. Keep readjusting until the print and screen view are as close as possible.

6. Your next step involves compensation for color casts. Any shifts in color from the monitor view to the print will need some compensation to bring them closer together. The Olé file is in a CMYK mode. Our adjustments will be made to each of the CMYK channels which will be made in the Levels dialog box. Bring up the Levels dialog box (⌘-L).

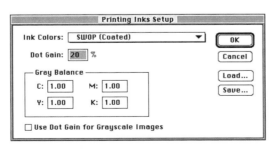

Fig. 13.38

The Printing Inks Setup dialog box.

(continues)

7. The Levels dialog box defaults to the CMYK composite channel. You need to adjust each of the individual channels by using only the middle gray slider for the input levels. Choose the Cyan channel from the Channels pop-up menu (see fig. 13.39). Move the gray slider and try to match the Cyan level in the screen image to the Olé print. Be certain the Preview box is on.

8. When the Cyan adjustment is made, move to the Magenta channel and perform a similar adjustment using the gray middle slider only. Move to the Yellow, and then the Black channel and

repeat the operation. You may have to go back and forth between the channels to fine-tune the adjustments. *Do not click OK.*

9. When the screen image matches the print, note the middle gray slider adjustment values for each channel on a piece of paper.

10. Click Cancel in the dialog box.

11. Open the File menu and choose Preferences, Printing Inks Setup. Enter the values noted from the Levels dialog box in the Gray Balance area for each channel (see fig. 13.40). Click OK after entering the values.

Fig. 13.39

Move the Levels slider to adjust for matching the Cyan level on the monitor to come as close as possible to the Olé No Moiré print.

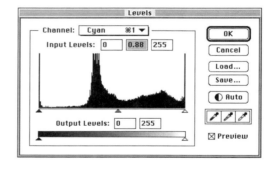

Fig. 13.40

The Printing Inks Setup dialog box with Gray Balance adjustments.

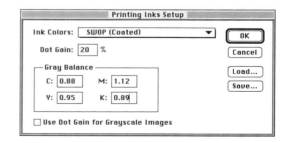

12. Open the File menu and choose Preferences, Separation Tables. The Separation Tables dialog box appears (see fig. 13.41).

13. The separation tables will have to be created from the settings just made. In order to create a custom separation table, you need to save the new printing inks adjustments. Click Save. A progress bar will display the progress in creating the separation table (see fig. 13.42).

14. After Photoshop creates the separation table, a dialog box is provided for naming and designating the location of the table. Provide a descriptive name and save the file to a new folder or the Separation Sources folder (see fig. 13.43).

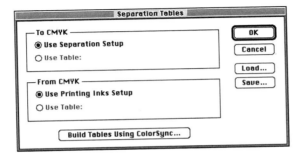

Fig. 13.41

The Separation Tables dialog box will default to the values in the Separation Setup dialog box. Before a table can be used, the Save button needs to be selected.

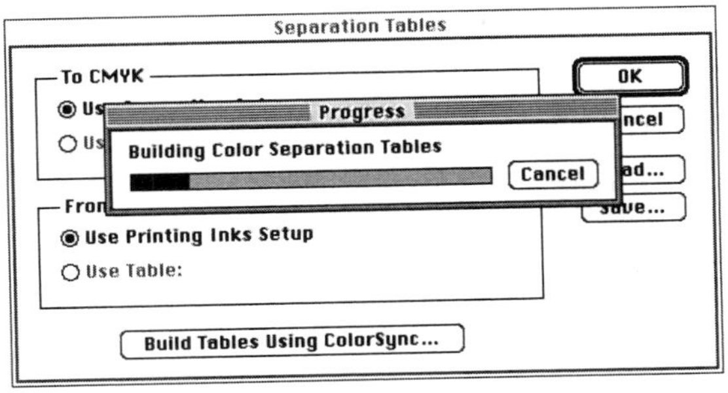

Fig. 13.42

When the Save button in the Separations Table is selected, a Progress Bar shows the progress on building the separation table.

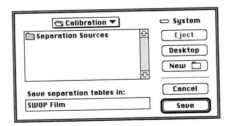

Fig. 13.43

When the separation table is built, save it as a custom table for later use.

(continues)

15. So far, you have created a custom separation table. When you open Photoshop and want to convert an RGB file to CMYK, you have the choice of using the separation table defaults or the custom table you created. If you want to use your table, it must be loaded prior to the conversion. Open the File menu and select Preferences, Separation Tables.

When the Separation Tables dialog box appears, you will need to Load the appropriate settings for the printing device to be used (see fig. 13.44).

16. When the table is loaded, the Separation Tables dialog box will indicate that the custom table is being used and not the Printing Inks Setup (see fig. 13.45).

Fig. 13.44

Each device for which a calibration is performed should be loaded prior to creating any RGB-CMYK conversions.

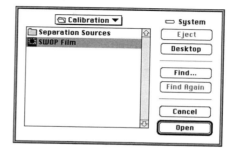

Fig. 13.45

The Separation Tables dialog box showing use of the custom table.

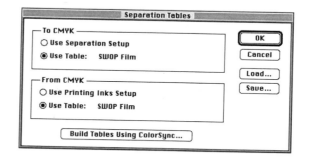

Every printing device you use should follow the same steps with separate tables created for each device. You will especially notice more dot gain on lower-end color thermal wax printers, sometimes color shifts with dye sub-printers, and certainly darker appearances on laser printers. When calibrating for grayscale images, select the check box indicating Use Dot Gain for Grayscale Images in the Printing Inks Setup dialog box.

Although not a perfect system, calibrating your monitor and printing inks will provide for much better results than using default settings generically for all devices.

Where To Go from Here

▶ Chapter 14, "Using Color Correction Tools," will be beneficial to all who want to gain better color results.

▶ Look at chapter 21, "Photoshop for the Desktop Publisher," and chapter 22, "Photoshop for the Digital Designer," for tips on printing and working with service bureaus.

▶ For color printing and looking at a number of different types of printers, check out chapter 24, "Photoshop for the Professional Photographer."

IV

Working with Color

405

Using Color Correction Tools

Correcting color in Photoshop means adjusting for changes in color that occur between input devices (scanners), monitors, and output devices (printers). Depending on the look you want for your image and the final output desired, modifications can be made to the range or levels of color, brightness and contrast, hue balance, and color depth.

by Elizabeth Brown Lawler

CHAPTER 14

Color Perception Overview

Color is perceived, displayed, and printed differently by different people, monitors, and output devices. This makes color matching a difficult, if not impossible process. As thoroughly discussed in chapter 13, "Understanding Color," images viewed on your monitor will look different when printed, even with careful monitor color calibration.

Monitor Calibration

Calibrating your monitor is an important first step for color correcting your images. The colors you see on your monitor will never exactly match the colors on printed material you produced from Photoshop, but the closest you can get will help you make good color correcting decisions. If your monitor is too dark or too light, or biased towards one color, then achieving good tonal range for your images will be more difficult. It's a good idea to follow the steps in chapter 13 for monitor calibration before proceeding with color correction tools.

Key Concept: Image Tonal Range

A 24-bit image should have a full tonal range of color with a white point, highlights, midpoints, shadows, and black points.

Tonal range is the distribution of color across the brightness spectrum. Color is made up of a mix of values of red, green, and blue, or percentages of cyan, magenta, yellow, and black, or other depend- ing on the color mode your image is in.

Each pixel also has a brightness, or luminance, depending on its color values. The color's tone is where the color falls in a brightness spectrum from black to white. An image with good tonal range has a full distribu- tion of pixels across the brightness spectrum from black to white.

If a scanner has flattened out the color, the black and white points may need to be reset. A white point is where pixels in an image are 100 percent white, and a black point is where they are 100 percent black. These points and ranges are adjustable. The brightness values of pixels determine what range the color falls in, and in a 256 color system, the range is the following:

	RGB	CMYK
White	255	0%
Highlights	129-254	1% - 49%
Midpoint	128	50%
Shadows	1-127	51% - 99%
Black Point	0	100%

Remember that with RGB mode, you are dealing with values of light on a monitor and with CMYK, you are measuring ink on "paper." RGB is additive color, and 100%, or 255 equals white. With CMYK "ink," 100% of ink equals black.

Evaluating Your Image

Before you begin making color adjustments, it is best to look at your image and evaluate what changes need to be made. Is the image too dark overall or too light? Is the color too flat looking and dull? Does it lean towards red, green, or blue?

When you begin reviewing your image, you can use the Histogram command in the Image menu to see how the pixels in an image are distributed. Follow these steps:

1. Select all or part of your image.

2. Open the Image menu and choose Histogram.

3. A graph of the distribution of pixels from the black point to the white point appears (see fig. 14.1).

The Histogram can show you if your image has good tonal range of brightness values of black to white. The black end of the histogram shows how many pixels are at the black point, and the white end shows how many are at the white point. In figure 14.1, the image used has more pixels in the range from black to midpoint (or threshold), than it does in the highlight areas, but it does have a white point.

Fig. 14.1

A histogram shows the distribution of pixels in each color channel from black to white.

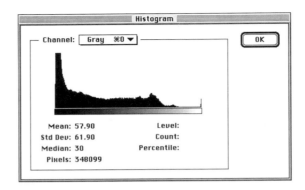

The histogram also tells you the mean, standard deviation, median, and number of pixels in an image. *Mean* is the average of the image's brightness values. *Standard deviation* is how much the pixels vary in brightness. *Median* is the middle brightness value of the pixels.

If a scanner has flattened the color in an image, it may not have any pixels at the black or white points and should be adjusted. See "Corrective Color Changes" later in this chapter for more information.

Another way to evaluate the tonal range of your image is to use the Eyedropper tool and the Info palette to see what numerical values are represented by the pixels in your image (see fig. 14.2):

1. Position the Eyedropper over the brightest point in the image, and look at the Info palette.

A white point should have RGB values of 255 and CMYK values of zero percent. If you cannot find any pixels with those values, then the white point may need to be reset to give an image full tonal range.

2. Position the Eyedropper over the darkest point in an image.

The Black point should have RGB values of zero and CMYK values of 100 percent. Once again, if no dark pixels are with this value, the black point may need to be reset.

If the Eyedropper shows that the lightest pixel in your image is not white and the darkest pixel is not black, you will want to reset your white and black points using Photoshop's color correction tools. Resetting white and black points in an image is important so that the image will have a good full tonal balance. If your image is muddy or flat, it probably does not have an even distribution of pixels from white to black. After the white and black points are reset, the brightness values of pixels are redistributed along the full brightness spectrum.

Eyedropper

Fig. 14.2

Use the Eyedropper and the Info palette to find white and black points in your image.

After you have looked at the brightness value distribution of pixels, you can check to see that no color casts exist. The Histogram or the Eyedropper will also show if there is commonly more red, green, or blue mixed in to the pixels.

Key Concept: Color Cast

Color cast means that the hue of the overall image leans toward one color over the others or the image is not balanced correctly in the shadow or highlight areas. Using the Histogram and looking at the other color channels will show the number of pixels represented by different hues.

Photoshop's tools can make adjustments to the color and tonal balance in your image and are described in the following two sections. All tools are available for RGB and CMYK images, some are available for Lab, Grayscale, and Duotone, but they do not work on Indexed Color images.

Don't forget to follow the steps in chapter 13, "Understanding Color," for calibrating your monitor as a good first step in correcting the color of your images. Then you will be ready to use color correcting tools.

Dramatic Color Changes

The Map submenu in the Image menu contains four options that change color and brightness values in an image (see fig. 14.3). They are normally not used for color correction, but for certain types of alterations and special effects.

Fig. 14.3

The Map submenu has four options that produce dramatic changes to your image.

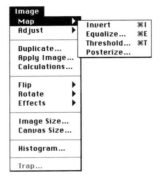

Tip

Using the Map Submenu

The tools contained in the Map submenu are not usually used for color correction. They contain functions that are used for dramatic color changes that are applied to your overall image, such as inverting the color, averaging brightness and contrast overall, and creating black-and-white images from color.

Invert

Invert creates a negative of an image. It is useful if you have scanned negative film and want to change it to a positive image. Every pixel in the image is converted to its inverse value; for example, white (255) is converted to black (0).

Equalize

Equalize redistributes the brightness values in an image to average out the light and dark balances. When you select an area, you can have it affect the whole image, or just your selection. If an image is too light, it will transform the darker pixels to an even darker brightness range to create an image that has an even dispersion of pixels in the highlight and shadow areas. This command, however, gives you little control over how the brightness levels are arranged and can produce unwanted results, as seen in figure 14.4.

Fig. 14.4

Equalize redistributes the overall brightness values in an image. This light image was made darker throughout.

Threshold

Threshold is the often the brightness midpoint you set in an image. Whatever threshold level you choose forces all colors brighter than that number towards white and all colors darker than that number towards black. This command converts a full-color image to black and white, depending on the threshold value you type. The default value is 128, the midpoint between black (0) and white (255). All pixels with brightness values higher than 128 will turn white, whereas all darker will turn black. If you are working in duotone mode, the colors will change to those in your duotone. Figure 14.5 shows an image before and after using Threshold.

Fig. 14.5

Threshold converts shadow and highlight areas to two colors.

Key Concept:
Threshold, Midpoint, and Gamma

Threshold is a term often used to mean the midpoint of the brightness values in an image. Threshold usually means a point where all pixels brighter are changed to white, or maximum brightness, and all points below it are changed to black or minimum brightness.

The *midpoint* of a tonal range is the point halfway between white and black, or the brightest and darkest points in an image.

Gamma is another term used to mean midpoint, but usually refers to a range of mid-level grays between the highlights and shadows rather than just one point. Adjusting gamma, which is possible in several of the color correcting tools, affects the brightness values of the midtones of an image without affecting the white and black points.

Posterize

Posterize is used when you want to force colors to a certain fixed number of brightness values. If, for example, you choose three, the full-color image will be transformed to an image with three brightness levels in each color channel. The result makes the image look made up of flat-color polygons, with different colors for shadow and highlight areas. A setting of three forces colors in each color channel towards the white point, the black point, and the midpoint. Figure 14.6 shows a Posterized image with a setting of three. With three colors in three color channels, the resulting image has a total of nine colors. Also see Fig. 14.6 in the color section, "Photoshop in Color!"

Fig. 14.6

Posterize forces colors to a fixed number of brightness levels. (Also see color section.)

Looking at the color channels in the histogram shows what the Posterize command does. Posterize is similar in function to Threshold, only it forces ranges of color to several fixed brightness points, instead of just white and black.

Key Concept: Posterizing an Image

When the term *posterize* is used anywhere not in reference to the Posterize command, it can mean to reduce the depth of tonal range in an image. Posterizing an image means to reduce the number of colors, force colors closer toward the white and black brightness values, or remove shading and create flat colors in an image.

The Posterize command can be used for special effects or for preparing spot color images. It can also be used for printing grayscale images on a laser printer.

Corrective Color Changes

The set of commands in the Adjust submenu under the Image menu are used for color correction. They allow you to alter the way pixels are distributed along the brightness spectrum to achieve good tonal range. Figure 14.7 shows the ten color-adjusting commands.

Fig. 14.7

The Adjust sub-menu contains Photoshop's color correction tools.

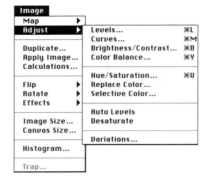

Levels

Levels brings up a histogram of the pixel distribution in an image along the brightness range. It enables you to adjust contrast and brightness in each color channel using sliders to reset black point, midtones (gamma), and white point. This tool is very helpful for increasing shadows and highlights, and bringing out color saturation in a muddy or flattened-color scanned image. To use the Levels command, follow these steps:

1. Select all or part of your image.

2. Open the Image menu, and choose Adjust, Levels, or press ⌘-L. The Levels dialog box appears, as shown in figure 14.8.

Fig. 14.8

The Levels command enables you to improve brightness and contrast in shadows, midtones, and highlight areas.

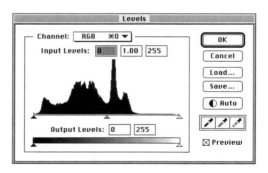

3. With the Preview button checked, first try clicking Auto to see if it gives you what you want. Auto automatically resets the white and black 0.5 percent from the edges of the histogram for each color channel. It uses the 0.5 so that it is not setting black and white points

based on only one pixel value. If you want to change that default, hold down the Option key, and the Auto button changes to Options where you can change the percentage.

If you want to cancel settings without closing the dialog box, hold down the Option key, and the Cancel button changes to Reset.

4. Try moving the black point (the black triangle slider on the left) in towards the edge of the histogram. This darkens the image and increases shadow areas.

5. Move the white point (the white triangle slider on the right) in towards the right edge of the histogram. This makes the image brighter and increases highlight areas. By moving both, overall contrast is increased.

6. Move the midpoint, or gamma, and see how it affects the midtones in the image.

7. If the color balance is not correct, you can repeat these steps for each color channel.

When you are done, try pressing ⌘-Z (Undo) a couple of times. It may look like a flat gray film has been removed from your image, as shown in the before and after image in figure 14.9. Also see figure 14.9 in the color section "Photoshop in Color!"

Fig. 14.9

An image before and after using the Levels command. (Also see color section.)

Another way to reset the black and white points in an image is to use the Eyedropper tools at the lower-right of the Levels dialog box.

1. Click the black Eyedropper tool and move it above your image.

2. Click on the darkest color in the image to make all pixels at the same brightness value become black.

3. Click the white Eyedropper and select the lightest color pixel in your image to set this and all pixels at the same brightness value to white.

4. You can use this same method to set the midpoint, but this is hard to do if you are working in all channels at once because it can offset the color balance. Use this method if you are editing each color channel, and use the Info palette to view the numbers of the midtone.

> **Note**
>
> Try using Auto to see what midpoint is suggested. Auto will set the midpoint so that there is an equal number of pixels above and below it. After you have used Auto, you can still alter the position of the midpoint, and the white and black points.

5. You can also double-click the Eyedropper tools to bring up the Photoshop color picker and set white, black, and midtone (gamma) points there.

Output Levels at the bottom of the dialog box controls what is the darkest and lightest color allowed in the image and can be used to decrease the levels and flatten color in an image. If you move the black point in to the right, then the darkest color that appears is the gray you choose, and no 100 percent black pixels appear in the image. If you move the white slider to the left, it darkens the entire image and allows no 100 percent white pixels in the image. This is useful if you are preparing images for video and don't want any 100 percent white pixels, or if you are decreasing contrast of a selection to use as a background.

Levels also enables you to view highlight and shadow areas as they are changed with your settings using Threshold mode. As the Threshold command converts an image to black and white based on the threshold (midpoint) value you choose, using Threshold mode in Levels can show you the new distribution of highlights and shadows that happen based on the settings in the Levels dialog box. To use the Threshold mode in the Levels dialog box, perform the following steps:

1. Make sure that the Preview box is unchecked.

2. Hold down the Option key and click the white triangle slider to see highlights or the black triangle slider to see shadows.

3. Try moving the sliders and checking again to see how it affects your image.

This function is also useful if you plan to convert your image to black and white with the Threshold command. You can get a good idea of what you will get if you set the Levels first.

Curves

Curves offers the most control over brightness and contrast of an image in each color channel, but it also is the most difficult to use effectively. Whereas Levels allows setting changes for the black, white, and midtone points in an image, Curves allows for changes along the complete tonal range of an image. The dialog box shows a line graph, and you can change any point or area along the line.

Often it is best to use Curves after you have made larger overall adjustments using the Levels or other commands.

> **Tip**
>
> **Use Curves for Best Tonal Correction**
>
> The Curves tool offers the most control for improving the tonal range of an image. The Curves dialog box allows you to change the brightness settings along the entire brightness spectrum of an image instead of just at three points, as Levels does, or for just the overall image, as with Brightness/Contrast. This is the best tool to master of all Photoshop's color correction tools.

To use Curves, follow these steps:

1. Open the Image menu and choose Adjust, Curves. The Curves dialog box appears, as shown in figure 14.10.

   The Curves dialog box shows a line that goes from black (0) on the bottom left to white (255) on the top right.

   You can move your pointer over the image and click and hold on pixels to see where they fall on the graph (do this before you select any Eyedropper tools). The input and output numbers on the bottom show the brightness level of the pixel.

Fig. 14.10

The Curves dialog box lets you change the levels of any area to affect the tonal range of an image.

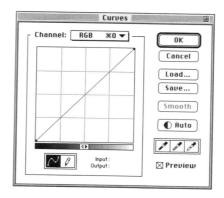

Tip

Using Curves in CMYK Mode

If working in CMYK mode, you can reverse the graph so that the graph goes from white on the left to black on the right, and the input and output values show as (ink) percentages. The default for Curves is set for RGB values, with black on the left and white on the right.

2. You can work in the composite channel or each channel at a time. If you select two channels before you bring up the Curves dialog box, you can work in those two channels at once (for example, red and green would read "RG").

3. Using the Curve tool (lower left curve icon) creates smooth curves for remapping pixels to the brightness range. Set points on the already existing lines and move them around. Try making the line start at the top left and go to bottom right to create an inverted image. This will give you an idea of how it works.

4. You can reset the black and white points for your image or selection in three ways. As with Levels, you can use the black and white Eyedropper tools to select the darkest and lightest points from your image; you can move the end points of the graph to new places; or you can click Auto. Holding down the Option key changes the Cancel button to Reset.

Editing Color Channels with Curves

Try clicking Auto and look at the separate color channels for an idea of where to start or what channels need the most editing. Sometimes because of the way Auto resets white and black points, it can create a color cast, so you may want to move the white and black points back closer to their origin to flatten that specific color.

5. You can anchor up to 16 points along the line with the Curve tool. To enhance contrast, it is best to anchor the midpoint and move the highlight areas up, which simultaneously moves shadows down a bit, resulting in an S curve, as seen in figure 14.11. This makes highlight areas brighter, shadow areas darker, and gives more detail in midtones. Figure 14.12 shows the result. Also see figure 14.12 in the color section "Photoshop in Color!"

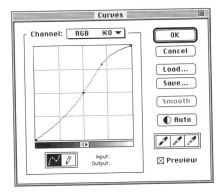

Fig. 14.11

Increasing contrast with the Curve tool.

Fig. 14.12

The contrast was enhanced in this image by first using Auto, which changed each color channel, and then drawing the S-curve in figure 14.11 in the composite channel. (Also see color section.)

You can also use the Pencil tool, called the *Arbitrary Map*. Click on it and begin drawing in the graph area to see what it does. This allows for more precise setting of isolated points and areas. Click Smooth to create a curve from your drawing.

If you click on the black or white point in the graph and move them horizontally, you are making more of the shadow or highlight area black or white, just as if you moved in the triangles in the Levels command. Moving the black and white points vertically (black point up, white point down) flattens the image and makes the darkest point allowable a dark gray value and the lightest point allowable a light gray value. This is similar to the Output Levels function in Levels.

When you create a Duotone, the Duotone dialog box has a Curves function very similar to the Adjust Curves tool. You can map colors to the image based on a graph of brightness levels to have color stronger or weaker in different areas. You can create settings for Duotone colors in the Curves tool; save them; then load them in the Duotone dialog box.

After you get used to working with both Levels and Curves, you will see that they offer the best options and results for remapping your pixels to create a better tonal range for your image than any of the other tools.

Brightness/Contrast

This is the easiest tool for adjusting the tonal range of your image. You can only adjust the overall image; there is no way to adjust certain areas, such as shadows, midtones, or highlights. This tool also only works on the composite channel, so you can't make adjustments to individual color channels.

Follow these steps to use Brightness/Contrast:

1. Open the Image menu and choose Adjust, Brightness/Contrast. The Brightness/Contrast dialog box appears, as shown in figure 14.13.

2. Simply drag the sliders for Brightness and Contrast, with the Preview button selected to see how it affects your image.

3. Click OK.

This tool is often used by beginning Photoshop users, but is really not best for image quality because it applies the same adjustments to shadows, midtones, and highlights. It can be interesting for effect when contrast is increased greatly, resulting in a highly saturated, posterized, sharp-edged image.

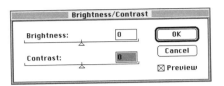

Fig. 14.13

Brightness/Contrast simply adjusts the overall image.

IV

Working with Color

Color Balance

Color Balance enables you to change the mix of colors in your image. Unlike the other Adjust commands discussed so far, it deals with colors, not tonal range or brightness. This can be used to produce a color cast, to bias the image towards certain colors and away from others, or to enhance or increase saturation of a muted color. This tool only works with the composite channel, but enables you to work on highlight areas, midtones, or shadow areas. To use Color Balance, perform these steps:

1. Open the Image menu; choose Adjust and then Color Balance. The Color Balance dialog box appears, as shown in figure 14.14.

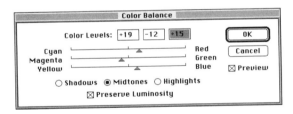

Fig. 14.14

Color Balance lets you change the mix of colors in an image.

2. Choose Shadows, Midtones, or Highlights.

3. Drag the triangles toward colors you want to increase in the selection and, with the Preview box checked, note how it affects your image.

4. Do this for all the colors you want to change.

5. Check Preserve Luminosity if you don't want the color change to affect the brightness balance in your image. See figure 14.15 for an example of changed color balances in an image.

Hue/Saturation

Hue/Saturation is a more precise method of making certain colors more or less saturated, biasing colors, or changing the overall hue or lightness of an image. It is similar in function to Color Balance, but gives you more control over which colors are biased towards other colors and gives controls for saturation and lightness of specific colors. It does not, however, allow you to change only highlights, midtones, or shadows of your image.

Fig. 14.15

Color Balance lets you change the mix of colors in an image.

You can either change the hue and saturation of all the colors in your image, or select a certain color by clicking on a color on the left side of the dialog box shown in figure 14.16.

Fig. 14.16

The Hue/Saturation dialog box allows you to change hue balance, saturation, and lightness in your image.

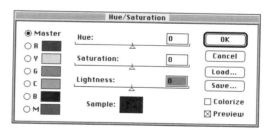

When Master is clicked, changes affect all colors of your image. The Hue slider rotates colors around the color wheel and affects the overall balance of color in your image. Changing Saturation and Lightness also affects all the colors in your image.

If you click on one of the colors on the left, the Hue slider reflects to show just that portion of the color wheel. For example, if the red in your image is too pink or too bright, you can edit just the red tones in your image. Choosing red changes the Hue slider to show Yellow (Y) on the left.

Moving the Red slider towards yellow (thus, away from magenta) decreases the pink bias in the red tones. Changing Saturation or Lightness while Red is selected only affects the red tones in your image.

The Colorize option allows you to change an entire image to one hue without losing brightness and saturation values. This is great for tinting grayscale images (although you must change them to RGB or CMYK to have Hue/Saturation available).

To use Hue/Saturation, follow these steps:

1. Open the Image menu and choose Adjust, Hue/Saturation. The Hue/Saturation dialog box appears, as shown in figure 14.16.

2. To change overall image colors, use the three sliders to change the hue, saturation, and lightness. With the Preview button clicked, you can see how it affects your image. If you want to change one color at a time, select it and use the sliders to make adjustments.

3. Use Colorize if your goal is changing the image to one tint.

4. Click OK to apply the results.

The numbers at the top of each slider reflect the change you are making. The Hue slider number represents the degree of rotation around the color wheel. The Saturation number is a percentage of increase or decrease, as is the number for Lightness. You can type directly if you know what value you want, and you can Save and Load settings for use on other images.

Hue/Saturation is great for enhancing, changing, or toning down certain colors in your image. Also, if you want a neon-looking special effect for your image, increase the Saturation greatly and move the Hue slider around. Decrease Saturation and increase Lightness for pastel tones. If you want an image with only a few color tones, you can desaturate all but those colors, or bias other colors towards your desired colors.

See figure 14.17 for an example of an image changed with Hue/Saturation.

Replacing a Color

New to Photoshop 3, the Replace Color function allows you to select a certain color and replace it with another color, saturation, and lightness. The Replace Color dialog box is similar to the Color Range dialog box, although a selection is not made. It shows a mask of your image, with the areas of the color you selected being white, and all deselected areas black, as seen in figure 14.18.

Fig. 14.17

The saturation and hue balance of color has been changed in the rose bouquet using Hue/Saturation

Fig. 14.18

The Replace Color dialog box lets you selectively change a color.

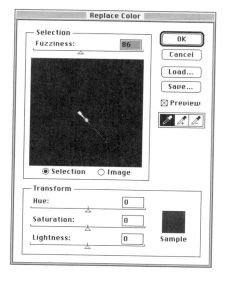

The Fuzziness slider controls how many colors are included in your selection, similar to the Magic Wand tool. The number represents how many pixels away in color value are included in the selection. For example if you chose 100 percent red, and your Fuzziness is "0," then only 100 percent red would be included. If the Fuzziness slider is higher, then more tones and brightness values of red would be included.

The Wand tools enable you to select a color, add more colors to the selection, or remove colors from the selection.

The Hue, Saturation, and Brightness sliders at the bottom determine the color you will fill in the selection.

To use Replace Color, follow these steps:

1. Open the Image menu and choose Adjust, Replace Color.

2. Move the pointer over your image, and it changes to an Eyedropper. Select a color. The mask will show in the dialog box.

3. Move the Fuzziness slider to enlarge or shrink your selection.

4. Add or remove other colors with the + or – Eyedroppers. You can click Image in the dialog box and add colors there if you can't see your total image.

5. After the selection is made, use the Hue, Saturation, and Lightness sliders in the Transform box to select a new color. The sample swatch shows you the color you've selected, and with Preview checked, you can see how it is applied to your image.

6. Click OK to apply.

Adjusting a Selective Color

Selective Color lets you adjust the amount of cyan, magenta, yellow, and black used to create different color tones. It is intended to emulate high-end scanners used in the printing industry. The Selective Color dialog box allows you to choose Reds, Yellows, Greens, Cyans, Blues, Magentas, White, Neutrals, and Blacks. Then, for the color group you choose, you can increase or decrease the amount of CMYK color "inks" that are mixed into the color. To use Selective Color, perform the following steps:

1. With the composite channel active, open the Image menu and choose Adjust, Selective Color. The Selective Color dialog box appears, as shown in figure 14.19.

2. Choose the color group you want to change from the pop-up menu at the top.

3. Adjust the cyan, magenta, yellow, and black percentages using the sliders.

Fig. 14.19

Selective Color lets you change CMYK ink amounts that make up different color groups.

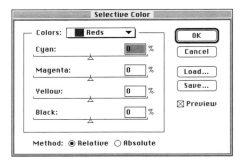

4. Choose Relative or Absolute. Relative adjusts the existing values by the percentage you choose. If you choose a pixel that has 20 percent cyan and you add 10 percent more cyan, it will add 2 percent (2 is 10 percent of 20). Relative will not affect white and black because there are no CMYK values to start with. Absolute replaces the percentage of a color in a pixel with the new percentage you choose.

5. Use the Preview button to see your changes and click OK to apply.

Auto Levels

Auto Levels is a quick one-step version of the Levels command, and has no dialog box. It will reset white and black points to the edges of the histogram of brightness values in an image. Then it will adjust 0.5 percent inwards so that the basis for the points is not made up of only one pixel brightness value. It will automatically redistribute all pixels in between the white and black points equally with the midpoint halfway in between.

This can be a good quick way to adjust a flat image, but using Levels will give you a preview and more adjustment controls.

Desaturate

Desaturate appears to convert an image to grayscale while keeping it in the current color mode. A new tool for Photoshop 3, the Desaturate option saves having to convert to grayscale and back to color if you want to tint a grayscale image.

Variations

Variations is a fun and useful color mixing tool that lets you see previews of your selection in a color wheel in its dialog box, as shown in figure 14.20. You can add and subtract colors in highlight, midtone, or shadow areas, or make them lighter or darker. Overall saturation can be increased or decreased also.

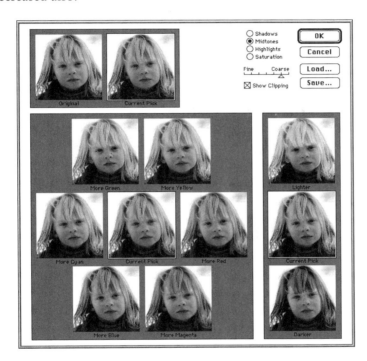

Variations lets you see your selection in a color wheel.

The top two images show your Original and a preview of the Current image according to your changes. The Fine to Coarse slider controls the amount of color added. The colors listed in the color wheel can be used to add color to or subtract color from your image. To use Variations, follow these steps:

1. Open the Image menu and choose Adjust, Variations.

2. Choose Highlights, Midtones, or Shadows.

3. Move the Fine to Coarse slider to adjust the amount of color added or subtracted each time you click.

4. Click on any one of the pictures as many times as you want in the color wheel to add color. To subtract a color, click on its opposite, across the color wheel.

When a color becomes too bright, dark, or oversaturated, it will look neon in your preview. Highlights that have been made too bright become white, and Shadows that have been made too dark become black.

5. To revert to your Original, you can click on the Original preview in the upper left window.

6. To apply the changes, click OK. To save the settings for use on other images, you can click the Save button, and later use Load. An image changed with Variations is shown in figure 14.21. Also see figure 14.21 in the color section "Photoshop in Color!"

Fig. 14.21

A fun example of changing colors with Variations. (Also see color section.)

Variations is a fun, but imprecise, method of color correction. It is a better tool for adding and subtracting hues than for adjusting tonal range of your image.

TACTICS RECIPE

Enhancing Grayscale Images with Monotone, Duotone, Tritone, or Quadtone Mode

In this tactics recipe, you'll learn the steps for creating a monotone, duotone, tritone, or quadtone. From here forward, the term *duotone* can be substituted for any of the four options. But first, let's cover some background and terminology.

Although, technically, there are 256 levels of gray (most of which you can probably see on your monitor), only about 50 of those different levels can be captured on the plates used by a printing press. This greatly reduces the clarity and available detail in any grayscale image. To increase the levels, and usually the quality, of a grayscale try creating a duotone from the other color of the printed job.

A *monotone* is a grayscale image printed in a non-black ink. Though this may give you a different look, you are still limited to the 50 levels. *Duotones* use two ink colors, *tritones* use three, and *quadtones* apply four different ink colors. With every added color you gain more available levels.

If you're having trouble imagining the concept, notice the difference between bitmap and grayscale images displayed on your monitor. Bitmap images have only two levels, black and white. Grayscale can have several or even many (usually 256) levels. With each additional level, the quality, clarity, and detail of the image increases.

Each of the colors used in a duotone is printed at a different angle. Usually the angles are 30° apart. Photoshop will automatically set the correct angle for each color of the duotone. There are, however, considerations for determining angle. Duotones should be created

with the darkest color first; and when creating tritones or quadtones, the remaining colors should descend in lightness. For instance, a duotone of black and cyan would be created with black as the first color.

Only grayscale images can be converted to duotones. Even though you have added other colors to the image when converting to a duotone, it is not a multichannel image as a CMYK or RGB would be. It is single channel and must be converted to multichannel for viewing the separate color plates. We'll get back to viewing plates in a moment. For now, remember that all duotones, tritones, and quadtones are single channel and that you *do not* convert them to CMYK for printing; they separate correctly on their own.

Creating a Duotone

Photoshop has made converting to duotones a completely automated process, modeled after the traditional methods. Generally, the color in a duotone adds dot ranges to the highlight (whites or light areas) and midtone (medium gray) dots of the grayscale image. The black, or darkest color, is used to produce the shadow (black or very dark area) dots. Photoshop allows you to

(continues)

specify exactly what percentage dot appears in each areas of an image. All of these functions are found in the Duotone dialog box, which is accessed through the Mode menu. To convert to duotone, follow these steps:

1. If your image is not grayscale already, choose Grayscale from the Mode menu. The image converts to the grayscale mode.

2. Choose Duotone from the Mode menu. The Duotone dialog box appears.

3. Choose Monotone, Duotone, Tritone, or Quadtone from the pop-up menu.

4. Click the Curves button to adjust the curves. (Refer to the section, "Adjusting Curves," later in this Tactics Recipe.)

5. Click the Ink Color button to choose a color. (Refer to the section, "Choosing Colors," later in this Tactics Recipe.)

6. Click the Overprint Colors button to change the way the colors overprint one another. (Refer to the section, "Overprinting Colors," later in this Tactics Recipe.)

7. Click the Load button if you wish to access Photoshop's

preset sample curves values. The preset curves are a good place to start experimenting. You can substitute the color you want in place of the color Photoshop chooses.

8. Click the Save button to save the curves you have adjusted.

9. Click OK. The image is then converted to the requested mode and the colors are applied.

Choose Save As from the File menu and select EPS to save the image as the specified duotone so that it separates correctly when it gets to your desktop publishing software. Do not return to the CMYK mode, or any other mode, as your plates will separate properly in the duotone mode.

Choosing Colors

When selecting colors for your duotone, you will nearly always choose the darkest color as color 1 and descend in order of lightness. This is standard for a duotone, but it is also the method that Photoshop uses to calculate the screen angles for a duotone.

In Photoshop 3, the most current version of the PANTONE Matching system is used. The names of the colors may not match older versions of other programs. This will become a problem, if you are trying to separate the colors of your duotone from another program. For instance, if you import the duotone into QuarkXPress and the names of the colors of the duotone do not match the available PANTONE names in QuarkXPress, Quark-XPress will create a third color, matching the longer name of the PANTONE color. Now instead of printing two plates for a two-color job, you're printing three. To avoid this, choose the Short PANTONE Names option in the More Preferences dialog box of Photoshop. Process colors are not a problem; simply define them as cyan, magenta, yellow, or black. Do not choose process colors from the PANTONE list. For example, PANTONE process cyan is not cyan. It does not separate as cyan in the page layout application.

Adjusting Curves

Working with the three areas of an image—the highlight, midtones, and shadow—you can adjust the amount of color added to an area. Generally, the colors are added to the highlight and midtone areas. For instance, if you want to add 20% cyan to the highlight dot (for instance, the 0% dot), you specify in the Curves dialog box that the 0% dot measures 20%. (To access this dialog box, click the Curves button in the Duotone dialog box next to the color you wish to adjust.) Although you are permitted 13 points on the curve, it's not necessary to specify each one. Specify only a few and Photoshop will calculate the intermediate values.

Use the Save button if you wish to save these values for use on other duotones. The Load button allows you to access predefined curves (Photoshop has included some examples) previously saved. Loaded curves can be further adjusted to suit your current needs and then re-saved if you should so choose.

Overprinting Colors

The order in which two unscreened colors print affects the final outcome of the resulting color. For instance, if you print yellow over red the resulting color will be orange. If you wish to view the colors, choose the Overprinting Colors button in the Duotone dialog box. You must first specify each of the colors.

The Overprint Colors dialog box displays the possible combination of colors based on the colors you have chosen for your duotone. If you are unhappy with the resulting colors that are created from your color combinations, click the Ink Color button for the color you wish to change and define a new color.

(continues)

433

The Overprint Colors dialog box does not affect the final printed piece. It only gives you the opportunity to view the possible results of creating a duotone with the selected color combinations. It is up to you to adjust colors as necessary to avoid possible undesirable combinations.

Viewing Color Plates

Unlike most other images with more than one color, a duotone is not a multichannel image. Therefore, you cannot simply select only one of the colors for viewing. It is possible to work around this restriction by first converting the image to multichannel, viewing the separate color using the Channels palette, and then reconverting back to the duotone mode. It is important that you do not save the duotone in the multichannel mode as it will not separate properly. If you want to save the multichannel image, rename it something other than your original image.

Using the other colors of your printed piece to add tonal range to your images through the use of duotones, tritones, and quadtones is very simple in Photoshop. You'll find yourself using these methods often to add quality, clarity, and tonal range to often flat grayscale images.

Modifying Indexed Color Images

When you want to convert a 24-bit image to 8-bit or below, you open the Mode menu, and choose Indexed Color. Lower bit depth creates smaller file sizes and is suitable for animations and multimedia or for position-only scans.

If you are working with an Indexed image, and want to color correct it, you need to convert it back to RGB or CMYK to use most of the color correction tools discussed in this chapter. Then you can change it back to Indexed color before you save it.

When you change an image to Indexed color, Photoshop will convert your image to a fixed number of colors. For example, if you are converting a 24-bit image to 8-bit, you are changing your image from one with 16.7 million colors to one with only 256 colors. Photoshop will find the best 256 colors from the image to convert it, either from the standard Mac System palette or a custom (Adaptive) palette. Dithering options control how the colors in your image are converted to a fixed number of colors in a color palette. Dither None will simply change each pixel to a new color from the palette. Pattern Dither, available only when the System palette is used, will convert the image by creating geometric patterns. Diffusion Dither will use spread out colors and blend to other colors using similarly colored pixels.

When you change an image to Indexed color, a Color Look-up Table, or CLUT is created. This is the palette of colors used in the image. For example, the Mac System 8-bit palette is made up of 256 colors. A 2-bit image only uses black and white.

Sometimes you will want to create a custom, or "Adaptive" palette that is created from an RGB or CMYK image. An 8-bit Adaptive palette will take the 256 most common or averaged colors from the image. If you are creating a series of images, like for an animation, and you want them to use the same palette, you can save the palette for later use.

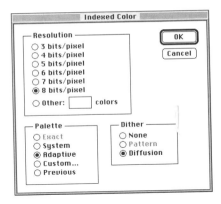

Fig. 14.22

In the Indexed Color dialog box, you can change bit depth of your image.

To create an Adaptive palette use the following steps:

1. With your RGB or CMYK image active, open the Mode menu and choose Indexed Color. The Indexed Color dialog box appears, as shown in figure 14.22.

2. Click on the bit depth you want and choose Exact or Adaptive. If the dialog box comes up with Exact, then the number of colors in your image is less than the number included in the bit depth. For example, if 200 different colors are in your image and you choose 8-bit, then Exact comes up as the default because the number is less than 256.

3. Then under the Dither option, you can choose None, Pattern, or Diffusion. If you aren't sure which looks best, try one; you can use Undo (⌘-Z).

4. Now open the Mode menu and choose Color Table. The palette you just created will show. You can save it for later use by clicking Save and naming it. The option to choose Color Table only shows if an Indexed color image is active.

5. As long as you have Photoshop open, this will be the active palette for Indexed color images (if you click Custom or Previous in the Indexed color dialog box), so you can apply it to other images.

Fig. 14.23

Color Table shows the current color look-up table of an indexed color image.

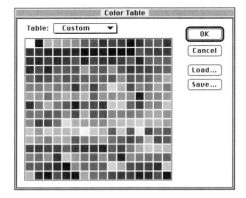

You can edit Color Tables after they are created. To edit a Color Table, follow these steps:

1. Open the Mode menu and choose Color Table. The current color table appears, as shown in figure 14.23.

2. You can double-click on any color to bring up the Photoshop color picker.

3. When you change colors, they are applied to your image. You must resave the palette, however, to record the changes.

> **Tip**
>
> **Designing for an 8-bit environment**
>
> You may need to convert 24-bit images to 8-bit because of monitor limitations or animation performance issues. Using Photoshop's Indexed color to convert an image is the best way to change the image to a lower bit-depth. It is best to create Adaptive palettes with Diffusion Dither for most images. With gradients, try Pattern Dither.

Previewing the Results of Color Changes

If you are preparing images for traditional printing and are working with RGB images, you can preview the image in CMYK by using CMYK Preview under the Mode menu. This doesn't convert your image, but it shows how the image will print with CMYK inks. If you are working with large file sizes, it can help to work in RGB mode because there are only three channels and they are smaller.

As discussed early in this chapter and in chapter 13, "Understanding Color," some colors can be displayed on a monitor but cannot be printed. These colors are called *out-of-gamut* colors. Usually they are brightly saturated colors that cannot be achieved with a mixture of CMYK inks. They should be corrected so that they will print properly. There are a few ways to identify and correct which colors are out-of-gamut by using Photoshop's gamut warning.

When the cursor is moved over an out-of-gamut color, a gamut warning appears. In the Info palette, exclamation points appear next to the CMYK values, if you have your Info palette set to show those values. In the Color Picker palette, the warning is a triangle with an exclamation point in it. Also, you can choose Gamut Warning from the Mode menu to display all the out-of-gamut colors in the image.

When you select a color with the Eyedropper tool that displays a gamut warning in the Color Picker palette, you can click on the gamut warning symbol or the swatch next to it, and it will change the foreground color to one that is acceptable and not out-of-gamut.

To determine out-of-gamut colors, follow these steps:

1. Open the image and make sure that the Color Picker palette and the Info palette are open.

2. Move the cursor or Eyedropper over color areas until you see the gamut warnings. These appear as exclamation points next to the CMYK values in the Info palette, as shown in figure 14.24. In the Color Picker palette, a triangle with an exclamation point appears when an out-of-gamut color is selected, as shown in figure 14.25.

Perform the following steps to display all out-of-gamut colors:

1. Open the Mode menu and choose Gamut Warning. This highlights all out-of-gamut colors in your image.

Fig. 14.24

Out-of-gamut colors appear with exclamation points in the Info palette.

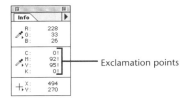

Exclamation points

Fig. 14.25

An Alert triangle with an exclamation point appears as a gamut warning in the Color Picker palette when an out-of-gamut color is selected.

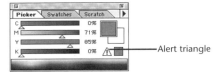

Alert triangle

2. The default color for displaying out-of-gamut colors is a neutral gray. You can change that color to a more contrasted, brighter color. Open the File menu and choose Preferences, Gamut Warning.

3. The Gamut Warning preferences dialog box appears. Click on the color swatch to bring up the Photoshop color picker and change it to the color you want. Change the Opacity level to your desired setting.

4. Open the Mode menu and choose Gamut Warning to preview out-of-gamut colors, as shown in figure 14.26.

Fig. 14.26

Gamut Warning highlights all the out-of-gamut colors in an image.

You can correct out-of-gamut colors in several ways, depending on how many colors need to be changed or how many areas of your image are out-of-gamut.

To change a few colors, follow these steps:

1. When you identify the color with the Eyedropper tool, you can use Color Range to select all of that same color. With the offending color chosen, open the Select menu and choose Color Range. Use the Fuzziness slider to include only that color or areas around it.

2. Click on the gamut warning in the Color Picker palette, and it changes the color to one that is in gamut.

3. Fill your selection with that color, using normal or saturation mode.

To change a large area that is out-of-gamut, perform the following steps:

1. Select the part of the image you want to change.

2. Open the Select menu and choose Color Range.

3. In the Color Range dialog box, choose Out of Gamut from the pull-down menu.

4. All the colors in your selection that are out-of-gamut are selected, as shown in figure 14.27.

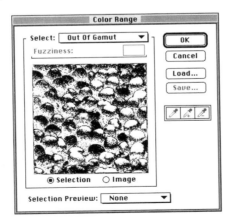

Fig. 14.27

Color Range can select all out-of-gamut colors in your selection.

5. The easiest way to correct the out-of-gamut colors is to use the Sponge tool to desaturate the colors. Wipe the sponge across your image, and it will affect only the selected out-of-gamut colors.

6. If you have Gamut Warning turned on, it will look like you are erasing the gamut warning color from your image as you apply the sponge, as shown in figure 14.28.

Fig. 14.28

Use the Sponge tool to desaturate out-of-gamut colors, and your gamut warning color disappears.

nectarines w/gamut warn (RGB, 1:2)

1.03M/1.03M

Of course, with all CMYK printing, as mentioned earlier, it is best to try tests with the output services you use most often, and always question their pre-press staff about concerns.

Where To Go from Here

▶ Chapter 13, "Understanding Color," helps you learn how to use color in a publishing environment.

▶ Chapter 15, "Using Photoshop's Plug-In Filters," tells you how to use filters to improve and touch up images.

▶ Chapter 21, "Photoshop for the Desktop Publisher," looks at using images for importing into DTP layouts.

▶ Chapter 22, "Photoshop for the Digital Designer," provides information aimed at digital designers.

PART
V

Filters, Plug-Ins, and Special Effects

Using Photoshop's Plug-In Filters

Filters are a powerful collection of tools that enable you to apply all kinds of special effects for your images. Many filters are included with Photoshop, and several more can be purchased from other vendors.

Located under the Filter menu are groups of filters arranged by category. Some provide controls for enchancing your images, while others are capable of applying complex effects. Photoshop filters include categories for blurring, sharpening, distorting, lighting, adding noise or texture, and applying stylistic effects among others.

Filters add a new dimension to your images and design process. Exploration is definitely encouraged!

by Elizabeth Brown Lawler

CHAPTER 15

The terms plug-in and filter are sometimes used interchangeably, but are actually slightly different. Plug-in refers to all add-in functions for Photoshop, including those that acquire and export files. Plug-ins do include Filters, which are add-ins that are used to manipulate images and refer to the multitude of choices under the Filter menu, as shown in figure 15.1. Many come with Photoshop, and many more are available by other software vendors. Photoshop's filters are often called "native" filters. Filters purchased by other companies are called "third-party" filters and are discussed in chapter 16, "Third-Party Plug-Ins."

Filters allow you to apply special effects to your images: for example, enhancing images, blurring or sharpening images, applying or reducing noise or texture, making painting effects, and turning images into geometric patterns. Photoshop's filters are organized into categories under the Filter menu (see fig. 15.1).

Fig. 15.1

To access Photo-shop's plug-in filters, open the Filter menu.

Using Filters in Photoshop 3

The new version of Photoshop comes with many additional features that can affect how you apply filters. The layering feature gives you more control over how filters are applied and you can preview effects of most filters that include dialog box controls.

Applying Filters to Layers

With Photoshop's Layers palette, a wide range of controls awaits you as you explore filters. You can apply different filters to different layers and then use different apply modes to affect how they look when composited. The variations are endless!

If you want to apply a filter to more than one layer at a time, be sure to merge them before applying the filter. This is because many filters evaluate all the visible pixels in an image to determine results, so no filter is applied the same way to different images. In other words, you can't expect to apply a filter to one layer and then a second layer to achieve the look of applying it to both layers at once.

When you float a selection, however, and apply a filter, it affects only the floating selection in which you are working.

> **Note**
>
> Don't forget, when your layer is floating, if you click another layer in the Layers palette, it moves that floating selection to whatever layer you click, even if it is not the one with which you started.

Previewing Filter Effects

In previous versions of Photoshop, you could set certain filters to preview your image in a dialog box. Photoshop 3 comes with this built in, and gives the feature to many more filters. Almost all the filters that have a dialog box include a preview window. The new preview window also allows you to zoom in and out of the image with plus and minus buttons, or move to preview other parts of the image by dragging across the window.

Overview of Filters

Photoshop comes with several filters built in. They reside in folders in the Plug-Ins folder in the Photoshop folder. Different categories of filters are organized by submenus under the Filter menu: Blur, Distort, Noise, Pixelate, Render, Sharpen, Stylize, Video, and Other. One filter that comes with the CD-ROM version of Photoshop adds a category called Synthetic.

You can learn about each filter by choosing About Plug-in from the Apple menu and selecting the filter about which you want to learn. Figure 15.2 shows the About Plug-In menu.

To use a filter, follow these steps:

1. Select the image or portion of an image you want the filter to affect.

2. Open the Filter menu and select the desired filter.

3. Choose your desired settings in the dialog box, if applicable.

4. Click OK.

Fig. 15.2

To learn more about Photoshop's plug-in filters, open the Apple menu and choose About Plug-In.

Tip

Using Filter Shortcuts

Remember keyboard combinations for faster filter usage. You can stop the application of a filter with ⌘-period. To apply a filter a second time with the same settings, press ⌘-F. Or, to bring up the dialog box of the same filter, press ⌘-option-F. To undo a filter after it is applied, press ⌘-Z.

The following section gives a description of each of Photoshop's plug-in filters. Many show a before-and-after image of how the filter affects an image. Don't be afraid to explore; however, you should realize that some of the filters take time to apply.

> **Tip**
>
> **Apply Filters to Floating Selections**
>
> To have more control over the way a filter is applied to your image, float your selection before applying it. Then you can use different apply modes in the Layers palette. Or you can duplicate your active layer and experiment before saving a final version.

Blur Filters

In the Blur submenu, there are five filters that are used in different ways for blurring (or softening) images or reducing noise or unwanted scanned patterns in images. The Blur category filters include Blur, Blur More, Gaussian Blur, Motion Blur, and Radial Blur.

Blur

Blur softens contrasting colors by smoothing the difference between them. It can be used to soften the look of an entire image, clean up noisy areas, or smooth edges between objects and the background.

Blur More

Blur More has just about the same effect as applying the Blur filter three or four times.

Gaussian Blur

Gaussian Blur gives you control over the amount of blurring you want in an image. In the dialog box that appears when you choose Gaussian Blur, you can type from 0.1 to 250.0 in the Radius box. Higher values blur more and take more time to process. Lower values blur less. The Gaussian Blur dialog box is shown in figure 15.3.

This filter is nice for creating a soft focus look, and is also quite effective for creating soft frames and shadows. See the section on "Filtering Techniques" later in this chapter for more information. See figure 15.4 for a photo affected with Gaussian Blur.

Fig. 15.3

The Gaussian Blur dialog allows you to set the amount of blurring you want to apply.

Fig. 15.4

Gaussian Blur creates a soft focus look for this photo.

Motion Blur

Motion Blur allows you to blur an image in a particular direction and strength (from 1 to 999). You choose the direction and strength in the Motion Blur dialog box. It gives the effect of a moving image or an image from a still camera with a long exposure time. For example, if you have a bike racing across a background, you can motion blur the background at a higher number, and the bike at a lower number. Figure 15.5 shows the Motion Blur dialog box and figure 15.6 shows a motion blurred photo.

Fig. 15.5

With the Motion Blur filter, you choose the direction and strength of blurring of an image.

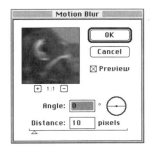

Fig. 15.6

Motion Blur makes subjects look like they're moving.

Radial Blur

Radial Blur makes an image look like it was shot with a camera that was zooming in or spinning around. In the Radial Blur dialog box (see fig. 15.7), you can select Spin to make the image blur along concentric circles out from the center. Zoom blurs the image as if the camera were moving in or out on the image. Figure 15.8 shows how Radial Blur makes an image look as if the camera is zooming in.

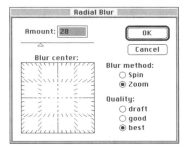

Fig. 15.7

The Radial Blur filter makes an image look like a camera is zooming in or spinning.

Fig. 15.8

Radial Blur creates a look that you are zooming in on a photo.

V

Filters, Plug-Ins, & Effects

Distort Filters

The Distort Filters are a set of nine filters that warp your image using geometric shapes. The process, often called mapping, forces your image onto a shape, like a sphere for a 3-D look, or into waves for a watery look. The Distort filters are Displace, Pinch, Polar Coordinates, Ripple, Shear, Spherize, Twirl, Wave, and ZigZag.

> **Tip**
>
> **Blending Distortion Effects**
>
> If you apply a Distort filter to an irregular selection, you can make the effect appear to blend into the rest of the image. Open the Select menu and use Feather to soften the selection at the edges. Then the distortion effect will be blended between the selection and the rest of the image.

Displace

Displace warps your image to a *displacement map* that you choose. Several come already made in Photoshop, or you can create your own. The map is actually a second image, and can be a texture, sphere, boxes, or other geometric shapes, waves, radials, and so on. The color value of a pixel in the displacement map image determines the amount of distortion—or shifting—of pixels in your target image. In the displacement map, a pixel color value of 255 causes the highest positive displacement, a value of 0 causes the maximum negative displacement, and a value of 128 causes no displacement.

In the Displace dialog box (see fig. 15.9), you can set the percentage of distortion—horizontally and vertically. The higher the number, the more warping happens—negative or positive depending on the color value in the displacement map. When the displacement map file is not the same size as your target image, you need to select Stretch To Fit or Tile, to either stretch out or tile the map to fit the size of your file. When the distortion happens, parts of your image are left blank, so you should choose Wrap Around to fill the blank space with content from the opposite side of your image, or Repeat Edge Pixels to fill the space with area from the edge of your image.

To create your own displacement map, you can create any Photoshop file except for a bitmapped file. Try grayscale files with spheres or boxes to experiment. Figure 15.10 shows an image displaced with a spherized displacement map.

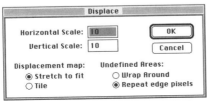

Fig. 15.9

Warp an image to your liking in the Displace dialog box.

Fig. 15.10

Displace applied to an image with a spherized displacement map.

Pinch

Pinch squeezes a selection toward or away from its center with a percentage value you choose. It can create strange looking warped effects. Figure 15.11 shows the Pinch filter dialog box and figure 15.12 shows a photo "squeezed" by the Pinch filter.

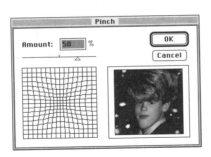

Fig. 15.11

The Pinch filter squeezes an image toward or away from its center.

Filters, Plug-Ins, & Effects

V

Fig. 15.12

Pinch applied to a photograph makes it look squeezed in the center.

Polar Coordinates

This filter takes a rectangular image and creates a circular one by making the horizontal edges meet at the top. Like the world map would look if you looked at it from the top of the north pole. It also takes a circular or spherized image and converts it back to a rectangular image, depending on which option you choose in the dialog box. Figure 15.13 shows a preview of how a flat world map can be rounded in the Polar Coordinates dialog box.

Fig. 15.13

With the Polar Coordinates filter, you can wrap a rectangular image around a "pole" or vice versa.

Ripple

Ripple is just like it sounds: it warps the image into a rippled or wavy pattern, horizontally and vertically. In the Ripple dialog box (see fig. 15.14), you can choose small, medium, or large ripples, and you can vary the intensity with a slider bar, from –999 to +999. Figure 15.15 shows how Ripple applies liquid effects to a photo of trees.

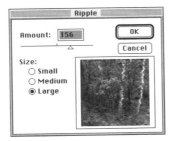

Fig. 15.14

The Ripple filter adds Small, Medium, or Large wave patterns to an image.

Fig. 15.15

Ripple applied to this image of trees makes it look like it's under water.

V

Filters, Plug-Ins, & Effects

Shear

With this filter, you define a curve you want applied to an image by making points along a vertical line, and it warps along that path. In the Shear dialog box (see fig. 15.16), you can click the straight line and move points by dragging the mouse. When the curve pulls an image away from the edges, you can choose Wrap Around to have the resulting space filled with content from the opposite side of the image, or choose Repeat Edge Pixels to have the space filled with the color of the pixels at the edge of the image.

This filter only allows you to plot a vertical line, so if you want to warp your image horizontally, rotate it 90 degrees before you apply the filter.

Figure 15.17 shows how a background image is made more interesting by warping the image to a curve with the Shear filter.

Fig. 15.16

The Shear dialog box lets you plot points of a curve to warp an image.

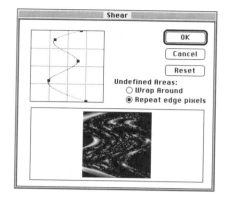

Fig. 15.17

Shear warps a background image to a curvy line distortion.

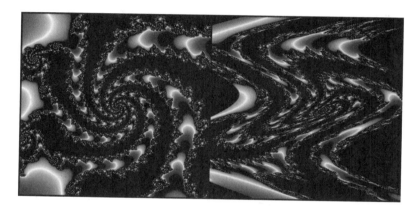

Spherize

Spherize creates a 3-D look by wrapping a selection around a spherical shape. In the Spherize dialog box (see fig. 15.18), you control the percentage (+/– 100) of the application and whether it is applied Horizontal only, Vertical only, or Normal (both). Figure 15.19 shows a "spherized" dollar bill.

Twirl

Twirl rotates a selection out from its center. In the Twirl dialog box (see fig. 15.20), you can control the spin amount. You can type in from –999 to +999 or just drag the slider control in the twirl window. Figure 15.21 shows how the Twirl filter can be used for humorous effects for photos.

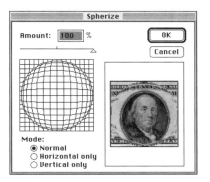

Fig. 15.18

The Spherize filter
creates a 3-D look.

Fig. 15.19

Spherize applied to
a dollar bill image.

V

Filters, Plug-Ins, & Effects

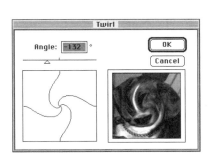

Fig. 15.20

The Twirl filter
creates a spinning
effect.

Wave

Wave is similar to Ripple, but gives you more control. It also warps more
diagonally than Ripple. Wave can be used to create all kinds of effects
because there is a wide range of controls. Figure 15.22 shows the Wave
dialog box with the various settings you can use.

Fig. 15.21

Twirl can create humorous effects for photos.

Fig. 15.22

The Wave filter gives you many controls to distort an image.

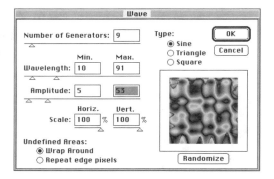

In the Wave dialog box you can vary the number of waves (generators), the length of the waves, their height (amplitude), the size (horizontal and vertical scale) and type of wave (sine [rolling], triangle, or square). You also can choose Wrap Around or Repeat Edge Pixels to control how the resulting blank spaces are filled. Figure 15.23 shows how a Wave affects a gradient background to create an interesting texture.

Zigzag

Zigzag allows you to create the look of a drop hitting the surface of water. In the Zigzag dialog box, you can choose Pond Ripples, Out From Center, or Around Center to create different looks. You also can vary the amount of rippling and the number of ridges in your image. Figure 15.24 shows the Zigzag dialog box and figure 15.25 shows how Zigzag can make a photo look like it's under water.

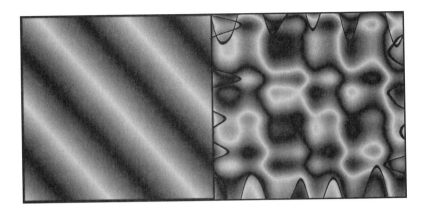

Fig. 15.23

Wave applied to a gradient creates a more interesting look.

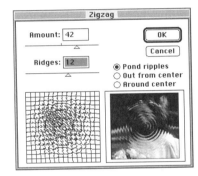

Fig. 15.24

With the Zigzag filter you can make an image look like it's under rippling water.

Fig. 15.25

Zigzag applied to a photo makes it look like it's under the surface of water.

V

Filters, Plug-Ins, & Effects

Noise Filters

The Noise filters add a contrasted or blended random speckling of pixels to give a grainy or blended look. The Noise filters include Add Noise, Despeckle, Dust & Scratches, and Median.

Add Noise

The Add Noise filter adds pixels to your selection to give it a rough, textured, or old look. You can vary the amount of noise, distribution of pixel colors, and color or monochrome in its dialog box. In the Distribution section, Uniform calculates random color values between 0 and +/– any number you specify. Gaussian distributes colors on a bell-shaped curve and is slightly less random. You can choose to have random color or monochromatic, which keeps the noise in the same hue as the colors in your selection. The preview box shows the effects of different choices. Figure 15.26 shows the Add Noise dialog box and figure 15.27 shows how a photo is given more texture with Add Noise.

Fig. 15.26

Add Noise produces a grainy or textured effect.

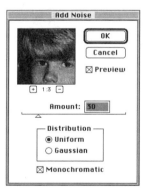

Fig. 15.27

Add Noise applied to a photo gives it texture.

> **Tip**
>
> **Using Noise for a Mezzo Look**
>
> Add Noise can produce interesting color mezzotint effects. Try high settings of noise amount, Gaussian distribution, and Monochromatic to keep underlying hues. This will give your photos an old, rough look. See "Filtering Techniques" later in this chapter for more ways to create color mezzotint looks.

Despeckle

Despeckle blurs an image except where edges or sharp contrast of colors occur. This filter is good for cleaning up scans to retain detail. You don't have control over how the filter is applied, however. Try Despeckle to help correct noisy scans. Figure 15.28 shows how Despeckle blurs areas of similar color without losing detail at color edges. Some settings of Despeckle can make the image look too blurred or oil painted.

Fig. 15.28

Despeckle applied twice to a low-contrast photograph blurs areas of similar color while keeping detail at color edges.

Dust & Scratches

Dust & Scratches is new to version 3, and is intended to help clean up defects in scanned images. It calculates how different the color of a pixel is in relation to the surrounding area, depending on the amount, or "threshold level," you choose in the dialog box. In the Dust & Scratches dialog box (see fig. 15.29), you can find where dust occurs in the preview window, and then drag the slider left and right until it disappears to find a good setting. The higher you set the Radius option, the more the image is blurred. Figure 15.30 shows how a dusty scanned image on the left was cleaned up using Dust & Scratches, with corrected detail shown on the right.

> **Note**
>
> *Threshold* refers to the level of difference between two colors. The lower the number you set, the more different the two colors have to be before Photoshop applies the filter.
>
> *Radius* refers to the number of pixels from a color edge (area of contrasting colors) that are affected by the filter. The higher the number, the farther from a color edge a filter affects.

> **Tip**
>
> **Best Dust & Scratches Settings**
>
> For images that have very light dust spots on a dark background, first try keeping radius as low as possible and threshold as high as possible. If that doesn't remove the dust and scratches, try lowering the threshold level until you see results.

Fig. 15.29

Dust & Scratches can help clean up spots in scanned images.

Median

Median calculates a middle value of a selection of pixels and replaces all those in a radius you choose with that value. In some ways, it is like posterizing little circles of colors, taking a section of color and filling it with an average of that color. The higher the radius, the more blurring and the larger the area of that middle color is applied. It is intended to balance bright and dark areas of an image. Figure 15.31 shows how a low radius setting in Median can create a soft-focus (or wet-paint) look.

Fig. 15.30

Dust & Scratches applied to detail of scanned image.

Tip

Using Median for a Painted Look

The Radius setting in Median controls how much color is averaged into a common color. Low radius settings can create a soft-focus (or wet-paint) look. Try Median with a low radius setting for a watercolor effect.

Fig. 15.31

Median calculates a middle color in a radius of pixels and fills that area with the resulting color. Some settings give an image a painted blurred look, as in this image that used a radius setting of 3.

Pixelate Filters

Before Photoshop 3, many of these filters were contained in the Stylize submenu, but now are separated to reflect their function. Pixelate refers to altering or drawing information from the color values of the pixels in an image to produce new shapes or effects. The Pixelate filter category includes Color Halftone, Crystallize, Facet, Fragment, Mezzotint, Mosaic, and Pointillize.

Color Halftone

This filter gives your image the look it will have as a printed halftone image. In printing a halftone, each color channel (cyan, magenta, yellow, and black) is printed in dots or other shapes at different angles to simulate the wide range of colors an image will have. You can see this if you look closely at color images in magazines or books. When the angles of the distributed color are off, it produces what is called a moiré pattern.

> **Note**
>
> If you scan images from a book or magazine, the halftone printed pattern, or moiré, shows up in your image, and you can reduce it with other filters as noted in this chapter.

In Photoshop, Color Halftone works in grayscale, CMYK, or RGB mode, and shows you a halftone effect on-screen. It works by examining areas of color in each color channel (or the black channel in grayscale images), and replacing that area with a dot. You can vary the size of the dot and the angles for each color channel. Figure 15.32 shows the Color Halftone dialog box and figure 15.33 shows an image before and after applying Color Halftone. Also, see figure 15.33 in the color section, "Photoshop in Color!"

Fig. 15.32

Color Halftone simulates the look of a halftone.

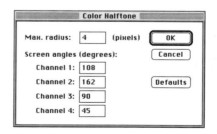

V

Filters, Plug-Ins, & Effects

Fig. 15.33

Color Halftone applied to a photo-graph gives it the look of a printed halftone on-screen. (See color section also.)

Crystallize

Crystallize examines the range of color pixels in your selection and creates polygons of one color calculated from that range for a flat, blocky, abstract look. You can vary the pixel size, or cell, of the polygon. See figure 15.34 for the Crystallize dialog box and figure 15.35 for an image affected by Crystallize.

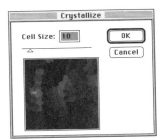

Fig. 15.34

Crystallize creates colored polygons in an image for an abstract look.

Fig. 15.35

Crystallize applied to an image changes it to colored polygons.

Facet

Facet is like Crystallize, but it takes into account the brightness and darkness in your image, and stays truer to the colors in your image. It can make your selected image look painted and, with several applications, quite abstract. There is not a dialog box or controls with this filter. The result can be subtle, even if applied three times, as shown in the before-and-after dollar image in figure 15.36.

Fig. 15.36

Facet applied to the dollar image shows that effects can be subtle; but on larger images, Facet can create a painted effect that doesn't blur the image or lose detail.

Fragment

Fragment duplicates your image four times and slightly offsets each copy up and to the right of your original. It then blends all of the copies. Fragment makes a picture look like the camera was shaking when the picture was taken.

Mezzotint

Mezzotint creates a grainy look, like old, rough photos. New to version 3, it used to be available only by third-party vendors. Mezzotint is widely used in printing and can produce images much better than halftones for newspaper. It is similar to a halftone. However, you have more control over different dot shapes in the filter's dialog pull-down menu, such as fine, medium, grainy, or coarse dots; short, medium, or long lines; and short, medium, or long strokes. The space between the dots or lines is filled with white. The Mezzotint dialog box is shown in figure 15.37.

For best results with the Mezzotint filter, try increasing contrast with Levels or Curves before applying the filters. A before-and-after example of Mezzotint is shown in figure 15.38. Also see figure 15.38 in the color section, "Photoshop in Color!"

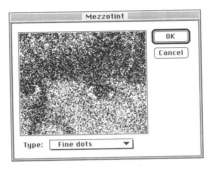

Fig. 15.37

The Mezzotint filter provides options for different Mezzo patterns to apply to your image.

Fig. 15.38

Mezzotint applied to a photograph creates a grainy, old look for images. (See color section also.)

Mosaic

Mosaic is similar to Crystallize, except that it uses square blocks instead of polygons. You can vary the cells from 2 to 64 pixels in size. Figure 15.39 shows the Mosaic dialog box as it changes a photograph into colored squares.

Pointillize

Pointillize simulates the look of a pointillist painting by breaking the image into randomly placed dots and filling the areas in-between with the background color you choose. The Pointillize dialog box (see fig. 15.40) gives you control over the size of the dots but not the placement. Figure 15.41 shows a before-and-after image of how Pointillize affects a photo.

Fig. 15.39

Mosaic breaks an image into colored squares.

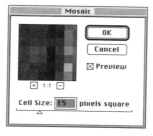

Fig. 15.40

Pointillize gives your image the look of a pointillist painting.

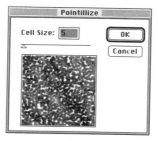

Fig. 15.41

Pointillize applied to a photograph breaks it into dots.

Render Filters

The Render category contains some filters that are new to Photoshop 3. The four filters do something special on top of your entire selection, like add lighting effects, texture, or a camera lens flare. The Render category contains Clouds, Difference Clouds, Lens Flare, Lighting Effects, and Texture Fill.

Clouds

The Clouds filter creates a random, soft, clouds pattern from the foreground and background color you choose in the toolbox or color picker. If you hold down the Shift key while applying the filter, you can get higher contrast and more dramatic shapes. Be sure to float your image selection or the filter replaces your image with the clouds. Also, floating your image gives you more control over how the filter is applied. Figure 15.42 shows how Clouds replaced a background.

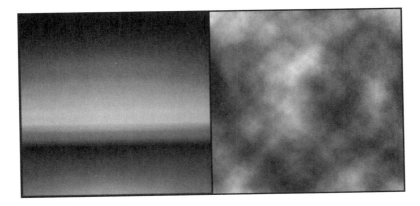

Fig. 15.42

The Clouds filter applied to a background.

Difference Clouds

Difference Clouds also calculates a cloud pattern from foreground and background colors, but automatically applies the clouds pattern to your image using difference mode. Try applying this filter more than once to create a marbled look with veins. Figure 15.43 shows the effect of Difference Clouds on a photo.

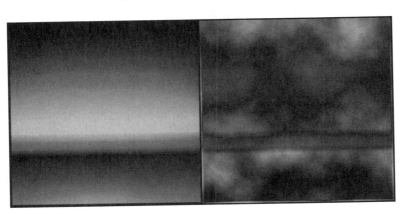

Fig. 15.43

The Difference Clouds filter applied to a photograph.

V

Filters, Plug-Ins, & Effects

Lens Flare

Lens Flare simulates a bright light on a camera lens in a photograph. The Lens Flare dialog box (see fig. 15.44) enables you to control the position of the flare, brightness percent (up to 300), and camera lens type (50-30mm zoom, 35mm prime, and 105mm prime). The preview window shows the different effects. The photograph in figure 15.45 shows how Lens Flare is applied.

Fig. 15.44

Lens Flare adds the effect of a light shown on a camera lens.

Fig. 15.45

Lens Flare applied to a photograph adds a light as if from a camera lens.

Lighting Effects

New to version 3, this filter lets you apply multiple light sources to your selection. You have control over the number of lights, the type of light, and the light strength and color. You also can add texture for special effects. Figure 15.46 shows the Lighting Effects dialog box with its multitude of settings for different light effects.

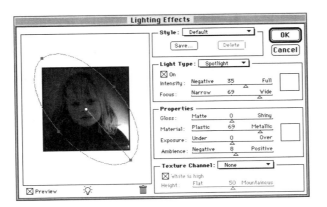

Fig. 15.46

The Lighting Effects dialog box has many controls to add different types of lighting to your image.

The Lighting Filter comes with several built-in styles. In the Lighting Effects dialog box (refer to fig. 15.46), check out the styles in the pull-down menu at the upper-right to see a variety of lighting looks.

To alter or create your own lighting styles, you can add up to 16 lights and change their type and properties. To add lights, simply drag the light icon from the bottom of the preview window, or Option-drag an existing light to duplicate it. To change the size and direction of the light, click and move the four points around the light for size, or click and drag the center line of the light for changes in direction.

Another way that Lighting Effects are applied is to create another layer and fill it with black. Apply Lighting Effects to this layer and set the apply mode to Screen in the Layers palette. Then, move the layer around to reposition the lights on your image.

Tip

Lighting Effects Shortcuts

Try these key combinations for faster, more effective Lighting Effects setting changes: Use Option-drag to duplicate an existing light. Use Shift-drag when changing the size of a light to keep the angle constant. Use ⌘-drag when changing the angle of a light to keep the size constant.

You can choose from the following three light types in the Light Type pop-up menu:

▶ **Spotlight** casts an ellipse-shaped light. With the spotlight only, you have the focus option, which controls how much of the ellipse is filled with light. Figure 15.47 shows an image before and after applying Spotlight.

▶ An **Omni** light is like a light bulb, shining down from above. Moving its line longer or shorter determines its distance away from the surface.

▶ **Directional** light is like a far away sun, and the only changeable control is its angle. The shorter the line, the brighter the light.

Fig. 15.47

Lighting Effects adds colored lights to a photograph.

After you add lights and choose their type, you can set the properties for each light (click a property to select). Light properties include the following:

▶ **Intensity.** A setting of 50 is normal. Less than 50 shines a black light. A setting of 100 is the brightest.

▶ **Color.** You can change the light color or ambient color by clicking the color swatches that bring up the Apple color picker. (The color swatches are the boxes to the right of the settings under Light Type and Properties.)

▶ **Gloss.** Determines how shiny the surface of the image is, from matte to glossy.

▶ **Material.** From plastic to metallic, this controls whether the surface reflects the color of the light or the color of an object.

▶ **Exposure.** This lightens or darkens overall.

▶ **Ambience.** A high number strengthens the effect of the light; a low number weakens it. Ambience refers to how much the light is diffused, as though there is another light in the room.

The Texture channel gives you the option of using a texture to affect the surface of your image. To use this option, create a channel in your image document and fill it with a texture (see the "Filtering Techniques" section later in this chapter for information on how to create textures). In the texture part of the dialog box, you have two options for how the texture affects the look. White Is High determines whether your image is embossed looking with bright parts of the texture rising up from the surface. White is Low creates the opposite, where light areas in the texture look like depressions in which the light shines down into the surface. You can also set the height of the texture from Flat to Mountainous.

After you create your own set of Lighting Effects, you can save them to use in other documents. Click the Save button and name your style. Remember, if you use a texture from a channel, that texture must be present in the same channel in your new document. Selecting a style and clicking Delete removes that style from the palette.

Texture Fill

Texture Fill, also new to Photoshop 3, fills a selection with a texture from a grayscale Photoshop 2.5 or 3 file that you previously created and saved. When you choose this filter, a find file dialog box appears for you to find the grayscale file to use as a texture. The CD-ROM version of Photoshop will come with several pre-saved textures for you to use.

This is another filter where it is best to float your selection before applying the filter. Use Photoshop's apply modes in the Layers palette for different effects. Try Overlay, Luminosity, and Soft Light for interesting applications of the texture. Figure 15.48 shows how the Overlay apply mode was used with a floating selection to apply a "crumpled-paper" texture.

Fig. 15.48

Texture Fill applied
a "crumpled-paper"
texture to this pho-
tograph using the
Overlay apply mode
from the Layers
palette.

Sharpen Filters

The Sharpen filters do the opposite of the Blur filters; they sharpen the
contrast between pixels of different colors. In general, sharpening can be
used to enhance and focus an image. The Sharpen category includes
Sharpen, Sharpen Edges, Sharpen More, and Sharpen Mask.

Sharpen

Sharpen brings out the detail in an image, especially where colors
contrast. It also helps reduce the flatness of scanned images.

Sharpen More

Sharpen More is the same as applying the Sharpen filter a few times.
If Sharpen More is used too much, unsightly patterns can be produced.

Sharpen Edges

This filter sharpens areas where colors are very different from each other,
such as the "edges" of color, and leaves the other areas alone. This brings
out the depth of an image without affecting the rest of the image.

Unsharp Mask

Unsharp Mask (see fig. 15.49) gives you more control over how the edges of color in an image are sharpened. The dialog box has controls for percentage of sharpening, size (radius) of sharpened areas from the edges, and level of difference in color at the edges (threshold).

This filter is intended to emulate photographic processes for sharpening images. It combines a blurred positive image with a sharp contrasting negative of the image to enhance the edges.

Unsharp Mask is great for enhancing scanned images, or for bringing out detail after you size an image down. Figure 15.50 shows a photo with increased contrast at color edges produced with Unsharp Mask. Some settings also can produce a posterized effect.

Fig. 15.49

Unsharp Mask gives you controls over how edges are enhanced in an image.

Fig. 15.50

Unsharp Mask was applied to sharpen contrast at color edges in this image.

V

Filters, Plug-Ins, & Effects

Stylize Filters

The Stylize filters offer a wide range of special effects, including embossing, diffusing the edges of an image, or creating geometric shapes out of your images. The Stylize filters are Diffuse, Emboss, Extrude, Find Edges, Solarize, Tiles, Trace Contour, and Wind.

Diffuse

Diffuse blurs the edges of color in an image in a more random and "sprayed" look than the Blur filter; it moves pixels away from color edges. It is similar to the way the Dissolve apply mode looks from the Layers palette. You can use this filter to soften the focus of an image in a rougher way than with blurring.

In the Diffuse dialog box, you can choose three ways to apply the filter: Normal, Darken Only, and Lighten Only. Darken Only replaces light pixels with dark ones, and Lighten Only replaces light pixels with dark ones. Use the preview window and move to an area of contrasting color, or an edge, to see the different effects, as shown in figure 15.51.

Fig. 15.51

Diffuse can blur the edges of an image with a "sprayed" look.

Emboss

Emboss makes the edges of an image look as though they are raised from the paper, just like traditional embossing. You control the angle of light direction, the height of the stamping, and the amount of color that results in the image. A low number turns the image gray. The Emboss dialog box is shown in figure 15.52 and an embossed photo is shown in figure 15.53.

Photoshop's Emboss works better on high contrast images. Third-party vendors also sell versions of this filter and can offer more controls. See chapter 16, "Third-Party Plug-Ins," for more information.

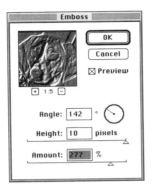

Fig. 15.52

Emboss makes an
image look raised
from paper.

Fig. 15.53

Emboss applied to
a photograph.

V

Filters, Plug-Ins, & Effects

Extrude

With Extrude, the color values are examined in an image, and then 3-D
objects are created from an average color in an area. In the Extrude dialog
box (see fig. 15.54), you can choose Blocks or Pyramids for the shape. You
also have control over the size of the shapes, their height (depth), and
whether the height is random or based on levels of brightness. Choose
Solid front faces to fill the top of the objects with the average color of the
area, and Mask incomplete blocks to hide objects that extend beyond your
selection area. Figure 15.55 shows how an image is changed to little 3-D
pyramids with Extrude.

Find Edges

Find Edges examines the image for sharp contrasting color "edges," draws
a dark colored line on those edges, and fills the rest with white. This filter
can be used just to create an outline, but it can also produce very

475

interesting effects if the selection is floated and different apply modes are used in the Layers palette. Figure 15.56 shows a before-and-after photo changed with the Find Edges filter.

Fig. 15.54

Extrude creates 3-D objects from an image.

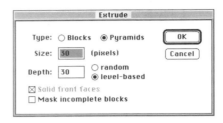

Fig. 15.55

Extrude changed this colored text on a background to a pattern of little 3-D pyramids.

Fig. 15.56

Find Edges creates a thick outline of the edges of an image and fills the rest with white.

Solarize

Solarize blends a positive and negative version of your image, creating a psychedelic effect. It is intended to emulate a photographic process in which a print is exposed to light during developing. Figure 15.57 shows a photo made psychedelic with Solarize.

Fig. 15.57

Solarize blends a positive and negative version of your image.

Tiles

Tiles changes your selection into an area of tiles, or boxes. You control the number of tiles, the size, how far they are offset from the original image, and how the spaces between the tiles are filled. Figure 15.58 shows the Tiles dialog box and the available settings.

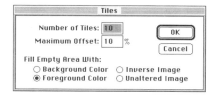

Fig. 15.58

The Tiles filter changes your image into boxes according to your settings in the Tiles dialog box.

Trace Contour

Trace Contour is similar to Find Edges; however, it gives you control over what level of color is traced in an image. The Trace Contour dialog box is shown in figure 15.59. For example, if you choose threshold level 0, or black, it draws a line wherever black edges occur. If you choose 255, it traces the areas where white edges occur. Threshold 128 traces all medium gray edges. The filter produces cyan, magenta, and yellow lines to show the threshold levels in each color channel. Figure 15.60 shows a clock traced by the Trace Contour filter.

Fig. 15.59

Trace Contour
traces outlines at
different levels of
color that you
choose.

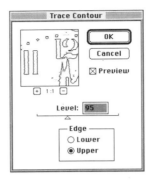

Fig. 15.60

Trace Contour
created cyan,
magenta, yellow,
and blue outlines
of the clock in
this picture.

Wind

Wind makes an image look as though it is being blown; it paints little strips
of color in a direction (left or right) and length you choose. The Wind
dialog box (see fig. 15.61) includes Wind, Blast, and Stagger. Figure 15.62
shows an image painted with the Blast option in Wind.

Fig. 15.61

Wind gives your
image a blown look.

Fig. 15.62

Wind applied to
a photo using the
Blast option.

Video Filters

Photoshop's video filters offer functions to help prepare your image for video use or to enhance images captured from video. The Video Filters are De-Interlace and NTSC Colors.

De-Interlace

Television monitors display video by flickering between odd and even fields. Capturing images from video can bring in defects from this motion and can look banded or noisy. De-Interlace deletes the odd or even field, and then replaces the information, either by duplicating the present field or interpolating between two bands (interpolation is best). If you don't know which one is missing, try both to see which looks better; this helps to reduce the banding.

NTSC Colors

NTSC, or National Television Standards Committee, created a standard for colors on a television monitor. Because of the way video is displayed, it cannot accept certain colors, such as 100 percent white or a bright red. You can notice when bright reds "bleed" or bright white flickers on television. The NTSC Colors filter restricts the colors in your image to those acceptable for NTSC standards, so you don't have problems associated with too bright or bold colors when the image goes to video. See chapter 24, "Photoshop for the Professional Photographer," for more discussion on producing images for video.

V

Filters, Plug-Ins, & Effects

Other Filters Submenu

The remaining set of filters is specialized for certain tasks. With these filters you can create filters, change the look of a mask, adjust colors for producing bitmaps, or move a selection. The Other Filter category contains Custom, High Pass, Maximum, Minimum, and Offset.

Custom

Custom allows you to change the brightness of pixels in your image according to mathematical operations. Often called *convolution*, or *kernels*, this filter operates similarly to the Apply Mode's add and subtract in the Layers and Brushes palette. You then can save your settings for use in later images.

To produce a Custom filter, type settings in the Custom dialog box (see fig. 15.63). A value typed in the center text box affects the center pixel. You can type in from +/– 999 to change the pixel's brightness. The boxes around the center affect the pixels next to the center one. The number you type here is a multiplication of the center number, or how many more times you want the adjacent pixels affected over the setting for the center pixel. Scale divides the sum of the values used in calculating the effect. Offset is a value that adds to the Scale calculation. It is difficult to describe how this filter works, but after you try it and get a feel for how it affects your image, you can gain a better understanding of how filter technology works.

Fig. 15.63

The Custom filter allows you to create your own Photoshop filters.

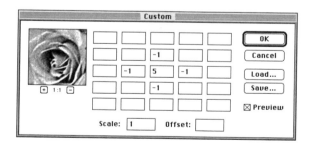

High Pass

High Pass strengthens bright areas in an image and removes shading except at edges where colors are in sharp contrast. This filter is good for bringing out large black-and-white areas when you convert a grayscale image to a bitmap. You control how much detail is kept or lost by setting the radius number either low (less detail) or high (more detail) in the High Pass dialog box (see fig. 15.64). Figure 15.65 shows a before-and-after image affected by High Pass. The flatter color areas have been brightened and flattened to light gray, while the detail at the color edges has been retained.

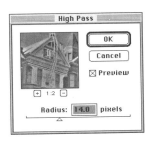

Fig. 15.64

The High Pass filter allows you to bring out bright areas in an image.

Fig. 15.65

High Pass was used on this photo to dull and lighten flat color areas while keeping color edges sharp.

Maximum

Maximum is used to spread white pixels in a channel mask. Maximum adds to the edges of a white area by the amount you choose (choking the black area). Maximum can be used on full-color images to spread highlight areas, but it's most useful for channel mask operations.

Minimum

Minimum is the opposite of Maximum; it adds to the edges of a black area in a channel mask by the amount you choose, thus spreading the black area. Minimum used on full-color images spreads out the shadow areas by the radius you choose.

Offset

Offset moves a selection horizontally and vertically by the amount you choose in the Offset dialog box (see fig. 15.66). For example, settings of horizontal 10 and vertical 10 move the image up and to the right 10 pixels. Negative values move the image to the left and down. The resulting space can be filled with the background color from the toolbox, or the edge pixels of the selection being moved, or the image can be wrapped to fill the space with content from the opposite side of the image. If you use Offset on a Layer with a transparent background, be careful to have Preserve Transparency deselected in the Layers palette, or part of your selection will disappear.

Fig. 15.66

The Offset filter lets you move a selection by the specific amount you choose.

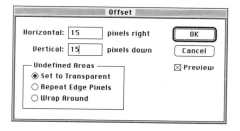

Filter Factory

Filter Factory, which ships only with the CD-ROM version of Photoshop 3, is a filter creator that goes even further than Custom to let you design your own filters. An understanding of filter technology and programming may be required to enable you to use this filter effectively; you have to type in algorithmic generators to affect pixels in an image with this filter. Photoshop documentation includes a 13-page electronic document on Filter Factory, but you don't need a strong background with filter creation. The Filter Factory dialog box (see fig. 15.67) includes a preview box that shows the effects of the filter. (Note that, in figure 15.67, the preview box appears black because Filter Factory was opened on an empty picture.)

Filtering Techniques

This section teaches you how to produce certain useful effects with filters for your images. Photoshop is a very deep program and mastering it never ends; this is due largely to the power of its filters. When you learn all the built-in filters, you still can buy more from third-party vendors!

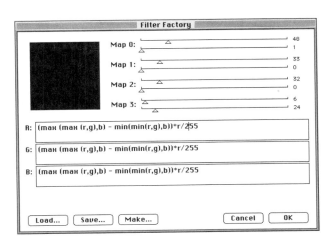

Fig. 15.67

Filter Factory gives you extensive control for creating your own filters.

Also, when using filters, don't forget that the key word is exploration. Although there are some steps provided here for achieving certain tasks, it is impossible to include all the effects available with 40+ filters and Photoshop's apply modes. The following sections provide you with guidelines to get started with your experimentation. With preview windows now available for most of the filters, you can view the effects of different settings before committing the time to apply the filter, so make use of those previews!

Using Filters for Masks and Shadows

You can create soft shadows with the Gaussian Blur filter, or change the look of masks for new selection options.

Creating a Soft Shadow

In earlier versions of Photoshop, creating a soft shadow underlying your image took several steps involving the use of channels. With the Layers palette in version 3, this process is simplified. To create a shadow under an image, follow these steps:

1. Select an object in your RGB or CMYK channel.

   If you want to apply a shadow to the entire image, make sure your Canvas Size is large enough to accommodate it.

V

Filters, Plug-Ins, & Effects

483

Tip

Making Backgrounds Transparent in Layers

There is no way to delete, or make transparent, an existing white background from images created in older versions of Photoshop. To take advantage of the transparency features in version 3 with layers, you may need to copy and paste your selection into a new document. When you create a new document, the New file dialog box appears. Make sure Transparent is selected in the Contents options. You may also want to make the document larger; it will default to the size of your copied selection. Then paste your image into the new document, and the background will be transparent.

2. Create a new layer by choosing Make Layer from the Layers palette.

3. Click the new layer if it isn't already active. Make sure Preserve Transparency is clicked in the Layers palette. With your selection still made, fill it with black. (Option-Delete fills a selection with a foreground color.)

   You can turn off the display of the other layer to see what is happening.

4. While in the new layer, Select All, and then use your arrow tools to move the box below and to the right of the original image. Or you can open the Filter menu, and Choose Other, Offset to type in the number of pixels to which you want to move the box. The best number varies with your preference and the resolution of your image.

5. Select All again (make sure the Protect Transparency box is not selected) and then open the Filter menu. Choose Gaussian Blur.

6. In the Gaussian Blur preview window, move to the edge of the black box and adjust the slider for the softness level you want. Again, the best number varies with preference and resolution.

7. Click OK.

8. If you follow these steps exactly, you might notice the shadow is on top of the image. Simply move the shadow layer in the Layers palette underneath the layer containing your original image. Figure 15.68 shows the result, with the shadow underneath the image.

Fig. 15.68

With Gaussian Blur, you create soft drop shadows.

Changing the Look of Masks

As you will learn in chapter 18, "Creating Special Effects with Channels," channel operations are a powerful and important feature of Photoshop. Filters give you a lot of control over channels that you can use as your selection masks.

To enlarge or shrink the edges of a black and white mask, follow these steps:

1. Go to the channel containing the mask you want to use as a selection.

2. Select All.

3. Open the Filter menu and choose Other Maximum to enlarge the white area (it enlarges your resulting selection). Choose the Other Minimum to enlarge the black area (it shrinks your selection).

4. Type in the number of pixels by which you want to enlarge or shrink.

5. Click OK.

6. Go back to your RGB or CMYK channel and load the selection to see how it has changed.

Figure 15.69 shows two masks. The selection on the left was enlarged with Maximum; the selection on the right was shrunk with Minimum.

Another way to change the look of a selection is to blur the edges. When you load the selection, you have a feathered effect.

1. Go to your selection channel and Select All.

2. Open the Filter menu and choose Blur, Gaussian Blur. Gaussian Blur blurs the area between black and white.

V

Filters, Plug-Ins, & Effects

3. Click OK.

4. Go back to the RGB or CMYK channel and load the selection. Invert the selection and change the background to see how the edges of the selection are feathered.

Fig. 15.69

Maximum and Minimum can change the size of a selection mask.

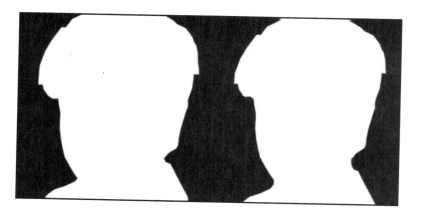

After you become comfortable using channels to affect selections, try other filters and see how they work.

Using Filters to Improve and Touch Up Images

There are several ways to use filters to enhance your images. As shown in Chapter 6, "Scanning Images," images that are scanned often show up with a flatness, noisy patterns, or defects. It's always a good idea to open the Image menu and Adjust Curves or Levels to remove some of the flatness. There are also a few filters that help improve your image.

Try each one of the following to see which works best. The method depends on the range of colors and brightness levels in your scan, the amount of noise or artifacts, and the resolution. Also, different filters do different things for your image depending on what your goal is. Use Undo (⌘-Z) if the filter does not produce your desired effect.

▶ **Blur** can help soften the look of noisy scans with an overall blurring effect.

▶ **Gaussian Blur** can soften an image, but has less effect on contrasting colors in your image. Using blur tools too much can make your image look unfocused.

▶ **Median** averages the color values of adjacent pixels in a size area you determine and can help soften rough areas. Using this filter at too high of a level produces a painted look.

▶ **Sharpen** improves overall contrast and detail to an image.

▶ **Sharpen Edges** brings out detail at color edges and leaves the rest unsharpened. This helps add depth to your image.

▶ **Unsharp Mask** gives you more control over what is sharpened. Try different settings and use the preview window to see how they affect your image.

Removing Scanned Patterns

If you scan an image from printed material, such as a magazine or book, instead of from a continuous-tone photograph, you also are scanning in the dot pattern used to print the image. (Don't forget that most images from books and magazines are copyright protected, unless they are over 75 years old or you have permission to use them). This pattern is often called a moiré pattern and can be very difficult to remove.

It is always best to scan at the highest resolution your scanner can provide and then size the image down to the size you want. This action alone takes care of some of the noise in the image. When you size an image down, it blurs the contrast or patterns in the image. You then can use one of the Sharpen filters to enhance any lost detail.

If you are not resizing an image, the basic method for removing noise is to use Blur filters to soften the patterns, and then Sharpen to bring out detail. There are a few steps you can take to help reduce the pattern in the image:

1. First, examine the color channels in your image. Determine which channel has the sharpest moiré pattern.

> **Note**
>
> Be sure to save your image, so that you can Revert if the steps you take don't give the desired effect.

2. In that channel, you can use Gaussian Blur, Blur More, or Median to blur the image.

3. After blurring the channel, use Unsharp Mask to sharpen it.

4. In each of the other channels, do the same thing at lower settings than you used on the first channel.

5. Go back to your RGB Image and view the results.

Another method for reducing noise is the new Dust & Scratches filter in Photoshop 3. To use this new filter, follow these steps:

1. Open the Filter menu, and choose Noise, Dust & Scratches.

2. Move your image in the preview window to show where dust occurs.

3. Change the radius and threshold settings to remove the dust and look at the preview of the overall image.

4. If the filter blurs the image more than you want, use a Sharpen filter to enhance detail without bringing back the unwanted dust.

Focusing a Blurred Image

Focusing a blurred image is pretty simple with the Sharpen filters. Just make sure you don't overuse the Sharpen tools to introduce noise or artifacting of colors.

1. Open the image. Open the Filter menu, and choose Sharpen, Unsharp Mask.

2. When the dialog box comes up, press the Minus tool in the preview window to view the selection to be focused.

3. Experiment with the Amount, Radius, and Threshold sliders until you get a desired level of sharpening.

Figure 15.70 shows an image focused using Sharpen filters.

Fig. 15.70

Focus images by using Sharpen filters.

Creating Backgrounds and Textures

There are several Photoshop and third-party filters designed to create interesting backgrounds. Experimentation is a must! In Photoshop, there are some simple steps you can use to begin creating a texture either for a background or as a texture to apply to an image:

1. Start with a New file and fill it with a color.

2. Open the Filter menu, and select Noise, Add Noise. Figure 15.71 shows how Add Noise creates a good starting texture.

3. Vary the options in the Add Noise dialog box until you get a colored, speckled pattern.

4. To enhance the brightness differences, you can adjust Levels, or use Hue/Saturation to change the color.

5. After you have this base image, try several of the filters for your desired effect—for example, Emboss, Crystallize, Extrude, or Find Edges.

6. Don't forget to experiment with floating images and different Apply modes from your Layers palette.

Several third-party filters can provide further options for backgrounds. See chapter 16 for more information.

Fig. 15.71

Noise can add texture for a good starting image to use as a background.

Creating Mezzotints, Textured, and Traced Look Images

Photoshop 3 gives you tools for creating mezzotint looks, tracing the outlines of images, and applying textures to images.

V

Filters, Plug-Ins, & Effects

A Mezzotint Look

Although Photoshop now provides a Mezzotint filter under the Pixelate submenu, as described in the previous section, there are other ways to achieve mezzotint-like effects that may suit your purposes better. Use the Noise filters to get these effects.

1. Make your selection and open the Filter menu. Choose Noise, Add Noise, and vary the options to view different applications.

2. Use Despeckle if you want to soften the effect overall without losing contrast.

3. Once again, don't forget to try floating your selection and using the different apply modes for different effects.

Figure 15.72 shows two variations of adding noise to photos to create a colored mezzotint effect. Also see figure 15.72 in the color section, "Photoshop in Color!"

Fig. 15.72

Adding noise to an image can create a colored mezzotint effect. (See color section also.)

Applying Textures to an Image

With the steps above, you easily can use apply modes for different ways to apply a noisy texture to an image. Photoshop 3 now comes with a filter called Texture Fill located in the Render submenu which allows you to open a pre-saved file to use as a texture pattern. But with the Layers palette, you can simply create textured patterns in another layer and apply them to an image. To experiment with different textures, follow these steps:

1. Open an image file and create a New Layer.

2. Fill this layer with a color and experiment with filters discussed in this chapter, especially those in the Noise, Pixelate, Render, and Stylize submenus. Also, combine filter effects by applying more than one for different textures.

3. While the new layer is active and above your original image in the Layers palette, use different apply modes to see how the texture affects the image.

4. If you're new to layers, you can simply float your image in the same layer and apply filters to that layer. You also can use different apply modes.

Figure 15.73 shows two examples of textures applied to images. Also see figure 15.73 in the color section, "Photoshop in Color!"

Fig. 15.73

Two examples of applying textures to images. (See color section also.)

Using Filters To Create Color and Lighting Effects

The new Lighting Effects filter, found in the Render submenu, can create all kinds of different looks for applying white or colored light to your images.

1. Open the Filter menu and choose Render, Lighting Effects.

2. First explore the different preset options under the Style pop-up menu to get an idea of what is possible.

3. You can change or expand on any of the pre-saved styles you choose to create your own lighting effects.

Be sure to try variations with light color and ambient light colors, direction, sizes, and textures. Then expand upon that by using Layers or floating your selection to take advantage of the Layers apply modes.

Using Filters for Effects with Type

Why have the same old, flat-colored type in your images? Filters can provide very interesting effects for headlines in your multimedia presentations or magazine layouts. Select type characters and follow the steps in other parts of this chapter to try out different effects.

Chapter 16, "Third Party Plug-Ins," shows you how to produce metallic-looking type, beveled type, type with gradations, 3-D-looking type, and more.

Using Filters To Create Other Special Effects

The various effects created by using filters are virtually limitless. Filters can be used to create popular, "real-life" looks, such as the traditional paintings and stained glass described in this section.

Painting Effects

Many of Photoshop's filters give your image a painted look. Experimenting with Median, or high levels of Unsharp Mask, can give oil painting or posterized looks to your images. Also try Pointillize for a pointillist effect. Figure 15.74 shows how Median can give an image a painted look. Also, see figure 15.74 in the color section, "Photoshop in Color!"

Fig. 15.74

Median can give your image a painted look. (See color section also.)

See the next chapter for a discussion on several third-party filters that are specifically designed to create anything from watercolors to charcoal drawings.

Stained Glass

Using Crystallize, or Mosaic, can produce stained glass effects for your images. To achieve this effect, use the following steps:

1. With your image selected, open the Filter menu and choose Mosaic or Crystallize.

2. Choose settings in the dialog box to adjust the size of the resulting polygons or squares. Click OK.

3. Now float your image (⌘-J).

4. Open the Filter menu and choose Stylize, Find Edges. Click OK.

5. In the Layers palette, your floating selection should still be active. Choose Multiply from the Mode pop-up menu in the Layer Options dialog box.

6. If the edges aren't strong or thick enough, open the Filter menu and choose Other, Minimum while your selection is still floating.

7. Adjust the desired width of the black edges by moving the Radius slider in the Minimum dialog box.

8. Click OK and voila! You have stained glass, as shown in figure 15.75. Also see figure 15.75 in the color section, "Photoshop in Color!"

Fig. 15.75

Mosaic and Find Edges were used to make this stained glass image. (See color section also.)

Combining Filters

Often when you use filters, you may start out with a goal in mind, then change it based on the extensive options you find when you experiment with different effects. Such is the beauty of digital manipulation! As stated earlier, there is no way to describe how many thousands of looks you can get by combining filters and apply modes. The best thing to do is simply start exploring. Start with any image, and apply filters to it. Apply one filter, and then another to the same image. Float your image, apply yet another filter, and try different apply modes. You will see that Photoshop is certainly not limited by anyone's imagination. (Just don't forget to eat and sleep!)

Where To Go from Here

▶ Chapter 1, "Touring Photoshop," teaches you about using multiple layers.

▶ Chapter 2, "Exploring What's New in Photoshop 3," discusses Dust & Scratches, new palette design, and previews in filters.

▶ Chapter 6, "Scanning Images," discusses scanning different types of images.

▶ Chapter 16, "Third-Party Plug-Ins," introduces you to several types of plug-in filters available from third-party software companies.

▶ Chapter 17, "Creating Special Effects with Video," explains how to create effects with video.

▶ Chapter 18, "Creating Special Effects with Channels," explains how to create effects with channels.

▶ Chapter 19, "3-D Modeling Special Effects," shows you how to make your images appear 3-dimensional.

▶ Chapter 20, "Text Special Effects," tells you how to apply effects to your text.

▶ Also see Part VII, "Learning from the Pros," for tips on how to use filters and other techniques to design for different media.

Third-Party Plug-Ins

There are several types of plug-in filters available from software companies. They are called *third-party* filters because they are created by companies other than Adobe, but were designed using Adobe's plug-in architecture to work with Photoshop. They range from art and effects filters to specialized filters for certain functions in certain industries.

Third-party filters range from art and effects filters to specialized filters that were designed for specific, narrow functions or industries. Art and effects filters enhance or apply special looks to images, while specialized filters work with certain file types used in the pre-press industry, or encode caption information for the newspaper industry. Filters are available to purchase from mail-order catalogs, or there are several shareware or freeware filters that can be downloaded from on-line services.

by Elizabeth Brown Lawler

CHAPTER 16

To use third-party filters with Photoshop 3, simply install or copy them into the *Plug-Ins* folder in the Photoshop 3 folder. Previous versions of Photoshop had all filters floating in the same folder, but in Photoshop version 3, you can have folders for different filter sets or function categories inside the Plug-Ins folder.

Once installed, the Filter menu changes to include all the third-party filters that are in the Plug-Ins folder. Figure 16.1 shows an example of the Filter menu with some third-party filters added.

Fig. 16.1

Installing third-party filters changes the look of your Filter menu.

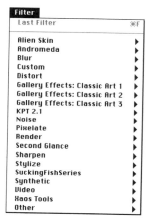

You use a third-party filter the same way as you use Photoshop's filters:

1. Select the image or portion of an image you want the filter to affect.

2. Open the Filter menu, and select the desired filter.

3. Choose your desired settings in the dialog box, if applicable.

4. Click OK.

You can stop the application of a filter with ⌘-period.

> **Tip**
>
> **Filter Shortcuts**
>
> Using key combinations will speed your use of filters. To undo a filter after it is applied, press ⌘-Z. To apply a filter a second time, press ⌘-F. Or, to bring up the dialog box of the same filter, press ⌘-Option-F.

Not only can third-party filters be added to Photoshop, but there are several other graphics programs that use the same plug-in technology, and can use Photoshop's filters and third-party filters in their programs. Other plug-in compatible painting and photo processing programs include Fractal Design Painter, and PixelPaint Pro. Desktop video programs that can access plug-in filters include Adobe Premiere and CoSA After Effects. A few 3-D programs can use filters after rendering images, including Stratavision and Ray Dream Designer.

The next section gives a description of many popular third-party filter sets. Each set comes with a manual with more information and often tips about using the filters. Check the Resources appendix to see how to contact the companies that make these filters.

Overview of Art and Effects Third-Party Filters

The most popular types of third-party filters are those that apply special effects to your images or make a photo look like art. Some have simply expanded and improved on functions available with Adobe's built-in filters, while others have ventured into completely new territory.

The Black Box

The Black Box filters, by Alien Skin Software, were created by Jeff Butterworth to automate several important functions in Photoshop. Available for Mac (including PowerMac native) and Windows, these filters make creating a drop shadow or embossing an object a one-step process!

Installing these filters creates a Filter submenu called Black Box. Each filter comes with its own dialog box with controls to vary your settings. To apply a Black Box filter, you must have an object selected, and it is *very important* to save your selection so you can load it again. Due to the way filter technology works, the selection disappears after the filter is applied. This is because filter technology is designed to affect what is *inside* a selection, and the Black Box filters affect what is *outside* a selection (like making a drop shadow under an object).

Drop Shadow

The time you save creating one-step drop shadows pays for this filter almost immediately. Although the Layers feature in Photoshop 3 makes it easier to create shadows as described in chapter 15, "Using Photoshop's Plug-In Filters," this filter automates in one step one of Photoshop's most widely used techniques.

The Drop Shadow dialog box, shown in figure 16.2, gives you control over how far offset the shadow is (horizontally and vertically). Moving the X or Y sliders to the right makes the shadow fall below and to the right of your object. Moving the sliders to the left take it up and to the left. You also have control over how blurred the shadow looks, how opaque or transparent it is, and what color it is. Figure 16.3 shows an image example of Drop Shadow.

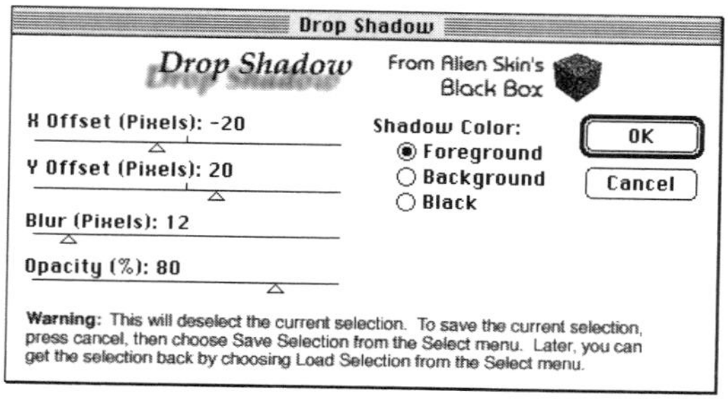

Fig. 16.2

Drop Shadow creates shadows below your objects in one step.

Note

When working with CMYK images for printing, if you want your shadow to be a Process Black, click Black/White for the colors in your toolbox before you open this filter. Then when you use the Drop Shadow filter, click Foreground color instead of Black. The Black in Drop Shadow is pure black "ink" and not process black.

Glass

The Glass filter makes your object look like glass on top of the rest of the image. It puts colored glass over your selection, and adds a bevel to raise it up from the rest of the image. The Glass dialog box, shown in figure 16.4, gives controls over bevel shape and highlights, light refraction, opacity, and glass color. Figure 16.5 shows how an object is turned into glass. Also see figure 16.5 in the color section, "Photoshop in Color!"

Fig. 16.3

Drop Shadow applied to an object.

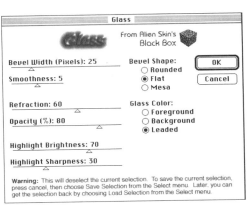

Fig. 16.4

The Glass filter puts a sheet of colored glass over an object.

V

Filters, Plug-Ins, & Effects

Glow

Glow puts a radiating glow around an object in the color and width you choose. Without this filter, a glowing effect could be achieved with several steps in Photoshop involving the use of channels or layers; however, in areas where your image is thin, the glow would be weaker. This filter applies the same strength and width of glowing around all edges of your object. The dialog box (see fig. 16.6) also gives you options for glow width, intensity, color, opacity, drop-off (how the glow fades out into the background), and anti-aliasing.

Fig. 16.5

An object turned into glass. (Also see color section.)

Glow is very effective for making type or other objects stand out against a background. When selecting type, try inverting your selection and make a dark-colored glow inside your type to give it a raised appearance.

Fig. 16.6

With the Glow filter, you can make objects appear to glow using the Glow dialog box.

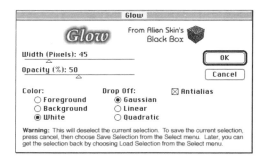

HSB Noise

In earlier versions of Photoshop, the Noise filter that came with Photoshop would add all kinds of different colored pixels to an image, making it look like TV static. Many third-party filter creators added options to produce noise without destroying color hues in your image. Photoshop version 3 now has the option of choosing Monochromatic to add noise, while retaining color values, but HSB and other third-party filters give different controls for how noise is applied.

HSB means hue, saturation, and brightness. The HSB Noise filter gives control over how much the hue, saturation, or brightness of pixels in a selection are varied with application of this filter. The HSB Noise dialog box is shown in figure 16.7

Fig. 16.7

HSB Noise gives a good starting texture for other effects.

Swirl

Swirl smears the area outside of your selection into randomly spaced whirlpools for a fluid look. With the Swirl dialog box (see fig. 16.8), you can set the whirlpool spacing, smear length (how much image is blurred), and whether the image smears around the whirlpool in rings or out of them like a fountain spray (using the Twist slider). Figure 16.9 shows how a cloverleaf background can be affected with Swirl.

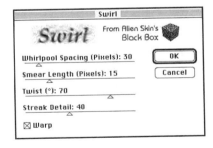

Fig. 16.8

The Swirl filter applies fluid-looking whirlpools to the area outside your selection.

The Boss

This is a very powerful filter for making objects look embossed in one step. You can set the bevel height, width and smoothing into the background, highlight brightness and sharpness, and overall opacity (see fig. 16.10). With certain settings of highlight brightness and sharpness, you can control how shiny the embossed object looks. Setting the opacity slider to transparent gives you an embossed shape of your selection. Figure 16.11 shows how text can be embossed with The Boss.

V

Filters, Plug-Ins, & Effects

Fig. 16.9

The Swirl filter applied to a back-ground creates whirlpools all over the image.

Fig. 16.10

The Boss is a powerful tool for creating embossed looks.

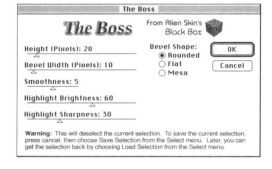

Fig. 16.11

The Boss was used to emboss the text in this image.

Kai's Power Tools

Award-winning Kai's Power Tools, created by HSC Software, is a powerful set of about 40 filters that are widely popular in the graphics industry. Version 2.0 hit top-ten best seller lists for graphics applications several times in 1993.

Many of the filters extend and improve functions available in Photoshop, like for blurring, noise, and tracing edges. However, Kai's Power Tools (KPT) goes beyond this with incredibly deep and specialized filters and beautifully intuitive dialog boxes designed by Kai Krause.

All KPT filters work in full 24-bit color as well as with monitor settings of 16- or 8-bit. Most work in RGB, CMYK, or Grayscale mode. Most filters have intensity controls by pressing numbers on the numeric keypad, with 1 as the lowest application of the filter and 0 (10) as the highest. For some filters these numbers do different things. Also, having Caps Lock pressed varies the effect, depending on the filter.

When you install Kai's Power Tools into the Plug-Ins folder, it creates a Filter submenu called KPT 2.1 which includes Gradient Designer, Texture Explorer, Fractal Explorer, Fade Contrast, 3D Stereo Noise, PixelBreeze, PixelStorm, PixelWind, Seamless Welder, and Selection Info. Other filters begin with the name "KPT" and are put into Photoshop's existing filter submenus, depending on their function. The description under each filter tells which submenu contains them.

Gradient Designer

Creating a two-color ramped blend is fairly simple in Photoshop. But what about a blend with three colors, or even 50 colors applied procedurally to an image to produce interesting colored lighting effects? This can take all day! Or what about a gradient applied in the shape of your selection with transparency levels at different settings for each area of the gradient? This is impossible without Gradient Designer.

Gradient Designer is a potent tool for creating complex color blends. It is a must for anyone wanting to create backgrounds for video and multimedia, but can be used intelligently to create effects for many image processing needs.

When you open the Filter menu and select KPT Gradient Designer from the KPT submenu, the Gradient Designer dialog box appears, as shown in figure 16.12.

V

Fig. 16.12

The Gradient Designer dialog box gives various controls for creating color blends.

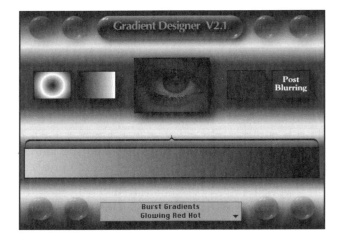

In the Gradient Designer dialog box, you find controls for all aspects of a color blend. The top-center box gives you a preview of the gradient applied to your image. The four boxes to the right and left of the preview window control the type of gradient, how it is looped, its direction, and how it is blurred.

The color bar, across the lower part of the dialog box, allows you to pick as many as 512 colors in one gradient, from several supplied palettes or from any image outside the dialog box. When you click the color bar, the KPT color picker appears, as shown in figure 16.13. The bracket above the color bar can be stretched, shrunk, or moved to allow changes in specific portions of the color bar. Portions of the color bar may be copied, pasted, cut, moved, flipped, or stretched however you want.

Fig. 16.13

You can access the KPT color picker by clicking on the color bar to change colors in the gradient.

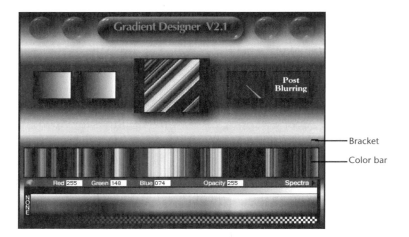

The pull-down menu at the bottom center contains hundreds of preset styles grouped in categories to get you started, or you can save or delete your own styles. Figure 16.14 shows the preset style pull-down menu.

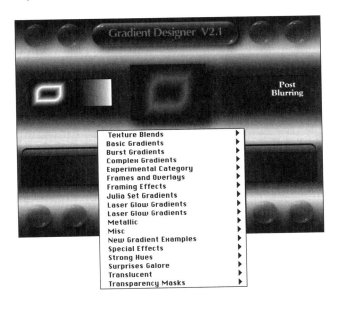

Fig. 16.14

Gradient Designer contains many preset styles.

V

Filters, Plug-Ins, & Effects

Tip

Gradient Designer Shortcuts

The Gradient Designer dialog box incorporates many key combinations as shortcuts you can use. The up- and down-arrow keys scroll through the preset gradients. Page Up and Page Down will jump to the next category of presets. Using the Tab key will scroll through the Apply Modes Under options.

Types of gradients include Linear Blend, Circular Sunburst, Elliptical Sunburst, Radial Sweep, Square Burst, Rectangular Burst, Angular Shapeburst, Circular Shapeburst, Angular Pathburst, Circular Pathburst, and Gradient on Paths. The Shapeburst warps the gradient to the shape of your selection, and Pathburst warps it to a path. Circular provides smooth curves at sharp contours of the selection, while Angular creates sharp edges.

Note

KPT Gradient on Paths used to be a separate filter but has been integrated as a choice into Gradient Designer.

With the looping control, you can make a gradient go from its origin to its end and back again (A to B to A), and from end to origin to end again (B to A to B). You can also repeat a gradient up to ten times, and you can warp it towards its origin or end for special perspective or rolling effects. Clicking the looping control box will apply your setting to the color bar. For example if you create a black to blue gradient, then want to loop it, black to blue to black, you can choose that in looping control, then click it to apply it to the color bar for further editing. If you want a gradient to repeat 20 times, you can use looping control to choose "repeat 10 times," click it to apply it to the color bar, then go back and choose "repeat twice" to make 20.

With transparency controls built into the color bar, you can make different portions of the gradient have different opacity levels. With the Options menu at the top right, you have even more control over how the gradient is applied to your image, much like the Photoshop's Layers palette, but with an additional option like Procedural Blend (which "wraps" the gradient to an image depending on the image's brightness intensity) and Reverse Blend (like Procedural but somewhat in reverse).

Help for all KPT filters is available by clicking the Help button. The Shuffle button allows you to randomly shuffle through different gradients.

Figure 16.15 shows examples of how Gradient Designer can create images. The left image shows a frame entirely made with the filter. Part of the power of Gradient Designer is that black and white gradients can be applied to a color with the Procedural apply mode to make an object look three-dimensional. The right image shows a background created with two radial gradients. Also see figure 16.15 in the color section, "Photoshop in color!"

Try applying this filter to the same image a few times in different ways for exciting effects. See "Filtering Techniques" later in this chapter for how to use the Gradient Designer to create 3-D looks and frames.

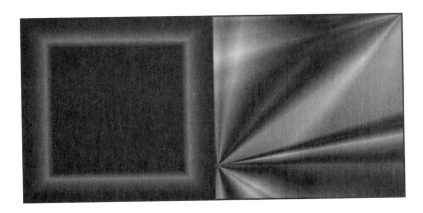

Texture Explorer

With KPT's Texture Explorer, you can create unlimited color textures for
backgrounds and image special effects. The creation of textures is based on
randomly calculated algorithms, so the results are practically infinite. The
preset styles contain many popular textures, like marble, paper, wood,
and liquid categories, but they also contain textures never before seen in
nature. You can explore the presets to get an idea of what types can be
created, and then expand on those by clicking different parts of the dialog
box.

When you select Texture Explorer from the KPT submenu, the dialog box
appears, as shown in figure 16.16.

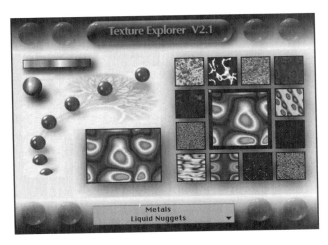

Fig. 16.16

With Texture
Explorer, you can
create an infinite
number of textures.

V

Filters, Plug-Ins, & Effects

The boxes on the right side of the dialog box show variations on a texture in the center. When you choose a different preset, the choice appears in the center, and the variation boxes change based on that choice. Clicking any of the outer boxes moves that choice to the center, and recalculates variations based on that image. The "mutant tree" on the left of the dialog box changes variations from very similar to very different as you click the different red balls moving upward from the bottom.

From the color bar in the upper left, you can access preset textures from Texture Explorer, as shown in figure 16.17. This is a great option if you want to restrict your texture to certain colors. For example, if you want to make a black and blue stone texture, you can create a black to blue gradient and save it as a style in Gradient Designer, then choose it to apply those colors to a texture in Texture Explorer.

Fig. 16.17

You can access colors from styles in Texture Explorer with the color bar.

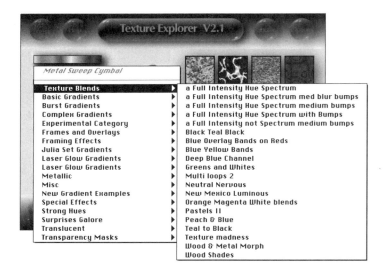

The Shuffle button allows you to shuffle through random textures. If you deselect Shuffle Colors in the Shuffle menu, you will shuffle through textures using the same colors as you've chosen in the color-choice bar.

There is a small preview window next to the mutant tree, but if you click the large center texture box, it will expand to show you a real-size preview (if your image selection is at least 512×512 pixels), as shown in figure 16.18. If you click and hold the center texture box, you can choose how large the texture will be in pixels when it is applied to your image. Pixel sizes smaller than your image size tile the texture across your image.

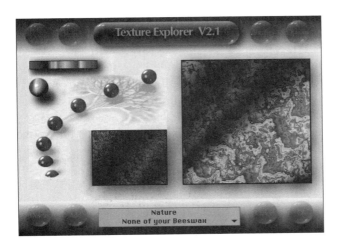

Fig. 16.18

You can preview your image at real-size by clicking the center texture box.

Texture Explorer contains an Options menu similar to the one found in Gradient Designer, for variations on how the texture is applied. Also included in the Options menu is the ability to create 3-D Stereo Noise, or *stereogram*, images. These are colorful images, increasing in popularity, where you focus on a point deep in the image and see two sides converge, like in a 3-D movie. Any texture can be applied to an image to create the 3-D stereo effect.

Once again, try applying textures more than once with different apply modes from the Options menu for even more interesting effects!

Figure 16.19 shows two examples of textures created with Texture Explorer. In both images, Texture Explorer was used more than once to create the result.

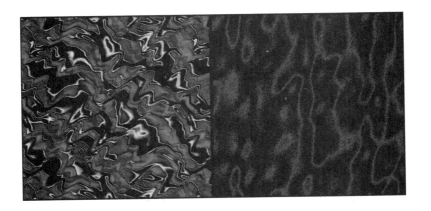

Fig. 16.19

Samples of textures created with Texture Explorer.

Fractal Explorer

This is a great fractal generator for fans of fractal images, but it also can add interest to any image or background. The Fractal Explorer dialog box, shown in figure 16.20, comes with several presets, and Mandelbrot or Julia Set fractals and hybrids. Color inside and outside the fractal is controlled by two gradient bars, which access presets from Gradient Designer. There is also looping, zooming, panning, spiral wrapping, radial spoke wrapping controls, and a real-time preview. Fractal Explorer has several apply modes, like in Gradient Designer and Texture Explorer, as well as a numerical input option for fractal experts.

Fig. 16.20

The Fractal Explorer dialog box.

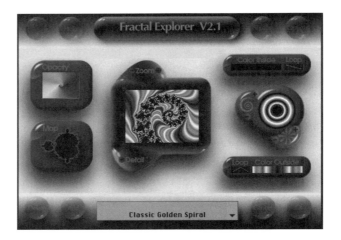

3-D Stereo Noise

This filter creates 3-D stereogram images from grayscale images by creating a black-and-white pixel pattern. By focusing on the two boxes created in the bottom center, some people can see the 3-D effect it creates. For colored stereogram images, see the description of KPT Texture Explorer in the previous section.

Fade Contrast

Fade Contrast desaturates and lightens a selection, like flattening the brightness levels. This is used to prepare images for use as backgrounds.

PixelBreeze, PixelWind, and PixelStorm

PixelBreeze, PixelWind, and PixelStorm apply diffusion across an entire image, instead of just color edges, like Diffuse or KPT Diffuse More. Each offers intensity control with the numeric keypad. PixelStorm scatters pixels 200 pixels, while Wind diffuses them 80 pixels and Breeze uses a 30 pixel area. PixelBreeze has a lightening effect and Wind brings out color saturation during application. Caps Lock offers fade out and blur control with feathered selections when using PixelWind and PixelStorm. These filters are also very useful for diffusing the edges of masks. Figure 16.21 shows an image with PixelBreeze applied to the edges.

> **Note**
>
> The term *color edges* refers to the lines where contrasting colors run into each other.

Fig. 16.21

PixelBreeze was applied to the edges of this image to give it a diffused look.

Gaussian Electrify, Glow, and Weave

Found in the Blur submenu, these three filters add a blurred glow around your image selection. Electrify blurs the image and reapplies it using Lighten Only apply mode, while Glow does the same thing with Darken Only apply mode. Gaussian Weave is a combination with horizontal and vertical blurs of the image done separately, then reapplied. Try variations with the numeric keypad, with 1 as the faintest application and 0 (ten) as the strongest.

Seamless Welder

Seamless Welder creates tiles from your selection so you can use them to create a texture. It takes information from the edges of your selection to make the tiles appear to match on all four sides. The resulting pattern will not have hard edges and will look naturally blended when you use it as a texture to fill an image.

Selection Info

Selection Info simply tells you the width and height of your selection. It also calculates the total number of pixels in the selection and the percentage of the total image that is selected.

Smudge Darken & Lighten, Left & Right

The Smudge filters are similar to Photoshop's Motion Blur, but offer more controls with direction, and use darken or lighten apply modes. Smudge Darken blurs the dark pixels into light areas and Smudge Lighten blurs the light pixels into dark areas. Choosing the Left or Right filter will smudge pixels in the corresponding direction. These filters are found in the Blur submenu.

Glass Lens Soft, Normal, Bright

The Glass Lens filters, found in the Distort submenu, create a highlighted sphere from your selection. Bright creates the most lighted and pronounced sphere, while Soft generates a soft bubble coming out from the image. You can control which direction the light is coming from by holding down a number on the numerical keypad when you select the filter. For example, pressing 7 makes the light shine from top left. You can use the Caps Lock key to control whether there is black or the image filling the background behind the sphere. Figure 16.22 shows how a photo is warped into a sphere using Glass Lens Bright.

Page Curl

KPT Page Curl, in the Distort submenu, makes your image look like a page that is being turned. You have control over which corner is "curled," and whether it is on the horizontal or vertical axis. Figure 16.23 shows the effect of Page Curl.

Fig. 16.22

Glass Lens Bright warps images into 3-D spheres.

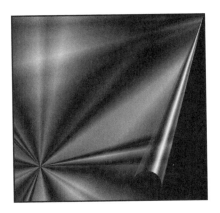

Fig. 16.23

Page Curl makes your image look like it's a page being turned.

Vortex Tiling

New to KPT version 2.1, this tiles several copies of your selection in a circular pattern out from the center. By pressing keys in the numeric keypad, you can control the number and size of the tiles: 1 is the lowest number of the largest tiles and 0 is the highest number with smaller tiles. Vortex Tiling is located in the Distort submenu. Figure 16.24 shows how a clock is tiled around a center point.

Grime Layer

Found in the Noise submenu, KPT Grime Layer adds a speckling of darkening pixels across your image, and has numeric keypad intensity control. For noise effects, it is best to experiment with different noise filters, because they are all applied in different ways.

Fig. 16.24

Fig. 16.24

Vortex tiling
applied to an
image.

Hue Protected Noise

KPT Hue Protected (H-P) Noise gives Photoshop users a way to add noise that takes into account colors in the underlying image. There are three H-P Noise filters, Maximum, Median, and Minimum, and each has 10 levels of application by pressing numeric keys.

Special Red, Green, and Blue Noise

These special noise filters get their colors from three preset gradients in Gradient Designer and can produce noise effects not available from any other noise filter. Different variations occur with different numeric keys and whether you use a feathered selection.

Sharpen Intensity

Sharpen Intensity works like the Adjust Levels tool, but it goes even further with increasing contrast and color in an image. Overuse can create loss of detail in dark areas, and a posterized effect. Try different numeric keys while applying this filter on scanned images to reduce the flatness caused by scanning. This filter is located in the Sharpen submenu.

> **Note**
>
> *Posterizing* color means to flatten shading and fill with one common, usually brighter and more saturated color. Very high posterization pushes light colors towards white, and dark colors towards black.

Diffuse More

Diffuse More takes Photoshop's Diffuse filter further by affecting a larger pixel area and provides intensity control with the numeric keypad. It spreads pixels at color edges of a selection. KPT Diffuse More is found in the Stylize submenu.

Find Edges Charcoal, Find Edges Soft, and Find Edges & Invert

These three filters are variations on Adobe's Find Edges filters and can be found in the Stylize submenu. Find Edges & Invert is just like the native Find Edges, but earlier versions of Photoshop did not include the option to invert the image while applying the filter. Find Edges Soft takes into account the brightness levels of pixels more, and creates softer, lighter edges around very bright pixel areas. Find Edges Charcoal creates light gray lines on white, and with some images can simulate a charcoal look. Numeric keys control the intensity of the lines, and using Caps Lock inverts the image.

Scatter Horizontal

Scatter Horizontal simply diffuses pixels horizontally with a lightening effect. Numeric keys control the intensity.

Cyclone

KPT Cyclone, located in the Video submenu, is like animating the Adjust Curves function for all channels randomly. When you choose this filter, color values and brightness levels begin changing before your eyes. Figure 16.25 shows a before and after image where the colors have been changed by Cyclone. You can speed up or slow down the change with the right-and left-arrow keys. Pressing numbers in the numeric keypad changes the algorithm being used to change the levels, and pressing "S" saves the settings for use in the Curves dialog box (the settings are called arbitrary maps and you can use the Load button in Curves to load the map). Holding down the Spacebar freezes the image, and pressing Return applies the color and contrast changes to your image.

V

Filters, Plug-Ins, & Effects

Fig. 16.25

Cyclone animates
the color look-up
table of an image.

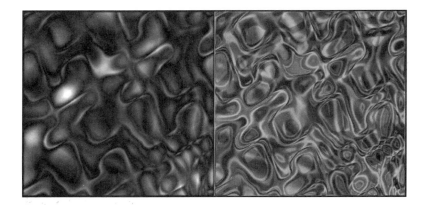

Gallery Effects: Classic Art, Volumes I-III

Created by Aldus Corporation (now owned by Adobe Systems), Gallery
Effects is so named because each filter gives your image a traditional art
look, like a charcoal drawing or watercolor painting. Photoshop users
who want quick and easy painting, drawing, noise, and several other
effects can really benefit from these filters.

Most of the 48 filters are intuitively named, and each has its own dialog
box (see fig. 16.26) with simple controls for how the filter will look. A
preview of your filtered image is supplied so you can explore different
options before applying the filter. Filter speeds are excellent, with the new
version taking advantage of PowerMac technology. The dialog boxes also
allow you to save your settings for later use. On-line help is also provided
in each dialog box, and some help screens offer tips for special ways to
apply the filter.

Fig. 16.26

Example of a
Gallery Effects
filter dialog box.

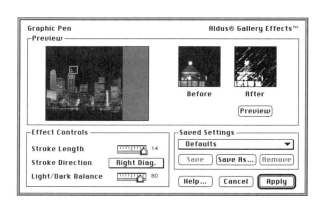

Gallery Effects also comes with a stand-alone desk accessory application for use outside Photoshop.

The sets are listed in order, with Set I comprising all the filters up to Watercolor. Set II contains filters from Accented Edges to Underpainting, and Set III is from Conte Crayon to Water Paper.

Chalk and Charcoal

When this filter is used with black and white as the current foreground and background colors, it looks like chalk and charcoal drawn on gray paper (see fig. 16.27). Darker areas are painted with the foreground color in one direction, and lighter areas are painted with the background color in the opposing stroke direction. With the dialog box's sliders, higher values for Chalk area and Charcoal area show less of the gray "paper" underneath, and higher Stroke Pressure shows less of the stroke detail.

Fig. 16.27

Chalk and Charcoal applied to an image.

Charcoal

Charcoal is similar to the previous filter, but uses the foreground color to stroke dark areas and the background color as the paper color. Controls determine how much of the image selection is stroked (light/dark balance), the charcoal thickness, and detail kept in an image.

Chrome

Chrome creates a polished metallic look from your image. Smooth, curvy highlights and shadows take the place of dark and light areas of an image. The Chrome dialog box gives control over the appearance of hills and valleys in the reflecting surface.

V

Filters, Plug-Ins, & Effects

Craquelure

By applying a random patterning of shadowed cracks, Craquelure creates the look that your image was painted on a cracked, plaster-like surface. The dialog box gives controls for crack brightness, depth, and spacing.

Dark Strokes

Dark Strokes paints the image with diagonal black-and-white brush strokes. It forces light colors to higher saturation and brightness approaching white, while it forces dark colors towards black. Balance control makes the light or dark areas larger (higher levels provide more detail). Two intensity controls for Black and White force colors closer to black and white. The image looks posterized and blurred at high settings.

Dry Brush

Dry Brush flattens out the color shading in an image, and paints each color area with one solid color. It creates an interesting, but difficult to describe, thick oil or acrylic paint look. Figure 16.28 shows the painted look Dry Brush can give to a photo.

Fig. 16.28

Dry Brush applied to a photo gives it a painted look.

Emboss

Emboss creates an image that appears raised up out of its surface without destroying the image's colors. Dark areas are made brighter so that the shading shows properly. Dialog box settings control emboss depth and light-source direction. This is one of the best embossing tools available. Figure 16.29 shows how Emboss affects a photo.

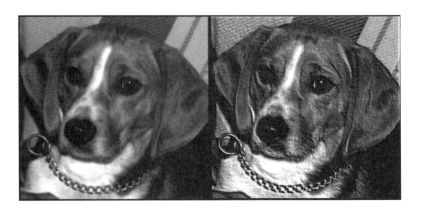

Fig. 16.29

Emboss gives an image a raised look without destroying color.

Film Grain

Film Grain is a noise filter that applies random noise to an image, while at the same time, giving control over how much a selection is brightened. Controls also determine the amount of noise added (grain). Try this for a different look from other noise filters.

Fresco

Fresco transforms an image into a thickly painted look, similar to Dry Brush, but with less detail and larger dark areas. The size of the brush, detail, and texture controls change the look. Texture setting 3 posterizes the colors, forcing lighter and darker colors toward black and white.

Graphic Pen

Graphic Pen changes your image into thin ink strokes that are "drawn" in a direction and length you choose. The dark areas are drawn with the foreground color, while light areas are filled with the background color. Settings give you control over the Light and Dark balance, Stroke length, and direction. Figure 16.30 shows how a black and white drawing can be created from a full color image.

Mosaic

Mosaic embosses an image with a random pattern of odd rectangular-like shapes, as shown in figure 16.31. Controls let you set tile size, grout width, and grout lightness.

V

Filters, Plug-Ins, & Effects

519

Fig. 16.30

Graphic Pen draws an image with thin lines.

Fig. 16.31

Mosaic embosses an image with a pattern of irregular rectangles.

Poster Edges

Poster Edges posterizes the color in an image and darkens and thickens color edges. It has an overall blurring effect while defining and strengthening color edges. Controls vary Edge Thickness, Edge Intensity, and Posterization.

Ripple

Ripple makes the image look as if it were under rippling water; warping the image and adding highlights. The dialog box gives settings for Ripple Size and Magnitude.

Smudge Stick

Smudge Stick smears dark color edges in downward-right short diagonal strokes. Strokes can be made longer and areas made brighter with controls.

Spatter

Spatter warps and sprays an image using a spatter airbrush technique, as shown in figure 16.32. At high settings the image almost looks like the viewer is underwater! At low settings it creates a pointillist effect.

Fig. 16.32

Low settings of Spatter give a pointillist effect.

V

Filters, Plug-Ins, & Effects

Watercolor

This changes an image into a painted watercolor look by using a medium-sized brush, flattening fine shading and smearing strokes with water. More "paint" appears at the edges of daubs. Dialog box controls include brush detail, shadow intensity, and texture (randomness of painting).

Accented Edges

Accented Edges creates a blurred, watery image and then adds lines at color edges. Brightness controls take the lines toward white or black. High brightness and smoothness controls create a white and pastel colored look while low brightness enlarges dark areas. Edge width determines how far the edges are blurred from their source, and Smoothness also controls blurring.

Angled Strokes

Angled Strokes paints straight diagonal strokes from colors in an image. The dialog box gives control over stroke direction, length, and sharpness. When the stroke direction setting is 50 (middle), lighter areas of the image are painted in one direction and darker areas are painted in the opposite direction. Figure 16.33 shows an image painted with Angled Strokes. Also see figure 16.33 in the color section, "Photoshop in Color!"

Fig. 16.33

Angled Strokes paints long diagonal brush strokes into an image. (Also see color section.)

Bas Relief

Bas relief changes an image to the foreground and background colors and creates the look that it has been carved. Light and dark color edges create the highlights and shadows. The dialog box gives control over light direction, detail, and smoothness.

Colored Pencil

Colored pencil draws color edges of an image in two-way diagonal lines at the stroke width and length you choose, in the colors of the underlying image. Flat color areas are reverted to paper color (the current background color).

Diffuse Glow

Diffuse glow adds a bright sprayed highlight in light areas, and mutes others with a grainy texture. The dialog box gives controls for Graininess, Glow amount, and Clear Amount (transparency).

Glowing Edges

Glowing Edges adds bright colorful neon lines to the color edges of your image while making the rest of the image dark. Figure 16.34 shows how Glowing Edges converts color edges to glowing lines.

Fig. 16.34

Glowing Edges creates colorful neon lines in an image.

Grain

Grain is a noise filter and is deeper than it first looks. Depending on the type of grain chosen in the dialog box's pop-up menu, the effects can be quite different. Also the controls for Grain Amount and Contrast vary with each grain type. *Regular* is very similar to Photoshop's Add Noise. *Soft* blends the speckling of noise into the colors of the image better. *Sprinkles* overlays the image with noise in the current background color. *Clumped* noise blurs into the image with big dots. *Constrasty* is similar to Clumped but gives the image higher contrast. *Enlarged* applies noise in larger, colored, blurred dots. *Stippled* changes your image into the foreground and background colors, applying noise in the foreground color to darker areas. *Horizontal* and *Vertical* apply patterns of noise similar to these options in halftone tools. *Speckle* darkens the color edges and posterizes the image before adding black noise. Figure 16.35 shows different types of grain applied with GE Grain.

Notepaper

Notepaper creates an embossed look made of the foreground and background colors for dark and light areas of an image. The texture of the "paper" is rough, and graininess can be controlled. Light/dark balance and relief are also controls in the dialog box. Figure 16.36 shows an example of Notepaper.

Fig. 16.35

Different types of Grain applied to an image, from left to right: Regular, Sprinkles, Clumped, Enlarged, Stippled, and Speckle.

Fig. 16.36

Create an embossed image on rough paper with Notepaper.

Palette Knife

This filter uses big, flat, hard-edged brush strokes to give the image a look as though it has been painted with a palette knife. Dialog box controls include stroke size, detail, and softness.

Patchwork

Patchwork turns an image into squares of color with highlights and shadows to give it a tiled or patchwork look. Figure 16.37 shows how Patchwork transforms an image into little tiles.

Fig. 16.37

Patchwork makes little raised tiles out of an image.

Photocopy

Photocopy posterizes the image into the foreground and background color. Choosing black and white gives the look that the image has been copied, losing most shading. Controls include detail and darkness.

Rough Pastels

Rough Pastels paints an image with long diagonal strokes on a rough texture using colors in your image. The pastel is thicker in light areas, while in dark areas more texture is revealed. You can choose stroke length and detail, as well as a texture from four preset textures, or a PICT file you choose. Figure 16.38 shows Rough Pastels applied to an image using the Canvas texture.

Fig. 16.38

Rough Pastels looks like thick pastels used on canvas or another texture you choose.

V

Filters, Plug-Ins, & Effects

Sprayed Strokes

Sprayed Strokes is similar to Spatter and gives a spattered airbrush look, but settings provide direction choices, stroke length, and spray radius for a more controlled effect.

Stamp

Stamp changes the image to a flat foreground and background color with smooth edges so that it appears to have been stamped with a rubber or wood stamp. Controls include light/dark balance and smoothness.

Texturizer

Texturizer applies your choice of textured surfaces (burlap, brick, canvas, sandstone, or any PICT file) to the image with control for texture size, relief, and light position. Figure 16.39 shows how a logo PICT file was used as a texture.

Fig. 16.39

You can use provided textures or your own PICT files in Texturizer. A logo PICT file was used to provide the texture in this example.

Underpainting

Underpainting applies the image to a textured background then paints the image over that. More texture shows in dark areas and at color edges, while more paint appears in flat color areas All the controls from texturizer are given, as well as brush size and texture coverage.

Conte Crayon

Conte crayon makes the image look as if it were drawn with a thick oil crayon on a textured background you choose. Dense application of the foreground color is used for dark areas and color edges. Midtones show the texture on dark gray and background color draws the lightest areas.

Crosshatch

Crosshatch paints opposing-angled strokes through the image to give a crosshatching look. Similar to Angled Strokes, but more detail is kept in flat color areas, it is less blurred overall, and adds texture and roughness to color edges.

Cut Out

Cut Out is so called because the resulting image looks like cut-out pieces of colored paper, as shown in figure 16.40. This filter flattens color areas into shapes with smooth edges. Controls allow you to set the number of levels from 2 to 8, as well as edge simplicity and fidelity (how true the edge stays to the original image). High contrast grayscale images appear as silhouettes.

Fig. 16.40

Interesting cut paper patterns emerge from your image with Cut Out.

Glass

Glass makes an image appear like it is being viewed through a type of glass you choose (frosted, blocks, tiny lens, canvas, or PICT file). The dialog box has controls for glass size, image distortions, and smoothness.

Halftone

Halftone screen applies a dot, circle, or line screen to the image. Dark, flat color areas fill with the foreground color, while light areas fill with the background color. Midtones and color edges reflect the halftone shape. Controls are given for halftone size and image contrast.

Ink Outlines

Ink outlines draws thin dark lines at color edges and paints the rest of the image with diagonal strokes in one direction. Stroke length, dark intensity, and light intensity are provided as controls. Figure 16.41 shows an image affected by Ink Outlines.

Fig. 16.41

Ink Outlines retains the overall color while providing thin lines at color edges.

Neon Glow

This filter first changes the image to foreground and background color, while retaining shading and detail. Midtones are the background color mixed with gray. Then a neon glow in a color you choose from within the dialog box is added at the brightest areas of an image. Glow size and brightness can also be set.

Paint Daubs

Paint Daubs paints an image with blobby thick paint. There is a widely varying set of brush types from which to choose: simple, light rough, dark rough, wide blurry, wide sharp, and sparkle. Brush size and sharpness also control how the effect will look.

Plaster

Plaster makes dark areas look raised and light areas sunken for a molded plaster effect. It uses the foreground and background colors with some shading, and gives controls for image balance (light/dark areas), light position, and smoothness.

Plastic Wrap

Plastic wrap makes the image look like it is coated in shiny plastic, as shown in figure 16.42. The filter adds rippled highlights to color edges, while keeping most detail. Controls are given for highlight strength, detail, and smoothness. The on-line help gives tips for how to use this filter to give the effect of a Polaroid that's been scratched.

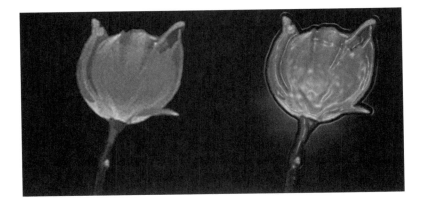

Fig. 16.42

Coat your image in plastic with Plastic Wrap.

Reticulation

Reticulation happens in traditional photographic processes when film emulsion is shrunk and distorted in a controlled fashion. This filter changes the image to foreground and background color, and applies a mottled circular grain. Controls determine density of the grain, white level, and black level (really background and foreground for light and dark areas). Figure 16.43 shows how Reticulation can change a photo into grainy 2-color art.

Fig. 16.43

Reticulation changes an image to grainy two-color art.

Sponge

Sponge flattens and fills areas with a common color, but keeps some shading, as shown in figure 16.44. It looks like water was blended in, but keeps sharp edges between paint daubs. You can set the brush size, detail, and smoothness in the dialog box. This look also resembles a watercolor.

Fig. 16.44

Sponge gives a wet, blurry painted effect.

Stained Glass

Stained glass converts the image to irregularly shaped panes of glass with lead borders in between. The panes, or cells get their color from the image, while the lead is the current foreground color.

Sumi-e

Sumi-e creates a very interesting look that mimics a Japanese style of brush and ink painting. The result is a dark, thick, but watery image with contrasted but blurred edges, and stronger dark areas. Controls provide settings for stroke width, pressure, and contrast.

Torn Edges

Torn Edges creates a two-color image of torn pieces of paper. It uses foreground and background colors for light and dark areas, and includes controls for image balance, edge smoothness, and contrast.

Water Paper

Water Paper uses watery brush strokes on textured paper, causing the colors to bleed across the texture. Paper fiber length, brightness, and contrast can be set.

Andromeda Series

Andromeda originally began creating filters because some well-known photographers wanted to use Photoshop to re-create special optical effects. The company has expanded on this, adding effects not possible with traditional tools. Series 1 includes nine filters capable of producing multiple images, rainbows, reflections, twinkling lights, patterns, mezzo effects, and motion looks. Series 2 is a powerful 3-D surface wrapping filter.

Each filter contains a dialog box with a preview and various controls to change how the filter is applied. Selection tools in the dialog boxes allow you to use part of an image as a source, or to apply the filter to a specific region of the image.

cMulti

A kaleidoscope effect is created by duplicating an image selection to a circle or square pattern around the original. The Circular Multiple Image (cMulti) dialog box, as shown in figure 16.45, gives control over size of source selection (radius), width of the copies, and number of wedges (areas). There are also sliders for transparency (intensity), and edge-feathering (transitions). Spoke transitions allow feathering between the edges.

V

Filters, Plug-Ins, & Effects

531

Fig. 16.45

cMulti duplicates
an image around
a source selection.

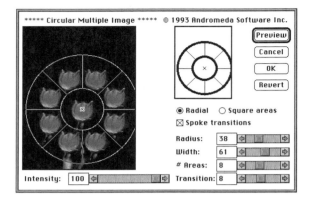

Designs

This filter overlays a pattern or fills your image with a mezzo texture. It has a variety of preset patterns and textures that can be altered in size, color, and transparency. Patterns may also simulate 3-D looks, as they can be warped in perspective to user-defined shapes, like planes, cylinders, and droplets. The Designs filter dialog box is shown in figure 16.46.

Fig. 16.46

The Designs filter
dialog box offers a
library of patterns
and a special
Mezzo feature.

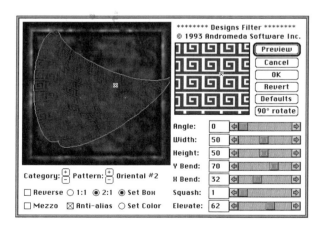

The mezzo feature offers more texture options than other mezzo-like filters. By clicking on Mezzo in the dialog box, you can select grains or patterns from the pattern library, and control size and grain intensity.

Diffract

Diffract simulates a diffraction camera lens and adds bright points of light with user-defined spectral rays, or spokes, out from the center. It is similar in function, but has more controls, than Photoshop's Lens Flare.

Halo

This diffuses bright areas of an image in the direction you choose, as shown in figure 16.47. The controls also let you set the brightness value affected (cut-off), light spread amount, and glow intensity. You can make the halo glow in all directions or one angle. This filter can also create an interesting watercolor look.

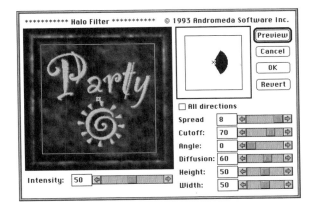

Fig. 16.47

Halo creates a glow from light areas in an image. In this image, it makes the text glow.

V

Filters, Plug-Ins, & Effects

Prism

Prism gives the effect that you are looking through a prism by stepping the red, green, and blue values of an image in the direction you choose. Low spread setting can simulate the look of an old 3-D movie.

Rainbow

This adds a rainbow to your image, as shown in figure 16.48. The Rainbow dialog box gives controls for the rainbow's origin, curvature, and intensity. There is also an option for adding a "Pot of Gold" at the bottom of the rainbow.

Fig. 16.48

Adding a rainbow
to your photo.

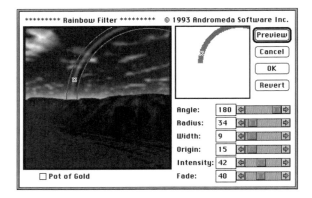

Fig. 16.48

Adding a rainbow
to your photo.

Reflection

With this filter you use the dialog box controls to create a reflection of the top part of an image into the bottom part. This is great for cityscapes or scenes that need a reflection on water.

sMulti

sMulti duplicates a selection into straight-lined steps. You select part of the image in the preview window and choose the source size (spacing) number of copies, angle of steps, intensity, and fade to make a repeated image.

Star

This filter puts 4, 8, or 16 point stars into an image, as shown in figure 16.49. Controls let you set the number of stars, color, brightness, position, size of star, halo, and length of spokes (points). It can create some beautiful specialized lighting effects for any image.

Velocity

Bright areas of an image are smeared in any direction, similar to Photoshop's Motion Blur, but with more controls. This filter can be used to blur or smear an image in one or two directions at once at a user-defined angle. The dialog box also lets you set how much the image is smeared (number of copies of the image), how blurred (spacing), and transparency of the blur (intensity). Velocity can also be used for interesting extruded effects.

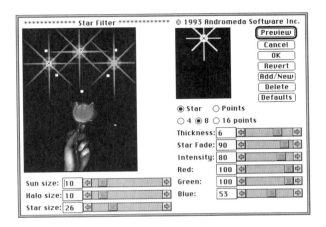

Fig. 16.49

Stars add interesting lighting effects.

3-D

This Series 2 filter is the first of its kind for 3-D creation and surface wrapping within Photoshop. It creates realistic 3-D images according to numerous controls in the dialog box (see fig. 16.50). Settings include shape (cylinder, box, plane, and sphere), colors (faces, cutout, and background), wrapped image size, viewpoint, light position, ambiance, spread, and glare. Figure 16.51 shows an image wrapped to a box. Also see figure 16.51 in the color section, "Photoshop in color!"

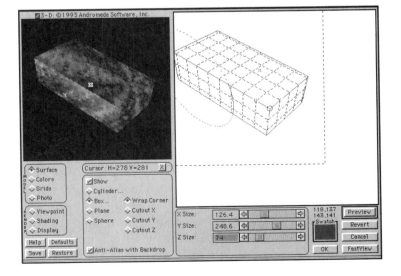

Fig. 16.50

Andromeda's 3-D filter wraps photos to 3-D objects within Photoshop.

V

Filters, Plug-Ins, & Effects

Xaos Tools

Xaos Tools produces several artistic software packages for digital artists on the Mac, PC, and SGI platforms. Their two sets of Photoshop filters include the popular Paint Alchemy, and just released Terrazzo.

Paint Alchemy

Paint Alchemy is a powerful set of 36 brush styles that can be painted into your image. Some might say it gives the image a painted look, but with the wide range of brushes and controls, there are all kinds of special effects that can be created with this very popular filter package. There are some more standard brush styles, like Oil Tip, Standard Stroke, and Stroke-Splatter, but imagine painting with a footprint or a funny little man shape (Man-Fred Fade).

Fig. 16.51

Any image can be wrapped to a box (shown), sphere, plane, or cylinder (See color section also.)

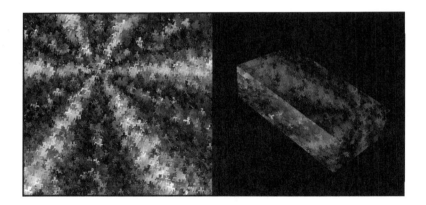

Also, you can create any PICT file and use it as a "brush." For example, paint an image with your own logo. Xaos also sells another 50 brushes called "Floppy Full of Brushes."

The Paint Alchemy dialog box gives you complete control over how the brushes are applied. Not only are there settings for brush color, size, angle, and transparency, but there are controls for how aspects of the underlying image affects the brushing application. For example, transparency can vary with the color saturation of your image, brush angle can vary with the hue, and brush size can depend on brightness in the underlying image.

With all the controls, brushes can have a strong or subtle effect, and the variations are unlimited. Figure 16.52 shows just two examples of this deep plug-in.

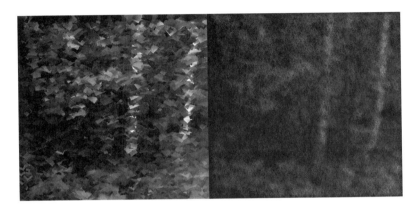

Fig. 16.52

Images painted with Paint Alchemy.

Terrazzo

Terrazzo produces 17 different types of patterns that create textures from areas selected in your image. With it you can create backgrounds, 3-D texture maps, kaleidoscope images, fabric, or wallpaper.

The Terrazzo dialog box, shown in figure 16.53, brings up a thumbnail of your selection, and you choose from 17 patterns, called *symmetries*, that are named after common patchwork quilt patterns. Depending on the pattern, you get a moveable and sizable rectangle, triangle, or polygon that you use to choose a part of the image to generate the pattern.

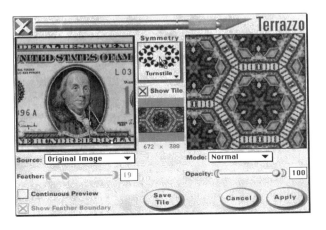

Fig. 16.53

Terrazzo creates patterns using images as the source.

The pop-up menu under the left window lets you use your current image selection, or another image. The pop-up menu under the right preview window gives you apply mode controls similar to those in Photoshop's Layers palette. With feathering control you can make your tiles hard-edged or seamless (edges blur into each other). You can save the tile you've created to use as a pattern in Photoshop's Define Pattern menu option (under the Edit menu). Samples of several patterns created from the image in the Terrazzo dialog box are shown in figure 16.54.

Fig. 16.54

Many patterns can be generated from one image with Terrazzo.

Second Glance Software

Second Glance Software produces several plug-ins designed to expand and improve on existing choices for color manipulation, spot color separations, color PostScript output, scanner settings, and color diffusion dithering. Their manuals are full of tips and techniques, including using these images with popular page layout programs.

Acetone

Acetone examines the color in an image and changes it to a spot color image by the number of colors you choose. When you choose this filter, a dialog box comes up to set the number of colors, then the user dialog box appears. The Acetone dialog box shows the resulting color palette and provides large, scrollable preview windows of the original image, and resulting spot color image. The Acetone dialog box is shown in figure 16.55. You can change the colors in the target palette by selecting from the Apple color picker (no Pantone support, unfortunately). You can further manipulate colors from side-by-side source and target palettes by selecting colors directly from the image. Figure 16.56 shows a 24-bit image converted to six spot colors.

After you use this filter, you can use Second Glance's Photospot to output the spot color separations. Acetone and Paint Thinner are similar, but Acetone is much quicker and performs color determinations for you.

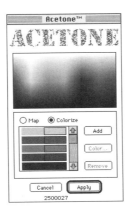

Fig. 16.55

Acetone creates quick and easy spot color images from Photoshop files.

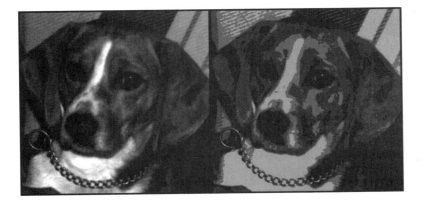

Fig. 16.56

Acetone changes a 24-bit image to a number of spot colors you choose.

Paint Thinner

Paint Thinner is more complex than Acetone but offers more control over what colors in your original image are combined into each spot color. This filter first converts a 24-bit image into an 8-bit (256 colors) image using a method similar to Photoshop's Indexed color, Adaptive palette, Diffusion, function. If you don't want diffusion, you can create the 8-bit image before selecting this filter.

The dialog box shows the preview image, source palette, and target palette. You can choose several similar colors from the source palette or image and click Add to combine them into a spot color. Paint Thinner calculates the chosen colors into a common color. As you go through doing this for each spot color, you can preview your image to show the original image, the "thinned" image, colors selected, or colors remaining to be selected. You can add or remove source colors from the target spot color or change it using the Apple color picker. Figure 16.57 shows the Paint Thinner dialog box.

Fig. 16.57

Paint Thinner offers complete controls for making spot color images in Photoshop.

Photospot

Photospot saves an image containing as many as 500 colors as spot color separations, in Tiff, Photoshop or EPS file formats. It allows you to choose which colors to save as plates, and to name the colors. This is intended to be used after Acetone or Paint Thinner create spot color images. The Photospot manual gives tips on how to use the separation files in QuarkXpress, PageMaker, and Freehand. Figure 16.58 shows the Photospot dialog box.

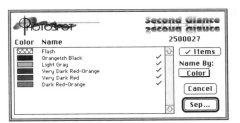

Fig. 16.58

Photospot exports spot color separations from Photoshop.

Turpentine

Turpentine uses a proprietary dithering function to transform continuous tone images to 8-color images. Photoshop can then be used to save the separations (cyan, magenta, yellow, black, red, green, blue, white). The result is a color bitmapped similar to what Bitmap, Dither, does for grayscale images.

> **Note**
>
> Photographs are referred to as *continuous tone* images. This is opposed to printed images that are made up of CMYK dots. For many printing applications, it is better to convert a continuous tone image to a halftone or other format.

Chromassage

Chromassage is a powerful filter for exciting color effects! It allows you to replace and cycle palettes of an image with real time preview. The dialog box brings up your image and its 256 strongest colors in the original palette. There are several preset palettes to choose from and you can apply colors from them to replace those in the image's palette. You can sort the colors several ways (variations on RGB, HSL, and so on) and then cycle them horizontally or vertically with jogging sliders. The preview window shows changes as you make them. This filter is similar in function to KPT Cyclone, but results are more controllable. Figure 16.59 shows the Chromassage dialog box.

V

Filters, Plug-Ins, & Effects

Fig. 16.59

Chromassage can replace and change palettes associated with an image.

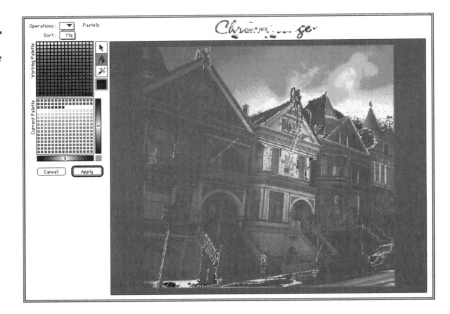

Other Graphics Filters

There are new filters being created all the time, and it would be impossible to comprehensively cover them all in this volume. A short description of some others available follows.

Knoll Software Cybermesh

Cybermesh is located in the File, Export menu. It takes grayscale images and creates 3-D maps from them based on luminosity. The maps can be exported as models in DXF and ElectricImage Fact formats.

Ring of Fire Fotomagic

Fotomagic includes several filters that manipulate color. Filters include Color Expander, Color Filters, Color Noise, Color Ranger, Color Ranger II, Color Reversal, Color Scaler, Color Shifter, and Color Switcher.

MicroFrontier Pattern Workshop

These filters build on and replace Photoshop's Define Pattern tool. The first allows you to choose a pattern from a library of 160 and apply it to your image with color and transparency control. The second filter lets you derive patterns from an image selection. Patterns may also be colored with gradients within the dialog box.

Razz Matazz Filters

From Performance Resources, this filter set is one of the oldest. The eight filters include effects that manipulate color and contrast, create frame looks, and perform trigonometric functions.

Shareware and Freeware Filters

There are several filters available to download from popular on-line services, like America Online. Shareware means the filter might cost from $10 to $20. This fee should be sent to its creator. Freeware means the filter is free.

Chris Cox

Chris Cox is a freelance programmer who distributes his filter collection over on-line services. Available now are 17 filters that perform a variety of useful functions, and a few thrown in for fun. He is constantly creating new ones so stay tuned.

- *Average,* which is located in the Blur Submenu, calculates and fills a selection with the average color. It is a way to create shapes and stained-glass looks.

- *UnAlias* blurs edges of an image with controls for threshold value (which determines what is considered an edge), and how much blurring. It is located in the Blur submenu.

- *Edge3×3* is similar to Photoshop's Find Edges, but works a little differently.

- *Erode* reduces the dark areas in a selection. It compares the sum of the color values of the pixels in the region to the threshold value chosen, then sets the pixel to white if the total exceeds the threshold. It can create a bright, posterized look.

▶ *Dilate* is similar to Erode, but it enlarges the dark areas, based on the threshold value chosen.

▶ *Skeleton* posterizes color, reduces the dark areas of an image, and strengthens centerlines. Using this filter repeatedly will continue to thin the centerlines. Figure 16.60 shows an image transformed by Skeleton.

Fig. 16.60

Skeleton strengthens the centerlines from color edges in an image.

The Edge3×3, Erode, Dilate, and Skeleton filters are located in the Custom submenu.

▶ *Total Noise* replaces an image selection with random noise. The noise replaces rather than adds, like Adobe's Add Noise filter.

▶ *Fractal Noise* fills a selection with a random "cloud" look, like Photoshop's Clouds filter. The noise varies with different setting combinations of Hue/Saturation, Curves, and levels.

▶ *Plaid* makes symmetrical patterns in each available color channel.

▶ *AddMoreNoise* is similar to Adobe's Add Noise filter, but offers some more options in RGB and CMYK color modes.

Total Noise, Fractal Noise, Plaid, and AddMoreNoise are located in the Noise submenu.

▶ *Psycho* applies random color maps to RGB and CMYK images. Each time you use it, the colors are different. Try it on simple gradients to see what it does. Psycho is located in the Stylize submenu.

▶ *BitShift* is located in the Other submenu. It rotates the image's bytes by a specified number of bits (1–7), and can create interesting psychedelic effects. Try it on a grayscale radial gradient, as shown in figure 16.61.

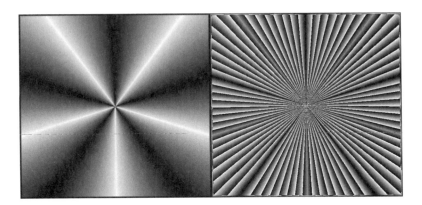

Fig. 16.61

BitShift applied to a 5-spoked radial gradient five times.

▶ *ColorKey,* which is located in the Video submenu, is similar to Photoshop's new Color Range selection tools. It makes a mask from the current foreground color by turning the image white wherever the foreground color appears, and black where it doesn't. You can set a tolerance value, similar to that used in the Magic Wand selection tool to choose only the color or a range based on the color from 0 to 999. Figure 16.62 shows a mask created from the image on the left with ColorKey, based on the color shown in the box.

Fig. 16.62

ColorKey creates a mask based on the current foreground color.

V

Filters, Plug-Ins, & Effects

▶ *ChromaKey,* also in the Video submenu, creates a mask based on the current foreground color as well, but gives tolerance controls for Hue, Saturation, and Value.

▶ *FastKey* is like Color Key but does not have a tolerance control. Only the exact same foreground color will be masked. It is located in the Video submenu.

FastKey, ColorKey, or ChromaKey are helpful for making alpha channels for video.

▶ *Grid* draws a grid of specified spacing and line width over the existing picture using either the foreground or background colors. This is great for experimenting with distortions and the Displace filter.

▶ *Checkers* draws a checkerboard pattern of specified width and height over the existing image.

Grid and Checkers are located in the Other submenu.

Jim Bumgardner

Jim Bumgardner is a programmer at Time Warner Interactive, and distributes a number of Mac programs as freeware over various on-line services. These include Expression, the arcade game "Cheese Toast," and the utility "Hex Edit."

Expression is a filter that creates colorful art and patterns based on mathematical expressions that are randomly applied each time it is used. The dialog box allows users to type in their own mathematical functions to affect the pixels in the image, or if you're not a math genius, it provides several preset options from which to choose. Figure 16.63 shows the Expression dialog box.

The manual that comes with the program gives descriptions of mathematical equations that can be used, and explains different algorithmic functions and how pixels are affected. The dialog box also includes a fractal generator. There is a variety of uses for Expression, including psychedelic images, wallpaper, patterns, textures, and fractal images.

Expression also works with Adobe Premiere and can make animations based on mathematical expressions. Animation features include Fractal zoom and other abstract movies and animated texture maps for 3-D rendering.

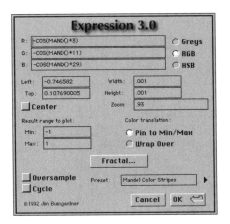

Fig. 16.63

Expression's dialog box comes with preset options, or you can type in your own equations.

Jeff Burton

BackSwap is a functional color-switch filter created by Plug-In Systems' Jeff Burton. It changes pixels with the current background color to the foreground color. Using the Option key replaces all occurrences of the foreground color with the background color.

Paul Badger

Paul Badger is an artist interested in image processing. He currently teaches at the Cleveland Institute of Art, and writes filters for fun and use in his own work. He is working on publishing a collection of filters.

▶ *VectorGraph,* located in the Stylize submenu, gives an image a ridged, 3-D like look by manipulating the shading in an image. It doesn't just take into account brightness values, but looks at the direction of shading contained in a region. The filter is best used on one color channel of an RGB or CMYK image but can be applied to all channels for a colorful effect. Try this filter on a floating layer and use the apply modes Color Only and Luminosity for variation.

▶ *Radar* adds a sweeping radar to an image, and is best used for animation. The radar has a white line, with a radial sweep from light to dark. The dialog box provides light control and others. The manual gives information about macros that animate this filter for several frames of a movie. It is contained in the Other submenu.

V

Filters, Plug-Ins, & Effects

▶ *Lumpy Noise* is a noise filter that gives you control over the size of the noise particles. The dialog box lets you set "Lump" size, and gaps (Between Lumps), Color Depth, and Color Divergence. Try this filter on a small area to test effects as it is very slow. A faster version is coming.

Watch for additional Badger filters that will be available soon.

David Hull

David Hull created and distributes two filters that dither grayscale images to black and white so that they can be printed better on a laser printer. PNDither and VGDither contain algorithms that are superior to Photoshop's halftoning and dithering, because they take into account the dot gain created by laser printers. *Dot gain* means that black pixels print larger than they "should" because the dots are round and must overlap to produce solid black. This creates output with less detail that is too dark.

VGDither uses an algorithm that clusters dots to minimize the effect of dot gain, while PNDither uses a physical model of a laser printer to produce results with better tone detail than produced by Photoshop's Diffusion Dither. Figure 16.64 shows the resulting image of both filters: VGDither on the left and PNDither on the right.

These filters work only on grayscale images. After using the filter, you should convert the image to a Bitmap using the 50 percent Threshold method so it will print as black and white.

Both filters are distributed free over on-line services, and provided documentation gives more information. David Hull is also at work on more halftoning and dithering filters.

Sucking Fish Series

The Sucking Fish (Koban Zame) filters are available as free mailware through the Asian E-mail address listed in the Resources Appendix. It includes two filters that create embossed boxes and brick, as described below.

▶ *Deko-Boko* creates 3-D look embossed boxes in one step. Simple, but very useful if you are used to creating them on your own.

Fig. 16.64

VGDither and PNDither convert grayscale images to better print on a laser printer by adjusting for dot gain.

▶ *Mr. Sa'Kan* creates brick patterns in an image, with controls for the pattern, brick size, depth, gap size, grain, and transparency (see fig. 16.65). It gives an image a raised box look rather than just applying a pattern on top of it.

Fig. 16.65

Mr. Sa'Kan "embosses" a pattern of bricks into your image.

Kas Thomas

Warm Contrast, created and distributed by Kas Thomas, is available on on-line services. The filter is a simple, one-step filter that enhances contrast in an image with warmer hues than are available using Photoshop's contrast features. The dialog box gives brightness controls, because this filter may give results that are too dark for some images.

Specialized Filters

Many filters and plug-ins have been designed for specialized functions and for certain industries. Following are descriptions of some that are available for dealing with special file types, communication, security, the pre-press industry, and using high-resolution files.

Filters for Acquiring and Exporting Special File Types

Several plug-ins exist for working with specialized file types, and specific input and output devices, such as scanners and special printers. Many come with a certain input or output device when it is purchased. Kodak Photo CD is one example of an Acquire plug-in, and it now comes with Photoshop 3.

Communication and Security

Plug-ins for communication and security uses are available, and are useful for certain industries. Multiple-location companies and newspapers will find the filters from IronMike helpful. One filter-set allows for modem sending of files from within Photoshop, and another filter creates and finds captions attached to images.

Candela's ColorCrypt offers security by locking Photoshop files with a password, scrambling the image unless the filter is used again and the password is entered.

Pre-Press

The use of Scitex equipment in printing is very prevalent. There are filters that take advantage of this by providing features similar to Scitex systems. In Software offers two filters that edit files and export in Scitex-compatible formats.

Other filters that may be useful for the pre-press industry are Image Xpress's ScanPrep for color separations, DPA Software's Intellihance filters for color correction and adjustments dependent on specific input and output devices, or Candela's filters for color-printer and scanner calibration.

Filters for High-Resolution Files

Alaris and Total Integration offer filters for editing parts of large high-resolution images. Their filters work with formats compatible with Scitex systems, which are often used in the printing industry.

Tips for Maximizing Filters

Simply applying a filter may not achieve the effect for which you are looking. Using Photoshop's other tools after the filter has been applied, or experimenting with different settings in the filter can dramatically change the way your filtered image looks. Try some of the tips that follow for variety.

Experiment with Filter Settings

Many filters contain dialog boxes with different settings, and many give you a preview of the effect on your image. Try varying the settings to see what they do so you can learn more about how the filter works and get the effect you want. Some filter option settings are very sensitive, and a slight change in the setting can vary the results dramatically.

Apply the Filter More Than Once

Because most filters work by applying mathematical calculations based on pixel color values, among other things, the second application of a filter may simply strengthen the effect, or produce unexpected and interesting results. Duplicate your image and experiment with small areas to see what happens.

Use Photoshop's Layers Palette

The Layers palette greatly expands the power of multiple effects. Now if you don't have transparency or other controls in the Filter dialog box, it doesn't matter! Either float your image or copy it to a new layer. Then apply the filter and experiment with the Layers palette apply modes and transparency. (Just don't forget to eat and sleep!) The variations are unlimited!

V

Filters, Plug-Ins, & Effects

Apply Filters to Different Color Channels

Some filters can create quite interesting effects when they are applied to one color channel rather than just the top RGB or CMYK channel. Or you can duplicate your image and make it a grayscale, run the filter, and paste it back into a new layer to apply all kinds of effects.

Use Feathered-Edge Selections

Feathering the edges of a selection can produce a blend of the filtered portion of the image into the unfiltered part.

Apply Filters Using Masks

As discussed in chapter 12, "Using Masks and Channels," masks can be a powerful selection tool. When you create a selection and save it as a mask or channel, you normally get a grayscale image, with white being the selection, black not being selected, and gray giving partially transparent levels of selection. Try applying a filter to a mask, and then using it as a selection to produce other effects, or use the mask as a selection before applying a filter.

Change Hue and Saturation

Some filters change the colors in your image, and may not give you the colors you want. After the filter is applied you can use the Adjust: Hue/Saturation, or use Photoshop 3's new Color Range tools to select and change colors.

Use Blur or Sharpen Tools

The results of a filter may produce edges that are too sharp and have artifacts, or produce an image that is too blurred. Adjust the image with the Blur and Sharpen filters (discussed in chapter 15, "Using Photoshop's Plug-In Filters") to achieve the desired look.

Change Levels or Curves

Once again, if the filtered image is too flat or needs enhancement, adjust the Levels or Curves after it is applied.

Experiment with Different Filter Combinations

This is the best part—applying different filters to the same image. Even just applying the same filter in a different way can produce particularly intriguing looks.

Filtering Techniques

Because there is such an unlimited range of results available with filters—especially if your collection includes the 100 or so listed in the preceding pages—this section is intended to guide you toward some suggestions. There are so many possibilities with different filters and combinations that it would be pointless to give step-by-step directions to achieve one outcome. Many different goals can be accomplished with many different filters, so the sections that follow give you some direction to which filters to try for certain special effects.

The time you spend experimenting pays off when you discover new and unique results for your images. Once again, the key word is *explore!*

Using Filters to Improve and Touch Up Images

Several add-in filters can improve the look of scanned or poor-quality images. KPT's Sharpen Intensity can enhance the brightness levels and color contrast, making it appear as if a flat, dull film has been removed from your image (see fig. 16.66).

Creating Painting Effects

The entire library of Gallery Effects (GE) was designed for art effects. If you are going for a thick, oil-painted look, try GE Dry Brush, Dark Strokes, Fresco, or Paint Daubs. For watery looks, try Watercolor, Sponge, or Sumi-E. A pointillist look can be achieved with low levels of Spatter.

Fig. 16.66

Enhancing an
image with filters.

Xaos Tools Paint Alchemy features many different brush types (made out
of grayscale PICT files) with which to "paint" your images. Brush styles
include Amoeba, Branch-Furry, Bubble, Doodle-Spiral, Footprint, Hurri-
cane, Oil Tip, Scratches, Smoke, Stripes, Triangle Cuts, and Vasili Tip.

Figure 16.67 shows three examples of painted looks you can achieve with
third-party filters. Also see figure 16.67 in the color section, "Photoshop in
Color!"

Fig. 16.67

These painted looks
were achieved with
GE Fresco, GE Paint
Daubs, and GE
Sumi-E. (Also see
color section.)

Creating Flat Shapes, Sketches, and Line Art

Photographic images may not look good for certain types of low-level
printing. Posterizing the color in an image, creating flat color shapes, or
creating sketches or traced images can transform a photo into another
type of art.

Flat Art Images

There are several filters that reduce the colors and create flat color shapes from an image. GE's Stamp, Photocopy, Bas Relief, Cut Out, and Torn Edges create distinct shapes from an image. Second Glance Acetone and Paint Thinner were designed to create spot color images, and change an image to flat color shapes. Figure 16.68 shows three flat art images created with filters.

Fig. 16.68

A few filters that create flat color shapes are GE Stamp, GE Cutout, and Second Glance Acetone.

Sketching

Sketched looks can be achieved with GE Graphic Pen, GE Chalk and Charcoal, and GE Charcoal. Also try Andromeda's Designs Mezzo for black-and-white sketching. If you want black-and-white images, choose those colors for foreground and background in the Photoshop tool window. Full color sketching includes GE Rough Pastels, and Colored Pencil. Figure 16.69 shows three different sketched looks applied to an image.

Fig. 16.69

Sketched art was created with Andromeda Designs: Mezzo, GE Colored Pencil, and GE Chalk and Charcoal.

Line Art and Tracing

To create tracing or line art (see fig. 16.70), it is best to first posterize, o: reduce the colors in an image, using the filters suggested previously; or Photoshop's Map Posterize tool. This also increases the sharpness of color

V

Filters, Plug-Ins, & Effects

edges from which to draw lines. For full color images with enhanced edges, try KPT Find Edge filters, GE Poster Edges, Accented Edges, or Ink Outlines. To achieve traced looks with fewer colors, or images that can be changed to black and white, try Chris Cox's Dilate, Erode, or Skeleton.

Fig. 16.70

Tracing images
with filters.

Noise, Mezzotints, and Halftones

Because mezzotint and halftone looks are so popular, there are several filters that produce different versions. Advertising agencies pay for converting photographs to images usable in newspaper and certain types of printing. By using the filters designed for adding noise, and producing different types of halftones and mezzotints, you may create the result you want in-house.

Noise and Diffusion

To apply a rough, grainy effect, you can use one of several noise filters. Adding noise in certain ways can also bring out the color edges and enhance dark areas for greater depth.

Early noise filters simply applied a random speckling of multicolor dots onto an image. Photoshop's Add Noise was one of these filters before it offered the Monochromatic option.

Now filters take into account the color in the underlying image, and can create the grainy effect without changing hues. KPT Hue Protected Noise offers 30 levels of noise with its three filters and numeric-keypad application controls.

GE Grain filters offer 10 types of noise. Some, like Regular, are reminiscent of old, colorful Add Noise. Others offer partial or total hue protection, and one even changes the image to two color and draws with a noise texture.

Speckled applies noise and creates almost an embossed look at high contrast. See the description of this filter earlier in this chapter for more information.

GE Film Grain applies a brighter colored noise and changes the image's contrast at the same time. KPT Grime Layer and GE Grain, Sprinkles, can add black noise to an image. The Black Box includes HSB noise with controls for how noise is applied based on hue, saturation, and brightness of the underlying image.

KPT Texture Explorer offers a preset category for noise and some are really great as alternatives to "traditional" noise filters. Try Lucid Polarized noise, tiled at 96×96 pixels, and take advantage of KPT's apply modes for variations.

Paul Badger's Lumpy Noise lets you choose the noise size, spacing and other variations for more controlled effects.

The Second Glance Turpentine filter changes an image into an 8-color dithered image. All the shading and detail in the image is made up of cyan, magenta, yellow, black, red, green, and blue dots on white.

An interesting trick to try, is to duplicate a grayscale image, and convert it to a bitmap using diffusion. Then recomposite the bitmap to a new layer in the original image, using Multiply mode. This keeps the continuous tone image, while adding a noisy diffusion pattern on top to enhance details.

Don't forget also, that by using Layers and different apply modes, you have complete control over how noise is mixed into your image. Figure 16.71 shows three examples of noise filters and how they change the appearance of an image. Also see figure 16.71 in the color section, "Photoshop in Color!"

Mezzotints

Mezzotints has long been a popular style of converting images to dot, line, or crosshatch type patterns, and effects can be used for several printing and art applications. Don't overlook the preceding section on noise, because a limitless range of mezzotint looks can be produced with the variety of noise filters available. There are only a few filters specially designed for mezzotints other than Photoshop's native option.

V

Filters, Plug-Ins, & Effects

Fig. 16.71

Noise effects vary widely as seen in this image using GE Film Grain, GE Grain; Clumped, and KPT Texture Explorer. (Also see color section.)

Andromeda's Designs filter has a mezzotint feature built-in. It offers access to 100 patterns (maybe 20 suitable for mezzo looks), and works on color or grayscale images. For color images, it might be best to use the Layer apply modes (try Overlay, Hard Light, or Multiply). Andromeda is currently working on an expanded Mezzo filter for its Series 3 filter package.

Two filters that could have been included as noise, but are closer to a mezzotint look are Gallery Effects' Grain and GE Reticulation. Using the Stippled grain type of Grain changes light areas to the background color, and draws dark areas and edges with dots in the foreground color. GE Reticulation converts an image to two colors and uses a noisy pattern for shading and color edges, yet has a larger and stronger texture in flat color areas. Figure 16.72 shows three images with different filters applied to emulate the look of a mezzotint.

Fig. 16.72

Different Mezzotint looks achieved with filters: GE Grain; Stippled, GE Reticulation, and Andromeda Designs; Mezzo.

Halftones

Halftones convert a continuous tone image to a pattern of dots, circles, lines, or other shapes, often used in process or black-and-white printing. Note that the noise and mezzotint suggestions previously discussed may produce a better image for certain types of printing than halftones. Photoshop's Bitmap, Halftone tool is great for grayscale images, letting you choose from six shapes, but the controls for Color Halftone only include dot size and color angles. Gallery Effects Halftone lets you choose dots, circles, or lines, and also has controls for size and contrast (see fig. 16.73).

V

Filters, Plug-Ins, & Effects

Fig. 16.73

Color Halftone with Gallery Effects.

Backgrounds, Textures, and Patterns

Many people originally thought of Photoshop as a photograph retouching program. Now, with the growing need for images for multimedia and for digital effects for printed pieces, Photoshop is recognized as a powerful tool for creating backgrounds, textures, and patterns. Any of the following suggestions can be applied to flat color images or photographs for use as backgrounds.

> **Note**
>
> The terms *pattern* and *texture* may be used similarly but are differentiated here. Textures are more blended and random, creating a more organic-looking surface. Patterns are often flat colors or tiles mapped in a predictable way.

Gradients

KPT's Gradient Designer is an incredible resource for creating color blended gradients for background material or for image special effects. Apply the filter more than once with different apply modes for more interesting gradient effects. See the description and samples earlier in this chapter (refer to fig. 16.15).

Textures

Several options now exist for creating and applying textures. Photoshop's Texture Fill lets you apply any grayscale image as a texture, and of course the Layers apply modes give you limitless control over how it is applied.

KPT Texture Explorer is an extensive resource for generating textures. Mentioned earlier in this chapter are its presets for standards like marble, wood, and liquid (See section on KPT, Texture Explorer, under "Art and Effects Filters"). Other preset categories include Animalia, Fabric, Metals, Sky, Papers, and Mirages, or you can save your own. The filter has several options for texture, size, color, and apply modes among others.

Gallery Effects Texturizer is a good option for applying a texture to an image, gradient, or flat color. It gives you Canvas, Brick, Sandstone, Burlap, or any PICT file, and gives control over light direction, texture size, and relief amount (see the earlier section on Gallery Effects Texturizer, "Art and Effects Filters"). Other GE filters that apply textures to an image include Craquelere, Rough Pastels, and Notepaper.

With Xaos Tools Paint Alchemy, you can save a texture as a grayscale PICT file, and then use the filter's broad controls as a paintbrush.

It's a good idea to save a folder called Textures in your Photoshop folder to keep textures for later use. Figure 16.74 shows three textures created with multiple applications of KPT Texture Explorer. Also see figure 16.74 in the color section of this book, "Photoshop in Color!"

Fig. 16.74

The power of third-party filters to create textures is virtually unlimited. These three examples were created with multiple applications of KPT Texture Explorer. (Also see color section.)

Patterns

There are two filters discussed in this chapter specifically designed to create patterns. Xaos Tools Terrazzo creates 17 different types of patterns from a portion of your image. See the description of Terrazzo earlier in this chapter for a sample image.

Andromeda's Design filter lets you overlay patterns in any color from its library of more than 100. It also lets you warp patterns into perspective planes, cylinders, and drops.

Other Background Options

If you are using a full-color image, use KPT Fade Contrast on a selected area to dim the image so you can overlay type. You can also darken and modify the image by applying texture to it using the Multiply and Darken apply modes.

If you are using most of an image as a background, but want to call attention to a certain part, you can darken and fade the rest of the image, and highlight the part you want to stand out. You can use KPT Gradient Designer to highlight a certain part while darkening other parts. Or you can add a glow or frame around that part of the image, as discussed in the following sections.

See the suggestions later in this chapter: "Making Glass" and "Creating Liquid Effects" to use on backgrounds.

Creating Lighting and Color Effects

Of course, Photoshop 3 includes the new Lighting Effects filter discussed in chapter 15, "Using Photoshop's Plug-In Filters." But there are several other options provided by third-party filters for color and lighting effects.

Lighting Effects

Several of Andromeda's Series 1 filters were designed for photographic lighting effects, including Diffract and Star that add lights to an image. In figure 16.75, the left image shows how Andromeda Stars adds lighted stars to an image.

KPT Gradient Designer can be used both for lighting and color manipulation. A light can be easily added by choosing a linear white-to-black gradient, Circular Sunburst (move origin point), and the Procedural, Lighten or Screen apply modes. After you see how this works, try it for other effects. Using the Add, Lighten, and Screen apply modes adds colored lighting effects as well. In figure 16.75, the right two images use KPT Gradient Designer. The center uses just a white-light Circular Sunburst, while the right uses a colored gradient.

V

Filters, Plug-Ins, & Effects

KPT Gaussian Glow, Electrify, and Weave can create halos around images, as can Andromeda's Halo. Gallery Effects Neon Glow adds bright glows in the current background color to light areas in an image.

KPT's Glass Lens filters also add lights to an image, but produce a 3-D spherizing effect at the same time.

Fig. 16.75

Lighting effects created with filters: Andromeda Stars, and two different applications of KPT Gradient Designer.

Color Effects

Colors in an image can be completely manipulated with Second Glance Chromassage. It is very similar to KPT Cyclone, in that it changes the color look-up table (CLUT) that affects the color of each pixel in an image. Chromassage offers more controls with real-time preview of changing palette colors and positions, while Cyclone animates color values in your image, letting you stop the animation when you see what you want.

The other Second Glance filters are intended to reduce the number of colors in an image to prepare for spot color separations, but can be used to replace and manipulate specific colors. Try Paint Thinner for this process.

Also, as noted in the earlier section, "Tips for Maximizing Filters," don't forget to try filters on different color channels for very interesting color looks.

Using Filters to Create Other Special Effects

Some other popular effects created with filters are making glass, creating liquid effects and simulating three-dimensional looks. With filters you can create many "real-life" looks in Photoshop, and these are just a few options when you realize the extensive power of filters for special effects.

Making Glass

Glass looks can be made with several filters. The Black Box Glass filter creates colored or leaded glass that makes an object look raised from an image surface. Glass surface looks can be created with GE Spatter, Glass, Plastic Wrap, KPT PixelBreeze, and KPT Diffuse More. GE Stained Glass makes panes with leaded grouts but the panes are equally lit and rather flat.

Figure 16.76 shows three images with glass-looking surfaces. They were created with GE Glass, GE Plastic Wrap, and KPT PixelBreeze.

Fig. 16.76

These glass surfaces were created with GE Glass, GE Plastic Wrap, and KPT PixelBreeze.

V

Filters, Plug-Ins, & Effects

Creating Liquid Effects

Creating liquid surfaces is simply a matter of distortion and lighting. Gallery Effects Ripple filter makes an image appear to be under rippling water. Spatter also works with a high spray radius and smoothness and almost looks like the viewer is underwater looking up. GE Chrome gives a liquid metallic look, as shown in the center image of figure 16.77.

KPT Gradient Designer and Texture Explorer are powerful filters for creating liquid effects. Try Procedural Apply with different versions of a black-to-white-to-black gradient. Repeat the gradient several times, use Pinch Left or Pinch Right, and move the origin around for a rippling water surface. Try experimenting with different gradient shapes, origins, transparencies, and distortions for more liquid effects. The left and right images in figure 16.77 show liquid applied with Gradient Designer and Texture Explorer, respectively.

Use the Liquid presets in KPT Texture Explorer and try different apply modes and sizes for variation.

Fig. 16.77

Liquid with third-party filters.

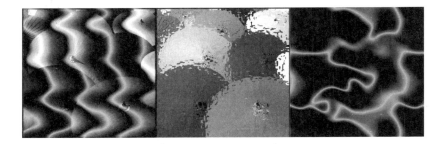

3-D Looks

There are several ways to make an image appear three-dimensional or raised off a surface. Making a two-dimensional image look 3-D is really just a trick of using light, shading, and image distortion.

Of course there's Andromeda's new 3-D filter that wraps images to 3-D objects. See the description earlier in this chapter for a sample image.

KPT Gradient Designer, as described in the Liquid Effects section, is a powerful warping tool that creates a black-to-white-to-black gradient, and repeats it several times using distort left. Use Circular Sunburst and move the origin to the corner. Use Procedural Apply and you've got a tunnel.

The same method can be used to create picture frames with Gradient Designer. With the same black-to-white-to-black gradient (or other dark and light colors) choose Circular Shapeburst. Cut the gradient and drag the color bar slider to the right, to about one-fifth of the total bar. Paste the gradient into that area. Use the Procedural or Multiply apply modes to frame your image. This is a simple rounded frame but once you get the hang of it you can experiment with all types. Check out the preset categories Frame and Overlays, and Framing Effects.

KPT Glass Lens Bright spherizes your selection, including light and shading to make it appear to be a bubble rising from a surface. Add a shadow to it, and it will look even farther off the surface.

Making soft drop shadows is a one-stop process with the Black Box Drop Shadow filter. With it you can control the shadow color, opacity, and amount of blur.

Andromeda's Reflection can also be used for duplicating the image and distorting its position to make the original appears it's standing. The Velocity filter can be used to make an object look extruded, as described in the Andromeda manual.

Embossing creates raised textures in an image. GE Emboss, Bas Relief, Plaster, and Notepaper each do it in different ways. The Black Box filter, The Boss, is a powerful embossing tool. Sucking Fish Series Deko-Boko creates instant raised, beveled boxes.

Figure 16.78 shows a 3-D looking tunnel with floating spheres created with three third-party filters. Also see the section "Art and Effects Filters" earlier in this chapter for sample images of other filters just mentioned.

Fig. 16.78

This 3-D looking image was created with KPT Gradient Designer, KPT Glass Lens Bright, and Alien Skin Drop Shadow.

V

Filters, Plug-Ins, & Effects

Creating Type Effects with Third-Party Filters

Every technique discussed in this section can be applied to type in an image. Create a glow around type with KPT Gaussian Glow or Andromeda Halo. Make type look extruded with Andromeda Velocity. Add drop shadows, make it look embossed or made out of glass with The Black Box filters. Fill it with a gradient. Make it look like it's bubbling out of the surface with the same technique for making frames with Gradient Designer. Fill it with the same texture you used in a background, only inside the text, use Difference apply mode. There are so many options, you can turn type into art. This is great if your photo budget is small. Figure 16.79 shows three text treatments created with several filters described in the caption. Also see figure 16.80 in the next section on Combining Filters for a type example.

Fig. 16.79

Many filters were used to create these type effects, including KPT Gradient Designer and Texture Explorer, GE Texturizer, Alien Skin, The Boss, and Andromeda Reflections.

Combining Filters

As suggested in the section, "Tips for Maximizing Filters," combining filters can lead to amazing and unique effects. You could spend all day just going between KPT Gradient Designer and Texture Explorer, so with 100 other filters, the combinations of effects are endless.

Every time you change the look of an image with a filter, the next filter is applied differently. That's because so many filters read the pixel values of an image to determine how the effect is applied. So even when you apply the same filter twice, it results in a different look.

Some filter combinations are useful for achieving certain results. For example, as suggested previously, creating flat color images before applying tracing filters gives a better line art image. This is also useful for simpler embossing effects. See figure 16.80 for two examples of filter combinations. Also see figure 16.80 in the color section, "Photoshop in Color!"

Fig. 16.80

Filter Combinations create new and unique effects. The Type image was created using KPT Gradient Designer, Texture Explorer, and Alien Skin Drop Shadow. The "Easter Fun" image was also created with KPT Gradient Designer and Texture Explorer. (Also see color section.)

Where To Go from Here

▶ Chapter 15, "Using Photoshop's Plug-In Filters," introduces you to plug-ins and explains the plug-ins that ship with Photoshop.

▶ Also see Part VII, "Learning from the Pros," for tips on how to use filters and other techniques to design for different media.

V

Filters, Plug-Ins, & Effects

Creating Special Effects with Video

Whether you're an amateur experimenting with QuickTime movies, or in a professional production environment, you will be able to apply expert effects with Photoshop 3. This chapter covers a few different techniques for rotoscoping, paint/filter effects, titling, and blue screen compositing. Working frame-by-frame in Photoshop, you can achieve image effects that will rival the big Hollywood studios—right on your desktop!

by Jeff Foster

CHAPTER 17

Creating a Filmstrip File in Adobe Premiere:

Working with video images, QuickTime movies, Filmstrips, and sequential PICT files in Photoshop requires other programs to record, import, composite, transpose, save, and export movies and files. Adobe Premiere, CoSA's After Effects, Apple's Movie Player, or Movie Shop can easily be used to get good results in most situations. If you are not using one of these programs already, you should carefully research them before you make your purchase, so you can get the application that best suits your needs.

This first example demonstrates using Adobe Premiere to create a Filmstrip file for adding frame-by-frame effects in Photoshop.

1. To create a Filmstrip file from a QuickTime movie in Premiere, open the File menu and choose the Open command to open the original movie file.

2. Open the Make menu and choose Movie to open the Movie dialog box (see fig. 17.1).

Fig. 17.1

Selecting the Make Movie dialog box in Adobe Premiere.

3. Click the Output Options button (see fig. 17.2).

Fig. 17.2

Selecting Output Options.

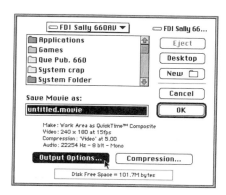

4. From the pop-up menu, select the Filmstrip File option, as shown in figure 17.3.

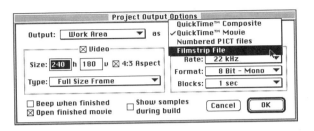

Fig. 17.3

Selecting the Filmstrip File option.

5. Choose the Compression button from the opened Make Movie dialog box. If you have hard disk space, and you're creating a movie/file to edit, it is suggested that you use the highest quality (Most) and lowest compression settings (None), as shown in figure 17.4. The other compression settings will determine how many frames per second your filmstrip will need to be, and if you need QuickTime compression. However, you will severely lose quality if you are working in less than the Millions of Colors quality settings.

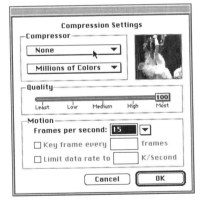

Fig. 17.4

Selecting the Compression quality settings.

Applying an Effect to a Filmstrip File in Photoshop

Now that you have a Filmstrip file created, you can edit it frame-by-frame in Photoshop. You can experiment with cutting out frames and re-sequencing them, painting on each frame with the Paintbrush or Airbrush tools, or using plug-in filters to create patterns and effects in motion.

V

Filters, Plug-Ins, & Effects

Many plug-in filters and paint effects can produce great results when animated. To learn more about applying plug-in filters and effects, refer to chapter 15, "Using Photoshop's Plug-In Filters."

The following steps demonstrate a painting effect that's applied frame-by-frame to a Filmstrip file. This is done with the simple application of a plug-in filter. You can use any video clip or animation that's been converted to a Filmstrip file.

Note

Make sure you are not working on the only copy of your video/animation file, as you can only save a Filmstrip without re-naming the file!

---

1. Open a Filmstrip file in Photoshop 3 to do any effects editing or rotoscoping. Open the File menu and choose the Open command. Because your Filmstrip file is probably rather large, it will be necessary to use the Zoom tool to zoom-in on the first frame that you want to apply the effect to (see fig. 17.5).

Fig. 17.5

Use the Zoom tool to gain a 1-to-1 view ratio.

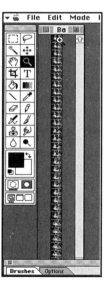

2. Using the Rectangle Marquee tool, drag-select the frame as close as possible to the edges of your image. Make sure that you select the entire frame (see fig. 17.6).

Photoshop in Color!

This special section provides color illustrations of many of the techniques explained in the text. The figure number or section head in the chapter is given so that you can easily refer to the text for step-by-step explanations.

Fig. 9.13
Red is selected and then yellow is added from the Color Range dialog box.

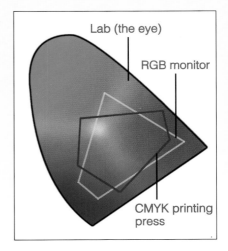

Fig. 13.29
The color gamut, or color range, of the three color systems you use when creating a color image for the press—Lab (or what can be perceived), your RGB color computer monitor, and a CMYK printing press.

Fig. 13.37
The Photoshop Olé No Moiré file printed on 60-pound coated stock can be used for preliminary calibration.

Fig. 14.6
Posterize forces colors to a fixed number of brightness levels.

Fig. 14.9
An image before and after using the Levels command.

Fig. 14.12
The contrast was enhanced in this image by first using Auto, which changed each color channel, and then drawing the S-curve (in figure 14.11) in the composite channel (see chapter 14, "Using Color Correction Tools").

Fig. 14.21
An image changed with variations.

Fig. 15.33
Color Halftone applied to a photo gives it the look of a printed halftone on-screen.

Fig. 15.38
Mezzotint applied to a photograph creates a grainy, old look for images.

Fig. 15.72
Adding noise to an image can create a mezzotint effect.

Fig. 15.73
Two examples of applying textures to an image.

Fig. 15.74
Median can give your image a painted look.

Fig. 15.75
Mosaic and Find Edges
were used to make this
stained glass image. (left)

Fig. 16.5
An object turned into glass.
(right)

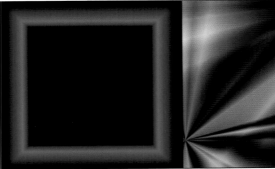

Fig. 16.15
Gradient Designer created
this frame and background.

Fig. 16.33
Angled Strokes paints long
diagonal brush strokes into
an image.

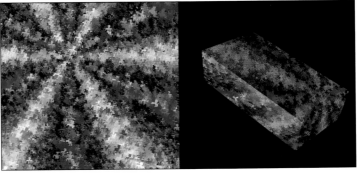

Fig. 16.51
Any image can be wrapped
to a box (shown), sphere,
plane, or cylinder.

Fig. 16.67
These painted looks were achieved with GE Fresco, GE Paint Daubs, and GE Sumi-E.

Fig. 16.71
Noise effects vary widely, as seen in this image using GE Film Grain, GE Grain (clumped), and KPT Texture Explorer.

Fig. 16.74

The power of third-party filters to create textures is virtually unlimited. These three examples were created with multiple applications of KPT Texture Explorer.

Fig. 16.80
Filter combinations create new and unique effects. The "Osiana" type image was created using KPT Gradient Designer, Texture Explorer, and Alien Skin Drop Shadow. The "Easter Fun" image was also created with KPT Gradient Designer and Texture Explorer.

With a blue screen you can buy or rent from a pro-photo supplier, you can shoot anything from 35mm stills to motion picture (cine) film, and composite with other footage or computer-generated scenes like the pros—well, maybe a little slower! (See "Blue Screen Compositing," in chapter 17, "Creating Special Effects with Video," p. 586.)

On the top is the first frame from a QuickTime movie; in the middle is the still image graphic with transparent background; and on the bottom is the composite image (see "Rotoscoping Quick-Time Movies in Photoshop 3," in chapter 17, "Creating Special Effects with Video," p. 584).

Fig. 17.30
Changing the light source positions on a KPT spheroid.

Fig. 17.33
Lens Flare filter in motion.

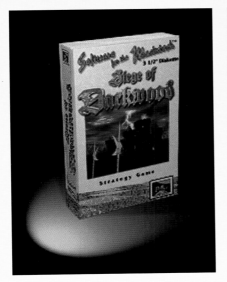

Fig. 19.5
Creating soft
shadows around
the box makes it
more believable.
(left)

Fig. 19.8
Creating a
3-D can. (right)

Examples
created with
KPT Page Curl
(see "Working
with Page Curl,"
in chapter 19,
"3-D Modeling
Special Effects,"
p. 623).

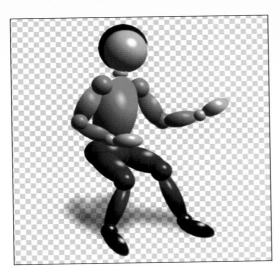

Fig. 19.31
The completed
"Molecule Mann"
character.

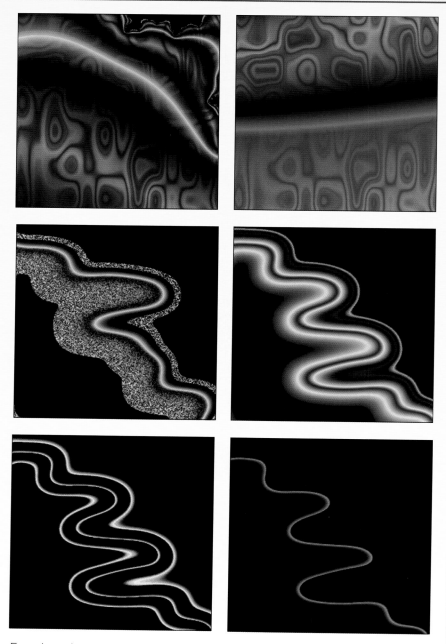

Experimenting with different settings in KPT will produce liquids, textures, glowing tubes, and so on (see "Creating Liquids, Glowing Tubes, and More!" in chapter 19, "3-D Modeling Special Effects," p. 629).

Fig. 19.38
The final image composited using
two Spheroid Filter effects.

Fig. 19.43
Creating surface texture.

Fig. 19.47
The final rendered
Bryce image.

Fig. 19.52
Bringing flat art work
to life!

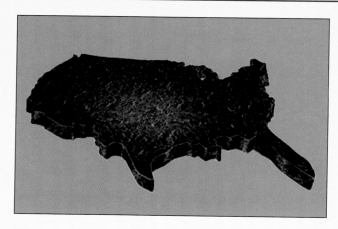

Fig. 19.57
It's easy to create
3-D graphics in
Photoshop.

Bringing life and
action to an image
(see "Do the Logo
Motion," in chapter
20, "Text Special
Effects," p. 680).

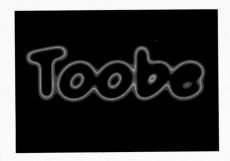

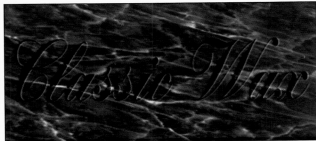

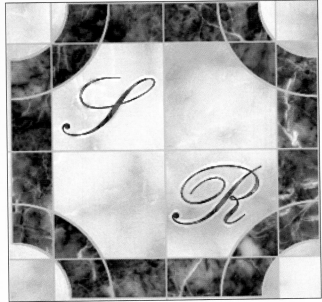

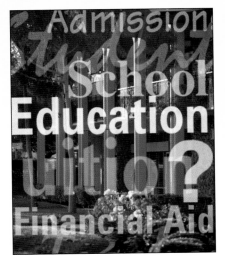

Interesting titling and logo effects you can create with type (see chapter 20, "Text Special Effects").

Fig. 22.9
If a screen printer lays down six or eight different colors, the separations need to be individual spot colors.

Fig. 22.10
Large presses with eight or more heads in an octopus-like configuration have separate color inks applied to many different types of material, the most popular being textiles and clothing.

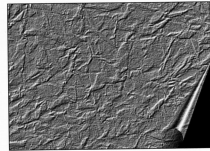

With help from Photoshop, you can add exciting backgrounds to your presentation. (See "Backgrounds," in chapter 23, "Photoshop for the Presenter," p. 748.)

Enhance photos for use in your presentation. (See "Photos and Graphics," in chapter 23, "Photoshop for the Presenter," p. 748.)

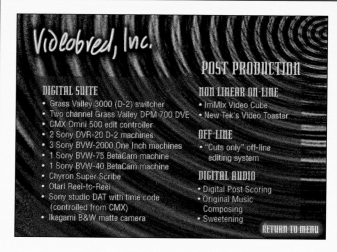

Fig. 23.3
Effects available in Photoshop can spice up your presentation.

Fig. 23.5
Dark backgrounds and light type are easier on the eyes.

Fig. 23.9
Often images will look just as acceptable at a lower bit-depth.

3. Now you can apply the paint or filter effect that you choose to this selected frame. Figure 17.7 shows XAOS tools Paint Alchemy. Notice the difference between the images on the left and right preview windows. The paint effect is shown in comparison from frame 1 and 2 of this Filmstrip in figure 17.8.

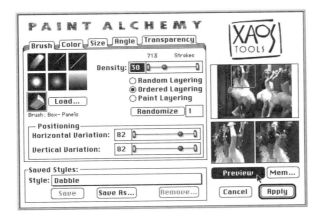

Fig. 17.7

Previewing the
selected paintbrush
style to apply.

4. The Brush Strokes should be animated from each frame to the next, as well as the actual sequence of frames, giving the effect of a hand-painted animation effect. To get this effect, click on the Randomize button in Paint Alchemy when applying this effect to each frame in the Filmstrip sequence.

Fig. 17.8

Viewing the
applied effect
to frame 1.

5. Examine the differences in the brush strokes between the two edited frames in figure 17.9.

Fig. 17.9

Viewing frames 1
and 2 respectively.

6. Once you have created the desired filter effect(s) to the frames you have chosen, open the File menu and choose Save. Do not make any changes to the Size, Mode, Name, or File type whatsoever.

> **Tip**
>
> **A Quick and Dirty Alternative Repetition**
>
> To expedite the paint filter application process, you could simply choose not to randomize the effect from frame-to-frame, and only apply the master settings to each frame, by simply pressing ⌘-F (Repeat Last Filter). This will allow the effect to remain in a stationary position, and the video image will appear to "move" behind the effect—similar to a moving oil portrait.

Now open your Filmstrip file in Premiere and continue your project or make a QuickTime movie. You can go back and forth between Premiere and Photoshop 3 as many times as you wish—as long as the file type does not change from the Filmstrip mode, and you save often!

Rotoscoping Sequential PICT Files

Rotoscoping is a process in which you take a frame out of sequence (whether it's video, cine (motion picture) film, or a QuickTime movie), edit it in some way, and place it back into sequence.

You can open any sequenced PICT files, whether created in Premiere or another program, or straight from the video digitizing software. You can then edit, color shift, filter, composite, paint...virtually anything you can do to a still image, you can apply to a series of video frames. Keep in mind that anything painted freehand, or pasted and placed by freehand, may have sketchy, often sloppy, hand-animated results IF NOT executed meticulously!

Using mask channels is only one part of rotoscoping an effect. You must have good control of your Airbrush and Paintbrush tools as well. Refer back to chapter 8, "Drawing, Painting, and Editing" to review the use of these tools.

If you wanted to add a wild zapping, animated, electrical light current to a character, here is a set of steps to follow.

1. Open the File menu and choose the Open command. Select a sequence of PICT files to be edited. Open several frames (about 10) at a time to keep a visual perspective on your rotoscoping progress.

V

Filters, Plug-Ins, & Effects

2. Starting with Frame 1, freehand airbrush a light path for a base to the moving light beams around the character by using the Airbrush tool and a white color at a 35 percent opacity setting (see fig. 17.10).

Fig. 17.10

Airbrushing the main light motion paths.

3. Select an area around each light path with the Lasso tool (feathered approximately 9 pixels), as shown in figure 17.11. Refer to chapter 9, "Selecting Objects in Photoshop," for information on how to feather a selection.

Fig. 17.11

Selecting a feathered section to colorize with the Lasso tool.

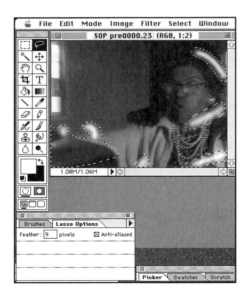

4. Open the Image menu and choose Adjust Levels. Adjust the amount of Blue (to approximately 2.00) and Red (to approximately 1.35) saturation inside the selection. This gives a glowing "electrical" effect (see fig. 17.12).

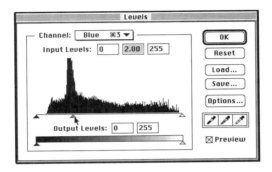

Fig. 17.12

Changing the color inside the selection with the Levels dialog box.

5. Open the Select menu and choose All.

6. Open the Edit menu and choose Copy. This places the dimensions of the frame you're working on to the clipboard.

7. Create a new file by opening the File menu and choosing New. This will be a mask file that you will paint through later on in this chapter.

8. Select the Grayscale Mode button, with a black background selection in the New File dialog box, keeping the default size of the clipboard's dimensions that will appear automatically.

9. Open the Filters menu and choose Noise, Add Noise. The Add Noise dialog box appears.

Set the Amount of noise to approximately 350 and apply to the New file (see fig. 17.13).

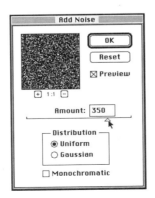

Fig. 17.13

Adding noise to the New file for use as a mask.

V

Filters, Plug-Ins, & Effects

577

10. Open the File menu and choose Save. Name this file Sparkle Mask.

11. Open the Select menu and choose All.

12. Open the Edit menu and choose Copy.

13. Return to the Frame 1 file and create a new channel in the Channels palette, by selecting New Channel from the palette pop-up menu.

14. With the new channel open, open the Edit menu and choose Paste.

15. Open the Select menu and choose Load Selection.

16. Choose the new channel for the target selection.

17. Open the Select menu and choose the Hide Edges command. This enables you to see where you will be painting your effect, instead of trying to see through the "marching ants" of the selection edges.

18. Set the Paintbrush tool at 60 percent opacity and paint white through the selection, creating a sparkling effect. This is visible in figure 17.14.

Fig. 17.14

Using the Paint-brush to add the final sparkle effect.

19. Open the File menu and choose Save As to save the Frame 1 file. Select a name for this file with sequential ending and leading zeros for the number of frames you will be applying the effect to.

Repeat steps 1 through 18 for all frames of your PICT file sequence. There is no need to change the Mask File for each frame as you will be hand-painting the effect very swiftly. The eye will never notice if it's a static pattern or not. You must have a great deal of patience and time to perform this task.

Creating a Graphic Image for Compositing

Adding graphic images such as logos, type, photo inserts, or graphic banners to QuickTime movies or video first requires an image file to import into a video compositing/editing application, or directly to the QuickTime movie itself, as is demonstrated later in this chapter. Refer to the first section in this chapter for some examples of video and QuickTime compositing/editing software.

Adding a Graphic

The example in this section shows how to create a graphic image for a mock TV news broadcast, only in a smaller QuickTime movie resolution. The steps that follow show you how to create an image to add to a video segment in Photoshop.

First you must determine the size of the QuickTime movie or video that you're going to add your graphic to. For instance, if you're working with full-frame video captured on your Mac, you'll be working with 640×480 pixels; so your graphic file must be the same size.

1. In Photoshop, create a new document by opening the File menu and choosing the New command. A dialog box appears.

   Select RGB Color in the Mode pop-up menu and make sure the dimensions match your sample image. The example in figure 17.15 shows the selection of 240×180 pixels, 72 dpi, and a Transparent background.

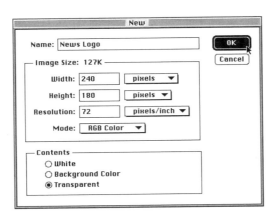

Fig. 17.15

Creating the New file for the graphic image.

2. In the pop-up menu in the Layers palette, select New Layer. Click OK. This will be Layer 1.

3. With Layer 1 selected, create a graphic shape. For this example, the Rectangle Marquee tool is used to define a small square near the upper-left corner of the file.

4. Using the Eyedropper tool, select a color from the Swatches palette.

5. Open the Edit menu and choose the Fill command.

   Select Foreground Color and choose 100 percent opacity in the Fill dialog box. Click OK.

6. Apply a special effect. If you have the "Sucking Fish" from Bill Niffenegger's "Photoshop Filter Finesse" CD-ROM sampler installed, you can open the Filter menu and choose Sucking Fish.

   If you want the selected graphic area to appear to be raised out like a mortise, choose the Deko mode with a 4-pixel wide bevels setting, as shown in figure 17.16.

Fig. 17.16

Applying the Deko filter to get a Mortised effect.

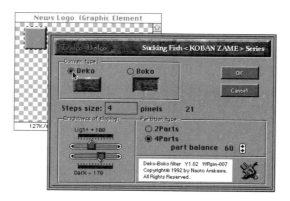

7. Create a new layer by selecting New Layer from the Layers palette pop-up menu. Click OK. This will be named Layer 2. Position Layer 2 below Layer 1 in the Layers palette.

8. With Layer 2 selected, create another graphic. This example uses the Rectangle Marquee tool and selects an area protruding to the right of the square created in step 2 on Layer 1.

9. Using the Eyedropper tool, select a color in the Swatches palette.

10. Open the Edit menu and choose the Fill command.

Select Foreground Color and choose 100 percent opacity in the Fill dialog box (see fig. 17.17).

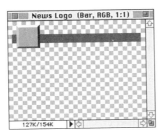

Fig. 17.17

Adding a new graphic element on a new layer.

11. Adjust the transparency of the graphics by selecting the layer and using the opacity slider in the Layers palette (see fig. 17.18).

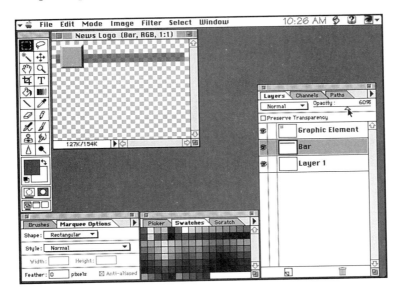

Fig. 17.18

Adjusting the transparency of the new layer with the Opacity slider.

V

Filters, Plug-Ins, & Effects

Adding Text to the Graphic

Using the graphic elements as a base, you can add text by following these steps:

1. Select New Layer from the pop-up menu in the Layers palette to add a new layer for the text. Click OK. This will be Layer 3. Position this layer on top of all the layers in the Layers palette.

2. Using the Eyedropper tool, select a new color in the Swatches palette.

3. Using the Type tool, double-click over the square graphic on Layer 1. Make sure that Layer 3, the newest layer, is the selected layer. A dialog box appears.

4. In the Type tool dialog box, type the text. Then pick a type style from the fonts list, and size it until the text fits inside the square box. Use the Edit menu and choose Undo Type Tool if you're not pleased with the size.

5. Open the Select menu and choose None.

6. Using the Eyedropper tool, select white in the Swatches palette.

7. Using the Type tool, double-click over the rectangular bar graphic on Layer 2. Make sure that Layer 3, the newest layer that was created, is the selected layer. A dialog box appears.

8. In the Type Tool dialog box, type the text. Pick a type style from the fonts list, and size it until it fits inside the rectangular bar, as shown in figure 17.19.

Fig. 17.19

Type added to the square and rectangular graphics.

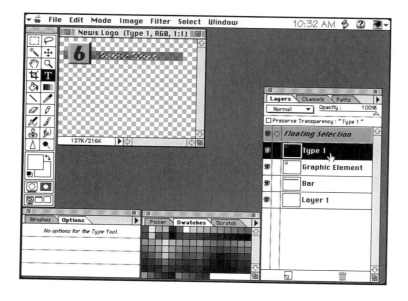

9. Open the Select menu and choose the None command.

Adding a Shadow Effect

When the text is positioned and correctly sized on a graphic element, you can add special effects to the text. The following steps show you how to apply a shadow effect:

1. Create a new layer by selecting New Layer from the Layers palette. This will be called Layer 4. Position this layer above Layers 1 and 2, but below Layer 3 in the Layers palette.

2. Using the Eyedropper tool, select black in the Swatches palette.

3. Using the Type tool, click over the rectangular bar graphic on Layer 2. Make sure that Layer 4, the newest layer that was created, is the selected layer.

4. In the Type Tool dialog box, type the same text for the rectangular bar. Pick a type style from the fonts list, and size it until it fits over the type on Layer 3 perfectly.

5. Open the Select menu and choose None.

6. Select the Move tool and position the type on Layer 4 just to the right and bottom of the type on Layer 3. This is the close drop shadow for the type on the rectangular bar.

7. Using the Airbrush tool, with an opacity setting of 7 percent (set in the Edit, Fill dialog box) and a small brush selected from the Brushes palette, airbrush a shadow on Layer 4 just under the type positioned over the square on Layer 1 (see fig. 17.20).

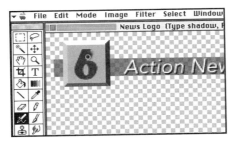

Fig. 17.20

Airbrushing directly to the shadows layer.

Merging the Layers

Once all the layers are complete, you are ready to compress the images to one layer. From the pop-up menu in the Layers palette, choose Merge Layers. Figure 17.21 shows the merged layers from the example with the graphic element LIVE added. Now you can import this document into Premiere to use as an element, or cut and paste it into single frames or QuickTime movies, as will be the example in the next section.

Fig. 17.21

Merging the Layers down to one.

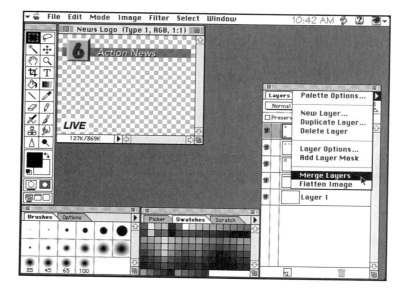

Rotoscoping QuickTime Movies in Photoshop 3

Sometimes you just want to do a simple, quick 'n dirty edit to a short QuickTime movie. This will work with large or small file sizes—depending on your machine and how much RAM it has.

Once you have both a QuickTime movie and a size-matched still graphic image with a transparent background available, you can proceed with the QuickTime rotoscoping process. You will need to have BOTH your QuickTime movie editing application AND a copy of Photoshop 3 open; it will be necessary to toggle back and forth between the two applications. Click the Application icon in the far right of your menu bar to select another application without quitting the one you're in. You can also get back to the Finder using this same method.

The following example is performed in Apple's Movie Player and Photoshop 3, using a small QuickTime movie, and the "News graphic" still image created earlier in this chapter. Be sure to check out the images created in the following example in the color section, "Photoshop in Color!" too.

1. Open the QuickTime movie in Apple's Movie Player.

2. With the first frame selected, open the Edit menu and choose Cut.

3. Select the Photoshop application, leaving the Movie Player application still active, and the cut image still in the clipboard.

4. Create a new file to the default dimensions of the clipboard by opening the File menu and choosing the New command.

5. Open the Edit menu and choose Paste to place the QuickTime frame into the new document, as shown in figure 17.22.

Fig. 17.22

On the left is the first frame from the QuickTime movie, and on the right is the still image graphic with transparent background, created in the last section.

6. Open the still image graphic created in the previous section by opening the File menu, choosing Open, and selecting the file.

7. Open the Select menu and chose All.

8. Open the Edit menu and choose Copy.

9. Return to the File that has the first frame of the QuickTime image on it, open the Edit menu, and choose the Paste command.

10. Open the Select menu and choose None. Notice how the transparency of the graphic still holds against the background image in figure 17.23.

11. Open the Select menu and choose All.

12. Open the Edit menu and choose Copy.

V

Filters, Plug-Ins, & Effects

Fig. 17.23

Pasting the graphic
image onto the
new file image.

13. Select the QuickTime movie application in the menu bar.

14. Returning to the first frame where you began in step 2, open the Edit
menu and choose Paste. The results are shown in figure 17.24.

Fig. 17.24

Pasting the new file
composite image
into the QuickTime
movie.

You can repeat this process (steps 2 though 14) for all following sequential
frames in the QuickTime movie. This may seem a bit complicated at first,
but you will quickly get the hang of it. It's really an easy step-by-step
approach to frame editing, without creating a lot of extra frames and
movies on your hard drive.

Blue Screen Compositing

Working with a blue screen used to be left up to motion picture studios
and TV stations. Now you can achieve the same great effects from the
company that pioneered the technology...right on your Mac! Ultimatte
has developed a plug-in for Photoshop called PhotoFusion. And guess

what? It really works! Sure, there's some okay "keying" effects and extensions to mask-out certain colors in an image, but what about the shadows? What about fine hair? What about glass, water, and smoke? Using a blue screen that you can buy or rent from a pro-photo supplier, you can shoot anything from 35mm stills to motion picture (cine) film, and composite with other footage or computer-generated scenes like the pros (well, maybe a little slower!).

A detailed explanation of how to work with this plug-in is beyond the scope of this book, but the following example gives you a taste of what can be done with PhotoFusion. See the color section, "Photoshop in Color!" for full-color images of the following example.

In the example, the original blue screen shot was done in a parking lot on a sunny day, with a 35mm motion camera (29.97 frames per second) on a boom. The footage was then cine-transferred to D1 (digital video), and brought in on 8mm Exabyte tape (still digital frames). This is the easiest way to get the digital frames from movie film onto the Mac, but it requires the professional (and expensive) expertise of a qualified service bureau.

1. In the first frame of the blue screen sequence, the Lasso tool (feathered 5 pixels) is used to select an area of motion the characters make against the screen (see fig. 17.25).

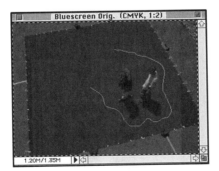

Fig. 17.25

Selecting around the figure's motion path.

2. The selection is Inversed and the Eyedropper tool is used to pick up the general color of the blue screen. A 100 percent fill of that color is added (see fig. 17.26). This selection and fill are copied to the clipboard and pasted on each frame sequentially. Each file (frame) is saved under a new name in the Photoshop format.

Fig. 17.26

Filling the
foreground color to
create a "Garbage
Matte" for all
sequenced frames.

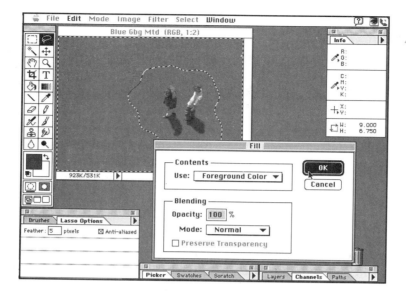

3. Next the Foreground image is loaded using the Acquire, PhotoFusion
command, and an area is selected for the Backing Color, as shown in
figure 17.27.

Fig. 17.27

Selecting the
background
color of the Fore-
ground image in
Ultimatte's Photo-
Fusion Acquire
plug-in.

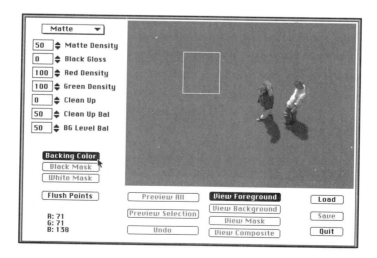

4. After you select the white part of the mask and click "White Mask,"
then proceed with the "Black Mask." The image mask is sufficient for
compositing figure 17.28, although the controls for edges and flare
suppression are incredibly accurate.

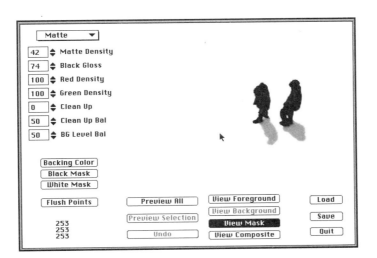

Fig. 17.28

Adjusting the mask settings.

5. The 3-D background image in this example, which was created in KPT Bryce, is loaded. The composite in Photofusion's window prior to saving is shown in figure 17.29.

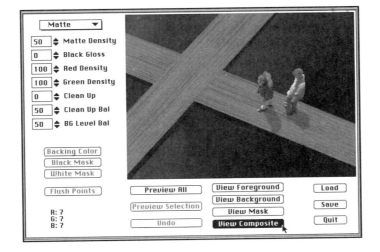

Fig. 17.29

Viewing the final composite image.

Again, this was done for a 10 second segment (approximately 300 frames). The final was then exported to 8mm Exabyte tape and transferred to Betacam SP (broadcast video). Patience and attention to detail are extremely important. There have been literally days lost on a project like this when only one frame got out of sequence!

V

Filters, Plug-Ins, & Effects

Sequential Application of Filter Effects

As you saw earlier in this chapter, XAOS tools' Paint Alchemy can be used to create animated, random brush patterns which provide an interesting effect to a section of video. The same can be done with other plug-in filters as long as there is some kind of sequential or numerical control between the individual frames. The next section presents a couple of examples.

Animating a Light Source

The controls for the light direction in this series of plug-ins from HSC are the number keys on your keyboard. If you are using an extended keyboard, then use the numerical keypad on your right, as this gives you a visual of what direction the light source will come from. Consider it as a type of joystick controller.

1. Open a new file by opening the File menu and choosing New.

2. Apply a simple KPT Fractal Explorer design by selecting the Filter menu and choosing the KPT, KPT Fractal Explorer.

3. Choose a design inside the KPT interface. (Refer to chapter 15, "Using Photoshop's Plug-In Filters," for information on how to use Kai's Power Tools' custom filters.)

4. Make a selection with the Elliptical Marquee tool, in the center of the file.

> **Tip**
>
> **I Want a Circle Selection...Not an Ellipse!**
>
> If you hold down the Shift key while drawing your circle, it will keep it concentric. Also, by holding down the Option key, you can draw from the center of your selection origin point. This really helps to center your circle selection to the file.

5. Open the Select menu and choose Save Selection to a New Channel.

6. Load the new channel selection, by opening the Select menu and choosing Load Selection.

7. Hold down the number 1 key on your keyboard, open the Filter menu and choose Distort, KPT Glass Lens Normal. This creates a spheroid with the light source coming from the bottom-left side.

8. Continue this process, working the light source around the spheroid in a clockwise direction, using the sequence of number keys 1, 4, 7, 8, 9, 6, 3, and 2. If you are using an extended keyboard, use the numbers keypad on the right, and you can visualize your light directions. See figure 17.30 to refer to the sequence. Also see figure 17.30 in the color section, "Photoshop in Color!"

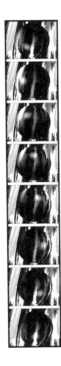

Fig. 17.30

Changing the light source positions on a KPT spheroid.

This effect works well for buttons and lights in multimedia applications. Check it out!

Animating with Lens Flare

Okay—you've seen it in many space movies and TV shows, but it's a versatile little plug-in that you can animate quite easily!

The following example starts with a single-frame scene, created in KPT Bryce, which we will add a "pseudo-sunrise" animation to. You may use any still image you have lying around on your hard drive.

1. With the original image open and with no selections current, select the Lens Flare filter, by opening the Filter menu and choosing Render, Lens Flare. The Lens Flare dialog box appears.

2. Place the crosshair in the preview box at the starting point of the light source path.

3. Select the Lens type and set the brightness down to 10 percent as the initial setting, as shown in figure 17.31. Click OK.

Fig. 17.31

Setting the initial location and brightness of the Lens Flare filter.

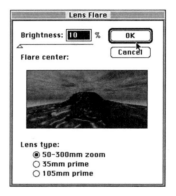

Note

It is important that you do not use your mouse to move the light source cursor from this point on, or you will have an uneven animation!

4. Open the File menu and choose Save As with a sequential numerical ending (for example, Lens.001) for animation.

5. Open the original image, by selecting the File menu and choosing Open.

6. Open the Filter menu and choose Render, Lens Flare.

7. If you want a fairly fast "sunrise" effect, then change the brightness levels by 5 percent increments in the Lens Flare dialog box for each frame you create by repeating steps 4-7.

Also, on each frame, move the positioning cursor in the Lens Flare dialog box preview window, with the arrow keys, clicking the up arrow and left arrow twice for each frame to move the effect upwards and across the sky. This is demonstrated in figure 17.32.

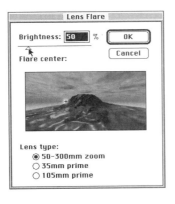 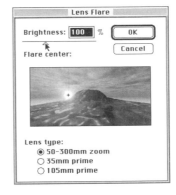

Fig. 17.32

Sequential movement through the Lens Flare filter dialog box.

Looking at the example sequence, you can see how the effect moves easily across the sky, and appears to be "peeking" out from behind the mountain, as shown in figure 17.33. Also see figure 17.33 in the color section.

Fig. 17.33

Lens Flare filter in motion.

This chapter didn't go into great detail with the landscape lighting, but you could very well move the light source in a 3-D application prior to using the Lens Flare filter, and match the motion control by sight.

V

Filters, Plug-Ins, & Effects

Where To Go from Here

▶ Chapter 9, "Selecting Objects in Photoshop," will familiarize you with making selections. If you are using Photoshop for the first time, you should check out this chapter.

▶ Chapter 15, "Using Photoshop's Plug-In Filters," covers many creative ideas for using plug-in filters.

▶ Much of the material covered in chapter 18, "Creating Special Effects with Channels," and chapter 19, "3-D Modeling Special Effects," can be applied in a frame-by-frame method to add 3-D effects to your QuickTime movies.

Creating Special Effects with Channels

In this chapter, you learn the mathematical process of calculating images between channels (also known as channel operations, "channel ops," or CHOPS). Channel operations are used for performing many functions in Photoshop including creating selections, special effects, simulating 3-D images, and creating photorealistic images. Using channel ops, you also create effects like glass, embossed paper, stamped metal, and more. Working with channel operations is an advanced area of Photoshop features. If you lack a basic understanding of what channels are and how to create them, you should first read chapter 12, "Using Masks and Channels." In this chapter, you'll explore how to use channels to create special effects.

by Ted Padova and Jeff Foster

CHAPTER 18

Using Photoshop for Macintosh

With Photoshop 3, you can utilize layers to create interesting effects through compositing or painting on each layer. In addition to the many layer functions you can perform with Photoshop, channel operations add many more features for editing and compositing images. When you combine the features of working with layers and channels, there is an infinite number of possibilities of how the images will appear.

Calculating in Channel Ops

The images you create with channel operations are the "Wow!" stuff you see in posters, ads, and printed material. They are the kind of images that you look at and say, "How did they do that?" Kai Krause of HSC software developed international notoriety for his work with channel operations a few years ago. He had a weekly forum on America Online and responded to users' questions from all over the world. Through Kai's work and followers, a special interest group developed for people who wanted to get the most from the 11 calculate commands used to perform channel operations in Photoshop 2.5. With all this interest and dedication to learning channel operations, you know there must be some important reasons for users to spend so much time mastering them.

This section explains how a typical channel ops process works so you can take advantage of using channels. Inasmuch as channel operations are considered to be reserved for advanced Photoshop users, this chapter presents a step-by-step process for working with channels. Even if you don't consider yourself an advanced user, try to follow the steps outlined in this chapter. Once you become familiar with the basic concepts, you will be able to accomplish some amazing tasks.

Some of the tasks you will perform include using some third-party filters such as Kai's Power Tools from HSC software and Gallery Effects from Adobe Systems. If you do not currently own some of these filters, this chapter provides some Photoshop alternatives so you can work through the process and understand the concepts.

Creating the Channels

There are three items that you use when working with channel operations. The first item you should become familiar with is the Channels palette. The Channels palette and Channels palette operations are discussed in chapter 12, "Using Masks and Channels." For your purposes here, you will want to open the Channels palette by opening the Windows menu and choosing Palettes, Show Channels. Keep this palette open during all the steps you perform in this chapter. The other two items involve commands in the Image menu. Channel operations are commands addressed by opening the Image menu and choosing either Calculations or Apply Image. Using these two commands is what is considered *channel operations*. Each command performs a different function and each will be explained as we use it.

One of the nice things about using channel operations is you don't need to have a photographic scan or image to perform the functions. In essence, you can start with a new document, create a text character or painted shape, and then proceed to create some amazing effects. This example starts by creating a new document and using a text character to explain some of the tasks performed with channel operations.

Before working with channel operations, you need to understand some fundamental principles. Channels can be added to an existing document, or they can be added to a second document. Whenever you work with channels between two documents, the documents must be the same size and resolution. If there is a one pixel difference between the documents, you cannot perform channel operations between the two documents. Some of the exercises in this chapter will be performed by adding channels to the same document. In some instances you'll use two documents. If you cannot perform channel operations between two documents, check to be certain that both documents are the same size and resolution. Let's start our exploration into channel operations by creating a new document.

1. Begin by setting the environment. Before you open a document, set the foreground color to white and the background color to black in the Photoshop toolbox. Open the Window menu and choose Palettes, Show Channels.

2. Create a new document by opening the File menu and choosing New. When the new document dialog box appears, enter 250 pixels for the width, 250 pixels for the height, and grayscale for the mode. Set the resolution to 72 ppi (pixels per inch). Set the Contents to Background. When the new document is created, a black background will appear.

    Note: The resolution has been set to 72 ppi for demonstration purposes only. If you intend to print the document on laser printers, imagesetters, or other devices, you should follow guidelines established for those printers. A thorough explanation of printing guidelines is offered in chapter 13, "Understanding Color," chapter 21, "Photoshop for the Desktop Publisher," and chapter 22, "Photoshop for the Digital Designer."

3. Create a text character. Select the Text tool in the toolbox and click in the new document window. For this example, we'll use a beta symbol. Choose Symbol for the font from the Font pop-up menu in the text dialog box. Set the point size to 220 point. Click the cursor in the window at the bottom of the dialog box and strike the B key on your keyboard; then click OK. Figure 18.1 illustrates the beta symbol, which appears white on a black background. The text character will appear white because you defined your foreground color as white when you set up the environment in step 1 above.

Fig. 18.1

A new document displays a white beta symbol on a black background.

Observe the Channels palette. The new document is a single channel file with the first channel appearing as black. When you open or create a grayscale document, the default channel will appear as black. When you print a document, only the black channel will print. All additional channels added to the document will be Alpha channels. Alpha channels can be used in a document as holding places or work areas, but they will not print when you send the Photoshop image to a printer. Photoshop 3 limits the total number of channels in a single document to 24.

4. Working with the Calculations dialog box, new channels can be created in several ways. You can, for example, click on the new channel icon in the Channels palette to create a duplicate channel. For these exercises, reserve your steps to using the Image menu and Calculations commands. By using the Calculations commands, you

can create a new channel and change the appearance of the image in a single dialog box. For example, at this point let's duplicate the text character and invert the image so the text appears black and the background appears white. This operation is easily handled by opening the Image menu and choosing Calculations. Figure 18.2 shows the Calculations dialog box and the number of choices available to describe the calculation functions used with channel operations.

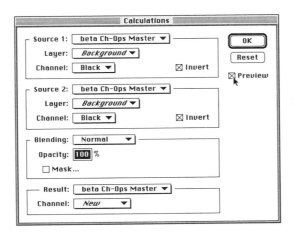

Fig. 18.2

The Calculations dialog box provides many choices to perform channel operations.

V

Before we go too far, let's examine each item in the Calculations dialog box.

▶ *Source 1*. Our new document is entitled "beta Ch-Ops Master." The Source is this document and appears as beta Ch-Ops Master in the pop-up menu for Source 1. If there are two documents of identical size, you may wish to perform calculations between the documents. In such a case, your Source 1 could be either beta Ch-Ops Master or a document of another name.

▶ *Layer*. In the example, there is a single layer document. If there are several layers, the Layer pop-up menu provides an opportunity to choose the layer you wish to use for your calculations.

▶ *Channel*. Thus far there is only a single channel in the document—the black channel. As you add new channels, the channels will be available in this pop-up menu and you can pick which channel you want to use for the calculations.

▶ *Invert.* When the Invert check box is enabled, the image will be inverted. In the example, if you want your beta symbol to appear black and the background to appear white, you can select Invert and accomplish this task.

▶ *Source 2.* This area represents the second image where you might perform calculations. If you wish to perform calculations on a single image as in this example, the Source 2 image will also be beta Ch-Ops Master. If you want to take the black channel in the image and perform a function to the same image, Source 1 and Source 2 will be the same image.

▶ *Source 2 Layer and Channel.* The same holds true for layer and channel in the Source 2 area of the dialog box. You can use the same document, the same layers, or different layers in the same document. You also can use the same channel or different channels in the same document.

▶ *Source 2, Invert.* You can enable Invert in the Source 2 channel much the same as you inverted the Source 1 image. The results of the inverting will appear differently depending on which channel is inverted. As you progress through the steps of using the Calculations dialog box, the results of inverting Source 1 or Source 2 will become more apparent.

▶ *Blending.* You can choose one of the blending modes to apply calculations between the channels which will affect the new channel created. If you are not familiar with the blending modes, see chapter 8, "Drawing, Painting, and Editing."

▶ *Opacity.* The opacity of the result image can be defined by choosing the opacity level.

▶ *Mask.* If you wish to mask a channel so the result is only applied to a portion of the image, choose Mask. When Mask is enabled, the dialog box will automatically expand to provide choices for how and where the Mask will be used.

▶ *Result.* The result is where you will place the end product of your calculations. You can place the result in a new document or in an existing document.

▶ *Channel.* The result channel can be a new channel in a new document, a new channel in an existing document, or you can overwrite an existing channel in either document. In addition, the result can be represented as a selection.

▶ *Preview.* With all these choices on how calculations can be performed and where the result will be placed, the number of possibilities are endless—which makes using them very confusing. Fortunately, Photoshop provides the capability to preview the results dynamically as you make choices in the Calculations dialog box. When you enable Preview in the dialog box, the results will be updated in the document window. As a standard practice, be certain to enable Preview for all your calculations work.

Tip

Adding More Viewing Area to Your Monitor

The Calculations dialog box takes up some precious space on your computer monitor. If you use a 13-inch or even a 17-inch monitor, the Calculations dialog box will prevent you from viewing much of the document below the dialog box. If you hold the Option key down while opening the Image menu and choosing Calculations, the dialog box will be presented in a smaller size.

---

5. Open the Image menu and choose Calculations. Use the Calculations dialog box to create a duplicate channel and invert the image so the text character appears black and the background appears white.

In the Calculations dialog box, choose beta Ch-Ops Master document for Source 1, Background for Layer, and black for Channel. Select the Invert check box. Source 2 should be beta Ch-Ops Master, Background for Layer, and black for Channel. The result will put the new channel back into beta Ch-Ops Master and the channel will be a New channel.

By choosing the above options, you are telling Photoshop to take the black channel, invert it, and put it back into the same document as a new channel. Figure 18.3 illustrates the final result of the new channel. This channel will become channel #2 and can be viewed in the Channels palette below our black channel.

6. Apply a Filter to the new channel. Be certain channel #2 is selected in the Channels palette. Selecting a channel in the Channels palette is achieved by clicking on the channel name in the palette. With channel #2 selected as the active channel, choose Filter, Other, Minimum. In the Minimum filter dialog box, enter 2 for the Radius. The minimum filter will enlarge the object according to the amount specified in the Minimum filter dialog box for the Radius setting. In this case, we will make our text character 2 pixels larger than the original character. Figure 18.3 shows channel #2 with the minimum filter applied.

Fig. 18.3

The minimum filter can be used to increase the size of the character in the second channel.

The text character in the black channel is now smaller in size than the channel #2 character. When you perform calculations between the channels, you can create many interesting effects. For example, you could take the black channel, which has the smaller text character, and carve it out of channel #2, which has the larger text character. The result would be an outline text character. Let's observe how we might use channel operations to create such an effect.

7. Create outline type with channel operations. At this point, we will take channel #2 and carve out the black channel. Choose Image, Calculations to present the Calculations dialog box. The Source 1 image is beta Ch-Ops Master and the Layer is the Background. These two options will remain the same for both the Sources and throughout this exercise. The only area of concern is what channels you use and whether you invert the operation. For the Source 1 channel choose black, and for the Source 2 channel choose channel #2. You should note that the reverse of this operation will create the same effect. In other words, you could choose channel #2 for Source 1 and black for Source 2. Either way the result will appear the same.

For Blending, choose Difference. The Difference blending of the two channels will take the black channel information, which is a white text character, and blend it with channel #2, which is a larger text character appearing black. The result will be a stroke character appearing as outline type. Since the channel #2 was larger than the black channel, all that will remain is the 2 pixel stroke you developed by using the Minimum filter. The result channel will be New to put our result in a new channel in the beta Ch-Ops Master document. When you click OK in the Calculations dialog box—presto, you have outline type, as illustrated in figure 18.4.

Fig. 18.4

Outline type can be easily created with channel operations.

V

Filters, Plug-Ins, & Effects

At this point, you could copy the new channel with the outline type, paste it into a layer and use it for some design purposes. You could then proceed to another document and use channel operations to create another effect. If you want several effects to be saved in a single document, you can continue performing channel operations to create more effects and save them all in the same document. For this exercise, just keep working on the same document and include more effects with your type character in the beta Ch-Ops Master document.

Perhaps the most radical change between channel operations in earlier versions of Photoshop and version 3 is the Duplicate command. In earlier versions, you open the Image menu, choose Calculations, and then Duplicate. Photoshop 3 has a command in the Image menu defined as Duplicate. This command simply duplicates a document and creates a copy. It provides no options for duplicating channels. Don't confuse the Duplicate command with using channel operations to duplicate a channel.

8. To duplicate a channel using the channel operations, open the Image menu and choose Calculations. At first, duplicating a channel may appear somewhat confusing since there is no command identified as

Duplicate. The Source and Layer information will remain the same for both sources. For Source 1, choose black for channel. Source 2 is incidental since you are taking the black channel and simply duplicating it into a new channel. Whatever channel you may have in the Channel pop-up menu for Source 2 will not affect your current operation. In other words, you can have any channel identified for Source 2, and the result will be the same. Choose Normal for the Mode. The Result is beta Ch-Ops Master and the Channel is New. When you click OK, Photoshop will duplicate the black channel and create a new channel. This new channel will become channel #4.

You duplicated this channel so you can perform some changes to it. If you wish to change any channel information and feel you need to preserve your original channel, always create a duplicate. You can make changes without disturbing the original channel. In this case, the black channel remains unedited while you work on the duplicate created as channel #4.

9. To move channel information by offsetting, choose Filter, Other, Offset. In the Offset dialog box, enter 4 for Horizontal and 2 for Vertical. Select the Wrap Around radio button for the Undefined Areas and click OK. Figure 18.5 shows the Offset dialog box with these settings.

Fig. 18.5

The Offset dialog box enables you to offset channels from their original position.

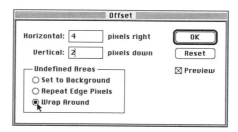

10. To blur channel information, be certain channel #4 is the active channel; then choose Filter, Blur, Gaussian Blur. In the Gaussian Blur dialog box, set the radius to 2.5 pixels by either typing in the value or moving the slider. Click OK to accept the values. Figure 18.6 shows the Gaussian Blur dialog box. When the blur is applied to the channel, the edges of the text character will be softened. By performing Offset and Blur filters to a channel, you can use Calculation commands to create many effects including embossing, neon, halos, drop shadows, and much more. From this point, you'll see how to create some embossed and neon appearances with channel operations.

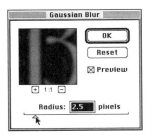

Fig. 18.6

The Gaussian Blur dialog box provides a preview of the blur amount applied by moving the slider or entering numeric values for the Radius setting.

11. To adjust Brightness and Contrast, open the Image menu and choose Adjust, Levels. To sharpen the contrast in this channel, in the Levels dialog box move the White Output slider in the lower-right corner of the dialog box to the left until it reads 170 for the white output level (see fig. 18.7). Click OK to accept the value. Figure 18.8 shows channel #4 after the Levels adjustment was applied.

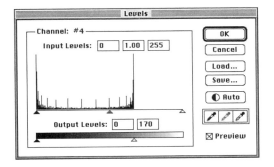

Fig. 18.7

Brightness and Contrast adjustments can be performed in the Levels dialog box.

Fig. 18.8

The results of contrast adjustments are easily noticed in channel #4.

V

Filters, Plug-Ins, & Effects

12. To create a new channel, open the Image menu and choose Calculations. This time you'll duplicate channel #4. For the Source 1 Channel, choose #4; for Blending, choose Normal; and for Result, choose New. Once again the Source 2 Channel is incidental. The new channel will be channel #5, as illustrated in figure 18.9.

13. To offset the channel information, choose Filter, Other, Offset. Enter 8 for the Horizontal and -5 for the Vertical, and choose the Wrap radio button.

Fig. 18.9

Channel #5 shows the results of the duplicated and then offset channel.

14. To blend the difference between channels, use the Difference blending mode. This gives a neon appearance to the image. Open the Image menu and choose Calculations. For Source 1, choose channel #4; for Source 2, choose channel #5. For Blending choose Difference, and for Result choose New. The Difference blending creates an effect similar to the one that you created earlier, using the outline technique (see steps 4 through 7). Here you create a blur and offset channels in different directions which results in a glowing or neon appearance. The effect will be much more apparent when the image is inverted.

15. To invert a channel, choose Image, Map, Invert or ⌘-I. Notice when you invert the selected channel, only the channel is inverted, leaving the rest of the document unchanged.

16. Adjust Brightness and Contrast, if the image needs a little contrast, using the Levels dialog box. Choose Image, Adjust, Levels. Move the White input levels slider on the right toward the center of the input levels until it reads 185. This will add a little more white to the lighter areas of the image (see fig. 18.10).

Fig. 18.10

Channel #6 after the Levels dialog box has been used to improve contrast.

You can use channels to render some interesting appearances that show depth in shapes as if they were created in 3-D applications. In order to create these effects, you need to progress through a series of steps, first to perform embossing and then to add depth to the image. This entire sequence will be performed using channel operations.

17. Choose Image, Calculations. For Source 1, choose the black channel; for Source 2, choose channel #4. For Blending mode, choose Add. Set the scale to 1 and the Offset value to 0. This is channel #7, as illustrated in figure 18.11.

Fig. 18.11

Channel #7 shows the results of using the Add blending mode in the Calculations dialog box.

Let's complete a few more calculations that will demonstrate some different effects. Some of these channels will also be used to complete exercises later for Floating Plastic images and Embossing Paper.

18. Choose Image, Calculations. Set Source 1 to the black channel, and Source 2 to channel #4. Set the Blending mode to Multiply, and the Result to New. This is channel #8.

V

Filters, Plug-Ins, & Effects

19. Type created with the Text tool appears static with no sense of dimension. You can use channel operations to add an appearance of depth by manipulating shadows and tones. Choose Image, Calculations to bring up the Calculations dialog box. For the Source 1 Channel, choose the black channel and for the Source 2 Channel, choose channel #4. Select the Invert check box for Source 1 and Source 2. For the Blending mode, choose Subtract, and set the Scale to 1 and the Offset to 120. The Result will be a New channel titled channel #9. Notice the shading on the image provides an appearance of depth (see fig. 18.12).

Fig. 18.12

Channel #9 shows the result of adding the appearance of depth to a shape.

By creating a number of variations with the calculations, such as dealing with different offsets, blending modes, blur amounts, and inverting channels, you can mold images into more three-dimensional appearances. Let's look at one example of using channels and filters to create an appearance of depth with our text character.

20. Choose Image, Calculations. Set Source 1 and Source 2 to the black channel. Set the Mode to Normal, and the Result to New. This action will duplicate the original black channel.

21. Choose Filter, Blur, Gaussian, and set the Radius in the dialog box to 2.5.

22. Choose Filter, Stylize, Emboss. In the Emboss dialog box, set the Angle to -60, Height to 2 pixels, and Amount to 120 percent. This will be channel #10 that will be used later to create an embossed paper image.

23. To create depth in shapes, choose Image, Calculations to access the Calculations dialog box. For the Source 1 Channel, choose #4; for the Source 2 Channel, choose #6. For Blending, choose Difference and for Result, choose New. To create the dimension in the character, choose Image, Map, Invert.

    At this point, you need to adjust the contrast. Choose Image, Adjust, Levels to open the Levels dialog box. Move the left black input slider to the right, so it reads 10 on the input levels.

24. Next, you will isolate the text character from the background. The text character will appear more dramatic as you add more contrast between the character and the background. To fill the background white, you can load a selection from another channel and fill it white. Choose Select, Load Selection. From the channels available in the Load Selection dialog box, choose channel #2. Channel #2 has our original text character appearing against a white background. When you load a selection, all the white in the channel will become the selection. The current foreground color will appear as white in the Photoshop toolbox. With the white foreground color active, press the Option key and strike the Delete key. The Option-Delete key sequence will fill a selection with the current foreground color. If white is the background color, simply strike the Delete key to fill the selection with white. When white appears around the image, the dimension created by the Calculate commands will appear more dramatic. Figure 18.13 illustrates the final image.

Fig. 18.13

Channel #9 appears with dimension after using a combination of calculations and fills.

From this point, you will be able to experiment with the new set of channels. There are thousands of combinations that you can use with these channels. You can create an unlimited number of new combinations or variations of the channels as well. You will refer back to them several times in the next couple of sections, as well as in chapter 19, "3-D Modeling Special Effects," and chapter 20, "Text Special Effects."

V

Filters, Plug-Ins, & Effects

Applying the Channels

As you will soon discover (most likely by a pleasant "accident"), there are an unlimited combination of channel effects in Photoshop 3. The best way to explore is to randomly select one channel at a time and apply others to it by using the Image, Apply dialog box.

To continue in the channels exploration process, here are just a few samples of some effects that can be developed from the series of channels created in the previous section.

Creating a Floating Plastic Image

At this point, you should have an understanding of the vast number of options that channel operations can provide for editing images. Using the Calculations dialog box, however, is only half the equation when performing channel operations. The other half relates to the Apply Image dialog box and the many functions you can perform with these commands. In this section, you will use the Apply Image dialog box to continue your journey through channel operations.

1. First, open the beta Ch-Ops Master channels file, created earlier. Open the File menu and choose New. Enter 250 pixels for the height and width, set the mode to RGB and the resolution to 72 ppi. When using Apply Image, you need to follow the same principles as those with the Calculate commands (the same physical size and resolution for both documents).

2. The example used here is from Kai's Power Tools. If you own the KPT Filter set, select the RGB image and open the Filter menu; then choose KPT 2.1, and KPT Texture Explorer. In the KPT dialog box, select Liquids from the texture options, and then Metals and Liquid Gold II. If you don't own the KPT filter set, open any texture or scan you may have on hand and crop the image to the same dimensions and resolution as the file size noted above.

Now that you have two documents of the same size and resolution, you can use the Apply Image command to combine information from a channel in one document to the selected document. Whenever you wish to use Apply Image, remember that you always want the active document window to receive the result of the calculations. If you wish the result to appear anywhere other than the active document, you must hold the Option key down when you open the Image menu and choose Apply Image. This action will include additional options to send the result to another document, a new document, or a new channel. To explore the Apply Image options, first create a simple blend between the beta Ch-Ops Master document and the new file created with the KPT texture. Once again, if you do not have the KPT filters installed, substitute your own image whenever the KPT texture is discussed.

3. Select the RGB image with the KPT Texture to make it the active window.

4. Choose Image, Apply Image. The first item in the Apply Image dialog box is the Source image. This option provides an option to apply an image from another document or the existing document. For the Source image, choose beta Ch-Ops Master. This choice enables you to apply a channel from your original document. The default Layer will be the Background. Because there are no other layers in either document, no choices are available. However, keep in mind when you work with the Apply Image command, you can take advantage of combining layers with channel operations for much more flexibility.

The Source Channel in the Apply Image dialog box enables you to choose which channel will be used with your application. When you select the Channel pop-up menu in the dialog box, all the channels from the beta Ch-Ops Master document will appear. You can apply any of the channels available. For your purposes here, choose channel #8. The next item is Blending, which behaves just like you observed when using the Calculations dialog box. Choose Multiply for your blending mode.

The final item to select is the Mask enabling check box. Click the check box to enable the mask. When you enable the mask, the dialog box will open and provide additional choices for the masking operations. The first set of pop-up menus deals with the document that contains the item to be masked. In this case, use beta Ch-Ops Master again because it contains all the channels you can use for masking. Background will appear as the default layer. The only item left for your selection is the channel. You can choose any channel to mask your image from the list available in the pop-up menu. For this example, choose channel #2.

Like the Calculations dialog box, a Preview check box will dynamically show results when it is enabled. You can view all the different applications of Apply Image as you choose different channels and sources when the Preview check box is enabled. To get a better feel for what happens to your image, experiment and look at the many applications when choosing different channels. Click OK to accept the choices in the Apply Image dialog box (see fig. 18.14).

Fig. 18.14

The Apply Image dialog box provides many choices for blending channels and documents.

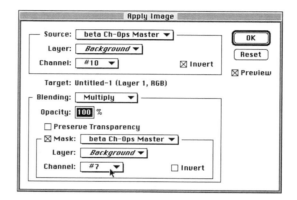

5. On Layer 1, choose Image, Adjust, Hue/Saturation, and select the Colorize check box. Adjust the Hue to -88. Enter a value of 50 for Saturation (see fig. 18.15). This gives the gray image a soft purple plastic appearance.

Fig. 18.15

The Hue/Saturation dialog box adds color to grayscale images when you enable the Colorize check box.

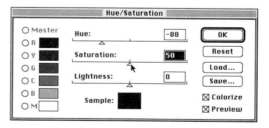

6. Choose Load Selection from the menu. In the Load Selection dialog box, choose Layer 1 Transparency in the Channel pop-up menu, as shown in figure 18.16. Copy the selection to the clipboard.

7. Next, click the Eye icon next to Layer 1 on the Layers palette window to make the image on Layer 1 invisible.

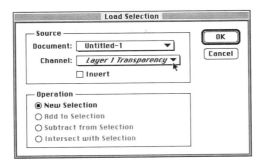

Fig. 18.16

The Load Selection dialog box enables you to create a selection from a shape on a transparent layer.

8. Now paste the image from the clipboard to a new Layer 2. Select the image, and choose Edit, Clear—without deselecting the image.

9. From the Select menu, choose Feather, 5 pixels.

10. Open the Edit menu and choose Fill with Black 100 percent. Click OK.

11. Deselect the image. Figure 18.17 illustrates the results.

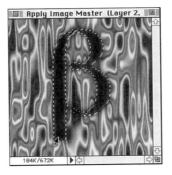

Fig. 18.17

Filling the Shadow Selection.

12. Move Layer 2 below Layer 1 on the Layers palette by clicking on Layer 2 and dragging it in the Layers palette.

13. Click the Eye icon on Layer 1 to make the Layer visible again.

14. Move the shadow into the correct position to match that shown in figure 18.18.

V

Filters, Plug-Ins, & Effects

Fig. 18.18

The composited "Plastic" image.

Creating an Embossed Paper Effect

In this exercise, you will use one of the Adobe Gallery Effects filters and create an image that looks like embossed paper. The Gallery Effects filters offer many effects that can render Photoshop images like fine art pieces. If you do not currently own Gallery Effects, you can use a simple texture to follow the steps outlined for using the calculations. The result will not be the same, but you will learn the process of using the Apply Image command.

1. Open the beta Ch-Ops Master image with the channels you created in the first exercise of this chapter.

2. Create a New RGB file by opening the File menu and choosing New. Enter 250 pixels for the width and 250 pixels for the height. Set the Blending mode to RGB, and enter 72 for the resolution. Remember the file attributes must be the same as our original file in order to apply the Calculations commands. Be certain the contents include white for the Background. Most filters cannot be applied to a transparent background.

3. Open the Filter menu and choose Gallery Effects #2; then choose GE Note Paper. Click OK to accept the defaults.

    If you do not have the Gallery Effects, filters follow these steps:

    a) Open the Filter menu and choose Noise, Add Noise with an amount of 60 and click OK.

    b) Open the Filter menu and choose Stylize, Emboss. Enter -60 for the Angle, 2 for the Height, and 400 for the Amount.

    c) Set the foreground color in the toolbox to white.

d) Open the Edit menu and choose Fill. Enter 70 percent for opacity and click OK.

e) Open the Edit menu again and choose Fill. Enter 50 percent opacity and click OK.

These steps will produce a texture similar to the Gallery Effects filter.

4. Next, choose Image, Adjust, Hue/Saturation, Colorize, to give the texture some smooth soft color.

5. Click the New Layer icon in the Layers palette to create a new layer titled Layer 1.

6. Choose Image, Apply Image. For the Source, choose beta Ch-Ops Master. For the Channel, choose channel #10. For the Blending mode, choose Normal. Enable the Mask check box. For the Channel Mask, choose channel #2. Enable the Invert check box.

7. Next, choose Image, Adjust, Brightness/Contrast (+25)/Contrast(+50) and set the Layer Opacity in the Layers palette to 20 percent (see fig. 18.19).

Fig. 18.19

The composited "Embossed Paper" image.

You may have to experiment with this technique a bit to get it just right. This is but a small taste of using the Calculations and Apply Image commands. For your individual purposes, it is best to comprehend the process just discussed. Try to experiment with documents by first creating channels and then opening a second file. Be certain both images meet the requirements for performing channel operations. They must be the same physical size and resolution. Work with the Apply Image command until you develop a sense of predictable results. From this point, you will be able to create your own spectacular images.

Where To Go from Here

▶ Check out chapter 12, "Using Masks and Channels," for an introduction to channels.

▶ Look at chapter 15, "Using Photoshop's Plug-In Filters," and chapter 16, "Third-Party Plug-Ins," for more information on the use of filters, which you can combine with channel operations.

▶ Review chapter 10, "Working with Layers," to help you understand some of the differences between layers and channels.

This chapter explores the ways you can create 3-D images and texture effects. The following topics are discussed:

▶ Mapping textures with plug-in filters

▶ Illustrating and manipulating with spheroids

▶ Creating simulated 3-D effects in Photoshop 3

▶ Making effective stereograms

3-D Modeling Special Effects

The virtual world is all around us—just look at our advertising, publications, and entertainment sources. If something can't feasibly be photographed, it can be created on a computer. That's where 3-D modeling and illustrating come into play. Although many stand-alone 3-D applications are on the market, you won't always need to rely on them for all your 3-D illustration requirements. In fact, few 3-D images ever totally bypass the need for interaction with Photoshop either before or after the rendering process. With tight production schedules, you may often need to expedite the 3-D process directly inside Photoshop.

Using Photoshop for Macintosh • *Using Photoshop for Maci*

by Jeff Foster

CHAPTER 19

Using Plug-In Filters

The first plug-in to be discussed in this chapter is the Andromeda Series 2 3-D filter. This is almost like having a 3-D modeler-renderer inside Photoshop. If you need to create previsualization of products and packaging for a client and can't afford the cost or the time to learn a 3-D modeling program, this would definitely be the ticket! It takes some time to prepare your surface map (think of it as a decal you apply all around the object shape) because you need to have all sides in one document. If you are familiar with other 3-D applications, you'll know that they all apply surfaces differently. Some use texture maps and surface maps that wrap similarly to the Andromeda plug-in, and some allow you to apply a different texture or surface map to each side independently.

Creating a Box

In this first example, you learn how to create a simple box with only one surface map. Add some lighting effects, and the results will satisfy the pickiest client! You may want to follow this step-by-step procedure with a photo image of your own. This can be an RGB or CMYK image. Andromeda Series 2 works with both.

> **Note**
>
> Most of the completed images in this chapter are shown in the color section, "Photoshop in Color!"

1. You can use a scanned image of several sides of a box to do this exercise. Try to obtain three separate images including a top, side, and front of a box. Position them as illustrated in figure 19.1. See how the surfaces butt-up next to each other. Remember to think of this image as a decal of sorts that wraps around the box.

2. With this surface map file open, select the Andromeda 3-D filter. To do this, open the Filter menu and choose Andromeda, and then choose 3-D.

3. Inside the Andromeda 3-D dialog box, select the Surface button and select Box, Cutout X. This is where you can experiment with your dimensions of both the box and the image you are applying to it. The controls allow you to make adjustments with slider bars, and the

preview window helps you see when it is locked into position (see fig. 19.2). For more detailed instructions on how to use the Andromeda 3-D interface, please refer to your Andromeda Series 2 user's manual.

Fig. 19.1

The image file for the Andromeda surface map.

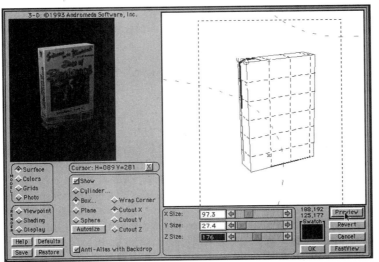

Fig. 19.2

The Andromeda dialog box with image layout and preview.

4. After you have the "decal" positioned over the box shape correctly (when it looks right in the preview window), click OK. Your new 3-D box should now appear in the original file's window, with a black background (default setting).

5. Using the Magic Wand tool, select the background black color.

6. Open the Select menu and choose Inverse. This allows you to select only the new box you created.

7. Open the Edit menu and choose Copy.

8. Open the Edit menu and choose Paste. In the Layers palette, you will see that a floating selection is now active.

9. Click on the Make Layer icon at the bottom left of the Layers palette. This will be called Layer 1. Your box should now be on its own layer.

Now you will create a background surface for your new box. It will look like a table top surface.

1. Create a new layer by selecting New Layer in the Layers palette. This will be called Layer 2.

2. Position this layer just below Layer 1 in the Layers palette.

3. Select an area on this layer with the Rectangular Marquee tool, just behind the box and into the foreground. This will be the surface on which the box is sitting.

4. Using the Eyedropper tool, select a medium brown color in the Swatches palette.

5. Hold down the Option key and again select the Eyedropper tool; select a dark brown color in the Swatches palette. You will now have two brown colors for the foreground color and the background color.

6. Select the Gradient Blends tool by double-clicking the icon and apply a gradient blend fill of 100 percent opacity. Click OK.

7. Drag the cursor inside the active selection on Layer 2, from top to bottom of the selection area (see fig. 19.3). This gives your surface some color.

Next, to add some studio light to the image and make the table top surface blend into the black background, follow these steps:

1. Open the Filter menu and choose Render, Lighting Effects.

Fig. 19.3

Applying a gradient
fill to a selected
new layer.

2. Apply a soft spotlight in the area just under the box by selecting the
Soft Spotlight command. Make sure that your size and angle look right
in the preview window (see fig. 19.4). Look at how the light is shining
on your box and try to imagine how the spotlight might actually look
on the surface around the box. It's just like taking a picture with your
camera!

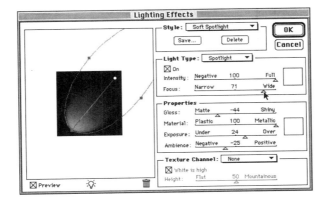

Fig. 19.4

The Lighting
Effects dialog box.

Now create some soft shadows around your box to make it more believable. Make sure that your shadow "makes sense" to the eye! Think of how
your light sources should all match—from the modeled image to your
spotlight to your shadows.

1. Select the Lasso tool and set the Feather amount in the options
window to approximately three pixels. This will vary with the resolution of the image you're working with, so some experimenting is
necessary here.

V

Filters, Plug-Ins, & Effects

2. Select an area of the spotlight layer with the feathered Lasso tool, making some imaginary foreground and side shadow areas. Holding down the Option key while using the Lasso tool allows you to release the mouse button and create straight lines.

3. Open the Image menu and choose Adjust, Brightness/Contrast to darken the shadow area to the desired effect (see fig. 19.5). Remember, imagine you're looking through the lens of a camera. Also, see figure 19.5 in the color section, "Photoshop in Color!" Figure 19.5 in the color section is the final image.

Fig. 19.5

The Selected Shadow area.

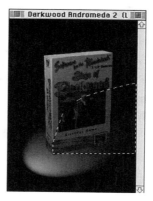

Creating a Can

Still using the Andromeda Series 2 filter, you can experiment with a more difficult image—a can! Actually, it's just a simple cylinder, but the hard work goes into making the surface map image. This requires some patience because it's almost a trial and error fit.

1. Create a "Decal" image. The example in this image is a KPT Bryce file. Use any similar type of file you may have if you don't use Bryce.

2. Next, to paste in a scanned image of a soda can top, open the Edit menu and choose Paste.

3. Create a new layer by clicking the Make Layer icon at the bottom left of the Layers palette. This allows you to move the soda can top easily into position for adjustments. Figure 19.6 illustrates the image to be mapped onto the model.

4. Save this as the "Master Decal" image file. Flatten your image prior to using the Andromeda 3-D filter by selecting Flatten Image from the pop-up menu in the Layers palette.

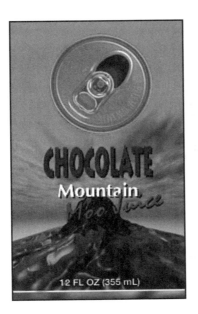

Fig. 19.6

The completed surface map image ready to wrap on the model.

5. Select the Filter menu; choose the Andromeda, and then choose 3-D.

6. Inside the Andromeda interface, select the Surface button and select Cylinder; Top, Lip and Side buttons. This is where you will want to experiment with your dimensions of both the can and the image you're applying to it. Refer to step 3 of creating the box earlier and figure 19.6 for positioning the image. You will probably need to go back-and-forth with your dimensions and placement several times because it's difficult to line everything up on the first pass.

7. Apply the effect when you're pleased with the placement; to save the finished image, open the File menu and choose Save.

Again, it requires a great deal of patience to correctly place and scale your image in the Andromeda 3-D plug-in (see fig. 19.7). This example uses the default black background (see fig. 19.8). Also see figure 19.8 in the color section, "Photoshop in Color!"

Working with Page Curl

The next plug-in filter—the KPT Page Curl effects filter—is also featured in chapter 16, "Third-Party Plug-Ins." I've gone a little wild with it—adding textures and creating individual images. Remember, if you can

V

Filters, Plug-Ins, & Effects

visualize it, you can create it in Photoshop! For this exercise, we'll take the KPT Page Curl beyond a simple application and combine the filter with some textures.

Fig. 19.7

The Andromeda dialog box with image layout and preview.

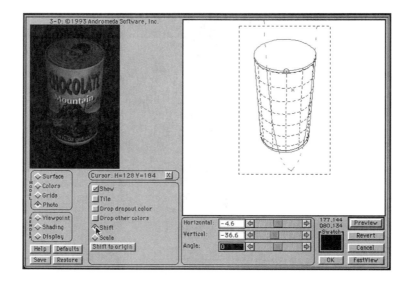

Fig. 19.8

The finished 3-D can. (See color section also.)

1. Select the File menu and choose Open. Select a textured image file. If you need to, create a new one with the plug-in examples listed in chapter 16, "Third-Party Plug-Ins."

2. Next, while holding down the number 3 key on your keyboard, select the Filter menu; then choose Distort and KPT Page Curl. This creates a curled edge from the bottom-right corner of your file. Remember that the keypad controls the angle from which your curls come up.

3. Select the "curled" part of the effect image with the Lasso tool. Holding down the Option key while using the Lasso tool allows you to release the mouse button and select straight lines.

4. Open the Filter menu and choose KPT; then choose KPT Texture Explorer.

5. Select a custom texture and click OK. The texture will be applied with the Procedural Blend option into the selection (see fig. 19.9). Again, if you need more information on the KPT Texture Explorer filter, please refer to chapter 15, "Using Photoshop's Plug-In Filters."

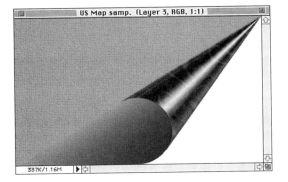

Fig. 19.9

The selected page curl with KPT Texture Explorer applied.

6. While the selection is active, choose Select, Float to create a floating selection.

7. Open the layers palette and choose Make Layer from the Layers palette options.

8. Select the Background image layer and, while holding down the number 7 key on your keyboard, open the Filter menu; then choose Distort, KPT Page Curl. This creates a curl from the top-left of your file.

V

Filters, Plug-Ins, & Effects

9. Repeat steps 3 through 8 on this second curl. You may want to use another effect on the second curl, such as XAOS Tools Paint Alchemy, instead of the KPT Texture Explorer.

10. Select the Background layer in the Layers palette. With the Magic Wand tool, select the white areas of the image behind both curls. Shift-click to select more than one area at a time.

11. To invert the selection, open the Select menu and choose Inverse.

12. Open the Edit menu and choose Copy.

13. Open the Edit menu and choose Paste.

14. Click the Make Layer icon on the bottom-left of the Layers palette. This will be Layer 3.

15. To open a new image to paste into the background, open the File menu and choose Open. This example used one created in KPT Bryce.

16. Open the Edit menu and choose Copy.

17. Open the Edit menu and choose Paste.

18. Click the Make Layer icon on the bottom-left of the Layers palette. This will be layer 4.

19. Position this layer just above the Background layer and under the other layers in the Layers palette, and position Layer 3 just above Layer 4.

20. You can now adjust the transparency of layer 3 with the Opacity Slider located at the top-right of the Layers palette (see fig. 19.10). Adjust enough to see the image on Layer 4, but still maintain your Layer 3 texture.

Look for the final image in the color section, "Photoshop in Color!"

To create a montage of KPT Page Curl images, start with a clean document and one curl against a white background. You can build from this single image and create several more to make an interesting 3-D effect.

The first set of steps describes how to create the tubes:

1. First, open the File menu and choose New.

2. While holding down the number 3 key on your keyboard, select the Filter menu; then choose Distort, KPT Page Curl (see fig. 19.11).

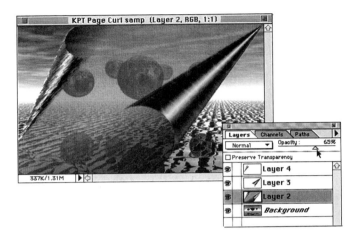

Fig. 19.10

Adjusting the transparency of the image layers.

Fig. 19.11

Creating a single page curl.

3. Select the white background with the Magic Wand tool and select the Quick Mask icon on the bottom of the toolbox. The selected area should be white, whereas the area not selected should be pink on your screen.

4. Click the Foreground/Background Color Switch icon on the toolbox to select Black as the foreground color.

5. Select the Airbrush tool and set the opacity in the Airbrush Options palette to 20 percent.

6. Using a brush size large enough to fit inside the "cone opening" of the page curl, airbrush a soft blend by freehand into the shadow area (see fig. 19.12).

Fig. 19.12

Painting in Quick
Mask around the
image.

7. Click the Standard Mode icon on the toolbox next to the Quick Mask
   icon.

8. Open the Select menu and choose Inverse.

9. Open the Edit Menu and choose Copy.

10. Create several new layers (this example used about seven), by select-
    ing the New Layer command in the Layers palette.

11. Open the Edit menu and choose Paste while selecting each layer
    individually from the Layers palette. This places one standard page
    curl image on each layer.

12. Select each layer one-by-one. Using the Move tool, position each layer
    into a "bouquet-like" arrangement. Use the Rotate, Free command in
    the Image menu to rotate each curl.

13. For each layer, open the Filter menu and choose KPT Texture Explorer.
    Apply a different texture to each layer, always using the Procedural
    Apply option in the KPT Texture Explorer interface (see fig. 19.13).

14. When you are pleased with the basic arrangement of the curls, choose
    Merge Layers from the Layers palette pop-up menu, with the Back-
    ground layer's Eye icon clicked-off. You want to maintain the trans-
    parency of the background at this point.

The second set of steps describes how to create the kaleidoscope effect.

1. Open the Select menu and choose All.

2. Open the Select menu and choose Float.

Fig. 19.13

Arranging the
textured curl layers.

3. In the layers pop-up menu, choose Make Layer.

4. Open the Image menu and choose Effects, Scale. You can resize the new layer's image to a smaller version of the main image.

5. Open the Edit menu and choose Copy.

6. Open the Edit menu and choose Paste.

7. Click the Make Layer icon on the bottom-left of the Layers palette. This will now be Layer 2.

8. Repeat steps 5 through 8 several times until you have almost filled the background and foreground with many curls, making a tubular kaleidoscope effect. You will have to use your judgment and design abilities to create a proportional image with a balanced perspective.

9. Select the Background layer in the Layers palette; then open the Edit menu and choose Fill.

10. Fill with the Foreground color (Black) at 100 percent opacity (see fig. 19.14).

See the color section, "Photoshop in Color!" for the final image.

Creating Liquids, Glowing Tubes, and More

Exploring the world inside KPT's Fractal Explorer and Gradient Explorer, you can find random kernels of 3-D looking liquids, patterns, and tubes. Remember that working with Kai's Power Tools is mathematically based, and you will never exhaust the resources inside.

Fig. 19.14

The completed
composite image.
(Also see color
section.)

1. Start by opening a new file. Open the File menu and choose New.

2. This example used a KPT Texture Explorer background with neutral earth tones (see fig. 19.15). You can use any textured background you choose.

Fig. 19.15

The background
texture from KPT
Texture Explorer.

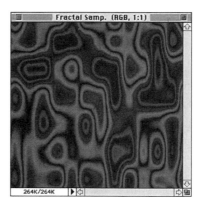

3. Open the Filter menu and choose KPT, KPT Fractal Explorer.

4. Inside the KPT Fractal Explorer (see fig. 19.16), find a nice mixture of light, shadows, and color to apply. Notice the naturally transparent areas in the fractal.

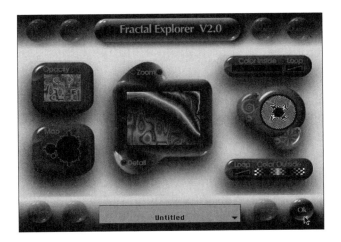

Fig. 19.16

The KPT Fractal Explorer interface.

Because this was a small example, it didn't take long to process. Kai Krause and the folks at HSC added an Estimated Time function to the Progress bar (see fig. 19.17). Sorry—no coffee break just yet! Our completed image effect has a translucent liquid feel to it (see fig. 19.18). Also see the color section, "Photoshop in Color!" to view the final image.

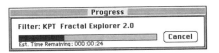

Fig. 19.17

Thank you Kai!

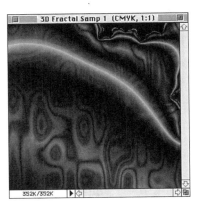

Fig. 19.18

The applied KPT fractal.

The next example was done similarly to the preceding steps 3 and 4, with the same background texture (see fig. 19.19), only this fractal created a glowing neon tube effect (see fig. 19.20). Also see the color section, "Photoshop in Color!" to view the final image.

Fig. 19.19

The KPT Fractal Explorer interface selection.

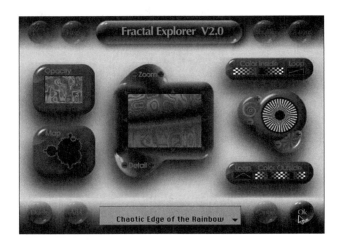

Fig. 19.20

The applied KPT fractal.

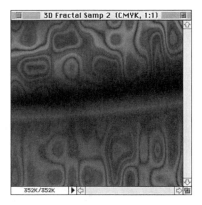

For more control of where you place your effects, try KPT Gradients on Paths. Now that Photoshop 3 has layers, you can easily draw a selection path with the Lasso tool and erase whatever part of the effect you don't want on that layer. Follow these simple examples to produce simulated 3-D paths:

1. To create a new file, open the File menu and choose New.

2. Start with a single selection (see fig. 19.21), using the Lasso tool. Make sure that the Feather rate in the options window is at least 10 to 15 pixels; otherwise, you will not see your path effect.

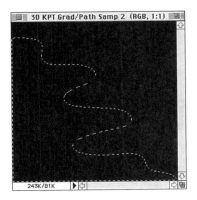

Fig. 19.21

The selection feathered at 15 pixels.

3. To create a new channel, select New Channel in the Channels palette.

4. To save this document as your Master, open the File menu and choose Save.

5. To load the selection, open the Select menu and choose Load Selection.

6. Open the Filter menu and choose KPT, KPT Gradients on Paths.

7. Apply a desired effect using the normal mode in Options. For more information on using KPT Gradients on Paths, refer to chapter 15, "Using Photoshop's Plug-In Filters."

The following examples (see figs. 19.22 and 19.23) were created in the same manner. Experimenting with different settings in KPT Gradients on Paths, produces liquids, textures, glowing tubes, and so on. These and other examples in this chapter are located in the color section, "Photoshop in Color!"

Line art from illustration programs like Adobe Illustrator is two dimensional. Using illustration programs for creating three-dimensional appearances to images is difficult. Sometimes we can use tools and commands in Photoshop to add depth to images. In this exercise, we'll look at opening an Adobe Illustrator file in Photoshop and use some of Photoshop's features to add a three-dimensional appearance to our image.

V

Filters, Plug-Ins, & Effects

Fig. 19.22

A smooth aqua on sand KPT Gradient on Path effect. (See color section also.)

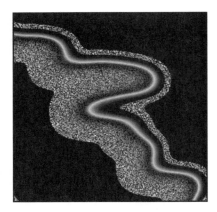

Fig. 19.23

A liquid gold KPT Gradient on Path effect. (See color section also.)

1. Open the File menu and choose Open to open a textured file.

2. Select New Layer in the Layers palette to create a new layer.

3. To import a design from Adobe Illustrator to a new file, open the File menu and choose the Open command (see fig. 19.24).

4. While the new file is open, copy the Illustrator image. Open the Edit menu and choose Copy.

5. Open the Edit menu and choose Paste to return to the textured background file and paste the image.

6. Click on Layer 1 in the Layers palette to deselect and paste the image to that layer.

Fig. 19.24

The Adobe
Illustrator design
imported.

7. Apply a texture to the graphic. Open the Filter menu, choose KPT, and then choose KPT Texture Explorer filter (see fig. 19.25).

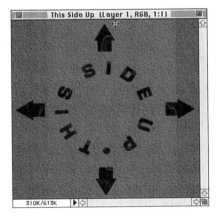

Fig. 19.25

The design layer
with applied KPT
Texture.

8. Open the Filter menu and choose Stylize, Emboss. The settings should be -45, three-pixel height, and an 80 percent effect amount. You only want to apply this effect to the graphic layer and not the background image layer.

9. Open the Select menu and choose Load Selection; then choose Level 1 Transparency.

10. Open the Select menu and choose Feather to the amount of three pixels.

11. Without deselecting, click on the Eye icon for level 1 in the Layers palette to hide the layer, and then select the background layer.

V

Filters, Plug-Ins, & Effects

635

12. To fill the selection with Black 80 percent, open the Edit menu and choose Fill. This creates a slight shadow around the inset embossed graphic.

13. Click the Eye icon back on for Layer 1 to view the final embossed effect (see fig. 19.26). Notice the "sunken in" effect the shadow gives the embossed image.

Fig. 19.26

The embossed image.

Next, you examine the Extrude filter, which was also covered in chapter 15, "Using Photoshop's Plug-In Filters." It has limited 3-D effect and is not too realistic, but is worth mentioning.

1. Open the File menu and choose Open. Select a stock marble background texture.

2. Open the Filter menu; then choose the Stylize, Extrude Filter, and click the radio button for Pyramids. The dialog box provides user definable size and depth values. Experiment with changing these values to view different results (see fig. 19.27).

3. Try applying the Random Blocks effect in the Emboss Filter dialog box to the marble image. This, too, will have several different results depending on the settings you choose to experiment with (see fig. 19.28).

The next filters sampled are the KPT Glass Lens and Spherize plug-ins. You can illustrate with the spheroids to create simple 3-D models, or combine the two filters to create type on a spheroid. It's a trick that can't be done by either filter alone (at least, being readable when you're done!).

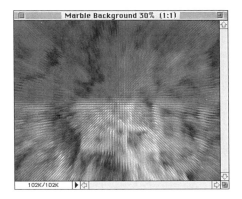

Fig. 19.27

The Applied
Pyramids effect.

Fig. 19.28

The Applied
Random Blocks
effect.

The following example is a quick illustration done in layers with just KPT Glass Lens spheroids. This could be easily animated in the layers as well, if you have the patience.

1. Begin with a line sketch on the background layer for the frame of your "Molecule Mann."

2. Next, to apply a colored spheroid to a new layer, open the Filter menu and choose the KPT Glass Lens filter.

3. Rotate the spheroid into position. Open the Image menu and select Rotate, Free (see fig. 19.29).

4. Apply a different-colored torso and legs to separate new layers, repeating steps 2 and 3 alternately (see fig. 19.30).

5. Continue creating spheroids and positioning them between the layers as if actually modeling in a 3-D application.

Fig. 19.29

The spheroid body and line-sketch of our character.

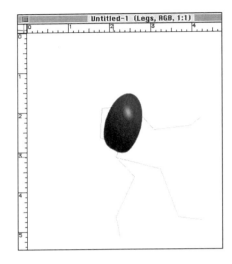

Fig. 19.30

More spheroids added to the character.

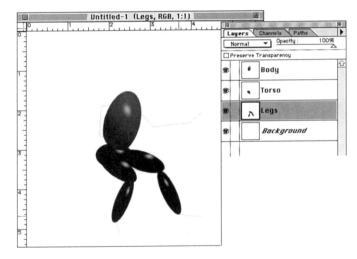

6. After completing the construction process, airbrush a slight shadow to the transparent background layer (see fig. 19.31). Also see figure 19.31 in the color section, "Photoshop in Color!"

This character takes all of about 15 minutes to create. You might want to consider creating something 3-D in Photoshop versus a stand-alone 3-D application. Rendering alone in a 3-D application would have more than doubled that time, let alone the model wireframe construction time that would be involved.

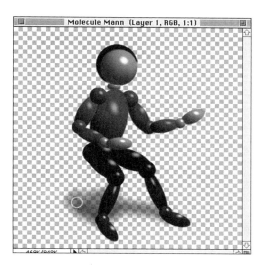

Fig. 19.31

The completed "Molecule Mann" character. (See color section also.)

The next example is another wacky KPT spheroid ball from Planet Zplatff. Only this time, type is added to the surface. This could be done in a stand-alone 3-D application as well, but the flexibility, speed, and ease of use working in layers in Photoshop 3 makes it much more practical for any print applications.

1. Begin with (what else?) a KPT Texture Explorer background by opening the File menu and choosing Open.

2. Select a concentric circle directly in the middle with the Ellipse Marquee tool (see fig. 19.32).

3. Save the selection to a new channel by opening the Select menu and choosing Save Selection.

4. Next, open the Filter menu and choose the KPT Glass Lens Soft, with the default lighting setting (see fig. 19.33).

5. Load the selection by opening the Select menu and choosing Load Selection.

6. Copy the spheroid by opening the Edit menu and choosing Copy.

7. Create a new layer by choosing New Layer in the Layers palette. This is Layer 1.

8. Paste the spheroid into Layer 1 by opening the Edit menu and choosing Paste.

Fig. 19.32

The selection on
the background.

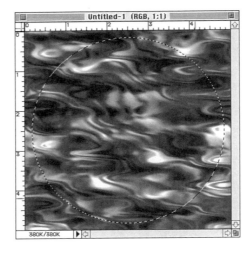

Fig. 19.33

The Applied
Spheroid effect.

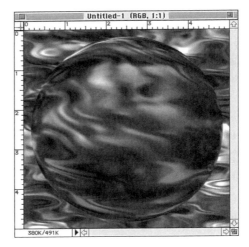

9. Select the background layer and load the selection by opening the Select menu and choosing Load Selection, channel #4.

10. Feather this selection by 25 pixels by opening the Select menu and choosing Feather.

11. Fill the selection with Black at 100 percent by opening the Edit menu and choosing Fill. This will be the shadow effect behind the ball (see fig. 19.34).

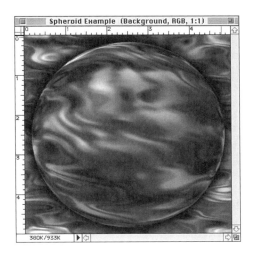

Fig. 19.34

The shadow
added behind
the spheroid.

12. Create a new layer by choosing New Layer in the Layers palette. This is Layer 2.

13. Select the Type tool from the toolbox and click over the sphere to place type on the new layer 2. Refer to chapter 8, "Drawing, Painting, and Editing," for more information on using the Type tool.

14. Load the selection to layer 2 by opening the Select menu and choosing Load Selection, channel #4.

15. Open the Filter menu and choose Distort, Spherize. I used 65 percent on this example (see fig. 19.35). This filter can control the amount of distortion—you want to keep the type readable (see fig. 19.36).

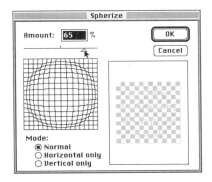

Fig. 19.35

The Spherize Filter
dialog box pro-
vides a dynamic
preview for ren-
dering a 3-D
appearance.

Fig. 19.36

The Spherize Filter effect applied to type.

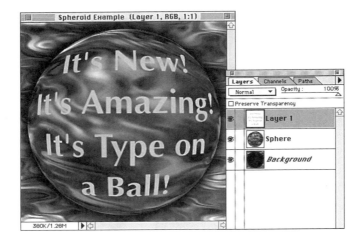

To make the type look like it is floating over the surface of the ball, and to make it more readable, create a shadow on a new layer below the type. Remember to do this after you distort the type so that it lines up correctly.

1. Create a new layer by choosing New Layer in the Layers palette. This is Layer 3.

2. Load the selection of the type layer 2 by opening the Select menu and choosing Load Selection, Level 2 Transparency.

3. Feather this selection by three pixels by opening the Select menu and choosing Feather.

4. Fill the selection with Black at 100 percent by opening the Edit menu and choosing Fill. This will be the shadow effect behind the type (see fig. 19.37).

5. Position layer 3 behind layer 2 in the Layers palette.

The final image is composited by using both Spheroid Filter effects applied to the texture and the type (see fig. 19.38). Also see figure 19.38 in the color section, "Photoshop in Color!"

The last spherizing example is applied to a texture. The example uses a burlap texture to illustrate the effect in Black and White the best way possible. This effect also works on photos to create bubbling or bulging surfaces.

1. To open the background texture, open the File menu and choose Open. Open any texture you may have on file to progress through this exercise.

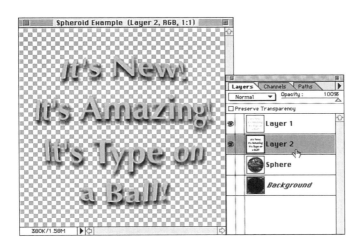

Fig. 19.37

Adding the soft
drop shadow layer.

Fig. 19.38

The composited
spheroid image
with type. (See
color section also.)

2. Make several circular selections using the Elliptical Marquee tool, feathered by three pixels in the options window.

3. Save each selection to separate channels by opening the Select menu and choosing Save Selection.

4. Load each selection by clicking on the Selection icon in the Channels palette. Apply the Spherize Filter, under the Filter menu, to each selection independently. Use level 70 percent or less, or the distortion will be too much and look like spheres rather than smooth bulges from the surface. Notice the distortion of the surface (see fig. 19.39).

Fig. 19.39

The distorted background texture.

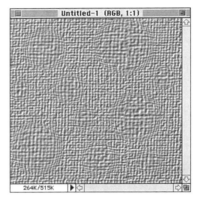

5. One-by-one, combine the channels into one channel, using the Load Selection Icon in the Channels palette and pressing the Delete key (white must be the background color).

6. Load the selection by using the Load Selection icon in the Channels palette.

7. Using the Dodge and Burn tool, apply the highlights and shadows by freehand. This method is great because you can adjust your simulated light source and amount manually (see fig. 19.40).

Another great filter 3-D paint effect is XAOS Tools Paint Alchemy. Some samples of this filter are covered earlier in chapter 16, "Third-Party Plug-Ins," and chapter 17, "Creating Special Effects with Video." The brushes work with the image or light sources generated in the brush itself. This example shows a custom brush pattern in Paint Alchemy applied to a woman's face, creating a fur effect (see fig. 19.41).

3-D Surface and Modeling Maps

Using Photoshop, you can create just about any surface texture or bump map for virtually any 3-D application. Most 3-D applications accept color or grayscale PICT files for bump, texture, and surface mapping. This section shows a few examples of how these techniques are used, although if you are a 3-D power-user, you'll already know these methods inside and out.

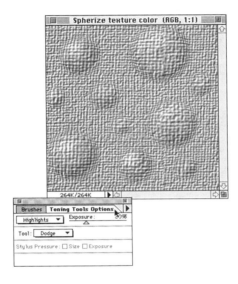

Fig. 19.40

The completed distortion.

Fig. 19.41

Paint Alchemy filter applied "Fur Woman."

Filters, Plug-Ins, & Effects

This first example is for adding a texture and bump map from the same image source into Strata Studio Pro.

1. Create a texture with Aldus Gallery Effects, Note Paper from the Filter menu, or use any texture you may have on file.

2. Colorize it to an antique off-white, using the Adjust, Hue/Saturation dialog box from the Image menu (see fig. 19.42). Try moving the Hue/Saturation sliders in the dialog box to create an off-white look to your texture.

Fig. 19.42

The texture map for 3-D application.

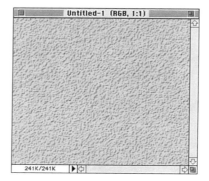

3. This step requires having Studio Pro software. Apply the texture onto the Studio Pro model's surface as well as its bump mapping. The two images (one color, one grayscale) are aligned inside the application's mapping architecture and can be rotated and scaled to fit. Use another texture to create the wood in this image (see fig. 19.43). Also see figure 19.43 in the color section, "Photoshop in Color!"

The next example shows how to generate a texture map for KPT Bryce, using simple type. Of course, any grayscale image will work—photos of faces, satellite photos, and so on—anything with light and dark areas can be imported in as a *mountain map*. Remember that the lighter areas will be raised and dark areas lowered.

1. Create the map with a simple type style, using the Type tool from the toolbox (see fig. 19.44). To create a smoother transition from light to dark, you can feather the edges or blur the entire image.

2. Open the bump editor in KPT Bryce and import the PICT type file, blending it slightly with the original bump texture (see fig. 19.45).

Fig. 19.43

The rendered image with the Photoshop map applied. (See color section also.)

Fig. 19.44

The Type Image bump map.

Fig. 19.45

The Bump Map editor/compositor in KPT Bryce.

3. Previewing the Bump wireframe in 3-D view mode (see fig. 19.46), you can see whether you need to smooth out the image. You also can see if you need to adjust the height or depth of the image to the ground plane.

Fig. 19.46

The 3-D View
Bump editor in
KPT Bryce.

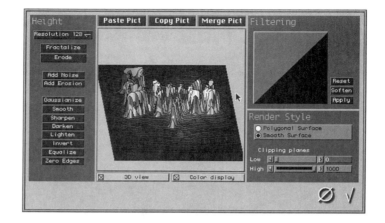

4. Choose a color texture to apply to the new "mountain" before
positioning and rendering the scene (see fig. 19.47). Also see figure
19.47 in the color section, "Photoshop in Color!"

Fig. 19.47

The final rendered
Bryce image. (See
color section also.)

3-D Stereograms and a Visit to the Mall

You see them everywhere—at malls, at gift shops, at tourist attractions.
It seems like 3-D stereograms came out of the woodwork overnight. Not
everyone can see these marvels of digital eyeball confusion—some say it's
just a hoax. But you have to admit they're cool if you CAN see them!

The biggest problem that most people have in creating stereograms with KPT Stereo Noise is determining the appropriate gray levels and how much detail to use when generating the grayscale image.

A good rule is to stay within the focal range of 50 percent gray. That is, don't let your *closest,* or lightest, part of the image be any more than 50 percent lighter than your *deepest,* or darkest, part of the image. (Use your info window to check the Black percent level.) For example, if you have a figure in the foreground at 20 percent gray, then your furthest point should be no more than 70 percent gray. Anything much more than a 50 percent difference will be too confusing and hard to focus on. I personally don't like to drop below 10 percent gray or go above 70 percent gray because it's too close or too deep into the image to focus on it well.

The following example is a good basic range of levels that I've found to be most consistent. Use it for a guide to making your own stereograms.

1. Create several separate layers in a Photoshop document with different percentages of gray for each number. Place the numbers 1 (10 percent gray), 2 (15 percent), 3 (20 percent), and 4 (25 percent) on separate layers against a 30 percent gray background. Then, place numbers 5 (35 percent), 6 (40 percent), 7 (45 percent), and 8 (50 percent) on separate layers (see fig. 19.48).

Fig. 19.48

The grayscale image to filter.

2. Make sure that you keep the numbers in the suggested range at 5 percent increments, by selecting with the Eyedropper tool from the toolbox on the Swatches palette (see fig. 19.49).

Fig. 19.49

Selecting the 5 percent incremental gray swatches.

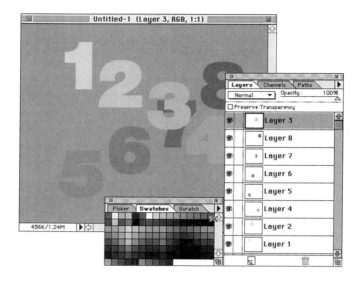

3. Select the KPT 3-D Stereo Noise filter from the Filter menu.

To view the image, de-focus your eyes until the two dots at the bottom become three and keep staring. The bottom of the number 6 will start to "move," so try to focus on that movement. After you focus on the stereogram, notice the progression of the numbers and the depth in the image (see fig. 19.50).

Simulated 3-D Illustrative Techniques

The most important part of making something look real is the lighting. If you're making 2-D cartoons or clip-art designs, you don't have to worry about light or shadows. But when you are doing production images, previsualization renderings, products, or packaging comps, you must be as accurate and detailed as possible. Of course, this requires more than a light source and a nice shadow, but hopefully you're beyond the basics if you're into this chapter anyway.

The next example brings to life some flat logo artwork brought into Photoshop from Illustrator.

1. Open a textured background image file, by opening the File menu and choosing Open.

Fig. 19.50

Image after
selecting the
KPT 3-D Stereo
Noise filter.

Bottom

V

Filters, Plug-Ins, & Effects

2. Import an Adobe Illustrator drawing of a logo similar to the basic logo in figure 19.51, by opening the File menu and choosing Open.

Fig. 19.51

Importing the Illustrator logo.

3. Open the Edit menu and select Copy to copy the logo to the clipboard.

4. Paste the logo to the textured background file, using the Edit menu and choosing the Paste command.

5. Create a new layer from the Floating Selection by clicking on the Make Layer icon in the Layers palette.

6. Open the Edit menu and choose Fill, 100 percent to paint the logo with 100% of the foreground color.

7. Using the Paintbrush tool, paint color into the logo layer.

8. Using techniques showed earlier in this chapter on spherizing, apply the Spherize filter to the center "globe" shape inside the logo.

9. Using the Dodge and Burn tool, manually dodge/burn the highlights and shadows inside the sphere.

10. Use the airbrush and paint White (10 percent) into the highlights and Black (10 percent) into the shadow areas to give a richer shadow effect (see fig. 19.52). Also see figure 19.52 in the color section, "Photoshop in Color!"

The following example is a very simple, illustrative approach to creating a quick 3-D graphic. It looks as though it was created in a 3-D application, but in all actuality, it took only about 20 minutes to create in Photoshop 3. Follow along with a similar graphic image:

Fig. 19.52

Adding the air-
brushed shadows
and highlights.

1. Import a graphic image of the Continental United States from Illustrator by opening the File menu and choosing the Open command.

2. Create a new layer for the background White by selecting New Layer
   in the Layers palette.

3. Next, paste a stock marble texture into the logo by opening the Edit
   menu and choosing Paste.

4. Open the Image menu and choose Effects, Perspective to distort the
   image at an angle (see fig. 19.53).

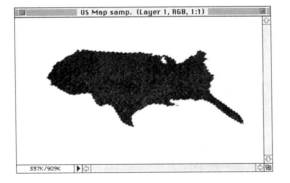

Fig. 19.53

Perspective
distortion of
the graphic.

5. Copy the logo by opening the Edit menu and choosing Copy.

6. Create a new layer behind the logo layer by selecting New Layer in the
   Layers palette. This is layer 2.

7. Paste the image to layer 2 by opening the Edit menu and choosing
   Paste.

8. Position layer 2 behind and slightly lower than the first image, (approximately as "thick" as you want to make the final image), using the Move tool.

9. On layer 2, use the Rubber Stamp tool, with the Clone aligned Option, to fill in the gaps at the edges of the image (see fig. 19.54).

Fig. 19.54

Cloning the gaps at the edges of the graphic.

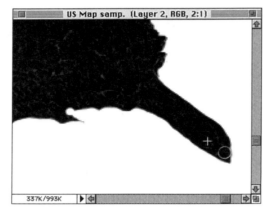

10. Create highlights and shadows by using the Dodge and Burn tool, working back and forth between highlights and midtones (see fig. 19.55). This is where you must decide on your light direction and reflectivity of the object you're illustrating.

Fig. 19.55

Airbrushing highlights with the Dodge/Burn tool.

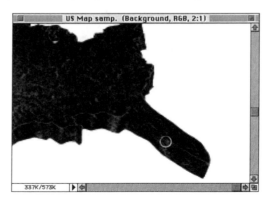

11. To add an overall light to the image, open the Filter menu and choose the Lighting Effects filter. I selected the Soft Spotlight button and aimed the direction in the middle of the image (see fig. 19.56).

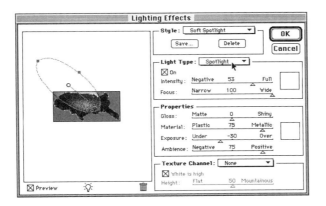

Fig. 19.56

The Lighting Effects dialog box provides several ways to create lighting in a Photoshop image.

12. After applying Unsharp Mask to the image, choose Merge Layers in the Layers palette and drop in a simple, colored, solid background (see fig. 19.57). Also see figure 19.57 in the color section, "Photoshop in Color!"

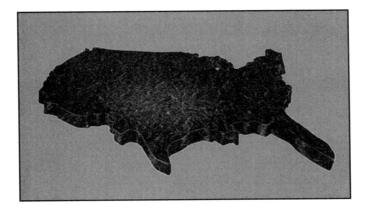

Fig. 19.57

The final 3-D graphic. (See color section also.)

V

Where To Go from Here

▶ This chapter has many images in it that just do not make as much sense in black and white, so be sure to view them as created in the color section, "Photoshop in Color!"

▶ Throughout the examples in this chapter we discussed using layers and channels. Chapter 10, "Working with Layers," takes a closer look at using layers.

▶ For additional information on working with channels, take a look at chapter 12, "Using Masks and Channels," and chapter 18, "Creating Special Effects with Channels."

▶ Filters are used in most of the examples in this chapter. For more information on using filters and third party plug-ins, check out chapter 15, "Using Photoshop's Plug-In Filters," and chapter 16, "Third-Party Plug-Ins."

▶ For additional special effects techniques, look at chapter 17, "Creating Special Effects with Video."

Text Special Effects

The creative application of type design is probably one of the most-used production practices today. It is also one of the easiest and most fun, because the possibilities are endless. Working creatively with type in a photorealistic environment is becoming even more popular in the multimedia, video, and print media environments. Whether it's used for titling, logo work, or just a design graphic, you're just a few steps away from virtually any effect you can dream up in Photoshop 3.

Thanks and kudos go out to those wonderful folks at Adobe—with Photoshop 3, you can now work with layers! Now when clients want to move everything around (and you know they always do!), you can oblige them with ease.

by Jeff Foster

CHAPTER 20

Vector-to-Raster Images in 3-D

A vector image is a postscript image that uses outline and fill data, (such as an Adobe Illustrator file). Images in Photoshop 3 are called raster images, because they are comprised of dots, or "pixels." When you open a vector image in Photoshop 3, it automatically converts to a raster image. No more fill or outline data.

So why do you even use Illustrator for importing type? Because it gives you incredible control over an outline vector image. You can distort, curve, manipulate, and mutilate it until Tuesday—and it still keeps the outlines crisp and clean. After you kern and distort your type design in Illustrator, you can open it at any resolution in Photoshop and it will be clean. No jaggies!

Sometimes it's not necessary to import all your type into Photoshop, as you will see later in this chapter. Usually, if it's a quick and simple low-resolution project, the Type tool is more than adequate.

Sometimes you will want to create realistic type and designs without sufficient stock images or very much time to do it. You can make your design believable and 3-D looking, starting with simple forms created in a vector graphic program, such as Adobe Illustrator. It's not always necessary to use a 3-D program to get these great looking results!

To show both an outline type and a drawn graphic design, this next example was created in Illustrator in two parts: the Type Logo and the Graphic files.

In the first part, you can take a type file and make it look like goldleaf embossed onto a marble slab. This would be useful when designing corporate logos, brochures, and advertising pieces.

1. First, open the File menu and choose Open. Choose a texture for the background image. A nice, stock marble texture was used for the example (see fig. 20.1).

2. Then create a new channel by selecting New Channel in the Channels palette. Channel #4 was used in the example.

3. Next, Place the Type that was created in Illustrator into channel #4 by choosing the File menu and selecting the Place command (see fig. 20.2). You can now size and place the type anywhere you want in the channel.

Fig. 20.1

The background image should be even-patterned, like this marble texture.

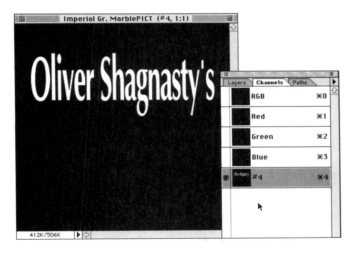

Fig. 20.2

The type graphic image of the imported name.

V

Filters, Plug-Ins, & Effects

4. Then create a new layer. Select New Layer in the Layers palette. This is Layer 1.

5. Load the channel #4 selection by dragging it on top of the Load Selection icon in the Channels palette.

6. Use the Eyedropper tool from the toolbar to select a color from the Swatches palette. The example used a 50 percent gray.

7. On Layer 1, fill the selection with the color by selecting the Edit menu and choosing Fill, Foreground, and then 100 percent.

8. Select the Airbrush tool from the toolbar and lightly paint a random pattern of Black 100 percent and White 100 percent over the gray logo image (see fig. 20.3). This will give a light/dark reflection pattern to the type.

Fig. 20.3

Airbrushing some reflection lines to the selected name.

9. Then, open the Filter menu and select the Aldus Gallery Effects Chrome Filter and apply it to Layer 1, with very high detail settings on the slider in the dialog box (see fig. 20.4).

Fig. 20.4

Adjusting the detail slider in the Gallery Effects Chrome filter dialog box.

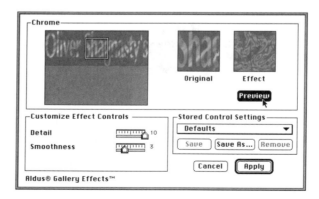

10. The next step is to emboss the type on Layer 1 only—without affecting the background layer. Open the Filter menu and choose Stylize, Emboss. The Emboss dialog box appears (see fig. 20.5).

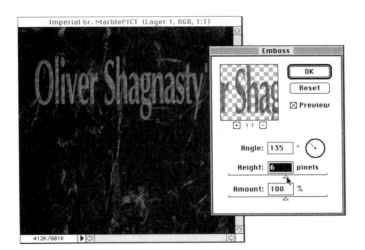

Fig. 20.5

Setting the light angle and detail amounts in the Emboss dialog box.

11. Then colorize the type image to give it a simulated gold leaf effect. Open the Image menu and choose the Adjust, Hue/Saturation command. The Hue/Saturation dialog box appears (see fig. 20.6).

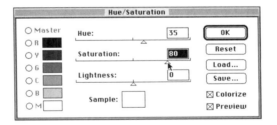

Fig. 20.6

Colorizing the type in the Hue/ Saturation dialog box.

12. Create a new layer by selecting New Layer in the Layers palette. This is Layer 2, and is positioned just under Layer 1 in the layers window.

13. Again, load the channel #4 selection by dragging it on top of the Load Selection icon in the Channels palette.

14. On Layer 2, feather the selection by 2 pixels by opening the Select menu and choosing the Feather command.

15. Then fill the selection with Black 100 percent. Open the Edit menu and choose Fill, Foreground, and then 100 percent. This is the embossing shadow on the background surface (see fig. 20.7). Make sure you don't offset this shadow from the Name layer; that makes it look like it's "floating" instead of slightly inlayed into the marble.

V

Filters, Plug-Ins, & Effects

Fig. 20.7

Adding the embossing shadow on a new layer, under the type.

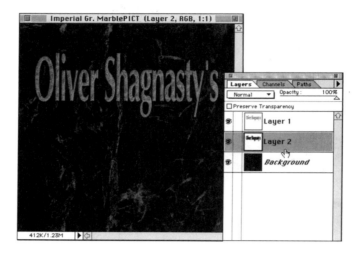

Tip

Paste It Now—Lose It Later.

Whenever you paint or paste anything to a new layer, and the image or paint is alone on that layer, always choose to apply it at 100 percent. Later, you can adjust the Layer Opacity with the slider on the Layers palette, but you can't make it more opaque at a later time.

The second part of this example is to add a simple Graphic image to the piece. The one used here was a simple design created in Illustrator. This will be given a rough stone texture to complement the marble and goldleaf. Remember, to make an impact with graphic type design, you need to have contrast—not only in color, but texture as well.

1. Now create a new channel by selecting New Channel in the Channels palette. In the example, this is channel #5.

2. Place the Graphic that was created in Illustrator into channel #4 by choosing the File menu and selecting the Place command. You can now size and place the type anywhere you want in the channel.

3. Then, create a new layer by selecting New Layer in the Layers palette. In the example, this is Layer 3.

4. On Layer 3, load the channel #5 selection by dragging it on top of the Load Selection icon in the Channels palette.

5. Open the File menu and choose Open. Select a stock rock texture for the graphic image.

6. Next, open the Edit menu and choose the Copy command.

7. Paste the rock texture to the Layer 3 selection by opening the Edit menu and choosing the Paste command (see fig. 20.8).

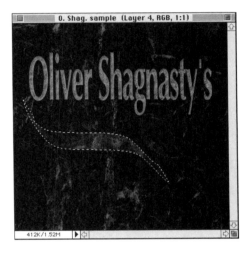

Fig. 20.8

Pasting a rock texture into the graphic layer.

8. Then, emboss Layer 3 by using the Stylize, Emboss filter in the Filter menu (see fig. 20.9).

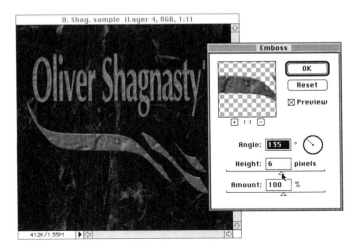

Fig. 20.9

Embossing the graphic layer to give the texture depth and dimension.

V

Filters, Plug-Ins, & Effects

9. Colorize the graphic on Layer 3 by opening the Image menu and choosing Adjust, Hue/Saturation.

10. Finally, create the embossing shadow for the graphic image in the same way that you did for the type image, shown in steps 12 through 15 in the first part of this example (see fig. 20.10). The marble layer is turned off in the Layers palette, to show the edges of the shadows in detail.

Fig. 20.10

The embossed graphics and shadows shown without the marble background layer.

Notice in this final composite figure that the shadows are directly around the top images, giving it a "sunken-in" look (see fig. 20.11). (Also see the color section for the final image.)

Note

The color images of all of these examples can be found in the color section, "Photoshop in Color!"

The next example is a simple layering engraved effect with an imported Illustrator file. This is an everyday use of imported type in Photoshop, and works with virtually any texture or photograph you apply it to.

1. For this example, start with another stock marble background texture. To do this, open the File menu and choose Open (see fig. 20.12).

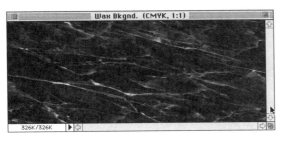

Fig. 20.12

The stock marble background texture used in this example.

V

Filters, Plug-Ins, & Effects

2. Place the type that was created in Illustrator into channel #5 by choosing the File menu and selecting the Place command. You can now size and place the type anywhere you want in the channel.

3. Next, load the selection on the background layer. To do this, drag channel #5 on top of the Load Selection icon in the Channels palette (see fig. 20.13).

4. Open the Edit menu and choose the Copy command.

5. Then create a new layer by selecting New Layer in the Layers palette. This is Layer 3.

6. Paste the clipboard to Layer 3 by opening the Edit menu and choosing the Paste command. Leave the image transparent in the middle.

Fig. 20.13

Dragging the
channel to the
Load Selection
icon.

7. Then open the Image menu and choose Adjust, Brightness/Contrast and darken the background image layer (see fig. 20.14).

Fig. 20.14

Adjusting the
background image
layer.

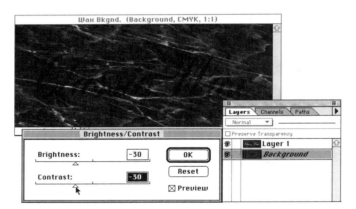

You can create subsequent layers in the same manner described above: lighten one layer, and then offset it down and to the right about four pixels each direction. The idea here, is to make a slightly darker edge for the shadowed edge of the engraved type, and a lighter one for the highlighting edge.

1. Create a new layer by selecting New Layer in the Layers palette. This is Layer 4.

2. By opening the Edit menu and choosing the Paste command, you can paste the clipboard to Layer 4, leaving the image transparent in the middle.

3. Then open the Image menu and choose Adjust, Brightness/Contrast. This lightens the image on Layer 4; it is the highlight layer.

Now that you've created a highlighting edge, continue to make the shadowed edge by following these steps:

1. Create a new layer by selecting New Layer in the Layers palette. This is Layer 5.

2. By opening the Edit menu and choosing the Paste command, you can paste the clipboard to Layer 5, leaving the image transparent in the middle.

3. Then open the Image menu and choose Adjust, Brightness/Contrast and darken the image on Layer 5. This is the shadow layer. Notice the placement of the layers in figure 20.15. The opacity slider was adjusted to blend the effect smoothly throughout the layers.

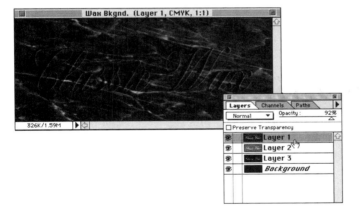

Fig. 20.15

Adjusting the layers into position.

4. Next, flatten the layers by selecting the Flatten Layers command in the Layers palette.

5. The image could be complete here, but in this example, a mortised edge effect was desired—like a plaque.

The Deko-Boko "Sucking Fish" filter (courtesy of Bill Niffenegger's "Photoshop Filter Finesse" CD-ROM), from the Filter menu, was added in the example (see fig. 20.16). This creates a mortised marble plaque effect (see fig. 20.17). Also see the color section for the final marble image.

V

Filters, Plug-Ins, & Effects

Fig. 20.16

Applying the Deko-Boko filter to the image edge.

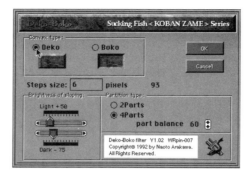

Fig. 20.17

The final engraved effect with a mortised edge.

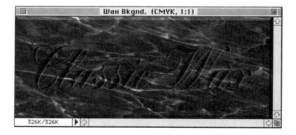

Ghosting Type Effects

Thanks to Photoshop 3's layering capabilities, you can now handle any type of ghosting or imaging with ease and without worry! Just by placing your type on separate layers, you can size, distort, ghost—or do whatever you want—and still be able to go back and edit it later. What a concept! What a life-saver!

The image in the following example is a photograph with several layers built on top. You can follow this example with any photo image and any type styles you choose! One caution: with all the layers building up, the file size gets large quite fast; so make sure you have plenty of hard drive space before building your file.

1. Open the File menu and select the Open command. Choose an original photograph with which to work.

2. To create a new layer, select New Layer in the Layers palette. This is Layer 1 in the example.

3. Using the Type tool from the toolbar, click the new layer and select the type for that layer. The example uses White 100 percent.

4. Repeat steps two and three, until you have seven layers of type (see fig. 20.18).

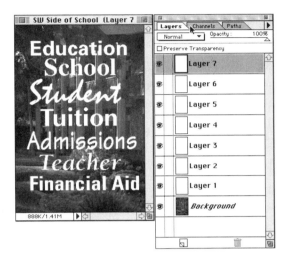

Fig. 20.18

Seven layers of type created independently.

5. Now, just adjust the scale of the title on each layer by opening the Image menu and choosing Effect, Scale.

6. Use the Move tool from the toolbar to reposition the title on each layer.

7. By selecting the Opacity slider on the Layers palette, you can change the opacity of each layer for a "montage" graphic effect (see fig. 20.19). Also see the color section for the final image.

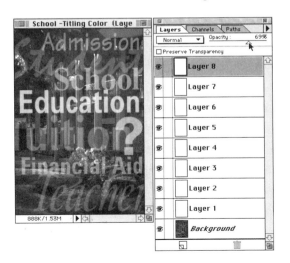

Fig. 20.19

The ghosted type on photo composition.

V

Filters, Plug-Ins, & Effects

It's really just that simple! This only takes about 10 minutes to create, and it's easy to edit later.

3-D Type Effects

This section covers various 3-D titling and logo effects. Though some can be quite simple, they are a very effective type of communication tool for print, video, and multimedia. You also can find similar techniques through Channel Ops in chapter 17, "Creating Special Effects with Video," and chapter 18, "Creating Special Effects with Channels."

You can add graphics to an existing tile arrangement, using components of the original tiles to create the type inlay. To create such a design, follow these steps:

1. The first step is to open a tile image file. Do this by opening the File menu and choosing Open (see fig. 20.20).

Fig. 20.20

The background tile image used for this example.

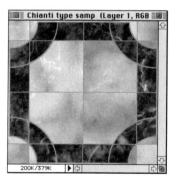

2. Next, make a new layer by selecting New Layer in the Layers palette. This is Layer 1.

3. Using the Type tool from the toolbar, click the new layer and select the title for that layer. The example, as seen in figure 20.21, uses Black 100 percent.

4. Then select a marble area from the tile background with the Rectangle Marquee (see fig. 20.22). Open the Edit menu and choose Define Pattern.

Fig. 20.21

The type posi-
tioned on a
new layer.

Fig. 20.22

Selecting the
pattern for marble
inlay design.

5. Select Layer 1, with the Preserve Transparency button on in the Layers palette and fill it with the defined marble pattern, by opening the Edit menu and choosing Fill, Pattern 100 percent (see fig. 20.23). Don't deselect the loaded selection.

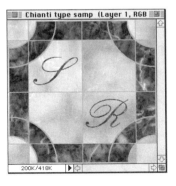

Fig. 20.23

The pattern pasted
into the initials.

V

Filters, Plug-Ins, & Effects

6. On the background layer, outline the selection from Layer 1 by opening the Select menu and choosing Outline at approximately three pixels.

7. Paint several colors from the surrounding grout inside the selection around the inlay with the Airbrush tool. This gives the image a nice photo-real effect (see fig. 20.24). It looks just like real inlay—but look Ma, no mess! Also see the color section for the final image.

Fig. 20.24

The finished tile inlay design.

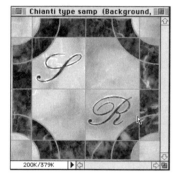

This next example is a simple alternative to more advanced techniques covered in chapter 17, "Creating Special Effects with Video." If you ever need to put graffiti on a brick wall, follow these easy steps:

1. Start with a brick background image, by opening the File menu and choosing Open (see fig. 20.25).

Fig. 20.25

A brick background image to apply the effect to.

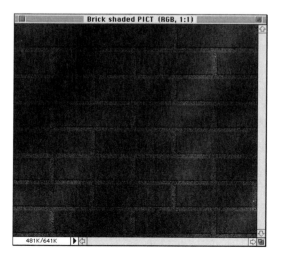

2. Next, select the mortar areas between the bricks with the Magic Wand tool. Press the Shift key while clicking the tool to select more areas (see fig. 20.26).

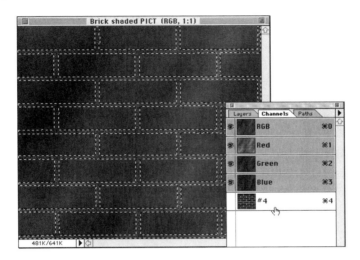

Fig. 20.26

Selecting the mortar areas between the bricks.

3. Create a new channel by clicking the Make Channel icon in the Channels palette. This is channel #4.

4. Select channel #4 from the Channels palette and hit the Delete key (with White as the background color). This saves the selection to this channel.

5. From the background layer, choose Select menu and select the Float Selection command.

6. Click on the Make New Layer icon in the Layers palette.

7. Create a new channel by clicking the Make Channel icon in the Channels palette. This is channel #5.

8. With the Type tool, choose a loose script-like font and type a message on channel #5.

9. Next, make a new layer by selecting New Layer in the Layers palette. This is Layer 2.

10. Load the selection of channel 5 by dragging the channel to the Load Selection icon in the Channels palette.

11. On Layer 2, feather the selection by approximately two pixels by opening the Select menu and choosing the Feather command.

12. Using the Airbrush tool set at about 35 percent White, loosely freehand spray-paint inside the selection, to create a hand-painted look (see fig. 20.27).

Fig. 20.27

Spray-painting inside the type selection.

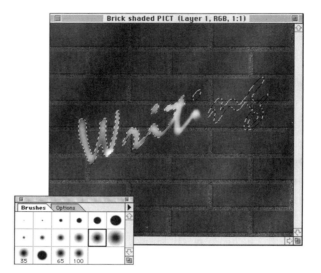

14. Now position Layer 1 (click the Eye icon back on) on top of Layer 2 in the Layers palette.

15. To create a sunken effect between the bricks, adjust the opacity of Layer 2 with the Opacity slider in the Layers palette (see fig. 20.28).

16. Finally, with the Airbrush and Paintbrush tools, freehand paint splatters and drips on the bricks (see fig. 20.29). Viola! Instant graffiti—just less destructive. (Also see the color section for the final image.)

The next effect is one of my favorites, and is next to impossible to get a believable result conventionally. It's Neon! "Yeah, sure," you say. You've seen it done a million times. But does it look real? I mean, like "Dad! stop-the-car!" real? This does. You do have to have good Airbrush control and skills to make it work realistically.

First, you'll need to start with these steps to make the actual neon "tubes":

1. Open the File menu and choose New to open a new file.

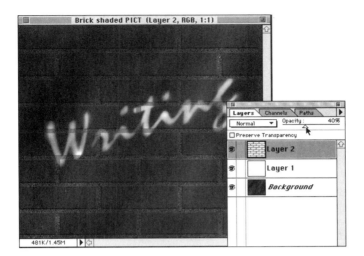

Fig. 20.28

Adjusting the mortar layer opacity.

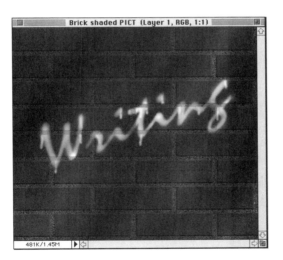

Fig. 20.29

Painting in the details freehand.

V

Filters, Plug-Ins, & Effects

2. Create a new channel by selecting New Channel in the Channels palette. This is channel #4 in the example.

3. Next, using the Type tool, create text in channel #4 (see fig. 20.30).

4. Load the selection from the background layer by dragging channel #4 to the Load Selection icon in the Channels palette.

5. To feather the selection, open the Select menu and choose Feather. The example is only 1 pixel—I worked on a 320 pixel-wide image, so you can experiment with higher resolution images.

Fig. 20.30

The type applied in
channel #4.

6. Then open the Filter menu and choose KPT Gradients on Paths. Select
a stock setting (Tubular Blues was used in the example) and apply
Normal in the options (see fig. 20.31). Make sure that you do NOT
deselect yet!

Fig. 20.31

The KPT Gradients
on Paths dialog
box.

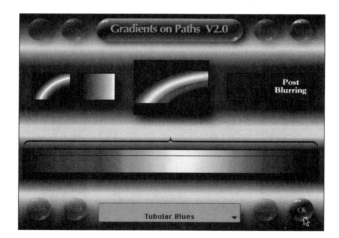

The final result is a tube that looks as though it was squirted from a tube
of toothpaste (see fig. 20.32). The next step is to add the "glow" around
the tubes. Do this by using the following steps.

1. Remember, you are working with the previous image, which you did
not deselect. So, open the Select menu and choose Modify, Border, at
a level of three pixels.

Fig. 20.32

The Gradients on
Paths applied to
the image.

2. Invert the selection by opening the Select menu and choosing the Inverse command.

3. Next, use the Eyedropper tool from the toolbar to sample the color that will be applied in the middle of the tube against the foreground color. You want a color that provides good contrast. The example used the brightest color possible.

4. Then use the Airbrush tool at 5 percent opacity to paint color by freehand around the tubes. This creates a glow effect.

> **Tip**
>
> **Airbrushing Help!**
>
> This is where you have to be careful not to paint too much or too dense. Slowly build-up until you can just see a thin, dark line around the tube. Try not to do it all at once! It's a natural tendency to "over-work" your image, so less is more!

5. Now, open the Select menu and choose None to deselect.

6. Make highlights by continuing to airbrush with a smaller brush.

7. Then choose a huge brush (about 100 pixels) from the Options palette, and lightly sketch over the entire glow image area once (see fig. 20.33).

The next step is to create "breaks" in the neon tubing where it goes into the sockets. To do this, follow these steps:

1. Using the Burn tool from the toolbar, select a small brush and about 15 percent Opacity in the Options palette.

V

Filters, Plug-Ins, & Effects

Fig. 20.33

Airbrushing the
glow around the
tube selection.

2. Finally, burn the image in small increments, working back and forth
   between the Highlights and Midtones settings (see fig. 20.34). (Also
   see the color section for the final image.)

Fig. 20.34

The finished neon
sign—just like the
one at the corner
market!

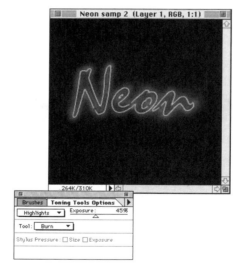

There it is, the finished product. You can now change the colors through
Levels or Hue/Saturation. Be sure to check out the final color image in the
color section.

The next example is quite similar to the Neon tube, except it can be done
much easier. It's a simple fat tube effect that looks convincingly 3-D and
plastic-like. To learn how to create a similar effect, follow these steps:

1. Start with a new file by opening the File menu and choosing New.

2. Select New Channel in the Channels palette to create a new channel. This is channel #4.

3. Next, use the Type tool to create text in channel #4 (see fig. 20.35).

Fig. 20.35

The selection channel image.

4. On the background layer, load the selection by dragging channel #4 to the Load Selection icon in the Channels palette.

5. Open the Select menu and choose Feather to feather the selection. The example feathered the selection by one pixel.

6. Then open the Filter menu and choose KPT Gradients on Paths. Select a gradient setting and color and then apply it in the normal mode to the selection (see fig. 20.36).

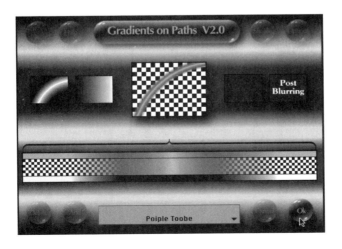

Fig. 20.36

The KPT Gradients on Paths dialog box.

7. Now, open the Select menu and choose None to deselect and enjoy! Figure 20.37 shows the finished example. (Also see the color section for the final image.)

Fig. 20.37

A plastic fat tube title design.

Do the Logo Motion

Trying to bring life and action to a logo or title on a still image can be a challenge. So what can you do besides make an image 3-D? You can put it in motion! Next, you'll experiment with Motion Blur on layers and I'll show you combinations of the following: a blurred background, a blurred logo foreground, and a wild combination that really moves (see the color section for these full-color images)!

1. Start with a background image by opening the File menu and choosing the Open command. The example uses an image created in KPT Bryce, which gives you a nice outside distance shot (see fig. 20.38).

Fig. 20.38

The KPT Bryce background image used in this example.

2. To open your logo or title image created in Illustrator, open the File menu and choose the Open command.

3. Using the Move tool, drag the Illustrator image from its window over to the Background image window.

4. In the Background image file, click on the Make New Layer icon in the Layers palette.

5. Fill the image on Layer 1, the example uses 50 percent gray. You do this by opening the Edit menu and by choosing Fill, Foreground, 100 percent, Preserve Transparency.

6. To emboss the image, open the Filter menu and choose Stylize, Emboss filter (the example is at about five pixels).

7. Then colorize it to a bright red by opening the Edit menu and choosing Adjust, Hue/Saturation (see fig. 20.39).

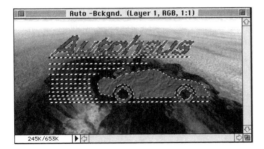

Fig. 20.39

The embossed graphic image created on top of the background image.

8. Next, on the background layer, apply Motion Blur. Open the Filter menu and apply the Motion Blur filter (see fig. 20.40).

Now you'll want to create a drop shadow under the graphic image by following these steps:

1. Create a new layer under Layer 1, by selecting New Layer in the Layers palette. This is Layer 2.

2. Load the selection of Layer 1 by clicking it in the Layers palette. Then open the Select menu and choose Load Selection, Layer 1 Transparency.

3. On Layer 2, feather the selection by about two pixels, by opening the Select menu and choosing the Feather command.

Fig. 20.40

Applying Motion
Blur to the
background image.

4. Open the Edit menu and choose Fill, Foreground color; the example uses Black 100 percent.

5. Offset the shadow slightly down and to the right, using the Move tool (see fig. 20.41). This is the background blur effect example. (Also see the color section for the final image.)

Fig. 20.41

The blurred
background effect.

As an optional approach to this, you may want to blur the foreground image, instead of the background, while still keeping it legible. To do this, follow the first eight steps of the above example and then continue with the following steps:

1. Move the Layer 1 graphic to the right, using the Move tool. This gives room for motion to the left (see fig. 20.42).

2. Copy the Logo image on Layer 1 to the clipboard by opening the Edit menu and choosing the Copy command.

Fig. 20.42

Moving the
graphic image
layer to make
room for zoom!

3. Create a new layer to go under Layer 2 by selecting New Layer in the Layers palette. This is Layer 3.

4. Paste the Logo to Layer 3 by opening the Edit menu and choosing Paste.

5. To apply Motion Blur to Layer 3, open the Filter menu and choose the Blur, Motion Blur filter (see fig. 20.43). (See the color section to view the final effect of the blurred logo.)

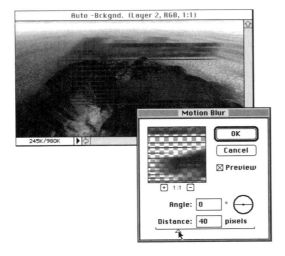

Fig. 20.43

Motion blurring
the new image
layer, underneath
the graphic image.

6. Load the selection of Layer 1 by clicking it in the Layers palette and choosing Load Selection, Layer 1 Transparency, under the Select menu.

7. Open the Select menu and choose the Feather command to feather the selection on Layer 2 by about 2 pixels.

8. To fill the selection, open the Edit menu and choose Fill, Foreground color (and the percentage of your choice). The example uses a foreground color at 100 percent.

9. Offset the shadow slightly down and to the right, using the Move tool. Then add the logo image layer and the drop shadow on top of the blurred logo (see fig. 20.44). Adjust the opacity of the blurred logo layer to a desirable level.

Fig. 20.44

Adding the drop shadow and logo layers.

In addition to the last effect, you can also blur both the foreground and the background layers; add Motion Blur to the background layer. To do this, open the Filter menu and choose the Motion Blur filter (see fig. 20.45). Make the background rate stronger than the foreground blur rate. This really makes the Logo pop off the page. Figure 20.46 shows the combination blur effect example. (See the color section for the blurred combo effect.)

Fig. 20.45

Blurring the background image layer in the Motion Blur dialog box.

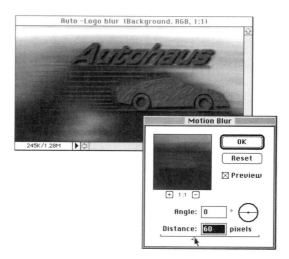

Fig. 20.46

The blurred combination logo effect.

Where To Go from Here

▶ You may want to look at the filters in chapter 15, "Using Photoshop's Plug-In Filters," for more effects ideas.

▶ Most of the effects in the preceding chapters (16, "Third-Party Plug-Ins," 17, "Creating Special Effects with Video," 18, "Creating Special Effects with Channels," and 19, "3-D Modeling Special Effects,") work well with type and imported vector-to-raster images.

V

Filters, Plug-Ins, & Effects

PART

VI

Publishing

This chapter on desktop publishing covers the following topics:

► Preparing images for layout

► File formats for desktop publishing

► Optimizing output

► Reproduction options

Photoshop for the Desktop Publisher

The term *desktop publishing* has come to mean many things since the term was first introduced around 1985. At that time, terms such as digital prepress, electronic design, digital designer, and so on were not yet developed. Today, most of us consider desktop publishing a different form of creating images, layouts, copy, and designs on computer systems than the sophisticated world of digital prepress. Desktop publishing is synonymous with office personnel creating in-house publications, newsletters, announcements, and material typically designed for output to laser printers, photocopiers, and desktop color printers.

by Ted Padova

CHAPTER 21

This is not to say that sophistication is not present in the world of desktop publishing. On the contrary, desktop publishers can make good use of high-end programs such as Adobe Photoshop 3 for the integration of photo images with their layouts. Where desktop publishing ends and digital prepress begins usually is determined by the type of output to be generated. This chapter is devoted to a discussion on output to office desktop machines (like laser printers) and high-end devices (like imagesetters) for grayscale imaging. Chapter 22, "Photoshop for the Digital Designer," explores the world of high-end digital prepress including color separations and output.

Preparing Images for Layouts

For the desktop publisher, images from Photoshop invariably are destined to be exported to another application where text and illustrations are combined for creating the layout. Preparing a file in Photoshop requires several considerations. What program to use to create the layout is important to understand because various programs accept different file formats. Knowing the appropriate file format is essential. File formats not supported by a program do not recognize the file and therefore, do not permit its placement in the program. Often, programs support several file formats which offer the user many choices.

The second consideration for preparing files is what printing device to use. Presuming you have a number of choices for importing files in a program, the issue then becomes what file format is easier or more successful when printing. Because many formats print on desktop printing devices, some image much faster than others. Knowing the requirements of the output device can save time and much aggravation.

Finally, the last choice to make when preparing files for other programs is determining the physical size and image resolution. In Photoshop, you can see an image occupying a full-screen document area. Sometimes the view on-screen can be misleading because the image can be amplified or reduced without immediate reference to page boundaries. Sizing images in Photoshop is much more desirable than sizing images in other applications.

Using Color or Grayscale

Whether files are prepared in grayscale or color, it is important to properly prepare the image. Obviously, a color image printed on a black-and-white laser printer is not the proper approach. Will the document be printed as several copies or a master for duplication? Will the file be prepared for offset printing or at the copy shop? Will color masters be printed on higher-end devices and then duplicated on color copiers? These are some of the questions to answer before the layout is completed. Some alternatives in preparing and reproducing grayscale and color images are explored in the following sections.

Preparing Grayscale Images

Preparing a grayscale image starts with the scanned file. Previous chapters presented material on scanning and obtaining good results from desktop scanners. A Photoshop image should begin with a good quality scan. Regardless of how good the original scan is, scans typically require some adjustments with brightness and contrast, which should be addressed in the Levels dialog box. Images adjusted on-screen may appear to be perfect; however, when run off a laser printer, the output may be distinctly different. This is easily understood if you can imagine your computer connected to 20 different laser printers. One can have a rich, black toner; another can appear dull in the black areas; one can be 300 dpi; while another is 800 dpi, and so on. In other words, the same wonderful looking image on-screen can have 20 different appearances on all those different printers.

Calibrating Dot Gain for Grayscale Images

So, how do you get within the range of predictable results? It all begins with calibration, as discussed in chapter 13. You have to adjust the image and move the screen image close to what you can expect from the printer. Assuming you have read the section "Calibration," in chapter 13, "Understanding Color," you can presume the Gamma, White Point, Black Point, and monitor settings have been adjusted. Therefore, you will work on adjusting the screen image to the printing device.

VI

Publishing

691

Before you can work on the screen image, you need a print of the grayscale file. If the final file is printed from Photoshop, you can exercise your Print command here. Often, the file is printed from another application. If this is the case, you have to save the scanned image for export to a layout application. If using PageMaker or QuarkXpress, save the grayscale image as a TIFF file. To create a sample image, import it into the layout document.

Tip

Control Variables When Test Printing

Because there may be no discernible variances with TIFF files printed from one application or another, it is best to eliminate every possible variable when running samples. If an image is to be printed from a specific application, always run all tests from the final application. With respect to calibrations, it is best to control and isolate every possible variable.

From PageMaker or QuarkXpress (or whatever layout program you use), print the image. After the document is printed, open the image in Photoshop. Examine the laser proof and hold it up to your monitor. Look carefully at the laser proof and the screen image. Many laser printers, especially those of lower resolution capacities, produce an image darker than the screen image. Presume for a moment that the laser proof is indeed darker than the screen image.

For now, you could readjust the levels, lighten up the image, and print again. The problem with this method is the adjustments applied will only be made for the image in question. Every time you scan a new image, adjustments have to be made in the same manner. If your monitor view differs greatly from the laser print, an adjustment to your view can bring them closer together, which eliminates the need for making the test print every time.

Rather than go to the Levels adjustment, open the File menu and choose Preferences, Printing Inks Setup. A dialog box appears, as shown in figure 21.1. Position the dialog box next to the image on-screen.

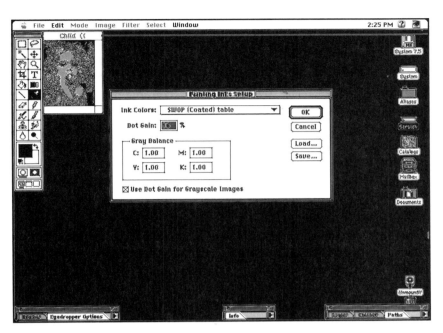

Fig. 21.1

Position the Printing Inks Setup dialog box next to the image on-screen.

With the sample laser print beside the monitor, adjust the dot gain. The dot gain adjustment ranges from –10 at the lightest setting to 40 at the darkest setting. Therefore, the higher the dot gain adjustment, the darker the image appears on-screen. Notice also that the check box for Use Dot Gain for Grayscale Images should be selected.

Unfortunately, Photoshop does not support dynamic previews with the Printing Inks dialog box. Some guesswork is needed to make the adjustments.

> **Tip**
>
> ### Use an Averaging Method To Determine Dot Gain Adjustment
>
> I always use an averaging formula for making dot gain adjustments. Start with the highest value—40—and click OK. If the image is too dark, average 20 (which was the original default) and 40 (the most recent adjustment), which results in 30, and use this value. If too dark again, average 20 and 30, or, if too light, average 30 and 40.

VI

Publishing

Keep adjusting the dot gain and click OK after each change until the image on-screen appears as close as possible to the printed piece. When the adjustment appears correct, go to the Printing Inks Setup dialog box and click the Save button. Navigate to the Calibration folder installed inside the Photoshop 3 folder and save the settings. If more than one laser printer is used, run tests for each device.

Try to understand exactly what you have accomplished. If you look at your monitor and see an image in Photoshop and that image appears too dark on the screen, then you will get a laser print equally as dark. You know this is true because you have adjusted your monitor and the printed piece to be as close as possible. It stands to reason, therefore, that if you adjust your screen image and lighten it up, your printed piece likewise appears lighter. To make these adjustments, use the Levels dialog box.

With the image open in Photoshop and the Printing Inks Setup dot gain adjustment made, open the Image menu and choose Adjust, Levels (or press ⌘-L) to bring up the Levels dialog box. Go to the gray balance slider in the center of the Input levels adjustment. Move the slider to the left to lighten the image and reveal more detail in the shadow areas. Adjust the slider with the Preview check box selected to dynamically view the results, as shown in figure 21.2. When the image appears to be right for the output, click OK.

Fig. 21.2

Move the slider in the Levels dialog box to reveal more detail in shadow areas.

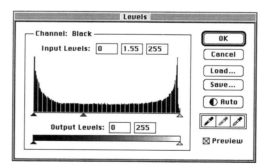

Every time a photo is scanned, load the Printing Inks Setup calibration and view the image when it is produced on the printer for which the calibration was made. When using multiple devices, calibrate for each device and load the appropriate settings.

Sharpening Images

Desktop scanners and low-end devices are CCD (charge-coupled devices), with CCD sensors that capture the color and grayscale values of images during the digitizing process. Low-end CCD systems usually produce images on the dull side and require some sharpening. Regardless of the output destination, desktop scans can be greatly enhanced with proper sharpening effects.

Photoshop provides several sharpening filters all noted under the Filter menu. The only filter recommended for improving image quality is the Unsharp Mask filter. Unsharp masking actually is built into higher-end scanners during the scanning process. With low-end flatbed scans, the unsharp masking takes place after the scan, when the filter is applied to the scanned image.

With your image on-screen, look at the Unsharp Mask filter. Open the Filters menu and choose Sharpen, Unsharp Mask. A dialog box appears for user definable settings. There are three items to adjust in the dialog box. First is the Amount option which adjusts the amount of sharpness applied to the image (see fig. 21.3).

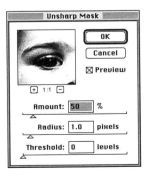

Fig. 21.3

The Amount option adjusts the amount of sharpness applied to the image.

VI

Publishing

695

As a standard rule, use one of three values for sharpening images. If you start with a good quality scan and it is relatively sharp, use a value of 60 in the Amount setting. For scans requiring a lot of sharpness, use 200 percent. For those in-between, use 100 percent. This, of course, is an area for testing and printing results on your own equipment. Use these values for your own testing as a starting point. Photoshop 3 shows a Preview option for all the changes applied in the Unsharp Mask filter with the dialog box still present. If the dialog box is placed beside the image, the dynamic preview shows amounts applied that can be too much or too little sharpening. Readjustments can be made easily without leaving the Filter dialog box.

Radius is the second setting in the Unsharp Mask dialog box. Use a standard constant to calculate the Radius amount. Take the dpi resolution of the image and divide by 200. If, for example, an image resolution is 150 dpi, the Radius will be .75. For good quality images, the Radius amount should not exceed 2.0. Too much Radius applied to an image creates a halo effect or white areas on either side of the sharpened pixels.

Threshold is the third option in the dialog box. Set this value to 3. The lower the threshold value, the more sharpening effect is applied. This may not be immediately recognizable. If you want to examine the effects of the Threshold setting, zoom in on the document and raise the slider to 255. You should see almost an elimination of the sharpening effect. Dropping the Threshold below 3 can have a subtle deterioration effect on the image in sharp contrast areas.

Adjusting Image Resolution

Images scanned can have resolutions determined at the time of scanning. This is often the case when the size requirements have been predetermined and the image is compensated for both size and resolution when it is scanned. Sometimes, you can scan an image and later determine the final output size. Then, you would resample the image in Photoshop to adjust the physical image size and final output resolution.

Output resolution can be determined on laser printers by performing repeated tests for yielding the best results. The standard rule is to settle on a resolution twice the halftone frequency. Often, this actually is more than sufficient for optimum results on a laser printer, but it's a good starting point for conducting your own tests and experiments. Therefore, if you print to a 300 dpi laser printer, the halftone frequency would be in a range between 53 and 60 lpi (lines per inch). On such a device, the image resolution would be no more than 120 dpi.

If you scan an image and want to resample it in Photoshop, you always should avoid resampling the image up in size. Doing so creates a higher resolution through interpolation. The image quality on grayscale and color images never is as good as rescanning the image at the desired size and resolution. When resampling images in Photoshop, the Image Size dialog box can be a good source to indicate when an image is interpolated. To observe the relationship between sizes and resolutions, open a grayscale image in Photoshop and choose the Image Size option from the Image menu. The Image Size dialog box appears (see fig. 21.4).

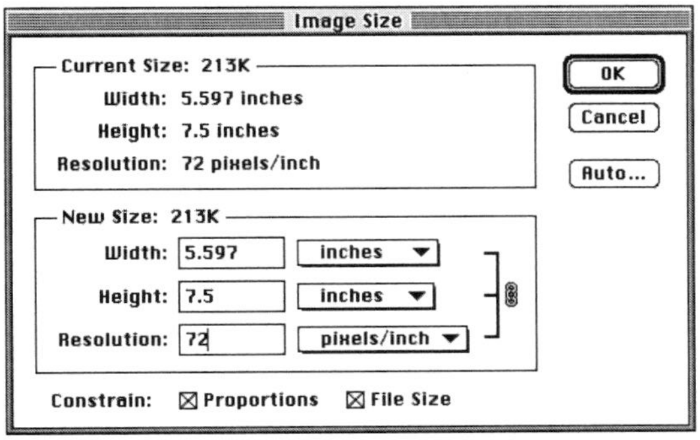

Fig. 21.4

See the relationship between sizes and resolutions in the Image Size dialog box.

The Image Size dialog box has user-definable ranges for Width, Height, and Resolution. At the bottom of the dialog box, the user can lock the proportion ratio so when either the width or height is changed, the other changes proportionately. Unless you want intentional distortion of an image, this box always should be selected. The other check box relates to file size and its relationship to the physical image size. When File Size is selected, the image resolution is locked to the size of the image. If, for example, a 100 dpi image at 3 inches by 3 inches is sized to 200 dpi with the File Size selected, the physical size of the image changes to 1.5 inches by 1.5 inches. Therefore, when the image resolution is doubled, the size is reduced 50 percent. Conversely, when the image is sized 200 percent, the resolution is reduced 50 percent.

VI

Publishing

The File Size option is excellent for determining whether you size with or without interpolation. In using the values in figure 21.4, suppose you want the width of the image to be 4 inches and the resolution to be 120 dpi. If you select the File Size check box and set either the width or resolution, the other tells you if you are in range (see fig. 21.5). By entering your width requirement, the resolution reports 100.75. This figure is less than your requirement of 120 dpi. If the File Size check box is not selected, you could enter 4 inches for the width and 120 for the resolution because the relationship between the two is broken when the check box is not selected. Doing so, however, means Photoshop recalculates the image size and adds pixels to the image through interpolation. In such an example, it would be better to rescan at a higher resolution.

Fig. 21.5

Selecting the File Size check box recalculates the image size.

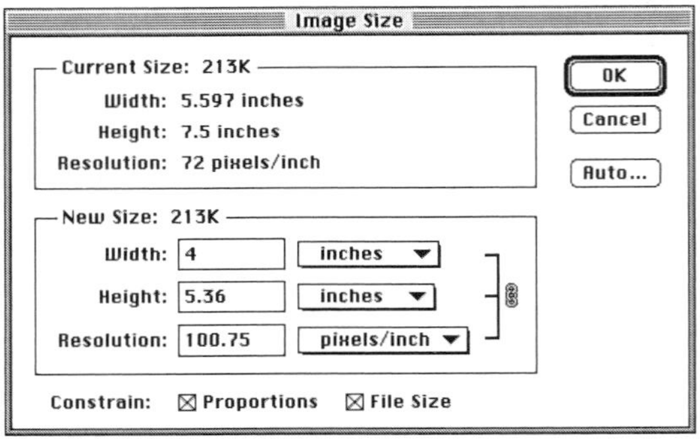

As a standard rule for preparing images for any output device, avoid interpolated resolutions and stay within ranges that provide for true or optical resolution.

Preparing Color Images

Preparing color images for printing in color follows many of the guidelines used for grayscale images with respect to sharpness and resolution. The same adjustments are made to color images regardless of the printer used. Calibration, however, follows the same principles used in chapter 13, "Understanding Color," on calibrating for color printing. Each device used should have separate color separation tables made for the RGB to CMYK conversions, as defined in chapter 13.

Besides the issues discussed for grayscale images, color image preparation involves the proper selection of the color mode to be used. Some color printing devices are RGB and others are CMYK. Knowing which color mode is preferred by the printing device should be determined prior to printing the file. When submitting files to service centers for color output, ask the service personnel which mode is best for the device to be used.

Acquiring the image for color output is another consideration. For grayscale scanning, many flatbed models perform well. For color images, there can be differences in the source material scanned. Slides, transparencies, negatives, and color prints can all be used to scan into the computer. Each material used can require different types of scanners. Slides and negatives, for example, yield better results from slide scanners rather than flatbeds with transparency adapters. If a flatbed scanner is the only scanner available, you can obtain color prints before scanning images. Slides require an internegative, and then a print for reflective scanning. You should weigh the costs against having a service bureau or photo lab scan transparencies over the costs of photographic prints. If the cost difference is not much, the higher-end scanners provide better results than low-end, flatbed scanners.

Output Type

Preparing images involves knowing what output device will be used, what software will eventually print the image, and how the image will be exported for output. For desktop publishers, Photoshop is usually an intermediary step in creating a layout. Images are prepared in Photoshop, and then exported to a layout application for integration of type and illustrations. If Photoshop files are imported into other applications, you must know the proper file format to achieve the best results. With the variety of file formats available, it is important to make the best choice for the application and printing device. There are several guidelines helpful in obtaining the best results and most efficient printing. Examine the most popular formats for the desktop publisher and discover how and why one format can be an advantage over another.

Bitmap Files

Bitmap formats contain two values, black and white. These formats most often are used with line art images, and therefore contain no gray values. In an office environment, some of the most common uses of a bitmap image are scanning and placing logos, icons, and line art drawings.

VI

Publishing

Tip

Scanning Line Art

Scanning line art on desktop scanners always should be performed at the highest interpolated resolutions of the scanning device. Line art, unlike grayscale images, can take advantage of interpolated resolutions. Therefore, if a scanner can achieve 1200 dpi resolution, for example, scan the image at that resolution.

Another use for bitmaps is creating templates for drawing programs. Programs like Adobe Illustrator, Adobe Streamline, and Aldus FreeHand can use bitmap images as templates for tracing. The traced image produces much cleaner on printers of all types and the file sizes are much smaller. Images used for export into illustration programs for tracing are determined by the formats supported by the illustration program. Adobe Illustrator, for example, can use either a paint file format, such as MacPaint, or a PICT file format. Aldus FreeHand can use either Paint, PICT, TIFF, or EPS. Adobe Streamline can use Paint, PICT, or TIFF formats. None of the formats have any impact on printing the final file because all are used as templates for tracing. The traced art typically is in EPS format and can be imaged on PostScript printers.

For importing images into programs that print the file, there are some important issues to understand. If, for example, a Photoshop image is imported into a program where a background color or image exists, the major concern is the surrounding white area. If a Photoshop file appears on anything other than a white background, all the white area of the image is visible and the underlying background is blocked out. To eliminate this problem, you have to make the white transparent.

To create a transparent background from a bitmap image, only the EPS format is usable. If the application accepting the file supports the EPS format, this is the easiest way to mask out the white areas. To save a file with Transparent Whites, open the File menu and choose Save or Save As. Choose EPS for the file format and a dialog box appears. Notice the option for selecting Transparent Whites (see fig.21.6). Select this check box and click OK. When the image is imported into another program and placed on top of another element, only the black area is visible. This is particularly helpful with presentation programs like Aldus Persuasion and Microsoft PowerPoint where background colors frequently are used.

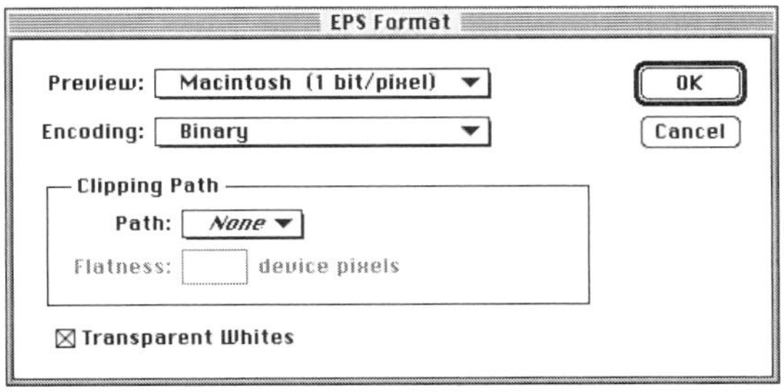

Fig. 21.6

Use the EPS Format dialog box to select the Transparent Whites check box to mask out white areas.

If Transparent Whites are not necessary, bitmap files also can be saved as PICT or TIFF images.

PICT Files

PICT files are native to the Macintosh environment. The PICT format first appeared in August 1984 with the introduction of MacDraw. Since then, many applications have supported the format, in addition to formats subsequently developed by Adobe Systems and Aldus Corporation. The format is available throughout the Macintosh world; however, it is a format that should not be used by the desktop publisher for output to PostScript printers.

To fully understand the complications with PICT formats, you must first look at printing devices. Printing files from Macintosh computers are generally available in two standards: QuickDraw and PostScript. The former is Apple's native format; the latter, Adobe PostScript, is the de facto standard in the design industry. PICT files are best suited for QuickDraw devices and not PostScript.

To understand complications related to printing PICT files on PostScript devices, use an analogy. Assume for a moment you have a conversation with another person in your native tongue. You discuss issues back and forth, and provide clarification when necessary to comprehend each other's thoughts. If, however, you speak English and your friend speaks French, you need an interpreter if neither of you is bilingual. Every sentence has to be translated back and forth. The communication proceeds, but it takes longer to complete the conversation.

VI

Publishing

PICT files sent to PostScript printers are much like language translations. The files can be imaged properly, but they always take longer. In the previous example, some key issues can be lost in translation. Likewise, some PICT files printed on PostScript printers may not image and create PostScript errors. This is particularly true of high-end imagesetters.

So, when are PICT files useful and why does a program like Photoshop support them? PICT files are best suited for screen views in using multimedia applications. Slide presentation programs, video, and interactive media are all good applications for PICT formats. In addition, the deviation with printing devices from PostScript is often found with film recorders for imaging 35mm slides and transparencies. If you create a slide show and want to have the slides output to a film recorder by a service bureau, it can be an advantage to create PICT files in Photoshop and export them to the presentation program.

TIFF Files

Photoshop images used in desktop publishing are most often saved in TIFF format. All of the popular layout, illustration, and PC Windows applications support TIFF, with the exception of Adobe Illustrator. For office environments as well as professional publishing studios and art departments, TIFF works well. Both grayscale and color images can be saved in a TIFF format and exported to layout programs for printing in black and white or color.

EPS Files

Encapsulated PostScript (EPS) files are necessary when halftone frequencies have to be embedded in the Photoshop image or the file is exported to programs accepting EPS and not TIFF. As noted, PICT files are of little use to the desktop publisher. Both TIFF and EPS formats are the desired file choice for anyone sending information to PostScript printing devices.

Frequencies can be embedded in a Photoshop file where the output result is different than the printing device's default. In the example of the 300 dpi laser printer, the default frequency is 60 lpi. If you want to image a Photoshop file at 45 lpi, you can instruct Photoshop to carry the output frequency with the saved image. To do so requires the EPS format.

Reproduction

Desktop publishers can develop mechanicals for offset printing, digital files for high-speed copiers, or multiple laser prints from high performance laser printers. Depending on the needs of the client and the quality desired, there are many options for choosing reproduction devices. When color is an issue, there are many choices for color output devices and many new technologies being developed. The following sections discuss a few options the desktop publisher can consider.

High-Speed Reproduction Systems

All the principles used for setting up files for output to laser printers can equally be applied to higher-end systems. Still within the definition of the tasks of the desktop publisher can be the need for volume documents produced on high-speed copiers. The ever-increasing world of technology continually bridges the gaps between computers and various mechanical devices. A good example is in the photocopier market. Service centers are offering reproduction on copiers direct from disk. The Xerox, Docutec, and Canon 550 series are examples of black-and-white and color copiers that use PostScript RIPs (Raster Image Processors) to feed the page description to the copier.

Preparation of files is much the same as for laser printers. The PostScript standard is mentioned because these devices are PostScript or PostScript clones. If you prepare a file for a non-PostScript printer, the document may need to be entirely reformatted before you send it to a copier center that uses PostScript RIPs.

All the issues related to image quality, frequencies, and resolutions apply to copier systems creating documents from computer files. The advantages of printing directly to copier systems are cost, particularly with low volume publications; speed, in terms of turnaround; and the capability to obtain a single copy for proofing before printing the entire job. Some of these advantages are cost prohibitive on a printing press. The corporate in-house art department or desktop publisher who prepares employee handbooks, procedure manuals, proposals, reports, and so on can make great use of services provided by large copy centers. Ten 100-page documents can be run directly from disk to a copier which reproduces halftone images, copies on card stock for the covers, and binds the booklet at the end of the run.

Like any other printing device, the user should investigate conventions for file formats, optimum resolutions, and file structure for facilitating the printing process. Ask the service personnel which file format is recommended for Photoshop images, what is the best dpi resolution to produce the most gray levels, and what programs are supported.

Imagesetter Output

The desktop publisher can use an imaging service bureau for higher-end output. When the laser printer proofs won't work for a particular job, then an imagesetter might be the necessary alternative. In dealing with imagesetter output, there are primarily two materials to purchase at the service bureau: film and paper. Film is used when taking a job to an offset printer. Reproduction equipment at copy shops won't make use of film for duplication unless the shop has a printing press. Resin-coated (RC) paper can be used for both offset press and photocopying. Even when duplication on copy machines fits the client's requirements, photocopying an original from an imagesetter can make a difference with the photocopies.

Laser printers are available supporting 600, 800, and 1200 dpi. Many are quite good and provide excellent results. The laser printer is a toner-based machine. As toner is applied to paper, the toner can flake and spread. This is most noticeable when examining small type under a magnifying glass. In a magnified view, the edges of the toner demonstrate flaking and imperfect shapes. Imagesetter output at 1200 dpi resolutions always appears tighter and more perfect without flaking on the edges of the dots. Therefore, the desktop publisher can choose to output masters on an imagesetter and visit the copy shop for duplication. Many higher-end copiers have a photograde feature to optimize photographic images during duplication. This feature provides some excellent results when photocopied from the imagesetter output.

When using RC paper for duplication, it is best to run some tests on halftone frequencies best suited for duplicating devices. A good frequency for photocopying images on Xerox 5090 copiers and similar devices is 75 lpi (lines per inch). If you use a different copier, performing some tests can establish criteria for your imagesetting output.

Laser Printer Output

Multiple copies from a laser printer are perhaps the least desirable forms of duplication. Many copy shops offer photocopying for three cents to six cents per copy. When you consider the cost of your laser printer and materials like toner and paper, photocopying at low rates makes good economic sense. Laser printers won't provide the bindery opportunities of many high-speed copiers that take time to collate and staple or bind multiple copies. Depending on the type of paper used, many curl and become more difficult to handle than photocopied stocks nicely bound. Laser printers are best suited to create a mechanical or original that is used at the print shop or on the photocopier.

Paper Types

With such a large laser printer market, there have been many paper manufacturers supporting different types of paper especially designed for laser printers. Laser printer paper comes in all forms, colors, sizes, and for specific uses. If the paper is used for a mechanical to be reproduced at the print shop or copy shop, there are some excellent papers suited to this need. If the paper is used for laser printing or photocopying, many preprinted papers designed for laser printers are available. In addition, a desktop publisher can decide to have some paper preprinted on one side in color and use the other side for laser printing.

Laser paper has been offered by paper manufacturers for several years. The types and varieties keep growing and more choices continually become available. For desktop black-and-white laser printers, the user can choose from the available paper designed for producing mechanicals, or original laser prints, or preprinted paper for a variety of uses. Paper such as Hammermill Laser Print is a clay-based, white paper producing good results for photocopying or as a mechanical for printing. Sometimes laser toner, especially in large areas of the document, appears dull. Toner can be made richer in the black areas by spraying with Krylon No. 1306 Workable Fixatif. The Fixatif not only renders the blacks darker, but also prevents some flaking and loss of the toner material. This is particularly useful with card stocks that can be printed on the laser printer for document covers. To preserve the cover, spraying with a coat of Fixatif helps.

VI

Publishing

Many distributors are offering preprinted paper for a variety of purposes including color borders, brochure and pamphlet covers, resumés, proposals, and so on. This paper can have a color design printed on the paper with white space left for individual text entries. Preprinted paper can be helpful for very low-end jobs where some flair to the design in color produces a better looking piece generated from a laser printer.

Optimizing Output

Regardless of the device used in imaging your Photoshop files or the material for which the file is printed, there are variables to control in obtaining optimum results. Understanding halftone frequencies, avoiding printing disasters, proofing files, and preparing files for other services help save time and money. Creating a great design on the computer does no good if it cannot be printed. Look at some important factors to understand how to achieve optimum results when printing.

Setting Halftone Frequencies

All images digitally produced and printed on laser devices produce dots. Dots in the printing industry are measured in lines per inch. Sometimes, dots cannot be easily detected without the use of a loupe or magnifying glass. Magazines such as *Architectural Digest* and *National Geographic* use high frequency values to produce stunning pictures. These pictures still have dots because they were produced from a printing press.

Compare these publications to the local Sunday newspaper. If you look at the images in a newspaper you can see the dots without the assistance of a loupe. The larger the dots the lower the frequency setting. Newspaper frequencies range between 85 to 100 lines per inch (lpi), and magazine quality is generally 133 to 150 lpi. By contrast, 300 dpi laser printers have maximum frequencies of 60 lpi. Some of the newer laser printers capable of achieving 600 to 1200 dpi can sustain frequencies from 85 to 120 lpi.

Halftone frequencies not only are important for the high-end professional who uses frequency values in every job, but also the desktop publisher who outputs to laser printers, copiers, and other office reproduction systems. If, for example, you output to a 300 dpi laser printer, the default frequency is 60 lpi. Saving Photoshop images at the default setting and printing from layout applications at their default values produces 60 lpi.

Presume you have made adjustments in a Photoshop image as previously discussed in this chapter, and the image looks fine until you attempt to photocopy it. When the master laser print is run from a photocopier, you notice the screens become darker in much of the gray areas. This can occur on older or lower-end photocopiers. To solve the problem, you can increase the size of the dot and white space between the dots by reducing the frequency setting and printing the original at a lower line screen value.

Changing halftone frequencies can be accomplished either in Photoshop or other applications where placed Photoshop images exist. Look at some of the popular layout programs that can help you control frequency settings. To print from a layout program, the Photoshop file has to be exported in a format acceptable to the layout application. For your purposes, use the TIFF format because it is acceptable to both QuarkXpress and Aldus PageMaker.

In QuarkXpress, the halftone frequency is set in the Page Setup dialog box. The box denoting Halftone Screen usually defaults at a laser printer's default screen frequency. For laser printers, the user can specify any frequency below the default value and obtain larger size dots on the printed image. Entering a value too high for many laser printers does not improve results and often renders the printed page less desirable than the default value. However, if a default frequency is not producing well on copiers or on stocks like newsprint, it can be advantageous to lower the frequency setting. In figure 21.7, the frequency has been set to 45 lpi for a 300 dpi laser printer.

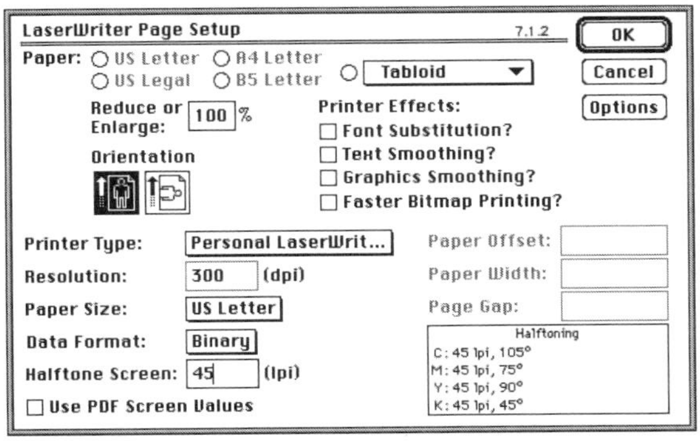

Fig. 21.7

The halftone frequency can be set in the Quark-Xpress Page Setup dialog box.

VI

Publishing

Aldus PageMaker 5.0 provides for user-definable halftone frequencies. In PageMaker's print dialog box, the Color button must be selected from the Print dialog box to navigate to the frequency setting. PageMaker's Optimized screen option registers a default setting every time the Color button is selected in the Print dialog box. If a frequency other than the default is desired, the Custom option from the pop-up menu must be selected. If Custom is not selected, PageMaker always prints the default screen value. In the case of a 300 dpi laser printer, that frequency may be 53 or 60 lpi. After Custom is selected, the user-definable Ruling option can be set to a value similar to the one you set previously in QuarkXpress. In figure 21.8, the ruling has been set to 45 lpi.

Fig. 21.8

The ruling is set to 45 lpi in Aldus PageMaker 5.0.

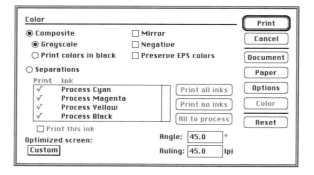

Photoshop files can be printed by either QuarkXpress or Aldus PageMaker at different frequencies as long as no frequency setting has been embedded in the Photoshop file. As a rule, always leave frequency settings alone in Photoshop and try to use the layout software to control the printing. This is especially true if you want laser prints at one frequency and imagesetter output from the service bureau at another frequency.

Preventing Output Disasters

There are some general rules for printing that should be followed with all Photoshop documents, especially when imported into layout and illustration programs. If you create documents that are ultimately to be printed, there are some important considerations, regardless of the printing device used.

Sizing and Rotating Images

The first safeguard to employ when preparing images for output devices is to perform proper sizing and rotating operations. The standard rule, regardless of where the image is printed, is to never size or rotate a placed image. Therefore, all sizing and rotating must be performed on Photoshop files from within Adobe Photoshop before they are placed in layout or illustration programs.

Most programs provide measurement tools, dialog boxes, or palettes to determine an image size or rotation. A layout can be created by sizing and rotating images, noting the precise reductions and angles of rotation, then reentering Photoshop to apply the values. Figure 21.9 is an image that has been sized and rotated in PageMaker 5.0. The Control palette shows the reduction percentage and the angle of rotation.

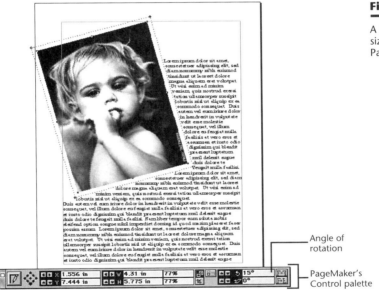

Fig. 21.9

A Photoshop image sized and rotated in PageMaker 5.0.

Angle of rotation

PageMaker's Control palette

The desktop publisher can manually size and rotate images to complete the design, then note the size and rotations on a piece of paper. Photoshop can be opened and the changes applied to the original image. For reductions, the Photoshop Image Size menu option should be selected, which displays the Image Size dialog box (see fig. 21.10).

VI

Publishing

709

Fig. 21.10

Reducing an image in Photoshop to 77 percent of the original size in the Image Size dialog box.

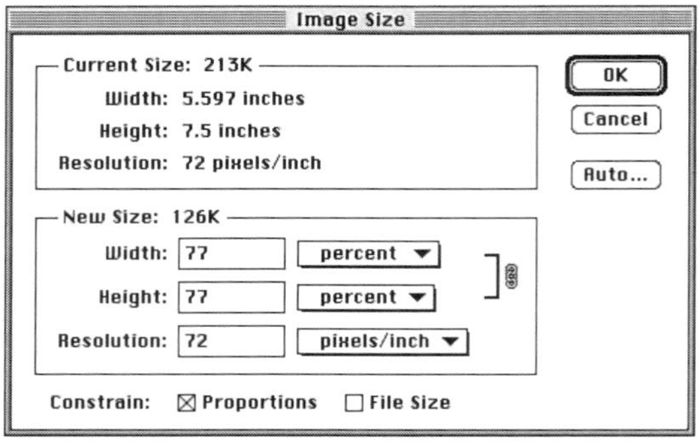

The Image Size dialog box provides for percentages of reductions that can be used to match the values in PageMaker's Control palette. In Photoshop, open the Image menu and choose Rotate, Arbitrary. The Arbitrary Rotate dialog box appears (see fig. 21.11).

Select the direction for clockwise (CW) or counterclockwise (CCW), and specify the angle of rotation from the value noted in PageMaker's Control palette (refer to fig 21.9).

Fig. 21.11

An image can be rotated in the Arbitrary Rotate dialog box.

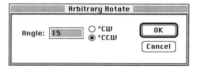

After the image has been prepared for placement at a 1:1 ratio, in terms of size and rotation, save it and place it again in the layout application. Performing such a task is time consuming and can appear unnecessary. The importance of approaching a layout in this manner cannot be overemphasized. In some cases, images do not print on some devices if rotations and sizing in the layout application are extensive. Other times, files can image, but the time to image them could be four to eight times longer. Extensive time to image files could result in overtime costs on an imagesetter and can make a job cost prohibitive.

Working with Gradients

Gradients and blends are subject to banding. *Banding* is a distinctly noticeable set of stripes of grays on a gradient where a smooth transition of tones was intended. Banding most often occurs on laser printers where image resolutions are lower than 1200 dpi. Sometimes banding can be controlled by lowering the frequency setting. The lower the halftone frequency, the smoother the blend appears. If gradients cannot be properly reproduced on a laser printer, output from the imagesetter produces excellent results.

Gradients created in illustration programs can be imported into Adobe Photoshop where they can be rasterized at an image resolution which is user-definable. Once in Photoshop, the gradient can be manipulated to yield some better results. Gradients can appear smoother by adding a little noise to the blend. Open the Filter menu and choose Noise, Add Noise. The Add Noise dialog box appears (see fig. 21.12). Photoshop 3.0 displays a preview of the noise filter applied to a gradient so adjustments can easily be made on-screen. To determine the level that works best for a given printing device, apply different amounts of noise to the image and print.

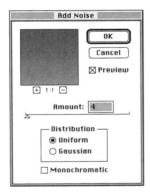

Fig. 21.12

Noise applied to a gradient can be adjusted on-screen.

Clipping Paths

Clipping paths can create printing problems, especially on printing devices with small RIPs. Clipping paths contain points on a path. The more points in the path, the more difficult the printing task. An imagesetter with a fast RIP and lots of memory can image a file that cannot be printed on a laser printer. Although the opposite also can be true, don't presume that anything imaged on a laser printer also can be printed on an imagesetter. The only way to develop some confidence in creating files you believe will print on any device is to avoid files with potential problems.

VI

Publishing

Clipping paths are used to mask out the surrounding area of an image when it is positioned on top of an element or another image. A good example is a human figure and a white background. To eliminate the white background, you can elect to create a clipping path around the human figure. The figure then can be placed in front of a texture, gradient, or another image without a white frame around the figure.

Clipping paths always have a difficult time printing to PostScript printers. There are two ways to minimize the problem: first, avoid the use of a clipping path whenever possible, and second, create paths with high tolerances. To avoid the use of a clipping path, you can create composite images in Photoshop. If a gradient is used in an illustration program, open the gradient in Photoshop. The rest involves merging two images into a single Photoshop file. A figure can be positioned on top of a gradient, texture, or another image in a composite Photoshop file. Now you can save the file and import it into another application as a single file.

Tip

Don't Be Fooled by File Sizes

If a composite image file size is greatly enlarged to accommodate a large background element, it is better than several small files with clipping paths. For example, if six images are .5MB each and are imported into another application where they are positioned over a gradient, the total file size of the document would be a little over 3MB.

If the gradient is opened in Photoshop and the six images are composited with the gradient, the file size could be much larger due to the size of the background element.

Printing a 3MB image with multiple clipping paths takes longer than a 20MB file with no clipping paths. In some cases, the file with clipping paths may not image at all and generate a PostScript error. File size in this case is not as important as the complexity of the file to be imaged.

If a clipping path is totally unavoidable, the second way to minimize problems is to never use a path tolerance below 2.0. Path tolerances are specified when creating a path in Photoshop. Figure 21.13 shows that when a selection is created, a path is made in the Channels palette by choosing Make Path.

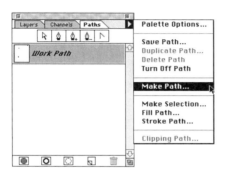

Fig. 21.13

Choose Make Path in the Channels palette to create a path.

When the Make Path option is chosen, a Make Path dialog box (see fig. 21.14) is presented for user-definable path tolerances. The tighter tolerance, represented by lower numbers, plots more points on a path.

Fig. 21.14

A Make Path dialog box appears when the Make Path option is selected.

Each point on a path is calculation intensive for PostScript RIPs. The more points on the path, the more difficult it is to print the image. By entering a tolerance value of more than 2, the number of points is significantly reduced. Figure 21.15 contains a path with a tolerance set to 1.0. Figure 21.16 is a path created with a tolerance set to 2.5. Notice the difference in the number of points plotted on the paths of each image. Figure 21.16, with its fewer points, images much easier on PostScript devices.

VI

Publishing

Fig. 21.15

Path created with
a tolerance of 1.0.

Fig. 21.16

Path created with
a tolerance of 2.5.

Preparing a Service Bureau Job

Files submitted to the service bureau for output follow the same principles in file preparation as those discussed for high-speed copiers and laser printers. All PostScript devices behave similarly and problems experienced with one typically are experienced with another. The service bureau images files on PostScript devices for most of the services rendered.

Exceptions to this rule are discussed in chapters 22, "Photoshop for the Digital Designer," and 25, "Automating Photoshop." For the purposes of the desktop publisher, using the service bureau usually involves output to material that is used by the offset printer or mechanicals created for photocopying.

Film or Paper

The first decision to be made when submitting a job for output on an imagesetter is whether to request film or paper. This determination is usually made in a discussion with a printer. If the printer wants RC paper or composed film to create plates for the printing press, he or she dictates to the designer what his or her needs are. In dealing with newspapers and magazines, you always should contact the source printing the job to determine the material needed for the press run.

Separations

Color separations also can be produced on RC paper or film. If a four-color job with a Photoshop image is used, the request from the service bureau must be film. Paper separations usually are reserved for spot colors and jobs without color photographs.

Running Proofs

Another way to avoid output disasters is to print files on a laser printer in the exact manner that they are imaged at the service bureau. If color separations are requested, it is best to print separations on a laser printer and examine the colors before submitting the job for imagesetter output.

Color separations typically are produced from layout applications. Separations can be created from Photoshop; however, if body text is included with an image, the text is integrated with the Photoshop images in a layout program. Programs like QuarkXpress and Aldus PageMaker permit creating separations from within the respective application. To observe printing separations from layout programs, examine the issues related to QuarkXpress and Aldus PageMaker.

Separations are made from files containing either spot colors or process colors. When using process colors, Photoshop images should be converted to CMYK. If the file remains in RGB, many programs do not separate the file. PageMaker 5.0, for example, does not perform an RGB-CMYK conversion while printing. If a separation of an RGB image is made, the Photoshop file only appears on the black plate. Regardless of what program separates an image, it is always best to let Photoshop perform the RGB-CMYK conversion and then import the image into the separating application.

In using both QuarkXpress and Aldus PageMaker, there is a danger in using predefined colors within the application. If a Photoshop CMYK image is imported into either application, and a color is used from the layout application's color palette, the resultant color appears as a spot value. When the document is separated, the four process colors print and the spot color images on a fifth plate. Printing laser separations shows the error. If a composite print is generated, there is no indication of spot values defined in a process job.

The best way to avoid any error with misassigning colors is to eliminate all predefined spot colors after the software is installed. This is easily performed in QuarkXpress and Aldus PageMaker. When the program is launched and before a new document is created, all changes made to colors change the program's defaults. These changes must be made without a document in view.

In QuarkXpress, the colors can be changed by opening the Edit menu and choosing Colors. The color selector is presented in a dialog box. All colors that can be deleted should be removed. Xpress does not permit elimination of process colors. Each color can be selected and the Remove button appears active for those that can be removed. Colors like red, green, and blue are spot values and they cause potential problems if used in process color jobs. By eliminating the colors, you can prevent the accidental use of these values. When spot colors are desired, they can be created in the document for which they are used (see fig. 21.17).

Fig. 21.17

Deleting spot colors from QuarkXpress in the Default Colors dialog box.

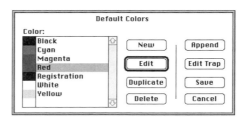

Likewise, PageMaker can have its color default values changed. In PageMaker, open the Element menu and choose Define Colors. As shown in figure 21.18, a dialog box appears and the colors similarly can be removed from PageMaker's palette by selecting the color and choosing the Remove button.

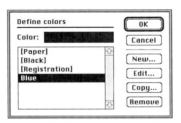

Fig. 21.18

Deleting spot colors from PageMaker in the Define colors dialog box.

Performing these steps in Xpress and PageMaker eliminates the need to convert all spot colors to process when printing a file. PageMaker, like QuarkXpress, permits the identification of spot colors to be created in a document. Always create new color values in either application with a document window open. Whenever a window is open, any changes made only affect the current document and do not change the default settings.

When printing separations on laser printers, all the image information does not appear unless the page size is smaller than the paper size. A letter-size document, for example, does not produce registration marks, color names, file names, crop marks, bleeds, and so on, because this information always prints outside the page boundaries. To reveal the document information on a letter-size page printed on a letter-size laser printer, it is necessary to print the file scaled down.

From either QuarkXpress or Aldus PageMaker, a document can be scaled to include the printer's marks and page information. On letter size pages, print the document as separations and scale to 85 percent. Tabloid pages can be printed at 60 percent to include all the information.

When submitting a job to any service center, always provide laser proofs and check them before submitting the job. Taking the time to print files the way you expect your output to be generated saves time and money.

VI

Publishing

Where To Go from Here

▶ If desktop scanning is part of your work, chapter 6, "Scanning Images," discusses obtaining good results from your scanner.

▶ Chapter 13, "Understanding Color," is important if you want to output to color devices or for color separations.

▶ Chapter 22, "Photoshop for the Digital Designer," is an extension of this chapter. Where you leave desktop publishing and venture into electronic design is not easily definable. Desktop publishers can see themselves performing many of the tasks discussed in chapter 22.

▶ For those who print to color printing devices, chapter 25, "Automating Photoshop," discusses many output options and devices for color printing.

▶ Refer to Part VII, "Learning from the Pros," for some specific design issues.

▶ Appendix E, "Swapping PC and Mac Photoshop Files," can be helpful to those preparing cross-platform files where exchanges between the Mac and PCs are needed.

Photoshop for the Digital Designer

The biggest problem facing designers today is not with artwork or creating artwork on computer systems. It is not related to type, illustration, or even understanding the use of the applications software. The problem is getting what is on the computer screen to a high-end imagesetter and getting it right the first time. This chapter looks at working with service bureaus and printers, and preparing files for high-resolution devices.

by Ted Padova

CHAPTER 22

Preparing Halftone Images

Halftoning a photograph is breaking apart the image into a series of dots. Traditional methods required a fine screen to be used to force light through the open areas of the screen, which then created dot patterns. In the digital process, where printing devices are connected to computers, halftoning occurs as the file is imaged on the printing device. Laser printers and high-resolution imagesetters produce halftone images.

Adjusting Image Contrast

Grayscale images designed for output to imagesetters that eventually go to a print shop for printing should be prepared according to the needs of the printer. The printer needs dots present in the white areas of an image to lay down ink. Conversely, if an area of an image is solid black, no dots exist and a loss of detail in the shadow areas occurs.

In making adjustments for any grayscale image that is to be printed on a printing press, you should assess the black-and-white areas for the amount of black present. The step-by-step process for performing this assessment is as follows:

1. Open the Image Menu and select Adjust, Curves (⌘-M).

2. Examine the lightest area of the image with the Eyedropper tool.

3. Increase any area less than six percent in the output readout to within six percent and eight percent.

4. Examine the darkest areas in the shadows.

5. Decrease any area more than 94 percent in the output readout to within 92 percent and 94 percent.

As an example, figure 22.1 shows a grayscale image on-screen with the Info palette adjacent to the image. The Eyedropper placed in the lightest area shows a readout of two percent. It is difficult for a printer to apply ink to any area less than six percent. To increase the amount of black in this area, follow the steps outlined in the previous list.

The Curves dialog box represents a linear position between the white point in the lower-left corner of the dialog box to the black point in the upper-right corner of the dialog box. Along this diagonal line are the 256 levels of gray. Any point on the line moved up darkens that level. Conversely, any point moved down lightens the level. As a point is moved up or down, it will be reflected as a percentage of the Input and Output of the brightness value.

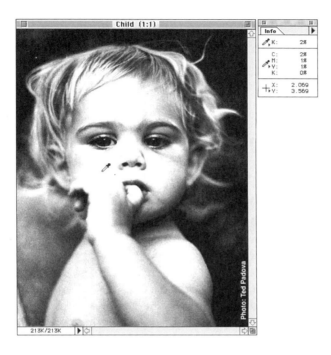

Fig. 22.1

The Info palette next to a grayscale image shows the black level in the lightest area.

To add more black in an image, the point in the lower-left corner should be moved upward. As the point is moved, a readout becomes visible in the lower-right corner denoted by Output. In this case, move the white point up to read between six percent and eight percent in the output area (see fig. 22.2). Moving the white point up will add some black to the lightest areas.

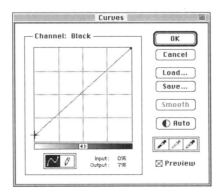

Fig. 22.2

In the Curves dialog box, adjust the white point to within six percent and eight percent.

VI

Publishing

Moving the point in the Curves dialog box, as described, adds more black to the image in the lightest areas. Performing this task creates a gray value of at least six percent, which provides the printer an opportunity to apply ink in areas that otherwise would reveal the paper color and the absence of ink.

After the white point adjustments have been made, the black point should be adjusted. Black point adjustments occur in the same manner, only using the upper-right corner of the Curves dialog box. If the assessment readout in the darkest area of the image is higher than 94 percent, the black point needs to be moved downward to within 92 percent and 94 percent.

Compensating for Dot Variations

Preparing an image for output to a service bureau is only half the task of creating halftone images for printing. After the prepress material is produced at the service bureau, you still should be concerned with the printing press. Different presses and paper types produce different quality images. Newsprint, for example, has a much higher absorption level than coated stocks. The dots created in the halftoning process have a tendency to swell as the ink is absorbed which creates more ink on the paper. This is typically referred to as *dot gain*. Roller pressure of presses also has an effect on image quality. If the pressure is too light, the dots tend to become smaller or disappear. Ideally, the designer creates sample images that are output to a service bureau and run on different presses used with various vendors. It is costly to start with arbitrary tests for every press and stock type used.

Knowing that paper stocks absorb ink differently, you can compensate for the amount of black applied to halftone images as a general guideline and starting point for performing some tests. There are primarily three types of stocks the designer uses: coated, uncoated, and newsprint. Each of these stock types has different absorption levels and requires more or less ink accordingly. You can make adjustments to the amount of black in the highlight and shadow areas in the Levels dialog box (see fig. 22.3).

Open any grayscale image. Open the Image menu and choose Adjust, Levels to access the Levels dialog box (⌘-L).

Note in figure 22.3 that the Output Levels values default at 0 and 255. To compensate for dot gain or loss, adjust the output levels for the different stock types. Table 22.1 shows recommended ranges for coated, uncoated, and newsprint stocks. This can only be used as a beginning for conducting tests and experiments. You cannot predict other variables, such as roller pressure and press variations of the printer.

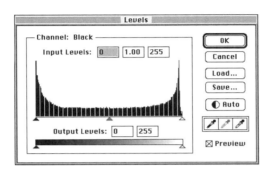

Fig. 22.3

Adjust the amount of black in the Levels dialog box with output levels at default 0 and 255.

Table 22.1   Stock Types and Output Levels Adjustments

Stock Type	Black Output Range	White Output Range
Coated	10–14	240–244
Uncoated	20–25	225–230
Newsprint	25–30	220–225

Recording values from table 22.1 can be entered in the output boxes numerically with the black point represented on the left side and the white point represented on the right side. Select appropriate values from table 22.1 and enter the black value in the left Output Levels box and the white value in the right box (see fig. 22.4).

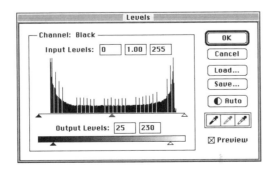

Fig. 22.4

The Levels dialog box with Output Levels adjusted for uncoated stock.

VI

Publishing

723

Midtone Adjustments to Grayscale Images

So far, you have adjusted black-and-white areas of an image to provide for the presence of dots and have made adjustments for dot gain or loss. After making these adjustments, you can notice that the image appears darker on-screen, especially in the midtone regions. Typically, all desktop scanning devices produce darker images. This is especially true of scanners with transparency adapters. They always appear too dark. There almost always is a need to lighten the image. To lighten a grayscale image, you again access the Levels dialog box. This time, the only adjustment is to the middle gray balance slider in the Input Levels. As the slider is moved left, the image becomes lighter, especially in the midtone ranges. The slider should be moved so the gray balance readout above the Input Levels is between 1.5 and 1.6. Figure 22.5 illustrates the midpoint slider adjusted to 1.55.

Fig. 22.5

The Levels dialog box with midpoint slider adjusted to 1.55.

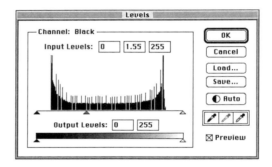

Depending on how well your monitor is calibrated to the printing device, the monitor view will be lighter than the image will print. In other words, if it looks perfect on screen, it probably will print a little darker than your monitor view. When making midtone adjustments, lighten the image a little more than the perfect view on-screen. Once again, running tests and printing results is invaluable in determining settings for your own equipment, service bureau, and printer.

Tip

Calibrate for All Printing Devices

Perform the image enhancement features noted previously beginning with white and black point adjustments, dot gain adjustments, and midtone adjustments. Print the image to a laser printer and examine the print against your monitor. If the image is too dark, adjust the dot gain as mentioned in the section "Calibration," in chapter 13. Print the file again and examine the results.

The final print should be a good quality image within the limitations of the laser printer. Use your laser printer to understand what is going on and how the dot gain adjustments affect your printed piece. When you get a handle on the dot gain adjustments in the Printing Inks Setup dialog box, run a print at the service bureau on film. Have a contact print made from the film. This will show the dots growing a bit, which simulates a dot gain. Bring the contact print back to your computer and compare the output to the monitor. Make the necessary dot gain adjustments and save the setting. Whenever outputting to the imagesetter, load the dot gain adjustment setting before submitting the file to the service bureau.

Preparing Color Images

The digital design professional should not use desktop scanners for color work. Printing separations from low-end scanned images produce less than desirable results. Drum scans and high quality scans purchased from service bureaus and prepress houses provide professional results. Trust me on this. I can't tell you the number of people I have worked with who initially cut corners on costs only to wind up paying almost twice as much for re-scanning and re-separating a job. With all the things known about Photoshop and how well it performs all the wonderful effects, everything still starts with a good quality scan. Even Photoshop has its limitations on improving poor quality images.

Placing a Drum Scan Order

Drum scans are best produced from transparencies. If you have a choice or are art directing a photo shoot, request 4-by-5-inch transparencies for scanning. Reflective art works well on drum scanners, but try to stay away

VI

Publishing

725

from negative film. In most cases, it is best to obtain a photographic print for scanning the negative. The designer should always check with the service bureau and discuss what the preferred source material should be before submitting an order or contracting with a photographer.

After you have discussed with the service bureau the material to be submitted for the scan, there are some considerations to be made about how the scan is used.

▶ *Physical Image Size.* If you have a 35mm slide to be scanned, what will the final image size be? The service bureau should know if the image will be sized up to preserve the appropriate image resolution.

▶ *Halftone Frequency.* When the scan is output, what line screen will be used? Knowing the halftone frequency determines the image resolution.

▶ *Color Mode.* If the scan will be color separated, typically the mode is CMYK. If you want RGB for some reason, like applying special filters such as lens flare or lighting effects, the scanning specialist should know. You can convert RGB images to CMYK, but once converted, you don't want to go back.

▶ *Cropping Instructions.* Specific instructions related to cropping the image should be supplied with the order. This can occur in a comment section in the form of a narrative, or preferably on a laser print with crops marked clearly on a low-resolution version of the scan. For low-resolution images where the image is a guide, you can use desktop scanners and laser prints.

▶ *Archiving.* Will your scan be used *as is* or will it be edited in Photoshop? If the scan is not edited, you can elect to have the service bureau archive the original scan and provide you with a low-resolution image for position only (FPO). When you place an order for film separations, the service bureau substitutes the original high-resolution image for the one you placed in a layout application. Or, if you elect to massage or edit the image in any way, you should have the high-resolution image.

▶ *File Format.* What file format will be used? The scan can be supplied in TIFF, EPS, or a Photoshop file format. Bureaus using Scitex prepress systems can save the file in Scitex CT format. The Photoshop format requires returning the original high-resolution image to you because native Photoshop files cannot be used for placement into layout applications.

Color correcting and image enhancement features are provided in some high-end service bureaus and prepress houses. High-end services use proprietary systems and can require the presence of the designer for making color adjustments as you view the screen while a technician operates the equipment. Specialized services like this are costly and reserved for high-budget jobs.

If you are new to placing high-end scan orders, talk to the people at your service bureau and request an order form (see fig. 22.6). Familiarize yourself with the form and request clarification on anything you don't understand. If you want the service bureau to be precise in filling your order, you must be precise in your request. Keep in mind, too much information is always better than not enough.

Graphic Traffic
S C A N N I N G
Ventura 805.650.9807
Thousand Oaks 805.494.1981
M-Th 8:00 - 8:00, Fri 8:00-6:00, Sat 9:00-5:00

Customer Company

SCANNING ORDER FORM

FULL SERVE FLATBED AND NIKON SCANNING:

Item (description of image)	Material Supplied (Slide, photo, artwork)	Output Resolution	Dimensions (final size)	Mode CMYK/RGB

HOWTEK DRUM SCANNING:

Item (description of image)	Include Dye-Sub	Material Supplied (Slide, photo, artwork)	Output Resolution	Dimensions (final size)	Mode CMYK/RGB

Graphic Traffic Use:
Order taken by: ________ Scanned by: ________
Date needed: ________ Dye-Subs printed by: ________

Billing info:
Scanning: ________

FAX: Ventura: 805.650.9824 Thousand Oaks: 805.494.7224
Prices Effective January 1, 1994

Fig. 22.6

Become familiar with a service bureau drum scanning order form.

Working with Color Images

Unlike grayscale images where you made adjustments for dot gain or loss, adjusted the levels, and compensated for paper stocks, color images acquired from drum scanners typically are not altered for image enhancement. The service bureau calibrates its devices so scanners, color printers, imagesetters, and proofing systems provide a consistent continuum with appropriate reproduction of color. If you or the designer make adjustments to color images on your monitor, you can find great disparity between the monitor view and the final, separated film. Color adjustments should only be made with extensive testing between you, the service bureau, and the print shop. Follow the steps outlined in this book for calibrating your monitor and perform the tests to verify your results.

The one major issue you do have to deal with in preparing color images for layout applications is deciding on the right file format. As a professional designer, you are probably used to using EPS and TIFF formats and you are hopefully avoiding PICT, Paint, and the like when printing to PostScript devices. With the choices available, when is it best to use one over the other?

TIFF Images

TIFF is a popular choice for images imported into layout programs. With the exception of Adobe Illustrator, TIFF files are accepted by the top design applications that professionals use. Although TIFF files can separate well and provide good results in high quality work, there can be minute differences in color when using this format over EPS.

TIFF files are great for grayscale and composite printing. Another advantage in using TIFF files is they require less disk space than EPS files. However, if you have the choice between the two, take a look at the description for EPS files.

Scitex CT Images

Scitex CT (continuous tone) format is a proprietary format for output to Scitex prepress systems. When ordering a drum scan in a Scitex shop, the service bureau saves the file in Scitex CT. Scitex CT can only be used with either CMYK or grayscale images. Photoshop can open or save in the Scitex CT format, but special software is needed to transfer these images to Scitex workstations.

Designers using Scitex CT formats should have the output prepared at a Scitex prepress facility or service bureau running Scitex systems.

EPS Images

EPS images can be saved in two formats. The EPS image can be exported as a composite or as a desktop color separation (DCS) file. If layout programs are used to separate files, both Aldus PageMaker and QuarkXpress support the DCS format.

When color separating scanned images from PageMaker or QuarkXpress, the DCS format is ideal on imagesetters. DCS creates five separate files. One file is a composite which is placed in the layout program and the other four include each of the four process color separations. When the file is printed as a separation, each of the four individual files is sent to the imaging device as the respective color is printed. At the time the film separations are ordered from the service bureau, all five files must be delivered to properly image.

Caution

Printing Proofs with DCS Files

When a color proof is needed prior to printing separations with DCS files, be certain to request that the color proof be imaged as a separation. Some desktop color proofing systems, like the 3M Rainbow dye sublimation printer, image a composite color print from a file printed as separations. If the file is printed as a composite, the 72 dpi FPO image is printed rather than the high-resolution image. It noticeably shows pixelation.

VI

Publishing

Key Concept: Understanding Frequencies, Resolutions, and Grays

Regardless of whether your output will be composite grayscale or separated color, there are some basic things to understand about halftone frequencies and image resolution in order to successfully place an order at a service bureau.

Halftone Frequencies

Halftone frequencies are dictated by your printer, the type of stock used, and material supplied from the service bureau to the printer. The first determinant in deciding which frequency to use is the type of stock required for the job. For coated stocks, the recommended frequencies range between 133 lines per inch (lpi) and 175 lpi. Uncoated stocks are printed with frequencies ranging between 85 and 133 lpi while newsprint is recommended between 65 and 85 lpi.

Some imagesetters can produce as many as 300 lpi, but only a handful of presses can hold more than 175 lpi frequencies. In almost every situation, it is best to talk to the printer first and ask about his or her press capabilities before requesting output from the service bureau.

Output Resolutions

You should tell the service bureau at what image resolution to print your file. High-end imagesetting equipment is capable of printing files from a selectable set of image resolutions. Unlike your laser printer, the imaging specialist can set the imagesetter to print at 1200 dpi, 2400 dpi, or 3600 dpi (with slight variations according to different manufacturers). When placing an order with a service bureau, you should specify at what resolution you want to have your file imaged.

Determining the frequency is pretty straightforward. You decide on the paper stock, discuss it with your printer, and use his or her guidance in choosing the frequency. Output resolution requires a little calculating to determine what resolution to image a file. It all begins with the maximum number of gray levels that can be imaged on PostScript devices.

Levels of Gray

PostScript, which is the defacto standard in the high-end output industry, has the capability of producing 256 levels of gray. Think of the gray levels applying to color images as well as grayscale. The objective, therefore, is to capture all gray values within the limits of PostScript. Imaging service bureaus base their rates on the time it takes to image files. At higher resolutions, the files take longer to print. As a result, 2400 dpi output is usually more expensive than 1200 dpi out-put, and 3600 dpi is higher in cost than 2400 dpi.

When placing an order at a service bureau, don't think more is better. Always ask the service bureau personnel if you are uncertain. Someone at the service bureau should be able to make recommendations on output resolution if you explain what you want and how it is to be printed.

Tip

Calculating Gray Levels

The formula to calculate gray levels is: Gray levels = (Output Resolution÷Halftone Frequency)^2 + 1. Using this formula, if you want to image a 133 halftone frequency at 1200 dpi, you can calculate the number of gray levels possible. Plugging the values into the formula, the total number of grays equals 82: (1200÷133 = 9), (9×9 + 1 = 82). The same file imaged at 2400 produces all 256 levels of gray: (2400÷133 = 18), (18×18 + 1 = 325). Because PostScript can only produce 256 levels of gray, anything over that amount is ignored.

If this file were imaged at 3600 dpi, it would appear no different than the 2400 dpi image. Because all 256 gray levels would be captured at 2400 dpi, you would waste your money for paying differences in cost for the higher resolution.

Trapping

There are many publications discussing or referring to trapping colors in pixel-based programs like Photoshop and vector-based programs like Adobe Illustrator and Aldus FreeHand. When two adjacent colors of different values are printed on a printing press, slight movement of the paper or shrinkage of the paper may cause a small area to not receive ink. A gap will exist and the color of the paper will be seen between the colors. *Trapping* colors is a way of overlapping two inks slightly so that they will compensate for the paper movement or shrinkage. If the overlap is too large, a third color will appear when the inks are mixed and overlay each other. The ideal is to create enough overprint on the inks to compensate for the paper movement without creating the appearance of an additional color. For more information about trapping, see Que's *Using PageMaker 5 for the Mac* and *Using QuarkXpress version 3.3 for Macintosh.*

Photoshop Trapping

Photoshop has a trap function that can be applied to CMYK images. The designer can trap a Photoshop file by opening the Image menu and choosing Trap (see fig. 22.7).

Fig. 22.7

A designer can trap a Photoshop file with the Trap command in the Image menu.

When the Trap command is accessed, Photoshop presents a dialog box for user-specified trap amounts available in pixels, points, or millimeters (see fig. 22.8).

Fig. 22.8

The Trap dialog box offers trap amounts in pixels, points, or millimeters.

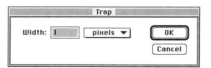

The question is, should you use Photoshop's trapping feature or not? If you request trapping to be performed at the service bureau, most bureaus will tell you not to trap anything and let them take care of all the traps. Photoshop trapping has little control and goes out to the image to trap abutting colors globally throughout the image. Other than the amount of trap applied, there is no provision for exercising conditions or creating specific trap zones. It is crude at best.

> **Caution**
>
> **Talk to the Professionals before You Apply Trap**
>
> Arbitrarily trapping files can present as much of a problem for the printer as files with no trap. Before trapping any document,
>
> talk to the printer and ask for recommendations. Then, talk to the service bureau and ask if they have samples of printed pieces where Photoshop trapping has been applied.

Service Bureau Trapping

If Photoshop images are imported into layout or illustration programs, trapping the Photoshop image only solves part of the need for creating trap. The rest depends on trapping solutions provided by the application used for the layout.

Service bureaus can create trap with proprietary systems, like Scitex, or with specialty software like Adobe TrapWise. Trapping solutions for service bureaus start at around $5,000 for software to trap image files. The control special trapping software can exercise is far greater than that available in either Photoshop or graphics applications software. In addition, service bureaus and prepress specialists ideally have knowledge about what colors to *choke* (bring in) or *spread* (push out) and where to create trap zones.

In traditional graphics art and printing, printers always controlled trap when shooting mechanicals. Through the advent of computer systems and the sophistication of design application software, designers are more aware of trapping issues and can create trap in files before they are imaged at service bureaus. Today, there is software available that deals specifically with trapping files. Service bureaus purchase the software to meet their clients' needs. As a result, you should see a shift away from the designer creating trap and the responsibility put back on the shoulders of prepress and printing specialists.

VI

Publishing

> **Tip**
>
> **To Trap or Not To Trap**
>
> If, in talking to your printer, it appears as though your files need to be trapped, always let the service bureau trap your files. If something goes wrong with the separations or printing, you can try to have your files reprinted at no charge, especially if someone who trapped or printed the file was in error. On the other hand, if you take on the responsibility of trapping files, you own the mistakes and any additional separations or printing are your responsibility.

One thing not obvious in selecting printers is knowing the capabilities of the strippers. You can discuss jobs with printing sales and estimating people and you can see the press operators at the time of a press check, but rarely will you come in contact with the stripper, especially in large shops where roles are maintained in specialized domains. If the stripper is locked up in a back room working on a table, you may never know who's back there working. Yet, one of the most important individuals at the print shop is the stripper. Shops with true craftspeople can make a world of difference with your printed piece. You can find shops that consistently print pieces with all knockouts and no trap flawlessly. Other shops consistently show trapping problems and complain of the pitfalls of digital film. If both shops receive film from the same service bureau, then the difference between them is the talent of the strippers. When looking for printers, try to find out as much as possible about their stripping department. Solicit information from other professionals and service bureaus. The word gets out fast and many know who are the best strippers in town.

Preparing Files for Screen Printing

Fig. 22.9

(See color section.)

Fig. 22.10

(See color section.)

Silk screeners often require special treatment of separated film. Rather than separating process color, many screen printers use spot colors. Large presses with eight or more heads in an octopus-like configuration have separate color inks applied to many different types of material, the most popular being textiles and clothing (see figures 22.9 and 22.10 in the color section "Photoshop in Color!"). If a screen printer lays down six or eight different colors, the separations need to be individual spot colors.

Using Spot Colors

Photoshop does not provide a mode to separate spot colors. If four colors or less are needed in a design, each individual color can be represented in a CMYK document. Duotones, tritones, and quadtones do not work because there are percentages of ink laid on top of each other. If the colors are solid, 100 percent Cyan will be in the Cyan channel, 100 percent Magenta in the Magenta channel, and so on. Figure 22.11 shows an image with the Channels palette indicating each of the four colors contained in the composite image. Because no tint values of any color are mixed together, each separation only contains 100 percent of the respective channel.

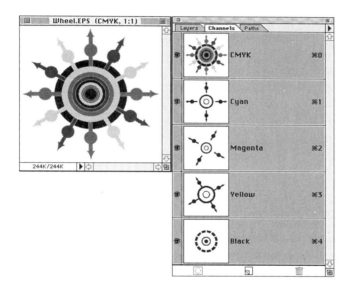

Fig. 22.11

The Channels palette indicates a four-color image with 100 percent values in each channel.

After the file is separated, any color ink can be applied to a separation. Green, for example, can be applied to the cyan separation, orange to the black separation, and so on. The screen printer burns a plate from the separated film and then the press person applies whatever color is appropriate to that plate. In other words, don't think that cyan ink needs to be laid on the cyan plate.

Creating Multiple Spot Colors

Using CMYK channels is fine for four-color documents, but how do you approach files needing eight, 12, or 16 spot color separations? This is a multi-step process. Figure 22.12 includes eight channels.

VI

Publishing

Fig. 22.12

An eight-color image with each color in a separate channel.

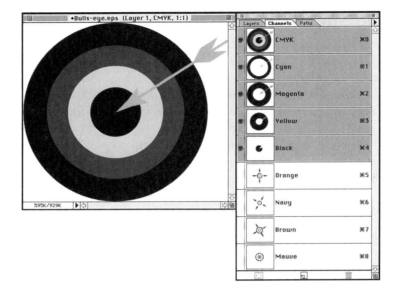

1. Save each color in a separate channel. All colors in the composite image must be saved into separate channels. Because the composite image is CMYK, much care is needed in selecting and saving selections.

2. Duplicate the image. After all channels have been created, use the Duplicate command to create a duplicate image.

3. Delete channels from the original image. The original image has been duplicated. All channels but the CMYK channels can be eliminated and the file saved. These are the first four colors to be separated.

4. Apply the alpha channels information to the CMYK channels. Two steps should be performed. The information in the CMYK channels should be deleted, and the alpha channels' information should be moved to the CMYK channels. Photoshop 3 accomplishes both tasks in a single operation. One of the CMYK channels must be the current active channel and the Apply Image command from the Image menu should be accessed. In the Apply Image dialog box (see fig. 22.13), it's a matter of choosing the desired channel to be applied. Photoshop replaces the CMYK channel with the alpha channel information.

5. Delete the alpha channels. When all four channels have been replaced, the alpha channels can be deleted and the CMYK information becomes a new document ready for separations.

6. Separate both files. When both images are separated, they should be in registration because the second image was an exact duplicate of the original.

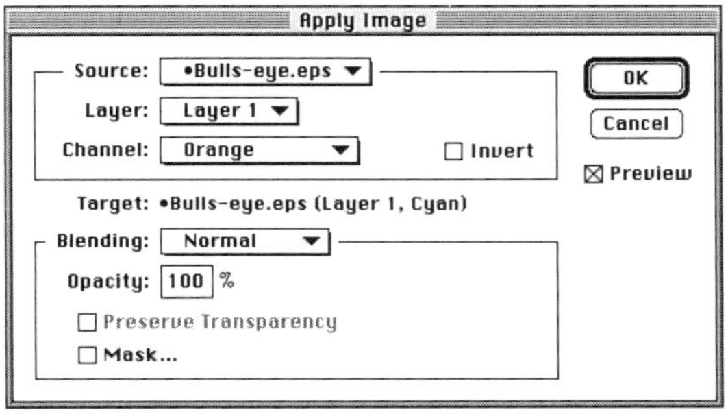

Fig. 22.13

Apply an image with an alpha channel (Orange) replacing the cyan channel.

If you create files regularly for screen printing, there are some third-party plug-ins that can simplify separating more than four colors. Photospot from Second Glance or Platemaker from In Software are designed specifically for separating spot colors from Photoshop.

As a final note about screen printing, the separations are not trapped. Screen printers want knockouts. Like anything else you do in digital imaging, you should talk to the printer first; but as a rule, don't create any trap on your files.

Creating Custom Screen Angles

Earlier, this chapter discussed process color separations at the service bureau that were prepared for the printer. Process separations are imaged at all frequencies with specific screen angles. Each color must have the dots at angles apart from each other. Failure to spread the angles results in a moiré pattern. For offset printing, the angles are usually set to C = 15°, M = 75°, K = 45°, and Y = 0°. With the angles set apart 30 degrees, the likelihood of a moiré is lower.

VI

Publishing

737

Screen printers typically specify color angles much differently than offset printers. Because most separating software and printer drivers default to the offset angles noted previously, screen angles must be user-defined to accommodate the screen printer. Photoshop provides an easy way of handling the selection of custom angles in the Page Setup dialog box. The Page Setup dialog box (see fig. 22.14) has a button to activate Screen; when selected, another dialog box appears.

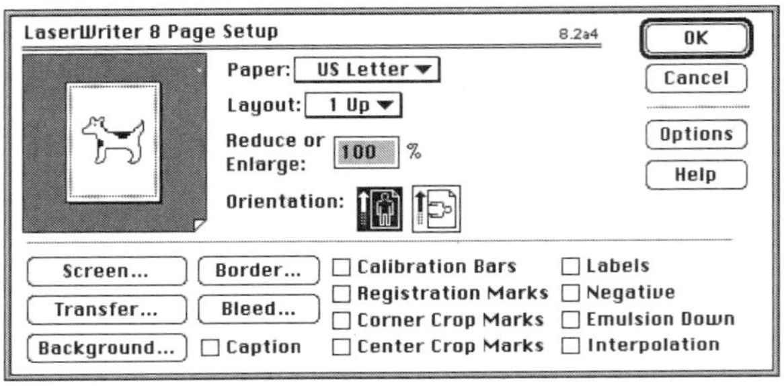

Fig. 22.14

The Page Setup dialog box handles selection of custom angles.

The Halftone Screens dialog box (see fig. 22.15) permits user-defined screen angles to be identified. In addition, custom frequencies also can be created. This feature is equally important because many screen printers use values anywhere from 30 lpi to 100 lpi.

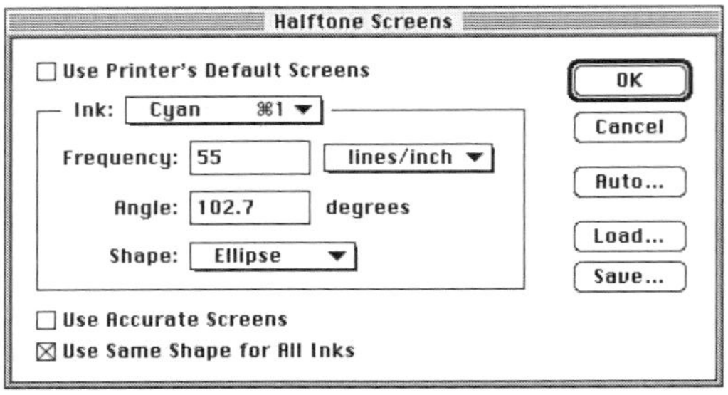

Fig. 22.15

The Halftone Screens dialog box enables identification of user-defined screen angles.

After the screen angles and frequencies are chosen, it is important to save the values with the image. The only format acceptable for saving screen angles and frequencies is EPS. When the EPS Format dialog box is presented, the Include Halftone Screen check box must be selected (see fig. 22.16). Selecting this box embeds the screen angles and frequency settings in the Photoshop image. Whenever they are placed in another application, these screen values supersede any settings requested by another application.

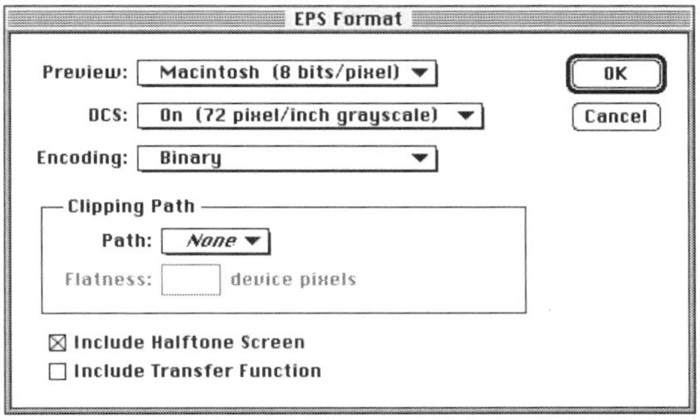

Fig. 22.16

Select the Include Halftone Screen check box in the EPS Format dialog box to embed screen angles and frequency settings in the Photoshop image.

Caution

Don't Save Files with Halftone Frequencies

Saving files with Halftone Frequency values should only be used when intentionally changing angles and frequencies from standard settings obtained in separating software. If you set the frequency to a default for a laser printer at 53 lpi, and save with the Halftone Frequency included in the document, it cannot be changed by another application. For example, if the file was placed in QuarkXpress where a 133 line screen is requested, all elements in the Quark document image at 133 lpi and the Photoshop image prints at the frequency setting that was included in the document. In this example, the frequency is 53 lpi. The only way to change the frequency is to open Photoshop and change the setting or save without the Include Halftone Screen box in the EPS dialog box. When the Include Halftone Screen is left deselected, any frequency within the capabilities of the separating software can be requested.

Understanding Dot Shapes

In addition to the frequencies, resolutions, and angles, you can alter the shape of the dot. The offset printer typically uses a round dot shape. Screen printers, on the other hand, often prefer elliptical dots. Photoshop provides an opportunity to select different shapes for dots in the Halftone Screen dialog box, shown in figure 22.17. Photoshop provides for selection of six different dot shapes. If a dot shape is needed beyond those available, there is a Custom setting in the pop-up menu for dot shapes.

VI

Publishing

Fig. 22.17

Select different dot shapes from the pop-up menu in the Halftone Screen dialog box.

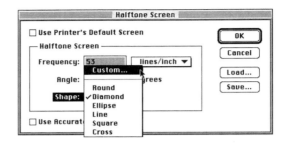

The Custom dot shape option is a window for entering PostScript code. Anyone experienced in PostScript programming can enter the code in this window to describe virtually any shape of dot. A sample of the description for a Triangle shape dot is noted in figure 22.18.

Fig. 22.18

Enter PostScript code to describe a triangle dot shape in the Custom Spot Function dialog box.

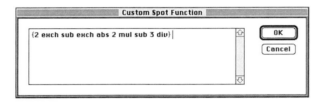

For the designer, it is not imperative to know PostScript programming. Descriptions of PostScript code for defining dot shapes can be found in books on PostScript programming. The user simply should key in the code in the Custom Spot Function dialog box and be certain to match the characters exactly. In addition, some service bureaus may have developed sets of custom dots for specific jobs.

Submitting an Order to a Service Bureau

After understanding the requirements for requesting output and having discussed the job with the printer, the service bureau order form should be filled out (see fig. 22.19). This is an important document in obtaining the correct material for the printer. It is important to fill out the order form accurately.

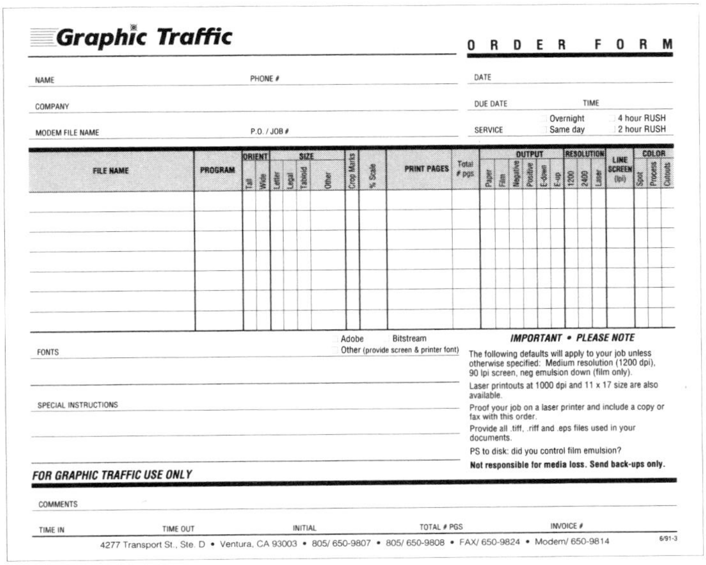
Graphic Traffic

ORDER FORM

NAME | PHONE # | DATE

COMPANY | DUE DATE | TIME

MODEM FILE NAME | P.O. / JOB # | SERVICE: Overnight / Same day / 4 hour RUSH / 2 hour RUSH

FILE NAME	PROGRAM	ORIENT: Tall	Wide	SIZE: Letter	Legal	Tabloid	Other	Crop Marks	% Scale	PRINT PAGES	Total # pgs	OUTPUT: Paper	Film	Negative	Positive	E-down	E-up	RESOLUTION: 1200	2400	Laser	LINE SCREEN (lpi)	COLOR: Spot	Process	Cutouts

FONTS — Adobe / Bitstream / Other (provide screen & printer font)

SPECIAL INSTRUCTIONS

IMPORTANT • PLEASE NOTE

The following defaults will apply to your job unless otherwise specified: Medium resolution (1200 dpi), 90 lpi screen, neg emulsion down (film only).

Laser printouts at 1000 dpi and 11 x 17 size are also available.

Proof your job on a laser printer and include a copy or fax with this order.

Provide all .tiff, .riff and .eps files used in your documents.

PS to disk: did you control film emulsion?

Not responsible for media loss. Send back-ups only.

FOR GRAPHIC TRAFFIC USE ONLY

COMMENTS

TIME IN | TIME OUT | INITIAL | TOTAL # PGS | INVOICE #

4277 Transport St., Ste. D • Ventura, CA 93003 • 805/ 650-9807 • 805/ 650-9808 • FAX/ 650-9824 • Modem/ 650-9814

6/91-3

Fig. 22.19

Fill out a service bureau order form completely and accurately.

Filling Out a Service Bureau Order Form

Unnecessary expenses can be avoided by filling out an order form completely and accurately. Imagine that an order is placed for color separations on a job. You expect to receive two pieces of tabloid film: Black and Pantone 144. The imaging specialist prints your job as separations and you get charged for Cyan, Magenta, Yellow, Black, Pantone 144, Pantone 144 CV, Red, and Blue. The service bureau wants to charge you for eight pieces of film; you want to pay for two. The service bureau's argument is you ordered a job to be separated and it provided film separations to you. And your argument is what? You expected them to guess which two of the eight separations you wanted? Unfortunately, it doesn't work that way. Someone is going to eat the extra film. If you are clear and accurate with your order, both you and the service bureau save money, time, and aggravation.

The following are some guidelines in placing orders with a service bureau:

▶ *Application File and Version:* Indicate in what program the imaged file was created and the version number. Example: Adobe Illustrator 5.5.

▶ *File Name:* Specify the *exact* name of the file to be imaged. Example: Brochure.PM5.

▶ *Page Size:* Indicate on what page size the document was set up. Example: Letter, Legal, Tabloid, 9 × 12, 13 × 22, and so on.

▶ *Page Number to Print:* If you have a PageMaker or QuarkXpress file and want pages 2, 5, and 9 to print, indicate the page numbers.

▶ *Total Plates To Be Received:* This is simply the quantity of material you expect to take away from the service bureau. If you want two pages printed with three colors on each page, the total is six.

▶ *Media Output:* Most often, this is film or RC paper.

▶ *Halftone Frequency:* What line screen do you want to have your file printed? If no screens exist, indicate N/A for not applicable.

▶ *Resolution:* What resolution do you want (1200, 2400, 3600, and so on)?

▶ *Emulsion:* E-Up or E-Down. This typically is the preference of your printer.

▶ *Positive or Negative:* Usually for film requests, this is another issue described by your printer. Offset printers usually want negative film. Silk screeners typically use positive film.

▶ *Fonts Used:* List all type fonts, including any used in images placed into the layout program. For example, if you use the Frutiger font in an Illustrator file and place the EPS into QuarkXpress, list that font in addition to all the fonts used in the layout application.

▶ *Type of Separation:* This can be composite, process separation, or spot separation.

▶ *Color Names:* List all colors to be printed for separations. Example: Black, Cyan, and Pantone 324 CVC. Be certain to provide the *exact* name of each color including upper- and lowercase in the spelling of the color names.

▶ *List All Linked Image Names:* Note any changes in link names that may have been renamed and indicate specific link names that should be ignored.

Following Successful Steps in Film Separations

If you consider yourself a design professional, you should maintain professional standards that help you obtain professional results. If you find yourself cutting corners and compromising your beliefs, it always comes back to haunt you. Usually, cutting corners results in extra costs.

There are six essential steps in producing good, four-color work. If your client is not willing to pay for all the steps and your fees, my advice is to walk away and go to the next job. If you cut corners and reprint material, you will find yourself losing money on the job and wishing you had turned it down.

Assuming you adhered to the advice presented earlier and followed the directions of your printer and service bureau, the following will give you good, cost-effective results:

▶ *Obtain the best quality input.* With images, this means high-scans for all your color work. Don't use flatbed scanners for color work or even mid-range CCD systems. Opt for the best and shop around for good prices on quality work.

▶ *Order a color proof of your final layout.* Find service bureaus that have desktop color proofers designed to come as close as possible to printed separations. Color printers that offer color which is brilliant, but distinctly different than separations printed on coated stock won't be useful to you, especially if you show the color print to your client. The client will be disappointed in the printed piece and so will you.

▶ *Print laser separations of your job.* If you have an extra color or a spot color that wasn't converted to process, it won't show up on the color proofer. Check your separations on a laser printer to be certain they are separating appropriately.

▶ *Order film separations according to the specifications of your printer.* If your printer requests trap, order the separations with trap. Always provide composed film and not paper, and use service bureaus that calibrate their instruments regularly.

▶ *Order a match print.* Many service bureaus have proofing systems and can provide a match print or Cromalin along with the composed film. If your service bureau or printer does not have a proofing system, then go to a third party and order one. If your printer has a two-color press,

VI

Publishing

order a color key so he or she is able to view the color combinations as they are laid down on the press.

▶ *Perform a press check.* All four-color work requires a press check. If it's 3:00 a.m. and the printer calls, rush down to the print shop. Don't let a press run happen unless you see the color that comes off the press.

Following these guidelines will save much time and money over the course of a year. Don't look at the individual costs of an item. Look at the whole job and calculate what the cost would be if something went wrong. Are you willing to pay for an extra set of film, redo all your scans after the first set of film and a match print, or pay for a second press run? Methodically following these guidelines keeps you in business as you watch the less fortunate disappear.

Where To Go from Here

▶ Review chapter 13, "Understanding Color." Predictable color results begin with calibrations. Follow the directions for calibrating as described in chapter 13.

▶ There are a number of different opinions regarding definitions of a desktop publisher and an electronic designer. Material covered in chapter 21, "Photoshop for the Desktop Publisher," will be helpful if you produce high-end work.

▶ Does your design work include presentations or multimedia? Chapter 23, "Photoshop for the Presenter," is a must for all designers interested in new and upcoming markets.

▶ If you create files or expect to create files output on film recorders or various color devices, as well as archiving all those intense drum scans, check out chapter 24, "Photoshop for the Professional Photographer."

▶ Design professionals will enjoy the material throughout Part VII, "Learning from the Pros," which includes chapters 26 through 30. These chapters are both inspiring and informative.

Photoshop for the Presenter

This chapter is designed to help the presenter, video designer, and animator prepare Photoshop files, and includes information on the following:

▶ Preparing Photoshop files for monitor presentations, slides, video, and animation packages

▶ Tips on color issues, memory size, and other issues relating to presentations, video, and animation

▶ Suggestions for using Photoshop's tools for special looks in presentations, video, and animation

Photoshop is widely used to create and prepare images for presentations, video, and animation. Even if you create your images in another program, such as an illustration or 3-D program, using some of the features in Photoshop can help provide images that look better, especially for video use.

by Elizabeth Brown Lawler

CHAPTER 23

Preparing for Monitor Display

Many computer professionals are accustomed to designing for print. Working in CMYK ink, scanning and outputting in the resolution demanded by pre-press imaging devices, using delicate lightweight typefaces, white space, and so on are all issues a good print designer knows. This is all different when you are designing for monitor presentations, video, or animation.

Size

For most monitors and for video, the standard size is 640 pixels wide by 480 pixels high, or 8.89 inches x 6.67 inches at 72 pixels (dots) per inch (dpi). Larger monitors vary and are up to 1152 x 870 pixels for 21-inch monitors.

Resolution

All monitors display information at 72 dpi. This is great for memory reasons—no more 100 MB files for one page! You can scan images in at 72 dpi unless you plan to enlarge them and then plan accordingly. For example, if you scan in a 4-inch x 3-inch portion of a photo and plan to enlarge it to full-screen, or about 200 percent, scan it in at 144 dpi. Some scanners allow you to keep the resolution at 72 dpi and scale the scan to 200 percent, thus saving you a step in Photoshop. If not, you can easily use Image Size in Photoshop to make the necessary change.

Color and Bit Depth

Monitors display color in red, green, and blue pixels (RGB). This also saves a little memory over images destined for print because CMYK images have four channels rather than three. It is important to know what color bit depth is supported by the monitor that will be used for presentations or animations. Usually it is best to design with 8-bit in mind, which is also better for speed and performance of interactive presentations or animation because the higher the bit depth, the bigger the image file. This does not apply to video, however, because after the file is transferred to video tape, the file size does not matter.

> **Note**
>
> *Bit depth* refers to how many colors are available on your monitor or video card. Eight bit is 256 colors, whereas 24 bit provides 16.7 million colors and usually requires that the monitor have a video card. You can use your monitor's control panel to find out your monitor's setting.

> **Tip**
>
> **Creating Images for Monitor Viewing**
>
> There are standards you should apply for most images destined for monitor viewing. Monitors show colors in RGB, or red, green, and blue. Monitor pixel resolution is 72 dpi, and most monitors are 640 x 480 pixels in size.

Specific issues related to presenters using slides, designers for video, and creators of animation are discussed in the following three sections.

Preparing Photoshop Images for Presentations

Several presentation packages are available for slide shows and monitor presentations. Many presenters use Photoshop for adding photos, special effects, and backgrounds to make presentations more interesting.

Most presentation packages accept PICT files for import into the program. For memory reasons, it is best to stick with 8-bit color depth unless a gradient looks too banded or dithered at less than 16 or 24 bit.

If the presentation is being shown on a monitor, the rules for size, resolution, and color in the preceding section apply.

VI

Publishing

Adding Interest to Presentations with Photoshop

Most presentation packages are designed with the corporate presenter in mind, with many automated template designs, backgrounds, and graphic effects. The illustration and graphics creation tools are usually pretty limited. Although you can certainly use the program's features to design a presentation, using Photoshop to add certain elements helps you avoid a cookie-cutter look.

Backgrounds

Often packages only offer two to three-color gradient backgrounds or a few stock textures for your images. Luckily with Photoshop, you can create interesting textures and gradients and even incorporate your logo into a background. Then save it as a PICT file and import into the background template of your presentation program.

For exciting gradient backgrounds, the best choice is Kai's Power Tools (KPT) Gradient Designer, which is described in Chapter 15, "Third-Party Plug-Ins." For textured looks, try Photoshop's Add Noise or Texture Fill to any image, KPT Texture Explorer, or Gallery Effects Texturizer. For interesting patterns, try Xaos Tools' Terrazzo. For stock image backgrounds and textures, try Xaos Tool's Artist's in Residence series Fresco™.

You also can make backgrounds out of photos. Using KPT Fade Contrast flattens and lightens the image so that dark text can be added on top. Photoshop's Emboss turns most of an image gray except at the edges. Experiment with all the filters, just make sure that you can read text on top of them if you use them as backgrounds. See figure 23.1 for examples of presentation backgrounds created in Photoshop. Also see the color section, "Photoshop in Color!" for examples of backgrounds.

Photos and Graphics

Graphics add interest in presentations. Add photos and graphic art whenever you can. When creating or manipulating an image in Photoshop, keep in mind the colors of the presentation and use complementary colors. Save the files without white space around them.

Fig. 23.1

With help from Photoshop, you can add exciting backgrounds to your presentation.

With Photoshop's tools, you can change a photo to match the look of your presentation. For example, if you are using dark blue, gray, and maroon, you can apply these colors to your image, or give a photo a painted look using these colors. Choose two of your presentation colors in the Photoshop toolbox and use Gallery Effects Chalk and Charcoal to paint an image using those colors. Use KPT Gradient Designer and choose the colors in your presentation; then apply a gradient procedurally to the image. Or create a texture in another layer and make it the colors of your presentation; then use the Layers palette apply mode: Color, to apply only the colors to your photo. You can also hand-tint grayscale images or create duotones. See figure 23.2 for examples of photos manipulated in Photoshop. Also see the color section, "Photoshop in Color!" for examples of the manipulated photos in color.

If you are importing an irregular-shaped graphic into your presentation, you will need to check what file formats the program accepts and how it deals with the rectangle around your graphic. Some can *key out* (make transparent) the white or color fill behind your image. Others might require an EPS file that has a clipping path. Refer to the program's documentation for details.

VI

Publishing

749

Fig. 23.2

Enhance photos
with Photoshop
for use in your
presentation.

Special Effects

Using Photoshop to create special looks for a logo or presentation title can really make a presentation sparkle. If your presentation has interactive buttons, you might want to create more interesting buttons in Photoshop than are available in the presentation program.

You can create softer, more realistic drop shadows in Photoshop than you can in the presentation program. Start with your background image and position the graphic or type where you want it. Then create a soft drop shadow as explained in chapter 15, "Using Photoshop's Plug-In Filters," or chapter 16, "Third-Party Plug-Ins." That way the drop shadow will blend into the appropriate background (you won't have a white box around it). Then you can cut out the picture and drop shadow to import into your presentation.

> **Note**
>
> If you are using a background from the presentation program, export it as a PICT file to use in Photoshop to make sure that the colors are the same around the drop shadow.

With your presentation title or section headlines, you might want to create special effects for type. See chapter 20, "Text Special Effects."

Figure 23.3 shows an example of a screen from an interactive presentation. The design used many Photoshop tools for the resulting look. Also see figure 23.3 in color section, "Photoshop in Color!"

Fig. 23.3

Effects available in Photoshop created this screen from an interactive presentation. (Also see color section.)

Using Monitors versus Slides

If you are creating images for a presentation that will be shown on or projected from a monitor, use the rules given earlier in the chapter about monitor color and bit depth, size, and resolution. If your presentation will be projected from an LCD panel or other projection system, check with your vendor for specifics on how it affects bit depth, resolution, and sizing.

For outputting to slides, the rules are different. When creating a presentation for output to slides, the files are sent through special imaging software to a film recorder that exposes the slide film. Then the slides are processed photographically. Often these film recorders are high in resolution, up to 8,000 lines-per-inch, so the 72-dpi rule for monitor display no longer applies. Depending on the film recorder, you can usually stick with images from 100 to 300 dpi, but double check with your slide service bureau for specifics.

Slides use a 3 x 2 size orientation. Because 640 x 480 is a 4 x 3 orientation, you need to adjust your image size in Photoshop accordingly. See figure 23.4 for an example. Overheads and handouts will also be different sizes. Make sure that you check the presentation software for default sizes for different types of output.

Screen size — Slide size —

Fig. 23.4

Slides are not the same size as screen presentations.

Also with slides, in some programs, transparent boxes or backgrounds image as black rather than white (because film is black). If you are used to printing, in which that non-filled space equals paper color, this might be a little different. It is best to designate all colors the way you want them. Some service bureaus also like to avoid imaging vertical orientation (3 x 4 ratio) slides.

Note

Don't forget that the higher the dots-per-inch resolution, the smaller the file is in inches. The number of pixels remains the same, but the amount of pixels fitting in one inch is different. For example, a 640 x 480 pixel file at 72 dpi is 8.89 x 6.67 inches; whereas at 144 dpi it is 4.45 x 3.34 (twice the pixels-per-inch equals half the number of inches). At 300 dpi, it is 2.13 x 1.6 inches.

Creating a Great Presentation

There are many things you can do to make your presentation more effective and more attractive to your audience. Following is a list of tips and design techniques to help you create a better presentation.

▶ Make sure that you are starting with the correct size.

Depending on whether you are creating for a monitor presentation or for slides, the size of your image may vary. Monitors use a 4 x 3 orientation, typically 640 x 480 pixels for a 13- or 14-inch monitor, up to 1152 x 870 for a 21-inch monitor. Slides use a 3 x 2 orientation. When you choose "slide" for your template in your presentation program, check what size it is (for example, Aldus Persuasion creates 10" x 6.67" default-size screens for slide output). Knowing this helps you not have to re-create or resize your Photoshop images later.

▶ Always double-check with vendors.

Get information before starting the work. Your service bureau or computer or monitor-projection vendor might have specific information that you need to know about how your images will look. For slides, get information about the resolution and possible file size limits of the service bureau's film recorder. If color matching is important, request color palette slides imaged on their film recorder.

▶ Use darker backgrounds and light type.

This is softer on the eyes of your audience because lighter colors project more light. Type stands out better and does not visually "bleed." Also, if using slides, dark backgrounds conceal any dust that may have gotten on the slide. Figure 23.5 shows the difference between light type on a dark background and dark type on a light background. Also see figure 23.5 in the color section, "Photoshop in Color!"

▶ Use sans serif typefaces when type is small.

Use interesting appropriate display typefaces for your headlines and titles, but when type is small, sans serif faces are more readable.

(continues)

VI

Publishing

753

Fig. 23.5

Dark backgrounds and light type are easier on the eyes. (Also see color section.)

▶ Be consistent with formats.

Especially when parts of a presentation are created by more than one person, double-check issues such as using bullets, boxes, or dashes for text callouts; initial caps on every word or just the first word in a sentence; and use of periods on bulleted lines. With Photoshop, you could even create more interesting bullets than the standards (add gradient boxes, spherize a small logo, or add a drop shadow).

▶ Use complementary colors.

To make your presentation look professional and modern, don't just drop in multicolor photos. Photoshop gives you the power to make them fit the look of your presentation program.

You could create duotones with the presentation's colors, or use other Photoshop tools to complement the look of the presentation.

▶ Use Photoshop to add special looks.

Don't forget to take advantage of the filters in Photoshop to apply special effects to your images. For example, for an old look, apply mezzotint variations on your images. Or turn all your photos into watercolors or oil painted looks. Use photos or icons as buttons for interactive presentations. With Photoshop enhancing the look of your presentation, be creative and break out of the standard, boring, typical presentation. You'll keep the interest of the audience much better.

Presentation Packages

Some popular presentation packages are Aldus Persuasion, Microsoft PowerPoint, Macromedia Action, or Gold Disk's Astound. Check out Appendix B, "Resources," to get more information.

Preparing Photoshop Images for Video

Tools for producing and manipulating video on the desktop are becoming better and faster, bringing the worlds of computer professionals and traditional videographers closer together. But there is a lot to learn, especially for people used to designing still images for printing.

Creating "broadcast quality" images on the computer can be difficult, but not impossible. Computers use high-quality monitors capable of millions of colors and high-resolution detail whereas video broadcast monitors must conform to a limited standard.

NTSC Standard

In the 1950s, the National Television Standards Committee (NTSC) developed a way for black-and-white televisions to display color, and a way for new color televisions to continue showing black-and-white images. While technology with computer monitors has advanced rapidly, this standard for video still exists and limits what NTSC monitors are capable of showing. Designers for video should be aware of the technical constraints imposed by NTSC to produce clean, quality graphics.

Interlaced Fields

Video monitors display an image in two sets of lines, or *fields*. They constantly alternate between showing the odd and even scan lines of an image. This method of alternating between two fields is called *interlacing*. The frames are redrawn at 30 full frames per second. Computer monitors, on the other hand, always display every line of an image (*non-interlaced*), and refresh, or redraw, the lines or frames of an image at a much higher rate, imperceptible to the human eye.

VI

Publishing

Color Issues

The colors in the image seen on a computer monitor may look vastly different on a video monitor. When the NTSC standard was created, issues like making flesh tone look good on screen were important and offset the balance of other colors. Also, rich color on a computer monitor may look washed-out on a video monitor because NTSC does not display highly-saturated color. Some bright colors will "bleed" out of their boundaries or into a neighboring color. This is commonly called *chroma creep* and can happen with colors such as bright red and green being next to each other. Bright 100 percent white can also create this problem.

Some colors are actually illegal and not displayable according to FCC regulations! This is because all the audio/visual information is contained in one signal. On a computer, you can separate color into red, green, and blue channels, and audio is entirely separated. Like the spectrum of light, only a certain range is viewable (the color spectrum), and other areas of the signal are reserved for audio and other things. Some saturations of color can mix into the audio portion of the signal. That is why, occasionally when a newscast displays a name across the bottom of the screen, you hear a buzz.

Size

Video monitors display images in a 4 x 3 ratio and can cut off as much as 20 percent of the edges of your image (see fig. 23.6). *Safe Titling Area* (STA) is the portion of the image that will not be cut off, and it is generally safe to include all the elements in the center 80 percent of the screen. Also, some television monitors may shift your image left or right, cutting off more on one side than the other. Test to be sure.

An understanding of these issues and others can help designers know what they are getting into when they design for video.

Creating Images for Video

Photoshop can be used to create images for placing in video or to enhance images captured from video. Some programs export *filmstrips* for editing several frames. Several Photoshop filters create interesting looks when played back in video. Some filters also have random applications—that is, they are applied differently to each frame and can create a great deal of motion.

Fig. 23.6

Images that fit in the computer monitor can be cut off on a video screen.

If you want to mask part of an image when it goes to a video editing system, you can create an alpha channel. Most video editors support this. An alpha channel is usually the fourth channel in an RGB image and is a grayscale image. Whatever is white will show on-screen, and whatever is black will not show. Gray will give the image levels of transparency, becoming more transparent as gray gets darker.

Designing Better Graphics for Video

TACTICS RECIPE

There are many issues to consider when creating graphics that are destined for video. The following tips will help you create better graphics for viewing on a video monitor.

▶ Use an NTSC TV monitor.

When you preview your computer-generated image on a video monitor the first time, you will see why having an NTSC monitor available for frequent viewing during the design process is important. Many changes in the way your image looks can occur when viewed on the video monitor.

(continues)

VI

Publishing

▶ Choose colors carefully.

As described earlier, NTSC is limited in the color saturation it can display. Photoshop provides the filter NTSC colors in the Video submenu to modify all the colors in your image to conform to this standard. Another color problem can happen when two incompatible colors are right next to each other, such as red and green. Make sure that you test on a video monitor to see how different color combinations are affected.

▶ Stay within the Safe Titling Area.

Make sure that your elements are contained in the center 80 percent of the screen.

▶ Avoid thin lines.

Because of field interlacing, a 1-point rule might be split across two scan lines of the monitor and because of the way nates between two fields, it can cause the line to "flicker"—appearing and disappearing very fast to look shaky. Make horizontal lines at least two pixels thick.

▶ Use anti-aliasing.

Sharp-edged graphics can also cause flicker because of where the edge may stop. Blurring or anti-aliasing the edges of your graphics helps alleviate that problem.

▶ Use heavier typefaces.

Traditional print designers are often fond of very lightweight fonts. This won't do on video because of the flicker.

▶ Avoid grids and patterns.

Creating grids or patterns with too much detail can cause a moiré pattern look on a video monitor. Black and white can look psychedelic because of the way video creates black or white from RGB dots.

Desktop Video Systems

A few Macintosh-based video editing and special effects programs are Adobe Premiere and CoSa AfterEffects. Systems that include specialized hardware are the ImMix VideoCube, Avid MediaSuite Pro, Media 100, and MoviePak. See Appendix B, "Resources," for more information.

Some video editing software uses Photoshop's plug-in architecture and can access Photoshop's filters. These include Premiere and CoSa After Effects. Try using the filters in these programs for exciting special effects!

Using Photoshop for Animation

Complex images used for animation are usually not created in the actual animation program, but in a drawing, painting, or 3-D programs. Photoshop is often used to create and enhance images or just convert them to the necessary PICT file format. Tools in animation programs are good for making simple polygons, type, or circles, but not for complex images.

Creating Pieces of an Animation

Photoshop is an excellent resource for creating backgrounds, logos, special type, and animated objects, or for enhancing drawn characters or diagrams. Using Photoshop's tools to change an image, and then saving the steps to the animation program, can create interesting animated effects.

You can apply filter effects repeatedly to an image to take an image from its original look to something wild. Or you can use a blurred, flat, low-contrast image for a background and "bring it to life" using Levels, Curves, and Sharpen functions. You can use Photoshop's Skew, Perspective, or Distort functions to change the look of an image. Figure 23.7 shows frames from an animation sequence that were created with effects in Photoshop.

Depending on how the animation and its pieces are used, there are special considerations.

Optimizing Speed and Performance

The speed and performance of an animation depends greatly on how fast the program can redraw each screen. Obviously, less complex images with smaller file sizes and fewer colors move the fastest. Some trade-offs always exist.

VI

Publishing

Fig. 23.7

Photoshop filters were used to create this animation sequence where the background transforms into folds and type rises into prominence. Then the whole scene "twirls" into a dissolve.

Memory Issues

The larger your animated objects, the slower they move, and the more memory (RAM) is required to run the animation. If outputting to video, there is little concern for this, but if many in your audience use Macintosh computers with 4 to 8 MB of RAM, this is a great concern. Every pixel in your image takes up memory, and images with 24-bit color depth use three times as much memory as 8-bit images. Sometimes you can bring in smaller files and enlarge them some in the animation program without increasing the file size (in Director, enlarging sprites as opposed to actual cast members). Check with your animation's program documentation for more tips on reducing memory requirements.

Image Use

If the image you are creating is used as a background, you can create it to fit the size of the screen. It can be larger in file size; it can possibly be 24-bit color if 8-bit doesn't look good.

For animated images, it is best to make them as small in file size as possible for faster movement. For objects smaller than an entire screen, this means cropping them as tightly as possible because in some animation programs, every additional pixel adds to memory use. If your object is not rectangular, you can make its background transparent. Figure 23.8 shows the same image created for use in an animation program, cropped and uncropped.

Tip

Using a Dark Background

If you are using Director to animate your files and your background screen is dark, it is best to use black or a darker color to fill in the background behind your irregularly shaped image, rather than white. If you use white and make white transparent, the anti-aliased edges will be light gray and will appear as light artifacts around your object. Instead, make the fill black or a dark color from the 8-bit 256-color palette, and make that color the background color in the tools window in Director to make it transparent.

Or, for even smaller file sizes, create the image on a dark background and use anti-aliasing to have the image blend at the edges. Then remove the outside fill color, while keeping the anti-aliased edge. Set your marquee to "0" and deselect anti-aliased to remove (fill with white) only the background before exporting it to your animation program. Don't forget to have the anti-aliased edge pixels dark, though. The white "background" will not be recorded into memory.

Fig. 23.8

Cropping images for animation helps improve speed and performance.

VI

Publishing

Also, screen redraw is faster when the number of moving objects is lower. Try to animate one object at a time. You can use certain tricks to make it appear that two objects are moving without actually setting them to move at the same time.

Color Depth

Animating 24-bit images is usually very slow. For anything other than video output, files should be converted to 8-bit color depth (or lower, for smaller file sizes) for better animation performance.

To convert files in Photoshop to 8-bit color depth, follow these steps:

1. Open the Mode menu and choose Indexed color.

2. Choose System palette and Diffusion Dither.

3. Try the other Dithering options to see which looks best for your image. For gradients, Diffusion dither blends the ramped colors more; no dither bands the colors.

4. For one-color objects, you can change them to 1-bit (black and white) and use the tools in the animation program to apply a color. Check your program's documentation to be sure.

Most images will look just as good at a lower bit depth, as shown in figure 23.9. Also see figure 23.9 in the color section, "Photoshop in Color!" In the color section, you can see that the only area that might be questionable in the 8-bit image is in the clouds. This is because there were more light blues and grays in this area of the image than was available in the 256 color (8-bit) palette that was used when the image was converted to Indexed color.

Fig. 23.9

Often images will look just as acceptable at a lower bit depth. (See color section also.)

24-bit   8-bit

Palettes

Managing palettes in your animation program can be a task. If the system palette doesn't work for your images, it is best to create a palette that includes all the colors you need. Then when you import the graphic, you get the option to import the palette as well. This takes up additional memory, however. To create a palette in Photoshop, you can take a 24-bit image with a wide range of colors and follow these steps:

1. Open the Mode menu and choose Indexed; then choose Adaptive palette and Diffusion dither, or whichever dither options work best for your image.

2. Click OK to create the Indexed color image, which creates the palette (color look-up table, or CLUT) at the same time.

3. Then go back into the Mode menu and choose Indexed, Custom.

4. The palette you just created will appear in the Color Table dialog box. Click Save to use your palette with other images.

Publishing the Animation

Determining where and how the animation will play affects how you create your images. Animations can be published and distributed on hard drives, CD-ROM, or floppy disks, or can be recorded to video. Each option has its own set of considerations that may affect your animation during the design process.

Hard Drive and CD-ROM

The advantages of creating animation or interactive presentations for hard drives or CD-ROM are obvious—large files can reside there. Hard disks are virtually limitless, and the available sizes of CD-ROM can hold up to 650 MB. Often hard drives are used for kiosks, whereas CD-ROM is used for games, large demos, and educational software.

Video Output

When creating for video, you don't need to be as concerned with the file size or speed of the animation. As a matter of fact, it is better to use 24- or 32-bit color for animations destined for video. See the tips for preparing for video in the preceding section.

VI

Publishing

Floppy Disk

With its limited size, obviously saving to floppy disk requires the most work with making images and animations small. Even if using a compression program, an animation program can quickly exceed the 1.4 MB limit. Every little bit helps—even going in and deleting unnecessary pixels at the edges of an object.

Designing for Better Animation

To prepare graphics in Photoshop for use in an animation, follow these tips.

Plan ahead. This may sound trite, but of course planning helps to prevent problems with having to recreate work at the last minute. Who is the audience for the animation? What platform will it be on? How will it be played?

Know where the animation will be played. What type of computer or monitor will be used? How much memory (RAM) will it have? Plan for the lowest common denominator—the slowest computer, the monitor with the lowest bit-depth, the lowest RAM available to your audience.

Know how the image will be used. If the image is a background image that stays in one place, it can be a larger file size. But for animated objects, you will be concerned with cropping the object and making its background transparent.

Check the animation program documentation. Look for tips on reducing memory requirements, managing palettes, and optimizing speed—each animation program is different. The methods suggested could affect how you create your Photoshop images.

Create anti-aliased objects in Photoshop. Even if your animation program has this option, it can run exceedingly slowly because it must create this look for every screen. When you create anti-aliased text and graphics in Photoshop, they can move more quickly because they don't require this calculation.

Avoid light-edged pixels on dark backgrounds. If you have an irregularly shaped object, you need to make its background rectangle transparent. Often Photoshop users new to animation create their object on a white background, and then choose white as transparent in the animation program. The problem is that the anti-aliased edge pixels are still being ramped to white; although white is transparent, these pixels are light gray and will show on a black background. You can avoid this in two ways. One is to make your images on a black background, crop them, and make black transparent. Another is to create on a black background, so that the edge pixels are dark and then delete only the 100 percent black (setting marquee to "0" and deselect anti-aliased). Fill only the black area with white and make white transparent, but your anti-aliased edge pixels will still be dark. Figure 23.10 shows anti-aliasing to a dark edge while deleting the background to white.

Use Photoshop tools. Take advantage of the effects Photoshop has to offer for your animation. For example, applying a filter several times and saving each image in steps can create some interesting looks in your animation. Depending on the program, you can also save textures and lighting effect looks in separate files and apply them in different ways in the animation. Also, in some programs you can animate gradients by cycling colors in the Color palette.

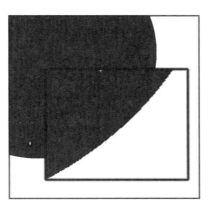

Fig. 23.10

Keep anti-aliased edge pixels dark while deleting the background.

VI

Publishing

Animation Programs

Some popular Macintosh animation programs are Macromedia Director and Macromedia Action. Many 3-D programs provide animation features, like Stratavision's Strata Studio Pro. Programs like Metaflo' and Morph can perform animated warping on an image or morph from one image to another.

Where To Go from Here

▶ Chapter 3, "Photoshop Basics," introduces you to other graphic formats, PICT, and color depth.

▶ Chapter 12, "Using Masks and Channels," helps you understand channels, alpha channels, and helps you work with the Channels palette and Channel palette pop-up menu.

▶ Chapter 17, "Creating Special Effects with Video," shows you how to create effects with video.

▶ Chapter 18, "Creating Special Effects with Channels," shows you how to create effects with channels.

▶ Chapter 19, "3-D Modeling Special Effects," gives you help creating and using 3-D effects.

▶ Chapter 20, "Text Special Effects," shows you how to apply effects to your text.

This chapter for professional photographers explores the changing role of photography today and examines the following:

▶ Understanding the changing role of the digital photographer

▶ Printing digital photographs

▶ Using digital tools for the professional photographer

▶ Archiving and cataloging digital photographs

▶ Creating digital portfolios

Photoshop for the Professional Photographer

As a professional photographer, you are among the fastest growing population of professionals entering the digital arena. Due to the way programs such as Photoshop can manipulate images, create different looks for an image, and totally alter an original, many photographers find themselves leaving the darkroom and using the desktop for photographic retouching. The commercial photographer who submits work to designers, editors, and art directors may find more requests for digital images than transparencies. To respond to the increasing demands for digital images, you need to understand the capabilities of digital systems.

Using Photoshop for Macintosh • Using Photoshop for Macintosh • Using Photoshop for Macinto

by Ted Padova

CHAPTER 24

If you jump on the digital bandwagon, you may be looking at a totally different approach to the type of work you perform. This chapter explores the changing role of the photographer, the many uses of digital photography, and the tools available to the electronic photographer.

Changing Roles

When you embrace digital methods, you must decide on the role you want to perform. Should you stay in the framework of using cameras and providing digital images to advertising studios and designers, or should you bridge the gap between photography and design? Should you perform digital photo retouching? Should you work with type and layouts? Because a digital photographer has a tool in the studio for creating designs, layouts, presentations, and media, should the new tools of the trade be used to venture into these areas?

In my work with photographers, I often see overlap and exploration into the design domain. As photographers become more familiar with the computer and applications software, they begin new experiences. On the other hand, there are many photographers looking over the shoulders of computer operators who can guide the photographers in such areas as color correction and digital photo retouching. Which role you decide to perform is a matter of individual preference; however, digital methods are here to stay. At the very least, you need to be educated in this area and must comprehend the various possibilities available in digital photography.

Working with Input Devices

If you perform your own digital retouching, you need to get what was exposed on film onto digital form. Digitizing images is performed on scanners. One question is whether to have a service bureau or photo lab perform the scans or to actually purchase a scanner. There are several types of scanners to choose from, if you decide to purchase a scanner. If you shoot transparency film, you need to look at transparency scanners. Similar to almost anything else in the electronic world, the more you pay, the better the performance. Here are some guidelines in shopping for scanners:

▶ **Run Scanning Tests.** Service bureaus and photo labs have many different types of scanners. You can look at the 35mm scanners such as Nikon, Leaf 35, Kodak, and so on. Try to find service centers that support these devices, and purchase scans from each device. Try to obtain several scans for the different film types and lighting situations you use, and for the different types of photography you perform (portrait, product, fashion, and so on).

▶ **Run Printing Tests.** If you are currently interested in obtaining color prints from digital devices, printing your test scans on different color printers may only satisfy your need today. If your work expands to color separations and offset printing, the tests performed may not be adequate. Try to perform tests on a complete range of devices for multiple purposes.

▶ **Attend Trade Shows.** Perhaps the best trade show in the industry is the Seybold Conference on Desktop Publishing. It takes place every year at the Moscone Center in San Francisco, usually in September. Admission to the exhibit floor is free. There are representatives from every major manufacturer of high-end equipment suited to the needs of professionals. Here, you can find the newest technologies available, and samples of output produced by many different devices.

▶ **Use Before You Buy.** Hardware devices are only half of what you get when you purchase a scanner or any other digital device. Computer-related hardware is like an automobile engine. You can have the best engine available, but if you don't have fuel you can't go anywhere. The same is true for computer systems. The fuel is the software; if it's not up to par with the hardware device, you can't go anywhere. If you're in the high-end market, you might be able to try out a system for a trial period. You can test the instrument and the software; if it's not what you expect, you can return it. You can find low-end devices in some service bureaus where you can rent time on a self-serve basis. Either way, try to log some time on a device you intend to purchase.

If purchasing a scanner is not cost-effective for you, you can buy scans from service centers. As discussed in chapter 23, "Photoshop for the Presenter," many service bureaus offer high-end scanning services. Or, you can look to the many photo labs acquiring digital devices. There are some advantages and some disadvantages to using one service or the other.

VI

Publishing

There are many advantages to using a service bureau. One is that its background is in prepress and film separations. Many have color printers for different types of composite printing, and they have been at it longer than almost any other type of digital service industry. Service bureaus usually have technically sophisticated people who can get files to print, understand application software, and work with computer systems. The downside is that service bureaus usually are not the most sophisticated in commercial photography, because they work with E-6 or C-41 processors or have photographic reproduction equipment.

As a photographer, you're in familiar territory with a photo lab. The photo lab can understand the photographer's needs, produce the material desired by the photographer, and process film as it is imaged to digital devices. This affords them the opportunity to regularly run tests and experiments and give feedback to their customers on film types, exposure settings, image resolutions, and so on. The downside of the photo lab is it may not have as technically astute computer people as the service bureau, it may have just begun working with digital equipment, and it may have purchased less sophisticated equipment.

These comparisons between a service bureau and a photo lab can vary from one community to another. Your area may have equally sophisticated establishments. The point is, you may work with one, the other, or both. Try to search out and use both types of service centers and draw your own conclusions on which will meet your needs.

Finding the Right Output Services

Similar to any other digital composition, you need some knowledge about the printing device in order to prepare images. Knowing what output device to use also dictates how the image may be scanned. If you purchase scanned images, it is essential to know what color mode and resolution is best suited to the output device.

Ideally, if you use the same service center for acquisition of the scan as well as output of the scan, the service center should be able to recommend file attributes best suited to their equipment. If, on the other hand, you like the scans from the photo lab and the output from the service bureau, you may have to perform your own tests. If you're fortunate enough to find a service bureau and photo lab that work well together, this can be an extra bonus. Simply ask the service bureau personnel's opinion about the photo lab's services and vice versa; this will tell you immediately how well they work together.

> **Tip**
>
> **Don't Get Caught in a Crossfire**
>
> You can find some fierce competition in the digital imaging industry. Some service centers may make claims about their services or the services of a competing center that are ludicrous and unfounded. Stay away from competing services that bash each other. Find shops that can work well together and have mutual respect for each other.
>
> If you have a deadline to meet and the equipment goes down at your bureau or lab, you may need a referral to another service to meet your deadline. Look to the local professional photographer's association and ask your colleagues where they find the best service.

When it comes to digital photographs that are prepared for printing presses, the service bureau most likely will fulfill your needs. In this regard, the services you use may be different than those you used for photographic prints. Don't assume that you can purchase scans for output to film recorders and use them for separations on imagesetters. There are distinct differences in equipment, and the requirements are not the same. In this scenario, the photo lab may be your source for purchasing scans for photographic prints, while the service bureau may be your source for scans going to film separations.

Digital Photography Printing

There are many avenues to explore with digital design tools and methods of working. As you become more familiar with working on digital devices, you may find yourself performing retouching services, providing digital photographs to your clients, or printing your images on digital equipment. Or, you may use a combination of both a digital and traditional process.

Become familiar with the various equipment available to help you decide how to deal with digital images and how they should be prepared for printing devices.

Using Film Recorders

Film recorders are printing devices that image on 35mm, 4×5, and 8×10 film. After it's processed, the film is the same as that exposed by your camera. All the traditional photographic processes are available in creating prints and enlargements. The advantage of outputting files to film recorders is the ability to perform photo retouching in Photoshop and print the edited image back to film. In many ways, you can create composite images much better than with traditional darkroom techniques.

The nature of film recorders is very different than other digital printing equipment. Film recorders are RGB devices and expose each of the Red, Green, and Blue colors on film. It's more important to know how the file must be prepared to achieve the best results than it is to know the technology of the device.

To obtain images scanned at service centers, the scan must be in the RGB mode. If the CMYK mode is used, the file can't print to the film recorder properly. With RGB, you have a much higher color gamut and can take advantage of the 24-bit color view on your screen. Because CMYK color is much narrower, many colors in this mode are lost. You can't convert from CMYK to RGB and expect to regain the colors. After the conversion from RGB to CMYK is made, colors not available to the CMYK gamut are lost. This presents a problem if you need to obtain photographic prints and color separations. There is some disparity in the view of the colors.

RGB output also requires setting your computer to a different gamma setting. In chapter 13, "Understanding Color," you will learn about using the Gamma Control Panel Device. Refer to the section "Calibrating" for further details on using the gamma settings. When you use the Gamma Control Panel to adjust gamma, use the highest 2.2 setting for RGB devices and video work. Notice the Gamma Adjustment in figure 24.1. This helps set up your calibrations between the output device and your screen view.

Film recorders use a different measuring system to determine resolution. Resolution is measured in lines—not dpi. Low-end film recorders are 2K and 4K (two thousand and four thousand lines of resolution). Medium-range film recorders are 2K, 4K, and 8K. High-end film recorders go to 16K. Most often, you find that service bureaus and photo labs use 8K film recorders. These film recorders are good for high-quality work and produce excellent results. If you need high resolutions, large imaging centers in metropolitan communities usually have 16K machines.

Machines with 4K usually don't meet the needs of the average photographer. These are fine for slide presentations with groups in a classroom setting, but don't produce resolutions high enough for good photographic enlargements.

Fig. 24.1

Gamma Control Panel set to 2.2.

Many film recorders are QuickDraw devices and not PostScript; therefore, the file format for Photoshop images is best produced from PICT files— TIFF or EPS. If photographic images are used in PostScript imaging programs like Adobe Illustrator or Aldus FreeHand, or if PostScript fonts are used, it may be wise to find service bureaus that have PostScript RIPS on their film recorders. Some service centers use software ripping with PostScript clones to image EPS files. Depending on the software, some files may or may not image. If you have difficulty printing EPS files, find a service with a true Adobe PostScript RIP. If PostScript programs are used, the Photoshop images should be saved in formats other than PICT.

Tip

Converting EPS to PICT

If illustrations from Adobe Illustrator are used with Photoshop images and the output goes to a QuickDraw device, composite the image in Adobe Photoshop.

Although Patterns and Tiles won't work, Photoshop 3 supports gradients and blends saved in EPS Illustrator 5 format. Open the Illustrator file in Photoshop to rasterize it at the desired resolution. Composite the Photoshop and Illustrator images while in Photoshop.

Sometimes saving the EPS file to a new file format corrupts the file. If this is a problem, duplicate the image using the Duplicate command in the Image menu and save the new document as a PICT file.

VI

Publishing

Another important consideration in dealing with film recorders is the physical image size. There are many different film recorders on the market, and each one requires a different image size to expose film in the entire printable area. The AGFA Fort film recorder, for example, requires 35mm film to be set up at 7.014 inches × 10.514 inches. This odd size is not standard in any slide presentation program or layout application. Before sending a job in for film recorder output, check with the service center on the recommended size that will image to the edges of the film.

Film types need to be discussed with services offering film recorder output. Some support a wider range than others. Typically, film recorder services provide output to Ektachrome and Vericolor III film. Many film recorders perform much better when exposing Ektachrome. If you find unsatisfactory results from Vericolor and need a negative for photographic enlargements, you may have to go to an inter-negative from the Ektachrome. At the very least, check with the services you use and ask which film types they can support and which film yields the best results.

Using Digital Printers

Photographic prints produced outside the darkroom and on digital color printers come in many varieties and sizes. If the end product is to be a photographic print, there are many devices from which to choose for producing astonishing results. If, on the other hand, the color proof is a composite for client approval and the images ultimately are color separated for offset press, you must be certain the device printing your file is designed to provide prepress proofs. There are many more color printers on the market than can be explained in this chapter, so only a few are explained in detail. Some investigation into the color printers used by your service centers is necessary, and it certainly would be wise to run some experiments on the machines.

Thermal Wax and Crayon Ink Printers

Thermal wax and crayon ink printers are low-end devices that are disappointing to those with a critical eye on color. These printers can be used for very rough comps where a design layout is created and some of the color ranges may be measured against the placement of graphics or text. Photographic images will not meet the standards of the professional photographer. There are some color printers, such as the Tektronix Phaser, that print on different stock types. These can be of interest to designers who want to see color prints on the stock that will be used for an offset press job.

Thermal wax printers are CMY or CMYK devices. The CMY printer creates a black from 100 percent of the CMY values. A ribbon in the printer applies the wax in three or four passes depending on the type of process it uses. Crayon ink type printers use a solid "crayon" type material which is applied with heat to the paper. In either case, the Photoshop image should be converted to CMYK before printing on these printers.

Dye Sublimation Color Printers

Dye sublimation (dye-sub) printers are continuous tone printers that produce excellent results from photographic images. There are many manufacturers of dye-sub printers; some perform better at producing good-looking color images, while others are marketed as desktop proofing systems. New low-end, dye-sub printers are priced under $1,500 while high-end printers are higher than $20,000. Depending on your needs, you might consider a continuous tone printer for use in the studio. If you perform proofing images regularly, some printers may be suitable for studio use in creating comps. When high-end proofing is needed, the service bureau or photo lab can be used. The distinction of printing a proof or looking at color as it comes off the printing press should always be considered. For film separations, many dye-sub printers fall short of predicting what printed images will look like on coated stock. The colors don't appear as brilliant when coming off press.

Perhaps one of the best color proofers around is the 3M Rainbow. This is a dye-sublimation color printer that brings the color print, the match print, and the press proof into very close resemblance. If film separations are to be ordered, a printer like the 3M Rainbow is an excellent indicator of what to expect from the print shop.

Similar to the dye sublimation process is Thermal Development and Transfer, which uses a photosensitive material exposed by laser diodes. A dye image forms with the aid of heat and transfers the dye to the finished print. This process is used in the Fujix Pictography 3000 printer developed by Fuji Photo Film Co. As a dye transfer process, it is mentioned here because it is more closely associated with dye-sublimation than any other process. The prints generated from the Pictography 3000 are astonishing;

VI

Publishing

they come as close to a photographic process as imaginable. For a final photographic print, this printer is one of the best on the market. If you want film separations at the end product, the color from this printer may be much more brilliant than prints coming off the press.

Dye-sub printers are also CMYK devices. The Pictography 3000 is a CMYK device which can create 16.7 million printable colors. Regardless of the printer used, all Photoshop images should be converted to CMYK before submitting a job for output. If a file eventually will be printed as a separation, some dye-sub printers will print a composite color print from a file printed as a separation. In this regard, the DCS format can be used to set up the file for printing. The advantage of printing a file as a separation is that trapping problems are more noticeable. The 3M rainbow printer is exceptionally good at showing trap problems when printed as a separation.

Ink Jet Color Printers

Ink jet color printers come in many varieties. The top of the line is the Iris color printer. Iris printers are excellent for a number of uses. The color falls between the Fuji and 3M Rainbow mentioned earlier. The Iris may not produce the best pre-press proofs because there is more brilliance to its look than the 3M Rainbow; however, it provides excellent quality output. Where the Fuji falls short, in image size limited to letter size pages, the Iris can image in 30×36 and larger formats. Also, the Iris can use a variety of material including special archival papers for fine art pieces, textured papers, and almost any paper used in offset press.

The Iris printer is also a CMYK device and all images should be converted to CMYK for output to this printer.

Oversized Color Printers

The technology of large-format color printers may be ink jet, plotter, electro-static, or other. Regardless of the technology, large-format color printers deserve a category of their own due to size capabilities. Printers in this category can image 35 inches to 42 inches wide and almost an indefinite length. Some are marketed at fixed lengths such as 108 inches or 112 inches or higher, but with files set on adjacent pages, they appear to be continuous and without limitation.

A rising star in this market is the LaserMaster DisplayMaker ink jet printer. This printer is capable of printing 35.5 inches wide by 110 inches long. It's an ink jet system with special dithering software to provide the appearance of continuous tone. The DisplayMaker can print on a polygloss material and translucent backlit material. The advantage of having access to this printer is that it provides photographic and design services for point-of-sale displays and convention banners. What's more, the lab that used to turn around Duratrans in a week can now output on backlit material in a matter of hours.

Oddly enough, printers like the DisplayMaker have the four CMYK inks to print the job, but the LaserMaster software prefers RGB files. During the ripping process, the software creates an RGB-CMYK conversion. Even grayscale images rip much faster when converted to RGB. Oversize printers have another consideration different from those mentioned earlier; image size is handled differently by these printers. Imagine that you want a 30-inch × 40-inch print of a Photoshop file. Obviously, creating a file that size presents a massive storage problem. Fortunately, these printers permit sizing at the printing step. Images can be sized up to 400 percent without loss of detail. Printing a Photoshop image at 30 inches × 40 inches from one 7.5 inches × 10 inches produces the same results as printing the file at a 1:1 ratio. The special dithering software of these devices ensures image quality when printing at amplified sizes.

Using Digital Tools

If you don't want to let go of your investment in Nikons and Hassleblads, shooting through traditional methods is still going to provide for excellent quality photography. Even if images need to be digitized, scanners provide good results. Digital cameras are continuing to develop and are providing solutions for many photographers who want to start with the digital process.

New cameras marketed today can offer professional photographers stunning results. As technology develops, you will see more photographers switching from traditional film to digital methods. Variety with film types, lighting, and shutter speeds are not yet available with digital devices. Although they are improving, the photographer may find times when the digital camera fills the need and other times when traditional photography is the best choice. It's important to realize that

VI

Publishing

developments in digital camera technology are growing at geometric rates. What may not be available today might be released in a few months. Film and camera manufacturers are pouring a lot of R&D dollars into research to bring products to market. If we go to a filmless society, many will be out of business if they don't venture into the digital arena. At the very least, the professional photographer must become aware of digital photography and explore some of the possibilities available.

Digital Camera Types

Digital cameras are modified from camera bodies and outfitted with a digital system and hard drive. Cameras like Kodak and Leaf use Nikon and Hassleblad bodies, respectively. The main body supports interchangeable lenses, and, for all practical purposes, works similar to the way photographers are used to shooting frames. When an exposure is made, rather than recording it on film, the image is dumped to a hard drive where it is stored. The mechanism is also outfitted with a SCSI connection so the image can be copied to the computer directly from the hard drive.

Until recently, the digital camera had two disadvantages. The first was the time it took to shoot each frame and record it on the hard drive. Some cameras took over four minutes to expose and save a 4M file. This made them unusable for portrait, action, or fashion work. The use of digital cameras was best reserved for still life and product shots. The second disadvantage was the quality of the image. Image resolution was too low for quality film separations.

Many of the previous limitations are continuing to be overcome by new developments in the technology of the digital camera. Eastman Kodak, for example, recently introduced a mega-pixel digital camera outfitted on a Nikon N90 body that is marketed as the world's highest resolution single-shot color device. The DCS 460 camera employs a full-frame CCD manager measuring 3060×2036 pixels. This resolution translates to a 7 inch $\times$ 11 inch image size over 266 dpi. Also, the camera overcame limitations of previous designs of time for exposures. After the DCS 460 is powered up, it takes 0.25 seconds for the first shot and 12 seconds to capture each subsequent shot. Storage also is extended to hard disk cards, or removable PCMCIA-ATA cards. These storage options enable photographers to shoot for extended periods by changing disks or cards. In addition, the high-power battery pack is good for 300 images per charge. Figure 24.2 shows the Kodak DCS 460 camera back on a Nikon N90 camera.

Fig. 24.2

The Kodak DCS 460 Digital Camera.

Digital Camera Uses

Until a number of manufacturers start producing high-quality digital cameras at competitive prices, the cost of these systems will remain extraordinarily high. The Kodak DCS 460 comes in at a suggested retail price of $27,995. With continued developments in digital cameras, the device you purchase today might be outdated next year. Fortunately, there is an alternative to purchasing a system. Many service bureaus and photo labs are renting digital cameras on a daily and weekly basis. Anyone first experimenting with digital cameras should consider renting a system for a day. When you measure the costs of shooting frames on a digital camera, or using film and purchasing drum scans, the former may be much more cost effective than the latter. Imagine the cost of 100 images scanned at $40 per image? For $4,000, you could rent a lot of time on a digital camera.

Digital cameras may not be suited yet for fine portrait or fashion photography. Traditional photographic methods may still be the best way to approach these areas. Areas like product catalogs, photojournalism, and still life images can be a cost-effective means of conducting photoshoots.

VI

Publishing

In addition to the DCS 460 mentioned earlier, Kodak also introduced the Associated Press NC 2000 digital camera specifically designed for photojournalism. Digital cameras are gaining acceptance for photojournalism and military use. During the Desert Storm campaign, for example, military photographers used digital cameras and transferred files over modems via satellite. Photographs were in a Pentagon briefing room within two hours of the shot. Photojournalists can accomplish the same task and have images on an editor's desk within hours of their shoots.

Archiving Digital Photographs

The photographer, more than any other digital imaging professional, needs to use sophisticated methods of archiving digital photographs. Drum scans acquired from the service bureau or photo lab can occupy between 20M and 80M of disk space. Storing images is well beyond the capacity of the computer's hard drive; storing images needs some serious planning and use of the right equipment. Regardless of the various models explained next, the only practical solution is storing images on CDs. Take a look at the hardware.

CD Hardware

CDs are written in two varieties: single session and multi-session. The single session is a one-write task of recording between 600M to 650M of data onto a CD. The one-write single session means any garden variety CD unit can read the information. If single session CDs are used, the CD reader can be purchased for as little as $99 through some mail order suppliers. If you use Bernoulli or SyQuest cartridges to store data, writing 600M of data to a CD pays for the CD unit and writing fees three to five times over the purchase of additional cartridges to support another 600M of storage space. In other words, you get a CD pressed, clear your cartridges, and you now have five to ten blank cartridges for use.

A single session CD reader can only read the first session of a CD; if a CD has been written to in a first session and another session is written on the same CD, only the first can be read. All subsequent sessions are not recognized by the reader. To read additional sessions, you need a multi-session CD reader.

Having multi-session CD readers means you can store images on a CD, add more sessions later, and continue doing so until the CD is full. It is important to know the services you use and the format of the CD writing before you purchase a CD unit. If you opt for a cheap solution and purchase a single session unit, you are stuck with writing CDs in single sessions. What's more, you may not be able to review any commercial CDs that were created in multi-session. Finally, you won't be able to take advantage of formats such as the Kodak Photo-CD technology.

Kodak Photo CDs

You've probably heard of the Kodak Photo-CD technology. This is a proprietary scheme developed by Eastman Kodak with an interesting philosophy behind it. The Kodak Photo CD is a process where you drop off your film (35mm to 4×5's) and instead of getting prints back, you get a CD with your images digitized. The cost of scanning the images is a fraction of the cost for high-end drum scans. Kodak Photo-CD scans can range from $1 to $5 per scan. Compare that to service bureau scans at $30 to $80 per scan, and you can see why many people choose to go this way.

Is there any difference in the quality of the images? The answer is yes. But assessing whether this technology works for you requires some testing and experimenting. Rather than discuss the technical process of the Kodak technology, look at the practical usage and differences between Photo CD and high-end scanning.

The first consideration is access. Kodak markets a complete system for creating CDs. This system costs between $100,000 and $150,000. Not every community has either photo labs or service bureaus that support the Photo-CD system. If it's not supported in your community, you may have to send your film to a servicer in a larger city where the Photo CD is offered. This creates a delay in turn-around. If you're constantly in a rush, you must weigh the costs and the time needed to use this process.

Next, quality is a consideration. Kodak created a system for fast turn-around to process hundreds of images in a short time frame. Your local service bureau may have a skilled technician working for an hour to get your transparency scanned. The Photo-CD operator may be processing many images during the same time frame. It's only obvious that one outperforms the other. It's like comparing the one-hour photo with the professional photo lab for processing film.

VI

Publishing

The question, then, is when does the Photo CD work and when do I need high-end scans? The only way to be certain is to run your own tests. When testing the performance of any equipment or process, you should stay away from demo files provided by manufacturers. You can obtain Photo CD demos, but these images are always the optimum photos designed to show off equipment. Your photography may be totally different than the samples provided on a Photo CD. To perform a critical test, send a roll of film with shots representative of the photography you do (indoor, outdoor, different lighting, product, action, and so on). When the CD comes back, output the files to the devices you use. If film separations are part of your work, output separations at your service bureau and obtain a match print from the separations. Pick a couple of images from your tests and have them drum scanned and perform the same output tests.

> **Tip**
>
> **Economizing Tests and Experiments**
>
> If you put four 4 inch × 5 inch images on an 8.5 inch × 11 inch page and use Photoshop's Include Halftone Frequency option, each image can be printed at different frequencies. Try saving files with 85 lpi, 100 lpi, 133 lpi, and 150 lpi. All four files when printed from QuarkXPress or Aldus PageMaker print at their respective frequencies on the same page. Each file needs to identify the frequency in the Screen dialog box and save it as EPS with the Halftone Frequency enabled. Although not suited for color printers, this procedure works well on film separations.

You may think these tests are costly and unnecessary, but imagine if you archived your photography on Photo CDs and the client wants everything redone because they're unwilling to settle for the quality of the images. Performing comparative tests guides you on when to use the Photo-CD process and when to use high-end scans.

High-End Scans

Archived high-end scans can be stored on CDs in either single or multi-session. If you use a service bureau or photo lab for acquiring high-end scans, the same service center may offer single and/or multi-session writing. You should always inquire about the type of CD-R (CD writer) the service has. If a single session writer stores an image on the CD, the CD cannot be used in additional writing sessions. Find out first if multi-session is supported.

If multi-session writing is available, you should also inquire about the writing standards of the software the service center uses. If they use the ISO-9660 standard, your naming conventions for file names have to be consistent with conventions used by DOS and PCs. These names are restricted to eight alphanumeric characters, a decimal point and a three-character extension. This means you can't use a Macintosh name of "my little scan" for the file name. When it comes back from the service center the name will appear as my_littl.esc. All the file names will appear rewritten to the point you may not be able to easily tell them apart.

The advantage of writing in the ISO-9660 standard is the CD can be read by both the Macintosh and PC. If you have clients using PCs, this can be a great advantage in supplying images without going through translations to DOS-formatted cartridges. Fortunately, Photoshop 3 has a preference setting to enable saving in Photoshop 2.5 formats. If your client uses Photoshop 2.5 on the PC, the files can be opened. If the file has been edited and Layers have been created, the Photoshop 2.5.1 format will read the document with the layers flattened. If you need to perform editing, stay away from layers and use channels when appropriate.

Document Archiving

Photoshop permits you to save files with a preview icon. This lets you see a mini view of the file to distinguish images when you forget the names. If there are several files similar in view, the mini icon hardly shows differences in appearance. Struggling through a 600M CD to find a specific image takes some valuable time and often proves very frustrating. The Kodak Photo-CD system provides a thumbnail view that can be scrolled and show images in a larger view than Photoshop's preview icon. When you use the Kodak system, this file is added or updated on the CD and makes file searches easy.

Ordering CDs from the service bureau or photo lab not supporting the Photo-CD system requires a little extra effort. Fortunately, there is a good cataloging program that works with Photoshop images and all high-end design applications. Aldus Fetch is superb in organizing the contents of CDs, hard drives, removable cartridges, and almost any storage medium.

Fetch provides an easy manner of creating thumbnail views and keyword references to all files on a CD.

When you order CD writing at service bureaus or photo labs in multiple sessions, try to leave 15 to 20M of free space on the CD. When the CD is full, catalog the files with Fetch. Fetch reads the CD and automatically creates thumbnails for each Photoshop image. You can add keywords and descriptions for each image on disk including any data for exposure settings, film used, lighting conditions, and so on. Remember that archive of negatives and transparencies you someday will get around to organizing? With CDs and Fetch, you'll find cataloging your photo archive to be a dream and you'll be more interested in getting the job done.

When the catalog is complete, you can take the file to the service center and have it written to the CD. Each time you read the CD, the catalog is available and you can quickly search by thumbnails in a scrollable window or perform a search on keywords. Figure 24.3 shows thumbnails of one Fetch catalog. To isolate images in logical categories, use the Find feature with a keyword to place thumbnails containing that word in view.

Fig. 24.3

The author's CD Fetch catalog.

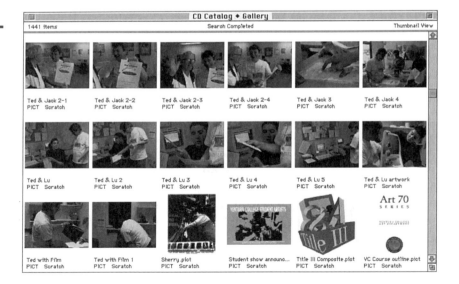

Another consideration when archiving images is protecting yourself against loss. Using CDs is a cost-effective means of storing images in digital form; thus, multiple CDs can be developed without degrading the quality. In the event of natural disaster or theft, losing all of your work from a single location can be devastating. When you store images on a CD, you can make duplicates to store in secondary locations. This is one of the most cost-effective means of insurance for a photographer.

Creating Digital Portfolios

In a world of Federal Express deliveries, faxes, telecommunications, and the Information Superhighway, you can have clients anywhere in the world. The book you are reading was written by a team of authors from all over the country, centralized in Indianapolis, Indiana, where manuscripts were delivered by overnight deliveries and via satellite to telecommunication services. In some cases, we had revisions at the editor's desk within hours of a phone call.

In today's world of high-tech communications, the photographer who embraces new technologies can take advantage of a world-wide marketplace. Of course, you may have to fly to locations for photoshoots (we haven't quite perfected the "beam me up Scotty" bit yet). Because your work is entirely visual, you may need to deliver portfolio samples of work to a prospective client. By providing a digital portfolio, your work can be viewed without the need for duplicating transparencies.

There are many applications to use for creating a presentation, many of which are discussed in chapter 23, "Photoshop for the Presenter." Depending on how sophisticated you want a presentation to be, you can choose from a number of presentation programs and multimedia applications. For a simple solution, you can download a file from America Online in the HSC Software library for Kai's Power Tools. Kai Krause developed a small application, 18K or so, called "KPT QuickShow" which previews PICT files on-screen. Figure 24.4 shows the Help screen of KPT Quickshow which provides keyboard strokes for viewing options.

To continuously view files one after another, you only need to place the application in a folder with PICT files and launch it. Anyone using it commercially should contact HSC software regarding restrictions; otherwise, it can be freely distributed.

VI

Publishing

785

Fig. 24.4

The keyboard commands for using KPT QuickShow.

For busy art directors, the easier your portfolio can be viewed, the better. An application showing your work should be launched and self-running, with no keyboard or mouse navigation. The person viewing your work may not be a sophisticated computer user and won't have the time to read a reference manual.

Tip

Using Viewers

Create a folder and copy all images saved as PICT files into the folder. Copy the QuickShow utility to the folder and place it at the top of the folder. Close the folder window so only the QuickShow application is visible. Rename the file **Double-Click Me.** When the disk is inserted, the application appears and the instructions are easily visible on-screen. Even a person with minimal computer skills should be able to launch the application. The rest is automatic.

Be certain to obtain permission to use an application and rename application files from the author. The QuickShow readme instructs the user not to disable the credit screen which appears after launch. No mention of renaming the file is included in the readme, but be certain to obtain permission for use. Figure 24.5 shows the application icon after it was renamed `Double-Click Me`.

One nice advantage of showing your portfolio in a digital setting is that the images only need to be 72 dpi to view them on-screen. Higher resolutions are unnecessary and a waste of space. When you create files for screen view, always use presentation applications that conform to monitor sizes. Test your viewer to make sure that the images can be viewed on 13-inch, 17-inch, 20-inch, or 21-inch monitors without losing any image area. Also, try to use viewers that blank out the background so that disturbances during your presentation are not visible. The KPT Quick-Show viewer, mentioned earlier, conforms to both of these needs.

Fig. 24.5

The application icon is displayed after QuickShow has been renamed Double-Click Me.

When you finish developing your presentation, have it pressed on a CD. Service centers charge about 25 cents per megabyte to write a CD, and the cost of the CD is between $12 and $15. So, for $30 to $40 you can send your portfolio to prospective clients and not worry about getting transparencies back undamaged. Don't have too many CDs made ahead of time because you may periodically change images. If you always keep an extra made, the client can see it the day after your telephone call via overnight delivery services.

Where To Go from Here

▶ Review chapter 13, "Understanding Color." Closely observe the differences between calibrating for RGB and CMYK devices.

▶ Material covered in chapter 22, "Photoshop for the Digital Designer," is helpful to photographers who work with graphic artists and designers and produce images intended for film separations.

▶ Does your photography work include presentations or multimedia? Chapter 23, "Photoshop for the Presenter," can help you understand the different design applications and file preparations used for these programs.

VI

Publishing

Automating Photoshop

In this chapter, you learn to use Publish and Subscribe, and how to:

- ▶ Share graphics with other documents
- ▶ Identify shared graphics
- ▶ Keep track of shared graphics
- ▶ Set preferences for the inclusion or exclusion of shared graphics
- ▶ Change and assign keyboard equivalents
- ▶ Process groups of graphics in Photoshop
- ▶ Record macros for automation of repetitive tasks

Though Photoshop is without question one of the most powerful programs for the Macintosh, it can become more so with the use of features from System 7, Photoshop plug-ins, and third-party software.

by Cyndie Klopfenstein

CHAPTER 25

In this section, you learn about the System 7 features, Publish and Subscribe. You will learn to use these features to keep graphics updated in your word processing or page layout documents. Publish and Subscribe are very much like cut, copy, and paste except that changes made to a published graphic are made to all of the documents where you place (subscribed to) the graphic.

For instance, when you place a graphic in a document, perhaps a QuarkXPress page layout, you usually want to have the most current version of the graphic. You can ensure that, regardless of the changes you make, they will always be included in the page layout by using Publish and Subscribe.

If you copy the graphic, paste the graphic, or import the graphic into a page layout program and then make changes to the original, the pasted (or imported) image is not affected. However, a graphic you create that is published updates changes in each of the documents to which it has subscribed.

Creating a Publisher from Photoshop

Publishing graphics from Photoshop is really very simple. Of course, you first must have a graphic to work with, which you can scan, open, or create from scratch. You must publish the entire item; you cannot publish a portion of a graphic you created.

Step-by-Step Publishing

If you want to publish a portion, select that portion, copy it, and paste it into a Photoshop document by itself. After you have the document open, follow these steps to publish the graphic:

1. From the Edit menu, choose Create Publisher. The Create Publisher dialog box appears.

2. Type a name for the item you are publishing.

3. Use the buttons to locate the folder where you want to store the item.

4. From the Format buttons below the name field, choose a format for the graphic. The options are PICT, EPS, and TIFF. See chapter 3, "Photoshop Basics," regarding image types if you need help deciding on a format.

5. Click the Publish button. This creates an *Edition* (a published item) in the location you chose.

The graphic, though it appears unchanged, is now a published item, or edition (see fig. 25.1). It can be subscribed to by any System 7 application that is System 7-Savvy. The term, *System 7-Savvy*, refers to an application that takes full advantage of the features of System 7.x. This includes System 7 Pro and System 7.5. Publish and Subscribe are a part of all System versions since 7.0, but not until recently have the majority of applications been fully savvy. You'll find that if you own the most recent version of your desktop publishing program or word processor, you now can subscribe to this graphic.

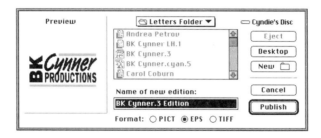

Fig. 25.1

Using the Create Publisher dialog box, you create a copy of the graphic to which you later will subscribe.

The Create Publisher dialog box can be referred to as the destination dialog box. It is requesting a destination and a name for the published item. This type of dialog box should be very familiar to those of you who are Macintosh veterans. A dialog box similar to this is used for Save, Open, Save As, and many other functions. The open folder icon and name of the folder appearing on the pop-up menu above the destination field shows the currently chosen location.

Storing Published Editions on Other Volumes

You may choose to store the edition on a *volume* (volume is a term for hard disks, floppy disks, and even other computers or servers to which you may connect) other than your internal hard disk. However, if the volume you

VI

Publishing

choose is not present when a document that has subscribed to the edition is opened, and you try to update the edition, a dialog box appears warning that the volume cannot be found or that the edition cannot be updated.

The PICT screen image still displays in the subscribing document, but the link between the edition and the document is temporarily shut down. You can update later by mounting the volume and using the Get Edition Now button, as described in the next paragraph.

System 7.5 is a bit smarter than its predecessors. If you store an edition on another computer or server on the network to which you are connected, System 7.5 attempts to reestablish the connection and ensure the current status of the edition. If the computer or server is not turned on, or is no longer a part of the network, you aren't notified until you choose Get Edition Now as described below. In earlier versions of System 7, you are warned that the volume is no longer available, but the system software made no attempt to log on to the computer or server.

If you store the edition on a floppy disk, a dialog box warns you that the volume is no longer available. Insert the disk and use the Get Edition Now button to update.

Recognizing Editions

After you publish an item, the icon representing the edition is surrounded by a gray outline. Look at the two icons in figure 25.2 and note that not only is there a gray outline around the icon on the right, but also that you are no longer afforded the preview of the file you see in the left icon (the original). The edition icon shows lines representing text and geometric shapes. This is the icon of an edition, regardless of the application used to create the edition.

Fig. 25.2

The icon on the left is a typical Photoshop icon. It is a thumbnail view of the contents of the file. The icon on the right is the published file, or edition.

the office edited

the office.5 Edition

> **Tip**
>
> **Quick Reports**
>
> To display information very quickly about an edition file, double-click the file. An information window appears with a brief description of the file. Click the Open Publisher button to travel to the publishing application (Photoshop).

Subscribing to Editions

Subscribing to an edition is the second half of Publish and Subscribe. It is the method for embedding editions into documents. It is also similar to the Paste function.

The most beneficial feature of Publish and Subscribe is that because they are System 7 features, they are available in all System 7-Savvy applications. This means that you can create a graphic in Photoshop and subscribe to it using a word processor or desktop publishing package. Photoshop, however, is a publish-only application; you cannot subscribe to graphics or text created in other programs from Photoshop.

As discussed earlier, Photoshop is unable to Subscribe to editions, so you must subscribe from some other application. Generally, you subscribe using a desktop publishing program such as QuarkXPress, or a word processing program such as Microsoft Word. The following steps are very general; your chosen application may have slightly different menu options or dialog boxes, but the concept is the same.

1. Save and close the document from which you created a publisher and launch the application for the document that will subscribe to the edition. For instance, save and close the Photoshop document and launch QuarkXPress. Open an existing QuarkXPress document or begin a new one.

> **Caution**
>
> **Save before Closing**
>
> It is possible to subscribe to a graphic that has not been saved or closed. However, if you subscribe and then close the document without saving, the link is broken and you are unable to edit the edition.

2. Choose the place where you want to place the subscribed item. (With QuarkXPress, draw a picture box; with Microsoft Word, place the cursor at the insertion point.)

3. From the Edit menu, choose Publishing, and from this pop-up menu choose Subscribe To. A new dialog box appears (see fig. 25.3). It looks very much like the Publish dialog box. A preview of editions to which you may subscribe is shown on the left of this dialog box.

Fig. 25.3

This is the subscriber dialog box from Microsoft Word 6.

4. Double-click the file name for the edition to which you want to subscribe. Any number of documents may subscribe to a published item. Notice that even in this dialog box, the edition is surrounded with the gray outline.

Tip

Photoshop's Graphical Text

Photoshop creates graphics files, even if they contain text. The text is not editable after it is placed, although published text from a word processor that was subscribed to is somewhat editable. You cannot make any changes that can be lost if the published edition is edited. You could make the entire edition bold, or change the size, and this would apply to an updated subscriber edition. Single or selected words with style changes are replaced with the formatting of the update.

Graphics published to a word processing subscriber can be scaled by the usual methods available to the subscriber, but not edited. This does not change the edition, so other applications or documents subscribing to that graphic may change the size also.

Changing the Options

Both Publish and Subscribe have a set of options to which they refer when creating or updating editions. You can change the options by choosing the item and then choosing Publisher or Subscriber Options from the Edit menu. With Photoshop, only the Publisher Options are available, but both are discussed in this section.

The Publisher Options Dialog Box

In Photoshop, after you publish an item, choose Publisher Options from the Edit menu. You cannot republish an item that was already published. For this reason, the Create Publisher option is dimmed in the Edit menu after the item is published. The Publisher Options dialog box appears, where you can choose from the following options (see fig. 25.4).

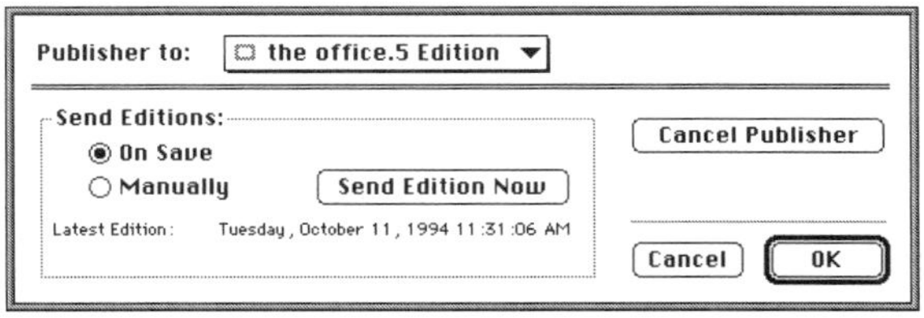

Fig. 25.4

The Publisher Options dialog box allows you to make changes, such as when to update.

▶ **Publisher To.** This pop-up menu shows the volume, or the nested folders in which you stored the published edition. Click this pop-up menu if you want to see the path or check which folder the edition is stored in.

▶ **Send Editions.** See the following descriptions:

On Save. Enable this option to update the edition for this graphic only when you save the document.

Manually. Subscribed editions are updated only when you click the Send Edition Now button.

▶ **Cancel Publisher.** This button stops future updates from occurring in Subscribing documents. This does not delete the edition file, so editions already embedded in documents using the Subscribe command aren't affected. However, those documents are no longer linked to the original published edition and changes made after this point do not update in subscribing documents.

VI

Publishing

795

Directly below the Send Editions options is the date and time that the published edition was last edited.

The Subscriber Options Dialog Box

Much like the Publisher Options, this dialog box allows you to view information pertinent to the currently selected Subscriber edition (see fig. 25.5). After selecting the item, choose Subscriber Options from the Edit menu.

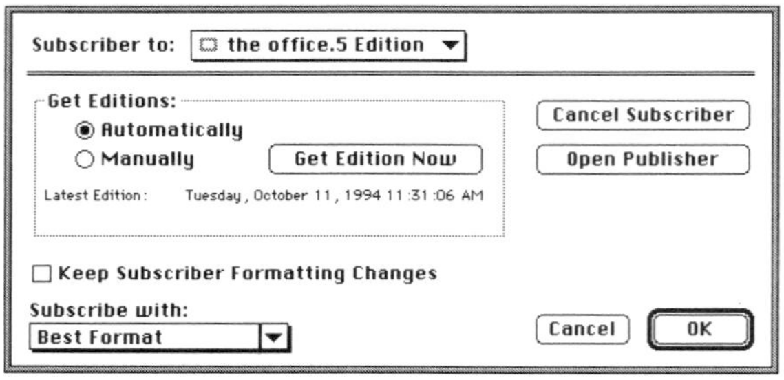

Fig. 25.5

The Microsoft Word 6 Subscriber Options dialog box is very similar to the Publisher Options.

The Subscriber pop-up menu at the top of the dialog box shows the volume or path of nested folders. Below that is the Get Editions area; here you can select whether you want editions to update Automatically (when they are saved in the original document) or Manually. Select Manually to allow no new changes unless you click the Get Edition Now button. The last update's date and time are displayed in the bottom of this boxed-in area.

Microsoft's dialog box may differ slightly from other dialog boxes of the same function in other applications. This dialog box can keep formatting changes, cancel the link, or travel directly to the Publisher. Click this button and you are transferred to Photoshop, assuming that was the publisher, of course.

Tip

Maintaining and Re-establishing a Link

When you subscribe to the item, the path name (where you placed the item) is embedded in the subscribing document. If you move the published item anywhere else on the same volume, Publish and Subscribe continue to maintain a link. If the edition is moved to another volume, then the link is broken and it's impossible to re-link to the same edition. Though the item remains in your document, it no longer updates as a Publish and Subscribe item would. It's easy to see when this happens; the Latest Edition line in the Options dialog box is dimmed.

To re-establish a broken link, open the original publishing document and select the graphic. Choose Create Publisher, use the exact name, and place it in the same place as the current edition. Click Yes to replace the existing file.

Talking to the Publisher

The Open Publisher button launches the application (Photoshop) and opens the file containing the original edition. You can edit the edition and then save it. Your subscribing document either updates automatically or, if you choose Manually in the Options dialog box, it only updates when you click the Get Edition Now button.

It is possible to edit the original graphics file and update the currently open subscriber without affecting other subscribing documents. To do this, use the following steps:

1. Select the subscribing item and choose Subscriber Options.

2. Click the Automatically button to update the edition automatically.

3. Click the Open Publisher button.

4. When Photoshop launches and the publishing document opens, choose Publisher Options from the Edit menu and click the Manual button.

5. Edit the graphic.

VI

Publishing

6. Again, open the Edit menu and choose Publisher Options.

7. Click the Send Edition Now button.

8. Close the original document without saving the changes.

The Subscribing edition file now is updated without affecting other subscribing documents.

The edition file cannot be edited directly. You must return to the original file where the published item was created. It's generally a good idea to save all the original files because this is the only way to edit. Deleting the original prevents you from making changes to the edition.

Learning where and when to use Publish and Subscribe may very well be the toughest feature. It's usually simpler just to use the import option of your page layout software. However, if you work on preliminary layouts or designs, you probably know first-hand how often a client can make changes to color, shape, and so on. Think how much easier the entire proofing and editing process could go if you didn't need to re-import, or copy and paste graphics with each edit cycle. Why do all that work? Let your Macintosh automate the mundane.

Earlier in this chapter, the shortcuts of Publish and Subscribe were discussed. This internal import/export automation can make updating graphics simple and seamless. But automation isn't limited to internal resources; you have the unlimited options of third-party vendors. These outside suppliers give you the opportunity to customize the type of automation you want, as with QuicKeys, or they may allow you to batch process a folder of graphics files, as with PhotoMatic.

The following sections take you on a brief tour through these two applications and give you some step-by-step instructions for making changes to the way Photoshop behaves, looks, and interacts.

Each of these applications are very complex and require much more room to detail their operations than can be afforded here. What you should come away with is a basic understanding of how the application works with Photoshop. Refer to the documentation that comes with the program if you need further assistance.

QuicKeys

QuicKeys is probably the most common macro utility on the market. A *macro* is a string of functions—such as changing font, size, and leading—that are stored and played back by a single keystroke or combination of keystrokes. QuicKeys is a standard in the industry and works quite well with all versions of the Macintosh operating system. QuicKeys allows you to record or write macros for not only Photoshop, but all programs on your Macintosh. Sometimes, you can store a macro that performs the same function in all or several applications. This is similar to the ⌘-S keystroke that invokes the Save command in most Macintosh applications. Other times, a macro is exclusive to that particular program, such as the Duotone command in Photoshop.

Keep in mind that QuicKeys ships with some equivalents already assigned. Some of these may conflict with keyboard equivalents in your program. Simply use the Sequence Editor to change the QuicKeys defaults to an equivalent you don't use.

In the next sections, you record and write macros for functions of Photoshop and, after you learn these skills, you apply them to other options with a small amount of creativeness.

Recording Macros

The Shortcuts of QuicKeys are actually keyboard equivalents for processes you normally find in a menu or series of menus in Photoshop (or other applications). You can record and edit a shortcut. Follow the steps below to record the macro and then continue on to learn how to edit a recorded macro.

1. Launch Photoshop.

2. Open a document so that you can access the menus of Photoshop.

> **Caution**
>
> If you want to record the sequence of opening a specific graphic, do not open the graphic before you choose QuicKeys from the Apple menu.

3. If you are applying the shortcut to a selected area, then select a portion of the graphic with a selection tool. If you are applying the shortcut to the entire document, Select All (⌘-A).

VI

Publishing

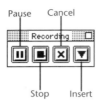

Fig. 25.6

The floating Record-
ing palette allows
you to stop the
recording without
making you use
the Apple menu.

Fig. 25.7

The Sequence
dialog box is where
you assign a name
and keystroke to
the macro you are
storing.

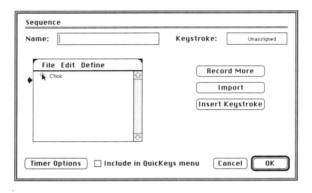

4. Choose QuicKeys from the Apple menu. A pop-up menu appears.

5. Choose Record Sequence. The Apple menu icon changes to a flashing microphone icon (it continues to flash until you stop the recording session), and the QuicKeys Recording palette appears (see fig. 25.6).

6. Perform the function or functions for which you want to assign a keystroke (or series of keystrokes).

7. Click the Stop button in the Recording palette. The recording stops and the Sequence dialog box appears (see fig. 25.7).

8. Type a name for the macro in the Name field.

9. Type the keyboard equivalent in the Keystroke field.

10. Click OK to dismiss the dialog box and accept the assigned name and keystroke.

The QuicKeys dialog box appears, as shown in figure 25.8, and displays a list of all stored macros and their keyboard equivalents. The QuicKeys menus are listed at the top of this dialog box. Click OK to dismiss this dialog box.

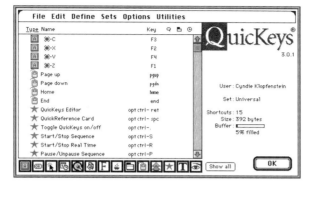

Fig. 25.8

This is the master QuicKeys dialog box. All stored macros and their keyboard equivalents can be viewed in the scrollable list.

Your keystroke or combination of keystrokes is now ready to use. This saved keystroke system is the macro. Apply the macro by selecting a portion of the graphic or selecting all and pressing the keystroke. The function that you stored is played or performed on the newly selected area.

Editing Macros

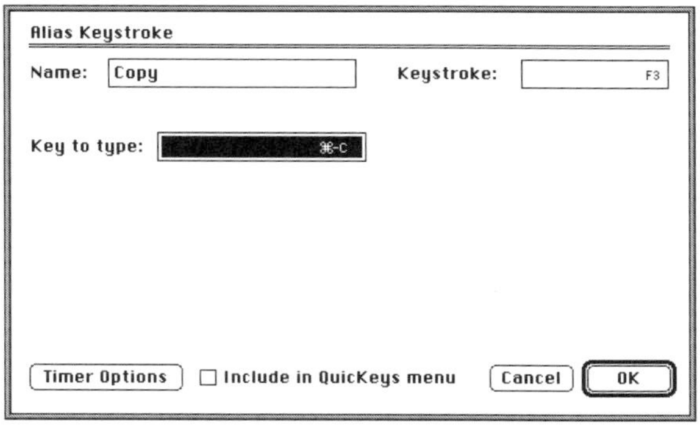

Fig. 25.9

The QuicKeys assignment for Copy is being edited.

To edit a sequence, you need to return to the QuicKeys dialog box. Open the Apple menu, select QuicKeys, and follow these steps:

1. Double-click the name of the macro you want to edit in the scrollable list. The Sequence dialog box appears. Depending on the type of macro you selected, the dialog box may look like the one in figure 25.9.

VI

Publishing

2. Click in the field you want to edit. Choose the Name field and type a new name if you want to change the name of the macro. Click the keystroke field if you want to assign a new keystroke (such as F3) and press the F3 key or keypad choice. Click the Key to Type field and press a new combination of keys to edit the keyboard combination.

3. Click OK. You return to the QuicKeys dialog box.

4. Click OK. You exit QuicKeys and the new combination or keystroke is ready to implement.

As was pointed out earlier, QuicKeys has a lot of power and, therefore, requires much more explanation than is possible here. Recording QuicKeys is the easiest way to use the application, but editing can go far beyond just a simple name or keystroke change. You also can alter the order in which functions are applied, delete portions of a macro, or, of course, delete the entire macro. Use this introduction as just that—an intro. Use the documentation that comes with QuicKeys for an in-depth look at ways to automate your programs.

PhotoMatic

The term *script* is very similar to the definition of a macro. PhotoMatic is said to perform tasks by following a script that you record. (Already this sounds like macros, and it is.) The primary difference between a script and a macro might be in the complexity. While the macros discussed in the previous section on QuicKeys were primarily a recording of trips made to the menus, scripts in PhotoMatic can include options that are not a part of the menus.

AppleScript is a scripting language that is included with System 7 Pro and System 7.5. The application, ScriptEditor, is the name of the program you use to write or record an AppleScript. Applications for which you can write or record an AppleScript are said to be *scriptable*, and while Photoshop is not scriptable, PhotoMatic is. PhotoMatic's scripting language can be augmented by AppleScript. This gives you the capability to write scripts that include functions that are outside PhotoMatic but within other applications that are scriptable.

This may all sound very intimidating, but you don't have to be a programmer, or even a good scripter, to record scripts in PhotoMatic. As soon as you install PhotoMatic on your computer, a new menu is added to the Photoshop menu bar. This Record menu has only four options: Start, Stop, Script Functions, and Play. That certainly seems simpler than all the previous programming jargon.

In the next sections, you learn how to Record and Play PhotoMatic scripts in Photoshop. We do not cover PhotoMatic to the extent of adding to its capabilities with AppleScript, but the System 7 Pro and System 7.5 discs both come with extensive Read Me files for AppleScript. Refer to these documents if you want to learn more about AppleScript. This next section provides an introduction to PhotoMatic.

Recording Scripts

Recording a PhotoMatic Script is very simple—as simple as it is for QuicKeys. When PhotoMatic is installed, a new menu appears to the right of the Window menu in Photoshop. Scripts do best when you use the keyboard rather than the mouse. Instead of double-clicking a field to select its contents, press the Tab key to highlight the field and then type the value. Rather than click OK, press the Return or Enter key. Keeping this in mind, follow these steps to record a script:

1. Open the graphic in Photoshop that is similar to the other images to which you are applying the script.

2. Choose Start from the Record menu. Record changes to Recording to indicate that you are in the midst of recording a script.

3. Perform the steps that you want the script to repeat. These don't need to be limited to menu operations, but they may include selections, drawing paths, changing modes, and so on. The time that you spend performing these tasks is not embedded in the script. The script performs the tasks at its own speed.

4. Choose Stop from the Record menu. The Save dialog box appears.

5. Type the name for the script in the Save Script As field, and choose a destination using the buttons to the right of the dialog box.

6. Click Save.

The Script is now recorded and ready to use on other graphics files.

VI

Publishing

Playing Scripts

After a script is recorded, it is ready to be applied to a new graphic. Make sure that you record the script while a graphic file that is similar to those on which you will play the script is open. For instance, if you want to apply the script to high-resolution files, be sure to record on a high-resolution file, otherwise you may achieve rather unexpected results when you play the script. The following steps explain how to play back a script:

1. Open a graphic file similar to the one you used when recording the script.

2. Choose Play from the Record menu. The Play Selection dialog box appears.

3. Double-click the file name for the script you want to play. The script is applied to the document.

If the script gives you the desired results, don't forget to save the graphic. After you finish saving, you're ready to open the next file and apply your script.

Script Functions

The final menu option of the Record menu is Script Functions. This area allows you to further control the way the recorded script behaves. The Script Functions pop-up menu provides the following four options:

▶ **Hide Photoshop.** This allows you to hide Photoshop and all its open windows while the script is being played. As with all applications, open windows require memory. Everything operates slower when the memory is being used elsewhere. Hiding Photoshop and its windows allows the script to run faster.

▶ **Show Photoshop.** Choose this option to redisplay all of the Photoshop windows that you have open. This also lets you view the progress that PhotoMatic is having on your script that is currently being played.

▶ **Work in Background.** Similar to Hide Photoshop, this command allows you to work in the foreground while PhotoMatic is playing a script in the background.

▶ **Work in Foreground.** This is the option for instructing PhotoMatic and Photoshop to work in the foreground.

Each of these four options are primarily for speeding up the process of playing scripts; there are other options that optimize script playing. Features such as drag-and-drop play and playing PhotoMatic locally are quick ways for implementing scripts. These features are explained more fully in the documentation for PhotoMatic where you also find other information on recording, editing, and playing your scripts.

If you didn't get enough of scripting, be sure to try out the AppleScripting features that also come with PhotoMatic. It's the only way to edit a script, and you learn a bit about ScriptEditor in the process.

Where To Go from Here

▶ Chapter 4, "Setting Up the Photoshop Environment," walks you through the defaults and how they can be changed before you begin editing them here.

▶ Chapter 5, "Importing and Exporting Images," helps you get other graphics into Photoshop to become a part of your published graphic.

▶ Chapter 6, "Scanning Images," helps you work with a scanned image or images in the batch processing of PhotoMatic.

▶ Chapter 8, "Drawing, Painting, and Editing," familiarizes you with the Photoshop tools that you will likely script using PhotoMatic.

▶ Chapter 15, "Using Photoshop's Plug-In Filters," is a primer to the plug-in functionality that you use when installing the PhotoMatic plug-in.

VI

Publishing

PART

VII

Learning from the Pros

Scanning Objects: Instant Art from Real Life

Denny Knittig, Knittig Design, Inc., Minneapolis, Minnesota

Denny Knittig started his career in art as a math major. That may not make immediate sense, but like many designers, he found his way to art in a round-about way. He was always good at math and it just seemed natural to pursue that interest as a career. That is, it seemed natural until he took his first course in calculus, which "seemed like a totally foreign language." Then, influenced by his artistic future mother-in-law and brother-in-law, he quickly calculated that a switch in career tracks was in order. At Iowa State University in Ames, Iowa, he flourished

by Rick Wallace

CHAPTER 26

as a commercial art major. Given the nature of his current food-oriented design practice, it's important to note that he has a Bachelor of Science degree in the applied arts program. At the Ames campus in the mid-60s, commercial art was a part of the home economics college. See? It all adds up.

Out of college, in 1968, Denny snagged a job as an artist with a custom publisher of magazines, newsletters, and cookbooks in Minneapolis. A project to produce a cookbook for a food processor manufacturer led him to join a local design firm which specialized in the food marketing area.

It wasn't long before he experienced the same epiphany as many designers before him. You know, the one

that goes something like, "If I'm going to work this hard, I might as well do it for myself." So he did, in 1978, and the result has been Knittig Design and a range of work for such food company giants as General Mills, Pillsbury, Land O'Lakes, and Borden.

Q You produce the *Fast and Healthy* magazine for Pillsbury?

Yes, we are responsible for the design, photography, and production of the magazine, and we deliver the publication in digital form to the printer.

Fig. 26.1

A two page spread, including the article title treatment produced by scanning a real maple leaf (also see color section).

Q I'm looking at this "Make Mine Maple" article. How did you create the title, with the leaf (see figs. 26.1 and 26.2)?

I guess you could say that you don't have to be an illustrator to create interesting art. We produce a lot of our art by scanning in a real object of some kind.

One of our team members, graphic designer Lori Korte, was working on this layout and picked some leaves off a tree behind our office. She was researching foliage for layout ideas. From there, it was a small leap to the idea of scanning in a maple leaf to use in the title.

Of course, this was the March/April issue, so the maple leaf was a golden color when we did the layout. We are usually working about six months out on an edition. Lori scanned the leaf and then used Photoshop to change the gold to a nice clean green that would snap nicely with the purple color of the title type and the texture of the wood table surface. The veins were already dark green, since the leaf hadn't fully changed color yet. We then traced a line around the leaf to highlight it, designating the outline as a clipping path.

I guess you could say that you don't have to be an illustrator to create interesting art.

We often set type in Illustrator and then add effects from Photoshop, or vice versa. Postscript object-oriented drawing programs have stronger type manipulation tools, I think. So, the leaf was saved as an EPS file, which we then imported into Illustrator. Inside Illustrator, for the type we used Tekton Bold for the top line, with an oblique effect applied. The word "Maple" is Goudy Extra Bold. All the type was converted to outline and then we roughed up the outline of "Maple" to give it a more rustic effect, and duped it to apply a white highlight.

Fig. 26.2

A close up of the title, showing the maple leaf scan as it was manipulated in Photoshop (see the color section also).

We used the leaf as a thematic art element in several other places in the multi-page article.

I wanted a heart to go with the subject of the article… So I drew one, simple as that.

Q How did you create the stylized heart you've used in this "good for your heart" layout (see fig. 26.3)? It doesn't look like the usual clip art thing.

Sometimes it is best to just be straightforward when you are working to get a job out on time. In this case, I wanted a heart to go with the subject of the article, which has a "heart-healthy" orientation. So I drew one, simple as that.

Fig. 26.3

A heart image, a piece of line art created by hand and scanned (see color section also).

There are lots of clip art hearts, the typical valentine-looking thing, but we wanted something nontraditional. That's why we went for the heavy texture, and why we left the

tail on. As with the leaf in the maple recipe article, the heart was used in several other locations in the layout, as a piece of imagery to pull the whole piece together.

I used a grease pencil on a heavily textured paper to get this look. First, I lightly outlined the shape with a pencil, then rubbed the grease pencil across the outline diagonally to get a consistent grain for the texture.

The paper was really nubbly, but I further enhanced the resulting textured effect by adjusting the contrast of the scan in Photoshop. I used very high contrast, which dropped out any lighter areas in the sketch, as well as the pencil outline.

The image was saved in a bit-mapped form because that allowed us to assign a color to the image in page layout. We primarily use QuarkXPress, but the same would be true in PageMaker.

Q Tell us about the paper effect in the *Fast and Healthy Editorial Profile* (see fig. 26.4). Judging from what you did with the leaf and the heart, you must

have just ripped up some paper and scanned it, right?

That's exactly what we did, but it was just a bit more complicated than that. For example, we knew our copy-fitting requirements, so we ripped up individual pieces of paper for each of these unusual copy boxes. The design effect was to subtly reinforce the idea that the comments were quotes that had been torn from letters.

We scanned each piece of paper, putting a black piece of paper behind each one to get a crisp, high contrast image of the torn edge from this light-colored paper.

What you may not have noticed is the other paper scan we used for this piece. The entire light background is a scan of the same paper we used for the quotes, with the colored threads in it. However, the two paper treatments were color adjusted in Photoshop. The paper was actually a dark buff color. For the quotes, we adjusted the buff to a light blue. We tuned the background image to bring out the colored threads embedded in the paper and to make sure it was light enough so that it wouldn't interfere with the readability of the type.

We made a number of trial runs until we got the colors just right.

Fig. 26.4

Scanned in paper, for quotes and for the subtle background (also see color section).

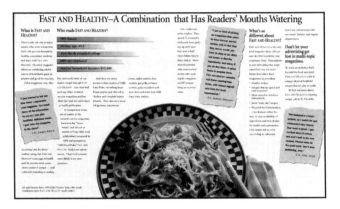

We scanned each piece of paper, putting a black piece of paper behind each one to get a crisp, high contrast image of the torn edge...

Q When you say you made a number of runs, do you mean proofing?

Yes, we have a color printer in the shop. I don't know how I would get along without it. No matter how experienced you are, there's always some uncertainty about the natural difference between what you see on your computer screen and what you get when the press applies ink to paper. No proofing can completely solve that, but with our Tektronix wax transfer printer we are able to make extremely educated guesses about colors. Because we've seen so many press runs, we have all developed an eye for what the press run will actually look like, compared to our proof.

That educated guess business is why I feel so strongly about letting prepress professionals do their specialty work.

That educated guess business is why I feel so strongly about letting prepress professionals do their specialty work. We're designers, not color separators. I always feel that when I start playing with photography, then I'm starting to become a separator. I don't know all there is to know about what it takes to get a good photograph on the press and I don't want to know. The same goes for trapping. The experts know what they are doing, so let them have the responsibility.

For this kind of high level slick magazine work, we do very little of the photographic scanning ourselves, at least for live art in the magazine. We scan the photographs, and get pretty good results, but they are FPOs, strictly for position only. The prepress shop inserts the high-end scans when the files arrive for production.

Deconstructing Reality: Photo Manipulation

Randy Sizemore, The Newsletter Factory, Atlanta, Georgia

"I've always been interested in any kind of design," Randy says, concerning his chosen career.

Since grade school, Randy dreamed of designing airplanes, and planned to specialize in aeronautics. But, according to Randy, by the time he got to high school, he "learned how much I hated math." Fortunately, about that time, his high school drafting

by Rick Wallace

CHAPTER 27

class held a design contest. All the entries had to be not only drawn, but also built as scale models or prototypes.

Randy's dad operated a furniture restoration business, where Randy often helped out after school; so it was only natural that he would design a sofa and then use dad's shop facilities to build his design in full-size form. But when Randy lugged the sofa into class, the instructor was a bit shocked at the size of it. The teacher hadn't meant for his students to take the word "prototype" quite so literally, so the sofa was disqualified from the contest as being too large. But, as Randy says, "It's a great sofa," and to this day it occupies a prominent (and useful) position in his home.

Designing the sofa convinced Randy that he should pursue a career in interior design. After all, he figured, airplanes and furniture both require thinking about design in three dimensions. He enrolled in the interior design curriculum at the Savannah College of Art and Design.

After a few courses, Randy realized that interior design was not his calling, any more than designing airplanes was. But, there was a course in graphic design built into the curriculum program. He took the course, and then another one, and another one. That was it. Graphic

design was Randy's new major, and he graduated in 1990.

Stops at ad agencies on St. Simons Island, Georgia, and Hilton Head, South Carolina, culminated in a return to Savannah, where he worked as a graphic artist for his alma mater.

Ultimately, he joined The Newsletter Factory, and is presently the organization's Senior Designer. The Newsletter Factory produces, as you might expect, newsletters for a wide variety of clients, large and small. They also consult with companies that wish to set up an in-house newsletter operation, and teach classes around the country on newsletter design.

Q You designed this newsletter according to basic Newsletter Factory principles, right (see fig. 27.1)?

That's right. For example, there's a clear statement of benefit built into the name plate, "Uniting Georgians Through Sport." The statement of benefit gives the casual browser a reason to go further and begin reading the newsletter copy. Plus, there's an eye-catching contents block to move the reader right into the interior of the newsletter.

Q Focusing on the Photoshop elements, the question mark silhouette picture looks like a simple item that would make a good place to begin our interview (see fig. 27.2).

The objective for this photo manipulation task was to graphically portray the story about the upcoming announcement of the Georgia Games' new mascot. I wanted to convey a sense of expectation and drama.

I began, of course, by using File Acquire to scan the image. I picked this photo because I knew the shape of the middle person's silhouette would be a simple one for me to cut out of the picture.

I hand-traced a path around the person, using the Pen tool. I like the Pen/Path approach because I find it easy to go back and edit the outline by grabbing handles on the Bezier curve points, making adjustments just like adjusting a path when working in Illustrator or FreeHand. This way, I get the advantage of a vector drawing program combined with the pixel level editing ability of Photoshop.

Also, once I have the path just right, I can call it back to make a mask or

perform other manipulations. In this case, I didn't need to perform any other manipulation, so I used the Paths menu to Make Selection and hit the Delete key to cut the silhouette out of the picture. Pretty simple.

There's an important thing to remember when using the Make Selection choice on the Paths palette. Be sure to feather the path. Double-clicking the Pen tool brings up a dialog box where the feather can be set. In this case, I used a 2 pixel setting. This does two things. It

Fig. 27.1

A newsletter front page displays some of the basic Newsletter Factory design techniques (see color section also).

softens the edge, of course. In addition, the feathering helps smooth any jaggies in curved lines if the image must be blown up to a larger size. Keep in mind, this will be a pixel-based digital image, not a vector style drawing, so it's easy to inadvertently produce an undesirable stair-step effect.

Fig. 27.2

Cutting a silhouette out of the picture helped tell the story of the impending announcement of a new mascot.

Then, when I brought the picture into the final QuarkXPress layout, I added the question mark just as I would set any other type on the page, centering it on the silhouette (refer to fig. 27.1).

I like the Pen/Path approach because I find it easy to go back and edit the outline by grabbing handles on the Bezier curve points.

Q Why wouldn't you use the Magic Wand to select the tones in the area you want to silhouette? Wouldn't that have been easier and faster than tracing the silhouette by hand?

This was such a simple shape, it really didn't take but a minute to trace it. But even so, the Magic Wand tool in this case would have selected contigious areas in the photograph—any section that matched the gray level in the area I actually wanted to cut out. It is true that I could then use Shift-Lasso to deselect certain areas, but I still would not be able to do the kind of fine tuning of the shape I can achieve by manipulating individual points and Bezier curves on a traced path.

Q Now let's have a look at the fancy duotone you created for the contents box. How did you get the image split like this (refer to fig. 27.1)?

That was easy. I simply colored the original image of the runner with a 30 percent tint of the PMS 286 spot color we used for this newsletter. When the project was put together in QuarkXPress, the monotone was placed behind the duotone, which was created in Photoshop. The duotone was then cropped to the size of the box, which produces an overall sensation that the duotone colors reverse when they fall outside the box boundaries, even though that's not actually true.

Tints, duotones, gradated screens—these things all can stretch the usefulness of a single spot color and add richness to the overall look of a newsletter or brochure. Stretching a spot color this way will make a project look twice as expensive at half the cost.

I was careful in creating this photo-based contents box design to make sure that the type would be readable. There was a danger that the photo might cloud legibility, but in this case the type and photo have been arranged so the type snaps out against the background. I put a drop shadow on the type to add contrast. Contrast is a critical factor for aiding legibility, needless to say, when setting type to go over any sort of background. If the reader couldn't decipher the type, the whole thing would be a waste of time, wouldn't it?

Stretching the use of a spot color this way will make a project look twice as expensive at half the cost.

Q **Now tell us about creating the duotone itself. Did you use the duotone mode in Photoshop (see fig. 27.3 and figs. 27.4 and 27.5 in the color section)?**

No, I didn't use the duotone mode. It's a powerful feature, and can be very useful, but not for this situation. The duotone mode means the designer must work blind to a certain extent, experimenting with the curve in the duotone dialog box without being able to get instant feedback on the results of the adjustments. To see the effects of changes, the designer must close the dialog box, assess the effect, and then reopen the dialog box to make further adjustments. Also, the duotone mode doesn't allow the application or removal of color in specific areas of the image.

Basically, I wanted more control than the duotone mode can ☆provide. I needed to create a hand-tinted duotone. Using this technique, I was able to add or subtract color at just the locations where it would help rather than hinder the legibility of the type.

The process begins, of course, by scanning the original image as a grayscale image (see fig. 27.3). Then, in Photoshop, convert it into a CMYK file. That will produce a four channel image, one of each process color (cyan, magenta, yellow, and black).

Use the Show Channels command from the Window menu to bring up the Channels dialog box. Click each channel in turn, and try to decide which of the two channels, when combined, will come closest to producing the desired effect. This may take some experimenting, so I always work on a copy of the image and stand ready to use the Edit Undo command. Generally, avoid working with the yellow channel, because the 90-degree screen angle in that channel is the most troublesome for moiré problems.

After choosing two channels, go to the unwanted channels and, in turn, select them. In each channel, use Select All and delete to remove all the information in the channel, but leave the empty channel in place. In the case of this duotone, I worked with the cyan and black channels and deleted magenta and yellow (refer to fig. 27.4 in color section).

By the way, always assign duotone colors in order, with the lightest one in the low numbered channel. This will help Photoshop assign screen angles properly. In this case, the blue color would go in channel one and the black in channel four. When making a tritone or quadtone, this ink order becomes even more important. To be safe, it's best to consult with your printer about the right sequence.

Click the eye icons to show both channels, but highlight only one of the channels at a time. Whichever channel is highlighted is the one that will be affected by work with the various tools. Both channels are still visible, however, so the designer can paint or otherwise manipulate one color while observing the effects of changes.

It is possible, of course, to select both channels and work on the entire image, in order to lighten or darken the entire duotone, for example.

When done editing, save the image and place it in a page layout program for final production of a publication (refer to fig. 27.5 in color section). The next step depends on whether the project is a spot or process color job.

If working in spot color—say, with black and one other color—use *cyan* as the name of the second color throughout the project. That way, when the job is separated and run to film, there will be two plates for each page and the duotone will automatically be separated. Just tell the printer what ink color to use (in our case, it was PMS 286) for all the plates that hold the name *cyan*.

For a process color job, again assuming the duotone is black plus a second color, the designer will probably want the printer to put the second color on a fifth plate. Work with the printer on this, but most likely the printer will strip out the duotone and put the duotone's *cyan* plate on its own fifth plate.

Basically, I wanted more control than the duotone mode can provide. I needed to create a hand-tinted duotone.

Q **This duotone image, and the color one we are going to speak about next, are a lot of flash for a table of contents box. Why put so much emphasis there?**

The flash attracts attention to the contents and we wanted that to happen—to really motivate readers to open up the newsletter and see what's inside, beyond the cover. Also, the design assignment was to execute the newsletter so that it carried the image of the Georgia Games—action and excitement oriented. Like any other volunteer organization, there are a lot of static photographs to run, as you might expect. This was an opportunity to put some bite into the design and still carry the required—and all important—handshake and awards photos.

Q **This tennis player looks like she's standing in a rainstorm of tennis balls. How did you achieve this effect (see fig.7.6)?**

Before we talk about the steps to get the effect, I want to mention one

Fig. 27.5

(See color section.)

thing about RGB versus CMYK editing. This image was an RGB TIFF when it came out of the scanner. I did all the editing in RGB mode, and as a final step converted it to CMYK. It seems like that approach would ordinarily make a lot of sense. After all, the monitor is in RGB and you would expect to get more accurate colors by working in the color space of the viewing medium. Unfortunately, there's a practical side effect of this approach. There's so much manipulation in this image that by the time I converted to CMYK, the colors went muddy. I believe this had something to do

with the way all the inks were laid down on paper. Anyway, the point is, there are times when it would be better to work in CMYK right from the beginning. One of those times is probably when you are doing a lot of heavy photo manipulation and aren't so worried about preserving the accuracy of the colors in the original photographic image.

I started creating this image by isolating the woman from the background. I made a clipping path, tracing around her in much the same way as I did in the question mark image. The difference here was the complexity of the image. I went to Quick Mask to test my clipping path. At the very bottom of the main toolbox, I chose the gray box with the white circle inside it. This mode shows what had been masked out. I can see the areas that are protected in red, a lot like the rubylith that strippers used in the X-acto knife days. See the triangular cutout in the handle of the racket? I hadn't traced that at first and this Quick Mask revealed the problem. In Quick Mask, I could easily solve the problem and not worry about ruining some of the work I'd already done, since the mask protects the areas under its transparent red mask.

After you have completed your mask, convert it to a selection and save it. Choose the Duplicate Channel command on the Channel palette and select a new document in

Fig. 27.6

A newsletter front page, shows a heavily manipulated image that is used to back up the table of contents box (see color section also).

the dialog. I don't always do this, but it might be a good idea to take the time to save the new document, and also to save the clipping path. That will make it easier to select the silhouette again if you have a crash or if you need to interrupt your work.

Now create a second new document, the same size as the original image. I used the Gradient tool to run a gradation from green to purple, from the top-left corner to the bottom-right corner, with green in the top portion of the image.

I then had three documents—the original, the clipped out woman, and the gradation (see figs. 27.7, 27.8, and 27.9).

Next, I needed to work on the gradient background to get the blobby tennis ball rain effect. This basically took a lot of experimentation, but in the end, here's what worked. I used Filter Distort Displace and chose Stretch Displacement To Fit, Tile, and Wrap Around. I then had a choice of displacement maps from the Plug in folder, and I chose Drops.

Next, I used Image Calculate and experimented to get the right effect, which in this case was Lighten, combining the original image with the gradation to get a new combined document full of raining tennis balls (see fig. 27.9).

Since I knew the image was increasing in size, I was afraid of getting pixelization so I applied some noise to this new document, the fourth of the set.

I then selected the tennis player image and pasted it into the new document (see fig. 27.10). If you keep all

Fig. 27.7

This photo shows the starting point; the original photo before manipulation in Photoshop.

Fig. 27.8

The tennis player is clipped out of her background.

Fig. 27.9 (left)

The next step is to use the Image Calculate Lighten combination.

Fig. 27.10 (right)

This is what the final Photoshop file looked like before it was stretched in QuarkXPress.

your images the same size, the pasted item will automatically go right in-to the old location. I also selected the tennis ball from the original image and enlarged it 300 percent and pasted it into the final image.

When I imported the completed image into QuarkXPress, I was experimenting with placing a horizontal format image into a vertical box, and I stretched the entire image to fit the contents box. We liked the effect so much, we went with it in the final product (refer to fig. 27.6).

The point is, experimentation has great value. You can get a lot out of using the standard filters and such that come with Photoshop if you just open yourself to the possibilities.

Achieving a Retail Vision: Product Design to Billboards

Scott Lipsett, FreeStyle USA, Camarillo, California

There must be hundreds, even thousands, of designers who first caught the graphics art bug the way Scott Lipsett did. He was the editor of his high school yearbook. In fact, his yearbook was one of the first to be done using electronic prepress techniques. The big yearbook publisher who had the school contract put an IBM PC at the school. The first year it was used just for setting the text. The next year, the publisher supplied a program that actually added page layout, using black boxes as place holders for the photos.

by Rick Wallace

CHAPTER 28

Scott headed off to the University of Southern California to study advertising and photography. A buddy who worked with him on the yearbook started a design firm. Before long, the buddy had more business than he could handle and asked Scott for help. And it wasn't very much longer before they went into business together.

That ultimately led to a job with one of their main accounts, a medical equipment company manufacturing specialized camera equipment. It was here that Scott further developed his skills in marketing, advertising, and product design.

These design cycles mean we are constantly under pressure to design our new product.

At FreeStyle USA, Scott was hired as a marketing coordinator, but the company had its eye on the computer skills displayed so prominently on his resumé. When Scott hired on with the 115 employee company, they had one PC and were doing their word processing in WordPerfect 3.1 for UNIX. Today, they have a full, computer-based graphics design department.

Q **Although watches are a consumer electronics item, they also are a fashion and, in your case, a sporting goods item. Does that mean there are seasons?**

Yes, we have two design cycles a year that are geared to product introductions—January for the Spring/Summer retailing season for sporting goods, and August for the Christmas retailing season. We do product introductions at trade shows like Surf Expo in Florida, the sporting goods Super Show in Atlanta, and Action Sport Retailer in San Diego.

These design cycles mean we are constantly under pressure to design our new product. We begin in mid-June, for example, to design the January product. We have to work that far ahead so the manufacturers we use in Asia have the time they need to produce the watches after we design them.

Q **So you actually design the product electronically, using Photoshop?**

Right, a scanner and Photoshop actually. The whole process begins when our management and design team get together to figure out what we need to meet the latest market trends and to fill in our product line.

Then, we go into our sample room. In that room, we've collected thousands and thousands of watch parts from our suppliers—watch bands, bezels, cases. Understand, they don't fit together. You couldn't actually make a watch out of these parts. We are just searching for the look we want.

![Q] If you can't assemble a watch from the parts, how do you put together your design?

We assemble the parts in Photoshop. I take the parts, put them on a scanner, and scan them in (see fig. 28.1).

Keep in mind that this is just for internal design purposes, so we are merely looking for the electronic equivalent of a sketch. I clean up the edges because there is a lot of flare and shadow when you scan a 3-D object like this. Then, in Photoshop, I can size the parts and "create" a watch design (see fig. 28.2). I will often change the type style or other markings on the bezel, the round facing that goes around the watch dial. On our sports-oriented watches, the bezel often has a marker or pointer on it which rotates to function as a timer.

I often create the dials in Illustrator, which I can then bring in to Photoshop. Also, you would not

Fig. 28.1

Scanning watch parts as a preliminary to "assembling" a watch design in Photoshop.

Fig. 28.2

The finished rough "design sketch" of a new watch, put together in Photoshop from the scanned parts.

believe the number of watch hands available. We do make analog watches in addition to digital ones, and we have hundreds of pairs of laminated cards with watch hands on them, which also can be scanned in with the assembled watch.

We assemble the parts in Photoshop. Keep in mind, this is just for internal design purposes, so we are merely looking for the electronic equivalent of a sketch.

![Q] How does this electronic paste up help you out?

For one thing, with manufacturing being done offshore, there is a language problem. We do the assembly in Camarillo, but the parts are made in Asia. Even with an office in Hong Kong, there can be confusion about what we want done. The Photoshop compiled picture leaps the language barrier. We even get good color matching this way.

Of course, it also helps us meet the demands of our product design cycles because we can very quickly produce a picture of what we want. Not only can we do it fast, we can also make a better decision because we have such an accurate, high quality image of what the finished watch will look like.

With manufacturing being done offshore, there is a language problem...The Photoshop compiled picture leaps the language barrier.

Very quickly, the vendor in Asia makes the watch, sending us the individual pieces for approval as they are completed. Once we have a complete sample, we have the prototype we need in order to complete our photography and produce a catalog for our trade show introduction.

Q Now in your business, I don't imagine this process stops with creating the product. You need a "look" or an "image" that delivers the product design to the consumer, right?

We create our look on an annual basis, and then embed that visual feeling throughout our line. Everything from the packaging, to the advertising, to the catalog gets the look.

The overall image of FreeStyle USA is of an active lifestyle company.

This particular year, the look revolves around a composited image approach. Being a sports watch line, we sponsor a lot of big name amateur and professional athletes in each of our competitive sports—surfing, volleyball, that sort of thing. Problem is, we aren't a clothing company. Watches are small objects. If you take a normal size image of an athlete, the actual watch on his wrist is pretty small.

The question was, how can we make the athletes an integral part of the message for this year, and still display the product? So, that marketing challenge led us to the look you'll see in the advertising materials. We composite together a big image of the watch, with an image of the athlete in action.

Q Tell us about compositing these images together. Do you use Photoshop for that too (see fig. 28.3)?

Yes, Photoshop has been essential for achieving our advertising "look."

Learning from the Pros

This special section gathers all the color illustrations from the Learning from the Pros chapters (chapters 26-30) together. The figure numbers in this section correspond to the figure numbers in the actual chapters of the book, so that you can easily refer to the text for more detailed information from the professional designer.

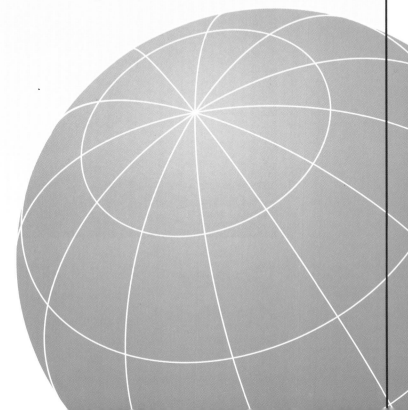

Denny Knittig

Photoshop is used by Denny Knittig, Knittig Design, Inc. to produce the "Fast and Healthy" magazine for Pillsbury. (See chapter 26, "Scanning Objects: Instant Art from Real Life.")

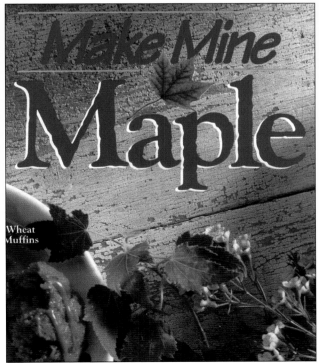

Fig. 26.1, Fig. 26.2

An article title treatment produced by scanning a real maple leaf and manipulating the result in Photoshop.

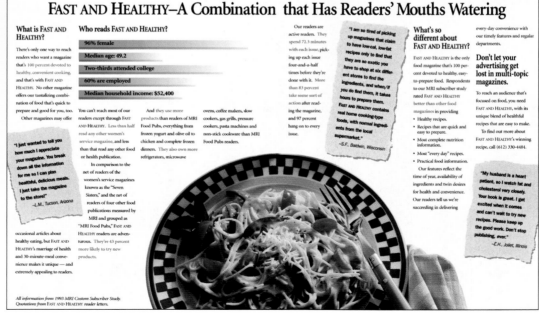

Fig. 26.3 (top)
A heart image; a piece of line art created by hand and scanned.

Fig. 26.4 (bottom)
Scanned in paper, for quotes and for the subtle background.

The Games

Uniting Georgians Through Sport

Georgians Play

Games to Hit Home Run with Mascot Introduction

The Georgia Games hopes to hit its first home run for 1994 with the introduction of their mascot at the Braves game on **May 9.**

A spectacular pre-game show introducing the newest member of the Games family starts an evening you won't want to miss. After the unveiling, the Braves play arch-rival **Philadelphia Phillies** for the first time since last season's National League Playoffs. Volunteers, sponsors and others associated with the Games can enjoy the Braves game together in a reserved section. Everyone is

Continued on page 4

The Georgia Games mascot will be welcomed at Opening Ceremonies by other mascots from around the state, such as "Doc" from Life College and "Buzz" the Yellow Jacket from Georgia Tech

Georgia Games Sponsors Dedicated to Amateur Sports

AT&T, Gold Sponsor of the Georgia Games, reached an agreement with the Atlanta Committee for the Olympic Games (ACOG) to become a Centennial Olympic Games Partner. AT&T will provide ACOG with the enormous amount of telecommunications support needed to stage this worldwide event. In addition, employees of AT&T will open their homes and serve as hosts to the families and friends of athletes from across the globe.

"AT&T is very excited and proud to continue our support of the Olympic movement. We look forward to bringing anytime, anywhere communica-

tions to the Olympics, and making Atlanta a showcase for the very latest in communications technology," said AT&T spokesman **Bill Blair.**

This agreement marks the sixth time a major Georgia Games sponsor has joined the family of 1996 Olympic Games sponsors. **WXIA-TV, 11Alive,** is the local NBC affiliate of the official network, **Coca-Cola** is the official soft drink, **PowerAde** is the official fluid replacement drink, **IBM** is the official computer and **Champion** is the official apparel of the 1996 Olympic Games.

For the third year, AT&T continues its role as presenting

sponsor for the seven District Sports Festivals (DSF). They will be joined by **Greater Atlanta Sports Medicine, Atlanta Gas Light Company,** IBM and the **Georgia Association of REALTORS** in making the DSF a success.

These major Georgia Games sponsors, along with **Courtyard by Marriott** and **Mead Corporation,** have dedicated themselves to amateur sports throughout Georgia. With continued support from these outstanding corporations, amateur sports will keep prospering and allow all Georgia residents an avenue to compete and participate in sport and fitness. ●

Randy Sizemore

Fig. 27.1

A newsletter front page, displaying some of the basic Newsletter Factory design techniques used by Randy Sizemore, a senior designer at The Newsletter Factory (see chapter 27, "Deconstructing Reality: Photo Manipulation").

Fig. 27.3
The starting point, the original photograph, scanned and ready to be manipulated into a hand-tinted duotone.

Fig. 27.4 (left)
The blue plate from the finished duotone.

Fig. 27.5 (right)
The finished duotone with the black and blue layers in composite form.

The Games

Uniting Georgians Through Sport

Georgians Play

Progress Unparalleled in Four Years

by Nick Gailey, Executive Director

Vol. 3 No. 2

Inside This Issue

N ot long ago, I was sitting at my desk, staring out the window and wondering how the first Georgia Games Championships could be created, coordinated, and conducted with a lead time of two months! The Georgia General Assembly had just created the Georgia State Games Commission and someone who knew State Games was needed—fast.

I was asked, and somehow said yes, realizing how much had to be done in so little time. But in those first days in 1990, if the windows on the 34th floor of the IBM tower opened, I might have jumped. They don't, I didn't, and last July 30,000 people participated in the fourth Georgia Games.

See *Progress,* on page 3

The Torch Run, which unites the state of Georgia through amateur competition, is a good example of the explosive growth of the Georgia Games.

Corporations Cash In on Sponsorship of Games

Community involvement, statewide media coverage, product exposure, and corporate networking are some of the reasons why corporations desire to support the Georgia Games.

In the wake of the excitement surrounding the 1996 Olympic Games in Atlanta, the Georgia Games, an Olympic-style sports festival, has developed into one of the largest state games programs in the country.

The Georgia Games offers corporate sponsors a way to promote their products and services to residents of Georgia in a dynamic fashion unparalleled by any other event.

As a sponsor of the Georgia Games, corporations have a unique opportunity to join athletes, volunteers, and spectators in celebrating amateur athletics throughout the state of Georgia. ◆

Fig. 27.6
Newsletter front page, showing heavily manipulated
image used as a background of the table of contents box.

Scott Lipsett

Figs. 28.6, 28.7

Two advertisements from FreeStyle USA where athletes are used as an integral part of the message for a line of sport watches. (See chapter 28, "Achieving a Retail Vision: Product Design to Billboards.")

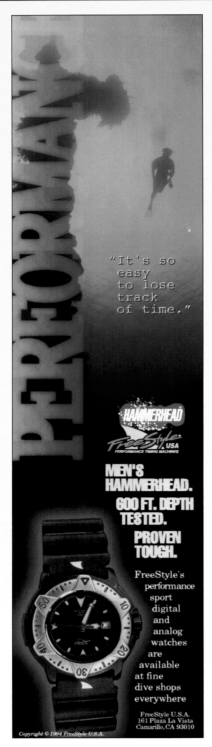

Fig. 28.8
A telephone kiosk billboard; this also shows the consistent delivery of the image message.

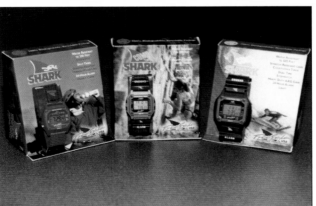

Fig. 28.9
The packaging embeds the actual watch into the athletic image.

Bert Monroy

Fig. 29.1

The point of photo-realism isn't to duplicate a scene like a photograph. It's to make a person feel as if they are in the scene. The completed painting, a photorealistic digital illustration of the Zanzibar Motel, in Reno, Nevada by Bert Monroy, Photo-realistic Illustrator. (See chapter 29, "Thinking Photo-realistically: Is It Real, or Is It Paint?")

Fig. 29.3
Bert fills in the sketch, working in fine detail by zooming in on each section of the scene. Here you see close-ups of the clouds, the motel doors, and the awning canopy.

Fig. 29.4
Photorealistic sign lettering often requires Photoshop.

Figs. 29.5 and 29.6

Applying texture to the detail work; in this case, the leafy bushes, the decorative metal panels, and the sidewalk and driveway.

Andy Fulp
of Kennickell Printing

Fig. 30.1

The "neighbor factor" happens when two abutting process color photos do not share a common color. This image shows what can happen. Notice the unsightly, untrapped seam between the two photos. (See chapter 30, "Designing Printable Pieces: When Paper Meets the Press.")

Fig. 30.2
In this example, the "neighbor factor" trapping issue was created when the designer laid orange-gradated type over a blue sky.

Fig. 30.5
A plugged up duotone.

Fig. 30.6
A duotone that has been tuned for proper ink saturation in the prepress process.

Fig. 30.7
An example of TIFF trash. The fix is to make a silhouette with a clipping path and save the image as an EPS.

Fig. 30.8
An example of an edge showing up on a silhouetted image because it was dropped into the layout on top of another image or background color.

Fig. 30.9
This image was assembled entirely in Photoshop, to eliminate the problems of hard-edged white rims around silhouetted images.

Fig. 30.10
An example of cropping overhang.

Fig. 30.11
Stairstepping jaggies, that could have been avoided by working more closely with the printer.

We get the control we want, and meet our deadlines on budget, because we can composite in-house.

We begin with a high quality drum scan of the athlete, in the size we need for the eventual finished advertising piece or catalog page. That's the basis for the eventual composited image. These are huge files, 20 to 30 megabytes, sometimes over 100 megabytes. We then crop the athlete photo to the area we want, and to the ad format.

Next, you increase the canvas size so that there's a blank where the picture of the watch will go. In the case of this catalog page, the blank was on the left-hand side of the "page." The total image size now

The question was, how can we make the athletes an integral part of the message for this year, and still display the product?

equals the ultimate size of the ad or catalog page.

Next, make a mask that will define the transition or blend area. Open an alpha channel and outline the area where the watch will go. Use the Lasso tool with a very large feather radius, maybe 250 pixels—as high as you can go. This will be very imprecise, but that's okay, because the wide feather is how you get the blending effect in the composite.

Fig. 28.3

The advertising look, achieved by compositing an athlete's photo with an enlarged image of the watch.

Photoshop has been essential for achieving our advertising "look." We get the control we want, and meet our deadlines on budget, because we can composite in-house.

After you have defined the mask area in the alpha channel, use the Selection Inverse command and fill the selection with black. This will be your mask. After completing this operation, you will have a large black area that transitions to white area along an uneven line.

Still working in the original document, the composite document, click the selection icon in the channel palette to bring the mask you have in your alpha channel into the main image.

Now you make the composite happen. Go to the watch photo and crop it to the proper size. Use Select All, copy the cropped watch image to the clipboard, and Paste it into the original document (the athlete photograph, in this example). Paste it into the composite image.

For this project, I touched up the edge where the two elements meet by copying and pasting parts of each image. (This project was done in Photoshop 2.51. In the new version of the software, it would be better to put the watch in a new layer and make a layer mast to achieve the blend between the elements.)

And the concept gets carried out throughout the product line, right? Consistency is part of the goal?

This image permeates everything. Even in the catalog, which has dozens of watches displayed, we have image pages scattered throughout the piece that constantly reinforce the look we created with this composite imagery.

In addition to the magazine ads (see figs. 28.4 through 28.7), and the catalog page (refer to fig. 28.3), we carry the look into point of purchase displays, and even into our billboards (see fig. 28.8). (See 28.6 and 28.7 in color section also.)

In a way, we also get the look into the packaging. If you look at this picture, you'll notice there's no composite of scans on the package. But the watch fits into a notch in the box that physically duplicates the look by having a smallish image of the athlete wedded to the full size actual watch (see fig. 28.9).

We integrate the athletic lifestyle and image with our product and we do it in every single thing we put out, including the product. It is this kind of visual continuity throughout the line, in large measure created through the use of electronic tools such as Photoshop, that helps me as a designer to deliver the company's image to the consumer.

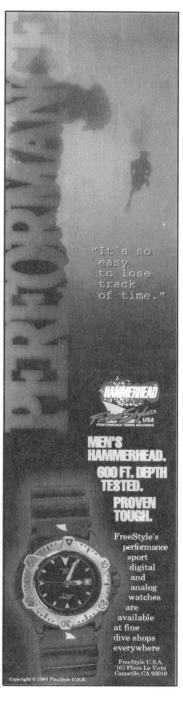

Figs. 28.4, 28.5, 28.6, 28.7

Four advertisements, carrying out the FreeStyle USA look.

This image permeates everything. Even in the catalog, which has dozens of watches displayed, we have image pages scattered throughout the piece.

Fig. 28.8

A telephone kiosk billboard, also showing the consistent delivery of the image message. (See color section also.)

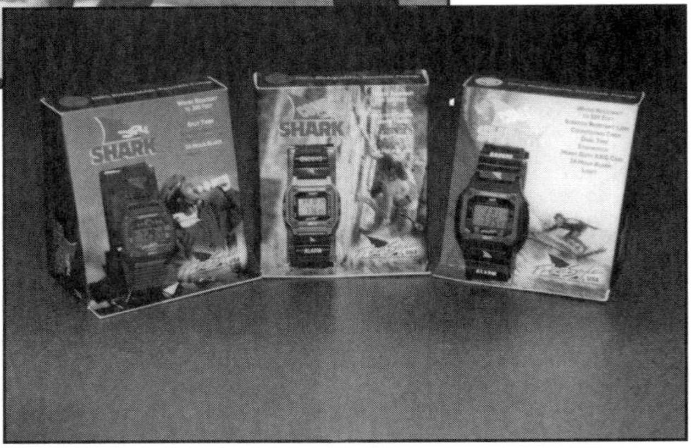

Fig. 28.9

The packaging embeds the actual watch into the athletic image. (See color section also.)

Thinking Photorealistically: Is It Real, Or Is It Paint?

Bert Monroy, Photorealistic Illustrator, Albany, California

More than anything else, photorealism is about drawing. And Bert Monroy always liked to draw. That was obvious to pretty much everyone around him, including one of the nuns who taught him back in eighth grade. As he was getting set to head off to high school, she had a talk with him, and told him he should go to a specialized school that would help him make the most of his artistic talents. Bert enrolled at the High School of Art and Design in New York.

by Rick Wallace

CHAPTER 29

Following his graduation from high school in 1967, his education was interrupted by some time in the service. After getting out of the Marine Corps, he returned to New York and attended college on the GI Bill at the School of Visual Arts.

Following college, Bert landed a job at a big ad agency, working in the "bullpen" doing mechanicals. After gaining some experience, he moved on to a smaller agency where he quickly worked up to the Art Director position.

During his ad agency years, he primarily worked on design and overseeing other artists. He also spent his spare time painting and sketching street scenes. At that time, he worked with the traditional paper-based illustration tools. He would lay down a base of color tones, using Dr. Martin's dyes, and work over the paper with pencil, felt tip markers, and a Rapidiograph pen.

However, it wasn't until he met the Macintosh that Bert launched into photorealistic illustration in a big way. In 1984, the year the Macintosh was first released, he was a partner in his own ad agency. His partner insisted that they had to computerize, and Bert's attitude initially was, "Fine, we'll get a computer, but I don't want to have anything to do with it." Then they went to the computer store to have a look at a demo model of the Mac (they weren't even shipping yet). "Something clicked," while playing around with MacPaint on that demo machine, he says, "I had found my medium."

Q Well, let's get one of the standard questions out of the way first. Are you sure you didn't scan any of this painting (see fig. 29.1)?

Right, well, here's the standard answer. There are no scans in this work, none whatsoever. This is about art, not scanning.

Scanning would defeat the purpose. The whole point is to illustrate in a photorealistic manner, not to duplicate a photograph. There's a difference between the two, a different way of thinking.

I guess I'd say that, like all my photorealistic illustrations, this painting asked to be done. I was driving down the road near Reno and saw this old motel, with the gaudy sign jutting up into the sky, and all those clouds in the background. I had to paint this scene.

Q **We aren't going to duplicate a couple of decades of training, experience, and drawing skill with this interview. But let's talk about the way of thinking you mention, the process you go through in creating a photorealistic illustration. How do you begin?**

As I say, the process begins when I spot a scene that somehow hits me so strongly that I feel like it is asking to be painted. At that point, I take a lot of pictures as a form of note taking. Like most artists, I don't work at the scene with an easel, or even my computer! I usually take some pictures of the overall scene, just to get the context. Then I take dozens of detail shots, to make sure I understand the scene completely. So this stage is note taking, and also part of my artistic observation process.

Now, I know what you're thinking. If you aren't going to scan in these pictures, why work on the computer in the first place? Why not just paint the scene?

I guess I'd say that, like all my photorealistic illustrations, this painting asked to be done.

Fig. 29.1

The completed painting, a photorealistic digital illustration of the Zanzibar Motel, in Reno, Nevada. (See color section also.)

Q Yeah, that is a good question. Why work on the computer instead of using pen, pencil, and paint?

For one thing, the computer isn't nearly as messy as painting!

Also, the computer is ideally suited for achieving the photorealistic effect. When I work on the computer I can zoom into an area and put in details that would never be possible with traditional illustration and painting tools. Once I did a futuristic scene of some cars flying through the sky, and if you zoomed in on that scene you would actually see that I had painted in a complete set of navigational controls on the dashboard of each of the cars. That kind of detail is part of achieving the photorealistic effect, but if I was painting or sketching I would only be able to put in some squiggles to suggest that kind of detail.

The point of photorealism isn't to duplicate a scene like a photograph.

It's to make a person feel as if they are there in the scene. For example, photographs have depth of field, but your eyes don't, at least not so that you can perceive it. Your brain and eye are working together to experience the scene. In the same way, my work has something of me in it. In the case of the Zanzibar painting we are discussing here, I distorted the perspective to put the viewer into the scene in a special way, so the person seeing this painting could share the experience that made me want to paint the scene in the first place.

Q Perspective plays a big part in establishing the feeling of being there, doesn't it?

Absolutely. And that's where I start, sketching in perspective guides and vanishing points, and establishing the basic shapes of all the major items in the illustration (see fig. 29.2).

Using a fine line in Illustrator, I sketch in all the perspective elements and outline the buildings and other big objects. This is where I create the fundamental composition. In the case of the Zanzibar, I exaggerated the perspective to make the sign stand out against the sky, and to draw the viewer's eye down

Fig. 29.2

The first step, a line drawing to establish perspective and outline major shapes.

the street on the far right of the image. It's a lot like working traditionally with pencil at this stage.

Q **With your compositional sketch completed, you no doubt bring the Illustrator file into Photoshop then. What's next?**

As you see in these zoomed in views of the painting, I select an area and blow it up very big so that I can get all of the detail (see fig. 29.3). At this point, I fill in colors and reflections—really all the detail. (See fig. 29.3 in color section also.)

I simply start filling in the painting, and I usually work from the background to the foreground and from the edges towards the center. The center foreground usually has the most detail of any location in the painting.

The first thing I did on this painting was the sky, which started as a blue gradient, and then I filled in the clouds. Then I moved to each area of the painting in turn, making the sketch come alive with detail.

Curtains must be painted into windows. Metal door frames must have reflections added, usually airbrushed streaks of gray or white, depending on what is being reflected.

That's where I start, sketching in perspective guides and vanishing points, and establishing the basic shapes of all the major items.

Fig. 29.3

Next, Bert fills in the sketch, working in fine detail by zooming in on each section of the scene. Here you see close-ups of the clouds, the motel doors, and the awning canopy.

As you see in these zoomed in views of the painting, I select an area and blow it up very big so I can get all the detail.

Q What about the lettering on the signs. Do you do them in Illustrator or in Photoshop?

I know it seems like Illustrator would be the right thing to use for type, but most of the type in this illustration was created in Photoshop. See, nothing in real life is a flat color. Everything has variations of color going through it, including signs (see fig. 29.4).

Fig. 29.4

Photorealistic sign lettering often requires Photoshop. (See color section also.)

That's why pretty much every object in this painting has been painted using a gradient, and there's almost no area where you could find a swatch of flat color. The computer, no matter which program I'm using, does make it easy to create any line art, such as type or wires and cables. But it's easier to produce the natural variations in surface color in a pixel-based program like Photoshop, as opposed to a vector-based drawing program such as Illustrator.

Q Okay, you've sketched perspective, and then filled in the sketch, working section by section, applying very fine detail. What's the next stage of creating the photo-realistic effect?

Texture comes next. For texture, you have to keep remembering as you work that nothing in real life is really smooth. This is a very experimental stage of producing the illustration. I apply patterns, add noise, use filters and effects, until I finally get the texture I need.

In the case of the Zanzibar painting, the bushes in the foreground needed a lot of texture (see fig. 29.5). They aren't just green. They are leafy bushes. I created a pattern, outlined the bush and masked in the pattern. I added noise just to reduce any unnatural sensation of flat uniformity. I then applied a faceting effect and worked the leaves over some more to get good color variation. The concrete sidewalk had to be worked over carefully, darkened in certain parts, so it looks like it has been walked on many, many times.

Q Nothing is all one color. Nothing is really smooth and flat. The idea seems to be that photorealism, for all its attention to fine detail, requires a lot of randomness.

That's right, and that's nearly the last step, introducing even more randomness. I go through the entire scene and carefully age the piece. Hardly any street scene has anything in it that is brand new. The decorative metal panels above the building had to be rusted. The sidewalk and driveway needed to be cracked and soiled (see fig. 29.6). It just wouldn't look real, otherwise.

Q You said nearly the last step. What's the last step, then?

I sign it. That's when I'm done and I can't touch it anymore!

Nothing in real life is a flat color. Everything has variations of color going through it, including signs.

Q There's no question you can draw after seeing all this. Is that the key for someone who wants to do computer-based illustration?

Of course. You have to learn how to draw; even art school is just the beginning of a long learning process. I published my first printed piece when I was 14-years-old, and that was a long way back. Just because someone gives you a palette full of paint or a computer, that doesn't mean you can draw or paint.

Fig. 29.5

The next step is applying texture to the detail work, in this case the leafy bushes. (See color section also.)

You have to learn how to draw; even art school is just the beginning of a long learning process.

I do think there are a lot of thought processes and techniques that will help anyone who does photo touch-up or manipulation. Even though I don't work from scans, the fact is it helps to understand that nature and life are random and that touching up a sky or the side of a building requires you to understand gradients, textures, and aging.

Fig. 29.6

Applying texture to the detail work, in this case the decorative metal panels, as well as the sidewalk and driveway. (See color section also.)

Designing Printable Pieces: When Paper Meets the Press

Andy Fulp, Kennickell Printing, Savannah, Georgia

It turns out that this is a small world indeed. During interviews, we discovered that Andy Fulp and one of the other "Pros" in this section, Randy Sizemore, went to school together at the Savannah College of Art and Design. In fact, following college they carpooled together two hours a day to and from work!

Long before ending up in Savannah, Andy studied architecture for a few years at the University of North Carolina at Charlotte (UNCC). He took one of the electives offered in his architecture curriculum—advertising. As Andy puts it, he "took to that like a duck to water." He switched his major to creative arts and within a few years received his bachelor's at UNCC.

by Rick Wallace

CHAPTER 30

Out of school, Andy worked at a textile printer in UNCC's art department. As Andy says, "If you could print it on a garment, we would do it."

Next, Andy received his master's degree from the Savannah College of Art and Design, followed by work with an illustration and design firm in Hilton Head. The firm had an in-house imagesetter and scanner, which gave Andy invaluable hands-on experience with the electronic prepress process. These skills led him to his current position as electronic prepress manager at Kennickell. It's a technically demanding job, because Kennickell runs both Macintosh and Scitex production workflows and is one of the few printers in the country to be certified by a team of auditors under the ISO 9000 standard for quality assurance.

Andy spends much of his time troubleshooting problem files submitted by clients. But, as with all the best printers, Andy says Kennickell has a philosophy that prevention is less expensive than administering a cure. Therefore, the company spends a considerable amount of time working with clients, educating them on Kennickell procedures so a job will go smoothly and produce predictable results on the press. In fact, Kennickell frequently sends Andy to work directly with a client to help sort out

any potential problems before jobs are sent to the shop. For example, he's been sent to Washington, D.C. for two days to conduct one-on-one personal training for a client.

It's in the spirit of prevention that Andy offered to help out with this section on common problems that designers unwittingly create when preparing their files for the press.

Q There must be about a hundred ways to design yourself into a corner when sending a job to the printer. Have you seen all of them?

I don't know if that's the right total for the number of ways a job can go wrong, but I can tell you this: Every time I think I've seen them all, the very next day I end up troubleshooting a new one.

Q Is there some common element among the problems—some magic issue—that could be solved?

The biggest generator of problems between designers and printers is communication. It's a collaborative effort, after all, and I find if the designer or artist sits down and talks with the printer about the project in advance, a lot of problems can be eliminated long before they turn into expensive problems with a deadline attached.

The specific issue may vary a great deal, from trapping tolerances to color correction to screen angles, but that's the common element—collaboration and communication.

I always try to help a client be specific when communicating about a job. If a client says "add noise" or "subtract some cyan" or some other direction of that sort, I search for a way to get some precision. The best way is for the client or designer to find some example of what they want; then our people can nearly always match the sample exactly. Failing some sort of sample I can use as a reference standard, I try to pin the client down to a number, like "5 percent less yellow," or "increase the magenta by 2 percent."

Getting the specifics pays off in a big way for the designer, too. When you are working for yourself, as so many designers are, all you have to sell is your time. So, the less time you spend redoing a job, the better off you will be. Obviously, there's also the possibility that a designer or a printer might have to "eat" an expensive job because it went bad and the client doesn't want to pay for something that's not his or her fault. Communication and collaboration can help make sure that doesn't happen.

The biggest generator of problems between designers and printers is communication. It's a collaborative effort, after all.

Q Let's move into some specific problems and examples. What about the subject of trapping?

Well, that's a communication issue, without a doubt. Many designers these days are trapping their own work. Both of the leading page layout programs have some level of trapping available at the end user level. QuarkXPress offers some rudimentary trapping of QuarkXPress objects, and PageMaker has released an Addition that's a limited version of the company's powerful TrapWise software.

This seems obvious, but the designer and client have to understand that the printer isn't responsible for trapping unless the printer actually performs the trapping work. As a designer who works at a printing company, I've never understood why a designer would want to take that responsibility, but some do. The charge is nominal—certainly a lot cheaper than blowing thousands of dollars on a job that gets rejected by the client.

Anyway, if you are thinking about doing your own trapping, you need to ask the printer for the trapping tolerances. Only the printer knows this number. We have very tight, sheet-fed presses and our standard trapping is .003 inch, which is 30 percent larger than the default value in QuarkXPress. It's also a number that might not be appropriate at all for another printer's presses.

Check with the printer about trapping issues raised by your design. For example, there's the "neighbor factor."

The other thing is to check with the printer about trapping issues raised by your design. For example, there's the "neighbor factor." Here's an example of two photographs that are "neighbors," meaning the designer has asked that they be kiss fit, so they fit seamlessly together. But the inset photo of the flowers has a lot of yellow because of those warm tones, and the sky of course has a lot of blue and no yellow at all (see fig. 30.1 in the color insert section). That means one of the basic process colors isn't shared between them. As a result, in the middle of a run if there's press slippage, you are liable to get a noticeable color artifact marring the effect where the pictures are supposed to join.

These photos should be trapped somehow, since this is a situation where it'll be difficult to get a common color going. No one is going to want to add some blue to their bricks and yellow flowers, or taint their blue sky with yellow.

You can create a "neighbor factor" color trapping problem almost any time you combine any two elements, not necessarily just in a situation where two photos come together. In this example, the designer placed some orange type over the blue sky (see fig. 30.2 in the color section).

All printers would like to be able to run jobs as kiss fit work, without traps, but inevitably somewhere in the run a kiss fit will slip and a seam like the one in these illustrations will be obvious to the naked eye, especially since the seams are at attention-getting visual points in the design.

The fix is to design around the problem and just plain avoid a kiss fit of two elements that have a neighbor factor color issue. Or, you can assemble the elements into one image in Photoshop and airbrush them together using a common color.

Q Okay, that's the neighbor factor issue. What about the pixel or vector issue?

It's surprising how many people understand the conceptual difference between a vector image and a

Fig. 30.1
(See color section.)

Fig. 30.2
(See color section.)

pixel image. But when it gets down to actually designing a piece, they seem to forget the issue. They'll send in a scanned piece of line art—a logo or something of that sort—and get upset because it isn't smooth when it comes off the press (see fig. 30.3)

The fix is to outline the pixel image, converting it to a vector image (see fig. 30.4). Streamline is astonishingly good at doing this quickly.

Q Now how about the "D" word—duotone?

The "D" word is right. We have lots of problems with duotones. This is one of those situations where you simply can't trust your monitor. You must go by the numbers to get predictable results. The monitor can't show you what the image will look like when it has been converted to layers of ink on paper.

Here are two versions of the same duotone. One is all plugged up, and the other one was adjusted during prepress to go down on press properly (see figs. 30.5 and 30.6 in the color section).

Here's the problem. Let's say your duotone is black plus a second color, and the second color has a fair amount of black in it. What's going to happen is the two are going to add together on the press, and you're going to end up with an extremely high density of black in some spots.

Fig. 30.3 (top)

This item of line art was sized up by the client, even though it is a pixel-based image.

Fig. 30.4 (bottom)

Here's the same item, outlined in a vector drawing program. You also can use Streamline to do a quick conversion from pixel to vector.

That's way too much—the duotone will come out blotchy and plugged up.

You must go by the numbers to get predictable results. The monitor can't show you what the image will look like when it has been converted to layers of ink on paper.

Fig. 30.5

(See color section.)

Fig. 30.6

(See color section.)

This gets to be an especially bad problem when you mix a process color that you use for one of the duotone colors. This imitation duotone often will literally add more of one of the process colors (usually black) and cause a plug. The safe thing to do is work with your printer and use a fifth plate and specify a Pantone spot ink for the second duotone color.

> **Note**
>
> Techniques for handling duotones are discussed in the interview with Randy Sizemore, in chapter 27 and in chapter 14, "Using Color Correction Tools."

In any event, you should consult with your printer to find out what the maximum and minimum dots should be for the specific press that will be running your job. For our two-color press, for example, we tell people we can hold maximum shadows at around 87 percent and highlights at 7 percent. Those are the measurements on the composite image. You can use the Information window in Photoshop to check this yourself.

With these settings, the pressman can always add more ink to get more saturation of color. But the pressman has a practical limit for how much he or she can starve back the ink to solve this problem and still avoid color shifts in the finished product.

The fix is to use Photoshop image control tools—such as levels, brightness, curves or contrast—to compensate until you get the right minimum and maximum dot values.

The basic concept here is that you should trust the numbers, not your computer screen. It is easy these days when designing with a personal computer to design something that looks great on-screen but will really disappoint the creator when ink meets paper on the press. It's just a practical side of our business—the printing press results can't always duplicate the colors you get on the computer screen.

Q You asked me to remind you to tell us about "TIFF trash." What's that?

TIFF trash happens because the Macintosh doesn't "know" transparency, or the absence of color. We will be getting transparency with a future system update, but it isn't here yet. When you clean up the background of a TIFF—using the Eraser or Magic Wand tool, or whatever—you may think you are removing stuff and creating a transparent background. You are really making white. The problem is, the imagesetter may pick up that white and make splotchy artifacts on your page, known as TIFF trash (see fig. 30.7 in the color section). This illustration with the purple streaks is one of the worst cases of TIFF trash I've ever seen. It isn't always quite this obvious.

The solution here is to silhouette the image with a clipping path after you have cleaned up the background. Save the path, and then save the image as an EPS before bringing it into your page layout program. For any PostScript program, like QuarkXPress or PageMaker, the clipping path will clearly delineate the image for the imagesetter, resulting in no more TIFF trash.

Q **Even when you use a clipping path, this transparency issue doesn't completely solve the problem does it? What about situations where a silhouetted**

image is laid over a background image or a background color?

That's right. The background image or the background color just highlights the rim of the imported image. Here's an example where you can plainly see the silhouetted image (the gray shadow behind the shell) because it was dropped into the page layout program over the top of a background color. That exposed the white edge around the gray shadow. (see fig. 30.8 in the color section).

The ideal fix here is to simply avoid the design problem. Design the publication so the silhouette will fall over white when it is imported, so the rim doesn't show so badly.

Fig. 30.7

(See color section.)

Fig. 30.8

(See color section.)

TIFF trash happens because the Macintosh doesn't "know" transparency, or the absence of color.

The problem here is that PostScript "knocks out" everything behind it. No matter how careful you are, your trace around the edge of the silhouette probably won't be perfect, leaving a white edge. Of course, the color of the background doesn't have to be white. That's just an easy color to match between Photoshop and the destination publication. The point is to make the backgrounds between the source and the destination match to make the edge less obvious.

The problem here is that PostScript "knocks out" everything behind it and no matter how careful you are, your trace around the edge of the silhouette probably won't be perfect, leaving a white edge.

Fig. 30.9

(See color section.)

Fig. 30.10

(See color section.)

As an alternative, compose the entire collection of images in Photoshop, where you are assembling the images in a pixel-based environment that will let you blend an edge, instead of working in the razor-sharp PostScript edge world (see fig. 30.9 in the color section).

You also can have the job run through a Scitex work station or have it hand-stripped using traditional Xacto knife techniques.

Q On this next example the picture seems to be badly cropped. What happened? (See fig. 30.10 in the color section.)

This is cropping overhang. The black frame, or even the sprockets, of a 35mm slide will show around the edges, or some similar cropping will show up. It often happens because of the difference in resolution between the computer screen, which is at 72 dots per inch, and the imagesetter, which will usually be at 2450 dots per inch.

Cropping overhang seems to be a particular problem when an image is shifted around in a QuarkXPress picture box.

There's one main way to fix this, and it is a good rule to follow for other reasons as well. Do your photo cropping in Photoshop, instead of trying to handle it in page layout. I always like to recommend handling all image manipulation before importing anyway, that way the raster image processor in the imagesetter doesn't have to process the image and then perform the manipulation. In addition to faster raster image processing in the imagesetter, QuarkXPress or PageMaker will run the job faster and will be able to feed information to the imagesetter much faster as well.

If you must do your cropping in QuarkXPress or PageMaker, try a couple of tests to see if there's a cropping overhang. Blow the image up very big on-screen, say 800 percent, and examine the edges. In QuarkXPress you can switch the picture to negative (unless it's an EPS)—the black frame line will be white and therefore easier to spot. Also, try laser printing the page the image is on at 800 percent. That would be equivalent to the resolution you get on the imagesetter.

Do your photo cropping in Photoshop, instead of trying to handle it in page layout. This approach generally makes the imagesetting operation run smoother.

Q How could a designer avoid the stairstepping jaggies that show up in this next example, on the sides of the letters (see fig. 30.11 in the color section)?

Well, the sides of the letters in "Savannah," where you can see the stairstepping problem, are at a shallow angle. That angle interacts with the standard screen angles in the CMYK process color technique. Black is at 45 degrees, yellow at 90, cyan at 75, and magenta at 105. This isn't a problem of a pixel-based versus a vector-based image, which also will create a problem with "jaggies." It's an interaction between

the PostScript type in the letters, the photo background, and the screen angles.

The designer fix for this one is to simply watch for and avoid shallow angles if they will be critical items in your design—items that will attract the eye and therefore be noticed. To avoid the problem altogether, consult with your prepress house or printer about your design before it goes to the shop. The experts will suggest what angles you can use to avoid the problem, or how you can adjust screen angles when the job is run.

This brings us around to where we started, I guess. The best solution is really to work closely with your printer to avoid problems on press.

Fig. 30.11

(See color section.)

PART

VIII

Appendixes

Photoshop and Your Hardware

I f you ask experienced Mac users what program requires the most powerful system, most say Photoshop. While this isn't entirely true (3-D programs and multimedia applications can be even more demanding), Photoshop is a system hog. The size and color depth of the images you edit determine how powerful your computer should be.

This appendix looks at the types of Macs that are most useful for image editing. When should you use a conventional Mac? When do you need a Power Macintosh? This appendix then looks at what you can do to the Mac to make it more suitable for running Photoshop.

by Bill Harrel

APPENDIX A

Which Mac?

Until early 1994, choosing a Macintosh on which to run Photoshop was easy. For the best results, you bought one of the fastest Quadras, such as an 800, 900, or 840AV (*AV* stands for *audio-video*). Granted, these systems still get bogged down when you apply certain filters to very large files; however, you had no choice but to learn to live with the power-hungry Photoshop, which sometimes required more power than the Macs were capable of. You simply waited.

Power Mac came to the rescue. A revolution now is occurring in the Macintosh image editing world. Apple released a new line of Macs based on IBM's PowerPC chip. Pundits in trade magazines are continually arguing whether most people really need this kind of power; most people probably don't. But Photoshop users need all the processing power they can get.

Based on a new type of processor, Reduced Instruction Set Computer (RISC), the Power Macintosh executes filters and commands at the speed of light. And, Photoshop 3 is written specifically to take advantage of the PowerPC chip. (Don't worry—it still runs on a conventional Mac.)

By the time this book is published (or shortly thereafter), whether to buy a Power Macintosh or not may be a moot point. Apple plans to phase out high-end Quadras. Soon, the only conventional Macs available will be the value-oriented home office machines, such as Performas. Frankly, you should not run Photoshop on a Performa; you won't be happy with the performance. If you're on a tight budget, you can always buy a used Quadra. With so many people upgrading to Power Macs, there are now plenty available.

The point is, if you're in the market for a computer on which to run Photoshop, you should get the most powerful Mac you can. You'll get much more work done. At the time of this writing, the most powerful Mac on the market is the Power Macintosh 8100, which sports an 80MHz PowerPC processor. But Apple has several other new models on the drawing board that promise to run even faster.

In fact, you may soon see a new line of Macs with 64-bit Peripheral Component Interface (PCI) local bus video ports. This video standard performed tremendous speed boosts on Windows machines and no doubt does wonders for the Mac. Video performance, as you see later in this appendix, is crucial to how fast Photoshop runs.

If you're new to Photoshop and in the market for a Mac on which to run it, you have a lot of choices and are most likely limited primarily by your budget. You can buy a 6100, 7100, or 8100 Power Mac now or wait a few months and pick up an even newer, more powerful model.

Photoshop and Memory

Whether you use a PowerPC or conventional Mac, there are a number of things you can do to improve Photoshop's performance. One of the most useful and fundamental methods is to add more system RAM to your computer. The more memory in your computer, the better Photoshop runs—up to a point. It also allows you to open more programs at one time during the same computer session. However, you should be careful when buying RAM. It improves performance only by reducing hard disk (virtual memory) access, which is substantially slower than memory. Depending primarily on the size of the images you edit, Photoshop uses only so much RAM. The rest of it just sits there.

Because only you can know what kind of work you'll be doing, it's difficult to make specific recommendations. Instead, take a look at how Photoshop uses memory. You can then make your own decision on how much RAM you need based on how you work.

Look at figure A.1. Notice that on my system (an 8100 with 32M RAM), the system software (System 7.5) takes about 4.3M of RAM. Because the computer has enough memory available, Photoshop grabs all the memory it can get—about 8.2M. This includes the program and all plug-ins in the Plug-ins folder. The numbers you see in the About This Macintosh dialog box reflect a default installation of Photoshop. I have not yet installed additional plug-ins.

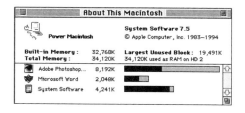

Fig. A.1

The About This Macintosh dialog box shows you how much memory applications are using.

If there wasn't enough RAM on my system, Photoshop would grab all it could (up to the Preferred size) as modulated by the system software (the Mac operating system does not let Photoshop have it all). Now you need additional RAM for image editing. A typical 6 × 5-inch full-color image at 200 dpi requires about 3.2M RAM. When you open the image, Photoshop sets aside another 3.2M to keep track of the way the image looked prior to your most recent edit or operation (in case you want to undo it). And, depending on the operation at hand, it sometimes requires yet another 3.2M to compute intermediary images required to create some special effects.

That's almost 10M of memory, even before you add Photoshop 3's 5M application code and plug-ins. Add that to the 4M for system software, and you're up to nearly 20M! Granted, your Mac can place much of this data in virtual memory (discussed in chapter 4, "Setting Up the Photoshop Environment"), but, again, RAM is faster.

Off the bat, you should have 12M RAM to run Photoshop. Anything less causes your system to run too slowly. If you edit large, full-color images, 16M is a must. Only high-end photograph editing and touch-up requires more than 16M. You must consider situations such as whether you plan to work on several images at once or large images (more than 10M), and how often you use Photoshop. In other words, does the increased productivity justify the expenditure?

Photoshop and Disk Storage

By itself, Photoshop doesn't require a lot of disk space, about 15M for a full installation. However, Photoshop files and desktop publishing files in general can quickly eat up hard disk real estate. If you lay out books, catalogs, or magazines, for example, the more disk space you have at your disposal the better. You need a large hard disk, and, if you take documents to a service bureau, you need a way to get them there, such as some type of removable media.

One beauty of the Macintosh is that its SCSI disk support allows you to easily add storage devices. This section looks at several of the most popular storage options, including hard disk drive and removable disks.

Hard Disks

When shopping for a computer, most people don't realize how quickly programs and documents can eat up disk space. Almost everybody finds themselves wishing they had purchased a larger hard disk with their system. This is especially true for Photoshop users. It doesn't take many color images to max out a 250M hard disk.

Fortunately, adding an additional hard disk to your system is easy, but a little expensive. If you need more disk space, what can you do? Depending on your Mac, you basically have two options: an external or internal drive. You also can choose between numerous sizes, ranging from about 80M to 2 or 3 gigabytes (G). Again, the decision is up to you—because only you know what kind of work you do or what your budget looks like. I have over 1G of disk space in my Mac and still find myself sometimes shuffling files. Keep in mind that you'll probably need to keep more than one project at a time on your system.

Some Macs don't have room for additional internal drives and some do. If you don't know whether yours does, Apple (1-800-SOS-APPLE) can tell you. There are advantages to both types. You easily can move internal drives around with your Mac, and you easily can transport external drives between Macs. Many desktop publishers and designers use external hard disks to transport documents back and forth to the service bureau.

If your work entails a lot of graphics editing and transporting large files between computers and locations, you should consider a large hard disk *and* some type of removable media, as discussed in the next section.

VIII

Appendixes

Removable Media

The most common removable media is the little 3.5-inch disk you slide into the front of your Mac. However, at 1.4M, it's not all that useful for desktop publishing and digital design. Most documents of this type are much larger. Graphics people get around this limitation with removable media. While several types are available, three are prevalent in the graphics and desktop publishing world: SyQuest, Bernoulli, and floptical.

> **Tip**
>
> **Use the Same Removable Drive as Your Service Bureau**
>
> I've been in the desktop publishing field for several years, and my equipment has evolved with it. Before removable high-capacity disks, we (my service bureau and I) had a hard time transferring large files. As soon as the first SyQuest drives hit the market, my service bureau snatched them up and advised its customers to use them also. Life got much easier. The point is, before investing in a removable media drive, call the service bureau where you get your imaging done and find out what it uses. Some use several different types, but some only support one type.

In addition to transferring data from computer to computer, many designers also use them for storage. However, the disks for these drives tend to cost considerably more than the tapes used in tape backup systems.

SyQuest Drives

SyQuests are one of the oldest removable media types. They are widely supported among service bureaus and production houses. Chances are, if you buy a SyQuest drive, you'll find somebody nearby to support it. There are several SyQuest drive manufacturers, and they're all compatible with each other. The drive uses large, plastic 5.25-inch disks ranging from 44M to about 250M, and they're getting larger all the time.

The one thing to remember about SyQuests is that they are not upwards-compatible. If you buy an 88M drive, it will read only 44M and 88M drives. You will not be able to read disks with larger capacity. Remember, also, that the larger the disks your drive supports, the more data you can squeeze on them.

Bernoulli Drives

Manufactured only by Iomega, Bernoulli drives use a thin, plastic disk somewhat sturdier than a SyQuest. They are also somewhat faster. Due to a recent vigorous promotional campaign by Iomega, Bernoullis have become a lot more prevalent in the DTP world. They come in several sizes, ranging from about 50M to over 200M. Also like SyQuest, they are not upward-compatible.

Floptical Drives

Floptical is a combination of the words *floppy* and *optical*. The disks used in floptical drives, therefore, are optical floppy disk drives. This really is the high-end elite in removable media. They are also faster and more reliable. However, you may have trouble finding a service bureau that supports them. And the drives and disks cost considerably more than SyQuests and Bernoullis.

CD-ROM Write Once/Read Often Drives

Perhaps you've noticed that nowadays almost all computers—PCs and Macs—come with CD-ROM drives. Software manufacturers, including Adobe, are using CD-ROM discs to distribute their wares. (You need a CD-ROM drive to access much of the extras in the package.)

CD-ROM is a double-edged sword. The discs have an enormous capacity— up to 650M—and they are highly reliable. They're also quite cheap, costing only a dollar or two each. About the only way to ruin them is to scratch or break them. Otherwise, data on a CD-ROM disc lasts virtually forever. However, they are what's known in the computer industry as "write once." You cannot erase them and use them over and over. Therefore, CD-ROM storage is useful only for storing static, finished documents.

Another drawback to using CD-ROM for storage is that the drives that write them are fairly expensive—between $5,000 and $10,000 and beyond. However, nowadays many service bureaus have writeable drives and charge reasonable fees for transferring data from hard disks and removables.

If you work in a high-volume design or production house, you may be able to justify the expense of a CD-ROM write-once drive. When looking at drives, be sure to determine whether they are single-session or multi-session. *Multi-session* drives allow you to write on the disk as many times as it takes to fill it up. *Single-session* drives are not as efficient at using disc space, because you only can write to the disc once, no matter how much data you put on it.

Mac Display Systems 101

Ever wonder how an image gets from your computer's CPU to the monitor? It's a three-step process. First, via the system software and CPU, Photoshop conveys the image to the video card. Then the video card deciphers the image to the monitor. Lastly, the monitor splashes the image out to the user.

Photoshop can use the maximum 16.7 million colors made available by your Macintosh system software. However, your Mac's display system—video card and monitor—may have limitations that restrict the number of colors you actually see.

Pick a Card

For this discussion, *video card* means any form of video output. It may be an internal video connector, like the one that goes directly to the built-in monitor on a Classic; a built-in video output port, as the one found in just about every Mac manufactured in the last four or five years; or a separately purchased NuBus or PDS video board. (NuBus and PDS are explained in the section, "Video Cards," later in this appendix.)

Regardless of all the different types of video adapters, you generally measure the capabilities of a video card by the number of colors it can display at one time on the monitor. Like image editing, image display comes down to a question of memory. Your video card has its own supply of memory, called *VRAM* (video RAM). That memory enables it to supply a certain amount of data to each pixel on the monitor, as measured in bits. The number of colors a video card can display is called its *bit* (or *bits-per-pixel*) *depth*. The standard bits-per-pixel depths are as follows:

▶ **1-bit.** 1 bit per pixel results in a black-and-white screen display. Each pixel is either off or on, white or black.

▶ **4-bit.** 4-bit displays provide 16 levels of gray. Each color is a *gray value*—a shade of gray. In other words, you see only variations of gray, not blues, greens, reds, and so on.

▶ **8-bit.** Macs with built-in video ports permit you to access at least 256 colors. You can edit color images on an 8-bit screen in Photoshop, but you won't get an adequate display of the colors. This standard is acceptable only if you use Photoshop to edit grayscale images.

▶ **16-bit.** Desktop Macs from the LC 11 and up provide (sometimes with VRAM upgrades) 16-bit color output for small- and medium-sized (13- to 16-inch) monitors. The 16-bit video cards provide 65,536 colors, which is the minimum standard for editing in Photoshop. Even with this many colors, some dithering occurs, giving you less-than-accurate color matches. For true color image editing, you really do need 24-bit color.

▶ **24-bit.** In most cases, you need to purchase a separate 24-bit video board to access the Mac's full 16.7 million colors. Only Quadras and Power Macs offer built-in 24-bit video capabilities, and even they require you to purchase additional video RAM. However, displaying 24-bit color at high-resolutions requires a lot of processing power. On-board VRAM is not as fast as some third-party display adapters, which are discussed in the next section.

▶ **32-bit.** You cannot get 32-bit pixel depth from most Macs. The few video boards that offer 32-bit capabilities allocate the additional byte of data for displaying analog images from videotape or laser disc, allowing you to layer 24-bit text and graphics over video images to add titles and animation to documents. The final byte of data buys you more functionality, not more colors.

Photoshop images are also measured by bits. Regardless of your video card's color capabilities, Photoshop allows you to open and view 24-bit images. The system software automatically dithers the display to match the limitations of your video card. Figure A.2 shows how Photoshop dithers an 8-bit image and displays it on a 4-bit monitor.

Video Cards

Full-color (24-bit) video boards come in two basic varieties: NuBus and PDS *(processor direct slot)*. Full-color NuBus boards are available from a wide range of vendors, including Apple, SuperMac, RasterOps, E-Machines, and others. To get 24-bit color on a Mac with PDS slots, you must use a NuBus adapter, which is not available for all Macs.

Be careful when you buy third-party cards. They range in price from about $500 to $4,000 and the makes and models change faster than I can type this. The important thing is to match color depth to resolution and monitor size.

VIII

Appendixes

Fig. A.2

Example of dithering. Left 4-bit, right 8-bit. Notice that the 8-bit image is much clearer.

You should also look at whether the card is Photoshop accelerated. If it is, an accelerated card can relieve the CPU of some of the Photoshop code processing. Whether they help much is debatable (and is debated often in the computer press), and certainly depends on the type of image editing you do.

Monitors

The resolution of your monitor is also important. Because the board devotes a certain amount of data (measured in bits) to each pixel on the monitor, the number of screen pixels (referred to as the monitor's *resolution*) affects the number of colors a video card can display. Full-color video boards in the $500 to $1,000 range tend to max out at 640 × 480 pixels—the resolution of a 13-inch monitor. If you want to view 24-bit color on a larger screen, you have to spend more money and, in most cases, abandon your old 24-bit card.

(An exception, of course, is the 24-bit on-board video built into Quadras and Power Macs. Quadras can support 16.7 million colors on monitors up to 16 inches, and Power Macs support 16.7 million colors on monitors up to 21 inches.)

What if you own a standard 13-inch monitor with a mid-priced 24-bit video card and you decide to splurge and upgrade to a 20-inch Apple monitor, which has a maximum resolution of 1152 × 870 pixels and a $3,000 retail price? But now you can't display more than 32,000 colors at a time, and even then, only when you set your system display to be lower than the monitor's maximum resolution. You're left with two choices: accept things as they are, or upgrade your video card that supports higher resolutions and also bundles Photoshop acceleration for another $3,000. Upgrades like this are usually only warranted if you work in Photoshop every day.

If you're used to 24-bit color and you're thinking of upgrading your monitor, keep in mind that you'll probably need to upgrade your video card as well. If you're not yet using 24-bit color, you may want to invest in a video card that provides high-resolution options. If and when you outgrow your present monitor, the upgrade fee won't be quite so high.

The software drivers that accompany most video boards let you switch resolutions regardless of the monitor you're using. For example, the standard resolution of a 21-inch monitor is 1152×870 pixels, but you can lower it to 1024 × 768 pixels (the standard 19-inch setting) or 832 × 624 pixels (the 16-inch setting). Granted, you're compromising the amount of information you can display on-screen, but it's a way to gain color depth.

VIII

Appendixes

Resource Guide

Product	Manufacturer	Address
5090 Copier	Xerox Corporation	100 Clinton Ave. S. Rochester, NY 14644 Tel: (716)423-4556 Fax: (716)423-5479
Accuset Imagesetters	AGFA Division, Miles, Inc.	100 Challenger Road Ridgefield Park, NJ 07660 Tel: (201)440-2500 Fax: (201)342-4742
Acetone	Second Glance Software	25381-G Alicia Parkway, Ste. 357 Laguna Hills, CA 92653 Tel: (714)855-2331 Fax: (714)586-0930

(continues)

APPENDIX B

Product	Manufacturer	Address
After Effects	Adobe Systems Incorporated	411 First Ave. South Seattle, WA 98104 Tel: 800-628-2320 Fax: (206)343-3360
America Online	America Online	8619 Westwood Center Dr. Vienna, VA 22182 Tel: 800-227-6364
Apertura	Alaras Corporation	PO Box 14562 Research Triangle Park, NC 27709 Tel: (919)544-1228 Fax: (919)544-7772
Artist in Residence: Fresco	XAOS Tools	600 Townsend Street Suite 270E San Francisco, CA 94103 Tel: 800-833-9267
Assorted Volume 1 Background Photo Library on CD	Vivid Details	8228 Sulphur Mountain Road Ojai, CA 93023 Tel: 800-94-VIVID Fax: (805)646-0021
Average	Chris Cox	110 Oakland Circle Madison, AL 35758 cc4b@andrew.cmu.edu chriscox@aol.com
Backswap Filter	Plug-In Systems	4578 Starboard Drive Boulder, CO 80301 Tel/Fax: (303)530-9344 E-mail: plugin@aol.com
Bernoulli Removable Drives	Iomega	1821 West 4000 South Roy, Utah 84067 Tel: (801)778-1000 Fax: (801)778-3450
BitShift	Chris Cox	See "Average"
The Black Box	Alien Skin Software	2522 Clark Ave Raliegh, NC 27607 Tel: (919)832-4124 Fax: (919)832-4065 alienskin@aol.com 72773.777@compuserve.com alien@vnet.net alienskin@eworld.com

Product	Manufacturer	Address
The Blue Ribbon Photography Series The Claudio Moure Collection	Pacific Publication Group	1030 Duane Ave., Suite D Sunnyvale, CA 94086
Canon 550C copier	Canon USA, Inc	One Canon Plaza Lake Success, NY 11042 Tel: (516)488-6700 Fax: (516)328-4929
ChromaKey	Chris Cox	See "Average"
Chromassage	Second Glance Software	See "Acetone"
ClickART® Studio Series Design™ Group CD	T/Maker Company	1390 Villa Street Mountain View, CA 94041 Tel: (415)962-0195 Fax: (415)962-0201
ColorCrypt	Candela, Ltd.	1676 E Cliff Road Burnsville, MN 55337 Tel: (612)894-8890 Fax: (612)894-8840
ColorKey	Chris Cox	See "Average"
Coolscan	Nikon Electronic Imaging	1300 Walt Whitman Road Melville, NY 11747 Tel: (516)547-4355 Fax: (516)547-0305
Cromalin	Dupont Printing & Publishing	Barley Mill Plaza Willington, DE 19880 Tel: 800-538-7668 Fax: (302)892-8306
CyberMesh	Knoll Software	P.O. Box 6887 San Rafael, CA 94903 Tel: (415)453-2471 Fax: (415)499-9322
D4000 drum scanner	Howteck	P.O. Box 9696 Rancho Santa Fe, CA 92067 Tel: (817)572-9688

VIII

Appendixes

(continues)

Product	Manufacturer	Address
Deko Boko	Sucking Fish	Koban Zane Naoto Arakawa <Wild River> Mailware: NIKKEJMTX: chuta NIFTY-Serve: GCA00443
Dilate	Chris Cox	See "Average"
DisplayMaker	LaserMaster Corporation	6900 Shady Oak Road Eden Praire, MN 55344 Tel: 800-933-5554 Fax: (612)944-0255
Docutec Copier	Xerox Corporation	See "5090 Copier"
Dolev	Scitex America Corporation	Eight Oak Park Drive Bedford, MA 01730 Tel: (617)275-3430
Duratrans	Eastman Kodak Company	343 State Street Rochester, NY 14650 Tel/Fax: (716)724-5629
Edge3x3	Chris Cox	See "Average"
Ektachrome	Eastman Kodak Company	See "Duratrans"
Erode	Chris Cox	See "Average"
Expression	Jim Bumgardner	jbum@aol.com, jbum@netcom.com
FastKey	Chris Cox	See "Average"
Forté Film Recorder	AGFA Division, Miles, Inc.	See "Accuset Imagesetters"
Fractal Design Painter	Fractal Design Corp.	335 Spreckels Dr. Suite F Aptos, CA 95003 Tel: (408)688-8800 Fax: (408)688-8836
Fractal Noise	Chris Cox	See "Average"
FreeHand	Adobe Systems Incorporated	1585 Charleston Rd. P.O. Box 7900 Mountain View, CA 94043

Product	Manufacturer	Address
Fujix Pictography 3000	Fuji Photo Film Co.	1285 Hamilton Parkway Itasca, IL 60143 Tel: (708)773-6251 Fax: (708)773-7999
GE Gallery Effects	Adobe Systems Incorporated	See "FreeHand"
Illustrator	Adobe Systems Incorporated	See "FreeHand"
Intellihance	DPA Software	913 Baxter Dr. Plano, Texas 75025 Tel: (214)517-6876 Fax: (214)517-2354
IronMike PIK	IronMike Software	4350 Georgetown Square Suite 717 Atlanta, GA 30338 Tel: (404)240-0331 Fax: (404)454-7719
IronMike SlingShot	IronMike Software	See "IronMike PIK"
Kai's Power Tools	HSC Software	6303 Carpinteria Avenue Carpinteria, CA 93013 Tel: (805)566-6200 Fax: (805)566-6385
Kodak Photo CD Sampler	Eastman Kodak Company	See "Duratrans"
KPT Bryce	HSC Software	See "Kai's Power Tools"
KPT QuickShow	HSC Software	See "Kai's Power Tools"
Leather Volume 3 Background Photo Library on CD	Vivid Details	See "Assorted Volume 1"
LineWorker	IN Software	2403 Conway Drive Escondido, CA 92026 Tel: (619)743-7502 Fax: (619)743-7503

VIII

Appendixes

(continues)

Product	Manufacturer	Address
Lumpy Noise	Paul Badger	11323 Hessler Road Cleveland, OH 44106 Tel: (216)791-2937 Pbadger@aol.com
MacPaint™	Apple Computer	20525 Mariani Avenue Building Mariana One Cupertino, CA 95014 Tel: 800-776-2333
MatchPrint	3M Company	Printing & Publishing Division 3M Center Buliding 223-2N-01 Saint Paul, MN 55144 Tel: (612)733-4299
Media Suite Pro	Avid Technology	Metropolitan Technology Park One Park West Tewksbury, MA 01876 Tel: (508)640-6789
Mezzo	Andramedia Software	699 Hampshire Road Suite 109 Westlake Village, CA 91361 Tel: (805)379-4109 Fax: (805)379-5253
Movie Player	Apple Computer	See "MacPaint"
Mr. Sa'Kan	Sucking Fish	See "Deko Boko"
PageMaker	Adobe Systems Incorporated	See "FreeHand"
Page Overtures 1&2	Form and Function	1595 17th Avenue San Francisco, CA 94122 Tel: (415)664-4010 Fax: (415)644-4030
Paint Alchemy	Xaos Tools	See "Artist in Residence: Fresco"
Pattern Workshop	Microfrontier	3401 101st, Suite E PO Box 71190 Des Moines, IA 50322 Tel: 800-388-8109 Fax: (515)278-6828
Persuasion	Adobe Systems Incorporated	See "FreeHand"

Product	Manufacturer	Address
PhotoDisc	21st Century Media	2013 4th Avenue, 2nd Floor Seattle, WA 98121 Tel: 800-528-3474
Photofusion	Ultimatte Corp.	20554 Plummer St. Chattsworth, CA 91311 Tel: (818)993-8007 Fax: (818)993-3762
PhotoMatic:	Daystar Digital	5556 Atlanta Highway Flowery Branch, GA 30542 Tel: (404)967-2077
Photoshop Filter Finesse CD	Photoshop Filter Finesse, Random House Electronic Publishing	201 E. 50th Street 3rd Floor New York, NY 10022
PhotoSpot (Paint Thinner)	Second Glance Software	See"Acetone"
Plaid	Chris Cox	See "Average"
PlateMaker	PraireSoft Software	P.O. Box 65820 West Des Moines, IA 50265 Tel/Fax: (515)225-2422
PlateMaker Photoshop Plug-in	IN Software	See "LineWorker"
PNDither	David Hull	1304 W Springfield Ave Urbana, IL 61801 E-mail: dlhull@uiuc.edu
Premiere Incorporated	Adobe Systems	See "FreeHand"
Professional Digital Design Seminars	Thunder Lizard Productions	1619 8th Avenue North Seattle, WA 98109 Tel: (206)285-0305
Psycho	Chris Cox	See "Average"
QuarkXPress	Quark, Inc.	1800 Grant Street Denver, CO 80203 Tel: (303)894-3556 Fax: (303)894-3399

VIII

Appendixes

(continues)

Product	Manufacturer	Address
QuickDraw™	Apple Computer	See "MacPaint"
QuicKeys	CE Software, Inc	1801 Industrial Circle West Des Moines, IA 50265 Tel: 800-523-7638
Radar	Paul Badger	See "Lumpy Noise"
Rainbow dye sub printer	3M Company	See "MatchPrint"
RayDream Designer	RayDream	1804 N. Shoreline Rd. Mountain View, CA 94043 Tel: (415)960-0765 Fax: (415)960-1198
Razz a Matazz	R&B Services	900 James Avenue Scranton, PA 18510 Tel: (717)346-8666
ResEdit	Apple Computer	See "MacPaint"
Scanmaker	Microtek	680 Knox Ave. Torrence, CA 90502 Tel: (310)297-5000 Fax: (310)538-3636
ScanPrep	ImageXpress	1121 Casa Nova Ct. Lawrenceville, Georgia 30244 Tel: (404)564-9924 Fax: (404)564-1632
SelectSet Imagesetters	AGFA Division, Miles, Inc.	See "Accuset Imagesetters"
Series 1 & 2	Andramedia Software	See "Mezzo"
Seybold Paris	Seybold Publications Division	Box 644 Media, PA 19063 Tel: 800-325-3838 Fax: (610)565-1858
Seybold San Francisco	Seybold Publications Division	See "Seybold Paris"
Seybold Seminars Boston	Seybold Publications Division	See "Seybold Paris"

Product	Manufacturer	Address
SilverScanner II	LaCIE Limited	8700 SW Creekside Place Beaverton, Oregon 97005 Tel: 800-288-9919 Fax: (503)520-9100
Skeleton	Chris Cox	See "Average"
Smartscan	Scitex America Corporation	See "Dolev"
Strata StudioPro	Strata Inc.	2 W. Saint George Blvd, Ancestor Square, Ste. 2100 St. George, Utah 84770 Tel: 800-678-7282 Fax: (801)628-5218
Strata Textures	Strata Inc.	See "Strata StudioPro"
StrataVision 3D	Strata Inc.	See "Strata StudioPro"
Streamline	Adobe Systems Incorportated	See "FreeHand"
Sucking Fish Filters	Photoshop Filter Finesse, Random House, Electronic Publishing	See "Photoshop Filter Finesse CD"
SyQuest Drives	SyQuest Technology	47071 Bayside Parkway Freemont, CA 94538 Tel: (510)226-4000 Fax: (510)226-4102
Tektronix Phaser III	Tektronix, Inc.	P.O. Box 1000, M/S 63-630 Wilsonville, OR 97070 Tel: (503)685-3092 Fax: (503)682-4948
Terrazzo	Xaos Tools	See "Artist in Residence: Fresco"
Total Noise	Chris Cox	See "Average"
Trapwise	Adobe Systems Incorporated	See "FreeHand"
Truchet	Paul Badger	See "Lumpy Noise"

VIII

Appendixes

(continues)

Product	Manufacturer	Address
Turpentine	Second Glance Software	See "Acetone"
U-Files	Plug-In Systems	See "Backswap Filter"
UnAlias	Chris Cox	See "Average"
VectorGraph	Paul Badger	See "Lumpy Noise"
Vericolor III	Eastman Kodak Company	See "Duratrans"
VGDither	David Hull	See "PNDither"
Warm Contrast	Kas Thomas	P.O. Box 625 Old Greenwich, CT 06870
Wrapture Reels 1&2	Form and Function	See "Page Overtures 1&2"
Wraptures 1&2	Form and Function	See "Page Overtures 1&2"

Installing Photoshop 3

f you're a seasoned Mac user, you probably think this is a needless appendix. Why didn't we just spare the poor tree that gave its life for this paper? Well, there are two reasons. The first is that not everyone who reads this book is a Mac Power user. The second is that the new version of Photoshop comes with a deluxe CD-ROM disc which provides a wealth of installation options that you, as a Mac Power user, might not know about. This appendix provides a brief overview of the installation process and briefly describes a few extras on the CD-ROM disc included with the Photoshop package.

by Bill Harrell

APPENDIX C

The Install Program

Whether you install from the floppy disks or the CD-ROM disc, installing Photoshop is essentially the same. (The frills and utilities alluded to in the introduction to this appendix have their own installation programs.) All you do is double-click the appropriate disk icon on your desktop and then double-click the Install Photoshop 3 icon. This opens the Install Adobe Photoshop dialog box, shown in figure C.1.

Fig. C.1

Use this dialog box to install Photoshop 3.

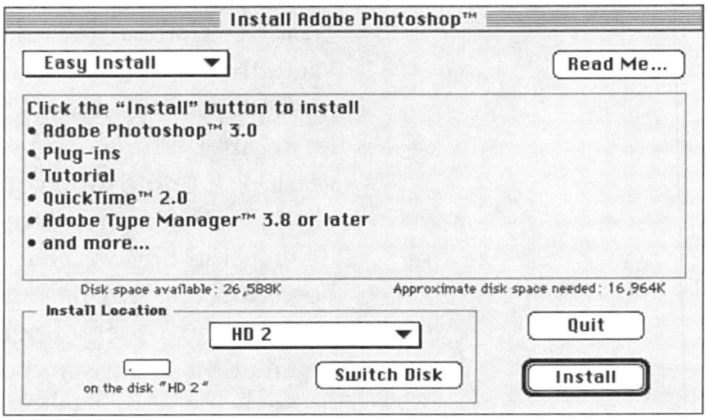

From this dialog box, you choose where to install the program and what components to install, such as QuickTime, Adobe Type Manager, and Type Reunion.

Where To Install

The default installation location is a folder named Adobe Photoshop 3 in the startup disk folder. If, for example, your startup disk is Macintosh HD, the install program creates an Adobe Photoshop 3 folder on that disk and then installs the program. You can change the destination disk and folder by clicking the Install Location pop-up menu (see fig. C.2). You also can change the target disk location by clicking the Switch Disk button to scroll through drives on your system.

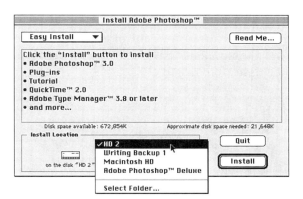

Fig. C.2

Choose a location for the Photoshop files.

Why change the installation location? It really depends on how you organize files on your hard disk. For instance, I have two hard disks. I keep applications on one disk and documents (my work) on another. When I install programs, I designate the applications disk for programs. (I also break programs down by function, such as Graphics, Utilities, and so on, and keep them in appropriate subfolders.)

What To Install

To take full advantage of all of Photoshop's features, you should install all the programs. However, complete installation requires about 22MB of disk space, which many Macs just can't spare. You can save disk space by customizing the installation.

If you have the disk space to spare, and aren't sure what components you may or may not use, select Easy Install from the pop-up menu in the upper-left corner of the dialog box, and then simply follow the directions. To pick and choose which elements to install, select Custom Install (see fig. C.3).

If you select Custom Install, the dialog box in figure C.4 appears. From here, you can scroll through the list of options and choose the ones you want to install. The Approximate Disk Space Needed message (above the

VIII

Appendixes

Quit button) keeps a running tally of the total disk space you need for your selections. The "I" button to the right of each option provides a brief message about the component. Use the descriptions and the following list to decide which options to install.

Fig. C.3

Select Custom Install to tailor the program to your needs.

Fig. C.4

Use this dialog box to choose from many custom options.

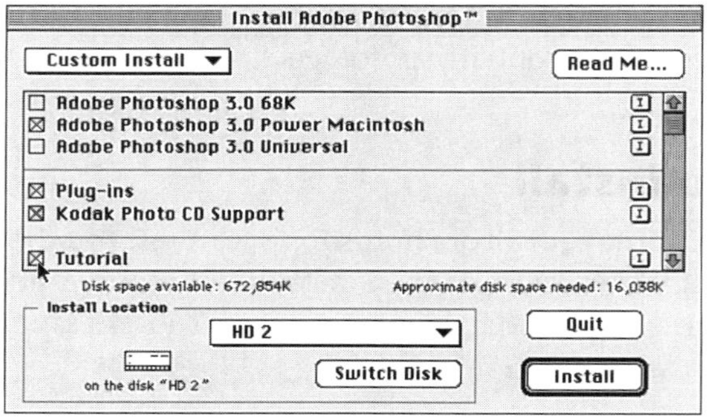

▶ **Computer Type.** Use the first three options to tell the installation program which computer you're using: Power Macintosh or a 68K-based Macintosh.

▶ **Plug-Ins.** Plug-ins are, of course, the filters and other modules that add functionality to Photoshop. Unfortunately, you can't choose which ones to install. After installation, you can go back and delete the ones you don't need.

▶ **Kodak Photo-CD Support.** This is a set of filters designed to work with Kodak's Photo-CD format. You can get a description of Photo CD in the "File Formats" section of chapter 3, "Photoshop Basics."

▶ **Tutorial.** These are images that correspond with the manual entitled *Adobe Photoshop Tutorial* included in the Photoshop package. Install them if you plan to go through the tutorial. You can always delete them when you finish. The install program places the files in the Tutorial folder.

▶ **Brushes & Patterns.** These are brush tips and pattern palettes. You really should install these.

▶ **Calibration.** This software helps you calibrate your monitor and other system components. You can never delete calibration files; the whole calibration process is dynamic and never ends.

▶ **Command Sets.** These prefabricated command sets are used with the new Commands palette. They include a command set for working with filters, color separations, and other functions.

▶ **Duotone Curves.** Duotones are special-effects for tinting grayscale photographs. Curves are preset instructions for creating duotones. These files are simply examples of duotones. Duotones are discussed in chapter 13, "Understanding Color."

▶ **Adobe Type Manager.** This is the latest version (3.8.1) of Adobe's premier Type 1 font manager. It is discussed in Appendix F, "Installing and Using ATM."

▶ **QuickTime.** Most likely, QuickTime is already installed on your Mac. It is the extension that allows you to run full-motion video on your computer. This is the latest, fastest version, QuickTime 2.0 (which also comes with System 7.5). You should install it, especially if you want to run the multimedia tutorial on the CD-ROM disc.

▶ **Adobe Type Reunion.** This extension speeds up the time it takes to launch Photoshop (and some other programs) on a system containing a large number of fonts. It also groups fonts into families that make your font menus smaller and better organized.

VIII

Appendixes

Installing the Frills

There are two types of software on the Deluxe CD-ROM disc: applications and utilities you install from the CD to your hard disk, and applications and utilities you access from the CD. For example, for speed and performance, you should install the Photoshop program itself on your hard disk. Most CD-ROM drives are too slow to run Photoshop with enough speed to keep you from pulling your hair out. The third-party stock photographs, on the other hand, are easily accessible from the CD.

> **Note**
>
> The on-line, multimedia tutorial contains several sound, movie, and animation files. Because it is so large, it's impractical to install it on a hard disk. The tutorial runs fine from a double-speed (or faster) CD-ROM drive. You'll be disappointed if you try to run it from a single-spin drive.

Installing Acrobat Reader

Besides Photoshop, you should also install Acrobat Reader on the hard disk. Acrobat Reader lets you read Adobe's Portable Document Files (PDF). After Acrobat Reader is installed, you can use it to access the on-line documentation on the CD-ROM disc. If you plan to use the on-line manual often, you will get much quicker access if you copy it to your hard disk; page turning and topic searches will execute much faster. The on-line documentation is located on the CD in the On-line Documentation folder.

Much of the other documentation for utilities on the CD-ROM disc is also in PDF format, including manuals for Filter Factory and the PostScript Printer Driver, version 8.1.1.

Installing Filter Factory

Filter factory is the plug-in that allows you to create your own custom filters, such as your own special effects filters. This is pretty high-powered computing, but if you think you're up to it, you can install this plug-in by dragging it from the Other Goodies/Filter Factory folder to the Adobe Photoshop 3/Plug-ins folder.

PostScript Printer Driver

Also located in the Other Goodies folder is the latest version of the PostScript printer driver, version 8.1.1. If you use System 7.5, you already have this driver. If not, you should run the installer to place the new driver in your Extensions folder. You will get faster and better printer results.

VIII

Appendixes

Keyboard Shortcuts

Some people just don't like mousing around. If you prefer accessing features and commands from the keyboard, use the shortcuts in this chapter. Here is a complete list of keyboard shortcuts. Also listed are ways to modify tool actions with keyboard-mouse combinations.

by Bill Harrel

APPENDIX D

Selecting

Action	Keyboard Shortcut
Constrain marquee to perfect circle or square	Shift-drag marquee select
Draw marquee from center	Option-drag and marquee select
Add to a selection	Shift-drag and marquee select
Subtract from a selection	⌘-drag any selection tool
Move copy of a selection	Option-drag a selection
Move selection border only	Option-drag Move tool
Move selection one pixel	Any arrow key
Move selection 10 pixels	Shift-arrow key

Selecting Tools

Tool	Keyboard Shortcut
Marquee	M*
Lasso	L
Magic Wand	W
Move	V
Cropping	C
Type	T
Hand	H
Zoom	Z
Paintbucket	K
Gradient	G

Tool	Keyboard Shortcut
Line	N
Eyedropper	I
Eraser	E
Pencil	P
Airbrush	A
Paintbrush	B
Rubber stamp	S
Smudge	U
Blur/sharpen	R*
Dodge/burn/sponge	O*
Switch background and foreground colors	X
Return to default colors	D
Toggle between quick mask modes	Q*
Switch between screen modes	F*

***Press continually to switch between modes or groups of tools.**

Viewing

Action	Keyboard Shortcut
Zoom and resize window in increments of 1	⌘- (+) or (-)
Zoom in by factor of 2	⌘-spacebar-click any tool
Zoom out by factor of 2	Option-spacebar-click any tool

VIII

Appendixes

Painting

Action	Keyboard Shortcut
Select background color	Option-Eyedropper
Fill a selection with background color or clear a layer	Delete
Display Fill dialog box	Shift-Delete
Replace a color in Swatches palette	Shift-any tool
Remove a color from the Swatches palette	⌘-any tool
Magic Eraser	Shift-Eraser
Constrain a stroke to a straight line	Shift-any paint or editing tool
Set paint opacity by increments of 10	Number key
Crosshair cursor	Cap Lock
Eyedropper	Option-any paint tool
Anchor Point Select	⌘-any paint or editing tool

Layers Palette

Action	Keyboard Shortcut
Select layer below currently active layer	⌘-[
Select layer above currently active layer	⌘-]
Select a layer containing a specific object	⌘-move-click
Temporarily turn off a layer mask	⌘-click layer mask
View contents of layer mask	Option-click layer mask

Miscellaneous

Action	Keyboard Shortcut
Increase or decrease a value in a dialog box by 10 units	Shift-up or down arrow key
Increase or decrease a value in a dialog box by 1 unit	Up or down arrow key
Reset dialog box	Option-click Reset button
Instant Hand tool	Spacebar-any paint or editing tool
Cancel	⌘-(.)
Open Last Filter dialog box	⌘-Option-F
Apply last filter	⌘-F

Menu Commands

File Menu	Keyboard Shortcut
New	⌘-N
Open	⌘-O
Close	⌘-W
Save	⌘-S
Print	⌘-P
Quit	⌘-Q

Edit Menu	Keyboard Shortcut
Undo/Redo	⌘-Z
Cut	⌘-X
Copy	⌘-C
Paste	⌘-V

VIII

Appendixes

887

Image Menu	Keyboard Shortcut
Map/Invert	⌘-I
Map/Equalize	⌘-E
Map/Threshold	⌘-T
Adjust/Levels	⌘-L
Adjust/Curves	⌘-M
Adjust/Brightness/Contrast	⌘-B
Adjust/Color Balance	⌘-Y
Adjust/Hue/Saturation	⌘-U

Select Menu	Keyboard Shortcut
All	⌘-A
None	⌘-D
Float/Defloat	⌘-J
Grow	⌘-G
Show/Hide Edges	⌘-H

Window Menu	Keyboard Shortcut
Zoom In	⌘-(+)
Zoom Out	⌘-(−)
Show/Hide Rulers	⌘-R

Swapping PC and Mac Photoshop Files

I t would be really nice if you didn't need this particular appendix. But, if you exchange any files between the Mac and DOS computer platforms, you *do* need this appendix.

Most Photoshop users have shared the fantasy of being able to perform completely transparent exchanges between the Mac and Windows versions of the program. Photoshop 3 comes closer than ever to making that fantasy a reality; any further improvements probably should wait for some fundamental changes in the operating systems. We aren't there yet, however, so use the tips in this appendix to save yourself some aggravation as you make your swaps.

by Bill Harrel

APPENDIX E

Computer Communication

Macintosh and DOS computers now can communicate in so many ways that it's hard to list them all. One of those ways is as steady as a rock, however, and probably your most reliable bet. Unless you have a network set up with both kinds of machines hooked together for easy communication, use one of the magic system extensions that lets your Mac's Super Drive read DOS floppies directly. If you have really big files to transfer, several of these extensions even let you read removable drives such as SyQuests.

Personal Communication

Sometimes the biggest headache in swapping between the two platforms has nothing to do with the machines; it's the people. When giving someone a file, be careful to avoid making assumptions about the other person's knowledge of your operating system. Make sure everything is clear. At least Photoshop 3 has moved the platforms closer together. The major documentation is exactly the same between the two systems.

Standard Photoshop Files

Across the board, or platform, Photoshop 3 files (files with a PSD extension on the Windows side), are completely compatible. They also maintain all layering and other functions specific to the program. If you think you might be editing an image more after going across platforms, you should save your files in Photoshop's native format.

Keep in mind, though, that Photoshop is the only application that can read Photoshop files. Desktop publishing applications (PageMaker, QuarkXPress, and others) cannot read or import the file format, and neither can other applications, such as word processing and presentation applications.

Stick with EPS and TIFF

Take the advice of the experts. If you swap between two platforms, use EPS and TIFF files exclusively. It is true that new filters make it possible for you to work between the two platforms, but that doesn't change the inherent differences in the natures of the two formats. EPS and TIFF were designed from the beginning as cross-platform formats.

Several filters that come with Photoshop translate between Macintosh and PC graphics files. Most other formats, however, are not as adept at maintaining artistic integrity or supporting color separations.

Again, you are better off sticking with EPS and TIFF formats, even though these formats do not maintain Photoshop's layers, masks, and so on. Also, if you know when you save the file that it is going to another platform, use Photoshop's platform specific switches. During the TIFF exporting process, for example, you are given the opportunity to choose PC or Macintosh, as shown in figure E.1.

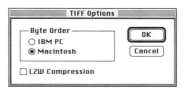

Fig. E.1

You can switch between platforms when you save a TIFF file.

VIII

Appendixes

When saving EPS files, make sure that the screen preview, or image header, is in the format for the specific platform. If it isn't, it won't display. In other words, if you save an image headed for a PC layout with a Mac header, you can import the image into the PC layout, but you won't see it on your monitor. This makes it difficult to place and resize. Figure E.2 shows the Mac and PC switches that appear during an EPS file export. For Macintosh, use one of the Macintosh settings. PC EPS files have TIFF image settings. To save an EPS file for the PC, select one of the TIFF settings.

Windows to Service Bureau

Maybe the most common Mac and Windows Photoshop swap takes place at the service bureau. Most service bureaus are heavily Macintosh-oriented, because that's where the desktop publishing revolution began. At the service bureau, all these cross-platform compatibility problems come to roost in a big way; it's time to go to expensive imagesetter output and you don't want it ruined.

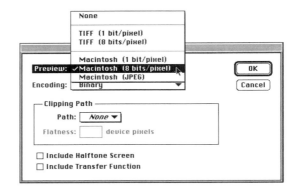

The best solution is for the Windows user to do a print-to-PostScript file. That file eliminates any worries about fonts and incompatibilities. Just be sure to tell the service bureau that your file is a DOS PostScript dump, because it does need to make a few adjustments.

Windows Printer Critical

In the Windows environment, the printer plays a big part in how a document looks. The importance of its role has to do with the basic nature of the print driver process, and that process in Windows is quite different from the process on the Mac. File swappers should agree on which printer they select inside Photoshop when doing work on the files. When all parties select the same printer, all the printer-dependent issues between the two platforms are common. You may not know it, but Photoshop includes most PPDs for the Apple laser printers in the Windows version of the program; so, this isn't as big a feat as it seems.

DOS File Names

File names in the DOS world are always eight characters or fewer, followed by a period, and then an extension of three letters or less. In Photoshop, if you send a Macintosh file to a Windows person, name the file with the three-letter extension of PSD. That's the Windows-world rough equivalent of the Macintosh file type and creator codes.

Installing and Using Adobe Type Manager

To get the most from Photoshop, you need to install Adobe Type Manager (ATM), which is included in the PhotoShop 3 package. ATM displays Type 1 PostScript fonts on your screen and renders fonts for non-PostScript printers. In other words, to use Type 1 fonts with a QuickDraw printer, you need to install ATM. When ATM is used with any type of printer—PostScript or non-PostScript—you must install the font outline in the Fonts folder inside the System folder for each font you intend to use, regardless of whether the font is resident in your printer.

Using Photoshop for Macintosh • *Using Photoshop for Macin*

Using Photoshop for Macintosh •

by Bill Harrel

APPENDIX F

> **Tip**
>
> If you use System 7.5, ATM 3.6 is included with QuickDraw GX. If you already installed QuickDraw GX, ATM is already on your system. However, Photoshop 3 comes with ATM 3.8.1, which is Power Mac native and slightly faster than the previous versions. Reinstall all the fonts and ATM after installing QuickDraw GX.

Type 1 Versus TrueType

Since the advent of System 7's (and Windows 3.1's) built-in TrueType font rendering system, many users have been confused about which type of font file is best. Even though they provide flexibility, too many choices can make computing difficult.

Actually, whether you use one font type or the other is not that critical. The speed and quality differences between the two formats are negligible; many people use both. The type you should use depends on what you do with your computer.

Both TrueType and Type 1 fonts are outline fonts. Font outlines use a font manager, such as Adobe Type Manager (ATM) and System 7.x's built-in TrueType manager, to *rasterize* or *render* fonts. Both terms simply mean reading information from a font file and then displaying type on a monitor, or sending font information to a printer.

Originally, Type 1 fonts were created for use with Adobe's PostScript page description language. The primary advantage of Type 1 fonts is that they have been around awhile and are the font of choice for desktop publishers and designers. Most desktop publishing service bureaus (establishments where users take their high-resolution printing, slides, and color-proofing jobs for printing) use them. This means that if you use Type 1 fonts in your documents, the service bureau is more likely to have those fonts.

This is not, however, as big a restriction as it may seem. An increasing number of service bureaus have TrueType font collections. For the most part, TrueType fonts are PostScript compatible. Still, most service bureaus prefer Adobe Type 1 fonts. Using them in desktop publishing and design work provides more reliability and fewer surprises. Whichever format you use, be sure your service bureau uses the same font. Don't use TrueType Times and let your service bureau use Adobe fonts, otherwise the font spacing may be wrong.

Installing ATM

If you choose the Easy Install option when installing Photoshop, the ATM control panel is automatically installed in the Control Panels folder in your System folder. If you choose Custom Install, you must select ATM from the list of options. Either way, the next time you start your system, you can see the ATM icon (see fig. F.1).

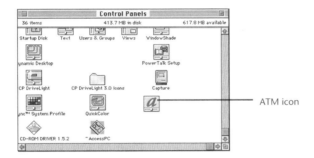

ATM icon

Fig. F.1

The Control Panels window shows the ATM 3.8.1 icon.

Using ATM

After it's installed, ATM hums along unnoticed and without a lot of interaction. You can fine tune the font manager from its control panel, shown in figure F.2. The ATM control panel icon is located in the Control Panels folder. You can open it by double-clicking it, or, in System 7.5, by choosing it from the Control Panels submenu on the Apple menu.

Fig. F.2

Custom tailor ATM in the Adobe Type Manager 3.8.1 control panel.

As you can see, the ATM control panel is not complicated. The following are brief descriptions of its three major components:

▶ **On/Off.** I can hear you sighing. Of course you know what this switch does. Right? Just remember this about ATM and Type 1 fonts: Adobe products are designed to work with ATM. Leave it on when working with Photoshop.

▶ **Font Cache.** A *cache* is a section of system RAM set aside for the last few lines of code used by the computer. The theory is that most likely the same lines of code will soon be needed again. Because memory is faster than a hard disk, the code waiting in memory can be processed faster. Make sense? The larger the cache, the more fonts can be stored and less hard disk accessing is required. Up to a point (about 512K), you should set your font cache to 1 percent of the amount of RAM in your system. More than 512K though, is really a waste of memory.

▶ **Preserve.** Preserve seeks to compensate for text in documents that are not created with ATM installed (or turned off). Line Spacing maintains line, paragraph, and page breaks. Character Shapes maintains the size and shape of characters. When working in Photoshop, you should keep Character Shapes turned on. Line Spacing has little or no application in image editing, because few Photoshop documents contain multiple lines of text. Line Spacing can affect word processing and desktop publishing documents—but you'll be hard pressed to find one that is created on a Mac without ATM.

Installing Type 1 Fonts

Unlike TrueType fonts, Type 1 PostScript fonts come in two parts—a bitmapped screen font and a mathematically defined, or *outline*, printer font. Screen fonts, of course, display on your monitor, and printer fonts are downloaded to the printer for output. All fonts are installed in the System/Fonts folder, shown in figure F.3.

Screen fonts are kept in suitcases and outline fonts are separate font files. In figure F.3, all the screen fonts for the typeface Helvetica (including weight and font types, such as bold, italic, and bold-italic) reside in one suitcase.

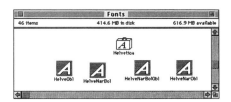

Fig. F.3

System 7.x stores fonts in the Fonts folder inside the System folder.

As shown in figure F.4, each suitcase contains screen fonts in several common sizes. ATM uses the screen fonts and outline fonts to render all font sizes smoothly on your monitor.

Fig. F.4

The contents of the Helvetica font suitcase.

VIII

Appendixes

Installing fonts is quite simple; you select the fonts and drag them into the Fonts folder inside the System folder. Make sure, though, that you leave the screen fonts in their suitcases. You should also make sure that you get all the printer fonts in a specific family. Most fonts come in four flavors—Normal (or Roman), Bold, Italic, and Bold-Italic. The availability of choices differs between fonts; some, such as Zapf Dingbats, have only one style, and others, such as Futura, have several.

Finally, if you didn't install ATM when you installed Photoshop, you can go back and install it by running the ATM 3.8.1 installation program, located either on the ATM Program disk or in the PhotoShop 3/Disk Images/ATM Program Disk folder on the CD-ROM disc (see fig. F.5).

Again, whether you use ATM or not isn't critical. However, Adobe products are designed to work with the font-managing system, as are most service bureaus. My advice is, use it.

Fig. F.5

The contents of the ATM Program Disk folder on the CD-ROM disc.

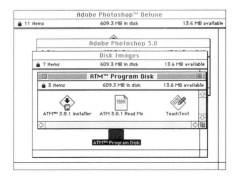

Symbols

INDEX

G

M

creating, 334
options, 336
subtracting from selections, 335-336
QuickDraw GX, 894
QuickDraw™, 872
QuicKeys, 799-802, 872
  editing, 801-803
  recording, 799-801
QuickShow utility, 786
QuickTime, 584-586, 879

R

Radar filter, 547, 872
radial blur, 449
radius (color), 460
Rainbow dye-sub printer, 872
Rainbow filter, 533
RAM, scratch disks, 108-109
raster image conversion, 658-667
Rasterize Adobe Illustrator Format
  dialog box, 73
rasterizing fonts, 894
raw file format, 133-135, 147
Raw Options dialog box, 134
RayDream Designer, 872
Razz a Matazz, 872
Razz Matazz Filters, 543
rearranging alpha channels, 343
recording
  QuicKeys, 799-801
  scripts, 803
Rectangular Marquee tool, 228-229
reference windows, 37-38
reflection filter, 534
removable media, 857-859
removing scanned patterns, 487-488
Render filters, 466-471
rendering fonts, 894
replacing colors, 64, 425-427
repositioning layers, 275
reproduction
  high-speed, 703-704
  imagesetters, 704
  laser printers, 705
  paper types, 705-706
resampling images, 162, 697
ResEdit, 872
resetting tools, 198
resin-coated paper, 704
resolution
  graphics, 85-86
  grayscale images, 696-698

line art, 165
monitors, 746
output, 730
Photo CD images, 181-182
printing issues, 93-94
scanning, 157, 161-165
  color scans, 164
  grayscale scans, 163-164
  line art, 162-163
retail design, 825-830
Reticulation filter, 529
Revert command (File menu), 43
RGB color, 90, 390-393
Ring of Fire Fotomagic, 542
Ripple filter, 452, 520
RISC processors, 854
rotating images, 709-710
rotoscoping
  filmstrips, 575-578
  QuickTime movies, 584-586
Rough Pastels filter, 525
round brushes, 222-223
Rubber Stamp tool, 24, 44, 214-216
rulers
  measuring objects, 39
  zero intersection point, 38

S

Safe Titling Area (STA), 756
sampled paint, 218
sampling images, 697
sans serif typefaces, 753
saturation, 423-425
  filters, 552
  increasing, 423
Save a Copy command (File menu),
  274
Save Path dialog box, 311-313
Save Selection dialog box, 242,
  340-341
saving
  channels, 353
  color sets, 196
  commands to New Commands
    palette, 55
  EPS files, 74-75
  paths, 311-312
  selections, 242-243
scaling options (scanning), 157
Scanmaker, 872
scanned image acquisition, 131
scanning, 695

U

PLUG YOURSELF INTO...

The MCP Internet Site

Free information and vast computer resources from the world's leading computer book publisher—online!

Find the books that are right for you!
A complete online catalog, plus sample chapters and tables of contents give you an in-depth look at *all* our books. The best way to shop or browse!

- ✦ **Stay informed** with the latest computer industry news through discussion groups, an online newsletter, and customized subscription news.
- ✦ **Get fast answers** to your questions about MCP books and software.
- ✦ **Visit** our online bookstore for the latest information and editions!
- ✦ **Communicate** with our expert authors through e-mail and conferences.
- ✦ **Play** in the BradyGame Room with info, demos, shareware, and more!
- ✦ **Download software** from the immense MCP library:
    - Source code and files from MCP books
    - The best shareware, freeware, and demos
- ✦ **Discover hot spots** on other parts of the Internet.
- ✦ **Win books** in ongoing contests and giveaways!

Drop by the new Internet site of Macmillan Computer Publishing!

To plug into MCP:

World Wide Web: http://www.mcp.com/
Gopher: gopher.mcp.com **FTP:** ftp.mcp.com

GOING ONLINE DECEMBER 1994